Art Law & Transactions

Art Law & Transactions

SECOND EDITION

Anne-Marie Rhodes
John J. Waldron Professor of Law
Loyola University Chicago
School of Law

Carolina Academic Press
Durham, North Carolina

ISBN 978-1-5310-1902-0
eISBN 978-1-5310-1903-7
LCCN 2021931922

Carolina Academic Press
700 Kent Street
Durham, North Carolina 27701
Telephone (919) 489-7486
Fax (919) 493-5668
E-mail: cap@cap-press.com
www.cap-press.com

Printed in the United States of America

David
James, Peter, and Cydney

Contents

Table of Cases

Boldface denotes principal cases.

Acknowledgments

Updating a book is a different undertaking than writing the original, but it is no less a task. Again, I was helped along the way with professional insights, endless encouragement, and research and technical assistance. I am enormously grateful to my professional colleagues at Loyola and elsewhere, my students, friends, and family, who gave generously to me. I thank all of them. I also thank Sotheby's for allowing me to use Sotheby's Conditions of Sale and Terms of Guarantee. A special note of thanks to the wonderful team at Carolina Academic Press for persevering with me on this second edition.

Above all, my husband, David.

Introduction

Welcome to *Art Law & Transactions*, a book written for law students and others interested in understanding how the law impacts art transactions.

This second edition continues to follow a transactional timeline, that is, the acquisition, ownership, and disposition of an artwork. The major doctrinal and policy issues confronting an art collector are discussed within this transactional arc. Sometimes those issues will nicely loop around, with the double dipping allowing us to revisit an issue from another angle. Like artistic perspective, what emerges and what recedes can be illuminating.

The book's primary perspective remains that of an individual collector. Collectors are one of the primary players in the art world and art market. The art world is a large one, primarily composed of artists, dealers, auction houses, museums, and collectors. It is supported by an even wider base, including curators, critics, conservators, art historians, art academics, fabricators, framers, installers and handlers, customs brokers, appraisers, authenticators, insurers, consultants, editors and writers, foundations, philanthropists, provenance researchers, governmental arts commissions, investment advisors, and yes, lawyers. This array of people parallels another reality for art law. There is no discrete area of law known as art law, rather it is law through the lens of art. Property, contracts, criminal law, civil procedure, torts, trusts and estates, intellectual property, tax, and other areas all play a role. Because art is the subject matter, sometimes the normal legal rules will apply and sometimes not. Art exceptionalism can allow or require a different, more tailored, rule to apply.

Being aware of art exceptionalism is one goal of this book. Another goal is for you to see and experience what it is that lawyers do. A necessary reminder for lawyers dealing with art is to keep your focus on the law. Do not be seduced by the art. To help develop that focus, there are drafting exercises sprinkled throughout the book. Try some of them.

Cases are edited down and generally presented without footnotes, citations, and concurring and dissenting opinions. Use of footnotes is equally restrained, with the hope of making the text easier on the eyes. Art law is dynamic, with noteworthy events and decisions happening seemingly every week. The materials are generally current through fall 2020.

Anne-Marie Rhodes
Chicago, Illinois
January 2021

Part One

Acquisition

Acquisition is the opening step in the transactional cycle of acquisition, ownership, and disposition. Viewed from the perspective of a collector, the three market venues—from an artist, from a dealer, and at auction—have a distinctive art market culture. That culture is at times beguiling, perhaps seductive, and always competitive. For a lawyer, contract law with its centuries-old principles and modern codifications dominates the acquisition process. The norms of contract are at times amplified by fiduciary concerns and may be modified by art market traditions.

Chapter 1 explores acquisition as a two-person transaction, a purchase by a collector directly from an artist through a commission. Chapters 2 and 3 present the more common acquisition structures involving a dealer or an auction house, usually as an intermediary between the buyer and seller. Chapters 4 and 5 move beyond the structure of the acquisition transaction to the buyer's core goals of authenticity and title. In the realm of art, authenticity is fluid, and title may rest on shifting sands. *Caveat emptor.*

Chapter 1

Acquisition by Purchase from Artist

Acquiring an artwork from an artist is a legal transaction directly between two parties: the buyer and the seller. If the acquisition is for an artwork not yet in existence, the simple transaction can be less simple. The lawyer's primary perspective in drafting a commission agreement is to protect her client's interest. The difficult part is to do so without too tightly circumscribing the artist's creativity, thereby jeopardizing the ultimate goal. It is a Janus-like task.

A. Private Commissioned Works

1. A Glimpse from History

Commissioning an artist to create an artwork has a rich historical legacy in the common law tradition. Early patrons of art were often the two main powers in society, the church and the state. Art was symbolic of power, stability, and greatness. Many great works of Western civilization are from Italian Renaissance masters, such as DaVinci, Michelangelo, and Botticelli. Millions know those artists' works, but few pause to consider the legal contracts that formalized their undertakings.

The following contract from 1481 is for the wall paintings of the Sistine Chapel in Rome. It is presented here as a historic link for art and law, as an example of what lawyers have done for centuries and still do today.

Sistine Chapel Contract*

On the 27th day of October, 1481, in the Apostolic Chamber at Rome, during the 11th year of the Pontificate of our Lord Pope Sixtus IV, the Most Holy Father in Christ.

At Rome, in the Apostolic Palace, the honorable Lord, Giovanni Pietro de'Dolci of Florence and living in Rome, supervisor and representative of the administration of the Apostolic Palace, proceeding, as he states, from a mandate and commission from our Most Holy Lord the Pope (in my presence, a public notary) commissioned

* Translated from the original Latin by the late Fr. Robert Araujo, S.J., John Courtney Murray, S.J. University Professor, Loyola University Chicago School of Law.

or agreed with the careful men: Cosimo di Lorenzo Filippo Rosselli, Alessandro Mariani [Botticelli], and Domenico di Tommaso Corradi [Ghirlandaio], all of Florence; and, Pietro [Perugino] Cristofano of Perugia—all painters presently in Rome—to paint the new, large chapel in the aforementioned Apostolic Palace from the top of the altar and downwards, with ten stories from the Old and New Testaments, accompanied by curtains below.

The paintings are to be executed with diligence and care, as each of the painters and their associates can do this in accordance with the work that has already been done.

And the aforementioned painters have promised to and agreed with the said Giovanni Pietro (de'Dolci), who is acting on behalf of our Most Holy Lord the Pope, to paint the ten stories with curtains, as already mentioned, by the fifteenth day of the next March, with payment at the amount paid to these painters for work already begun in this chapel, under the penalty of fifteen gold ducats of the Chamber for any breach, which penalty they have freely imposed, and which, if they breach this agreement, they will willingly pay to the administration of the Chapel.

And these painters have obligated themselves and pledged all their goods that are presently or will in the future be present for breaches. . . .

In the presence and witness of the venerable Lord Mario de Monte etc. in the Apostolic Palace and before me, Giovanni Gerones, the notary of the Chambers.

A few months later, on January 17, 1482, there was another agreement, now to value the work that was completed. A six-person panel of "arbiters and judges" made the decision. They determined that the painters "ought to have from . . . the Pope for the said four stories with the said curtains, frames and Popes, 250 ducats of the Chamber at the rate of 10 *carleni* to the ducat, for each story. And the said painters there present praised, approved and proclaimed the sentence and declaration, etc."

2. Private Commissions—Cases

Wolff and *Brockhurst* present a common example of many private commissions today, the portrait. In *Wolff*, the question is the meaning of satisfaction as used in the parties' written agreement; hence, the issue is one of contract interpretation. *Brockhurst* involves an oral contract, a not-uncommon occurrence in the art industry, because some artists refuse to sign a written contract. The case therefore raises the fundamental question of whether there is an enforceable contract at all. Pay particular attention to the affirmative defenses of the statute of frauds and the statute of limitations asserted by the defendant, as these defenses are key in art litigation.

Wolff v. Smith

25 N.E.2d 399 (Ill. App. Ct. 1940)

DOVE, J. This suit was instituted to recover the alleged contract price of a portrait and frame therefor. A trial was had resulting in a verdict for the plaintiff for $460, upon which judgment was rendered and defendant appeals.

The evidence discloses that appellee is a professional portrait painter having a studio in New York City. Appellant is an officer of the Smith Oil and Refining Company and resides in Rockford. Appellant and his brothers were desirous of having appellee paint a portrait of their deceased father to hang in the offices of the Company and in January, 1937, appellee was in Rockford and on the thirteenth of January, while in the offices of the Company, dictated, signed and delivered to appellant the following letter: "As per our conversation in your office January 12th, I beg to say that the portrait of your father will be painted entirely on my own responsibility and request with no obligation involved. I am sure of the happy result of this portrait and that it will be most satisfactorily accepted as an accurate and vivid likeness of the elder Mr. Smith. The price will be $500.00 for the canvass if my work is found to be to the entire satisfaction of all concerned." Appellee painted and delivered this portrait and it was accepted and paid for by appellant and his brothers. At the time this portrait was delivered appellant stated to appellee that some time in the future he would like to have a portrait similar to the one that had just been accepted to hang in his own home. On August 2, 1937, appellee was in Rockford, had lunch with appellant at the Faust Hotel, quoted a price of $400 for a second portrait and $60 for the frame, and, according to appellant's testimony, stated that he would paint the second portrait under the same terms as the first, that he would paint it upon his own responsibility and without any responsibility upon appellant's part to accept it and subject to appellant's full acceptance.

According to the testimony of appellee there was nothing said in this conversation about the terms upon which the second portrait was to be painted. Appellant, however, gave appellee a colored photograph of the first portrait and the next day appellee, while en route to his home in New York, wrote appellant from Toledo, Ohio, as follows:

> "My Dear Mr. Smith: I feel very much indebted to you for the courtesy and favor of calling at the Hotel Faust last evening to meet me. Please be assured that I will do all in my power to make the second portrait of your dear father as outstanding and exact a likeness as the first one and to your entire satisfaction. And herewith beg to reiterate my statement to you last evening that I am very pleased to paint this second portrait on my own initiative and request and no obligation at no time. The price to be $400.00 for the canvass (portrait) and additional cost of frame to be $60.00. And needless to say that a very fine appropriate frame will be selected to meet with your entire approval. Size of portrait 20 Inches by 24 Inches."

Appellee returned to his studio, painted the portrait and about October 20, 1937, brought it to Rockford and displayed it in appellant's living room and asked appellant for an expression of an opinion. According to appellant's testimony he then and there told appellee that his father's eyes were brown as shown in the first portrait and in the colored photograph but in the second portrait they were painted blue, that the clothing in the first portrait was gray instead of black, that appellee had given the figure a collapsed appearance, that the eyes were not right but were heavy and there was a cloud behind the glasses, that the whole portrait seemed to lack the vigor and vitality that the subject had and which was painted in the first portrait and that there were certain lights and shadows on the face which gave it an unnatural appearance. According to appellee's testimony appellant at this time stated that the second portrait was a very good one but that there was difference in the color of the eyes and clothing. That appellee told appellant that he would be glad to make the changes as he had his paint box with him and thereupon, at appellant's home, did make some corrections. The next day the first portrait was brought to appellant's home from the company's office and appellee testified that in comparing them he, appellee, found that in the second portrait the lines on the forehead were accentuated and on the face the lines were a little too hard and that these needed changing and the background needed a little deepening in tones. Appellee made these changes. According to the testimony of appellant, he, appellant, told appellee that the portrait was still unsatisfactory and that where corrections were made he felt that when a painting was once completed, it can never be satisfactorily corrected, that this criticism was not only his opinion but the opinion of art critics and that the picture as corrected was not satisfactory as it was not a good likeness of his father and that he was sorry the second portrait was not as satisfactory as the first. Appellant further testified that he told appellee that if appellee so desired the second portrait could hang in appellant's home until after the holidays when his sister would visit him and that he would try to overcome his objections to it but that if he felt, after the holidays, as he felt then, he would return the picture to appellee. According to appellant this arrangement was satisfactory with appellee. Appellee testified, however, that after he had made the corrections appellant did not say that he was still dissatisfied with it but on the contrary said it was all right and for appellee to send him a bill before he left Rockford and that appellant would remit him within a few days. Appellee thereafter mailed appellant a statement and on November 3rd and 10th wrote appellant, to which appellant replied on November 18th and appellee answered on November 22nd, 1937. From this correspondence it is apparent appellant was not satisfied with the portrait and appellee was equally insistent upon being paid.

* * *

Counsel for appellee argue that the contract which forms the basis of this suit was made with reference to the first portrait, which was the standard by which the second was to be judged, that the evidence discloses that appellee did all in his power to make the second as outstanding and exact in likeness as the first, that the second portrait is substantially like the first one and appellant can not arbitrarily reject it but he must be satisfied therewith inasmuch as the word satisfaction as employed in this contract means a reasonable and not an arbitrary satisfaction.

It is appellant's contention that this contract is one involving a matter of fancy, taste or personal judgment and that appellee agreed that the second portrait would be satisfactory to appellant, that therefore appellant is the sole judge of his satisfaction and when he asserts he is not satisfied there can be no recovery. Instructions embodying these theories were submitted by counsel to the trial court who gave those in accordance with appellee's theory and rejected those of appellant.

In 13 C.J. page 675 it is said:

> "Contracts in which one party agrees to perform to the satisfaction of the other are ordinarily divided into two classes: (1) Where fancy, taste, sensibility or judgment are involved: and (2) where the question is merely one of operative fitness or mechanical utility. In contracts involving matters of fancy, taste, or judgment, when one party agrees to perform to the satisfaction of the other, he renders the other party the sole judge of his satisfaction without regard to the justice or reasonableness of his decision, and a court or jury can not say that such party should have been satisfied where he asserts that he is not."

In a note cases illustrating and supporting the text are cited and the statement is made that contracts have been held to fall within the first class and support the rule stated in the text where they have related to portraits, a portrait bust, . . . and others.

* * *

Zaleski v. Clark, 44 Conn. 218, 26 Am.Rep. 446 . . . , was an action by a sculptor to recover the contract price of a bust of the defendant's deceased husband which he had modeled. In its opinion the court said: "Courts of law must allow parties to make their own contracts, and can enforce only such as they actually make. Whether the contract is wise or unwise, reasonable or unreasonable, is ordinarily an immaterial inquiry. The simple inquiry is, what is the contract? and has the plaintiff performed his part of it? In this case the plaintiff undertook to make a bust which should be satisfactory to the defendant. The case shows that she was not satisfied with it. The plaintiff has not yet then fulfilled his contract. It is not enough to say that she ought to be satisfied with it, and that her dissatisfaction is unreasonable. She, and not the court, is entitled to be the judge of that. The contract was not to make one that she ought to be satisfied with. * * * Nor is it sufficient to say that the bust was the very best thing of the kind that could possibly be produced. Such an article might not be satisfactory to the defendant, while one of inferior workmanship might be entirely satisfactory. A contract to produce a bust perfect in every respect, and one with which the defendant ought to be satisfied, is one thing; an undertaking to make one with which she will be satisfied is quite another thing. The former can only be determined by experts, or those whose education and habits of life qualify them to judge of such matters. The latter can only be determined by the defendant herself. It may have been unwise in the plaintiff to make such a contract, but having made it, he is bound by it."

* * *

In his letter to appellant from Toledo on August 3rd, 1937, appellee wrote that he would do all in his power to make this second portrait as outstanding and exact a likeness of appellant's father as the first one, that he was pleased to paint it on his own initiative without obligation on the part of appellant and added "and to your entire satisfaction". Under the foregoing and many other authorities, under this arrangement appellant must be held to be the sole judge whether he would accept the portrait and the trial court erred in not so instructing the jury.

* * *

For the error in instructions, however, the judgment must be reversed and the cause remanded.

Reversed and remanded.

Brockhurst v. Ryan

146 N.Y.S.2d 386 (N.Y. Sup. Ct. 1955)

GELLER, J. Plaintiff, Gerald L. Brockhurst, a renowned portrait painter and artist, brings this action to recover from the defendant, Clendenin J. Ryan, the sum of $17,000, alleging that the defendant agreed to pay plaintiff that sum for painting three portraits and that defendant has breached his agreement. The action was tried before the court without a jury.

* * *

In February, 1945 plaintiff entered into an oral agreement with defendant, whereby the plaintiff agreed to paint five separate portraits of the defendant, the defendant's wife, and the defendant's three children, Caryn, 6 years of age, Clendenin J. Ryan, Jr. (referred to in the testimony as 'Mike'), 5 years of age, and Cyr, 2 years of age. The defendant agreed to make himself and his family available for sittings and to pay $6,000 for each of the children's portraits and $5,000 for each of the parent's portraits, a total of $28,000.

The sittings for the portraits commenced shortly after the making of the contract and continued thereafter with frequent interruptions and delays. Plaintiff completed the portraits of defendant's wife and his daughter Caryn by August, 1946. Defendant paid the agreed price of $11,000 for the two completed portraits in August, 1946. Plaintiff substantially completed Mike's portrait and did some preliminary work on the portraits of defendant and his son Cyr. The last sitting on any of these portraits was on Mike's and took place in September, 1946.

I find that the plaintiff has established by a fair preponderance of the evidence that there was a valid oral contract between the parties, as alleged in the complaint and as set forth above, that the plaintiff was at all times ready, willing and able to and did perform his obligations thereunder (except as he was prevented by defendant from performing and except as noted below with respect to the portrait of Cyr), and that defendant breached the contract by failing to make himself and his children Mike and Cyr available for sittings, thereby preventing plaintiff from completing his performance of the contract.

These findings dispose of and necessarily reject defendant's contentions that the engagement was for plaintiff to paint only three separate portraits, namely, of defendant's wife, and his children Caryn and Mike.

On these findings and subject to the affirmative defenses hereafter discussed, the plaintiff would be entitled to recover the full amount of $17,000 sued for herein (less the small cost to plaintiff of completing the contract). However, I find that the contract in suit, insofar as it involves the portrait of defendant's youngest child, Cyr, was abandoned by the parties and hence the plaintiff is not entitled to recover the $6,000 fixed as the agreed price for Cyr's portrait. . . . And in a letter dated April 20, 1948, written at the plaintiff's request by Mr. Martin G. Jennings (who testified as a witness of Knoedler), and placed in evidence by plaintiff, Jennings stated:

> 'When I talked with Mr. Brockhurst yesterday, he told me he was very anxious to complete the portraits of you and your eldest son. He feels that the younger boy will have changed so much that he would have to forget about this one. . . .
>
> 'In order that we may close this transaction with Mr. Brockhurst, we would appreciate it very much if you would advise either of us just when you could, without too much inconvenience to yourself, arrange for this. He would like very much to finish both of these portraits before you and your family go to the country for the summer, and in view of its long standing, I hope very much you will be able to arrange this.'

* * *

The contract of the parties is clearly a divisible contract . . . ; 3 Williston on Contracts (Rev. ed.) Secs. 860a, 862. This is confirmed not only by the terms of the contract between the parties but as well by their intentions as demonstrated by the fact that two of the five separate portraits contracted for were completed and paid for at the separate contract prices therefor. Defendant's failure to cooperate in the performance of the contract by not producing Cyr for further sittings and plaintiff's acquiescence therein, as demonstrated by the aforementioned letter of April 20, 1948, establish, in my opinion, an abandonment of that part of the contract with respect to the painting of Cyr's portrait. The court may (and in this case does) infer such abandonment from the conduct of the parties and the attendant circumstances (6 Williston on Contracts (Rev. ed.) Sec. 1826). . . . Accordingly, and notwithstanding that defendant breached the agreement by failing to produce Cyr for sittings, the plaintiff is not entitled to recover the $6,000 which was agreed to be paid to him for Cyr's portrait.

This brings the court to the affirmative defenses of the statute of frauds and statute of limitations.

Defendant claims that the agreement in suit is unenforceable under the statute of frauds in that by its terms it was not to be performed within one year from the making thereof, Personal Property Law, § 31, subd. 1. The courts have held that if an oral agreement admits of performance within one year, although unlikely to be so performed, it is not within the prohibition of the statute of frauds. . . . The evidence establishes, and I find, that the parties contemplated completion of all of the portraits within a relatively short time; that plaintiff painted as many as 30 portraits a year, and that the contract was clearly capable of being performed within one year. Consequently, I hold that the defendant has not sustained his burden of establishing his defense of the statute of frauds.

The parties appear to agree, and the court decides, that the applicable statute of limitations is the six year statute, Civil Practice Act, § 48. The action was instituted on June 24, 1954 and hence would be barred by the statute of limitations if the cause of action accrued prior to June 24, 1948. The basic question to be determined, therefore, on the statute of limitations issue, is when the plaintiff's cause of action accrued.

The parties appear to agree, and the court decides, that where, as in the case at bar, no date or time of performance is specified in the contract, the parties have a reasonable time to perform and the cause of action accrues and the statute begins to run as soon as such reasonable time has expired. . . . It is, of course, clear that 'Reasonable time is not an inflexible term. It depends commonly upon the circumstances of each case.' . . .

Since the action was tried without a jury, the court must decide as a question of fact whether the cause of action accrued within or without the six year period prior to the institution of the action. It will be borne in mind that the transaction here in suit was not a commercial transaction. The evidence establishes that time was not considered by the parties to be vital or of the essence. The contract in suit was negotiated and performed (to the extent not aborted by the acts of the defendant) in an atmosphere of unhurried leisure. There were frequent cancellations and postponements of sittings at the request of the defendant and his family. Although the contract for the portraits was made in February, 1945, the second of the two completed portraits paid for by the defendant was not completed until August, 1946 and, as noted above, the last sitting (on Mike's portrait) took place in September, 1946. The portrait of defendant's wife, which had been completed by plaintiff in August, 1946, was not framed until the Spring of 1947.

At no time did the defendant give notice to the plaintiff of repudiation of the contract or of his intention not to submit himself and his family for further sittings. In the Spring of 1947, when the plaintiff and the defendant met at a cocktail party, the defendant requested the plaintiff 'When are we going to get down to these portraits?' and the plaintiff replied 'Any time you make a date'. While no inference is, or need be, made concerning defendant's failure to reply to the above quoted letter of April 20, 1948, I find that in the latter part of 1948 or the early part of 1949, Jennings, the writer of said letter, in a telephone conversation with the defendant, advised defendant that plaintiff had contacted Jennings with regard to further sittings and that defendant stated to Jennings that defendant would be in touch with plaintiff directly.

Since performance by defendant required affirmative action on his part, i.e., producing himself and his family for sittings, there can be no doubt that their failure to appear or arrange for sittings, if continued beyond a reasonable time, would constitute notice to plaintiff of defendant's repudiation and a cause of action would then have accrued. I am unable to find in this case that such reasonable time had expired by June 24, 1948.

* * *

In the court's opinion, a reasonable time for performance had not expired and the statute of limitations, therefore, did not begin to run until subsequent to June 24, 1948....

The damage recoverable by the plaintiff in this action is the contract price, less payments made and less the cost of completion.

Notes and Questions

1. *Satisfaction Standard.* In *Wolff,* the court simply held the artist to his written promise to the buyer that the portrait would be "to your entire satisfaction." Its decision is fully consistent with traditional contract doctrine and case law in upholding a subjective interpretation of satisfaction for cases involving "fancy, taste, sensibility or judgment." The artist attempted to push the interpretation of satisfaction "in this suit" to a more commercial and objective one because of the prior portrait. Simply stated, if the second portrait was substantially similar to the first, the buyer cannot arbitrarily reject it. Wolff argued, in essence, that a subjective interpretation of satisfaction is appropriate *only* in the first instance when the parties had not yet dealt with each other. The court was not persuaded.

If Wolff's letter to Smith only promised to "do all in my power to make the second portrait ... as outstanding and exact a likeness as the first one" and did not add "to your entire satisfaction," do you think that the decision would have been different? Why did the Sistine Chapel contract not contain a satisfaction standard?

Striking a proper balance between the artist's desire to be compensated for time and effort spent and the buyer's desire to buy something that is personally desirable is not an easy task, but it is a routine one. The commission agreements discussed below reveal one common approach. See Subpart 3. Private Commission Agreements, *infra*.

2. *Oral Art Commissions. Brockhurst*'s oral agreement is in line with the art world's casual tradition of handshake agreements. Despite the oft quoted "an oral contract is not worth the paper it's written on," an oral contract does not necessarily mean no contract. As long as the parties are competent, the subject matter is proper, there is consideration and a meeting of the minds, an oral agreement can be enforced. The party wishing to enforce the oral agreement must prove its terms, generally by showing the parties' actions with respect to each other, statements to others, and any written materials, including checks and letters. Having a written contract moves the discussion past these preliminary points. Brockhurst was, however, able to prove the contract relatively easily based on the actions of the Ryans in sitting for the portraits, the $11,000 payment for the completed portraits, and statements to others. Questions of contract formation based on oral understandings and the statute of frauds will resurface in more detail in Chapter 2, *infra*. One relevant point in the commissioning of an artwork is whether that agreement involves a good or service for purposes of the statute of frauds under relevant local law.

In deciding the statute of limitations issue, the court states the transaction was not a "commercial" transaction. What accounts for such an assertion? It seems somewhat odd given three objective indicia of commerce: the artist was a professional artist, the artist apparently had an agent, and the $28,000 price tag was a significant sum in 1945 ($404,229 in 2020). The "unhurried leisure" of performance may have something to do with it; if so, that characterization may be under revision. Today many portraits are done from photographs, not sittings. Does the substitution of photographs for sittings change the proof—either qualitatively or quantitatively—required to establish an oral contract?

The more likely reason for viewing art contracts as non-commercial is the theory of art exceptionalism, i.e., that art is different and therefore an exception to the normal rules of the marketplace. This view of art as noncommercial is currently challenged by the staggering prices some works can command and the parallel commodification and monetization of art. This evolutionary process is uneven, and the perception of art sales and contracts as qualitatively different from regular commercial contracts lingers. A lawyer needs to be aware of art exceptionalism, because it is a widely recognized theory, and sometimes, it happens to be true. Art exceptionalism is an important theme that will appear throughout this book.

The affirmative defenses of the statute of frauds and the statute of limitations are basically de rigueur for an oral agreement case, and we delve further into those defenses in Chapters 2 and 3. *Brockhurst* introduces the doctrine of abandonment and the notion of divisible contracts. Both concepts will resurface later. What would it take to make the *Brockhurst* transaction commercial? Would a written contract do it?

3. Private Commission Agreements

Transactional lawyers tend to agree with Professor Lon Fuller on the importance of observing contractual formalities in ordering business affairs. Lon Fuller, *Consideration and Form*, 41 Colum. L. Rev. 799 (1941). Having a written contract serves three principal functions: as evidence of the agreement's terms, as a cautionary mechanism against hasty actions and promises, and as a gate-keeping device for efficient use of judicial resources. Many working artists understand the utility of having a written agreement.

Consider the following two agreements. The first is an artist-drawn contract prepared by artist Robert Huitt, originally placed on his website, and used here with his permission. As you read through his agreement, notice what is important to him. The second art commission agreement is drafted by an attorney for his client the buyer. Not surprisingly, it has a decidedly different tone and a wider scope than Mr. Huitt's contract.

[Artist-Drawn]
Commission Agreement Between Artist and Client (Sample)

1. **Agreement**. This is an agreement between Robert Huitt ("the artist") and _______ ("the client") for the creation and transfer of the art work. All rights and liabilities of either party shall be governed by this agreement.

2. **Description of the work.** This work, to be created by the artist, shall be a portrait of ______ painted in oil on canvas, approximately _____ by ____ inches, unframed.

3. **Obligations of the artist and client.**

a) The artist shall create the work and pay for all necessary materials and supplies.

b) The artist shall deliver the work to the client and shall bear the expenses of crating and shipping the work, if any.

c) The client shall be responsible for framing the work.

4. **Start and completion dates.** The artist shall undertake the creation of the work on or about _______, and shall complete the work by _______.

5. **Fee and schedule of payments.** The client shall pay to the artist the sum of _____ in total payment for the work. The amount of ______ (25% of total) shall be paid at the time this agreement is signed by both parties. The balance of ______ (75% of total) shall be paid within ten days of the client's acceptance of the work.

6. **Acceptance of the work.** If the client is not satisfied with the completed work, the artist shall make reasonable changes in a good faith effort to satisfy the client's objections. If, following such changes, the client does not accept the work, the artist shall keep any portion of the fee already paid and shall retain ownership of the work.

7. **Title of ownership.** Title of ownership in the work shall pass from the artist to the client upon the client's full payment of the artist's fee.

Signature of the artist ________________________________ Date__________

Signature of the client ________________________________ Date__________

[Lawyer-drafted]
AGREEMENT TO COMMISSION ARTWORK

This Agreement (the "Agreement") is made and entered into as of the ___ day of ______, 20XX, by and between _________ ("the Artist") and _________ ("Buyer").

WHEREAS, the Artist is a recognized professional artist, and;

WHEREAS, the Buyer desires the Artist to create a work of art ("the Artwork") in the Artist's unique style, and;

NOW, THEREFORE, in consideration of the representations, warranties, covenants and agreements contained in this Agreement, the Artist and Buyer hereby agree to the foregoing and as follows:

1. **Description of the Artwork.** The Artist agrees to create the unframed Artwork, tentatively entitled View from the Porch, described as a landscape painting of the view from the front porch of the Buyer's ranch home in State A, in oil on canvas, approximately 36″ × 72″.

The Artist agrees to prepare a preliminary design by way of sketch or drawing of the Artwork for the approval of the Buyer. If approved by the Buyer, the preliminary design shall be deemed part of the Artwork.

2. **Price.** The Buyer agrees to pay the Artist the sum of US $100x for the Artwork, in accordance with the following schedule:

US $10x Upon the signing of this agreement;

US $15x Upon written approval of the preliminary design; and

Balance (plus any applicable sales tax) Upon completion of the work and its final approval and acceptance by Buyer.

3. **Time of Completion.** The Artist agrees to complete the preliminary design for the Artwork within _____ days of the signing of this agreement. The Artist further agrees to complete the Artwork within ______ days of the Buyer's written approval of the preliminary design. Notwithstanding the foregoing, in the event of the Artist's inability to timely complete the Artwork due to illness or other emergency, the Artist agrees to set a new date of completion but not more than ___ days beyond the original date of completion. In the further event of the Artist's inability to complete the Artwork (by the new date) due to death or other circumstance, this agreement shall terminate, and if the preliminary design has been approved by the Buyer, the Artist shall retain the payments made pursuant to Section 2, and the Buyer shall be entitled to the ownership of the preliminary design and the Artwork (to the extent that it is completed) without additional payment.

4. **Copyright.** Upon final approval, acceptance and payment in full by the Buyer, the Artist agrees to transfer the copyright to the Artwork to the Buyer in writing.

5. **Insurance.** The Artist agrees to keep the Artwork fully insured against loss or damage due to fire, theft or other casualty until final approval, acceptance and delivery to the Buyer.

6. **Warranty.** The Artist warrants that the design of the Artwork is the original product of said Artist's creative efforts. The Artist warrants that the artwork is unique, that it is an edition of one (1), that it has not been accepted for sale elsewhere, and that Artist has full authority to transfer the Artwork to the Buyer free of liens, claims, encumbrances, or interests of any person or entity.

7. **Approval and Acceptance.** The Buyer shall have the right in the Buyer's sole discretion to approve or reject the preliminary design in writing within ____ days of receipt of the preliminary design. The Buyer, in lieu of approval or rejection, may propose changes to the preliminary design, and the Artist shall have the right in the Artist's sole discretion to accept or reject such proposed changes within ____ days of receipt of such proposed changes.

If the Artist accepts any proposed change, the Artwork shall not be deemed a joint work, but shall remain the sole creation of the Artist.

The Buyer shall have the right in the Buyer's sole discretion to accept or reject the Artwork in writing within ____ days of being notified by the Artist of the Artwork's completion. If the Artwork is rejected by the Buyer, (a) the Artist shall retain payments made pursuant to Section 2, and the preliminary design and the completed Artwork shall be the property of the Artist, and (b) the Buyer shall not be required to make any additional payment.

8. **Integration and Governing Law.** This agreement contains all the covenants, promises, agreements, and conditions, either oral or written, between the parties and may not be changed or modified except in writing signed by the parties or their authorized representatives. The law of State B shall govern this agreement.

IN WITNESS WHEREOF, the parties have executed this agreement as of the date first set forth above.

______________________	______________________
Artist Signature	Buyer Signature
123 Main St.	456 Central St.
Anytown, State A	Thistown, State B
Telephone/email	Telephone/email

Notes and Questions

1. *Basic Contract Structure.* Comparing these two agreements with the 1481 Sistine Chapel Contract reveals structural similarities. Considering the over 500-year time difference, the representation of three different legal systems (civil law, canon law, and common law), and the identity of the drafting party (the buyer or the artist), the structural similarity is remarkable. The essence of all three contracts—across time, legal systems, and parties—is the same: this artist paints an artwork for this buyer. All contracts share the basics: the date, the parties involved, a description of the service, a time frame for completion, and a price (or, as in the Sistine Chapel contract, a recognized valuation mechanism).

No doubt you noticed that the modern contracts specifically deal with the buyer's satisfaction in a manner different from *Wolff*'s subjective "to your entire satisfaction" standard. The artist-drawn contract, for example, takes a pragmatic approach, agreeing to make "reasonable changes in a good faith effort" to address objections. This is exactly what Wolff tried to do with remedying the disparity in eye color, clothing, and so forth. The practical difference between the two is that Huitt protected his downside. He receives a 25% deposit upon the contract's execution that he retains. Wolff was to be paid only upon acceptance. In contrast, the Sistine Chapel Contract did not have a satisfaction standard or an agreed upon price, rather, an after-the-fact evaluation made by a panel of arbiters would determine value. That approach was consistent with prior practice and custom. Today, it is hard to imagine a commission agreement leaving price as an open term, yet the technique of having a panel of appraisers is commonplace in valuation disputes.

The artistic legacy of the simple Sistine Chapel Contract is an irreplaceable masterpiece of Western civilization; in this sense, the contract worked. Perhaps a more accurate assessment is that the contract, like most contracts, was not tested. The parties honored their agreement and worked out whatever questions arose in the course of the undertaking. Notice that the modern agreements reflect an acknowledgement that there could be differences of opinion on the acceptability of the artwork, and evidence an openness to working through disputes by providing a mechanism for approval and acceptance. The agreements go a step further and stipulate the parties' rights to monies paid and ownership of the work in the event of non-acceptance.

2. *Discussion Points for Commission Agreements.* At this introductory level of reviewing commission agreements, a good exercise is to compare the terms of the two agreements. The additional terms of the lawyer-drafted agreement reflect years of the lawyer's professional experiences as well as additional laws, cases, and human experiences. The following discussion points are not exhaustive but generally illustrate major themes.

a. Artist or buyer orientation. Do you think that the lawyer-drafted agreement is more pro-artist or pro-buyer in its form? Why? Remember, contracts are open to negotiation and negotiations need not be adversarial or hostile. For forms that "favor the artist," see Tad Crawford, BUSINESS AND LEGAL FORMS FOR FINE ARTISTS (4th ed. 2014); for a different perspective, see Ralph E. Lerner & Judith Bressler, 1 ART LAW: THE GUIDE FOR COLLECTORS, INVESTORS, DEALERS & ARTISTS (4th ed. 2013).

b. Description of artist. The lawyer-drafted agreement states that the artist is a recognized professional artist. Similarly, the agreement states the buyer wishes an artwork in the artist's unique style. What is the significance of these statements?

c. Description of artwork. The description of the artwork is critical but, unlike the proverbial commercial grade widgets, too closely describing the commissioned artwork can destroy the artistic impulse. Conversely, being too light on the description can result in a buyer's disappointment. But see Ellen Gamerman, *The Changing Face of Portraits*, WALL ST. J., Aug. 5, 2011 ("You have to understand that at least 50% . . . don't like [their] portrait," quoting Peter Brant). See also Taylor Dafoe, *Ringing in a New Era in Presidential Portraits*, ARTNETNEWS, Feb. 12, 2018, at https://news.artnet.com/exhibitions/obama-portrait-national-portrait-gallery-122162 (reporting how President Obama jokingly "unsuccessfully tried to negotiate 'less gray hair' and 'smaller ears'" with his portraitist Kehinde Wiley). An experienced buyer, already familiar with the artist's style, requires and pays for a preliminary design before the artist begins major work. This modest trust-but-verify measure helps both parties identify disagreements before larger sums of money and time are invested. See, e.g., the GSA-Alexander Calder contract description in Part B, *infra*.

Imagine you were the papal lawyer drafting the contract for Michelangelo's painting of the Sistine Chapel ceiling. How would you describe the ceiling painting? When Michelangelo began the initial "program" of the Apostles for the ceiling, "it seemed to come out poorly and I told the Pope that [the program] . . . seemed to produce a poor work." The Pope "then commissioned me to do what I wished." Thank goodness. Valerio Morriani, MICHELANGELO THE PAINTER 46 (1964), quoting from LETTERE DI MICHELANGELO BUONARROTI 121, 123 (G. Papini, preface 1913). See also Michelle O'Malley, *Subject Matters: Contracts, Designs and the Exchange of Ideas between Painters and Clients in Renaissance Italy*, in ARTISTIC EXCHANGE AND CULTURAL TRANSLATION IN THE ITALIAN RENAISSANCE CITY 32 (Stephen J. Campell & Stephen J. Miller eds., 2004) ("The evidence is that neither party considered the subject matter of a contract to be binding. . . .").

d. Secondary descriptive concerns. The type of artwork may require tweaking of the agreement. First, a description of a portrait, painting, sculpture, video, or photograph should include certain basics (medium, size, dimension or time, general content or style). Non-artistic presentation elements should be agreed upon; for example, framed or unframed for a painting or photograph, or a stand or base for a sculpture. Note that for some artworks, frames may be integral to the artwork and be considered part of the artwork.

Second, a piece, particularly a large one, may require installation expertise. If the piece is exposed to the elements, material specifications and maintenance requirements are important. Liability for improper installation is another consideration.

Third, the costs of fabricating and delivering a sculpture (and if it is a temporary installation, the costs of removing) can be significant. Clarifying who bears these costs is important. Structural engineers may need to be a part of the process.

Fourth, a buyer's privacy concerns, say for a child's portrait, may conflict with the artist's copyright and desire to promote his or her work.

e. Taxes briefly. The lawyer-drafted agreement specifically mentions that the buyer is to pay any applicable sales tax; the artist-drawn agreement is silent. In drafting the agreement, it is prudent to address sales tax. Two points are important. The first is the nature of the pertinent sales tax and the classification of a commission agreement. Sales tax in the U.S. is a matter of state and local law, not federal law. Consequently, there is a variety of approaches. Some jurisdictions impose a sales tax only on the sales of goods, and not on services; others impose the tax on both goods and services but create exclusions. In jurisdictions that do not tax services, if a commission agreement is deemed a service and not a sale of a good, no sales tax is due. Conversely, if it is deemed a sale of a good, i.e., the portrait, a sales tax could be due. In jurisdictions that tax services, however, sometimes an artist's service may be excluded.

The second point involves the interstate application of state and local sales taxes. In general, if a resident of State A makes a purchase from State B and takes delivery only in State A, without more, State B does not impose its state and local sales tax. State A, however, may impose a use tax on its resident buyer. In 2016, New York refined its view on when possession is transferred from a dealer to an out-of-state buyer for sales tax purposes. Gagosian Gallery Inc. paid a $4.28 million settlement to New York because, in selling significant amount of art from its New York gallery, it used specialty art handlers that were not considered common carriers. As such, delivery to those art handlers was deemed delivery to the buyer in New York. Consequently, the state's sales tax should have been collected. New York State Attorney general Press Release, A.G. Schneiderman Announces $4.28 Million Settlement with International Art Dealer Gagosian Gallery for Failure to Collect and Remit New York Sales Tax (July 11, 2016), at https://ag.ny.gov/press-release/2016/ag-schneiderman-announces-428-million-settlement-international-art-dealer. Do not avoid or evade local sales tax by phantom shipping to another location out of state, such as a vacation home. See, e.g., Timothy L. O'Brien, *Corporate Art Lovers Who Hate That Big Tax Bill*, N.Y. Times, May 9, 2004, at B1 (describing New York authorities' 2002 criminal investigation into New York art market's sales tax compliance).

A variation on this second point involves the use of special art storage facilities situated in locations that are tax-advantaged. Geneva, Switzerland is one of the oldest freeports. For art purchases that are more investment oriented than a personal collection, placing artworks in freeports typically avoids the payment of import and export taxes and affords safe and secure storage. Sam Knight, *The Bouvier Affair*, New Yorker, Feb. 8, 2016, at www.newyorker.com/magazine/2016/02/08/the-bouvier-affair. Domestic art storage facilities also exist. Graham Bowley, *Art Collectors Find Safe Harbor in Delaware's Tax Laws*, N.Y. Times, Oct. 26, 2015, at www.nytimes.com/2015/10/26/arts/design/art-collectors-find-safe-harbor-in-delawares-tax-laws.

f. Governing law. An agreement should specify the governing law. A related matter concerns specifying the forum for resolution of disputes—should litigation be the presumed option? Some believe disputes may be better served by alternative methods such as arbitration or mediation. What factors would you consider in choosing litigation over alternative methods for disputes involving art commissions? The Court of Arbitration for Art (CAfA) in The Netherlands is a recent addition for art disputes. See www.cafa.world.

3. *Non-commissioned Purchases from Artist.* Not all acquisitions directly from an artist are commissioned pieces; many are works from the artist's existing inventory. Buying an artwork already in existence is a very different experience than commissioning a new work. The decision to buy is totally independent of a contractual obligation, and therefore voluntary from the buyer's perspective. One contractual concern may be the artist's right to sell—the artist may have entered into an exclusive sales arrangement with a particular dealer or gallery. If so, the sale by the artist of his own work may be a breach of that exclusive sales agreement. The legal consequence is not generally to the buyer, but to the artist who may be liable for damages to the dealer or gallery. There is a related issue, however, from the opposite perspective. An artist may impose a resale restriction on the buyer, such as prohibiting a sale within three years. That could impact a buyer's decision to dispose of the

artwork. See, e.g., MAFG Art Fund, LLC. v. Gagosian, 2014 WL 359341 (N.Y. Sup. Ct. 2014), Chapter 2, *infra*.

4. *Permissive Certificates*. A more complex state of affairs concerns conceptual art that is covered by permissive certificates. These certificates, some dating from the 1960s, can purport to authenticate an unconstructed artwork and instruct the buyer how to realize the artwork and install it. The artist Felix Gonzalez-Torres's work, *Untitled* 1989/1990, is two stacks of paper about 26 inches in height that is printed fresh for each exhibition. Each paper in each stack bears one line of authorized text. The artist intends for people to take a sheet from the stacks, which is why there is authorization to reprint and repeat the process. The Certificate of Authenticity and Ownership for the artwork served to "reassure owners who found it difficult to see how an idea could be a unique work of art." These certificates that grant the right to reprint the Gonzalez-Torres stacks have sold at auction for $770,500 and $1.65 million. Peter J. Karol, *Permissive Certificates: Collectors of Art as Collectors of Permissions*, 94 WASH. L. REV. 1175 (2019); see also Alessandra Donati, *The Legal Relevance of Documentation for Contemporary Art: The Authenticity of Documents and Artworks*, in ARTISTS' ARCHIVES AND ESTATES: CULTURAL MEMORY BETWEEN LAW AND MARKET/ARCHIVI D'ARTISTA E LASCITI: MEMORIE CULTURALI TRA DIRITTO E MERCATO (Alessandra Donati et al. eds., 2018). The artist's moral right of attribution can also be involved. See Noland v. Janssen, 2020 WL 2836464 (S.D.N.Y. 2020), Chapter 7, *infra*.

5. *A Celebratory Commission*. Richard Polsky is an independent art dealer and the author of I SOLD ANDY WARHOL (TOO SOON) (2009). He tells a particularly engaging story of a client couple's quest that culminates in the couple's purchase of *Sunset* by Roy Lichtenstein. To mark the deal and celebrate his 30th anniversary in the business, he "wracked (his) brain thinking about what to treat (him)self to." As he savored his wine and music, he looked at a favorite painting of his and inspiration hit. He called the artist.

> "Hello Bill, I was just enjoying *Rain on the Mesa* and would like to commission you to do a small painting for me. Perhaps you could return to the same spot, just as the sun is setting, maybe give it a *warm yellow*?"

Richard Polsky, I SOLD ANDY WARHOL (TOO SOON) 249 (2009).

Happily, Bill Anton accepted the commission, and Richard Polsky has a new painting, *Morning at Sycamore Canyon*. There was no written contract. Polsky believes the highly personal nature of the business equates written agreements with a lack of trust, and that in turn, would destroy the spirit of the deal. E-mail from Richard Polsky (Jan. 10, 2011, 9:53 A.M.).

B. Public Commissions

1. *Brief History of Federal Commissions.* Direct public support of the arts through artists' commissions is part of U.S. history. The federal government, a majority of states, and many municipalities today have programs for the purchase or commissioning of artworks for public buildings and spaces.

At the federal level, the first program of fine arts in federal buildings began in 1855 when Congress hired Constantino Brumidi to paint committee rooms for $8 a day, and later, the 4,664 square foot fresco in the Capitol dome for $40,000.* The next significant federal effort occurred during the Great Depression. Artists such as Jackson Pollock, Mark Rothko, and David Smith worked at one point or another for the most well-known program, the Works Progress Administration (WPA).

The wartime economy halted the federal arts programs in the 1940s. In 1949, the newly created General Services Administration (GSA) received control of the federal buildings arts program. It wasn't until 1962 that the program attracted strong political support such that the GSA announced the policy that one half of one percent of estimated construction costs of new federal buildings over $250,000 would be allocated for fine art. This worked well until 1966, when funds were again frozen for economic reasons. In 1972, the fine arts program was restored to the GSA. See GSA News Release, Fine Art in Federal Buildings (April 20, 1973). The GSA reserves one-half of one percent of the estimated construction cost of each new federal building for the Art in Architecture Program. See www.gsa.gov/real-estate/design-construction/art-in-architecture-fine-arts/art-in-architecture-program. A panel of experts select the project artists from GSA's National Artist Registry, which is open to all American artists. Under the GSA's Art in Architecture Policies and Procedures, the parties will use the Art in Architecture Contract template that can be supplemented if necessary.

2. *Calder and Serra: A Tale of Two Commissions.* On April 16, 1973, GSA commissioned Alexander Calder to create an outdoor sculpture for the new federal plaza in Chicago. It was the first commissioned artwork under the new federal percent for art program. The contract "GS-00-B-2057 (PCCS)" consisted of a two-page fill-in-the-blank form that described Calder's $250,000 work as follows:

> This project will consist of the creation, production, and delivery of an art form, generally described as a stabile, to the Federal Center Plaza in Chicago, Illinois, immediately north of the Federal Office Building now under construction at West Adams and Dearborn Streets as indicated on Attachment Y of this contract. The red painted steel stabile will a.) be approximately fifty (50) feet high, b.) conform generally to the maquette shown in Attachments X and Y of this contract, c.) be delivered unassembled to the

* That Rotunda painting, the Apotheosis of George Washington, played an important role in Dan Brown's 2009 novel, THE LOST SYMBOL.

site for subsequent installation by the Government, and d.) be executed in an artistic and professional manner befitting fine art.

This form incorporated by reference another standard federal form, General Provisions (Architect-Engineer Contract), with modifications and special provisions for the Calder artwork. Those special provisions included a detailed scope of Calder's services, time specific schedule (for submissions, inspections, and payments), reproduction rights to government, insurance requirements, and guarantees as to structural integrity. In October, 1974, as the stabile *Flamingo* was ready for installation, the parties modified the contract to switch the installation responsibility from the GSA to Calder. *Flamingo*'s "bold cut relates well to all the Miesian geometry surrounding it. It . . . best suits its site." Franz Schultze, *Picasso, Calder and Chagall in Chicago*, ARTNEWS 52 (Dec. 1974).

The GSA's 1979 commission agreement with Richard Serra for *Tilted Arc* (a 120-foot long steel sculpture, 12 feet high, weighing 73 tons) was not as smooth. Serra v. U.S. General Services Administration, 847 F.2d 1045 (2d Cir. 1988). Serra's $175,000 "site specific" sculpture was installed in Federal Plaza in lower Manhattan in July 1981. Its placement cut "a swath across the center of Federal Plaza, dividing it in two," creating controversy almost immediately. After years of debate and a public hearing, GSA decided to relocate the sculpture in 1986. Serra sued claiming breach of contract, copyright and trademark violations, state law violations, and free speech and due process violations. The court determined that it lacked jurisdiction to hear Serra's contract, copyright, trademark and state law claims, because the United States did not waive sovereign immunity. In affirming the trial court's dismissal of Serra's complaint on the constitutional challenges, the Second Circuit emphasized the parties' contract:

> "Tilted Arc" is entirely owned by the Government and is displayed on Government property. Serra relinquished his own speech rights in the sculpture when he voluntarily sold it to GSA; if he wished to retain some degree of control as to the duration and location of the display of his work, he had the opportunity to bargain for such rights in making the contract for the sale of his work.

847 F.2d. 1045, 1049 (2d Cir. 1988).

> Serra has no protected property interest in the continued display of "Tilted Arc" at Federal Plaza. Pursuant to Serra's contract, the sculpture is the property of the GSA, not the artist.

Id. at 1052.

In March 1989, *Tilted Arc* was finally removed from Federal Plaza. Relocating the site-specific work to another location was apparently not possible; it was sent to a Brooklyn warehouse. Do you think Serra understood the contract he signed? Is there anything his attorney could or should have done differently? The court noted that Serra could have bargained for some degree of control. For some artists, whether it is possible to have equal bargaining power with the federal government may be debatable. In 1990, the United States enacted the Visual Artists Rights Act of 1990 (VARA). It recognizes an artist's moral rights, an ongoing nonpecuniary interest in certain artworks, specifically including the right of integrity. Today, Serra's concerns about his site-specific work and his ongoing nonpecuniary interests in it could receive a very different reception under VARA. See Chapter 7, *infra*.

3. *Presidential Portraits: A Blend of Public and Private.* The National Portrait Gallery includes the exhibit American Presidents. It is the only place outside the White House with a complete collection of presidential portraits. Since the presidency of George H.W. Bush, the portraits are paid for by private donations. Current commissioning practice is to have the President and First Lady select their portraitists from portfolios presented by the Portrait Gallery. President and Mrs. Obama, for example, chose Kehinde Wiley and Amy Sherald for their respective portraits. They are the first African-American artists so selected. The cost of the Obamas' portraits was reportedly $500,000, including costs for the unveiling ceremony and future care. See Roberta Smith, *Why the Obamas' Portrait Choices Matter*, N.Y. Times, Oct. 17, 2017, at C1.

4. *Public Monuments.* Cities across the nation often have public monuments on public land. Controversy over some monuments have led to some being defaced, toppled, or destroyed; while others have been removed by authorities. When a public monument or artwork is commissioned by a public body, what factors should be considered by the commissioning body? See, e.g., National Endowment for the Arts v. Finley, 524 U.S. 569 (1998) (discussing government speech and viewpoint discrimination).

First Drafting Exercise: Commission Agreement

To: Junior Associate

From: Senior Partner

Our client, Mr. Smith, wishes to commission Ms. Jameson, a well-known sculptor, to create a private memorial to his deceased wife, Mrs. Smith. He envisions the sculpture will initially be installed at Mr. Smith's lake home in the outdoor sculpture garden. He currently envisions the sculpture will be donated to a local arts center, college, or church at some point in the future.

Mr. and Mrs. Smith had contracted previously with Ms. Jameson for a work that was a source of great beauty and pleasure to the entire Smith family. For Ms. Jameson, that work was also a source of professional pride, as it received critical acclaim. Mr. Smith, who is now 80, wants the sculpture completed and installed by June 15 of next year, which would have been Mrs. Smith's 75th birthday.

He and Mrs. Smith had in the past opened their lake home and sculpture garden to the public as part of various fundraising efforts for local charities. Mr. Smith hopes to continue doing so.

Mr. Smith and Ms. Jameson are both residents of State X. Mr. Smith's lake home is in State Y. Assume the agreed upon price for the artist's services is $100X. Please draft a contract for my review and give me a heads-up on any nonobvious assumptions you have made.

Chapter 2

Acquisition by Purchase Involving Dealer or Gallery

For centuries, art has been bought and sold through dealers and galleries. The cultivated tradition of image, dignity, and gentility was largely based on a cultural norm that a gentleman's handshake sealed the deal. The market tradition is yielding to modern commercial norms, although not without transitional gasps of confusion. Fitting the oral contract tradition into the documentation model of modern business law requires an understanding of the statutory and common law elements of contract formation. Those contracts may be domestic or international in scope. In addition, a dealer's conduct may raise concerns about breach or scope of authority from the buyer's perspective.

A. Proving the Contract

1. Domestically

Hoffmann and *Marvin Inc.* provide eyewitness-type accounts of how art dealers manage their U.S. markets. *Hoffmann* involves a highly prized New York gallery exhibition where the plaintiff believes his conversation and actions with the dealer, in light of his prior dealings, created an oral agreement to purchase. In *Marvin Inc.*, a dealer momentarily changed sides; he acts as a buyer alleging the existence of an oral agreement. In neither case is the alleged oral contract upheld, because neither plaintiff could overcome the statute of frauds defense.

Hoffmann v. Boone

708 F. Supp. 78 (S.D.N.Y. 1989)

MUKASEY, J.

* * *

I. Background

Other than agreeing that no written contract exists, the parties concur on few of the specifics surrounding the alleged oral contract. Mary Boone states that, at an exhibition of Marden's works mounted by her gallery, Paul Hoffmann approached her and asked whether "Grey # 1" was for sale. Boone quoted a price of $125,000.

According to her, Hoffmann "neither offered to purchase 'Grey # 1' for $125,000 nor did I agree to sell 'Grey # 1' to Hoffmann at any price. At most, Mr. Hoffmann and I discussed entering into a sales contract but no specific terms were agreed on." Boone further avers that her gallery ordinarily sends an invoice after an agreement is made; no such invoice exists here. Finally, the painting remained on display for the remainder of the exhibit.

Paul Hoffmann's version of the events, needless to say, is very different. Hoffmann claims he came at defendant's request to view the exhibition before its opening. The Hoffmanns in the past had purchased 16 paintings from the gallery at a total price of $500,000, including a Marden—all pursuant to oral agreements. On April 7, Hoffmann flew to New York from Florida. At the gallery, Hoffmann asked defendant the price for "Grey # 1;" defendant quoted a price of $120,000. Hoffmann then placed a "reserve" on the painting ensuring that defendant would not sell the painting without contacting him. Hoffmann told defendant that he needed approval from his wife and would call the gallery on April 9. Back in Florida, he arranged to have his wife see the painting. On April 15, he and his wife met defendant at the gallery. Having secured his wife's approval, Hoffmann told defendant that he wanted the painting; defendant agreed to sell it. . . .

Several days after the April 15 meeting, defendant called Hoffmann and told him that she and Marden felt a different painting, "Blue," would be more appropriate for Hoffmann's collection. Hoffmann "requested that [defendant] sent [*sic*] transparencies of both paintings to me for review." After looking at the transparencies, the Hoffmanns decided they preferred "Grey # 1" and so informed defendant. On May 3, Mr. Hoffmann tried unsuccessfully to meet with defendant to arrange to ship the painting, but received no response.

II. Discussion

Both sides agree that this alleged oral contract is governed by the Uniform Commercial Code (UCC), as enacted into law by the New York legislature, because it involves the sale of goods at a price in excess of $500. Defendant contends that the statute of frauds, UCC § 2-201(1) (McKinney 1986), bars enforcement of the oral agreement:

> (1) Except as otherwise provided in this section a contract for the sale of goods at a price of $500 or more is not enforceable by way of action or defense unless there is some writing sufficient to indicate that a contract has been made between the parties and signed by the party against whom enforcement is sought. . . .

Plaintiffs assert the applicability of only one of the UCC's exceptions to the writing requirement: an oral contract is enforceable if the party against whom enforcement is sought admits in his court pleadings or testimony that the contract was made. UCC § 2-201(3)(b). Defendant, however, has filed an affidavit explicitly averring that no agreement was entered into. Judge Posner, faced with the same situation in *DF Activities Corp. v. Brown*, 851 F.2d 920, 922 (7th Cir.1988), held that a plaintiff cannot survive summary judgment by contending that the defendant might change her tune at trial or at a deposition and admit that an oral agreement was in fact made. I find Judge Posner's view compelling and adopt it.

Plaintiffs also contend that defendant is barred by the doctrine of promissory estoppel, Restatement of Contracts Second, § 217A, from relying on the statute of frauds. A threshold question is whether New York recognizes estoppel in UCC cases. A number of state courts have ruled that estoppel principles are inapplicable in contracts governed by the UCC because, otherwise, the explicit exceptions to the writing requirement, which exceptions appear in § 2-201, would be undermined. Other jurisdictions allow promissory estoppel to prevent the statute of frauds from being used as an instrument of fraud.

Although the New York Court of Appeals has yet to address this issue, several appellate and trial court decisions have simply applied estoppel principles to UCC actions without acknowledging that such application is itself a matter of dispute. In the absence of contrary state court precedent, federal courts applying New York UCC law have assumed that estoppel principles are applicable to UCC-governed contracts. Unless and until the New York Court of Appeals rules otherwise, I shall follow the decisions of the intermediate courts, *Commissioner v. Estate of Bosch,* 387 U.S. 56, 465, 87 S.Ct. 1776, 1782–83, 18 L.Ed.2d 886 (1967), and hold that estoppel principles are applicable to UCC contracts, a result that accords generally with the UCC's stated goal of preserving common law principles of equity like promissory estoppel. UCC § 1-103.

The elements of promissory estoppel in New York are (1) a clear and unambiguous promise; (2) reasonable and foreseeable reliance on that promise; and (3) an unconscionable injury. Plaintiffs contend that all their previous agreements with defendant were never reduced to writing, thus satisfying the reliance requirement at this stage of the pleadings.

Plaintiffs also allege that defendant made a clear promise, although Hoffmann's own account of his actions belies somewhat his contention that a clear and unambiguous promise was made. If he believed that he had already purchased Grey # 1, one would imagine that he would reject outright defendant's suggestion that he consider a different painting instead. However, because defendant might conceivably guarantee that one painting was Hoffmann's while still offering him the chance to purchase another in its place, I find that plaintiffs have adduced sufficient facts at this stage to suggest a clear and unambiguous promise.

Plaintiffs claim several injuries to meet the last requirement necessary to make out an estoppel-unconscionable injury. First, plaintiffs traveled to New York from Florida three times in order to settle the contract. Second, plaintiffs included the painting in listings for a planned exhibition of their collection at Chicago's Museum of Contemporary Art in December 1988. Finally, plaintiffs aver that Grey # 1's "special characteristics led us to purchase this particular painting and not to purchase other unsold Marden works which were part of the Exhibit at the Gallery or to wait until the next Marden exhibition to purchase a Marden painting."

New York courts, however, do not regard such injuries as unconscionable, even assuming *arguendo* that they are all traceable to the alleged promise. Thus, "[a] change of job or residence . . . by itself is not sufficient to call promissory estoppel into play. . . ." *Swerdloff* [*v. Mobil Oil Corp.*, 427 N.Y.S.2d 266, 270 (2d Dep't.)]. Foregoing other business opportunities similarly is not enough. *Id.* Nor is a claim that a plaintiff worked "endless hours" in the expectation of a dealership sufficient to invoke estoppel. *Id.* Plaintiffs' failure to purchase another Marden and their embarrassment in connection with the show at the Chicago museum are nothing more than part of the usual disappointment that attends a failed deal.

There is simply no evidence here that plaintiffs expended significant resources in reliance on the agreement. . . . Granting plaintiffs every conceivable inference in their favor, as I must on a motion for summary judgment, they have shown only two instances of injury in any form. Mr. Hoffmann's trip to New York to visit the gallery on May 3, to the extent that Hoffmann traveled solely to meet with defendant, and any possible costs involved in reprinting the catalog for plaintiffs' showing at the Chicago museum, to the extent that Hoffmann rather than the museum paid for the catalog, are minor and thus insufficient without more to meet New York's requirement of an *unconscionable* injury. That this alleged deal involved art rather than vans and trailers, and therefore engaged esthetic and perhaps egoistic considerations in addition to crass economic ones, is legally irrelevant in my view.

* * *

Accordingly, summary judgment for defendant is appropriate. The complaint is dismissed.

Marvin Inc. v. Albstein

386 F. Supp. 2d 247 (S.D.N.Y. 2005)

BATTS, J. * * * At the center of this dispute . . . is a Painting ("the Painting"), described minimally as "a superior work from a highly desired period" in a "well-known" artist's oeuvre, so as to "minimize the potential damage to the Painting's reputation and value." It became known to Plaintiff that Iris W. Albstein ("I. Albstein") was the representative of the owner of the Painting. . . .

. . . Mr. de Sarthe, President of Marvin Inc., contacted I. Albstein and began discussions for purchase of the Painting. Drafts of a proposed written contract were passed back and forth between the Parties. . . .

Parties agree that there was no final written contract for the purchase of the Painting. However, Plaintiff alleges that on or about January 20, 2004, after Mr. de Sarthe inspected the Painting, I. Albstein orally agreed to sell Plaintiff the Painting for $250,000. Based upon this agreement between the Parties, Plaintiff states that it agreed to sell the Painting to one of its clients for an amount higher than $250,000. Plaintiff alleges that Defendant knew of this agreement to resell the Painting.

Plaintiff then attempted to obtain written wire instructions from I. Albstein but I. Albstein "offered a variety of excuses and pretexts" for failing to do so, and on February 19, 2004, communicated to Plaintiff's attorney that the purchase price of the Painting was $300,000, not $250,000.

Mr. de Sarthe placed several telephone calls to I. Albstein, which he recorded. Plaintiff highlights one particular conversation that demonstrates, according to Plaintiff, that I. Albstein "repeatedly acknowledged the Agreement and the commitment to sell the Painting to Mr. [de] Sarthe for $250,000." That conversation, held on February 19, 2004 is excerpted below:

> de Sarthe: We did have an agreement for $250,000 to purchase [the Painting] and I got a call from Mr. Stern telling me now that you want 50,000 more.
>
> Albstein: Right. No, that's—that's correct, because of some other things that had happened. I—I—I wanted him to discuss it with you and instead I got back a barrage of threats. . . .
>
> de Sarthe: I wanted to call you because, I mean, we did have an agreement and a price that we have agreed to. The only thing I was waiting for was the bank information and a signed contract.
>
> Albstein: That's right. And a signed contract. And so what—my brother got some additional information and had asked me to open this up for discussion and instead what I received were absolute inappropriate threats.
>
> de Sarthe: I don't know. Mr. Stern was not authorized to—I just found out what you are saying. . . . In this case, we had an agreement. Somebody changed the terms of the agreement at the last minute. [. . .]
>
> Albstein: If you remember when we first spoke, you—we had talked about 300,0000.
>
> de Sarthe: Yes, but it—
>
> Albstein: I know it changed afterward. I am not saying no.
>
> de Sarthe: You accepted $250,000.
>
> Albstein: Right. I understand that, but the threats were really unnecessary. I was forced to convey them—[. . .]
>
> de Sarthe: You know we had an agreement at $250,000.
>
> Albstein: Right. . . . Unfortunately I guess or fortunately in time something else comes up in between, and that's why you know something—in—in—you know, you're not bound until something is in—is in writing, um, which I am sure he—[. . .]
>
> de Sarthe: You are the one who told me "Will you pay 250,000?" and I said yes, and we have agreed—
>
> Albstein: Right.

de Sarthe: — to the price. . . .

On February 20, 2004, I. Albstein informed Mr. de Sarthe that the Painting would not be sold to Plaintiff. [On that same day, Plaintiff filed his complaint requesting specific performance and damages. — Ed.]

* * *

II. Discussion

Defendant moves to dismiss the Amended Complaint on the ground that the claims are barred by the Statute of Frauds, and for failure to state a claim.

* * *

3. Statute of Frauds

Under § 2-201(1) of the New York Uniform Commercial Code, "a contract for the sale of goods for the price of $500 or more is not enforceable by way of action of defense unless there is some writing sufficient to indicate that a contract for sale has been made between the parties and signed by the party against whom enforcement is sought or by his authorized agent or broker."

However, there are several exceptions to the Statute of Frauds defense. The exception applicable to this matter, also known as the "Judicial Admissions" exception, is contained in § 2-201(3) of the New York Uniform Commercial Code. Section 2-201(3)(b) states that even if there is no written contract, a contract is nonetheless enforceable "if the party against whom enforcement is sought admits in his pleading, testimony or otherwise in court that a contract for sale was made."

Courts have allowed actions to go forward despite the assertion of a Statute of Frauds defense if it appears that the Judicial Admissions exception may apply. . . .

However, if there has been an opportunity for an admission, courts have found the Judicial Admissions exception inapplicable and dismissed the action as barred by the Statute of Frauds. *See Hoffmann v. Boone,* 708 F.Supp. 78, 80 (S.D.N.Y.1989) (holding that UCC § 2-201(3)(b) did not render a contract enforceable because the defendant had filed an affidavit stating that no agreement had been entered into). . . . Where a Defendant "has filed an affidavit explicitly averring that no agreement was entered into . . . a plaintiff cannot survive summary judgment by contending that the defendant might change her tune at trial or at a deposition and admit that an oral agreement was in fact made." *Hoffmann v. Boone,* 708 F.Supp. at 80.

Plaintiff relies upon one particular telephone conversation with Iris Albstein that took place on February 19, 2004, as the basis for asserting that the Statute of Frauds defense does not apply in this case. In the conversation, Plaintiff claims I. Albstein told Mr. de Sarthe that there was an agreement to purchase the Painting for $250,000.

I. Albstein has submitted an affidavit where she states that:

> It was always my understanding that no binding contract would exist until a written agreement was fully negotiated and executed by each of the

> parties. Nor was I authorized to bind Defendant to sell the Painting without a signed written agreement.... No contract for the purchase of the Painting was ever signed by Defendant.... It was never my belief or understanding that a binding contract for the purchase of the Painting had been formed. Nor did I make such a representation to Mr. de Sarthe or any of his representatives.

Plaintiff responds to the affidavit by stating that if faced with the transcripts of the telephone conversation in a deposition, I. Albstein "will have to 'change her tune.'"

The Court finds that the Judicial Admissions exceptions is not applicable. I. Albstein has submitted an affidavit clearly rejecting that she entered into a binding agreement with Plaintiff. There is no reason to believe that I. Albstein will "change her tune" in a deposition after she has submitted a sworn affidavit, and after she has become aware that Plaintiff recorded her conversations with Mr. de Sarthe. Furthermore, the Court's own examination of the telephone conversation between Mr. de Sarthe and I. Albstein reveals no indication that Ms. Albstein admitted to such an agreement. In fact, the conversation, when read as a whole, indicates that I. Albstein understood that she would not be bound by any contract until a written contract had been signed by the Parties.

As there is no written contract between the Parties, the Statute of Frauds defense applies. Defendant's Motion for Summary Judgment dismissing the claims alleging breach of contract and requesting specific performance is GRANTED.

B. Promissory Estoppel

Under New York law, a plaintiff must prove three elements to succeed on a claim of promissory estoppel: "(1) a clear and unambiguous promise, (2) reasonable and foreseeable reliance by the promisee, and (3) unconscionable injury to the relying party as a result of the reliance."

Plaintiff argues that I. Albstein made a clear and unambiguous promise to Mr. de Sarthe to sell the Painting for $250,000 on January 20, 2004, upon which Plaintiff reasonably relied upon in its contract with a client to resell the Painting. The injury is unconscionable, according to Plaintiff because of the "severe financial loss," and the loss of one of its most important clients.

The Court finds that there was not a clear and unambiguous promise upon which Plaintiff reasonably relied upon. Furthermore, Plaintiff, an art dealer, entered into negotiations to purchase the Painting, for the purpose of reselling the Painting to one of its clients. The unenforcement of the agreement would clearly result in the inability to resell the Painting. The Court finds that Plaintiff has failed to allege unconscionable injury that does not naturally flow from the unenforcement of the agreement.

Defendant's Motion to Dismiss the promissory estoppel claim is GRANTED.

* * *

III. Conclusion

For the foregoing reasons, Defendant's Motion for Summary Judgment [and] Defendant's Motion to Dismiss the fraud and promissory estoppel claims are . . . GRANTED.

Notes and Questions

1. *Statute of Frauds Defense.* In both *Hoffmann* and *Marvin Inc.*, the plaintiffs alleged the existence of an oral contract to purchase a painting, and the defendants moved to dismiss based on the statute of frauds. In terms of contract litigation, this description is pretty unremarkable. It would be surprising if an allegation of an oral contract was not met by the defense of the statute of frauds.

This procedural routineness highlights the difficult reality of proving an enforceable oral contract to purchase an artwork. If you cannot survive a motion to dismiss, you cannot tell your story at trial. In this context, the following five notes concerning the statute of frauds in the art market context deserve special attention.

2. *Tradition and Culture in Dealer Transactions.* The tradition and culture of the art industry contribute mightily to the statute of frauds defense in dealer transactions. The lack of a written contract is the most obvious factor, but the combination of a dealer's market-making, art's fluid value, and a seller's expectation of a discrete confidentiality, create uncertainty for a buyer. For example, a gallery's representation of an artist in the primary market can mean the artist's new works are initially offered exclusively at that gallery. For unique works of a highly-prized artist, that exclusive arrangement can make the actual acquisition by a buyer more challenging. Two buying protocols are illustrative. First, unlike a relatively common ten percent gallery discount, there is little or no room for price negotiation. In this instance, art from a highly-prized artist in the initial offering conforms to normal purchases, i.e., the store's written price is the price. The second point is buyer-specific and feels undemocratic. In an exclusive representation, a dealer may prefer a sale to one party rather than to another because of the party's elevated status as a discerning collector. Having the cachet of that party's name on the work's provenance is an imprimatur for the artist and the work's value and desirability. That, in turn, supports and perhaps enhances the market for the artist's works. It is straightforward market-making. See Sarah Thornton, SEVEN DAYS IN THE ART WORLD (2008), for a highly readable picture of the "statusphere" of the art market.

In *Marvin Inc.*, the painting's identity was confidential to minimize potential damage to its reputation and value. How does identifying the painting in the court case damage its value? Is there a generic taint associated with litigation or is it that the alleged sales price is now known and no longer speculative?

Let's consider why a seller chooses to sell through a dealer instead of at auction, and also consider the multiple sources for the artworks a dealer offers for sale. Those two considerations interact to create uncertainty for a buyer.

Art owners who sell privately through a dealer do so for a number of legitimate reasons. Private sales can be more efficient than auction sales in terms of time and expense, because private sales are not tied to the auction calendar and its significant expenses. *See* Chapter 9, *infra*. Many prefer the quiet, confidential marketplace of a private sale precisely because they do not want the greater art world to know of the sale. This could be for personal reasons, including personal and household safety or a fear that a public sale could signal financial weakness. It could also be for market valuation reasons. In times of economic uncertainty, sellers may prefer to avoid the additional uncertainty of the auction process. Failure to sell at a public sale or auction could damage a work's value; the artwork is deemed burnt. Because of these concerns, confidentiality agreements are important. This confidentiality, however, can blur the lines between the sources of a dealer's art and undermine the seller's ownership interests when entrusting the work to the dealer for sale. See Lindholm v. Brant, 925 A.2d 1048 (Conn. 2007), *infra*. The layers of confidentiality may also compromise the buyer's acquisition.

The artworks offered for sale by a dealer primarily come from three sources. First, a dealer may represent an artist, as in *Hoffmann*. Second, a dealer may represent a secondary owner on a consignment basis or as a broker. Third, a dealer may own the artwork outright. There can be slippage between a work on consignment with a dealer and the dealer's offering it for sale as his own, as was the case in *Lindholm, infra*. In *Marvin Inc.*, the slippage was due to an anticipated flip, i.e., de Sarthe's plan to sell the artwork to a client even before de Sarthe owned it. Because the buyer is not historically privy to the work's current ownership status, any slippage (whether due to theft, conversion, or flipping) can create uncertainty for the buyer. Ultimately, the confidentiality undermines the integrity of the market.

3. *Applicability of UCC § 2-201(1).* The alleged oral contracts in *Hoffmann* and *Marvin Inc.* were for the purchase of paintings for more than $500, which neatly seems to fit the requirements for the UCC's statute of frauds. Historically, some expressed doubt as to the applicability of the UCC to artworks. One argument was that the UCC deals with tangible personal property and an artwork is more than tangible personal property, it also includes intangible rights. Cf. Fink v. DeClassis, 745 F. Supp. 509 (N.D. Ill. 1990) (Article 2 of UCC deemed not applicable to sale by one corporation of its product line to another corporation where, under the dominant purpose test, the assets of an intangible nature, including trademark, logos, and artwork, are deemed not goods for Article 2 purposes). Another argument against UCC applicability concerns the timing of the statutes. Specific statutes on art, artists, and dealers began to develop about the same time as the UCC and, consequently, those specific art statutes should displace the more general UCC. See Franklin Feldman, et al., II Art Law 4–5 (1986). These two arguments reflect a philosophy of art exceptionalism, similar to *Brockhurst*'s non-commercial view of a portrait commission agreement. Nevertheless, the applicability of UCC § 2-201(1) was not at issue in *Hoffmann* or *Marvin Inc.*; the proponents of the UCC apparently prevailed.

On the other hand, UCC § 2-201(1) does not always apply to art contracts. Commissioning an artwork is often considered the provision of a service and not a purchase of a good. In National Historic Shrines Foundation Inc. v. Dali, 4 UCC Rep. Serv. 71 (N.Y. Sup. Ct. 1967), the plaintiff, a nonprofit corporation, alleged an oral contract with the acclaimed surrealist artist Salvador Dali. Dali was to paint a picture on a television show and to donate the painting (which could allegedly have been worth $25,000) to the charity. It would thereafter sell the painting at a public sale. After participating in two promotional events sponsored and paid for by the plaintiff, Dali refused to proceed with the planned television program. One of Dali's defenses was that the alleged contract was unenforceable under the UCC's statute of frauds. The court held that the commission was for the rendition of services and not a sale of goods within the meaning of the statute of frauds. Hence, the UCC defense was inapplicable.

It is also worth pointing out that the statute of frauds is not a universal norm. England abolished it in 1954 and the United Nations Convention on Contracts for the International Sale of Goods ("CISG") eliminated it. Choice of law can have a dramatic impact on questions for contract formation, as we will continue to see.

4. *Judicial Admission Exception.* In *Hoffmann*, the judge summarily adopted Judge Posner's view on the judicial admission exception as expressed in DF Activities Corp. v. Brown, 851 F. 2d 920 (7th Cir. 1988). Interestingly, that case involved an alleged contract to purchase a chair designed by the American architect Frank Lloyd Wright. The plaintiff was controlled by a "passionate enthusiast for the work of Frank Lloyd Wright," who desired to acquire the Wright-designed chair owned by Mrs. Brown, known as the Willits Chair. DF's art director began negotiations in September 1986 with Mrs. Brown to purchase the chair. In a telephone conversation with Mrs. Brown on November 26, DF alleged that Mrs. Brown agreed to sell the Willits Chair to DF for $60,000, payable in two $30,000 installments. About a week later, DF sent a letter confirming the sale, followed shortly thereafter by a $30,000 check. Mrs. Brown returned the check and letter with a note saying that because she hadn't heard from DF, she made other arrangements for the Willits Chair. Consequently, it was no longer available for sale to DF. In fact, Mrs. Brown later sold the Willits Chair to a third party for $198,000, more than three times the $60,000 sales price allegedly proffered by DF.

Mrs. Brown moved to dismiss based on the UCC statute of frauds and attached an affidavit denying she ever agreed to sell the Willits Chair to DF and denying any recollection of a conversation on November 26. The trial court granted the motion and dismissed the case. DF appealed based on the judicial admission exception. DF's argument was not based on the handwritten notes but rather that if DF were allowed to depose Mrs. Brown, she might admit to the November 26th agreement.

In the 2-to-1 decision, Judge Posner wrote:

> There is remarkably little authority on the precise question raised by this appeal—whether a sworn denial ends the case or the plaintiff may press

> on and insist on discovery.... Many cases hold ... that the defendant ... cannot block discovery ... simply by moving to dismiss ... or by denying in the answer ... that a contract had been made.... There is also contrary authority.... But where as in this case the defendant swears in an affidavit that there was no contract, we see no point in keeping the lawsuit alive. Of course the defendant *may* blurt out an admission in a deposition but this is hardly likely.... Stranger things have happened, but remote possibilities do not warrant the parties and the judiciary to proceedings almost certain to be futile.

In the course of the opinion that discussed the back-and-forth history of the judicial admission exception, Judge Posner stated the exception is now "firmly established." Some disagree. See James J. White & Robert S. Summers, 1 Uniform Commercial Code 79 (5th ed. 2006), where Summers, but not White, believes that defendants should not be able to simply deny the existence of an oral contrast in a sworn affidavit to effectively end the matter. He points to the language of UCC § 2-201(3)(b) that contemplates an admission in "open court" or cross-examination. See also Wayne R. Barnes, *The Judicial Admissions Exception to the Statute of Frauds: A Curiously Gradual Adoption*, 55 Wake Forest L. Rev. 475 (2020).

The plaintiff in *Marvin Inc.* attempted to use the transcript of the recorded telephone conversation as the defendant's admission, even though the defendant had submitted an affidavit denying the existence of a contract. The court determined that the telephone conversation did not indicate an agreement, and "in fact, the conversation when read as a whole, indicated that [the defendant] understood that [he] would not be bound by any contract until a written contract had been signed by the Parties." Thus, the judicial admission exception did not apply.

Look again at the telephone conversation. If Mr. de Sarthe had asked for your advice before the conversation, what would it have been? Do you think that the defendant knew the conversation was being recorded? In some jurisdictions, recording a conversation without notice is illegal.

5. *Promissory Estoppel.* The plaintiffs in *Hoffmann* and *Marvin Inc.* asserted the equitable doctrine of promissory estoppel in response to the statute of frauds defense. A threshold question noted by Judge Mukasey in *Hoffmann* is whether the equitable doctrine is applicable in a UCC statute of frauds case where the statute itself provides for explicit exceptions. Noting that UCC § 1-103 preserves common law principles unless displaced by particular provisions and that many courts "simply applied estoppel principles ... without acknowledging that such application is itself a matter of dispute," Judge Mukasey held common law estoppel principles are applicable to UCC contracts. 708 F. Supp. at 81.

The three requirements for promissory estoppel are (1) a clear and unambiguous promise, (2) reasonable and foreseeable reliance on the promise, and (3) unconscionable injury to the relying party. They demand a high quantum of proof, especially as to unconscionability. Both courts zeroed in on the plaintiff's alleged injuries and held that the injuries, including lost opportunity, embarrassment, and disappointment, were not unconscionable. The argument that unconscionability in the art world requires a different application (the art exceptionalism theory) was not well received. "That this alleged deal involved art rather than vans and trailers and therefore engaged esthetic and perhaps egoistic considerations in addition to crass economic ones is largely irrelevant in my view." *Id.* at 82.

6. *Statute of Frauds—A Writing.* The most direct way to defeat a statute of frauds defense is to produce a writing sufficient to prove the contract. Some acquisitions of artwork from dealers do involve writings. The question becomes the sufficiency of the writing to remove the case from the statute of frauds.

In Phoenix Ancient Art S.A. v. Kimball Art Foundation, 2003 WL 22705119 (S.D. N.Y. 2003), "snippets from various documents" offered by the art dealer plaintiff were deemed insufficient to establish a contract against the art museum defendant. The parties were both experienced in art transactions and had prior dealings with each other, which were reduced to writings. The documentation at issue had an express reservation not to be bound absent a written contract. Similar to the *Marvin Inc.* court's analysis of the recorded telephone conversation, the court held that the "snippets," whether considered singly or collectively, only evidenced continuing negotiations and not a completed deal.

A slightly different theme was involved in Jafari v. Wally Findlay Galleries, 741 F. Supp. 64 (S.D.N.Y. 1990). The plaintiff alleged that he had a contract for the sale of a Dali painting based in part on the dealer's handwritten note on the dealer's letterhead. That note was written hastily during negotiations in a car. The stated price for Dali's *Grand Opera* was $210,000. When the plaintiff failed to timely tender payment, defendant sold the work to another party, who then consigned the painting to Sotheby's for auction. Plaintiff was the successful bidder at auction, paying $330,000. The lawsuit was to recover the difference in price. For purposes of summary judgment, the court assumed the note, written and initialed by the defendant, was sufficient for statute of frauds purposes. Nevertheless, defendant's motion for summary judgment was granted because the plaintiff breached his part of the assumed contract by failing to tender payment.

2. Internationally

The art market's reluctance to written contracts is eroding. As the next case illustrates, when the artwork is sufficiently expensive and commands international attention, the buyer demands transactional formalities.

Faggionato v. Lerner

500 F. Supp. 2d 237 (S.D.N.Y. 2007)

PRESKA, J.

* * *

I. Background

Faggionato is a citizen of the United Kingdom and a dealer in paintings. Lerner is a citizen of the United States and a resident of New York City. This lawsuit alleges the breach of a contract to purchase a painting of a haystack ("meule" in French) by the painter Claude Monet (the "Painting") and seeks damages in the sum of $13 million, the alleged sales price of the Painting. . . .

Lerner maintained a relationship with an established New York art dealer Curt Marcus ("Marcus") and informed Marcus of his desire to purchase a Monet haystack. In May, 2005, Marcus sought Faggionato's help in locating such a painting. In November, 2005, Faggionato informed Marcus that she had located an early Monet haystack, the Painting, which had not been included in the Wildenstein Institute's comprehensive catalogue of Monet's works. The Wildenstein Institute ("Wildenstein") is an expert on Monet paintings and the publisher of the comprehensive catalogue raisonné of Monet's paintings. A document issued by Wildenstein (often called an "attestation" or "certificate") attesting that a painting is or will be listed in the Wildenstein catalogue raisonné is evidence of a painting's authenticity.

Between November 30, 2005, and January 10, 2006, Faggionato and Marcus exchanged a series of e-mails concerning the Painting, including Lerner's questions about the Painting. These questions concerned the authenticity of the Painting, its provenance, condition, ownership, and the reason for its absence from the Wildenstein catalogue raisonné. On September 8, 2005, the Wildenstein Institute executed an attestation letter stating that the Painting would be included in an upcoming supplement to the catalogue raisonné.

On December 22, 2005, Marcus wrote to Faggionato, stating that Lerner sought a confirmed date to view the Painting. . . .

Also on January 4, 2006, Douglas C. Jacobs, an accountant for Lerner, executed a "letter of intent" stating that Lerner is "prepared to purchase the Monet 'Meule' painting in the amount of U.S. $13 Million, subject to his viewing and approval, and the receipt of customary documentation."

On January 7, 2006, Marcus wrote to Faggionato stating that he had two questions: "1. Was the painting originally purchased from the artist or through a dealer? 2. Will my client receive a bill of sale from the owner? Will we know the original owners [sic] identity?" Faggionato responded that the first purchase would be "disclosed in 'Provenance' and can be checked in due course (through Wildenstein Institute)." However, as to the second question, Faggionato replied that Lerner would not receive a bill of sale from the owner, but would learn of his identity "in due course." Also on January 7, 2006, Marcus wrote to Faggionato expressing Lerner's concern "as to what recourse he would have, should he receive a letter one day from a collector in Paraguay stating that they are the actual owners . . . if he does not have a bill of sale from either the owners/seller or from a company that traditionally deals with this kind of transaction/money." Faggionato replied, "Fret not my friend[] the painting has been in the same family for the last 100 years, Art [L]oss Register ha[s] no record, I am working on the disclosure issue and the pigment analysis has already been done."

. . . On January 9, 2006, Lerner's lawyer, Joseph DeCampo wrote to Marcus describing the type of documentation De Campo wanted but also noting that if Lerner liked the Painting, the "next step would be to document the sale either in the form of a sales contract or bill of sale which we assume would be a direct contract between the sellers and our client, individually. It is this document that the seller will make various representations and warranties."

On January 10, 2006, Lerner inspected the Painting at the offices of Art Transit in Paris. That day, Lerner asked Faggionato for the Painting's provenance. Faggionato replied that "she could not guarantee that she could convince the owners to reveal their identities on official documents." Faggionato claims that on January 10, 2006, at 5:00 pm, Lerner orally announced to Faggionato and Marcus, "I have made my decision. I am buying the painting." . . . Faggionato claims that based on Lerner's agreement to purchase the Painting, and the terms of sale, she advised the owner's representative that the painting had been sold and she discontinued any further effort to sell the painting.

On January 11, 2006, Marcus wrote to Faggionato that "Randy [Lerner] put many wheels in motion based on our initial suggestion of urgency" and also reported on his conversation with DeCampo "to reiterate" that they now needed more time "to get the documents reviewed and confirmed once they are all in hand." On January 13, 2006, Marcus e-mailed Faggionato a series of "concerns about a number of points of authenticity" that Lerner had raised, including asking for the owners' name to be placed on the Certificate of Authenticity (issued by Wildenstein), were there other interested parties, and whether Lerner could hire another expert to view the Painting. On January 14, 2006, Faggionato answered Lerner's questions, explaining that she had not encountered a false or revoked Certificate of Authority; that she would ask whether the owners' names could be listed in the upcoming supplement to the catalogue raisonné. Also, Faggionato explained that if Lerner were to proceed with a new expert viewing the Painting, it could "suggest to the sellers a wavering by Lerner with uncertain results."

On January 17, 2006, Marcus wrote to Faggionato that Lerner did not have the "comfort level" that he had requested to proceed with an immediate deposit and desired further proof. On January 21, 2006, Marcus advised Faggionato that Lerner continued to love the painting but did not like buying it without "more transparency" and was seeking more documentation and clarity.

On February 2, 2006, Faggionato wrote to Marcus stating that the Painting "finally has a full set of documents," alleging that the conditions Lerner had requested in terms of documentation had been met. Marcus replied that day to Faggionato commenting on the "terrific news" but also reminding Faggionato that there were documents that Lerner had still requested for full documentation of the Painting, including a written bill of sale. . . .

On February 6, 2006, Marcus reported to Faggionato that Lerner had chosen not to purchase the Painting in part because "we were not forthcoming with his requests [for documents] and the lawyers needs." On February 9, 2006, Faggionato sent the full-provenance of the Painting to Marcus.

On February 10, 2006, Kendris Private [the company working with Faggionato in implementing the transaction] caused an invoice for $13 million, the Painting's Passport, an Art Loss Register document, and the provenance of the Painting to be sent to DeCampo. On February 13, 2006, DeCampo wrote to Kendris Private rejecting the sale documents and stating, "Mr. Lerner had abandoned any attempt to purchase this painting several weeks ago and we have had no communication regarding this transaction in over a month."

* * *

Discussion

Jurisdiction and Venue

This Court has subject matter jurisdiction over this action under 28 U.S.C. § 1332, diversity jurisdiction, as Faggionato is a citizen of a foreign country, and Lerner is a United States citizen. Venue is proper in that Lerner resides in the Southern District of New York.

* * *

Choice of Law

A federal court with diversity jurisdiction applies the choice of law rules of the forum state. New York courts apply the law of the jurisdiction with the "most significant relationship with the occurrence and with the parties." With respect to a case alleging breach of contract, New York applies a "center of gravity" or "grouping of contacts" analysis which allows a court to consider a spectrum of significant contacts.

* * *

Here, the most significant contacts and events occurred in France. Lerner traveled to France in order to view the painting, which was located in France. At least some of the negotiations took place in France, and many of the required documents were obtained in France from either French governmental authorities or French companies. The only connection to New York is Lerner's United States citizenship and domicile.

In the choice of law analysis, New York courts also determine whether there is an actual conflict between the substantive laws of the jurisdictions involved. As described below, the Court accepts the opinions of the French law experts and, based on their analysis of what may be used under French law to prove a contract, concludes that there is a substantive difference between applicable New York law and French law. For example, under French law, Article 1347 of the French Civil Code allows testimonial proof of contract formation if the party can demonstrate that there has been a beginning of proof in writing, which serves as an exception to the formal writing generally required to prove a contract. (*See infra.*) New York law does not offer an explicitly equivalent exception to the Statute of Frauds for a contract for sale of goods worth $500 or more. Federal Rule of Civil Procedure 44.1 provides that "[t]he court, in determining foreign law may consider any relevant material or source, including testimony, whether or not submitted by a party or admissible under the Federal Rules of Evidence." Fed.R.Civ.P. 44.1. Rule 44.1 grants the district court wide latitude in resolving issues of foreign law, and the court's determination shall be treated as a ruling on a question of law. . . .

French Law Analysis

The Court's interpretation of French law, as set forth below, is based on the expert law declarations submitted by both parties.

* * *

Both experts agree that any contract involving an amount greater than 1500 euros can be proved formally only through a writing that records the terms of the contract. However if there is no such document, under Article 1347 of the French Civil Code, there is an exception to the writing requirement if there exists a "beginning of proof in writing." Under this exception, a written document issued by the person against whom the claim is made or by a representative agent of that person, may be used to prove the beginning of proof in writing. . . .

[The court reviewed three possible relationships that under French law could give rise to a contractual relationship. The first is a contract of agency ("mandat") in which an intermediary enters into a legal transaction on behalf of and in the name of another person. The second is a "declaration de command," where one person asks another person to enter into a contract on the behalf of the former as buyer, and the seller in the transaction must be informed of the relationship but not the identity of the true buyer until after the transaction is concluded. The third is a convention of prête-nom, in which a strawman agrees to act in his own name on behalf of another because that person does not want to disclose his or her identity.—Ed.]

* * *

Faggionato Lacks Standing

In order to assert a claim in federal court, a plaintiff must be able to demonstrate that she has standing. . . . Where the claim asserted is contractual and the plaintiff is not a party to the contract or a third party beneficiary of the contract the claim must be dismissed.

* * *

Under French law, as described above by Professor Larroumet and accepted by the Court, Faggionato was not a proper party to the contract and thus cannot seek relief on her claims. The Court accepts Professor Larroumet's conclusions as persuasive.

Professor Larroumet pointed out that Faggionato was not a proper agent under the theory of mandat because Faggionato did not show that she had been granted powers to conduct the sale for the owners and because the identity of the owner (principal) was not revealed to the third-party (Lerner). Also, Professor Larroumet explained that a declaration de command was not applicable in this transaction because that type of transaction is used to hide the identity of the buyer only, not the seller. Professor Larroumet concluded that Faggionato could not rightfully be labeled a prête-nom in a convention de prête-nom because it was not clear who would play the role of intermediary between Lerner and the actual owners, Faggionato did not know the name of the actual owner at time the oral agreement was allegedly entered into, and one cannot have the capacity of a prête-nom if a contract had not been entered into. Professor Larroumet examined the requirements for a contract under French law and determined that no valid contract ever existed and that there was not sufficient beginning of proof in writing to permit Faggionato to give more evidence through testimony. Since Faggionato did not fill any of the roles necessary to be a proper party to the contract, including not being the owner of the Painting at the time of the alleged contract negotiations or properly representing the owners, she lacks standing under French law.

Facts Do Not Support Faggionato's New Claim of Ownership

In her opposition papers on this motion, Faggionato asserts a new claim that she had a conditional right to own the Painting because she was acting as a "middleman" in a back-to-back sales transaction that would enable her to resell the painting to Lerner. However, Faggionato failed to assert such a relationship and related transaction in her Complaint.

* * *

While in many cases, repleading might be permitted, the documents integral to the alleged transaction here demonstrate that repleading to articulate a claim consistent with Professor Molfessis' legal theory that Faggionato was to be the seller to Lerner and that she had the legal right to acquire the Painting from the owner would be futile. Faggionato's new allegation that she is the seller/owner is flatly contradicted by the documents that reflect the interaction between the parties.

* * *

Conclusion

Based on the Complaint as well as an examination of the documents relied on by Faggionato in her Complaint, with the aid of the declarations of the French law experts, the Court finds that Faggionato lacks standing to sue.

* * *

The Clerk of the Court shall mark this action closed and all pending motions denied as moot.

SO ORDERED.

Note and Questions

Faggionato shares procedural similarity with *Hoffmann* and *Marvin Inc.* All three cases were federal diversity cases in the Southern District of New York before the courts on motions to dismiss, all of which were granted. *Faggionato* provides new and significant perspectives as well.

First, *Faggionato* mixes the roles of the parties. It is a case in which an intermediary for the seller sues the buyer. The transfer of the painting is no longer at issue, although originally, there was a claim for specific performance. The prayer for relief includes damages for loss of Faggionato's reputation. The world of internationally-reputable private dealers for multi-million dollar Impressionists and Old Masters is finite, and unsuccessful dealings can reverberate in a tight-knit world.

Second, the case adds two interrelated legal issues: a motion to dismiss based on lack of standing (not the statute of frauds) and a choice of law determination. In order to proceed, Faggionato must prove her standing by establishing a contractual relationship with the unnamed owner of the Monet. The elements necessary to prove a contractual relationship depend on the law of the appropriate jurisdiction. When sitting in a diversity jurisdiction case, the federal rule is to apply the choice of law rule of the forum state, here New York. Under New York's choice of law rule, the law of the jurisdiction with the "[m]ost significant relationship with the occurrence and with the parties" controls. Because the painting was in France, Lerner went to France to view it, some negotiations took place there, and necessary documentation would come from the French government or French companies, French law governs. Under that law, Faggionato was unable to prove the necessary contractual relationship with the owner. Her attempt to amend her complaint to proceed as a direct owner (via a back-to-back sales transaction, a flip, as in *Marvin, Inc.*) was equally unsupported by the facts.

Third, *Faggionato* brings the international dimension of the art world into focus. Globalization is a reality for the art market, and consequently, for lawyers as well. Should Lerner's New York counsel have contacted local French counsel? If not, and assuming the deal advanced, is there a point at which French counsel should have been engaged? How do you decide if and when? In this regard, consider Rule 1.1 of the ABA Model Rules of Professional Conduct on Competence: "A lawyer shall provide competent representation to a client. Competent representation requires the legal knowledge, skill, thoroughness and preparation reasonably necessary for the representation."

Were you surprised that the Convention on Contracts for the International Sale of Goods (CISG), which both France and the US have adopted to some degree, was not mentioned in the case? Article 2 of CISG provides that the convention does not apply to sales "of goods bought for personal, family or household use, unless the seller at any times before or at the conclusion of the contract, neither knew nor ought to have known that the goods were bought for any such use. . . ."

Fourth, the case introduces the vocabulary of contractual assurances and documentation that buyers of artworks are coming to expect with respect to authenticity and title. As a prospective buyer, Lerner raised basic questions concerning the "authenticity of the Painting, its provenance, condition, ownership and the reason for its absence from the Wildenstein catalogue raisonné." These legal concerns will be more fully developed in Chapters 4 and 5 on Authenticity and Questions of Title, respectively, but a brief discussion of provenance and catalogue raisonné is warranted here.

A standard dictionary definition of provenance is "the listing of ownership of a valued object or work of art," much like a chain of title for real estate. For lawyers, this definition is slightly off, because ownership—as opposed to possession—is a legal conclusion, not one of art history. Nevertheless, a verifiable provenance is a starting point for determining the legal questions of title and ownership, with gaps in provenance or certain controversial or questionable holders in the past raising red flags. Gaps in personal record keeping combined with the historic tradition of privacy demanded by many art owners—whether as buyers or sellers—means that gaps in provenance are common, especially with older works. See, e.g., Jonathan Harr, The Lost Painting: The Quest for a Caravaggio Masterpiece (2005) (detailing the years-long, multi-country provenance search for Caravaggio's 1602 masterwork, *The Taking of Christ*).

A catalogue raisonné is a scholarly and comprehensive annotated listing of all known works of an artist, either in a particular medium or all media, sometimes from a particular period. Ideally, a catalogue raisonné would provide the title, date of creation, description of the medium used, dimensions, condition, provenance, and an exhibition and literature bibliography for each catalogued artwork. Inclusion in a catalogue raisonné is often seen as a mark of authenticity; yet a catalogue raisonné may not be comprehensive, sometimes due to privacy concerns. Like provenance, a listing in the pertinent catalogue raisonné provides a reference point for title and authenticity.

B. Breach of Written Contract

Contracts for the purchase of artworks are becoming more common today, especially for high-end artworks. The existence of a written contract does not eliminate all disputes as, the following case shows.

MAFG Art Fund, LLC v. Gagosian

2014 WL 359341 (N.Y. Sup. Ct. 2014)

Barbara R. Kapnick, J.:

This action arises from the purchase of various sculptures and paintings by plaintiffs MAFG Art Fund, LLC (the "Art Fund") and MacAndrews & Forbes Group LLC ("MacAndrews") from defendants Larry Gagosian ("Gagosian") and Gagosian Gallery, Inc. (the "Gallery").

* * *

Factual Allegations

I. The Popeye Sculpture

Plaintiffs allege that on May 12, 2010, MacAndrews and the Gallery executed a "Purchase Agreement," whereby MacAndrews agreed to a purchase price of $4 million in exchange for the rights to a black granite sculpture entitled "*Popeye*," created by world renowned artist Jeff Koons (the "MacAndrews Purchase Agreement").... The $4 million was to be paid in five installments of $800,000, with final payment due upon completion of the sculpture, which was then "estimated" to be on December 15, 2011.

Under the MacAndrews Purchase Agreement, the Gallery "irrevocably and without condition or reservation of any kind, [sold], transfer[red] and convey[ed]" the *Popeye* sculpture to MacAndrews, including "all right to possession and all legal and equitable ownership of the Work, to have and to hold the Work unto [MacAndrews], his successors and assigns, forever." The Gallery represented that, "upon delivery ... of the Work and after [MacAndrew's] receipt of the Purchase Price, good, valid and marketable title and exclusive and unrestricted right to possession of the Work, free of all Claims ... will pass from [the Gallery] to [MacAndrews]." The Gallery further represented that as of the "Delivery Date," the Gallery "is able, subject to Artist's reservation of rights in the work as set forth herein, to transfer the Work to [MacAndrews], free and clear of any and all rights or interests of others, claims, liens, security interests or other encumbrances held or claimed by any person and relating to the Work (collectively, 'Claims')," and that neither the Gallery nor Jeff Koons had "any knowledge of any Claims threatened or pending with respect to the Work." ...

In addition, MacAndrews agreed that it had "no right to sell the Work or the right to receive the Work before it has been paid for in full and delivered ... and any such sale shall be deemed null and void." The Agreement identified Jeff Koons as a third-party beneficiary.

Plaintiffs claim that, in reality, the Gallery had no rights to the *Popeye* sculpture at the time the Gallery entered into the MacAndrews Purchase Agreement, as evidenced by a separate but subsequent agreement entered into between the Gallery and Sonnabend Gallery, Inc., dated June 1, 2010. Under the Sonnabend Purchase Agreement, Sonnabend sold the Popeye sculpture to the Gallery under the same payment terms as the MacAndrews Purchase Agreement between the Gallery and MacAndrews; namely, a purchase price of $4 million to be paid in five equal payments of $800,000. The Sonnabend Purchase Agreement provided that the final $800,000 payment was due "[u]pon completion ([e]xpected to be December 2011)," and the Gallery acknowledged that "the estimated completion date for the Work is not firm and may be changed from time to time by [Sonnabend] due to delays in fabrication or other reasons." The Sonnabend Purchase Agreement further represented that "Jeff Koons, LLC" was "the sole and legal owner of the Work."

The Sonnabend Purchase Agreement also provided that, "if [the Gallery] sells the Work to a third party within 2 years after the date of this Agreement for a Profit . . . , then [the Gallery] will pay Artist an amount equal to 70% of such Profit," defining "Profit" as "the amount by which the Work's price in a Secondary Sale exceeds the Purchase Price" of $4 million. The Gallery also agreed to pay a 50% resale commission to Jeff Koons, LLC in the event that it sold the *Popeye* sculpture "to a third party and subsequently . . . resold [it] within 5 years after its original delivery to such third party."

As is apparently well known in the art world, Koons' works of art appreciate immediately after delivery to the first purchaser, often by multiples of the original purchase price.

Plaintiffs claim that Gagosian and the Gallery as Koons' exclusive dealer, were unwilling to be involved in any future resales of the *Popeye* sculpture as long as the profit-sharing provisions of the Sonnabend Purchase Agreement remained in effect. Thus, the plaintiffs contend that the Sonnabend Purchase Agreement destroyed their rights under the MacAndrews Purchase Agreement, and prevented them from exchanging or reselling the sculpture for fair market value once delivered. Plaintiffs also maintain that in June 2011, defendants informed them that the sculpture would not be completed until July 2012, approximately seven months after the estimated completion date, thereby breaching the MacAndrews Purchase Agreement.

II. The Exchange Transactions

Plaintiffs further claim that in April 2011, they sought to mitigate their damages . . . by entering into two transactions. In each transaction, the Art Fund acquired a work from the Gallery, or from a seller represented by the Gallery, and paid for the work with a combination of cash and a transfer or consignment to the

Gallery of certain works of art, including the *Popeye* sculpture, thereby receiving a credit for the purported value of those works. In the first Exchange Transaction . . . , the Art Fund acquired . . . [Cy Twombly's "*Leaving Paphos Ringed With Naves* (1)", 2009] painting for $10.5 million, which plaintiffs claim was an artificially high price for the work set by defendants ("Twombly Painting"). Plaintiffs assert that Perelman first viewed the Twombly Painting at the Gallery on or about April 28, 2011. The parties' negotiations lasted for several months, until they allegedly reached an oral agreement around the end of September 2011 on a purchase price of $10.5 million, and the Gallery delivered the painting to the Art Fund on October 7, 2011. . . .

In exchange for the Twombly Painting, the Art Fund was to pay $250,000 [and] exchange four works of art, including the *Popeye* sculpture. [The other three works of art were two Willem de Kooning oil paintings, "*Untitled*, 1974" credited at $3.6 million and "*Untitled*, 1970"; and the Roy Lichtenstein painting, "*Brushstrokes in Flight*, 1983."] Plaintiffs allegedly received a $4.25 million credit for the *Popeye* sculpture, minus the $1.6 million for its failure to make the last two installment payments of $800,000 each.

. . . [I]n the second Exchange Transaction, the Art Fund acquired [Richard Serra's "*Junction*, 2011"] steel sculpture for $12.6 million. In exchange for the Serra Sculpture, plaintiffs allegedly paid $4.75 million . . . and exchanged five unidentified works of art. [Roy Lichtenstein's painted aluminum sculpture, "*Brushstroke Nude*, 1993," credited at $4.5 million (the "Lichtenstein Sculpture"); Marino Marini's "*Cavaliere*, 1947"; Damien Hirst's "*Emperor Maximilian*, 2007" and "*The Premier Rose*, 2006"; and Richard Prince's "*Eden Rock*, 2006".] . . .

I. Breach of Contract and Breach of the Covenant of Good Faith and Fair Dealing (MacAndrews Purchase Agreement) (First Cause of Action)

* * *

Plaintiffs' first cause of action alleges that "[t]he Gallery breached the express and implied terms of the MacAndrews Purchase Agreement." The provisions allegedly breached by defendants included defendants' failure to comply with the "estimated" completion date of December 15, 2011, and the Gallery's alleged failure to convey the *Popeye* sculpture irrevocably and unconditionally, free and clear of any encumbrances, with valid and marketable title and exclusive rights to possession.

While the Amended Complaint identifies particular provisions of the contract which defendants allegedly breached, plaintiffs fail to explain how those provisions were, in fact, breached. The MacAndrews Purchase Agreement expressly identified the sculpture's completion date as "estimated", and plaintiffs fail to allege that time was of the essence. Therefore, the change in the completion date of *Popeye* cannot constitute a breach of the MacAndrews Purchase Agreement.

Next, the profit-sharing provisions of the Sonnabend Purchase Agreement required the Gallery to pay resale commissions to Jeff Koons upon subsequent sales of *Popeye*, but this obligation was the Gallery's alone, as it related to the Gallery's potential future commissions. The Sonnabend Purchase Agreement transferred the *Popeye* sculpture to the Gallery "free and clear of any and all rights or interests of others, claims, liens, security interests, [and] other encumbrances held or claimed by any person and relating to the Work." Plaintiffs' argument—that the profit-sharing provisions diminished the value of *Popeye* for a significant period of time following its delivery to MacAndrews, and effectively crippled plaintiffs' ability to exchange or subsequently sell *Popeye* at fair market value presupposes that defendants would be involved in any subsequent sale of the *Popeye* sculpture, given Gagosian's role as Koons' representative and the foremost dealer in Koons' work. Plaintiffs assert that based on the course of dealings between the parties, Gagosian and the Gallery knew it was plaintiffs' right and expectation that they would be able to sell *Popeye* or exchange it for other works of art. However, the MacAndrews Purchase Agreement contains no such obligation on defendants' part, and the Court, in the guise of contract interpretation, may not add this obligation to the parties' Agreement. Therefore, defendants' alleged refusal to be involved in future sales of the *Popeye* sculpture as a result of the profit-sharing provisions of the Sonnabend Purchase Agreement does not constitute an encumbrance, and is not a breach of any express or implied term of the MacAndrews Purchase Agreement. In short, plaintiffs fail to identify any conditions in the Sonnabend Purchase Agreement that constitute a breach of the MacAndrews Purchase Agreement.

* * *

Nor does plaintiffs' claim make sense chronologically. The Amended Complaint asserts that plaintiffs entered into the Exchange Transactions in April 2011, in an "effort to mitigate their damages" caused by the Sonnabend Agreement. However, plaintiffs claim that "at the time of the Exchange Transactions," the Sonnabend Purchase Agreement was "undisclosed" by defendants. Plaintiffs concede that defendants' refusal to be involved in "subsequent sales of *Popeye*" occurred "[o] ver a year and one-half after the parties entered into the MacAndrews Purchase Agreement." . . . The Amended Complaint fails to explain how plaintiffs could have known to mitigate their damages in April 2011, at a time when they had not yet discovered the very Agreement and conduct by defendants that caused the damages plaintiffs allegedly sought to mitigate. Plaintiffs also admittedly did not know about the delayed delivery date until June 2011, at which point they had already relinquished their rights to the *Popeye* sculpture, thereby undermining any allegation that plaintiffs sought to mitigate damages resulting from the delay.

* * *

In essence, plaintiffs' breach of contract cause of action alleges that, "'with the benefit of hindsight, it appears to have [entered into] a bad bargain'" but plaintiffs fail to plead a cognizable breach of contract claim that would entitle them to damages.

Plaintiffs also argue that the profit-sharing provisions of the Sonnabend Purchase Agreement breached the implied covenant of good faith and fair dealing.

Specifically, plaintiffs claim that at the time they entered into the MacAndrews Purchase Agreement, MacAndrews reasonably expected that Gagosian and the Gallery would be involved in any subsequent sale of the *Popeye* sculpture. Plaintiffs also claim that the Sonnabend Purchase Agreement permitted Sonnabend to unilaterally delay the completion date of the *Popeye* sculpture, further frustrating the parties' reasonable expectations under the MacAndrews Purchase Agreement that it would be delivered by December 15, 2011 or within a reasonable time thereafter.

. . . In any event, plaintiffs fail to identify any terms of the MacAndrews Purchase Agreement that could be construed to create an expectation concerning defendants' involvement in future sales of the *Popeye* sculpture, and "no obligation can be implied that 'would be inconsistent with other terms of the contractual relationship.' Accordingly, for all of the foregoing reasons, plaintiffs' first cause of action must be dismissed.

II. Breach of Fiduciary Duty (Second Cause of Action)

Plaintiffs' cause of action for breach of fiduciary duty is based upon defendants' alleged superior knowledge of contemporary art and the value of the artwork at issue herein, the longstanding friendship between Gagosian and Perelman, Gagosian's position of trust in advising Perelman and plaintiffs regarding art acquisitions and value, and defendants' various roles as consignee, seller, buyer, broker, bidder, and agent with respect to plaintiffs' artwork. Plaintiffs claim that defendants breached their fiduciary duties by entering into the Sonnabend Purchase Agreement, and by incorrectly valuing the artworks that were the subject of the Exchange Transactions. Defendants argue, that there was no fiduciary relationship among the parties, and that plaintiffs fail to allege that defendants engaged in any misconduct that would have constituted a breach of any purported fiduciary duties.

"The elements of a cause of action . . . for breach of fiduciary duty are (1) the existence of a fiduciary relationship, (2) misconduct by the defendant, and (3) damages directly caused by the defendant's misconduct." Two "essential elements" of a fiduciary relationship are "de facto control and dominance." However, "'[a]llegations of superior knowledge or expertise in the art field are per se insufficient to establish the existence of a fiduciary relationship.'"

* * *

Here, the Amended Complaint expressly states that "[p]laintiffs are art collectors and investors" with 20 years of experience making art investment decisions, having purchased and sold "nearly 200 works" of art through defendants alone. Plaintiffs concede that they are not "static collectors of art. Rather, they bought, sold and exchanged pieces frequently" with an express "art investment strategy." In short, plaintiffs are business entities admittedly engaged in the business of art investments, they had "staffs to work out the paperwork" and were represented by counsel, and plaintiffs are owned by the renowned businessman, Ronald Perelman.

* * *

Thus, plaintiffs' allegations make clear that they were experienced and sophisticated business investors who entered into negotiated, arm's-length transactions with defendants, which does not give rise to a fiduciary relationship.

Moreover, plaintiffs' reliance on the fact that Perelman and Gagosian were friends for 20 years, . . . had "worked together" previously and invested together, to establish a fiduciary relationship is unpersuasive, as . . . even a "longstanding relationship of fifty years" is insufficient to establish a fiduciary relationship "'where parties deal at arms length in a commercial transaction.'" At most, plaintiffs assert "'subjective claims of reliance on defendants' expertise,'" which do "not give rise to a 'confidential relationship' whose 'requisite high degree of dominance and reliance' was not in existence prior to the transaction giving rise to the alleged wrong."

For the foregoing reasons, . . . plaintiffs' second cause of action for breach of fiduciary duty is dismissed.

III. Fraud (Third Cause of Action)

Plaintiffs next allege that defendants possessed unique and superior knowledge concerning the value of the artwork included in the Exchange Transactions, and that defendants fraudulently misrepresented the value of this artwork, causing plaintiffs to overpay for the Twombly Painting and the Serra Sculpture and be undercompensated for the value of some of the exchanged works. Plaintiffs also assert that defendants falsely represented that the values they ascribed to the exchanged works were their true market values (less Gagosian's customary commission) and that those values were supported by market data, including non-public market data such as recent private sales and information gathered from the artists or their estates. Defendants argue that this cause of action should be dismissed, because the alleged representations about the value of artwork are not actionable, were not false or knowingly false, and because plaintiffs fail to allege justifiable reliance.

To state a cause of action for fraudulent misrepresentation, plaintiffs must allege "a misrepresentation or a material omission of fact which was false and known to be false by defendant, made for the purpose of inducing the other party to rely upon it, justifiable reliance of the other party on the misrepresentation or material omission, and injury". . . .

* * *

While generally, misrepresentations concerning value are considered matters of opinion which are not actionable, in certain circumstances they can be regarded as a representation of an existing fact, which is sufficient to support a fraud action. *See Cristallina v. Christie, Manson & Woods Intl.*, 117 A.D.2d 284, 294–295, 502 N.Y.S.2d 165 (1st Dept 1986). A person making such a representation must do so truthfully. Here, plaintiffs allege that Gagosian repeatedly stated that the values ascribed to the works implicated in the Exchange Transactions reflected their true market values, supported by market data which included recent sales and information gathered from customary sources, including artists' estates and his knowledge of private market sales. However, according to plaintiffs, Gagosian's statements as to the existing facts were knowingly false. Although plaintiffs concede that these values were based in part on market data, which is not "uniquely" within defendants' knowledge, they also claim that Gagosian's assessments were supported by information gathered from private market sales, which was not peculiarly within defendants' knowledge.

Defendants contend that the fraud claim fails to explain how defendants misrepresented the value of the artwork.... According to defendants, plaintiffs' explanation for defendants' overvaluation of the Twombly Painting and Serra Sculpture, and defendants' purported undervaluation of the works exchanged by plaintiffs, is based upon speculation and conclusory allegations.

As discussed *supra*, plaintiffs were credited $4.5 million for the Lichtenstein Sculpture and plaintiffs concede that they "ultimately accepted the value set by defendants of the works being traded in," based on defendants' representation that the values ascribed to the works being exchanged were "based on their true market value (less [defendants'] standard 10% commission." Thus, defendants' valuation could be false only if the Lichtenstein Sculpture were sold for more than $5 million (or $4.5 million once the 10% commission was subtracted). Defendants submit redacted copies of an Invoice showing that the Gallery sold the Lichtenstein Sculpture to Phillips de Pury & Company for $4.8 million, or $200,000 less than the value ascribed to it by defendants. This document suggests that defendants, in fact, overvalued the Lichtenstein Sculpture, giving plaintiffs the benefit of a higher trade-in value.

Similarly, defendants submit a redacted Invoice from the Gallery itself purporting to show that the Willem de Kooning painting, for which plaintiffs received a $3.6 million credit, was actually sold for $3.5 million, again giving plaintiffs the benefit of a higher trade-in value than anticipated by defendants. However, these Invoices are not the type of conclusive documentary evidence upon which the Court generally relies on a pre-answer motion to dismiss.... Plaintiffs also question whether these Invoices reflect bona-fide sales to third-parties, or some other arrangement, something which they have not been able to explore at this stage of the proceeding, prior to discovery. As such, this Court finds that plaintiffs have sufficiently alleged, for purposes of this motion to dismiss, that defendants made knowingly false misrepresentations.

Defendants also argue that plaintiffs' fraud claim is legally defective because plaintiffs have not, and cannot, allege justifiable reliance.

> If the facts represented are not matters peculiarly within the party's knowledge, and the other party has the means available to him of knowing, by the exercise of ordinary intelligence, the truth or the real quality of the subject of the representation, he must make use of those means, or he will not be heard to complain that he was induced to enter into the transaction by misrepresentations.

As discussed above, plaintiffs' allegations make clear that they were experienced and sophisticated business investors who entered into negotiated, arm's-length transactions with defendants. "As a matter of law, a sophisticated plaintiff cannot establish that it entered into an arms length transaction in justifiable reliance on alleged misrepresentations if that plaintiff failed to make use of the means of verification that were available to it."

... However, plaintiffs have alleged ... that defendants had superior and unique knowledge concerning the art market that was not available to plaintiffs. For instance, plaintiffs allege that Gagosian has enormous power to influence, and even set, the markets for the artists he represents because of his impressive roster of artists and his access to and knowledge of the largest private art collections in the world. Therefore, even though the plaintiffs are sophisticated art collectors and investors, the Court cannot say, as a matter of law, that plaintiffs' alleged reliance on defendants' representations regarding the art market and intrinsic value of particular works of art was *per se* unreasonable or unjustified.

Accordingly, that portion of defendants' motion seeking to dismiss the third cause of action for fraud is denied.

IV. Breach of the Covenant of Good Faith and Fair Dealing (Fourth Cause of Action)

Defendants next seek dismissal of plaintiffs' fourth cause of action for breach of the covenant of good faith and fair dealing with respect to the Exchange Transactions. This claim is based upon defendants' alleged fraudulent overvaluation of the Twombly Painting, and their undervaluation of the works exchanged for the Twombly Painting and the Serra Sculpture.

... "The duty of good faith and fair dealing, however, is not without limits, and no obligation can be implied that 'would be inconsistent with other terms of the contractual relationship.'"

As discussed above, the parties negotiated the prices ... in what plaintiffs claim were "valid and binding contractual arrangements." In essence, plaintiffs improperly seek to alter the prices ... that formed the basis of the Exchange Transactions, thereby rendering plaintiffs' claim inconsistent with pricing terms that were central to the parties' agreement. Accordingly, plaintiffs' fourth cause of action is dismissed.

V. Unjust Enrichment (Fifth Cause of Action)

Plaintiffs' fifth cause of action for unjust enrichment is based upon defendants' alleged improper valuation of the artwork that comprised the Exchange Transactions, whereby defendants made millions of dollars of illicit profits at plaintiffs' expense....

"Unjust enrichment is a quasi contract theory of recovery, and 'is an obligation imposed by equity to prevent injustice, in the absence of an actual agreement between the parties concerned.'" ...

Here, plaintiffs allege that the Exchange Transactions were governed by "valid and binding contractual arrangements" .... Therefore, plaintiffs' unjust enrichment cause of action is ... dismissed.

* * *

Accordingly, it is hereby

ORDERED that defendants' motion to dismiss the Amended Complaint is granted as to all the causes of action, except for the third cause of action for fraud which is severed and continued.

Notes and Questions

1. *Aftermath*. In December 2014, the case was affirmed on appeal by the Appellate Division with one modification. The fraud cause of action was also dismissed. 998 N.Y.S.2d 342 (N.Y. App. Div. 2014). Its short opinion was also very direct:

> The parties operated at arm's length when they negotiated (e.g. over the price of the $10.5 million painting). Thus, fiduciary obligations did not exist between them. Moreover, even read liberally, the complaint does not establish that defendants exercised control and dominance over plaintiffs-limited liability companies who, by their own description, frequently purchased, sold, and exchanged works of art as investments.
>
> The amended complaint alleges that defendants misrepresented the value of certain works of art and that the values were supported by market data, when they were not. As to the latter, the complaint fails to state a cause of action for fraud because plaintiffs did not allege justifiable reliance. As a matter of law, these sophisticated plaintiffs cannot demonstrate reasonable reliance because they conducted no due diligence; for example, they did not ask defendants, "Show us your market data". As to the claim that defendants misrepresented the value of certain art works, statements about the value of art constitute "nonactionable opinion that provide[s] no basis for a fraud claim".
>
> In light of the above disposition, it is unnecessary to consider defendants' argument that the documents they submitted refute plaintiffs' fraud claim.
>
> Plaintiffs contend that, when plaintiff MacAndrews & Forbes Group, LLC and defendant Gagosian Gallery, Inc. entered into a contract whereby MacAndrews bought a sculpture from the Gallery, defendants knew that plaintiffs expected to resell the sculpture. Plaintiffs allege that defendants breached the covenant of good faith and fair dealing implicit in the MacAndrews Purchase Agreement by entering into a subsequent agreement that decreased their incentive to be involved in resales of the sculpture, because without defendants' involvement, plaintiffs would not realize

> as high a price on the resale. However, the essence of the MacAndrews Purchase Agreement was that MacAndrews was going to buy a sculpture, not that it would later resell it. As important as defendants' involvement in the resale was to plaintiffs, the parties did not include it in the MacAndrews Purchase Agreement, and we will not interpret the agreement as impliedly stating it.

2. *Transactional Takeaway.* There are four important transactional takeaways from the appellate decision for buyers. First, the parties' negotiations were at arm's length; hence, "fiduciary obligations did not exist between them." Second, fraud allegations regarding the asserted art values were not supported. "As a matter of law, these sophisticated plaintiffs cannot demonstrate reasonable reliance because they conducted no due diligence." Third, statements about the value of artworks are "nonactionable opinion." Fourth, defendants' subsequent resale-limitation agreement with another did not violate the implicit covenant of good faith and fair dealing with plaintiffs. The plaintiffs did not include their resale expectation in the contract; theirs was an agreement to buy, not one to sell. See Daniel Kokhba, *Of Koons, Twombly, Perelman and Gagosian: Lessons to be Learned* (Part II), CENTER FOR ART LAW (Jan. 20, 2015), available at itsartlaw.org/2015/01/20/of-koons-twombly-perelman-and-gagosian-lessons-to-be-learned/.

Plaintiffs' sophistication in the art market was highly determinative for the appellate court in its analysis. The back and forth of the negotiations undercut an argument that there was unequal bargaining power. Yet plaintiffs' acceptance of the values asserted by Gagosian for artworks does suggest an asymmetry on market data. The court's remedy is self-help: ask for the data, don't blindly accept. In a word, investigate. There is a practical and recurring problem here: some highly relevant sales data is from confidential private sales. It is not to be disclosed. The gap between market insiders and those outside is real and can be easily exploited. How would you address this from a buyer's perspective?

3. *Participating in Post-Sale Upside. MAFG Art Fund* provides an insider's view of the purchase of a highly-prized artist's work. Artist Jeff Koons retained a 70% interest in profits generated by a future sale within two years and a 50% resale commission if sold again by the gallery within five years. Why? Is this another aspect of asymmetry in market data or knowledge? No. Unlike private market sales and transactions that have already occurred, the details of future sales are unknown by all. Simply, no one knows the future. Certainly, some may have more data on which to make predictions, but that itself is not certainty. Because of his recognized status as an artist, Koons has bargaining power. He is able to participate in future profits from his creations through provisions included in his sales contracts. This contractual approach allows Koons effectively to create a private parallel to artist

resale royalties that are available to artists in certain countries by law. See Chapter 7, *infra*.

C. Good Faith Buyer

One truism committed to memory by first year property students is that a thief cannot convey good title. It turns out that pithy statement is not always the case. *Lindholm* sets forth the entrusting exception, that special exception for a good faith buyer from a merchant to whom the property was entrusted. As you read the case, note how procedural safeguards often failed the plaintiff due to Malmberg's duplicity.

Lindholm v. Brant

925 A.2d 1048 (Conn. 2007)

SULLIVAN, J.

* * *

... The plaintiff [Kerstin Lindholm] was introduced to Anders Malmberg, a Swedish art dealer, in the late 1970's or early 1980's during the course of her marriage to Magnus Lindholm (Lindholm). Throughout the next thirty years, Malmberg ... handled all of the Lindholms' purchase and sale transactions for works of art.

In 1987, the plaintiff purchased Red Elvis from Malmberg for $300,000. The only written documentation evidencing the plaintiff's purchase of Red Elvis was the invoice that she received from Malmberg, written on Malmberg's stationary. During the process of purchasing Red Elvis, the plaintiff relied entirely on Malmberg to complete the transaction.

In 1989, the plaintiff, with the assistance of Malmberg, loaned Red Elvis to the Museum of Modern Art in New York to be included in a Warhol exhibition. A label affixed to the painting indicated that it was owned by a "[p]rivate [c]ollector" and had been loaned to the Museum of Modern Art "[c]ourtesy Anders Malmberg." The defendant visited the exhibition, viewed Red Elvis and saw its label, thereby becoming aware that Malmberg was associated with Red Elvis and its owner.[4]

In 1996, the Guggenheim Museum (Guggenheim) decided to sponsor an exhibition of Warhol paintings that would travel to several European venues....

In late summer of 1998, Germano Celant, a curator of the exhibition, met with the defendant to discuss loaning some of his Warhol artwork to the exhibition. In addition, Celant asked the defendant to assist him in obtaining loans of other

4. The Defendant had purchased Red Elvis in or around 1969, when he was a young college student and had owned the painting for a brief period of time.

Warhol artwork for the exhibition, including Red Elvis. The defendant advised Celant that he believed that Red Elvis was owned by a Swedish woman and that Celant should contact . . . Stellan Holm, a Swedish art dealer . . . for more information.

* * *

Through the efforts of Holm, who had contacted Malmberg, the plaintiff agreed to lend Red Elvis to the exhibition. . . . Malmberg helped the plaintiff to complete the loan forms, in which the plaintiff requested that the exhibition display Red Elvis with an identification plaque that read "'Private Collection, Courtesy Anders Malmberg, Malmo, Sweden.'" The defendant assisted the Guggenheim with the shipping arrangements for Red Elvis. . . . Accordingly, as of September, 1998, the defendant knew . . . that the plaintiff owned Red Elvis and that it was on loan to the Guggenheim for a Warhol exhibition.

In 1998, Lindholm initiated divorce proceedings against the plaintiff in Connecticut. Because of a shortage of funds, the plaintiff enlisted Malmberg to assist her in selling certain works of art. . . . On December 6, 1999, the family court issued an order . . . enjoining the plaintiff "from selling property without a court order. . . ." On December 8, 1999, the plaintiff's divorce counsel wrote a letter to Malmberg notifying him of the court order, thereby putting Malmberg on notice that he no longer was authorized to sell any property of either the plaintiff or Lindholm.

During this same time period, Holm, who had been working closely with the defendant . . . advised the defendant, on the basis of a conversation with Malmberg, that Malmberg had purchased Red Elvis. . . . Soon afterward, the defendant met with Holm and Malmberg at the defendant's residence. When Malmberg and Holm repeated that Malmberg had purchased Red Elvis from the plaintiff and asked whether the defendant would be interested in purchasing it, the defendant indicated that he would.

On or about February 2, 2000, the defendant agreed to pay Malmberg $2.9 million dollars for Red Elvis. Malmberg gave the defendant an invoice for the $2.9 million sale, indicating that a $900,000 deposit would be required immediately and that the balance would be due by a certain date. Although the defendant wired the deposit money to Malmberg, he objected to paying the balance prior to delivery of the painting without first entering into a formal contract with Malmberg. The defendant retained counsel to draft a contract and to conduct the necessary lien searches to identify any claims that Lindholm, who was in the midst of a bitter divorce and was reputed to be litigious, might have to the painting. During the contract negotiations, the law firm . . . conducted a lien search and an Art Loss Register[6] search relating to Red Elvis. Neither search revealed a claim or lien by Lindholm or any other individual. The defendant's counsel cautioned the defendant, however,

6. The Art Loss Register is a permanent international database of stolen and missing works of art recognized as the best mechanisms for determining whether a piece of art is stolen.

that these searches only provided "minimal assurances" that Malmberg had good title to the painting.

The defendant and Malmberg exchanged numerous drafts of the contract during the negotiations, which were completed on March 20, 2000. Ultimately, Malmberg agreed to delay payment of the balance until the delivery of Red Elvis to a bonded warehouse in Denmark.

During the negotiations, Holm served as a messenger between Malmberg and the defendant's counsel. In an effort to address the defendant's concerns about Lindholm's potential claims, Holm prepared a letter (the Swedish-English letter) to be signed by the plaintiff stating that she had good title when she sold the painting to Malmberg. The letter would be treated as confidential unless Lindholm made a claim to Red Elvis. Holm showed the letter to the defendant, but the letter was never signed by the plaintiff. When the defendant's counsel requested a copy of the signed letter, Holm refused, stating that it was none of the defendant's business. The defendant's counsel communicated Holm's response to the defendant.

The defendant also was concerned that . . . Malmberg had not yet acquired title to the painting or that this transaction was going to be a "flip."[7] The defendant's counsel . . . requested a copy of the invoice from the plaintiff to Malmberg. Malmberg denied this request on the ground that such invoices are not normally and customarily disclosed in the context of an art transaction.

On February 17, 2000, during the contract negotiations between the defendant and Malmberg, the Guggenheim notified the plaintiff, as a lender to the Warhol exhibition, that the exhibition would be terminating prematurely. At that point, the plaintiff agreed, at the suggestion of Greene [a Guggenheim curator—Ed.], to lend Red Elvis to the branch of the Guggenheim located in Bilbao, Spain. After Malmberg advised the plaintiff that Red Elvis would get better exposure at an exhibition at the Louisiana Museum in Copenhagen, Denmark, the plaintiff agreed to lend the painting to the Louisiana Museum. The plaintiff did not inform Greene that she had changed her mind about displaying the painting in Bilbao until Greene called her on March 17, 2000.

Also on March 17, 2000, the defendant spoke with Elissa Myerowitz, a registrar employed by the Guggenheim, to inquire when his Warhol works of art would be returned to him. The defendant also asked about the current status of Red Elvis. Myerowitz indicated that the painting was being returned to the plaintiff, who was listed as the lender on the loan forms. The defendant advised Myerowitz that the plaintiff no longer owned Red Elvis and that she should contact the new owner, Malmberg, because it was his understanding that Malmberg wanted Red Elvis to

7. "Flipping" is a term of art in the art industry that refers to a situation in which the purchaser of a painting immediately sells the painting for a higher price. The second purchase is often conditioned on the new owner's concealing the sale from the original owner. To prevent flipping, owners will often ask purchasers to agree not to resell the painting for a period of one year.

go to Denmark. The defendant believed that Red Elvis was going to be shipped to Denmark because, at that time in the negotiations, he had agreed to accept delivery there. Myerowitz then told Greene about her conversation with the defendant, after which Greene called the plaintiff. During this conversation, the plaintiff informed Greene that she had changed her mind and had decided to lend the painting to the Louisiana Museum. The plaintiff also informed Greene that Red Elvis should be released to Malmberg's custody because he was going to arrange for the shipment of the painting to Denmark. Greene advised the plaintiff that she would have to provide the Guggenheim with a letter authorizing the Guggenheim to release Red Elvis to Malmberg, which the plaintiff did on March 20, 2000. Greene then informed Myerowitz of the substance of Greene's conversation with the plaintiff, confirming that Red Elvis was to be released to Malmberg for shipment to the museum in Denmark. On March 21, 2000, the defendant called Myerowitz to inform her about the shipping arrangements to Denmark.

On April 12, 2000, after execution of the purchase contract, the defendant ... took possession of Red Elvis. On April 27, 2000, the defendant had the painting ... shipped from Denmark to the United States. The defendant then allowed Red Elvis to be shown in a traveling exhibition from May, 2000, through the end of 2002, doing nothing to conceal ... that he owned the painting.

From March, 2000, until the fall of 2000, the plaintiff took no steps to verify that Red Elvis was on display at the Louisiana Museum but, instead, relied on Malmberg's representations that the painting was there. In the fall of 2000, Malmberg informed the plaintiff that Red Elvis had not arrived at the Louisiana Museum in time to be a part of the exhibition. Thereafter, following an inquiry from Malmberg, the plaintiff authorized the sale of Red Elvis for $4.6 million to a Japanese buyer. ... In January, 2001, the plaintiff met with Malmberg and delivered an invoice conveying title to Red Elvis to one of Malmberg's companies, Eagle Eye Art Investments, Inc. The plaintiff agreed to have the sale proceeds sent directly to Malmberg's bank account. When the plaintiff agreed to sell Red Elvis for $4.6 million, she believed that she still owned Red Elvis, and was unaware that Malmberg already had sold the painting to the defendant in March, 2000.

In June, 2001, while awaiting her $4.6 million payment from the sale to the Japanese buyer, the plaintiff read a magazine article that reported that the defendant had purchased Red Elvis from Malmberg. When the plaintiff telephoned Malmberg, he told her ... that the defendant actually had bought a different painting, which was referred to as Green Elvis. For more than one year from the time that the plaintiff learned that the defendant had purchased Red Elvis, the plaintiff unsuccessfully sought the return of the sale proceeds from Malmberg.

On April 5, 2002, counsel for the plaintiff sent a letter to the defendant informing him that Malmberg's purported sale of Red Elvis to the defendant had not been authorized by the plaintiff and that title in the painting had not passed to the defendant. He further stated that, if the defendant did not return the painting to the plaintiff, she would commence proceedings against the defendant in the United States to recover the painting.

* * *

Following a trial to the court, the trial court . . . concluded that the defendant had satisfied his burden of proving that he was a buyer in the ordinary course of business, and rendered judgment in favor of the defendant.

* * *

. . . The plaintiff claims that the trial court improperly concluded that the defendant took good title to Red Elvis as a buyer in the ordinary course of business because: (1) the defendant was an art merchant who had valid concerns about Malmberg's ability to convey title; (2) applicable commercial standards of fair dealing required the defendant to "investigate [the transaction] scrupulously"; (3) the investigation conducted by the defendant's counsel provided only "minimal assurances" that Malmberg had good title; (4) Malmberg refused to provide documentary proof that he owned Red Elvis; and (5) the defendant could have discovered that Malmberg did not have good title and that a court order precluded the plaintiff from selling the painting if he had telephoned the plaintiff, the plaintiff's counsel, Lindholm, or Lindholm's counsel. We disagree and, accordingly, affirm the judgment of the trial court.

* * *

The plaintiff claims that the trial court improperly found that the defendant had established his affirmative defense that he was a buyer in the ordinary course, and, therefore, took all of the plaintiff's rights to Red Elvis. "It is an elementary rule that whenever the existence of any fact is necessary in order that a party may make out his case or establish his defense, the burden is on such party to show the existence of such fact." . . . Therefore, the burden was on the defendant to show the existence of such facts as would entitle him to the status of a buyer in the ordinary course pursuant to § 42a-2-403.

Section 42a-2-403(2) provides that "[a]ny entrusting of possession of goods to a merchant who deals in goods of that kind gives him power to transfer all rights of the entruster to a buyer in ordinary course of business." "'Entrusting'" is defined as "any delivery and any acquiescence in retention of possession regardless of any condition expressed between the parties to the delivery or acquiescence and regardless of whether the procurement of the entrusting or the possessor's disposition of the goods have been such as to be larcenous under the criminal law." General Statutes § 42a-2-403(3).

There is no dispute in the present case that the plaintiff's March 20, 2000 letter authorizing the Guggenheim to release Red Elvis to Malmberg constituted an entrustment under § 42a-2-403(3), or that Malmberg, an art dealer, is a merchant dealing in "goods of that kind"—works of art—under § 42a-2-403(2). Under the plain language of § 42a-2-403(2) and (3), therefore, Malmberg, as a merchant dealing in art entrusted with the painting, had the power to transfer all the rights of the entruster to a buyer in the ordinary course of business.

A "'[b]uyer in [the] ordinary course of business'" is defined as "a person that buys goods in good faith, without knowledge that the sale violates the rights of another person in the goods, and in the ordinary course from a person . . . in the business of selling goods of that kind. A person buys goods in the ordinary course if the sale to the person comports with the usual or customary practices in the kind of business in which the seller is engaged or with the seller's own usual or customary practices. . . ." General Statutes § 42a-1-201(9).[9] A person buys goods in good faith if there is "honesty in fact and the observance of reasonable commercial standards of fair dealing" in the conduct or transaction concerned. General Statutes § 42a-1-201(20).[10]

We are required, therefore, to determine whether the defendant followed the usual or customary practices and observed reasonable commercial standards of fair dealing in the art industry in his dealings with Malmberg. As we have indicated, the defendant presented expert testimony that the vast majority of art transactions, in which the buyer has no reason for concern about the seller's ability to convey good title, are "completed on a handshake and an exchange of an invoice." It is not customary for sophisticated buyers and sellers to obtain a signed invoice from the original seller to the dealer prior to a transaction, nor is it an ordinary or customary practice to request the underlying invoice or corroborating information as to a dealer's authority to convey title. Moreover, it is not customary to approach the owner of an artwork if the owner regularly worked with a particular art dealer because any inquiries about an art transaction customarily are presented to the art dealer rather than directly to the principal. It is customary to rely upon representations made by respected dealers regarding their authority to sell works of art. A dealer customarily

---

9. The trial court in its analysis relied on the current version of § 42a-1-201(9). At the time of the sale from Malmberg to the defendant, a buyer in the ordinary course of business was defined as "a person who in good faith and without knowledge that the sale to him is in violation of the ownership rights or security interest of a third party in the goods buys in ordinary course from a person in the business of selling goods of that kind but does not include a pawnbroker. . . ." General Statutes (Rev. to 1999) § 42a-1-201(9). Neither party contends that the trial court used the wrong statutory standard for determining whether the defendant is a buyer in the ordinary course of business. We also note that the second sentence of the current version of § 42a-1-201(9), which was added to the statute by Public Acts 2001, No. 01-132, § 135, can be interpreted as codifying the standard in existing case law, that a sale must comport with the usual or customary practices in the kind of business in which the seller is engaged. For convenience and consistency in our analysis, we refer to the current version of § 42a-1-201(9).

10. The trial court in its analysis used the version of the statute in effect at the time of the sale, which provided that "'[g]ood faith' in the case of a merchant means honesty in fact and the observance of reasonable commercial standards of fair dealing in the trade." General Statutes (Rev. to 1999) § 42a-2-103(1)(b). That language currently is codified at § 42a-1-201(20). See Public Acts 2005, No. 05-109, §§ 7 and 23. Because both definitions contain identical language, we refer to the current definition of good faith in § 42a-1-201(20) for convenience.

is not required to present an invoice establishing when and from whom he bought the artwork or the conditions of the purchase.

We are compelled to conclude, however, that the sale from Malmberg to the defendant was unlike the vast majority of art transactions. The defendant had good reason to be concerned that Lindholm might have claims to the painting. Several courts have held that, under such circumstances, a handshake and an exchange of invoice is not sufficient to confer status as a buyer in the ordinary course. [Court discusses Porter v. Wertz, 416 N.Y.S.2d 254 (1979), aff'd 439 N.Y.S.2d 105 (1981); Howley v. Sotheby's, Inc., 195 N.Y.L.J. 6 (Feb. 20, 1986); Cantor v. Anderson, 639 F. Supp. 364 (S.D.N.Y. 1986), aff'd 833 F.2d 1002 (2d Cir. 1986); and Morgold, Inc. v. Keeler, 891 F. Supp. 1361 (N.D. Cal. 1995).—Ed.]

* * *

We agree with these courts that a merchant buyer has a heightened duty of inquiry when a reasonable merchant would have doubts or questions regarding the seller's authority to sell. We further conclude that the steps that a merchant must take to conform to reasonable commercial standards before consummating a deal depend on all of the facts and circumstances surrounding the sale. In the present case, the defendant had concerns about Malmberg's ability to convey good title to Red Elvis because he believed that Lindholm might have had a claim to the painting. The defendant also was concerned that Malmberg had not yet acquired title to the painting or that the transaction might be a "flip."

Because of his concern that Lindholm might make a claim to Red Elvis, the defendant took the extraordinary step of hiring counsel to conduct an investigation and to negotiate a formal contract of sale on his behalf. He also insisted on and obtained a formal contract containing representations and warranties that Malmberg had title to the painting. In addition, during the course of the investigation, the defendant's counsel conducted both a lien search and an Art Loss Register search that revealed no competing claims to Red Elvis. Although the defendant was cautioned that the searches provided only minimal assurance that Malmberg had good title to the painting, such searches typically are not conducted during the course of a normal art transaction and, therefore, provided the defendant with at least some assurance that Lindholm had no claims to the painting.

Moreover, the evidence was sufficient for the trial court reasonably to conclude that at all times during the transaction, both Malmberg and Holm had reputations as honest, reliable, and trustworthy art dealers.... The defendant had little reason to doubt Malmberg's claim that he was the owner of Red Elvis, and any doubts that he did have reasonably were allayed by relying on Holm's assurances that Malmberg had bought the painting from the plaintiff because she needed money due to her divorce.... The defendant established at trial that it is customary to rely on the assurances of respected art dealers when conducting a transaction, and the defendant had no reason to depart from this practice.

The defendant's concerns were further allayed when Malmberg delivered Red Elvis to a bonded warehouse in Denmark, the delivery location the parties had agreed to in the contract of sale. At the time of the sale, the painting was on loan to the Guggenheim, whose policy it was to release a painting on loan only to the true owner, or to someone the true owner had authorized to take possession.... We conclude that these steps were sufficient to conform to reasonable commercial standards for the sale of artwork under the circumstances and, therefore, that the defendant had status as a buyer in the ordinary course of business.

We recognize that the customary practice in the art industry of not requiring a merchant buyer to obtain documentary proof that the seller owns the work of art whenever there are reasonable doubts or questions regarding the seller's authority to sell imposes risks on persons who entrust art to an art dealer. Section 42a1-201(9) evinces a legislative desire, however, for courts to respect "the usual or customary practices in the kind of business in which the seller is engaged...." We are not entitled to impose the type of business practices that we would prefer.

Moreover, the evidence presented at trial established that the reason that documentary proof of ownership customarily is not required is to protect the confidentiality of the owner and the buyer. Requiring a merchant buyer to obtain an invoice or other supporting documentation proving the seller's ownership would in every transaction destroy the privacy and confidentiality that buyers and sellers have come to desire and expect. Accordingly, only when circumstances surrounding the sale cast severe doubt on the ownership of the artwork are merchant buyers required to obtain documentary assurance that the seller has good title. In this instance, the Swedish-English letter was produced at Holm's suggestion to give the defendant assurance that the *plaintiff* had good title when she sold the painting to Malmberg. In light of the customary practices in the industry, the defendant reasonably could have concluded that Malmberg was unwilling to produce a signed copy of the letter because of his desire to protect the owner's expectation of confidentiality in their transaction. The purpose of the letter was not to give the defendant assurance that *Malmberg* had good title to the painting, and any concerns about Malmberg's title that could be inferred from the refusal to show the defendant a signed copy of the letter were quickly allayed by Malmberg's subsequent delivery of the painting to Denmark. Accordingly, we conclude, on the basis of all the circumstances surrounding this sale, that the defendant's failure to obtain an invoice from the plaintiff to Malmberg or a signed copy of the Swedish-English letter does not strip him of his status as a buyer in the ordinary course of business. For the same reasons, we conclude that the defendant was not required to contact directly the plaintiff or other parties who might have had knowledge concerning Red Elvis' title.

We conclude that the trial court properly determined that the defendant was a buyer in the ordinary course of business and, therefore, took all rights the plaintiff had to the painting pursuant to § 42a-2-403(2).

The judgment is affirmed.

Notes and Questions

1. *Aftermath.* In 2008, Ms. Lindholm was sued by her lawyers for their legal fee. Proskauer Rose, LLP v. Lindholm, 45 Conn. L. Rptr. 503 (Conn. Super. Ct. 2008). She sued them for malpractice and overcharging. Lindholm v. Proskauer Rose LLP, No. FST-CV 09-5011095-S (Conn. Super. Ct. 2009).

In 2002, Stellan Holm sued Malmberg and Mr. Lindholm over the ownership of another painting. Stellan Holm, Inc. v. Malmberg International Art, AB, 2002 WL 392294 (S.D.N.Y. 2002). In 2003, Anders Malmberg was convicted in Sweden of stealing *Red Elvis* from Ms. Lindholm and sentenced to three years in prison.

2. *UCC Good Faith Analysis and the Duty to Inquire. Lindholm*'s legal question was straightforward. There was no dispute as to the applicability of the state's version of UCC § 2-403(2). The question was simply one of the sufficiency of the evidence. Were the facts presented at trial sufficient to establish Brant's status as a buyer in the ordinary course of business?

Generally, one cannot sell what one does not own ("*Nemo dat quod non habet*"), but UCC § 2-403(2) makes an exception when a party entrusts the good to a "merchant who deals in goods of that kind." That merchant is able to transfer all of the entrustor's rights in the good to a buyer in the ordinary course of business. The policy behind the UCC entrusting exception is clear. It promotes the reliability of the marketplace and places the risk of loss on the entrustor, who voluntarily and consciously chose the merchant.

The entrusting exception requires a buyer to be a buyer in the ordinary course of business. The UCC § 1-201(9) definition has three components, two focusing on the buyer and one on the market. The buyer must (i) buy in good faith and (ii) without knowledge that the sale violates another's interest. In addition, the sale must be (iii) in the ordinary course from a person (excluding a pawnbroker) in the business of selling goods of that kind. For UCC purposes, knowledge means actual knowledge. A significant focus in many cases is the buyer's good faith.

The UCC definition of good faith has varied over time. Previously, UCC § 1-201(19) defined good faith as "honesty in fact in the conduct or transaction concerned." Current UCC § 1-201(20) defines good faith as "honesty in fact and the observance of reasonable commercial standards of fair dealing." This discrepancy (between having a subjective standard and combining a subjective with an objective standard) was somewhat muted in *Lindholm* because of Brant's deemed status as a merchant buyer. Article 2 of the UCC as then in effect had a bifurcated approach to many of its rules, one for merchants and one for non-merchants. If a person was deemed a merchant (and that term is defined expansively), then good faith for purposes of Article 2 was governed not by the general definition of good faith but by an internal Article 2 standard: "honesty in fact and the observance of reasonable commercial standards of fair dealing in the trade." The *Lindholm* court observed (in footnote 10) that the new UCC good faith definition and the prior Article 2 merchant good faith definition contained "identical language." It was "required, therefore, to determine whether the defendant followed the usual or reasonable commercial standards of fair dealing in the art industry. . . ." Consequently, Brant presented the court with evidence of the customs and traditions of the art industry: transactions based on handshakes, without requests for underlying invoices, without corroborating information as to ownership or authority, and relying on the verbal representations of reputable dealers.

Under *Lindholm*'s interpretation, a buyer is entitled to rely on the particular industry's traditions, assuming the buyer has no notice or reason to suspect the dealer's ability to convey good title. The court concluded, however, there were sufficient warnings in this case (the plaintiff's divorce proceedings and the possibility of a flip) to put Brant on alert; therefore, the circumstances compelled a duty to inquire on his part. Brant discharged this higher duty by taking the "extraordinary step of hiring counsel" to investigate possible liens and claims, and to negotiate and draft a written contract. To the argument that Brant should have obtained documentary assurances that the seller had good title, the court states that "only when circumstances surrounding the sale cast severe doubt on the ownership of the artwork are merchant buyers required" to do so. Within this legal and factual context, Brant was deemed a buyer in the ordinary course of business.

The court's opinion suggests using a sliding scale to determine a buyer's good faith. If there are no warning signs as to the dealer's ability to convey good title, the buyer can rely on the customs and traditions of the art market. Graffman v. Espel, 1998 WL 55371 (S.D.N.Y. 1998), *aff'd*, 201 F.3d 431 (2d. Cir. 1999) ("As a matter of law, the Does had no obligation to investigate the provenance of the painting. . . . The Does are not art dealers and are under no obligation to adhere to commercial standards. . . ."). If there is a warning sign, then the buyer has a duty to inquire. How probing that inquiry must be depends on how "severe" the doubt is. What constitutes severe doubt? See Interested Lloyd's Underwriters v. Ross, 60 UCC Rep. Serv. 2d 558 (S.D.N.Y. 2005) ("Whether the delay of four months between contract and delivery and the [10%] differential between the purchase price and the market value of the Painting constitute a 'red flag' to an art dealer" is a question of fact, barring summary judgment); Brown v. Mitchell-Innes & Nash, Inc., 68 UCC Rep. Serv. 2d 599 (S.D.N.Y. 2009) (Plaintiff's "failure to allege any warning signs means that [art merchant] Defendants are buyers in the ordinary course of business and fall within the protective scope of N.Y. U.C.C. § 2-403."); Morgold, Inc. v. Keeler, 891 F. Supp. 1361 (N.D. Cal. 1995) ("both Adler and Keeler responded to the available information reasonably. There were no warnings which required them to do further investigation.").

3. *A Contrary View on the Duty to Inquire.* The duty to inquire is generally attributed to Porter v. Wertz, 416 N.Y.S.2d 254 (App. Div. 1979), *aff'd*, 53 N.Y.2d 696

(1981). Porter was the owner of an art collection that included a Maurice Utrillo painting. He had had art dealings with Harold Von Maker, a man who also used other names, one of which was Peter Wertz. In the course of those art dealings, Von Maker expressed an interest in the Utrillo. Porter agreed to lend the painting to him temporarily to hang in his personal residence on approval. Porter visited the home and saw the Utrillo there. When after a period of time he had not heard from Von Maker about the Utrillo, Porter sought the painting's return, but he was unable to reach Von Maker.

Shortly thereafter, Von Maker sent a check to Porter regarding another sale, but the check was dishonored. When this happened, Porter "commenced an investigation" and discovered that he was dealing with Von Maker, not Peter Wertz, and that Von Maker had been sued many times, had outstanding judgments against him, had an extensive arrest record, and had been convicted of various crimes.

Learning this, Porter contacted the FBI about the dishonored check, but did not mention the Utrillo because Porter did not realize that Von Maker had already sold it. Porter had his attorney contact Von Maker's attorney and the two attorneys negotiated an extensive agreement concerning several paintings (including the Utrillo) delivered to Von Maker by Porter. Von Maker said the Utrillo was on consignment with another client but that within 90 days, he would either return the Utrillo or pay Porter $30,000. At the very time that Von Maker signed this agreement, he had already sold the painting for $20,000. Von Maker had directed the true Peter Wertz, an employee of a gourmet New York grocery store over whom Von Maker "cast his hypnotic spell," to take the Utrillo to the Feigen gallery. That gallery sold the Utrillo to another defendant, who in turn sold it to someone from Venezuela.

Feigen, the dealer who purchased the Utrillo from Wertz, asserted two primary defenses: statutory estoppel based on UCC §2-403 and common law equitable estoppel. The trial court dismissed the complaint based on Feigen's defense of equitable estoppel. The appellate division reinstated the complaint and found in favor of Porter:

> In order to determine whether the defense of statutory estoppel is available to Feigen, we must begin by ascertaining whether Feigen fits the definition of a "buyer in the ordinary course of business." Feigen does not fit that definition, for two reasons. First, Wertz, from whom Feigen bought the Utrillo, was not an art dealer—he was not "a person in the business of selling goods of that kind." If anything, he was a delicatessen employee. Wertz never held himself out to be a dealer. ... Second, Feigen was not "a person * * * in good faith" in the transaction with Wertz. ... Although this definition by its terms embraces the "reasonable commercial standards of fair dealing in the trade," it should not—and cannot—be interpreted to permit, countenance or condone commercial standards of sharp trade practice or indifference as to the "provenance," i.e., history of ownership

or the right to possess or sell an object d'art, such as is present in the case before us.

* * *

We note that neither Ms. Drew-Bear nor her employer Feigen made any investigation to determine the status of Wertz. . . .Had Ms. Drew-Bear done so much as call either of the telephone numbers Wertz had left, she would have learned that Wertz was employed by a delicatessen and was not an art dealer. Nor did Ms. Drew-Bear or Feigen make an effort to verify whether Wertz was the owner or authorized by the owner to sell the painting he was offering. . . . Thus, it appears that statutory estoppel provided by subdivision 2-403 of the Uniform Commercial Code was not, as Trial Term correctly concluded, available as a defense to Feigen.

We disagree with the conclusion of the trial court that the defense of equitable estoppel raised by Feigen bars recovery.

We pause to observe that although one may not be a buyer in the ordinary course of business as defined in the Uniform Commercial Code, he may be a good-faith purchaser for value and enjoy the protection of precode estoppel. . . .

In general terms: "Equitable estoppel or estoppel in pais is the principle by which a party is absolutely precluded, both at law and in equity, from denying, or asserting the contrary of, any material fact which, by his words or conduct, affirmative or negative, intentionally or through culpable negligence, he has induced another, who was excusably ignorant of the true facts and who had a right to rely upon such words or conduct, to believe and act upon them thereby, as a consequence reasonably to be anticipated, changing his position in such a way that he would suffer injury if such denial on contrary assertion were allowed. An estoppel in pais can arise only when a person, either by his declarations or conduct, has induced another person to act in a particular manner. The doctrine prohibits a person, upon principles of honesty and fair and open dealing, from asserting rights the enforcement of which would, through his omissions or comissions, work fraud and injustice." (21 NY Jur, Estoppel)

* * *

In the case at bar, Porter's conduct was not blameworthy. When the first promissory note was dishonored, he retained Bishop's investigative service and informed the FBI of the financial transactions concerning the series of notes. His attorney obtained a comprehensive agreement covering several paintings, within which was the assurance (now proven false) by Von Maker that he still controlled the Utrillo. Although Porter had permitted Von Maker to possess the painting, he conferred upon Von Maker no other indicia of ownership. Possession without more is insufficient to create an estoppel.

* * *

> Finally, we must examine again the position of Feigen to determine whether Feigen was a purchaser in good faith.
>
> * * *
>
> The Feigen claim that the failure to look into Wertz' authority to sell the painting was consistent with the practice of the trade does not excuse such conduct. This claim merely confirms the observation of the trial court that "in an industry whose transactions cry out for verification of the * * * title * * * it is deemed poor practice to probe." Indeed, commercial indifference to ownership or the right to sell facilitates traffic in stolen works of art. Commercial indifference diminishes the integrity and increases the culpability of the apathetic merchant. In such posture, Feigen cannot be heard to complain.

The appellate division's decision was appealed to the Court of Appeals of New York, which affirmed the judgment, but specifically did not reach the significant issue of a duty to inquire:

> The Appellate Division opined that even if Von Maker had duped Feigen into believing Peter Wertz was an art dealer, subdivision (2) of section 2-403 of the Uniform Commercial Code would still not protect his defective title because as a merchant, Feigen failed to purchase in good faith. Among merchants good faith requires not only honesty in fact but observance of reasonable commercial standards.... The Appellate Division concluded that it was a departure from reasonable commercial standards for the Feigen Gallery to fail to inquire concerning the title to the Utrillo and fail to question Peter Wertz' credentials as an art dealer. On this appeal we have received *amicus* briefs from the New York State Attorney-General urging that the court hold that good faith among art merchants requires inquiry to the ownership of an *object d'art,* and from the Art Dealers Association of America, Inc., arguing that the ordinary custom in the art business is not to inquire as to title and that a duty of inquiry would cripple the art business, which is centered in New York. In view of our disposition we do not reach the good faith question.

So the question lingers, is there an affirmative duty to inquire or not? Perhaps the most accurate assessment is from Interested Lloyd's Underwriters v. Ross, 60 UCC Rep. Serv. 2d 558 (S.D.N.Y. 2005):

> Many lower courts have held that to be a purchaser in the ordinary course within the meaning of § 2-403 an art dealer must investigate the provenance of a work of art being purchased, even if the work is being purchased honestly and from a reputable dealer.... The New York Court of Appeals, however, declined to endorse this position in affirming the lower court's

> decision in *Porter*. . . . Whether or not a duty of inquiry exists in New York in these circumstances is accordingly unclear.

4. *Another Finicky UCC Point?* The UCC does not stand still. In 2001, a revised version of Article 1 of the UCC was promulgated that notably included a new unitary definition of good faith meant to be applicable generally throughout the UCC, to merchants and non-merchants alike. As previously noted, this new unitary definition of good faith adopted the general approach of Article 2's merchant good faith by requiring both a subjective "honesty in fact" standard and an objective standard of "observance of reasonable commercial standards of fair dealing." In moving the good faith definition to Article 1, the words "in the trade" that were used in the Article 2 merchant good faith definition were dropped. Is this meaningful for art law purposes? If one can particularize the determination of "reasonable commercial standards of fair dealing" to the art industry, with its tradition of discrete confidentiality, informality, and lack of transparency, then this objective reasonableness standard may be set too low. That was the view of the appellate court in *Porter* when the court rejected defendant's defense of following the art trade practice. If, on the other hand, the determination is one of a general objective commercial reasonableness (after all, the definition uses the words "reasonable commercial standards of fair dealing"), while it may not be a realistic match with the traditional art industry, it can push the art industry to develop a more modern business-like approach. See James J. White & Robert S. Summers, 1 Uniform Commercial Code 18, n.17 (5th ed. 2006) ("This change presumably will exclude industry-specific commercial standards.").

Is that push already happening? In *Faggionato* and *Lindholm*, the buyer was represented by a lawyer. Each lawyer, as lawyers typically do, requested documentary evidence of authenticity and title from the seller. Lack of documentation satisfactory to the buyer ended the *Faggionato* transaction but it shifted the *Lindholm* transaction back to custom and tradition. Based on the statutory language for the merchant's good faith "in the trade" in effect at the time of the transaction, the *Lindholm* decision fits within case law precedent. Whether it will be authoritative going forward is unclear.

It is worth remembering that the UCC as adopted by a state can vary from the UCC model and states may not adopt revisions in a timely fashion. Therefore in a jurisdiction with the original good faith definitions, a non-merchant buyer's good faith is subjectively determined, without regard to objective commercial standards, and a merchant's good faith is subjectively and objectively determined with due regard for the practices of the trade. As of 2020, the revisions to UCC Article 1 were adopted by virtually all jurisdictions. Nevertheless, some states retained the good faith definition of the pre-revised UCC Article 1. Those states include Alabama, Arizona, Hawaii, Idaho, Illinois, Nebraska, New York, Rhode Island, Utah, Virginia, and Wisconsin.

5. *Form Contract for a Simple Sale.* The five principal cases in this chapter present the monetary divide in the art market. *Faggionato, Lindholm,* and *MAFG Art Fund* involved art worth millions, while the art in *Hoffmann* and *Marvin* was in the hundreds of thousands. Lawyers were present in the former, but not the latter, cases. Certainly monetary values are a consideration for this divide, but art culture plays a role as well. Few would think to buy a home, at any price, without a contract or a lawyer.

Consider the following form contract for a simple sale from a domestic gallery to a customer of an existing artwork by a living U.S.-based artist. Compare this form to the lawyer-drafted commission agreement from Chapter 1. You should note many similarities. As you gain more familiarity with other topics in art law, you may gain insights that would cause you to refine this form.

Sales Agreement

This agreement is entered into as of the ____ day of ____, 20XX, by and between Great Gallery ("Seller") and __________ ("Buyer").

1. **Sale.** Seller hereby agrees to sell to Buyer for the sum of $ _________ U.S., subject to the terms and conditions of this agreement the following work of art ("Work"):

Artist:

Title/Date:

Medium:

Dimensions:

Signature:

2. **Payment and Transfer of Title.** Buyer agrees to pay Seller the purchase price in full by ____________, 20XX. Buyer also agrees to pay applicable sales taxes, if any. Transfer of title to the Work from Seller to Buyer shall not occur prior to the complete payment of the purchase price by Buyer. Seller agrees to give Buyer a Bill of Sale as evidence of the transfer of title upon Buyer's complete payment of the purchase price.

3. **Delivery.** The Work shall be delivered to Buyer by a mutually agreed upon common carrier and such delivery to Buyer shall occur as mutually agreed to by Buyer and Seller, but in no event shall such delivery be later than 7 days after the complete payment of the purchase price. Expenses of shipping and delivery shall be born equally by Buyer and Seller.

4. **Seller's Warranties.** Seller hereby represents and warrants that:

(a) The Work is authentic and it is in accord with the description in Paragraph 1.

(b) The Work is free of liens, claims, encumbrances, and interests of any other person or entity, of any kind or nature, and will remain so at time of transfer.

(c) Seller has full legal authority to enter into and make this agreement to sell the Work and to deliver to Buyer a Bill of Sale transferring good, marketable title to the Work.

(d) Except as just expressly provided, Seller makes no other representation or warranty, whether express or implied, with respect to the Work.

Seller hereby agrees to indemnify and hold Buyer harmless from any and all demands, claims, judgments, and suits arising by reason of Seller's breach of any representation or warranty in this agreement.

5. **Integration and Governing Law.** This agreement contains all the covenants, promises, agreements and conditions, either oral or written, between Buyer and Seller and may not

be changed or modified except in writing signed by Buyer and Seller or their authorized representatives. The law of State A shall govern this agreement.

IN WITNESS WHEREOF, Seller and Buyer have executed this agreement as of the date first set forth above.

___________________________	___________________________
Great Gallery, Seller 123 Main Street Anytown, State A Telephone/email	Buyer 456 Central Street Thistown, State B Telephone/email

Second Drafting Exercise: Purchase through a Dealer

To: Junior Associate

From: Senior Partner

A few months ago, our client Mr. Smith (resident of State X) decided to buy a work by contemporary artist Lee Colors. He contacted his art consultant Paul Johns to get the process started. Last week, Johns finally located a work suitable for Mr. Smith's collection at a reputable gallery in State Z that represents Colors in that area. Johns has personally inspected the work and is satisfied as to its quality and authenticity.

The work *Untitled* dates from 10 years ago, and the gallery-provided provenance shows only one owner, "Private collector/State Z", who was the original purchaser from Colors. *Untitled* is a 32 × 39 1/2, unframed, mixed media work, signed and dated (verso) by Colors. The agreed upon price is $100x. The gallery was just going to use a receipt (I've included a copy of it below) for the purchase, but I believe we should have better documentation for the $100x transaction.

Please draft a contract for my review that will protect our client, Mr. Smith. Let me know of any non-obvious assumptions that you make and if you have any suggestions for additional steps to take.

Gallery of Distinction
1234 Washington St. Its Town, State Y

Receipt

Dated: XX/XX/XXXX

Sold to:	Mr. Smith c/o Paul Johns 789 Adams St. His Town, State X
Description:	Lee Colors Untitled, 20XX Mixed Media 32 × 39 ½ inches Signed and dated (verso)
Price:	$100x
	M. Mitchell, President

Chapter 3

Acquisition at Auction

Art auctions, one of the three primary marketplaces for the acquisition of art, were designed to be exciting experiences. The participant was meant to be dazzled by the sales room and the competitive, dramatic bidding process. This finely constructed world, matching a seller with potential buyers for a unique artwork at a single point in time, was built over centuries. Christie's and Sotheby's, the world leaders in fine art auctions, were each founded in the 1700s in London. That common origin may explain the familiar feel of the law relating to auctions. Nevertheless, the traditional auction world is evolving to address, if not totally accommodate, the 21st century. Technology, global concerns over ownership and money-laundering issues, and the high stakes monetizing and commodification of art all bear on the auction market today and, consequently, the law as well.

A. Auction Process

Let us begin with the auction process to understand what is expected of the three players—seller, auction house, and buyer. For each of the three players, the business purpose of the auction (a sale) and the timeline each player follows have basically remained constant over the centuries. In a typical fine arts auction, the seller starts the process by deciding to sell the artwork. Death, divorce, and debt (sometimes referred to as the three D's) tend to be the reasons for selling. The seller's belief that the excitement of a competitive auction will yield the highest price is generally the reason for choosing an auction as the sales venue. After deciding upon an auction house as the sales venue, the seller negotiates the consignment agreement with the auction house, including the reserve price, if any. See Chapter 9, *infra*, for a detailed discussion of consignment agreements.

The auction house then performs its two primary business responsibilities: to generate business for the auction and to conduct the auction. The final actor is the buyer, who must decide to buy the item, usually after inspecting the item and reviewing the Conditions of Sale. Thereafter the buyer must bid (in person, by proxy, on the phone, by advance written bid, or online) and, if successful, pay and take delivery. This thumbnail sketch belies the sharp legal disputes that can arise when any one of the parties believes the process was compromised.

Auctions operate under Conditions of Sale specific to that auction. While one can discern a common template, variations in Conditions of Sale can and do exist, even within the same auction house. Variations reflect the variety of auctions, such as location, items up for auction, and format of the auction (e.g., live, online, hybrid). The Conditions of Sale reproduced below is from Sotheby's Prints & Multiples Evening Sale in New York on October 22, 2020. As you read Sotheby's Conditions of Sale, notice the extent to which the historically simple roles of each party are now carefully delineated and where discretion lies. Many provisions are the result of regulatory actions and case law; some can reflect current conditions, such as the limited access to Sotheby's New York office because of the 2020 pandemic.

Sotheby's Conditions of Sale

The following Conditions of Sale and Terms of Guarantee are Sotheby's, Inc. and the Consignor's entire agreement with the purchaser and any bidders relative to the property listed in this catalogue.

The Conditions of Sale, Terms of Guarantee, the glossary, if any, and all other contents of this catalogue are subject to amendment by us by the posting of notices or by oral announcements made during the sale. The property will be offered by us as agent for the Consignor, unless the catalogue indicates otherwise.

By participating in any sale, you acknowledge that you are bound by these terms and conditions.

1. **As Is** Goods auctioned are often of some age. The authenticity of the Authorship (as defined below) of property listed in the catalogue is guaranteed as stated in the Terms of Guarantee and except for the Limited Warranty contained therein, all property is sold "AS IS" without any representations or warranties by us or the Consignor as to merchantability, fitness for a particular purpose, the correctness of the catalogue or other images or descriptions of the physical condition, size, quality, rarity, importance, medium, frame, provenance, exhibitions, literature or historical relevance of any property and no statement anywhere, whether oral or written, whether made in the catalogue, an advertisement, a bill of sale, a salesroom posting or announcement, or elsewhere, shall be deemed such a warranty, representation or assumption of liability. We and the Consignor make no representations and warranties, express or implied, as to whether the purchaser acquires any copyrights, including but not limited to, any reproduction rights in any property. We and the Consignor are not responsible for errors and omissions in the catalogue, glossary, or any supplemental material. Sotheby's will not be responsible or liable for damage to frames and glass coverings, regardless of the cause.

2. **Inspection** Prospective bidders should inspect the property before bidding to determine its condition, size, and whether or not it has been repaired or restored. Property will be available for viewing by appointment only at our New York premises, or such other location as we may indicate from time to time. You can schedule a viewing as indicated on our website.

3. **Buyer's Premium; Overhead Premium** A buyer's premium and an overhead premium will be added to the hammer price and are payable by the purchaser as

part of the total purchase price. The buyer's premium is 25% of the hammer price up to and including $400,000, 20% of any amount in excess of $400,000 up to and including $4,000,000, and 13.9% of any amount in excess of $4,000,000. The overhead premium is 1% of the hammer price.

4. **Withdrawal** We reserve the right to withdraw any property before the sale and shall have no liability whatsoever for such withdrawal.

5. **Per Lot** Unless otherwise announced by the auctioneer, all bids are per lot as numbered in the catalogue.

6. **Bidding** We reserve the right to reject any bid. The highest bidder acknowledged by the auctioneer will be the purchaser. The auctioneer has absolute and sole discretion in the case of error or dispute with respect to bidding, and whether during or after the sale, to determine the successful bidder, to re-open the bidding, to cancel the sale or to re-offer and re-sell the item in dispute. If any dispute arises after the sale, our sale record is conclusive. In person bidding is not available for this auction. Bidders are encouraged to submit bids online on Sothebys.com or through the Sotheby's App. In order to bid online, you must register an account with Sotheby's and provide requested information. In our discretion we will execute order or absentee bids and accept telephone bids and online bids via the Online Platforms as a convenience to clients who do not submit their bids online; Sotheby's is not responsible for any errors or omissions in connection there-with. Prospective bidders should also consult sothebys.com for the most up to date cataloguing of the property in this catalogue.

By participating in the sale, you represent and warrant that any bids placed by you, or on your behalf, are not the product of any collusive or other anti-competitive agreement and are otherwise consistent with federal and state antitrust law.

By participating in the sale, you represent and warrant that:

(a) The bidder and/or purchaser is not subject to trade sanctions, embargoes or any other restriction on trade in the jurisdiction in which it does business as well as under the laws of the European Union, the laws of England and Wales, or the laws and regulations of the United States, and is not owned (nor partly owned) or controlled by such sanctioned person(s) (collectively, "Sanctioned Person(s)");

(b) Where acting as agent (with Sotheby's prior written consent), the principal is not a Sanctioned Person(s) nor owned (or partly owned) or controlled by Sanctioned Person(s); and

(c) The bidder and/or purchaser undertakes that none of the purchase price will be funded by any Sanctioned Person(s), nor will any party be involved in the transaction including financial institutions, freight forwarders or other forwarding agents or any other party be a Sanctioned Person(s) nor owned (or partly owned) or controlled by a Sanctioned Person(s), unless such activity is authorized in writing by the government authority having jurisdiction over the transaction or in applicable law or regulation.

In order to bid on "Premium Lots" you must complete the required Premium Lot pre-registration application. Sotheby's decision whether to accept any pre-registration application shall be final. You must arrange for Sotheby's to receive your pre-registration application at least three working days before the sale. Please bear in mind that we are unable to obtain financial references over weekends or public holidays.

Sotheby's may require such necessary financial references, guarantees, deposits and/or such other security, in its absolute discretion, as security for your bid(s).

7. Online Bids via an Online Platform Sotheby's may offer clients the opportunity to bid on sothebys.com or through the Sotheby's App, or on any other online platform through which bidding may be made available for selected sales. By participating in a sale via any of the Online Platforms, you acknowledge that you are bound by these Conditions of Sale as well as the Additional Terms and Conditions for Online Bidding ("Online Terms"). By participating in a sale via any Online Platform, Bidders accept the Online Terms, as well as the relevant Conditions of Sale. Online bidding may not be available for Premium Lots.

8. Bids Below Reserve If the auctioneer deter-mines that any opening bid is below the reserve of the article offered, he may reject the same and withdraw the article from sale, and if, having acknowledged an opening bid, he determines that any advance thereafter is insufficient, he may reject the advance.

9. Purchaser's Responsibility On the fall of the auctioneer's hammer, the contract between the consignor and the purchaser is concluded, and the winning bidder thereupon will immediately pay the full purchase price or such part as we may require. Title in a purchased lot will not pass until Sotheby's has received the full purchase price in cleared funds. The purchaser's obligation to immediately pay the full purchase price or such part as we may require is absolute and unconditional and is not subject to any defenses, setoffs or counterclaims of any kind whatsoever. Sotheby's is not obligated to release a lot to the purchaser until title to the lot has passed and any earlier release does not affect the passing of title or the purchaser's unconditional obligation to pay the full purchase price. In addition to other remedies available to us by law, we reserve the right to impose from the date of sale a late charge of the annual percentage rate of Prime + 6% of the total purchase price if payment is not made in accordance with the conditions set forth herein. Please note Sotheby's reserves the right to refuse to accept payment from a source other than the buyer of record.

Sotheby's New York office is currently open on a limited basis by appointment only. All collections and deliveries for purchased property will be handled by Post Sale Services in coordination with purchasers after the auction. Unless otherwise agreed by Sotheby's, all property must be removed from our or our vendor's premises (as indicated on the invoice) by the purchaser at his expense not later than 30 calendar days following the auction. Purchasers are reminded that Sotheby's liability for loss of or damage to sold property shall cease upon the earlier of (a) 30 calendar days after the date of the auction and (b) our release of the property to the purchaser or the purchaser's designated agent. Upon the expiration of such 30 calendar day period or upon such earlier release, as applicable: (i) the purchaser bears full liability for any and all loss of or damage to the property; (ii) the purchaser releases Sotheby's, its affiliates, agents and warehouses from any and all liability and claims for loss of or damage to the property; and (iii) the purchaser agrees to indemnify and hold Sotheby's, its affiliates, agents and warehouses harmless from and against any and all liability for loss of or damage to property and any all claims related to loss of or damage to the property as of and from and after the time Sotheby's liability for loss or damage to the property ceases in accordance with this paragraph. If any applicable conditions herein are not complied with by the purchaser, the purchaser will be in default and in addition to any and all other remedies available to us and the Consignor by law, including, without limitation, the right to hold the purchaser liable for the total purchase price, including all fees, charges and expenses more fully set forth herein, we, at our option, may (x) cancel the sale of that, or any other lot or lots sold to the defaulting purchaser at the same or any other auction, retaining as liquidated damages all payments made by the purchaser, or (y) resell the purchased property, whether at public auction or by private sale, or (z) effect any combination thereof. In any case, the purchaser will be liable for any deficiency, any and all costs, handling charges, late charges, expenses of both sales, our commissions on both sales at our regular rates, legal fees and expenses, collection fees and incidental damages. We may, in our sole discretion, apply any proceeds of sale then due or thereafter becoming due to the purchaser from us or any affiliated company, or any payment made by the purchaser to us or any affiliated company, whether or not intended to reduce the purchaser's obligations with respect to the unpaid lot or lots, to the deficiency and any other amounts due to us or any affiliated companies. In addition, a defaulting purchaser will be deemed to have granted and assigned to us and our affiliated companies, a continuing security interest of first priority in any property or money of or owing to such purchaser in our possession, custody or control or in the possession, custody or control of any of our affiliated companies, in each case whether at the time of the auction, the default or if acquired at any time thereafter, and we may retain and apply such property or money as collateral security for the obligations due to us or to any affiliated company of ours. We shall have all of the rights accorded a secured party under the New York Uniform Commercial Code. You hereby agree that Sotheby's may file financing statements under the New York Uniform Commercial Code without your signature. Payment will not be deemed to have been made in full until we have collected good funds. Any claims relating to any purchase, including any claims under the Conditions of Sale or Terms of Guarantee, must be presented directly to Sotheby's. In the event the purchaser fails to pay any or all of the total purchase price for any lot and Sotheby's nonetheless elects to pay the Consignor any portion of the sale proceeds, the purchaser acknowledges that Sotheby's shall have all of the rights of the Consignor to pursue the purchaser for any amounts paid to the Consignor, whether at law, in equity, or under these Conditions of Sale.

10. Reserve All lots in this catalogue are offered subject to a reserve, which is the confidential minimum hammer price at which a lot will be sold. No reserve will exceed the low presale estimate stated in the catalogue, or as amended by oral or posted notices. We may implement such reserve by opening the bidding on behalf of the Consignor and may bid up to the amount of the reserve, by placing successive or consecutive bids for a lot, or bids in response to other bidders. In instances where we have an interest in the lot other than our commission, we may bid up to the reserve to protect such interest. In certain instances, the Consignor may pay us less than the standard commission rate where a lot is "bought-in" to protect its reserve.

11. Tax Unless exempted by law, the purchaser will be required to pay the combined New York State and local sales tax, any applicable compensating use tax of another state, and if applicable, any federal luxury or other tax, on the total purchase price. The rate of such combined tax is 8.875% in New York City and ranges from 7% to 8.625% elsewhere in New York.

12. Export and Permits It is the purchaser's sole responsibility to identify and obtain any necessary export, import, firearm, endangered species or other permit for the lot. Any symbols or notices in the sale catalogue reflect Sotheby's reasonable opinion at the time of cataloguing and are for bidders' general guidance only; Sotheby's and the Consignor make no representations or warranties as to whether any lot is or is not subject to export or import restrictions or any embargoes.

13. Governing Law and Jurisdiction These Conditions of Sale and Terms of Guarantee, as well as bidders', the purchaser's and our respective rights and obligations hereunder, shall be governed by and construed and enforced in accordance with the laws of the State of New York. By bidding at an auction, whether by agent, order or absentee bid, telephone, online or other means, all bidders including the purchaser, shall be deemed to have consented to the exclusive jurisdiction of the state courts of, and the federal courts sitting in, the State of New York. All parties agree, however, that Sotheby's shall retain the right to bring proceedings in a court other than the state and federal courts sitting in the State of New York.

14. Packing and Shipping Neither we nor our vendors are responsible for the acts or omissions in our or our vendors' packing or shipping of purchased lots or of other carriers or packers of purchased lots, whether or not recommended by us. Packing and handling of purchased lots is at the entire risk of the purchaser.

15. Limitation of Liability In no event will the aggregate liability of Sotheby's and the consignor to a purchaser exceed the purchase price actually paid.

16. Data Protection Sotheby's will hold and process your personal information and may share it with its subsidiaries and affiliates for use as described in, and in line with, Sotheby's Privacy Policy published on Sotheby's website at www.sothebys.com or available on request by email to enquiries@sothebys.com.

Under European data protection laws, a client may object, by request and free of charge, to the processing of their information for certain purposes, including direct marketing, and may access and rectify personal data relating to them and may obtain more information about Sotheby's data protection policies by writing to Sotheby's, 34-35 New Bond Street, London W1A 2AA, or 1334 York Avenue, New York, NY 10021, Attn: Compliance, or emailing enquiries@sothebys.com.

Please be aware that Sotheby's may film auctions or other activities on Sotheby's premises and that such recordings may be transmitted over the Internet via Sotheby's website and other online platforms. Online and telephone bids may be recorded.

Notes and Questions

1. *Registering to Bid.* If one wants to participate in an auction, it is necessary to register in advance of the auction as a bidder. For decades, this registration for many auctions could often be accomplished the day of the auction in a rather informal manner. For marquee auctions, there was more to the process, but it was relatively straightforward. Today the registration process can be more involved.

In the early 2000s, concern in the E.U. and the U.S. over money laundering and terrorist activity led to new restrictions in the financial sector. The Know Your Customer rule (KYC) requires affected firms in the financial sector to perform due diligence on their customers, including officially verifying identity and reporting suspicious activities (SARs). Today, a similar and sobering concern confronts the art market. Money gained through illegal activity may be laundered through the acquisition of art, some of which may be acquired at auction. In April 2018, the European Union passed the Fifth Anti-Money Laundering Directive (AML) requiring "persons trading or acting as intermediaries in the trade of works of art, including . . . art galleries and auction houses, where the value of the transaction . . . amounts to EUR 10,000 or more" to conduct customer due diligence and to notify authorities of suspicious activity. See Council Directive 2018/843, art. 1, 2018 O.J. (L 156/53) (EU); Timothy E. Burroughs, *US and EU Efforts to Combat International Money Laundering in the Art Market are no Masterpiece,* 52 Vand. J. Transnat'l L. 1061 (2019); Hannah Purkey, *The Art of Money Laundering,* 22 Fla. J. Int'l L. 111 (2010). These new rules of the Fifth Directive were to be implemented fully by January 10, 2020. With Brexit and the 2020 pandemic, the U.K. paused its full implementation, allowing affected firms to register with the government by June 10, 2021. Other compliance, however, is not paused. See Naomi Rea, *The UK Has Extended the Deadline to Register Under Its New Anti-Money Laundering Rules, Giving Art Dealers a Welcome 5 Month Reprieve,* Artnetnews (Aug. 25, 2020), https://news.artnet.com/market/uk-delays-anti-money-laundering-rules-1903930.

In the U.S., AML rules for the financial sector are generally found in the Bank Secrecy Act and have not officially applied to the art industry. Nevertheless, the four major auction houses voluntarily imposed their own AML rules for auction sales. Notice in Sotheby's Conditions of Sale, section 6 on Bidding, in order to bid on Premium Lots, registering to bid must be done a minimum of three days in advance and requires verifying the bidder's identity and financial references. This is a version of KYC. Despite the U.S. auction industry's voluntary measures, there is growing scrutiny on the unregulated art market and its culture of confidentiality. Some suggest it is time to include dealers in art and antiquities to the requirements of the Bank Secrecy Act. See Staff of S. Perm. Sub-Comm on Investigations, 116th Cong., *The Art Industry and the U.S. Policies That Undermine Sanctions* (July 29, 2020), providing a case study documenting how certain Russian oligarchs have used art transactions to evade U.S. sanctions. That suggestion was heard. In January 2021, the Bank Secrecy Act was amended to include "dealers in antiquities," effective after final regulations are issued, presumably in 2022. 31 U.S.C. § 5312(a)(2).

2. *Unsuccessful Bidders.* Unsuccessful bidders at auction sometimes move beyond their disappointment and file litigation, but unsuccessful bidders are generally equally unsuccessful in litigation. The auction houses, bolstered by UCC § 2-328, grant discretion to the auctioneer to determine the successful bidder. There are two scenarios involving bidding disputes for an unsuccessful bidder.

a. Re-opening bids. The first involves the auctioneer "re-opening" a bidding process that the unsuccessful bidder believes was completed by his bid which was "hammered down." In Callimanopulos v. Christie's Inc., 621 F. Supp. 2d 127 (S.D.N.Y. 2009), the plaintiff sought a declaratory judgment that he had a binding contract with Christie's for the sale of the painting *Grey* by Sam Francis. The plaintiff participated in the spring 2009 auction by telephone, connected to a Christie's employee who conveyed his bids to Christie's auctioneer Christopher Burge.

After the plaintiff's bid of $3 million, "Burge surveyed the room for other bids" and seeing none, dropped the hammer, announcing "sold to the phone." The Christie's employee told the plaintiff he was the successful bidder, but seconds later told him bidding was re-opened. The plaintiff challenged the re-opening, but Burge rejected the challenge. The sale was called to another buyer who bid $3.2 million.

The successful bidder was represented by an agent in attendance at the auction and she was seated in the front row to the right of the auctioneer. She raised concerns that day about that seat being a blind spot for the auctioneer; consequently two Christie's spotters paid particular attention to her during the auction. As Burge announced the sale to the plaintiff, the spotters signaled to Burge the new bid. Burge admitted that he did not see the new bid as he hammered down the sale "to the phone." Two employees of the plaintiff were also present at the auction, also seated in the front row, and they did not see the bid.

The court reviewed a videotape of the auction that confirmed the bid seen by the spotters but not the auctioneer or the plaintiff's employees. The court noted that, consistent with governing New York UCC § 2-328 and Christie's Conditions of Sale, the auctioneer had the discretion to re-open the bidding when another bid is being made while the hammer falls. Moreover, and contrary to plaintiff's argument, Burge was not required to actually see the bid in order to exercise his discretion; he could rely on spotters, a customary practice in the auction industry.

How important do you think the videotape was to the court? Are you surprised that the auction was being videotaped? Should Burge have reviewed the videotape before rejecting Callimanopulos's challenge? Historically, the auctioneer's duty is to get the seller the highest price. Does that put a thumb on the scale in favor of re-opening the bidding if there is a dispute? Is there something slightly disingenuous about bidding through an employee of Christie's but not allowing Christie's auctioneer to rely on Christie's spotters? Note again the importance of "custom" and "common practice" in the art industry in resolving disputes. See also Marx v. Sotheby Parke-Bernet, Inc., 476 N.Y.S.2d 482 (App. Div. 1983) (where plaintiffs were the successful bidders twice—at the initial fall of the hammer for $22,000 and at the subsequent fall of the hammer for $34,000 after the auctioneer re-opened the bidding because spotters noted another bid, but the court refused their suit to pay only the first hammered down price of $22,000, relying on the UCC and Sotheby's Conditions of Sale granting the auctioneer discretion to re-open bidding).

Assuming there is an "error or dispute" relative to the bidding, how long does the auctioneer have to exercise the discretion? Both Sotheby's and Christie's Conditions of Sale provide "whether during or after" the auction.

b. Mishandled bids. The second scenario involves mishandled bids, a phrase encompassing a variety of circumstances that includes plain mistakes. Consider the bidding arrangement a dealer reportedly made with Christie's in advance of a 1965 auction for a Rembrandt:

> When Mr. S is sitting down he is bidding. If he bids openly he is bidding. When he stands up he has stopped bidding. If he sits down again he is not bidding until he raises his finger. Having raised his finger, he is bidding until he stands up again.

Brian W. Harvey & Franklin Meisel, Auctions Law and Practice 224 (3d ed. 2006), quoting Daniel & Katherine Leab, The Auction Companion (1981).

Mr. S (allegedly Norton Simon) was ultimately the successful bidder, but only after the bidding process was re-opened because of his confusing signals. Sara Campbell, *Standing by his Bid—Unless He Sat*, ARTnews 90 (June 2010). Today, bidders at an auction are required to register in advance to bid. The tradition of making special arrangements for private bidding signals may be disappearing as auctions are increasingly using online or hybrid platforms. But see C. Hugh Hildesley, The Complete Guide to Buying and Selling at Auction 186–87 (1997) ("One of the most sophisticated that I have observed is that of a dealer who arranged that he would be bidding on a certain lot as long as he was *not* in the salesroom. . . . Such a bid is now only legal if the auctioneer has been given a preset upper limit of bid.").

Not all bidders are present in person or by a representative in the auction salesroom. Some submit written absentee bids in advance, and those bids are entered into the auctioneer's book. Occasionally, the absentee bids (also known as order bids) do not get entered or properly entered into the book due to human error. Telephone bids are usually handled by auction house employees staffing a phone bank in the salesroom. They are to call the telephone bidders as their desired lots come up for sale. Each of us knows that not all telephone calls go through or have clearly heard connections. What recourse does the absentee bidder have if the absentee bid was or would have been higher than the hammered down bid? What about the seller? See Nass v. Sotheby's Inc., No. 11229/91 (N.Y. Sup. Ct., Aug. 19, 1991). Does the auction house have a duty to notify the seller about the mishandled bid? See Cristallina v. Christie, Manson & Woods International, Inc., 502 N.Y.S.2d 165 (N.Y. App. Div. 1986), Part C, *infra*.

The auction houses did not easily embrace online bids. That changed as online bidding is desired by buyers and recognized by the auction houses for an increasing number of auctions. The coronavirus pandemic accelerated the shift to online bidding. Some auctions were shifted to online only and, more importantly, they were deemed successful. Some hiccups, of course, occur. Eileen Kinsella, *Sotheby's Livestreamed Paris-to-London Hybrid Sale Pulled in $90 Million, Led by a Picasso and Banksy's Irreverent Twist on Monet,* ArtnetNews (Oct. 21, 2020), available at https://news.artnet.com/market/sothebys-to-london.

3. *Successful Bidders.* Successful bidders at auction sometimes fail to follow through and pay for the property. Putting aside questions of authenticity and title, the reasons for non-payment include liquidity, mistake or misrepresentation, statutory violations, and political protest.

a. Liquidity. The plaintiff in Hessel v. Christie's Inc., 399 F. Supp. 2d 506 (S.D.N.Y. 2005), described himself as being "in the difficult position of having successfully purchased paintings that he desperately still wanted to own, but without the immediate cash resources to necessarily pay for them." *Id.* at 510. Bidding by phone, Hessel had the high bid of $1.5 million for a Jeff Koons painting (*St. Benedict*) on May 11, 2004 and the high bid of $600,000 for a Jean Michel Basquiat painting (*The Whole Livery Line*) on May 12, 2004. Christie's promptly sent invoices for the two works, and within a month, sent another set of invoices. Those invoices specifically noted that payment was overdue, that additional charges for storage and interest were applicable, and that the title would not pass until there was full payment. In June and July 2004, Hessel sent funds totaling $1,003,750 and began discussions with Christie's through an intermediary to gain more time for payment. Later that year, in response to a Christie's request, Hessel sent to Christie's an untitled painting by Damien Hirst as collateral but not the requested $500,000. Christie's indicated it would sell the Koons and Basquiat, but discussions continued. In March 2005, Hessel sent an additional $195,000 to Christie's. On September 2, 2005, Christie's informed Hessel that it intended to sell the Koons and Basquiat paintings at the November 2005 auction. One week before the advertised auction, Hessel brought an action seeking an injunction to prevent the sale of the three works and a determination that the additional charges for the storage and interest were inapplicable to him.

Hessel argued that Christie's Conditions of Sale did not apply to his telephone bids because no one mentioned them to him by telephone and because the terms were not on Christie's website (or he did not see them) when he viewed it. The court held that although this was a question of fact, it was unlikely that Hessel would prevail on the merits. Under New York law, the conditions of a public sale announced by the auctioneer are binding on a purchaser regardless of whether he knew or heard them. Moreover, Hessel had purchased from Christie's "at least ten times before." Additionally, UCC § 2-309(1) governing the sale of goods at auction provides for a "reasonable time" for delivery, and eighteen months is not reasonable. The court rejected Hessel's claim that by its actions Christie's waived or modified its rights.

Hessel's final argument that he stood to lose irreplaceable and unique pieces of artwork and that Christie's "would suffer absolutely no hardship" did not move the court. Noting that Hessel delayed bringing the injunction "until a few days before the auction," the court decided that Christie's would in fact suffer harm if required to withdraw the works at such a late date. The decision is straightforward contract law.

In this case, Hessel brought suit to prevent a "resale" of the works by Christie's at auction. A resale is one of the options available to the auction house under the Conditions of Sale, but whether a later offering is a sale or a resale can be important. See Christie Manson & Woods International, Inc. v. Brown, 214 N.Y.L.J. 29 (Aug. 28, 1995), where the court denied Christie's suit to recover from the nonpaying successful bidder the deficiency between his 1990 bid and the lesser sum paid in 1993 by a third party, when the items were next auctioned by Christie's. The court reasoned that because Christie's had voluntarily paid the original seller the amount of the 1990 bid shortly after the 1990 auction, the 1993 sale at auction was not a "resale." It was "merely a sale undertaken by the auctioneer, as the owner."

b. Mistake or Misrepresentation. Stavros Mihalarias, on behalf of his company, was the successful bidder at a Christie's auction in 2005 for a series of ten screenprints of Marilyn Monroe by Andy Warhol. Christie's Inc. v. Dominica Holding Corp., 2006 WL 2012607 (S.D.N.Y. 2006). He was also the successful bidder for eleven additional lots at the same auction. When he returned to Christie's the day after the auction to arrange for payment and shipping, he was surprised to learn that the Marilyn Prints were permanently glued to their supports and therefore could not be removed from their frames. In the catalogue, the Marilyn Prints had been described as "taped to the support" and "three examined out of the frames." Mihalarias declined to pay for the Marilyn Prints because the condition materially decreased their value but offered to pay for the other items. Christie's refused this offer at that time and reiterated that refusal in a subsequent exchange of letters. Christie's sued based on breach of contract, and Mihalarias counterclaimed for fraudulent inducement, breach of contract and lost profits. Christie's motion for partial summary judgment and dismissal of the counterclaims was denied.

It was undisputed that a sale was completed when Mihalarias was the high bidder. The question was whether the misrepresentations at issue would constitute fraudulent inducement thereby rendering the sale unenforceable. Under the governing New York law, a specific disclaimer normally bars a defense of fraudulent inducement, but not where the misrepresented facts are peculiarly within the knowledge of the seller. Christie's Conditions of Sale included a specific waiver. Did the exception apply, that is, did the misrepresentation involve information peculiarly within Christie's knowledge, such that the defects would not have been discovered upon inspection without great effort or difficulty? Mihalarias, a sophisticated art dealer for over 35 years, "simply viewed one of the Marilyn Prints in the hectic time immediately preceding the auction rather than examining it closely." Such a "cursory viewing" is not a careful examination of the type required by the courts to activate the exception to the waiver. Nevertheless, the court determined that it was unclear on the record before it whether Mihalarias *could* have conducted a thorough inspection of all the Marilyn Prints "without extraordinary difficulty, or even if he had whether he would have discovered the flaws." Consequently, his failure to conduct a thorough inspection was excused.

In his counterclaim, Mihalarias also claimed Christie's breached its contract to accept his payment and to deliver to him the additional lots on which he bid successfully. He alleges that each bid resulted in a "separate and distinct" contract. Recall a similar claim in Brockhurst v. Ryan, 146 N.Y.S. 2d 386 (1955), Chapter 1, *supra*. What provision in the Conditions of Sale would support Christie's refusal? What policy reason is there for Christie's not to accept payment for the undisputed lots? Christie's had resold these prints by the time of oral argument for a higher price. Do you think the owner-consignors of the undisputed works could force Christie's to complete those sales?

c. Statutory Violations. See Sotheby's Inc. v. Minor, 2009 WL 3444887 (S.D.N.Y. 2009) (discussed in Note 4 following *Veazie v. Williams*, *infra* in Part B), for discussion of whether the auction house's non-disclosure affects a successful bidder's duty to purchase. Also see William J. Jenack Estate Appraisers and Auctioneers Inc. v. Rabizadeh, 22 N.Y.3d 470 (2013), *infra*, for a buyer's allegation that an auction house violated the statue of frauds by not disclosing the identity of seller as required by New York statute.

d. Political Protest. In February 2009, Christie's held a highly publicized and a highly successful auction in Paris of property from the estate of fashion designer Yves St. Laurent. Chinese art dealer Cai Mingchao was the high bidder at $40 million for two 18th century Chinese bronze animal head sculptures. He allegedly refused to pay as an act of political protest. The two bronze animal heads (one a rat, the other a rabbit) were part of an 18th century fountain designed by a Jesuit missionary for the summer palace outside Beijing. The palace was sacked by French and British troops during the Second Opium War (also referred to as the War of Humiliation) in 1860, and the animal heads disappeared at that time. St. Laurent purchased the two sculptures decades before his death from a well-known French dealer.

Shortly before the auction, an action was brought in France on behalf of the Chinese government to prevent the auction of these two sculptures. The Chinese claimed ownership of the sculptures as national patrimony. The French court denied the claim of superior ownership. One irony of Cai Mingchao's actions is that one of the underbids was reportedly from another Chinese national who intended to repatriate the sculpture to China. See Chapter 5 and Chapter 6, *infra*, for a fuller discussion of repatriation of cultural property and customs enforcement of treaty obligations involving antiquities.

4. *Auction as Performance Art?* Sotheby's London auction in October 2018 created a unique art history moment. The last lot of the auction, *Girl with Balloon*, by the anonymous British street artist Banksy, had just hammered down at one million pounds ($1.4 million) when an alarm went off. The painting, slipped partially below the frame, was shredded by a remote-controlled mechanism in the back of the painting. It was reported that a man in the salesroom appeared to have operated an electronic device hidden in a bag; he was escorted from the building by Sotheby's security. The artist later posted a video showing his hiding a shredder in the frame and saying, "I secretly built a shredder into a painting in case it was ever put up for auction." The intent was to completely shred the artwork, but a malfunction occurred.

Some have wondered if Sotheby's knew of the shredder given that it was the last lot of the sale, the frame was presumably heavier than expected, and the work was placed on a wall for bidding and not on the podium as is the norm. Sotheby's denied prior knowledge. Scott Reyburn, *Banksy Painting Self-Destructs After Fetching $1.4 million at Sotheby's*, N.Y. Times, Oct. 7, 2018, at A18.

Is there any legal liability? There are several layers to consider. If a work was damaged by an auction house's negligence, there would be liability. What is the measure of damages? Banksy renamed the partially shredded *Girl with Balloon* as *Love Is in the Bin*, in effect creating a new artwork. The buyer agreed to purchase the newly-created artwork, which many believe is now worth more than she paid. "At first I was shocked but I realized I would end up with my own piece of art history." *Woman to keep Banksy Girl with Balloon painting*, BBC News, October 11, 2018.

5. *Auction Rings.* Section 6 on Bidding in Sotheby's Conditions of Sale provides that bids are not to be "the product of any collusive or other anti-competitive agreement." Auction rings (also known as bidding rings, bid pooling, or chill bidding) are a traditional example of such behavior. See Bunch v. Com., State Board of Auctioneer Examiners, 620 A.2d 578 (Pa. Commw. Ct. 1993). Usually, an auction ring occurs when dealers in the trade agree not to compete against each other at auction, thereby probably depriving the seller of the true value of the item. If the ring was the successful bid, there can be another auction held among the group. The differential in price is then split among the members of the group. Is there an argument that an auction ring is not *per se* anti-competitive? Does the size of the ring matter? Does intent matter? What if you and your friend agree not to compete for the same item? See Brian W. Harvey & Franklin Meisel, Auctions Law and Practice 264–274 (3d ed. 2006).

6. *Some Numbers.* The art market, including auctions, is a global business that can generate billions of dollars in annual sales. As an industry, auctions are not

immune to global downturns, yet record high prices can still be established in rough economic times. Some theorize that in times of economic downturns, the high-end art market will pay a premium for truly outstanding artworks that come to market. Some numbers from Christie's and Sotheby's are instructive.

In the first half of 2008, worldwide auction sales at Christie's and Sotheby's were reported at $3.2 billion and $3 billion, respectively. One year later, these figures for the first half of 2009 were $1.5 billion and $995 million, representing drops of 52% and 67%, respectively, reflecting the global economic downturn. The gap between Christie's and Sotheby's for 2009 is largely attributed to the Yves St. Laurent auction held in Paris in February 2009, which generated a record breaking $484.4 million in auction sales. For the first half of 2010, Christie's sales were $2.57 billion and Sotheby's were $2.2 billion. Both auction houses' results included world record prices for a single piece of art sold at auction.

In the decade since 2008, the growth in the global art market was described as "anemic." Deloitte & ArtTactic, ART & FINANCE REPORT 27 (6th ed. 2019). Nevertheless, the 2018 art market was estimated at $67.4 billion, which represented a 9% increase since 2008, while the 2019 art market was estimated at $64.1 billion, representing a year-over-year decline. Art Basel & UBS, GLOBAL ART MARKET REPORT (3d ed. 2019).

Despite the anemic decade since 2008, the art market can still offer some dazzling results. On November 15, 2017, Christie's set the world record for a single artwork ever sold at auction. In 20 minutes of bidding, Leonardo da Vinci's *Salvator Mundi* sold for $450.3 million (including the buyer's premium) to an anonymous bidder by telephone, against a reputed $100 million guarantee. There is speculation that the anonymous bidder was acting on behalf of Saudi Arabian crown prince Mohammed bin Salman. Early reports suggested the painting would be on display at the Louvre Abu Dhabi in fall 2018. A year later, the Louvre in Paris hoped the work would be part of their 500th anniversary exhibition commemorating Leonardo's death in 1519. Neither Louvre has shown the work. The whereabouts of *Salvator Mundi* remain uncertain. Some doubts as to the authenticity of the work have surfaced.

The major auction houses also conduct private sales or private treaty transactions through wholly owned subsidiaries. This integration provides the major auction houses with another venue of the art market to smooth art economic cycles. It also provides access to dealers' customers and entrée to dealers' art fairs. With such sales numbers and penetration of the art market by auction houses, dealers may have reason to be concerned about their survival as an independent part of the art market.

7. *Digital Art and Cryptocurrency Payments*. Christie's began a new era in auctions with its $69.3 million sale of Everydays: The First 5000 Days, a digital collage by Mike Winkelmann (aka Beeple) on March 11, 2021. The digital image was accompanied by non-fungible tokens (NFTs) that serve as a certificate of authenticity and effectively transfer ownership. The successful bidders negotiated in advance with Christie's to pay in cryptocurrency. Digital payments for digital art as well as for

physical art may become acceptable across auctions in the near future. Kelly Crow, *Sotheby's Considers More Cryptocurrency Payments*, Wall St. J., Mar. 17, 2021, at B1.

B. Seller's Anonymity

Anonymity of the seller's identity is for many an important attribute of auction sales. It is a time-honored part of auction's custom and tradition. *Jenack* directly challenged this paradigm.

William J. Jenack Estate Appraisers and Auctioneers, Inc. v. Rabizadeh

22 N.Y.3d 470, 5 N.E.3d 976 (2013)

Rivera, J.

* * *

. . . The central issue . . . is whether the sale of the auction item to Rabizadeh is memorialized in a writing that satisfies the statute of frauds.

As is common practice in public auction houses, Jenack permits bidding online and by telephone, or "absentee bidding," in addition to traditional in-person bidding. . . . At all times relevant to this appeal, Jenack's website set forth information about the auction process, as well as terms of sales for absentee bidders. . . . It informed any and all prospective bidders of payment obligation by stating "if your bid is successful you are legally responsible to make payment according to the terms set forth here."

* * *

Several days prior to a September 21, 2008 auction, Rabizadeh submitted a signed, absentee bidder form wherein he provided, as required by Jenack, his name, email address, telephone numbers, fax number, address, credit card number, and a list of items that Rabizadeh intended to bid on by telephone. Rabizadeh's list included the item at issue in this case, . . . "Item 193," and described in the online and printed catalogue as a "Fine Russian silver/enamel covered box with gilt interior, signed I.P. Khlebnikov, 19th Century Height 1 1/2"; top 1/2 × 3 5/8 (Estimate $4000–$6000)." Upon receipt of this form, Jenack assigned bidder number 305 to Rabizadeh, and included this number on the top of the form.

At the September auction, Rabizadeh submitted a $400,000 bid on item 193, and successfully outbid a competing bidder. . . . [T]he chief clerk recorded the winning bid on Jenack's "clerking sheet." This clerking sheet sets forth . . . a running list of the items presented at the public auction, with a separate line for each item that includes the item's lot number, catalogue description, and the number assigned by Jenack to the consignor. At the top of the clerking sheet Jenack's name and title are set forth as "William J. Jenack Appraisers/ Auctioneers." On the line for item 193, the chief clerk filled in Rabizadeh's previously assigned bidding number to reflect him as the buyer, and the amount of his winning bid, $400,000.

Shortly after the auction, Jenack . . . sent Rabizadeh an invoice for $497,398, which reflected the bidding price, the 15% "buyer's premium" and applicable taxes. When Rabizadeh failed to pay, Jenack commenced this action. . . .

Rabizadeh moved for summary judgment claiming . . . there was no writing memorializing any contract . . . as required by the statute of frauds. . . . Supreme Court denied Rabizadeh's motion and . . . entered judgment in favor of Jenack for the principal sum of $402,398.

Rabizadeh appealed. The Appellate Division, Second Department, reversed, concluding . . . Jenack failed to comply with General Obligations Law § 5–701(a)(6) because the clerking sheet did not include "the name of the person on whose account the sale was made," as required by the statute. . . .

On appeal, Jenack contends . . . the documents related to Rabizadeh's $400,000 bid satisfy the statute of frauds. Jenack and Rabizadeh dispute whether the clerking sheet constitutes the writing required by General Obligations Law § 5–701(a)(6), and whether any other document commemorates an agreement between them to purchase item 193.

* * *

To successfully establish his entitlement to summary judgment . . . , Rabizadeh must show that the record is bereft of documentation establishing such agreement, as provided for under the law. . . . [W]e conclude that Rabizadeh has not met his burden because there exists sufficient documentation of a statutorily adequate writing.

The statute of frauds is designed to protect the parties and preserve the integrity of contractual agreements. It is meant "to guard against the peril of perjury; to prevent the enforcement of unfounded fraudulent claims." . . . "In short, the purpose of the Statute of Frauds is simply to prevent a party from being held responsible, by oral, and perhaps false, testimony, for a contract that the party claims never to have made."

. . . As relevant to this case, the General Obligations Law sets forth a special provision for the auctioning of such goods:

"§ 5–701. Agreements required to be in writing

> "a. Every agreement, promise or undertaking is void, unless it or some note or memorandum thereof be in writing, and subscribed by the party to be charged therewith, or by his lawful agent . . .
>
> "6. Notwithstanding section 2–201 of the uniform commercial code, if the goods be sold at public auction, and the auctioneer at the time of the sale, enters in a sale book, a memorandum specifying the nature and price of the property sold, the terms of the sale, the name of the purchaser, and

> the name of the person on whose account the sale was made, such memorandum is equivalent in effect to a note of the contract or sale, subscribed by the party to be charged therewith."

Thus, in the case of a public auction, a bid may satisfy the statute of frauds where there exists . . . a memorandum in satisfaction of General Obligations Law § 5–701(a)(6). . . .

It is well established that the statutorily required writing need not be contained in one single document, but rather may be furnished by "piecing together other, related writings." Therefore, . . . a court may look to documents relevant to the bidding and the auction.

* * *

We construe the terms of a statute that are clear and unambiguous, "so as to give effect to the plain meaning of the words used." The General Obligations Law states clearly that the memorandum must include names. It makes no provision for an alternative to a name, including some other mode of identification . . . such as, in this case, numeric identifiers. . . . Thus, the numbers assigned by Jenack to represent the buyer and seller/consignor on the clerking sheet do not satisfy General Obligations Law § 5–701(a)(6).

Our analysis does not end with . . . the clerking sheet . . . because we must consider whether there are "related writings" that supply the required names, and which may be read, along with the clerking sheet, to provide the information necessary to constitute a memorandum in accordance with General Obligations Law § 5–701(a)(6). We agree with the Appellate Division that the absentee bidder form, along with the clerking sheet, provide the necessary information to establish the name of Rabizadeh as the buyer. . . .

In addition to the buyer's name, the General Obligations Law requires disclosure of "the name of the person on whose account the sale was made." Jenack urges a reading of the statute that would not require disclosure of the seller's identity, and that would permit it to continue to honor a seller's request to remain anonymous throughout the consignment and bidding process. Jenack and amici argue that the auction business is important to New York State and that it is a time honored and necessary custom and practice of auction houses to maintain the confidentiality of the seller. It is their contention that a requirement that the seller's identity be divulged would undermine the industry. However, the General Obligations Law does not reference the "seller," making it clear that the seller's name need not be provided in order to satisfy the requirement of "the name of the person on whose account the sale was made."

More than a century and a half ago, the New York Supreme Court of Judicature, then the highest common-law court in the state, held "the legislature intended it should not be necessary to insert the name of the real owner, but that it should be sufficient to insert the name of any person having legal authority to sell". It is well settled that an auctioneer serves as a consignor's agent. [*S*]*ee also Cristallina v. Christie, Manson & Woods Intl.,* 117 A.D.2d 284, 292, 502 N.Y.S.2d 165 [1st Dept.1986]....

Here, the clerking sheet lists Jenack as the auctioneer, and ... therefore, provides "the name of the person on whose account the sale was made" and satisfies General Obligations Law § 5–701(a)(6).... Thus, Jenack established an enforceable agreement....

It bears repeating in such a case as this that

> "'The Statute of Frauds was not enacted to afford persons a means of evading just obligations; nor was it intended to supply a cloak of immunity to hedging litigants lacking integrity; nor was it adopted to enable defendants to interpose the Statute as a bar to a contract fairly, and admittedly, made'".

Using the statute of frauds as a "means of evading" a "just obligation" is precisely what Rabizadeh attempts to do here, but the law and the facts foreclose him from doing so.... He cannot seek to avoid the consequences of his actions by ignoring the existence of a documentary trail leading to him.

Accordingly, the order of the Appellate Division should be reversed, with costs, and judgment of the Supreme Court reinstated.

Chief Judge Lippman and Judges Graffeo, Read, Smith, Pigott and Abdus-Salaam concur.

Notes and Questions

1. *Aftermath.* In 2010, the item was resold at auction for $50,000, one-eighth of the contested $400,000 bid in *Jenack* but a ten-fold increase from the original low estimate. Interestingly, the seller, Jonathan A. Thompson said, "I didn't ask to be anonymous. I didn't think about it at all." Tom Mashberg, *Lawyers Fight to Keep Auction Sellers Anonymous,* N.Y. Times, Feb. 3, 2013, at https://www.nytimes.com/2013/02/04/arts/design/battling-to-keep-auction-sellers-anonymous.html.

2. *Assessing Seller's Anonymity.* The auction industry has operated with seller's anonymity as the norm. In its unanimous *Jenack* decision, the New York Court of Appeals upheld this custom and tradition of the auction market in the nation's leading auction market. That is significant. To the extent anonymity is an important consideration for sellers, the New York high court's decision calmed the market that was somewhat roiled by the appellate court's contrary decision. The appellate court's decision created uncertainty in New York's auction market. Fears included losing auction business to other states, buyers reneging on their successful auction bids, and sellers leaving the auction market for private sales. By confirming the tradition, those fears were allayed. Yet every decision carries a cost. What is the cost of this anonymity?

Some argue that seller anonymity impairs data collection on antiquities looting and stolen property, increases the market for fakes and forgeries, hampers restitution efforts, and hurts efforts at artist resale royalties. See, e.g., Derek Fincham, *Assessing the Viability of Blockchain to Impact the Antiquities Trade*, 37 CARDOZO ARTS & ENTER. L. J. 101, 110 (2019); Guy A. Rub, *Experimenting with State-Enacted Resale Rights*, 107 KY. L.J. 651 (2019). Others posit that anonymity may allow stolen and looted art to resurface and consequently create visibility that can assist in restitution efforts. Cf, Solomon R. Guggenheim Foundation v. Lubell, 569 N.E.2d 426 (N.Y. 1991), Ch. 5, *infra*.

C. Seller's Bidding at Auction

One of the most vexing auction process questions is the role of the seller during the auction. Bluntly, can the seller participate and bid on his own property? Balancing seller's and buyer's concerns within a framework of market integrity has a long past and an active present. *Bexwell* and *Veazie* provide a centuries-deep perspective on the importance of good faith in auctions.

Bexwell v. Christie

Saturday, Feb. 3d, 1776, 1 COWP. 396
98 Eng. Rep. 1150

LORD MANSFIELD.—The matter in question is in itself of small value; but in respect of the principles by which it must be governed, it is a question of great importance. . . . The question is, whether a bidding by the owner of goods at a sale under these conditions, namely, "that the highest bidder shall be the purchasor" . . . is a bidding within the meaning of such conditions of sale?

There is no express undertaking on the part of the defendant, nor is it, as has been ingeniously said, a direction that there should be no bidding under 15l. which might be fair: but the direction given to the defendant is, "not to let the horse go under 15l;" which implies there might be a bidding under that sum. The question then is, whether the owner can privately employ another person to bid for him?—The basis of all dealings ought to be good faith; so, more especially in these transactions, where the public are brought together upon a confidence that the articles set up to sale will be disposed of to the highest real bidder: that could never be the case, if the owner might secretly and privately inhance the price, by a person employed for that purpose; yet tricks and practices of this kind daily increase, and grow so frequent, that good men give into the ways of the bad and dishonest in their own defence. But such a practice was never openly avowed. An owner of goods set up to sale at an auction never yet bid in the room himself. If such a practice were allowed, no one would bid. It is a fraud upon the sale, and upon the public. The disallowing it is no hardship upon the owner. For if he is unwilling his goods should go at an under price, he may order them to be set up at his own price, and not lower: such a direction would be fair: or he might do as was done by Lord Ashburnham, who sold a large estate by auction ; he had it inserted in the conditions of sale, that he himself might bid once in the course of the sale: and he bid at once 15,000 and 20,000l. Such a condition is fair; because the public are then apprised, and know upon what terms they bid. . . .

The question then is, is such a bidding fair? . . . What is the nature of a sale by auction? It is, that the goods shall go to the highest real bidder. But there would be an end of that, if the owner might privately bid upon his own goods. There is no contract with the auctioneer. He is only an agent between the buyer and seller. He may fairly bid for a third person who employs him, but not for the owner.

* * *

Therefore, upon full consideration, I am of opinion, that a bidding by the owner in the manner contended for, and agreeable to the directions given in this case, would have been a fraud upon the sale: and consequently, that this action against the defendant as auctioneer, cannot be maintained.

Veazie v. Williams

49 U.S. 134 (1850)

Mr. Justice Woodbury delivered the opinion of the court.

* * *

. . . [T]he bill asked the rescission of a sale at auction . . . of certain mills . . . on the alleged ground . . . of puffing or by-bidding, so as to advance the price about $20,000 above what it otherwise would have been. In their answer, the respondents denied any such bidding by their procurement . . . and that any claim to relief by the plaintiff is barred by the lapse of time since the sale.

* * *

The relief here is . . . sought for a fraud practised in augmenting the price; or, in other words, for taking false steps to enhance it; and it is the consequence and injury caused by these unfair means that the plaintiff would avoid.

* * *

It is conceded . . . that some other bids than Veazie's went nearly to $40,000, and as no person is shown to have made them but the auctioneer, it follows that they must have been real bids by him for himself, or fictitious ones by him, with a view to increase the price to be obtained by the respondents, and to increase his own commissions on a sum so much larger than had been anticipated when the sale began.

Looking to the supposition that the bids were real and for himself, that idea is not supported, but rather disproved, by the testimony. The auctioneer does not appear to be a man of wealth, able to buy so valuable property for investment, nor was such a purchase in the line of his business or profession, nor does he seem to have had the means or disposition for speculation, and especially on so large a scale; and he must have well known that the true value of this property was not considered by the owners above $14,500, nor its value to [another bidder] Wadleigh as enhanced by its locality in his dispute with Veazie, as above $18,000.

The weight of the testimony, then, is decidedly against the correctness of the supposition, that the bids above $20,000, except the plaintiff's, were by the auctioneer for himself and on his own account.

Had it been otherwise, it would be very questionable whether, in point of law or equity, an auctioneer can be allowed to bid off for himself the very property he is selling. It has been laid down that he cannot. The principles against it are stronger, if possible, and certainly were enforced earlier in courts of equity than of law. An opposite course would give to an auctioneer many undue advantages. It would tend, also, to weaken his fidelity in the execution of his duties for the owner. He would be allowed to act in double and inconsistent capacities, as agent for the seller and as buyer also; and the precedents are numerous holding such sales voidable, if not void, and at all events unlawful, as opposed to the soundest public policy. That an auctioneer is a general agent for the owner usually, though questioned in the argument, cannot be doubtful. He is so till the sale is completed. And though he may be agent of the buyer after the sale for some purposes, such as to take the case out of the statute of frauds, yet this does not affect the other principle, that till the sale, and before it, he acts for the vendor alone....

* * *

Veazie being thus situated so as to be more easily duped ... and his condition and fears and anxieties being probably known to [the auctioneer] Head, if not to [owner's agent] Stephen H. Williams, the auctioneer, by the means before described, procured for his employers nearly treble what they expected or what had been agreed on as the minimum price. The next inquiry is, if such a transaction renders the sale ... void, either for fraud or mistake. In ... the civil law, a buyer of immovables is ... entitled to a rescission of the sale if it turn out, though without fraud, that the price was more than fifty per cent above the true value. Here the price was at least a hundred per cent above,—yet there must in this country be fraud also, or a mistake.

Though no evidence is seen of fraud practised by the respondents in person, nor by their express directions, yet a fraud was evidently perpetrated by the auctioneer, as agent for the respondents ... and the respondents have taken and still retain the benefit of it. This conclusion is indisputable....

Does this state of things, then ... require the sale to be relieved against, on sound principles of equity and public morals?

By-bidding or puffing by the owner, or caused by the owner, or ratified by him, has often been held to be a fraud, and avoids the sale. He may fix a minimum price, or give notice of by-bids, and thus escape censure. But this shows that, without such notice, it is bad to resort to them. . . .

The by-bidding deceives, and involves a falsehood, and is, therefore, bad. It violates, too, a leading condition of the contract of sales at auction, which is that the article shall be knocked off to the highest real bidder, without puffing. It does not answer to apologize and say that by-bidding is common. For, observed Lord Mansfield, 'Gaming, stockjobbing, and swindling are frequent. But the law forbids them all.' Cowp., 397. In *Bexwell v. Christie,* Cowp., 396, the pole-star on this whole subject, it is said,—'The basis of all dealings ought to be good faith. So more especially in these transactions, where the public are brought together in a confidence that the articles set up for sale will be disposed of to the highest real bidder.'

* * *

Nor does it lessen the injury or the fraud if the by-bidding be by the auctioneer himself. He, being agent of the owner, is equally with him forbidden by sound principle to conduct clandestinely and falsely on this subject. Cowp., 397. All should be fair,—above-board.

Indeed, in point of principle, any fraud by auctioneers is more dangerous than by owners themselves. The sales through the former extend to many millions annually, and are distributed over the whole country, and the acts accompanying them are more confided in as honest and true than acts or statements made by owners themselves in their own behalf, and to advance their own interests. Great care is therefore proper to preserve them unsullied, and to discourage and repress the smallest deviations in them from rectitude.

Here the auctioneer virtually said to his hearers, when he made a fictitious bid,—'I have been offered so much more for this property.' But he said it falsely, and said it with a view to induce the hearers to offer still more. He averred it as a fact, and not an opinion; and as a fact peculiarly within his knowledge. . . .

Some cases, and some reasoning found in them, attempt to sanction a contrary doctrine, if the by-bids were made merely to prevent a sacrifice of the property,—a 'defensive precaution,'—but not otherwise.

These exceptions still concede that the by-bidding, when an artifice to mislead the judgment and inflame the zeal of others . . . is fraudulent and makes the sale void.

* * *

But they are held liable on ground beyond and apart from all this, and as well settled in England as here, that if a principal ratify a sale by his agent, and take the benefit of it, and it afterwards turn out that fraud or mistake existed in the sale, the latter may be annulled, and the parties placed *in statu quo;* or they may, where the case and the wrong are divisible, be at times relieved to the extent of the injury.

* * *

The sale thus made here, was adopted and carried into effect by the respondents; and hence, on account of the fraud involved in it, they should either restore the consideration, and take back the mills, or indemnify the purchaser to the extent of his suffering.

* * *

Notes and Questions

1. *Auction Law's Roots in Equity. Bexwell* and *Veazie* reveal the deep roots equity laid down in auction cases, largely due to the public nature of the auction sale. Lord Mansfield's concern for the integrity of the market transaction—"basis of all dealings ought to be good faith"—was heightened because "the public are brought together." To allow an owner's undisclosed bidding would be a "fraud upon the sale, and upon the public." *Veazie* echoed a similar concern for the public—"any fraud by auctioneers is more dangerous than by owners themselves. The sales extend to many millions annually . . . over the whole country. . . ."

This historic concern for integrity in the auction marketplace because of the public nature of auctions continues today. In the next principal case, *Cristallina*, the plaintiff argued for the imposition of punitive damages because "the business of an auctioneer has always been affected with a public interest."

This concern is not limited to judges and case law; it underlies legislation as well. For example, the New York City legislation governing auctions and auctioneers is found in the City's Rules, Title 6 Department of Consumer Affairs, 6 R.C.N.Y. §§ 2-121 et seq.

2. *Disclosure.* In *Bexwell*, Lord Mansfield was not troubled by the practice per se of an owner (or his agent) bidding on his own property, but by doing so secretly. He offered two alternatives for an owner. First, the owner could direct a reserve price, and presumably the existence (but not the amount) of a reserve would be revealed to the public. Second, the owner could "insert [. . .] in the conditions of sale, that he himself might bid." Because there is disclosure, the condition is fair.

Consider Sotheby's Conditions of Sale. Is it likely that an individual owner could change these terms? Regardless of the answer, Lord Mansfield's suggestions now rule the day. Today most items offered in art auctions have a reserve price, and most buyers at auction are fully aware of that. More important, the Conditions of Sale (section 10 on Reserve) provide the auctioneer may bid on behalf of the owner and, if the auction house has an interest in the item, on its own behalf, up to the reserve price. The Conditions of Sale effectively link Lord Mansfield's two suggestions. Allowing a seller to bid on his own property through the auctioneer at auction remains a controversial issue today in theory and in practice. It is complicated by the various, sometimes interlocking, financial interests and financing methods of the parties.

In theory, an auction establishes the true value of an item, because it was based on competitive bidding. Of the two main duties of the auctioneer, the conduct of the auction requires the auctioneer to spark and then manage an electric atmosphere for competitive bidding among the participants. Understandably, the auctioneer can view her ability to bid "off the chandelier," whether merely to get the action started or to keep it moving upward, as an important tool for her craft. Equally understandable is the skepticism of a buyer whose bid was the only genuine bid in response to a series of phantom bids. If there is no genuine bid, one can believe that competitive bidding to establish value was manipulated. This is especially important because, in bidding at auction, a bidder can view her economic exposure as merely the incremental difference between the prior bid and her bid. Without a genuine underbid, the economic exposure is greater.

Balancing this tension between the interests of the seller and the buyer, New York City's statutory law favors the seller by expressly permitting the practice with disclosure but recognizes the bidder's concern by capping this right to bid up to the reserve price only. Because the reserve price is a confidential number that cannot exceed the minimum estimated sales price, bidders are effectively on notice that until bidding reaches that minimum estimate, the bidding may be just the auctioneer doing the seller's bidding.

3. *Auction Houses and Guarantees.* In addition, an auctioneer can place bids on behalf of the auction house up to the reserve price with disclosure. Why would an auction house do this? One reason involves the fierce competition for top works and the financial incentives given to sellers to induce them to consign their works to the auction house and not to a rival. See Chapter 9, *infra*. In the early 1970s, as auction houses expanded their geographic and social reach, auction houses began to offer minimum price guarantees to certain sellers. In exchange, the seller would pay a larger percentage, up to 40%, of any successful bid beyond the guarantee. Disclosure of a guarantee is now required by statute. What impact does a guarantee have on auction prices or on the auction house? With the 2008 economic downturn roughly coinciding with the fall auctions, Sotheby's and Christie's were seriously impacted by outstanding guarantees. Guarantees, in turn, became less readily available for a period of time. They did not, however, disappear. By 2018, for example, guarantees in post-war and contemporary evening auctions were estimated at a record $1.29 billion. This "invisible hand" in the art market remains an important negotiation point in consigning artworks for auction. Deloitte & ArtTactic, Art & Finance Report 27 (6th ed. 2019).

In the early 1990s, two other financial incentives for seller-consignors emerged: non-refundable advances and nonrecourse loans. If the property fails to sell under a non-refundable advance, the consignor must pledge additional collateral to the auction house; but under a nonrecourse loan, the only recourse for the auction house is to re-offer the artwork later. Unlike the guarantee, neither the non-refundable advance nor the nonrecourse loan transfers title to the auction house if the property fails to sell. Does this difference affect the disclosure required by the auction house?

4. *Non-Disclosure of Guarantee.* Halsey Minor was the successful bidder for Edward Hicks's *The Peaceable Kingdom with the Leopard of Serenity* and Childe Hassam's *Carriage in Winter, Paris* at Sotheby's May 2008 auction. About three months before the auction, Minor contacted Dara Mitchell, Sotheby's Director of the American Paintings Department, for advice. She allegedly agreed to advise him about American art and assist him in purchasing it. Over the three months, Mitchell discussed the Hicks painting with Minor and suggested he purchase it. Minor did so by telephone bid through Mitchell. Subsequent to the auction, Minor discovered that Sotheby's had a security interest in the Hicks painting and the Hassam painting. Neither painting carried a disclosure symbol in the catalogue, nor had Mitchell disclosed Sotheby's interest to Minor. The auction catalogue stated that if "Sotheby's owns the lot in whole or in part or has an economic interest in the lot equivalent to ownership," a triangle symbol would be used. As neither work carried the symbol, Minor refused to pay. Sotheby's sued Minor, and he responded with a counterclaim.

On Minor's motion for leave to amend his counterclaim, the court denied his attempt to add a deceptive practices claim, which requires "consumer injury or harm to the public interest." Sotheby's, Inc. v. Minor, 2009 WL 3444887 (S.D.N.Y. 2009).

> There is no logical connection between Sotheby's failure to disclose a security interest and any actual or potential injury to either Minor or the public. Minor does not allege that the security interest otherwise decreased the value of the works. Furthermore, he does not allege that the paintings were auctioned at an inflated price because of the failure to disclose the security interest. To the contrary, because the paintings were sold at auction, Minor set the price for the paintings.

Id. at *6.

Minor's request to add a breach of fiduciary duty claim was also denied "because (Minor) does not adequately plead the existence of a fiduciary duty." *Id.* at *9. Noting the general rule that an auction house acts as an agent of the consignor, the court determined that neither Sotheby's role as an auction house nor Michell's alleged role as an art advisor, consultant, and telephone bid taker, created any sufficiently "extraordinary circumstances" to upset the general rule. In 2010, Minor was ordered to pay Sotheby's $6 million in damages. Sotheby's and Christie's have barred him from bidding at their auctions.

Another variation on financing is third party guarantees, some of which may include the auction house as one of the guarantors. If there is a third party guarantee that does not include the auction house, can the guarantor participate in the bidding? With or without disclosure? How would that work? This is largely uncharted territory, but one can readily see the difficulties for maintaining Lord Mansfield's good faith in the auction process.

5. *Evolution of Legal Relationships.* In *Bexwell*, the plaintiff was the owner of the item sold at auction and the defendant Christie was the auctioneer. According to Lord Mansfield, their legal relationship was modest: "There is no contract with the auctioneer. He is only an agent between the buyer and seller." 98 Eng. Rep. at 1151. Almost 75 years later in *Veazie*, the legal relationship between the owner and the auctioneer progressed to a principal-agent relationship: "That an auctioneer is a general agent for the owner . . . cannot be doubtful. . . . [T]ill the sale, and before it, he acts for the vendor alone. . . ." 49 U.S. at 152. Today, there is a written contract between the auction house and the owner, and there is no doubt that the auction house and the owner are also in a fiduciary relationship, as the next case makes clear.

Characterizing the relationship between the buyer and the auction house today is discussed in the Notes after *Cristallina*.

6. *A Nod to Civil Law.* In *Veazie*, the Supreme Court noted the civil law principle that a buyer is entitled to rescission, if the price paid for immovables exceeds the true value by more than 50%.

C. Evolving Duties of Auction House

The following case is brought by the seller, not a buyer, of artworks auctioned by Christie's. Like *Bexwell*, it admittedly does not fit squarely within the acquisition perspective. It is included here to give a fuller transactional understanding of the modern auction process and a sense of some of the behind-the-scenes pressures. *Cristallina*, a unanimous decision, confirms that fiduciary principles are not irrelevant.

Cristallina v. Christie, Manson & Woods International Inc.

502 N.Y.S.2d 165 (N.Y. App. Div. 1986)

SULLIVAN, J. At issue is the responsibility, if any, of an auction house to the consignor of works of art for sale at public auction. Cristallina S.A., a Panamanian corporation engaged solely in the purchase and sale of works of art, consigned for sale eight Impressionist paintings to Christie, Manson and Woods International, Inc., the international auction house. The auction was a conceded failure, and as a result Cristallina brought this action against Christie's and its former president, David Bathurst, for monetary redress, including punitive damages. Cristallina claims, *inter alia*, that Christie's and Bathurst intentionally or negligently misrepresented the sum the paintings would bring at auction and failed to advise it of the risks inherent in such a sale. The matter is before us on appeal from a grant of summary judgment dismissing the complaint.

In January 1981, Cristallina, anxious to raise $10,000,000 to purchase additional paintings, contacted Christie's about the possibility of selling several Impressionist paintings that it owned, and a meeting with Bathurst, an expert on Impressionist art, was arranged.

At a February 10, 1981 meeting in Switzerland with Cristallina's representative, Dimitry Jodidio, Bathurst inspected a group of 11 paintings, tentatively appraising the value of each and eventually recommending that 8 of them be put up for sale at a public auction. To demonstrate the advantage of a public auction, Bathurst prepared a memorandum showing what the paintings would obtain at auction as opposed to private sale. According to Jodidio, Bathurst played down the lowest anticipated private sale figure of $7,850,000, as well as the lowest auction estimate $8,500,000, to focus on the high auction gross figure of $12,600,000. On the strength of Bathurst's advice, Jodidio agreed to a public auction and, after subsequent negotiations, Cristallina consigned the eight selected paintings to Christie's for sale in New York City on May 19, 1981. Christie's commission was set at 4%. In the event, however, the total sales did not exceed $9,400,000, Christie's was to forego its commission entirely and accept, instead, a buyer's premium, which would amount to much less. Since it was also agreed that the seller's identity was not to be disclosed, Bathurst was instructed to use code words in referring to Cristallina and Jodidio.

Christie's proceeded to advertise and generate curiosity and interest in the sale, designated as "Eight Important Paintings from a Private Collector." It is undisputed that it placed advertisements, solicited and supplied information for articles, directly contacted collectors and compiled a color catalogue of the paintings. It also released sale estimates of possible selling price ranges to the media and the public.

After returning to New York, Bathurst undertook to reach agreement with Jodidio on the reserves which would be set for each of the paintings. Besides monitoring the art market and speaking to other auctioneers, dealers and collectors, Bathurst, in contemplating the reserve prices, also consulted Christopher Burge, the head of Christie's Impressionist paintings department. In his first conversation with Jodidio on the subject on February 23, 1981, Bathurst recommended a reserve totaling $9,300,000, and prepared a memorandum to that effect listing the reserve assigned to each painting. The next day Christie's picked up the eight paintings in Switzerland and shipped them to New York for research and cataloguing. In arranging for insurance, Christie's assigned a specific value to each of the paintings based on Bathurst's appraisals. Jodidio also wrote Bathurst on that day and set forth his understanding of the agreement reached on reserves. Jodidio's reserves matched the insurance values Christie's assigned to the paintings, and exceeded the total of the reserves recommended by Bathurst on February 23rd by $700,000.

Noting the discrepancies in their respective views as to the reserves, Bathurst contacted Jodidio and they agreed that since the auction was still several months away the final setting of reserves would be deferred until just before the auction. As of March, Bathurst still believed that the reserves contained in his February 23rd memorandum were appropriate, but the parties understood that his view of the appropriateness of the reserves was subject to change in the event Christie's concluded that market conditions had changed.

When the paintings arrived in New York in early March, Burge, who had "broadly concurred" with the values placed on them by Bathurst, began his research and cataloguing of them. Although he did not change his view as to their value, he disagreed with Bathurst as to the auction appeal of the selected paintings. Many of the paintings, he believed, irrespective of their true value, would be "difficult" to sell at auction since "a prettier picture will be easier to sell than a tough picture, even though the tough picture is important." For example, Burge considered the Cezanne to be "a tough picture" while Bathurst predicted possible proceeds as high as $3,200,000, a figure which Burge dismissed as "unobtainable". Burge had even less faith in the Morisot and the Van Gogh "Rats", which he dismissed as being "pretty horrible". Burge's concerns were never reported to Jodidio. At the time, the paintings had not been catalogued or a public announcement of the sale made, and thus the sale could have been canceled without the harm to their value which apparently would result if they were withdrawn from sale after they had been catalogued and placed on the public market.

Among Burge's assignments with respect to the auction was the responsibility for advising potential purchasers of the high and low presale estimates for each of the paintings. These estimates reflected Christie's belief as to the range within which the paintings would sell. Christie's quoted presale estimates on May 4, 1981 for seven of the paintings reveal a substantial difference in amounts from the figures quoted to Jodidio by Bathurst on February 10th. On May 4th, just weeks before the auction, the total of the high estimates for the seven paintings (excluding the Monet) was $8,550,000. In contrast, on February 10th, Bathurst had stated that with respect to the same paintings, the high estimates totaled $10,800,000. Moreover, for the same seven paintings, Bathurst had in February recommended reserves totaling $8,500,000—a figure which was barely under the high estimates ($8,550,000) quoted on May 4th.

In giving the low and high presale estimates, Christie's apparently violated its long-standing policy, stated in every catalogue which it published, not to set reserves higher than the announced high presale estimates. For example, in February the Van Gogh "Houses" reserve was initially set at $2,200,000. At Bathurst's recommendation, that reserve was raised on May 18th to $2,300,000. Yet, the high estimate for that painting was only $2,000,000. In other cases, in violation of normal practice, the high estimates and the reserves coincided exactly. As Burge noted: "Ideally, reserves should be around 80 percent of our published estimates." No discussion was had with Jodidio about the high and low presale estimates being quoted to the public, nor did Jodidio ever approve any specific high or low presale estimate.

As the May 19th auction date approached, Burge and Bathurst continued to discuss the Cristallina paintings. Burge told Bathurst in early May that the Monet and Cezanne estimates were high. Indeed, according to Burge, he and Bathurst agreed that the $3,200,000 Cezanne estimate quoted to Jodidio "was unobtainable". On May 12, 1981, Christie's public relations officer, who received her information from Burge, wrote to CBS in connection with her promotional activities for the upcoming auction, stating that Christie's expected to receive between $5,000,000 and $9,000,000 for the paintings. Thus, eight days after its May 4th quote setting forth the high and low estimates and only one week before the auction, Christie's was advising the media that the paintings were worth even less than the estimates quoted on May 4th.

Apparently, sometime during the month of May, rumors began to circulate with regard to Jodidio's supposed ownership of the eight paintings. In fact, on May 15, 1981, Jodidio was named in a *New York Times* article as the owner. According to Cristallina, the emergence of Jodidio's name may have given rise to questions about the ownership of the paintings and title thereto. An *International Herald Tribune* article which appeared shortly after the auction stated that the Cristallina sale "appears to have been the object of a hostile rumor campaign reportedly started by one of the world's leading dealers in old and modern masters." While Christie's denies having had any knowledge of these rumors, its denial is at least subject to challenge on the basis of a May 11, 1981 telex from its Geneva office indicating that, on the basis of information obtained from two different clients, Bathurst had notice of the "mystery and the doubts" concerning Cristallina. In any event, Cristallina was never aware of the rumors.

During the period between May 4th and May 18th, according to Bathurst, the public's reaction to the paintings "was quite favorable". Burge confirmed this by testifying that initially "there was considerable interest in a number of the [paintings]." While, ordinarily, this positive public reaction would cause him to revise the reserves upwards, Bathurst wanted to lower the reserves based on a negative "feeling" he had developed about the outcome of the auction. At his final meeting with Jodidio the day before the auction, Bathurst recommended reserves totaling $9,250,000, which was only $50,000 less than the reserves recommended by him in the February 23rd memorandum. This gross reserve figure was, of course, inconsistent with Christie's prior advice to the media that the paintings would earn between $5,000,000 and $9,000,000 and the fact that the bidding public had already been given, as high presale estimates, figures which were lower than the reserves Bathurst was recommending.

A comparison of the February reserves with the May reserves shows that Bathurst had increased the reserves on both the Gauguin and the Van Gogh "Houses" by $100,000 each. When this was noted at his deposition, he sought to justify the increase on the ground that those two paintings were the ones he "thought would do best." In discussing the reserves at the May 18th meeting, Bathurst did not advise Jodidio that Christie's had publicly announced that the paintings would sell for between $5,000,000 and $9,000,000 or that the recommended reserves, in violation of Christie's own policy, were greater than the high estimates. Not having this information available to him, Jodidio alleges that he agreed to the reserves recommended by Bathurst.

According to Bathurst, he was also given the unilateral right to add to the total reserve of $9,250,000 an additional $150,000 (the "floating reserve"), which he could use to increase the reserves on whichever paintings he felt were appropriate. Jodidio has denied that any agreement was ever reached with respect to the $150,000 floating reserve. The addition of the $150,000 floating reserve not only increased the reserves beyond what they had been in February, but was at odds with Bathurst's stated position that the reserves as of May should be lowered, not increased. When asked why he suggested that there be a floating reserve, Bathurst stated that he "was trying to meet Mr. Jodidio's insistence to obtaining this, as near to this $10,000,000 figure as possible." As even Bathurst conceded, however, an auctioneer does not increase his chances of obtaining better sale results by raising reserves. In his deposition Bathurst testified, "By raising reserves on a specific painting, that increases the chances of the item being bought in."

As matters turned out, Bathurst decided, several hours before the auction, to add the $150,000 floating reserve to two of the paintings. Without advising Cristallina, he increased the reserve on the Gauguin from $1,300,000 to $1,350,000 and the Van Gogh "Houses" from $2,300,000 to $2,400,000.

The sale was held during a week of intensive activity at Christie's and Sotheby's. According to preauction publicity, sale proceeds were expected to equal or surpass the large sums collected in previous sales of this magnitude. Despite extensive publicity, media coverage and a sell-out crowd, the sale went badly. Seven of the eight paintings were not sold. The one painting which was sold, the Degas, fetched a record $2,200,000. The Gauguin was hammered down at $1,300,000, which was the reserve price agreed to by Christie's and Cristallina. Christie's, however, has refused to acknowledge the sale, claiming that because Bathurst had decided to add $50,000 to the reserve, the $1,300,000 bid was below the reserve.

Immediately upon the completion of the auction, Bathurst advised Christie's press office that three paintings had been sold, the Degas, the Gauguin for $1,300,000, and the Van Gogh "Houses" for $2,100,000. Two weeks later, on June 1, 1981, Christie's issued a formal press release, approved by both Bathurst and Burge, confirming these sales. No other press release on the subject has ever been released. Bathurst's explanation for this deception is that it was for "the benefit of [Cristallina] and the art market."

Apparently, changes in the art market were not a factor in the auction's failure. Indeed, as reported in a *New York Times* article dated June 7, 1981, Christie's main competitor, Sotheby's, enjoyed record sales within days of the May 19, 1981 auction and the auction market for that month was as strong as ever.

Cristallina commenced this action in May 1982, asserting eight causes of action grounded in, *inter alia*, fraudulent misrepresentation, negligence, breach of contract, and breach of fiduciary duty. In essence, Cristallina claims that the auction's failure was due to Bathurst's selection of paintings lacking in auction appeal, the failure to bring vital information to its attention, Christie's advice to the public and the media that the value of the paintings was substantially less than the values given to Jodidio, and the recommendation of reserves in violation of Christie's public policy of not setting reserves higher than the high estimates. In sum, Cristallina contends, Christie's and Bathurst, by their own actions, created an environment which could only lead to failure. Almost one year after the case had been placed on the Trial Calendar, Christie's and Bathurst moved for summary judgment, which Special Term granted. Since we believe that factual issues exist which bar the grant of summary judgment, we reinstate the complaint....

Christie's concedes, as it must, that an auction house acts as an agent on behalf of its consignors. The auctioneer is the agent of the consignor. As an agent, Christie's had a fiduciary duty to act in the utmost good faith and in the interest of Cristallina, its principal, throughout their relationship. When a breach of that duty occurs, the agent is liable for damages caused to the principal, whether the cause of action is based on contract or on negligence.

Cristallina argues that Christie's and Bathurst withheld information which materially affected its interests. They cite the failure to disclose that Burge strongly disagreed with Bathurst's assessment of the auction appeal of the consigned paintings. Although Burge was of the opinion that they had a value of $10,000,000, he also believed that the paintings would be difficult to sell at auction. Had this information been conveyed to Cristallina, it could have avoided any potential damage by, *inter alia*, withdrawing the paintings from auction prior to their being catalogued. "[A]n agent is subject to a duty to use reasonable efforts to give his principal information which is relevant to affairs entrusted to him and which, as the agent has notice, the principal would desire to have and which can be communicated without violating a superior duty to a third person." Restatement [Second] of Agency § 381, at 182....

Cristallina also argues that Christie's and Bathurst failed to inform it of the information Christie's released in May 1981 to members of the public and the media shortly before the time Bathurst and Jodidio met to set the final reserves. Christie's, a self-avowed expert, inexplicably advised the public and the media that the values of the paintings were less than what it knew the reserves to be. Besides prejudicing Cristallina, those actions also violated a policy set by Christie's that reserves were not to exceed the high estimates. Based on the public and media disclosures, Christie's and Bathurst knew or should have known that it would be virtually impossible to sell the paintings unless the reserves were lowered. Yet, at his May 18th meeting with Jodidio, Bathurst failed to recommend that the reserves be substantially lowered below those recommended in February. Instead, he recommended that certain of the reserves be increased, which was done, with the result, Cristallina claims, that the paintings were bought in and their value thereby adversely affected.

Moreover, where, as here, an agent is selected because of its special fitness for the performance of the duties to be undertaken, the principal is entitled to rely on the agent's judgment and integrity. An agent has an "implied good faith obligation [to] ... use his best efforts to promote the principal's product". While an auctioneer, acting as the agent of an art seller, is not required to guarantee the results of a sale or, for that matter, even predict the price that a particular item will bring, he is nonetheless held to a standard of care commensurate with the special skill which is the norm in the locality for that kind of work. Thus, the breach of contract, negligence and breach of fiduciary duty causes of action should not have been dismissed since sufficient evidence has been shown to present a factual question as to whether Christie's and Bathurst acted in a manner commensurate with their skill and expertise.

In support of its cause of action for misrepresentation, Cristallina claims that Bathurst, by placing a value on each of the paintings that he knew was not and could not be true, improperly induced it to agree to a sale of the paintings at public auction. Moreover, Cristallina alleges, Bathurst failed to disclose the risks attendant to such an auction. Had it been made aware of these risks and the paintings' lack of auction appeal, it would never have agreed to a public auction. Christie's and Bathurst argue that the representations as to the estimated value of the eight paintings were mere expressions of opinion and not representations of existing fact.

Even assuming that Bathurst, in advising Cristallina as to the value of the paintings and setting reserves, was merely expressing an opinion, which is not actionable, rather than a representation as to an existing fact, which is, he had an obligation to render such opinion truthfully. Thus, his selection of eight paintings, many of which, according to Burge, would be difficult, if not impossible, to sell and the dissemination of estimates at variance with the reserves and his earlier predictions, raise serious questions as to whether Bathurst misrepresented the prices which could be obtained at public auction. Statements of value can, in certain circumstances, be regarded as a representation of existing fact. An expression or prediction as to some future event, known by the author to be false or made despite the anticipation that the event will not occur, "is deemed a statement of a material existing fact, sufficient to support a fraud action."

As further justification for its dismissal of the complaint, Special Term, citing the failure to present any expert affidavit as to the paintings' present value, found that Cristallina's claim for damages was speculative. The paintings' preauction value may, of course, be established by estimates, including Bathurst's, and the value Christie's placed on them for insurance purposes. The measure of damages is the difference between the paintings' preauction value and their value after the auction. Appraisals and bona fide sales are indicative of value and may serve as the basis of a damage award. (*Matter of Rothko*, 43 N.Y.2d 305, 322–323.) As the record discloses, four of the paintings have been sold since the auction, three in September 1982 and another, the Gauguin, in 1984, at significantly less than Bathurst's preauction appraisal figures. In each case, Cristallina advised Christie's of the offer and afforded it the opportunity to match or better it. In any event, "the difficulty of ascertaining damages does not excuse their determination."

Cristallina's claim for punitive damages . . . also should stand at this stage of the litigation. The complaint pleads the requisite allegations of recklessness and conscious disregard of Cristallina's rights. Whether the alleged misconduct warrants the imposition of a punitive damage award should, in the circumstances, be left for the trier of the facts. Cristallina argues that punitive damages are particularly appropriate in this case since "the business of an auctioneer . . . has always been affected with a public interest." *Biddles, Inc. v. Enright*, 239 NY 354, 365. . . .

* * *

Accordingly, the order . . . granting defendants' motion for summary judgment dismissing the complaint should be modified, on the law, to deny the motion as to the first, second, third, fourth, sixth and eighth causes of action, and, except as thus modified, affirmed, without costs or disbursements.

All concur.

Notes and Questions

1. *Aftermath.* On remand, the *Cristallina* case went to trial, but within a week, the two sides settled for an undisclosed amount. In addition, Christie's paid an $80,000 fine to the New York Department of Consumer Affairs for violating its statutory obligation by publishing false information about the auction prices and sales, and the auctioneer licenses of Bathurst and Burge were suspended. Following *Cristallina*, New York amended its auction regulations, *inter alia*, to require auctioneers to announce "bought-in" lots upon the fall of the hammer and to provide explanations and disclosures regarding estimates and reserves. 6 R.C.N.Y. § 2-123. For New York auctions, reserves now may not exceed the minimum estimated value. 6 R.C.N.Y. § 2-123(d). See Patty Gerstenblith, *Picture Imperfect: Attempted Regulation of the Art Market*, 29 Wm. & Mary L. Rev. 501 (1988).

2. *Duty to Communicate. Cristallina* emphasizes the traditional fiduciary duty that an agent owes to its principal: "to act in the utmost good faith and in the interest of . . . its principal." 502 N.Y.S. 2d, at 171. This basic duty of fidelity or loyalty can manifest in many ways. In the particular context of *Cristallina*, Christie's fiduciary duty was essentially to communicate to its principal its reservations about the likelihood that the paintings would sell at auction at their set reserves. Its duty was not to guarantee a successful auction, rather just to provide pertinent and relevant information in a timely manner to its principal. Is the agent's duty to communicate or the level of its communication linked to the expertise of the agent? Presumably, yes.

If the agent claims to have special skills or knowledge, the agent's duty of care, competence, and diligence is measured against that higher specialist standard. Restatement (Third) of Agency § 808 Duties of Care, Competence, and Diligence, and § 8.11 Duty to Provide Information (2006). Is that duty similarly linked to the sophistication of its principal? This is unclear. See Stuart Bennett, *Fine Art Auctions and the Law: A Reassessment in the Aftermath of Cristallina*, 16 Colum.-V.L.A. J. L. & Arts 257 (1992). Dealing with the asymmetry in experience and knowledge between industry insiders and others is a constant issue. See, Weisz v. Parke-Bernet Galleries, Inc., 325 N.Y.S.2d 576 (1971), *rev'd*, 351 N.Y.S.2d 911 (1974), Chapter 4, *infra*; see also MAFG Art Fund LLC v. Gagosian, 998 N.Y.S.2d 342 (N.Y. App. Div. 2014), Chapter 2, *supra*.

The duty to communicate to the principal stands in contrast to the muted communication to the buyers. Did you notice that the seller's identity was not to be disclosed? Was there something particular about this seller that argued for anonymity? There is a general perception that works owned by a dealer offered at auction do not have the appeal, or perhaps romance, as those coming fresh to the market. As artworks become commodified for their investment potential, this perception may weaken. On the other hand, to the extent the reported rumors circulating about Jodidio as the seller prompted pointed questions about the ownership and title of the artworks, the lack of communication is troubling. Receiving good title to artworks is crucial for any buyer. See Chapter 5, *infra*.

3. *Seller's Commission and Buyer's Premium.* As a consequence of the principal-agent relationship, a seller historically paid the auctioneer by means of a seller's commission, which is a percentage of the final selling price, often at declining graduated rates. When Christie's opened in New York in the 1970s, it introduced the buyer's premium to the U.S. auction market. The buyer's premium is an additional charge imposed on the buyer and paid directly to the auction house by the buyer. Initially highly debated and contested, the buyer's premium survived legal and industry challenges. Which part of the art industry would challenge the buyer's premium? It also increased over time and is differentiated for different auction segments and locations. Today it is common to see a rate of 25% up to $400,000, 20% on the amount between $400,001 and $4,000,000 and 13.5% thereafter. Comparatively, recall in *Cristallina* that the seller's commission was "set at 4%" and the buyer's premium was "much less."

Another charge to auction buyers emerged as of August 1, 2020. Sotheby's charges an additional 1% of the hammer price as an overhead premium to all auction buyers in their global sales rooms and online sales. It remains to be seen if other auction houses will follow suit.

The buyer's premium changed the dynamic of how the auction house is paid and unwittingly led to a criminal antitrust action discussed next. It also raises fundamental questions as to the legal relationship between the buyer and auctioneer. See Benna Adler, *The International Art Auction Industry: Has Competition Tarnished Its Finish?*, 23 Nw. J. Int'l L. & Bus. 433 (2003).

4. *Sotheby's and Christie's Antitrust Case.* In 2002, former Sotheby's Chairman, A. Alfred Taubman was sentenced to federal prison after being convicted by a jury of conspiring to fix commissions. Taubman was released from prison in 2003 and died in 2015 at the age of 91. He proclaimed his innocence in his autobiography, THRESHOLD RESISTANCE: THE EXTRAORDINARY CAREER OF A LUXURY RETAILING PIONEER (2007). His counterpart at Christie's, Sir Anthony Tennant, was liable for arrest if he entered the U.S.; he died in 2011.

Both Sotheby's and Christie's had published seller's commission rates. The fierce competition between them, however, to attract the premier pieces for auction meant those published seller's commissions were routinely lowered or waived. Consequently, the ever-increasing buyer's premium became the main source of auction revenue. Moreover, in order to clinch the seller's consignment, Sotheby's and Christie's not only waived the seller's commission but also began offering a nonrecourse loan or a guarantee to the seller. The financial pressure on the auction houses' revenue due to these concessions to sellers was severe. In 1993, secret negotiations began between Sotheby's and Christie's to develop nonnegotiable seller's commissions. By September 1995, Christie's and Sotheby's published sellers commission rates were essentially the same, and neither auction house practiced offering enticements to sellers, such as lowering or waiving the commission.

The Department of Justice launched an investigation in 1997. In late 1999, as part of his severance negotiations, a former Christie's CEO turned over his files to Christie's. Those files detailed his illegal activities. In early 2000, Christie's announced its cooperation with the DOJ, thereby taking advantage of the DOJ's conditional amnesty program. Soon thereafter, individual and class action lawsuits were filed against the auction houses by buyers and sellers. The consolidated class action lawsuit settled for $512 million in cash and certificates. In re Auction Houses Antitrust Litigation, 2001 WL 170792 (S.D.N.Y. 2001), *aff'd*, 2002 WL 1758897 (2d Cir. 2002). See Orley Ashenfelter & Kathryn Graddy, *Anatomy of the Rise and Fall of a Price-Fixing Conspiracy: Auctions at Sotheby's and Christie's*, 1 J. COMPETITION L. & ECON. 3 (2005), for an economic analysis of the price-fixing scandal. See also Christopher Manson, THE ART OF THE STEAL: INSIDE THE SOTHEBY'S-CHRISTIE'S AUCTION HOUSE SCANDAL (2004), for a riveting account of the conspiracy. Sotheby's pled guilty to Sherman Act violations and paid a $45 million fine.

Chapter 4

Authenticity

Authenticity and good title are the two core legal concerns for the buyer in the acquisition of artworks. Unraveling questions of authenticity and title can involve the lawyer in a rogue's gallery of con artists, the complex sweep of war plunder and history, and plain human error. This chapter and the next will address these two fascinating topics and attempt to fashion a lawyer's template of issues and approaches. Like the auctioneer cautions, take fair warning; clarity and certainty are elusive.

A. Forgeries

Authenticity sounds simple, direct, and permanent: the object is or is not what it is described to be. Were it so. Legal questions of authenticity arise from three scenarios. Intentional deceptions, such as forgeries, promptly come to mind, followed naturally by honest mistakes or misattributions. Those are the two primary scenarios for authenticity. The third is harder to label and reflects the uncertainty that some works exhibit. For example, a work that was clearly authentic may be challenged if there was an overzealous restoration. This is a topic that has relevance for the artist's moral rights discussed in Chapter 7, *infra*. Or a work may be reevaluated as "not-authentic-enough," if, for example, scholarship detects more studio assistants on a work. The legal template for authenticity disputes is grounded in contract and tort. This template continues to evolve, pushed by equitable and public policy considerations, such as fiduciary duties, consumer protection, and market and anti-competitive concerns. The prosaic statute of limitations is another important practical concern.

The process of determining authenticity requires two related inquiries: who determines authenticity and on what evidence? An important reality in the art world is that authenticity is not permanent. At best, a consensus emerges over time, but new scholarship or advances in scientific methods may raise questions. When authenticity shifts, a severe economic loss can lead to litigation. See Leila A. Amineddoleh, *Are You Faux Real? An Examination of Art Forgery and the Legal Tools Protecting Art Collectors*, 34 Cardozo Arts & Ent. L.J. 59 (2016).

State of New York v. Wright Hepburn Webster Gallery, Ltd.

314 N.Y.S.2d 661 (N.Y. Sup. Ct. 1970)

FEIN, J. This is an application by the Attorney General for an order granting the appointment of a receiver pendente lite of approximately sixty-eight paintings made by one David Stein, and the proceeds of any sale thereof, which are in the possession of defendant Wright Hepburn Webster Gallery, Ltd. ("Gallery").

* * *

This novel application by the Attorney General is based on the bizarre career of defendant, David Stein, who has not been served with process. In 1967, Stein, a former art dealer, was convicted in this county, on his plea of guilty, of six counts of counterfeiting art work and grand larceny. He had mastered the styles of such great artists as Chagall, Picasso, Matisse, Braque, Klee, Miro, Cocteau and Roualt, to such an extent that he was able to and did sell as the original works of such artists, watercolors, gouaches and other paintings which he himself had created.

After serving his jail sentence, Stein was deported to France where he was arrested and subsequently convicted for selling art forgeries in that country. Stein is now in jail in Paris where he has apparently been permitted by the French authorities to produce paintings "in the style of" such renowned artists as Chagall, Matisse, Picasso, Braque and others, subject to the proviso that they bear his own signature, "Stein, D.", rather than the simulated signatures of these masters as had been his prior practice.

In April, 1969, Gallery's affiliate in London exhibited and sold a number of such paintings made by Stein during his confinement.

Gallery is now exhibiting in its New York showroom approximately 68 such paintings made by defendant Stein. Gallery has placed a sign in its windows advertising: "Forgeries by Stein". However, each painting bears the signature of Stein. Attached as exhibits to the moving papers are a circular and press release issued by Gallery announcing the date for an "official" exhibition of "Master Forger David Stein" paintings. Both promotion pieces clearly indicate that the paintings are by Stein and are offered to the public as being "in the style of" "Chagall, Picasso, Matisse, etc.". The circular states: "Master Forger David Stein Presents Braque, Klee, Miro, Chagall, Matisse, Picasso".

The underlying action on behalf of the State of New York demands that the court (1) declare these paintings a public nuisance to be abated; (2) enjoin their sale or transfer; (3) appoint a permanent receiver over them with appropriate instructions to turn them over to a museum or similar institution for use in research, identification and education in the detection of art forgeries and not to be disposed of in such a manner as to circulate in the art market and not to eradicate Stein's signature.

The Attorney General contends that Stein's name can easily be removed from these paintings and that they will eventually find their way into the art market as original works of Chagall, Picasso, etc. The Attorney General argues that because of the ability of Stein to simulate the works of the aforementioned great painters, Stein paintings constitute a continuing, potential threat and hazard to the cultural welfare of that segment of the public which buys, sells and collects art and to art lovers and the cultural institutions which exhibit the works of the artists that Stein is simulating.

The issues presented by this application involve a case of first impression. The court is asked to find that the possible harm to the public from the sale of paintings made by a convicted forger "in the style of" acknowledged great painters warrants preventing this man from earning a livelihood by utilizing his peculiar and unusual artistic talents. It cannot be disputed that whatever Stein's motives, he is an artist, both in terms of dictionary definitions and as a matter of practical application. His work in perfecting the style of the masters may properly be ascribed to that special talent with which true artists are uniquely endowed. Otherwise it cannot be argued seriously that harm could result from the sale of his works.

No claim is made by the Attorney General that Stein is guilty of some criminal behavior by offering the subject paintings for sale to the public. However fraudulent or criminal his past transgressions have been, they cannot militate against Stein's right as an artist to sell his own works, acknowledged as such. Although Stein's prior deceptive practices cannot be completely overlooked in weighing the allegations that the same result will occur if his works are permitted to be sold commercially, at this juncture the court is merely presented with the possibility of the future commission of a crime, by Stein or some purchaser of his works. A court of equity will not enjoin the commission of a crime as such, much less a possible crime, although a nuisance may be enjoined, albeit the activity enjoined is also criminal.

Not one iota of proof has been submitted that anyone is now engaged or about to engage in the removal of Stein's name for the purpose of passing off his work as an original work of one of the masters. It is difficult to perceive how these paintings constitute a public nuisance on the basis of the possibility or suspicion that this may occur.

* * *

The current Penal Law does not specifically define the term "public nuisance". Instead, Section 240.45 simply provides:

> A person is guilty of criminal nuisance when: (1) By conduct either unlawful in itself or unreasonable under all the circumstances, he knowingly or recklessly creates or maintains a condition which endangers the safety or health of a considerable number of persons; or (2) He knowingly conducts or maintains any premises, place or resort where persons gather for the purposes of engaging in unlawful conduct.

It is manifest that Stein cannot be charged with the crime of nuisance....

The relief sought here is novel and drastic. It should not be granted in the absence of a clear showing that defendants have committed some public wrong amounting to a nuisance.

It may well be that Stein's paintings "in the style of" the masters are an attempt to appropriate ideas not his own and that the law should not permit one to profit who "is endeavoring to reap where (he) has not sown; * * *." (*International News Service v. Associated Press*, 248 U.S. 215, 239, 39 S.Ct. 68, 72, 63 L.Ed. 211.) However, such conduct does not constitute a public wrong. Stein's work may, under the circumstances, run afoul of some appropriate copyright law, or may even constitute a violation of General Business Law, Art. 12-E, Section 224, limiting the right to reproduce works of fine art. If so, the rights violated are private and do not form a basis for action by the Attorney-General.

In this context, perhaps consideration should be given to Goethe's query:

> "People are always talking about originality, but what do they mean? As soon as we are born the world begins to work upon us, and keeps on to the end. What can we call ours, except energy, strength, will? If I could give an account of what I owe to great predecessors and contemporaries, there would be but a small remainder." (Eckermann, Conversations with Goethe in the Last Years of His Life, p. 147).

So it must seriously be doubted whether the court, at the instance of the State, should prevent conscious appropriation of knowledge where no deception of the public is proven.

In essence this is acknowledged by the Attorney-General. He concedes that the case does not fall within any of the sections of the Penal Law. . . .

* * *

There remains only to consider the significance of defendant's window sign and other publicity describing the exhibit as being "Forgeries By Stein". Both sides concede these paintings are not forgeries, as well they must. The essence of forgery . . . is the utilization as a "means of defrauding another" of that which "purports to be in all respects an authentic creation of" or "fully authorized by its ostensible maker". The signature of Stein on these paintings establishes there is no forgery even if a painting could be considered as within the condemnation of the article.

On this count, the advertising by defendant "Forgeries By Stein" is false, although when read in context this "tag line" is manifestly only an exaggerated form of "puffing", a sales "gimmick", like all too much advertising. This does not appear to violate the Penal Law or any other statute. Nor does the Attorney-General make any such claim.

Neither this advertising nor the possibility or suspicion that in the future someone may remove Stein's name and substitute the name or signature of one of the masters is a sufficient basis for finding that the exhibition and sale of these paintings is a public nuisance.

* * *

Accordingly, plaintiff's application is denied, the temporary restraining order is vacated, and the complaint is dismissed. Settle order.

Notes and Questions

1. *Aftermath.* David Stein, one of the 20th century's master forgers, died in October 1999 in France. His common law wife Anne-Marie wrote an unapologetic book about their time together, THREE PICASSOS BEFORE BREAKFAST: MEMOIRS OF AN ART FORGER'S WIFE (1973). "What David Stein perpetrated upon the art world was a brilliantly engineered, masterfully executed hoax. It was illegal, but he did not deserve to be treated like a criminal. . . ." *Id.* at 11. But does he deserve to be treated like a "true artist," as the judge apparently thought ("His work . . . may properly be ascribed to that special talent with which true artists are uniquely endowed")? Both views are regrettable.

In 1971, the decision was affirmed on appeal. State v. Wright Hepburn Webster Gallery, 323 N.Y.S.2d 389 (N.Y. App. Div. 1971).

2. *Forgery as a Defense?* The story of Han van Meegeren (1889–1947), another 20th century master art forger, has an unusual twist. During World War II, one of van Meegeren's agents sold a forged Vermeer to Reichsmarschall Hermann Göring, who prominently displayed it at his home. After the war, van Meegeren was arrested as a collaborator for selling Dutch cultural patrimony to the enemy. As this would be an act of treason punishable by death, van Meegeren soon confessed to forgery. To prove his defense, he painted his last Vermeer in the presence of court-appointed witnesses and reporters. As a result, he became a folk hero for deceiving Göring. Van Meegeren was convicted of forgery and sentenced to one year in prison. He died of a heart attack before serving his sentence.

3. *Originality.* Goethe's comment on originality reveals an important aspect of art. Much of art is intentionally based on or incorporates others' works. Copying great works of art is a traditional, and usually benign, form of art instruction. Consider the following passage on Michelangelo from Vasari's LIVES:

> There he . . . set for himself to make from another piece of marble a Cupid that was sleeping, of the size of life. This, when finished, was shown . . . to Lorenzo di Pier Francesco as a beautiful thing, and he, having pronounced the same judgment, said to Michelagnolo: 'If you were to bury it under ground and then send it to Rome treated in such a manner as to make it look old, I am certain that it would pass for an antique, and you would thus obtain much more for it than by selling it here.' It is said that Michelagnolo handled it in such a manner as to make it appear an antique; nor is there any reason to marvel at that, seeing that he had genius enough to do it and even more. Others . . . say that Milanese took it to Rome and buried it in a vineyard . . . , and then sold it as an antique to [a] Cardinal. . . . [B]ut afterwards, . . . the Cardinal contrived to learn the truth . . . and so went to work that Milanese's agent had to restore the money and take back the Cupid. . . . This affair did not happen without some censure attaching

> to [the] Cardinal . . . , in that he did not recognize the value of the work, which consisted in its perfection. . . . What greater vanity is there than that of those who concern themselves more with the name than the fact? But of that kind of men, who pay more attention to the appearance than to the reality, there are some to be found at any time.

Giorgio Vasari, 2 Lives of the Painters, Sculptors and Architects 650–51 (Gaston de Vere trans., Everyman's Library, 1996) (1568).

Although the *Cupid* has disappeared, art experts debate the attribution of another marble sculpture, that of a boy. Some believe it is by a young Michelangelo, and perhaps a deliberate forgery of a classical sculpture. Ann Landi, *Little Archer, Big Mystery*, ARTnews 46 (Dec. 2009). The issue is unlikely to be resolved soon.

Beyond the attribution question, art that directly incorporates the works of others can pose difficulties in other areas of the law, such as copyright and moral rights. See Chapter 7, *infra*.

4. *Establishing Authenticity.* David Stein's forgeries included works of popular living artists. Allegedly it was Marc Chagall who verified a forgery for the New York authorities that led to Stein's arrest. Van Meegeren preferred Old Masters, including Vermeer (1632–1675), and it was only Van Meegeren's own confession that unmasked the deception. This reveals two cautionary, important points about forgeries — they can be from any time period, including contemporary, and detecting expert forgeries is difficult. There are three primary bases for determining the authenticity of artworks: documentary evidence, scientific evidence, and connoisseurship. Relying on any one basis for proof is not wise, as none of these can conclusively prove authenticity, although inauthenticity may be conclusively proven by one.

Documentary evidence of the provenance, the history of ownership or possession and of exhibition, can be important. When dealing with older works, this evidence (such as bills of sale, will bequests, tax records, insurance records) can be spotty or non-existent, and of course, if a work is counterfeit, the documentation can be equally counterfeit. In a well-publicized case, the records of the Tate Gallery in London were secretly altered to include forged works, so that a prospective buyer could be directed to use the Tate's records to verify provenance. Laney Salisbury & Aly Sujo, Provenance: How a Con Man and Forger Rewrote the History of Modern Art (2009). See also United States v. Schultz, 333 F.3d 393 (2d Cir. 2003), Chapter 6, *infra,* where an illegally exported item from Egypt had "a false provenance" created for it so it could be sold. Moreover, the documentary evidence may be truthful for the true work, but the proffered work is a substitute, or if not a substitute, it has been degraded by restoration, overpainting or damage. Relying solely on documentary evidence is not appropriate. In the case of Greenberg Gallery, Inc. v. Bauman, 817 F. Supp. 167 (D.D.C. 1993), *aff'd*, 36 F.3d 127 (D.C. Cir. 1994), however the court quoted art experts' opinions that a Calder mobile's flawless provenance was "the best proof of authenticity" and that provenance is accepted "in the art world as persuasive evidence of a work's authenticity."

Scientific evidence can assist in authentication and may prove that a work is inauthentic. The methods are varied, sophisticated, and can be expensive, but science can allow the dating of the materials used in the work and reveal internal and external structures not visible to the naked eye. The methods can involve teams of experts using interdisciplinary approaches. For example, the *Archaic Mark*, a prized holding of the University of Chicago Library, thought to be an early illustrated Byzantine manuscript, was proven in 2009 to be a counterfeit by an interdisciplinary examination of the material components of the *Archaic Mark*. One scientist analyzed samples of parchment, ink, and paints by polarized light, energy dispersive X-ray spectrometry, the scanning electron microscope, X-ray diffraction, Fourier Transform infrared spectroscopy and Raman spectroscopy to determine that the *Archaic Mark* was created after 1874, using materials not available until the late 19th century. A medieval book expert and preservationist reconstructed the forger's steps and detailed specific ways those varied from traditional Byzantine procedures. A third expert provided a textual critique based on an 1860 edition of the Greek New Testament. The University of Chicago press release stated that "collective efforts have achieved what no single scholar could do."

In some instances, scientific analysis can point to authenticity. For example, the Rembrandt Research Project used sophisticated scientific methods to re-authenticate works previously deauthenticated or at least to attribute them to the Rembrandt workshop. See, e.g., Ernst Van Du Wetering, *Thirty Years of the Rembrandt Research Project: The Tension Between Science and Connoisseurship in Authenticating Art*, 4 IFAR J. 14 (2001). Going forward, science may provide more proven techniques to combat forgeries. Tom Mashberg, *Eyeing DNA as a Tool to Ensure Art's Authenticity*, N.Y. Times, Oct. 13, 2015, at C3.

Connoisseurship, the visual inspection by a trained eye, is the most subjective of the three bases, but it is often the primary method. The art expert who offers stylistic judgment and opinion does not always easily fit the notion of an expert for legal purposes. Courts have expressed frustration with art experts who are not able to articulate reasons for their opinions. See Hahn v. Duveen, 234 N.Y.S. 185 (N.Y. Sup. Ct. 1929), Part E. Liability of Authenticators, *infra*. Art experts who spent years viewing and studying a particular artist, art, or period, in fact may have internalized artistic nuances and can credibly bring their accumulated knowledge to bear in the blink of an eye. Malcolm Gladwell, the author of Blink: The Power of Thinking Without Thinking (2005), chose to open his book with the story of the Getty Kouros.

In 1985, the J. Paul Getty Museum acquired its Archaic Kouros, a marble statue of a nude youth in classical pose, for $7 million. The Getty had received positive documentary evidence of provenance, had successfully completed scientific analysis, and gained approval of its experts. When other experts viewed the work, doubts were expressed, including by Thomas Hoving, then Director of the Metropolitan Museum of New York. Hoving's first thought was "fresh," which is not a good thought for a 2,500 year old statue. His second thought was that the Getty should undo the deal. Further examinations of the provenance documents revealed forgeries, and examinations of the scientific evidence revealed the possibility of modern manufacture. The Getty sponsored an international symposium to consider the statue's authenticity; it was inconclusive. For years, the caption for the Kouros read "Greek, about 530 B.C., or a modern forgery." In 2018, the Kouros was deemed inauthentic and placed in storage. The Getty is not alone. Some speculate that 10% to 60% of museums' holdings are inauthentic and smaller museums may be more vulnerable. For example, a small French museum discovered that 82 of its 140 pieces were inauthentic. See *"Catastrophe": French Museum Discovers Half Of Its Collection Are Fakes*, The Guardian, Apr. 29, 2018, at www.theguardian.com/world/2018/apr/30/french-museum-discovers-half-collection-fake.

5. *Why Authenticity Matters.* Viewing forgeries as a hoax or a joke is an attempt to minimize their destructive nature. Similarly, romanticizing forgers as folk heroes shifts the focus away from the criminal acts. What is lost in this redirection is the harm to the individual true artist and the conception of her work as she alone envisioned it as well as the harm of economic loss to the deceived buyers. There is also a collective harm to culture as our understanding of the artist, the art, and the time period is distorted.

Whatever one's views on the philosophical question of authenticity, it is undisputed that the art market values the authentic over the inauthentic. It is precisely this value differential that the forger exploits for his personal gain, and intentionally does so through deception. The seemingly ever upward arc of prices in the art market is what attracts forgers. Lord Mansfield's pronouncement that the basis of all dealings ought to be "good faith" is clearly breached. Bexwell v. Christie, 98 Eng. Rep. 1150 (1776), Chapter 3, *supra*. The integrity and efficiency of the market is compromised by the deception.

B. Misattribution: Opinion or Warranty?

Although there is no criminal intent or deception in situations of mistake or misattribution, there is likely economic harm, and the parties need to allocate that risk. When such disputes arise, the legal construct generally centers on the contract law of warranties, sometimes accompanied by allegations sounding in tort. As contract law marched from common law to statutory law, art authenticity disputes similarly followed. The hoped-for commercial certainty in allocating the risk of inauthenticity remains elusive. This lack of certainty is largely due to the dynamic nature of authenticity. Authenticity, as a working notion, is a perception or belief of authenticity at a particular point in time; it is not a permanent notion.

The cases in the next two sections show how the legal system with its core mandate to decide disputes struggles with the fluid notion of art authenticity.

1. Early Cases

Jendwine v. Slade

170 Eng. Rep. 459 (N.P. 1797)

* * *

This was an action brought to recover damages on the sale of two pictures, one of which was said to be a sea-piece by Claud Loraine, the other a fair by Teniers, which the defendant had sold to the plaintiff as originals, when in fact they were copies.

The defence relied on was, that they were sold under a catalogue, not amounting to an absolute warranty, but upon which the buyer was to exercise his own judgment; and further, that a bill had been filed by the defendant, two years ago, to compel the plaintiff to complete the sale; to which he had put in no answer, but paid the money, and that therefore he could not now seek to rescind the contract after such acquiescence.

The plaintiff's counsel answered this objection, by insisting that the name of the artist put opposite any picture in a catalogue was a warranty; and if the article sold did not correspond with it, it avoided the sale; and as to the transaction in respect to paying the money, that the plaintiff was deceived, but had brought his action as soon as he discovered the fraud.

Several of the most eminent artists and picture-dealers were called, who differed in their opinions respecting the originality of the pictures.

When the evidence was closed, Lord Kenyon said, It was impossible to make this the case of a warranty; the pictures were the work of artists some centuries back, and there being no way of tracing the picture itself, it could only be matter of opinion whether the picture in question was the work of the artist whose name it bore, or not. What then does the catalogue import? That, in the opinion of the seller, the picture is the work of the artist Whose name he has affixed to it. The action in its present shape must go on the ground of some fraud in the sale. But if the seller only represents what he himself believes, he can be guilty of no fraud. The catalogue of the pictures in question leaves the determination to the judgment of the buyer, who is to exercise that judgment in the purchase.

With respect to the bringing of the action, his Lordship added, that if any fraud has been committed in a sale, if the party comes recently after discovery of the deception, he is not barred by circumstances having taken place, such as were stated.

Power v. Barham

111 Eng. Rep. 865 (K.B. 1836)

In assumpsit for breach of a warranty of pictures, it was proved, among other things, that the defendant, at the time of the sale, gave the following bill of parcels:—"Four pictures, Views in Venice, Canaletto, 160l." The Judge left it to the jury upon this and the rest of the evidence, whether the defendant had contracted that the pictures were those of the artist named, or whether his name had been used merely as matter of description, or intimation of opinion, the jury found for the plaintiff, saying that the bill of parcels amounted to a warranty: Held, that the question had been rightly left to the jury, and that the verdict was not to be disturbed.

Assumpsit.... On the trial before Coleridge J. at the sittings in Middlesex after last term, it appeared that the defendant sold the pictures to the plaintiff for £160, and at the time of the sale, gave the following bill of parcels and receipt:—

"Mr. N. Power.
"Bought of J. Barham.
"May 14th 1832.

"Four pictures, Views in Venice, Canaletto, ...	£160	0	0
Settled by two pictures ...	£50	0	0
And a bill at five months ..	110	0	0
	£160	0	0

"J. Barham ."

A carver and gilder, who had been employed by the plaintiff to procure original pictures for him, gave evidence of previous representations by the defendant to him and to the plaintiff, that the pictures were genuine; some doubt, however, was raised as to the expressions actually used. The witness stated that the pictures were in the manner of Canaletti, and, at the time of the sale, appeared to him worth the money. A witness experienced in paintings stated that he considered the pictures not to be Canaletti's, and valued them at about 8l. each; and some other evidence was given on this point. For the defendant it was contended that the bill of parcels was not a warranty, but only an expression of opinion; and *Jendwine* v. *Slade* was cited. The learned Judge, in summing up, told the jury that the pictures were admitted not to be Canaletti's, and that the only question on the pleadings was, whether the promise was made; and he submitted to their consideration, upon the whole of the evidence, whether the defendant had made a representation, as part of his contract, that the pictures were genuine, not using the name of Canaletti as matter of description merely, or as an expression of opinion upon something as to which both parties were to exercise a judgment, but taking upon himself to represent that the pictures were Canaletti's. His Lordship noticed the argument on behalf of the defendant, as to the bill of parcels; and said that the words of Lord Kenyon, in the case referred to, must be considered, not as a general rule of law, but as a direction to the jury on the circumstances of that case. The jury found a verdict for the plaintiff, saying, "We think the bill of parcels is a warranty."

Sir J. Campbell, Attorney-General, now moved for a new trial on the ground of misdirection. The question was, whether the defendant had entered into a binding contract that the pictures were Canaletti's. The jury ought to have been told that the words in the bills of parcels did not amount to a warranty. *Jendwine* v. *Slade*. It is not necessary to contend here, that there could not be a warranty of a picture as Canaletti's; but there was no evidence of any. No fraud is imputed. No positive undertaking could be implied, from the bill of parcels, that the pictures were by Canaletti. It only implied that they passed for and were believed to be that painter's; that the vendor had bought them as his, and thought them so. It cannot be contended that every description given in a bill of parcels is a warranty. [Coleridge J. Do you say that the writing ought not to have gone to the jury?] Not as evidence, by itself, of a warranty. [Coleridge J. I said that it was to be considered with all the attendant circumstances.]

Lord Denman C.J. I think that the case was correctly left to the jury. We must take the learned Judge to have stated to them that the language of Lord Kenyon in *Jendwine* v. *Slade* . . . was merely the intimation of his opinion upon such a contract as was then before him. It may be true that, in the case of very old pictures, a person can only express an opinion as to their genuineness; and that is laid down by Lord Kenyon in the case referred to. But the case here is that pictures are sold with a bill of parcels, containing the words "Four pictures, Views in Venice, Canaletto." Now words like these must derive their explanation from the ordinary way in which such matters are transacted. It was, therefore, for the jury to say, under all the circumstances, what was the effect of the words, and whether they implied a warranty of genuineness, or conveyed only a description, or an expression of opinion. I think that their finding was right: Canaletti is not a very old painter. But, at all events, it was proper that the bill of parcels should go to the jury with the rest of the evidence.

Littledale J. The case was rightly sent to the jury; though, as to their decision, I think that all the auctioneers in London would be alarmed if they thought that such words as these were to be understood as a warranty.

Williams J. The words in question might be a mere expression of opinion, or might amount to a warranty; it was for the jury to say which they imported. The language ascribed to Lord Kenyon seems to imply that, if a master is very old, there can be no means of saying that a certain picture is his, and, therefore, no warranty. The Attorney-General admits that this is not correctly applicable to the present case. If a person will undertake to sell these things as the productions of a particular master, he must take the consequences.

Coleridge J. concurred.

Rule refused.

2. More Recent Cases

Weisz v. Parke-Bernet Galleries, Inc.

325 N.Y.S.2d 576 (N.Y. Civ. Ct. 1971)

SANDLER, J. On May 16, 1962, Dr. Arthur Weisz attended an auction conducted by the Parke-Bernet Galleries, Inc., where he ultimately bought for the sum of $3,347.50 a painting listed in the auction catalogue as the work of Raoul Dufy. Some two years later, on May 13, 1964, David and Irene Schwartz bought for $9,360.00 at a Parke-Bernet auction a painting also listed in the catalogue as the work of Raoul Dufy.

Several years after the second auction, as a result of an investigation conducted by the New York County District Attorney's office, the plaintiffs received information that the paintings were in fact forgeries. When this was called to Parke-Bernet's attention, Parke-Bernet denied any legal responsibility, asserting among other things that the Conditions of Sale for both auctions included a disclaimer of warranty as to genuineness, authorship and the like.

Following a formal demand by the plaintiffs for return of the purchase price, these two lawsuits were commenced against Parke-Bernet. . . .

In each case, several causes of action are set forth, all of them quite closely interrelated, and all ultimately turning on the identification by Parke-Bernet of the paintings as the work of Dufy.

In the first cause of action, which adequately presents the issues to be resolved, the catalogue listing "Raoul Dufy" is asserted to constitute an express warranty, as that term was defined under the former Sales Act, in effect when the auctions took place.

* * *

As to the actions against Parke-Bernet, I find that the following facts were quite clearly established by the evidence.

(1). Each of the plaintiffs bought the paintings in question in the belief that they were painted by Raoul Dufy, had formed this conclusion because Park-Bernet so stated in the respective catalogues, and would not have bought the paintings if they were not believed to be genuine.

(2). At the time of the auctions Parke-Bernet also believed the paintings ascribed to Dufy in the catalogues were his work.

(3). Neither of the paintings was in fact painted by Dufy. Both are forgeries with negligible commercial value.

The most substantial of the defenses interposed by Parke-Bernet is that the Conditions of Sale for the auctions, appearing on a preliminary page of each catalogue, included a disclaimer of any warranty and that the plaintiffs are bound by its terms.

This issue embraces two separate questions. . . .

First, did the plaintiffs in fact know of the disclaimer, and, if they did not, are they legally chargeable with such knowledge.

Second, if the answer to either part of the first question is yes, was the disclaimer effective, under all the circumstances of the auctions, to immunize Parke-Bernet from the legal consequences that would normally follow where a sale results from a representation of genuineness that is thereafter disclosed to be completely inaccurate.

* * *

The catalogues open with several introductory pages of no direct relevance to the lawsuits. There then follows a page headed "Conditions of Sale", in large black print, under which some 15 numbered paragraphs appears, covering the side of one page and most of a second side. These provisions are in clear black print, somewhat smaller than the print used in the greater part of the catalogue.

Paragraph 2, on which Parke-Bernet relies, provides as follows:

> "The Galleries has endeavored to catalogue and describe the property correctly, but all property is sold 'as is' and neither the Galleries nor its consignor warrants or represents, and they shall in no event be responsible for, the correctness of description, genuineness, authorship, provenience or condition of the property, and no statement contained in the catalogue or made orally at the sale or elsewhere shall be deemed to be such a warranty or representation, or an assumption of liability."

The next page in each catalogue is headed "List of Artists", and contains in alphabetical order, one under the other, a list of the artists with a catalogue number or numbers appearing on the same line with the named artist. The implicit affirmation that the listed artists are represented in the auction and that the catalogue numbers appearing after their names represent their work could scarcely be clearer.

The name Raoul Dufy is listed in each catalogue, together with several catalogue numbers.

* * *

Turning in each catalogue to the catalogue numbers for the paintings involved in the lawsuits, there appears on the top of the page a conventional black-and-white catalogue reproduction of the painting, directly under it the catalogue number in brackets, and the name RAOUL DUFY in large black print followed in smaller print by the words "French 1880–1953".

On the next line the catalogue number is repeated together with the name of the painting, a description of it, and the words, "Signed at lower right RAOUL DUFY." Finally, there appears a note that a certificate by M. Andre Pacitti, will be given to the purchaser.

The procedure followed at both auctions was to announce at the beginning of the auction that it was subject to the conditions of sale, without repeating the announcement, and at no point alluding directly to the disclaimer.

As to the first auction, I am satisfied that Dr. Weisz did not in fact know of the Conditions of Sale and may not properly be charged with knowledge of its contents. I accept as entirely accurate his testimony that on his prior appearances at Parke-Bernet auctions he had not made any bids, and that on the occasion of his purchase he did not observe the Conditions of Sale and was not aware of its existence.

The test proposed for this kind of issue by Williston, quite consistent with the decided cases, is whether "the person * * * should as a reasonable man understand that it contains terms of the contract that he must read at his peril." 1 Williston on Contracts Sec. 90D (1937).

The most obvious characteristic of the two Parke-Bernet auctions is that they attracted people on the basis of their interest in owning works of art, not on the basis of their legal experience or business sophistication. Surely it is unrealistic to assume that people who bid at such auctions will ordinarily understand that a gallery catalogue overwhelmingly devoted to descriptions of works of art also includes on its preliminary pages conditions of sale. Even less reasonable does it seem to me to expect a bidder at such an auction to appreciate the possibility that the conditions of sale would include a disclaimer of liability for the accuracy of the basic information presented throughout the catalogue in unqualified form with every appearance of certainty and reliability.

For someone in Dr. Weisz's position to be bound by conditions of sale, of which he in fact knew nothing, considerably more was required of Parke-Bernet to call those Conditions of Sale to his attention than occurred here.

The cases relied upon by Parke-Bernet where buyers were held to be bound by conditions of sale in auction catalogues are not at all apposite. For one thing, in only one of the cases does the opinion recite that the buyer flatly denied knowledge of the provision. . . . More importantly, these auction cases for the most part concern business auctions, in which sellers and buyers were part of a business grouping in which a general knowledge of the governing rules and usages was reasonably to be anticipated.

As to the Schwartz case, I am satisfied from the evidence that Mrs. Schwartz knew of the Conditions of Sale, and that both Schwartz plaintiffs are chargeable with that knowledge since they both participated in the purchase.

This factual conclusion leads to consideration of the extremely interesting question whether the language of disclaimer relied upon as a bar to the actions should be deemed effective for that purpose. No case has come to my attention that squarely presents the issue raised by the underlying realities of this case.

What is immediately apparent from any review of the evidence is that notwithstanding the language of disclaimer, Parke-Bernet expected that bidders at its auctions would rely upon the accuracy of its descriptions, and intended that they should. . . .

* * *

Where one party in a contractual relationship occupies a position of superior knowledge and experience, and where that superior knowledge is relied upon and intended to be relied upon by the other, surely more is required for an effective disclaimer than appears here.

After reassuring the reader that Parke-Bernet endeavored to catalogue the works of art correctly, there follow highly technical and legalistic words of disclaimer in a situation in which plain and emphatic words are required. And this provision, in light of the critical importance to the buyer of a warning that he may not rely on the fact that a work attributed to an artist was in fact his creation, is in no way given the special prominence that it clearly requires.

* * *

In denying legal effect to the disclaimer I am acting consistently with a whole body of law that reflects an increasing sensitivity to the requirements of fair dealing where there is a relationship between parties in which there is a basic inequality of knowledge, expertness or economic power.

* * *

Judgment may be entered for the plaintiff Weisz against Parke-Bernet in the sum of $3,347.50, and for the plaintiffs David and Irene Schwartz in the sum of $9,360.00, both judgments of course with appropriate interest and costs.

Weisz v. Parke-Bernet Galleries, Inc.

351 N.Y.S.2d 911 (N.Y. App. Div. 1974)

PER CURIAM: Plaintiffs' purchases by competitive bids, at a public auction were made in 1962 and 1964. At that time neither the statutory nor decisional law, applicable to such purchases, recognized the expressed opinion or judgment of the seller as giving rise to any implied warranty of authenticity of authorship. (See Memorandum of the State Dept. of Law (McKinney's 1968 Session Laws, vol. 2, pp. 2284–2285) recommending remedial legislation (now secs. 219 and 219-a of the General Business Law) to change the then existing law).

Additionally defendant's auction-sale, catalogue listing, describing and illustrating these paintings gave leading and prominent place, in its prefatory terms of sale, (explaining and regulating the conduct of the auction) to a clear, unequivocal disclaimer of any express or implied warranty or representation of genuineness of any paintings as products of the ascribed artist.

One of the factors necessarily entering into the competition among bidders at the public auction was the variable value of the paintings depending upon the degree of certainty with which they could be authenticated and established as the works of the ascribed artist. Since no element of a wilful intent to deceive is remotely suggested in the circumstances here present the purchasers assumed the risk that in judging the paintings as readily-identifiable, original works of the named artist, and scaling their bids accordingly, they might be mistaken. They will not now be heard to complain that, in failing to act with the caution of one in circumstances abounding with signals of *caveat emptor*, they made a bad bargain. The judgments are reversed with $30 costs and the complaints dismissed.

Notes and Questions

1. *Opinion or Warranty?* Comparing *Jendwine* and *Power* with *Weisz I* and *Weisz II* seems an exercise in déjà vu, albeit with tumbled results. Is it an opinion? Is there a warranty? Is there an effective disclaimer? Is there a time limit? The judicial approach of *Jendwine* and *Weisz II* is straightforward and categorical; their determinations favor sellers. Buyers should be vigilant and not rely on sellers' apparent pronouncements of authenticity. *Caveat emptor.* On the other hand, *Power* and *Weisz I* back away from the categorical approach in favor of a subjective or facts and circumstances one, a determination that can favor the buyer (or, at the very least, allow the buyer to survive a motion for summary judgment). This opinion-warranty redux by the judiciary underscored the need for another approach to promote the longed-for certainty in authenticity for buyers.

2. *Statutory Approaches.* The primary statutory approach on express warranties is UCC § 2-313. Because of New York's status as one of the world's leading art markets, its specific legislation on warranties in the art market is equally significant on this issue. N.Y. Arts & Cult. Aff. Law § 13.01. A few other states have followed New York's lead. See, e.g., Iowa Code Ann. § 715B.2 to .4; Fla. Stat Ann. § 686.504; Mich. Comp. Laws § 442.321 to .325.

a. UCC § 2-313 Express Warranties by Affirmation, Promise, Description, Sample. UCC § 2-313 provides in pertinent part as follows:

(1) Express warranties by the seller are created as follows:

> (a) Any affirmation of fact or promise made by the seller to the buyer which relates to the goods and becomes part of the basis of the bargain creates an express warranty that the goods shall conform to the affirmation or promise.
>
> (b) Any description of the goods which is made part of the basis of the bargain creates an express warranty that the goods shall conform to the description.

* * *

> (2) It is not necessary to the creation of an express warranty that the seller use formal words such as "warrant" or "guarantee" or that he have a specific intention to make a warranty, but an affirmation merely of the value of the goods or a statement purporting to be merely the seller's opinion or commendation of the goods does not create a warranty.

Because art authenticity is often imprecise and inconclusive, the application of UCC § 2-313 to authenticity questions is an ill fit. The section simply cannot provide the desired certainty to the art market that it provides to other markets, and we are quickly back in the *Jendwine* and *Powers / Weisz I* and *II* scenario. "Authentication in the trade context generally is the dealer's representation of authorship, i.e., 'This painting is by Van Gogh.' The problem with authenticity is that it can be interpreted simultaneously as guarantee . . . and as opinion under UCC Section 2-313." Jessica L. Darraby, 1 Art, Artifact, Architecture & Museum Law § 4:18 (2009 ed.). Nevertheless, for many jurisdictions, UCC § 2-313 is the governing law for express warranties of authenticity.

b. New York's Art Market Legislation. In 1966, New York enacted specific art market legislation that equated a "written instrument, which in describing the work, identifies it with any author" to an express warranty of authenticity. The goal was to eliminate the opinion-versus-warranty debate.

The current version of the New York legislation (N.Y. Arts & Cult. Aff. Law § 13.01), on Express Warranties dates from 1984. It provides as follows:

Notwithstanding any provision of any other law to the contrary:

> 1. Whenever an art merchant, in selling or exchanging a work of fine art, furnishes to a buyer of such work who is not an art merchant a certificate of authenticity or any similar written instrument it:
>
> (a) Shall be presumed to be part of the basis of the bargain; and
>
> (b) Shall create an express warranty for the material facts stated as of the date of such sale or exchange.
>
> 2. Except as provided in subdivision four of this section, such warranty shall not be negated or limited provided that in construing the degree of warranty, due regard shall be given the terminology used and the meaning accorded such terminology by the customs and usage of the trade at the time and in the locality where the sale or exchange took place.
>
> 3. Language used in a certificate of authenticity or similar written instrument, stating that:
>
> (a) The work is by a named author or has a named authorship, without any limiting words, means unequivocally, that the work is by such named author or has such named authorship;

(b) The work is "attributed to a named author" means a work of the period of the author, attributed to him, but not with certainty by him; or

(c) The work is of the "school of a named author" means a work of the period of the author, by a pupil or close follower of the author, but not by the author.

4.(a) An express warranty and disclaimers intended to negate or limit such warranty shall be construed wherever reasonable as consistent with each other but subject to the provisions of section 2-202 of the uniform commercial code on parol or extrinsic evidence, negation or limitation is inoperative to the extent that such construction is unreasonable.

(b) Such negation or limitation shall be deemed unreasonable if:

(i) the disclaimer is not conspicuous, written and apart from the warranty, in words which clearly and specifically apprise the buyer that the seller assumes no risk, liability or responsibility for the material facts stated concerning such work of fine art. Words of general disclaimer are not sufficient to negate or limit an express warranty; or

(ii) the work of fine art is proved to be a counterfeit and this was not clearly indicated in the description of the work; or

(iii) the information provided is proved to be, as of the date of sale or exchange, false, mistaken or erroneous.

C. Cases Involving Warranty Statutes

Dawson concerns the application of the earlier version of the New York legislation on art market warranties. In rejecting the buyer's request for a strict interpretation of the express warranty of authenticity, the *Dawson* court is clearly mindful of the "customs and usage of the trade."

Dawson v. G. Malina Inc.

463 F. Supp. 461 (S.D.N.Y. 1978)

BONSAL, J. Plaintiff Joseph M.A.J. Dawson ("Dawson"), a resident of Jersey, Channel Islands, is suing defendants G. Malina, Inc. ("GMI"), a New York corporation, and Gerald Malina ("Malina"), a resident of New York, individually, for rescission, or alternatively, for damages for breach of warranty with respect to certain objects of Chinese art which Dawson purchased from GMI in 1974. This action was tried to the Court without a jury....

* * *

The dispute arises from the purchase in 1974 of eleven objects of Chinese art by Dawson from GMI for a total purchase price of $105,400. The items purchased, which included both Chinese ceramics and jade sculptures, consisted of items Dawson had seen on the occasion of a visit to GMI on March 25, 1974 as well as items which Malina had recommended to him in correspondence between the two subsequent to his visit.

[Malina shipped the items to Dawson. Upon receipt Dawson showed one vase to various experts in London, all of whom concluded the vase was not authentic. Dawson later brought the remaining items to London for appraisal. Based on that appraisal Dawson consulted with his London solicitor and this lawsuit resulted.—Ed.]

* * *

Discussion

I. Plaintiff Dawson's Claim for Breach of Warranty

In suing for breach of warranty, Dawson relies primarily[3] upon § 219-c of the New York General Business Law, which provides in pertinent part as follows:

"§ 219-c. Express warranties.

> "Any provision in any other law to the contrary notwithstanding: 1. Whenever an art merchant, in selling or exchanging a work of fine art, furnishes to a buyer of such work who is not an art merchant, a written instrument which, in describing the work, identifies it with any author or authorship, such description (i) shall be presumed to be part of the basis of the bargain and (ii) shall create an express warranty of the authenticity of such authorship as of the date of such sale or exchange. Such warranty shall not be negated or limited because the seller in the written instrument did not use formal words such as 'warrant' or 'guarantee' or because he did not have a specific intention or authorization to make a warranty or because any statement relevant to authorship is, or purports to be, or is capable of being merely the seller's opinion.
>
> "2. In construing the degree of authenticity of authorship warranted as aforesaid, due regard shall be given to the terminology used in describing such authorship and the meaning accorded to such terminology by the customs and usage of the trade at the time and in the locality where the sale or exchange took place. . . ." (McKinney Supp. 1977.)

---

3. Although Dawson also relies on § 2-313 of the New York Commercial Code (McKinney 1964) which provides for the creation of express warranties, any benefit that Dawson might derive from this provision is embraced by § 219-c of the New York General Business Law set out in the text above. Indeed, § 219-c was enacted at least in part to eliminate questions as to whether an art dealer's representations with respect to the authorship of a particular work of art were to be considered an affirmation of a fact, in which event the description would create an express warranty under the Uniform Commercial Code, or merely the expression of the dealer's opinion which would not give rise to such a warranty. See Comment, Regulation of the New York Art Market: Has the Legislature Painted Dealers into a Corner?, 46 Fordham L.Rev. 939, 953–59 (1978).

Citing the above provision, Dawson contends that Malina and GMI expressly warranted that the objects were in conformity with the description provided by Malina in letters, invoices, and the final bill of sale, which were sent by Malina. Dawson contends that Malina's descriptions as to these five objects were inaccurate in material respects and that, therefore, Malina and GMI are liable for breach of warranty.

Defendants appear to concede that the descriptions of the objects cited by Dawson constitute express warranties under § 219-c of the New York General Business Law. Nevertheless, defendants deny that the representations made with respect to these objects were inaccurate in any significant respect, and maintain that they are not liable for breach of warranty. Thus, the issue presented here is whether the five objects which still remain in dispute were in fact what they were represented to be by defendants.

Dawson maintains that in order to prevail on his claim for breach of warranty here he need only establish that the works of art failed in any respect to conform to the descriptions which, under the New York General Business Law § 219-c, defendants warranted as being accurate. Stated conversely, Dawson argues that unless it can be found that these works of art were unqualifiedly what defendants represented each of them to be, he is entitled to relief for breach of warranty. Dawson seeks adoption of this standard arguing that defendants unqualifiedly and unequivocally represented these pieces to have been made during specific periods of Chinese antiquity, aware that such attributions have special significance in terms of the quality of workmanship and the value of the piece. Dawson contends that when measured against this standard the expert testimony of the witnesses called by both plaintiff and defendants establishes defendants' breach of warranty with respect to each of these items. Dawson points to the testimony of the experts whom he called to testify at trial as conclusively demonstrating that the objects in issue here were not in conformity with defendants' descriptions. Dawson further maintains that the testimony of defendants' experts, taken as a whole, fails to establish that the pieces were unqualifiedly of the period to which they were attributed by defendants.

Defendants, on the other hand, urge the adoption of a less stringent standard. Citing that portion of § 219-c of the New York General Business Law which directs that "(i)n construing the degree of authenticity of authorship warranted as aforesaid, due regard shall be given to the terminology used in describing such authorship and the meaning accorded to such terminology by the customs and usage of the trade at the time and in the locality where the sale or exchange took place," defendants contend that any standard applied here must take cognizance of what the experts testified was the inexactitude of the process of attribution where works such as those in issue here are involved. Accordingly, defendants maintain that unless Dawson has conclusively established by a preponderance of the evidence, that the representations made by them were in fact inaccurate, his claim for breach of warranty with respect to these pieces must fail.

Neither side has cited nor has the Court discovered any reported cases involving the precise legal question presented here. There do not appear to be any cases brought under § 219-c of the New York General Business Law; nor do there appear to be any cases based either on the Uniform Commercial Code or common law fraud or misrepresentation which would provide the Court with guidance on this issue.

In considering the standard to be applied in determining whether the objects of art in issue were in accord with the descriptions furnished by defendants, the Court must bear in mind that, as the experts called by both plaintiff and defendants conceded, the process of attributing any of the works of art involved here to a particular period of Chinese antiquity is by its very nature an inexact science. As the testimony of all of the experts makes clear, a determination as to the proper attribution for any of these pieces is to a substantial extent a subjective judgment based upon whether an expert finds a given piece to be aesthetically consistent with other works of the period on the basis of such elusive characteristics as the quality, character, form or "feel" of the piece. For these reasons, it is obvious that any attempt to ascribe any of the works of art involved here to a specific period of Chinese history must necessarily be imprecise.

Accordingly, it would clearly be unjust for the Court to adopt the strict standard proposed by Dawson. Guided by what the Court conceives to be the spirit and purpose of the New York statute quoted above, it appears that the proper standard to be applied here in determining whether defendants are liable for breach of warranty is whether the representations furnished Dawson by Malina with respect to each of these objects can be said to have had a reasonable basis in fact, at the time that these representations were made, with the question of whether there was such a reasonable basis in fact being measured by the expert testimony provided at trial. Since the plaintiff has the burden of proof on the issue of breach of warranty, the issue presented here, when reduced to its simplest terms, is whether plaintiff Dawson has established by a fair preponderance of the evidence that the representations made by Malina were without a reasonable basis in fact at the time that these representations were made. The Court now turns to the five objects which are in dispute.

[The Court determined that three of the five representations of authenticity were without a reasonable basis in fact at the time. — Ed.]

Balog v. Center Art Gallery — Hawaii, Inc.

745 F. Supp. 1556 (D. Haw. 1990)

[While on vacation in Hawaii, plaintiffs purchased artworks at the defendant's art gallery. The works were represented by the gallery to be exclusive originals or limited editions by Salvador Dali. The purchases, which began in 1978 and ended by 1981, were for a total purchase price of $36,200. After the sale, the gallery mailed the plaintiffs updated "Confidential Appraisal—Certificate of Authenticity" for each of their purchases on five separate occasions from 1978–1987. In 1988, the plaintiffs became aware of allegations of fraud and criminal activity against the defendant.

After investigating, plaintiffs brought suit, alleging a breach of express warranty of authenticity under the UCC. The defendants contend there was no express warranty and moved to dismiss based on the statute of limitations.

As a prelude to the UCC discussion, Judge Pence presented an overview of the various methods of art forgery and the two methods of authenticating (connoisseurship and scientific analysis). He noted that the cost of authenticating an artwork may be prohibitive for less expensive items. Judge Pence agreed that the UCC was applicable to the case but noted its specific shortcomings in the context of art authenticity.—Ed.]

* * *

PENCE, J. . . . [T]his case deals with allegedly counterfeit artwork which was sold to the plaintiffs based on the defendants' representations that it was genuine. The plaintiffs have claimed that, among other things, they have a cause of action for breach of an express warranty under the Uniform Commercial Code since by selling them fake artwork, the defendants breached the express warranties which are outlined in the Code; they claim that the defendants are therefore liable for the damage caused the plaintiffs through the defendants' sale of non-conforming goods. The defendants contend that no warranties were made explicitly and that the plaintiffs had an obligation to discover the non-conformity and bring any claim based on the allegations of forgery long before now. . . .

* * *

The sale of artwork presents a unique area for the application of these two [UCC] statements, since a dealer's statement that a work is the product of a particular artist can never be more than an educated guess or opinion (excluding, of course, the possibility that the dealer was an eyewitness to the work's production.)

This problem is not one which was created solely by the drafting and adoption of the U.C.C. In fact, it was the dispositive issue in the case of *Jendwine v. Slade*, decided almost 200 years ago. . . .

However, Lord Kenyon's opinion does not come down to this court as the only authority on this issue. The case of *Power v. Barham* [is another]. . . .

Two modern cases have also dealt with the issue. The first is *Weisz v. Parke-Bernet Galleries Inc.* . . .

* * *

The second modern case which has dealt explicitly with the issues is *Dawson v. G. Malina, Inc.* 463 F. Supp 461 (S.D.N.Y. 1978). . . .

* * *

This court would view [the *Dawson*] standard as an appropriate one to be applied in the instant case. . . . [T]herefore, to the extent that the evidence indicates that such representations do not possess a reasonable basis in fact, at the time these representations were made, this court finds that the party offering those representations will have violated the express warranties provided for under H.R.S. § 490:2-313.

D. The Statute of Limitations Under the U.C.C.

Even if the plaintiffs were ultimately able to prove that they possessed a claim for violation of the express warranties of § 2-313, the question remains whether or not the plaintiffs have brought their claim in a timely fashion. . . . H.R.S. § 490:2-725(2), the relevant statutory section, states that:

> [A] cause of action accrues when the breach occurs, regardless of the aggrieved party's lack of knowledge of the breach. A breach of warranty occurs when the tender of delivery is made [except where the warranty] *explicitly extends* to future performance of the goods and discovery of the breach must await the time of such performance. [Emphasis added.—Ed.]

* * *

§ 2-725(2) provides that the "cause of action accrues when the breach occurs." Breach usually occurs upon tender of delivery, due to the fact that the condition of the goods at the time of delivery is central to the question of their acceptance, fitness, and conformity to contract. Unfortunately, not all breaches are apparent, or even discoverable at the time of delivery.

Additionally, there are instances, such as the instant case, where one of the parties has taken steps which served to prevent the discovery of the breach by the recipient of the goods. These cases of "fraudulent concealment" will be dealt with in detail below. Suffice to say that in those cases where the breach is not immediately apparent, or has been concealed through affirmative conduct on the part of one of the parties to the agreement, litigants have urged the use of the "discovery rule," under which the limitations period does not begin to run until a buyer could discover the breach. . . .

The plaintiffs have raised a similar argument in this case. However, the defendants assert that the plaintiffs' claims by their nature fall under the statute of limitations provided by § 2-725, since their cause of action accrued upon tender of delivery, due to the fact that the artwork was not authentic and was thus overvalued (according to the plaintiffs' allegations.) (sic) Since the breach could have been discovered by the plaintiffs at any time, the defendants maintain that there is no way the plaintiffs could claim that their cause of action fell into the "future performance" exception.

The defendants point to three cases out of the First, Second and Third Circuits wherein purchasers of artwork who belatedly discovered that the items they had purchased were frauds were time-barred from pursuing their claims against the galleries which sold them the artwork. In *Wilson v. Hammer Holdings, Inc.*, 850 F.2d 3 (1st Cir.1988), a painting was purchased in 1961 and guaranteed as genuine by the gallery which sold it. The plaintiffs discovered in 1984 that the painting was a fake and sued in 1987; the First Circuit held that § 2-725 would provide the applicable statute of limitations and bar the claim since the plaintiffs were just as capable of discovering that the painting was a fake at the time they bought it as they were later on. The same result was reached in *Rosen v. Spanierman*, 894 F.2d 28 (2d Cir.1990) where the plaintiffs purchased a painting in 1968 and then discovered in 1987 that it was a fake and filed suit. The Second Circuit applied the same 4-year statute of limitations and held that the warranty did not extend to future performance and that the plaintiffs could have discovered the breach just as easily immediately after the sale as later. Finally, in *Firestone & Parson, Inc. v. Union League of Philadelphia*, 672 F.Supp. 819 (E.D.Pa.), *aff'd*, 833 F.2d 304 (3rd Cir.1987), the defendant sold a painting to the plaintiffs in 1981 which was allegedly produced by a renowned artist and worth $500,000. In 1985–86 it was discovered that another artist had done the painting and it was only worth $50,000. When plaintiffs filed suit in 1986, the court applied the 4-year statute holding that the "[p]laintiffs' claims, if any, accrued at the time of sale. The limitations period is four years. This action is time-barred." *Id.* at 822.

* * *

1. *Statute of Limitations—the Discovery Rule* As the defendants pointed out in the hearing held on this motion, the adoption of the discovery rule in application of the statute of limitations would require this court to reject contrary holdings in the cases of *Wilson v. Hammer Holdings, Inc.*, 850 F.2d 3 (1st Cir.1988); *Rosen v. Spanierman*, 894 F.2d 28 (2d Cir.1990); and *Firestone & Parson, Inc. v. Union League of Philadelphia*, 672 F.Supp. 819 (E.D.Pa.), *aff'd*, 833 F.2d 304 (3rd Cir.1987). The court made it quite clear that it was prepared to do so. This court is not bound by decisions coming out of the First, Second or Third Circuits except insofar as decisions emanating from courts within those circuits supply sound reasoning which the court may want to adopt. In the view of this court, far from being based on sound reasoning, these decisions flow from a too-literalistic application of the Code which takes no cognizance of the unique problem presented by the application of the U.C.C. to artwork and other collectibles; this is particularly true with works valued below the six-figure level. While this court recognizes the demand of uniformity when applying broad statutes of commercial application like the U.C.C., it rejects the defendants' invitation to simply apply the letter of the law with no thought whatsoever about the ramifications of such an application, a practice which, in the view of this court, was engaged in by the courts in *Hammer Holdings*, *Rosen*, and *Firestone*.

This court is in strong disagreement with the approach taken by its brethren in other Circuits. . . .

* * *

... [I]n the view of this court the decision in *Hammer Holdings* was based on a very literal reading of §2-725. The court in that case wrote that in order for the statute of limitations not to apply, they would have to "ignore the literal language of the statute requiring an *explicit* promise of future performance." 850 F.2d at 5 (emphasis in original). The court felt that any exception which would make works of art the type of good which by its very nature continued to "perform" in the future by virtue of being an authentic Dali, or Vuillard (the artist in *Hammer Holdings*) would be a decision for the legislature. This court disagrees.

In two cases, noted by the *Hammer Holdings* court, courts inferred a warranty of future performance even where one was not specifically stated in the language used to make the warranty. The first is *Mittasch v. Seal Lock Burial Vault, Inc.*, 344 N.Y.S.2d 101, 42 A.D.2d 573 (1973). There, the warranty for a burial vault promised "satisfactory service at all times." The court reviewing such language held that "the very nature of the product" suggested future performance which would take the case out of the strictures of §2-725. 344 N.Y.S.2d at 103.

The second case is *Moore v. Puget Sound Plywood, Inc.*, 214 Neb. 14, 332 N.W.2d 212 (1983). There, the parties agreed that "the description of the goods as 'siding' carried with it the representation that it would last the lifetime of the house." 332 N.W.2d at 214–215. That representation, according to Nebraska law, created an express warranty that the goods would conform to the description, resulting in the court's conclusion that the defendant seller had promised future performance, specifically during the lifetime of the house. *Id.*

This court recognizes that, as a general statement of law on implicit warranties of future performance, these decisions might be viewed as the minority viewpoint. However, this court does not now hold that the defendants' warranty of authenticity created an implied warranty as to future performance. Rather, this court holds that in the case of artwork which is certified authentic by an expert in the field or a merchant dealing in goods of that type, such a certification of authenticity constitutes an explicit warranty of future performance sufficient to toll the U.C.C.'s statute of limitations. U.C.C. §2-725(2).

* * *

However, this court wants to make clear that its holding applies narrowly to artwork as it comes under the regulation of the U.C.C. But with respect to artwork, this court views it as the type of thing about which questions as to authenticity normally arise only at some future time, usually the time of resale.

Since artwork does not "perform" in the traditional sense of goods covered by the U.C.C., and since the authenticity of a work of art, i.e. its "performance", would not change over time, Center Art's warranty necessarily guaranteed the present and future existence of the art as authentic works of Salvidor Dali. To force buyers to secure an additional warranty of future performance after an expert had certified a piece as genuine would be not only redundant, but ridiculous. The "Certificate of Authenticity" should be understood to provide what it said it did, an explicit warranty that the work was, and would be in the future, a Dali original. Based on such an explicit warranty of future performance, the statute is tolled until such time as the defect in the product was, or reasonably should have been, discovered.

* * *

This court notes that the decision of the court in *Lawson v. London Arts Group,* 708 F.2d 226 (6th Cir.1983) adopted the discovery rule for application of the statute of limitations in a case, similar to the instant case, where a dealer had made a warranty of authenticity of a painting purchased by the plaintiff. This case was different from the instant case in that it took place in Michigan, and the court was asked to construe Michigan's Warranty in Fine Arts Statute, and specifically the applicable statute of limitations under that law, M.C.L.A. § 600.5833. Under that statute, the claim accrued at the time the breach of the warranty was discovered or reasonably should have been discovered. This is the same rule of law which this court adopts today.... For the reasons outlined above, this court now holds that in the case of artwork, a warranty of authenticity given by a merchant constitutes an explicit warranty of future performance sufficient to toll the statute of limitations provided in § 2-725 and that the cause of action for breach of that warranty and for breach of the warranty provided under § 2-313 of the Code. In instances such as those, the limitations period of a claim of a party seeking damages for breach of such warranty accrues at the time when the breach is discovered or reasonably should have been discovered.

De Sole v. Knoedler Gallery, LLC

139 F. Supp. 3d 618 (S.D.N.Y. 2015)

Paul G. Gardephe, District Judge.

* * *

Background

I. Facts

A. The Knoedler Gallery, Ann Freedman, and Glafira Rosales

The Knoedler Gallery was founded by Michael Knoedler in 1846 and operated continuously for the next 165 years. Until it closed in 2011, the Knoedler Gallery was one of New York City's most venerable and respected art galleries.

In 1971, the gallery was purchased by Armand Hammer, the grandfather of Defendant Michael Hammer, and since that time the Hammer family has been directly responsible for the operations of the Knoedler Gallery....

* * *

Defendant Ann Freedman joined Knoedler's corporate predecessor in 1977.... In 1994, she became president of M. Knoedler & Co....

In the mid-1990s, Jaime Andrade, a longtime Knoedler employee, introduced Glafira Rosales to Freedman. Rosales was a Long Island art dealer who claimed to have access to a collection of previously undiscovered works by certain well-known Abstract Expressionist artists. . . . Rosales told Andrade that she had a Mexican client who wanted to sell a collection of Abstract Expressionist artworks, but to do so anonymously. . . .

Over the next fifteen years, Rosales provided Knoedler with dozens of previously unknown "masterworks" by well-known Abstract Expressionist artists, and Knoedler sold these paintings to its customers. All of these paintings are forgeries.

In early 1994, Rosales consigned to Knoedler what she represented to be five paintings by Richard Diebenkorn. . . . Knoedler sold these paintings to its customers at large mark-ups without submitting them to the Diebenkorn catalogue raisonné committee for authentication. During a series of meetings in 1994 and 1995, members of the Diebenkorn family informed Freedman that at least two of the five purported Diebenkorns Rosales had provided did not appear to be authentic. The Diebenkorn family also expressed concern about the lack of documentation for one of the paintings—which the family viewed as highly suspicious—given that the artist and his family kept meticulous records of his work. All of the Diebenkorn paintings were later discovered to be forgeries.

Between 1995 and the spring of 1998, Knoedler sold three other works that Rosales had supplied. . . . These paintings—all of which were forgeries—were allegedly from the collection of a man whom Rosales, Freedman, and others at Knoedler referred to as "Mr. X." Each painting was sold at a large mark-up.

Freedman testified that Rosales initially told her that these paintings belonged to a friend. The record is not clear as to what else Freedman had been told about these paintings before Knoedler sold them. The Knoedler invoices for two of these works state that they were initially acquired directly from the artist, and all three invoices state that the works were from a private collection in Mexico. Knoedler's invoice for the purported Rothko states that the work is "[t]o be published in the forthcoming catalogue raisonné: *Mark Rothko: Works on Paper*, by David Anfam, (London: Yale University Press)."

* * *

At a June 18, 1998 meeting with Rosales, Freedman and Knoedler's head of research "ask[ed] [Rosales for] more details about . . . the collector and his family." At this meeting, Rosales told Freedman that—as a child in Mexico—she had met a couple who were Jewish émigrés from Europe. The husband—"Mr. X"—made frequent business trips to the United States between the late 1940's and 1970's. During his visits to the United States, Mr. X purchased artworks directly from American painters. The couple died in the early 1990s, leaving these paintings to their children.

According to Rosales, the current owner of the collection—Mr. X's son—lived in Mexico City and Zurich. He and his sister both had paintings from their father's collection, but neither was interested in art, and they had been selling the works gradually. Rosales reported that the collector's son "remembers seeing artists in his father's home." Rosales also told Freedman that the deceased collector had corresponded with various artists, but that these letters had been "disposed of" after his death. Accordingly, there was no documentation for Mr. X's paintings.

* * *

Within two weeks of the June 18, 1998 meeting, Knoedler sold two purported Rothkos supplied by Rosales, both allegedly from Mr. X's collection.

* * *

Over the next eighteen months, Rosales brought three more Mr. X paintings to Knoedler, and Knoedler sold these paintings to its customers. The invoice for one of these paintings—a purported Rothko—described its provenance as follows:

> *Provenance & Exhibition History*
>
> Acquired from the Artist
>
> Private Collection, Switzerland

The invoice also states that the work is "[t]o be included in the forthcoming catalogue raisonne of Mark Rothko's works on paper, currently in preparation by the National Gallery of Art, Washington, D.C." Freedman began referring to Mr. X as "Secret Santa."

At some point between June 1998 and January 2000, the name of Alfonso Ossorio—an Abstract Expressionist artist with close ties to many other Abstract Expressionist artists—began to be associated with the Rosales Paintings. Freedman initially testified that it was Rosales who had first associated Ossorio with Mr. X's collection. Freedman later stated, however, that it was Freedman and Knoedler who first "surmised" that Ossorio had assisted Mr. X in purchasing the works in Mr. X's collection.

During a January 10, 2000 meeting with Freedman, Rosales "confirm[ed] that the family knew Ossorio well. There may be correspondence. [Mr. X's son] confirmed that [Mr. X] purchased through Ossorio." Knoedler began conducting research on Ossorio in or around 2001, but was not able to find evidence of a link between Ossorio and the paintings from Mr. X's collection.

At a May 26, 2001 meeting, Rosales told Freedman that:

> 1. the works were "acquired in the 1950s from Pollock, Rothko, Still, Kline, Motherwell, etc. At that time [the artists] did not have contracts with dealers . . .";
>
> 2. "It's not clear if the works were purchased from Ossorio (who purchased them directly from the artists) or, with Ossorio's direction and advise, from the artists themselves"; and

3. "All purchases were paid for in cash. The son of the collector remembered seeing his parents pay in cash to one of the artists.... Correspondence was probably lost or thrown out by the daughter after the deaths of her parents. She had much of the paperwork."

In December 2001, Rosales told Freedman that "Gerzso" was a "family name" connected to Mr. X, but was not his name. Knoedler then researched—without success—whether there was a connection between Mr. X and Gunther Gerzso, a well-known Mexican artist. Knoedler's research never uncovered a name for Mr. X.

B. The 2001 Sale of the "Green Pollock"

In late 2001, Freedman and Knoedler sold a purported Jackson Pollock—*Untitled 1949* (the "Green Pollock")—to Jack Levy for $2 million. Knoedler had purchased this work from Rosales in March 2001 for $750,000. Knoedler included in the provenance of the painting a reference to Ossorio.

* * *

The sale of the Green Pollock was conditioned on a favorable review of the work's provenance and authenticity by the International Foundation for Art Research ("IFAR"). On October 9, 2003, IFAR issued its report on the Green Pollock (the "IFAR Report"). The IFAR report rejects Knoedler and Rosales' claim that Ossorio had been involved in the acquisition of the Green Pollock, and notes that there are "disturbing" differences between the materials used to create the Green Pollock and the materials used to create a known Pollock from the same year. The report also states that "IFAR's own extensive archival and other research has turned up no documentary material of any kind linking the painting to Pollock, or Ossorio." The conclusion of the IFAR report reads: "given the several strongly negative opinions [from Pollock experts about the authenticity of the work] and the lack of information as to prior ownership, and with no documentation or other evidence to override the concerns of those who do not accept it as a work by Pollock, we cannot currently support its addition to the artist's *oeuvre*." Based on the IFAR Report, Levy returned the Green Pollock to Knoedler in late 2003, and the Gallery refunded his full purchase price of $2 million.

* * *

C. Substitution of David Herbert for Ossorio in Knoedler's Provenance for the Rosales Paintings

Freedman testified that, "after the IFAR report, I pressed Glafira Rosales for more information, and she went back to Mr. X and called me, I believe it was the following month [November 2003] ... and she said, I have information. The advisor was David Herbert."

Knoedler never informed IFAR that Knoedler had concluded that David Herbert—and not Ossorio—had acted as Mr. X's advisor. Moreover, Knoedler's search of archives relating to Herbert revealed no evidence of a connection between Herbert and any of the Rosales Paintings.

D. The De Soles' December 2004 Purchase of a "Rothko"

In the fall of 2004, the De Soles called Freedman and Knoedler to arrange a meeting to discuss the possible purchase of a painting by Sean Scully. The De Soles were aware of Knoedler and Freedman's excellent reputation, having been referred to Knoedler by a friend who collected art. During the meeting at Knoedler, Freedman told the De Soles that she did not have any Scully works available, and she instead showed them works purportedly created by Rothko and Pollock. Rosales had brought both of these paintings to Knoedler.

Freedman told the De Soles that both works "were owned by a Swiss collector that was a client of Knoedler and he had died and his son had decided to sell the paintings." Freedman also stated that the Rothko had been authenticated by Christopher Rothko and David Anfam, the author of the Rothko catalogue raisonné.

The De Soles decided to purchase the "Rothko." On November 30, 2004, Knoedler sent the De Soles' agent an invoice—either by Federal Express or by U.S. Mail—for the sale of the work, seeking a payment of $8.3 million. The invoice states:

Mark Rothko (1903–1970)

> *Untitled*
> 1956
> Oil on canvas
> 50 1/8 × 40 1/4 inches
> Signed and dated on verso
> A 12322
> ***Provenance***
> The Artist
> Private Collection Switzerland
> By descent to present owner
> ***Literature***
> To be included in the forthcoming supplement to the 1998
> Rothko catalogue raisonné under preparation by the National Gallery of Art, Washington, D.C.

An earlier draft of the invoice states that the Rothko is from a private collection in "Mexico and Switzerland." The Rothko had been consigned to Knoedler in December 2002.

Domenico De Sole asked Freedman to put in writing everything she had told the De Soles about the painting. On December 11, 2004, Freedman sent a letter to Laura De Sole that contains the following statements:

1. "This classic Rothko painting was acquired from the artist through the advice and counsel of David Herbert."

2. "The original owners of the Rothko, a couple whose residences included Switzerland, are now deceased and [the work] was inherited by their son."

3. Knoedler was "anticipating a loan request from Oliver Wick of the Fondation Beyeler."

4. "The painting has been viewed by a number of eminent scholars on Rothko as well as specialists on the Abstract Expressionist movement," including David Anfam, E.A. Carmean, Jr., Jack Flam, Laili Nasr, Stephen Polcari, Christopher Rothko, Irving Sandler, Bonnie Clearwater, Earl A. Powell III, Oliver Wick, and Dana Cranmer.

5. "Importantly, Laili Nasr, manager of the Rothko *catalogue raisonné* project for the National Gallery of Art in Washington, D.C., has written to us about her inten[t]ion to include the Rothko in the forthcoming *catalogue raisonné* supplement."

6. "Knoedler warrants the authenticity and good title of the painting, *Untitled, 1956,* and confirms its 'remarkably good condition.'"

With respect to the Rothko experts cited by Freedman, Eleanore De Sole believed that Freedman was indicating that "these people had said that [the] painting was real." After the De Soles received Freedman's letter, they instructed their agent to make payment to Knoedler. On December 17, 2004, the De Soles' agent wired Knoedler the purchase price of $8.3 million.

E. Rosales' May 2005 Refusal to Attest to the Authenticity of the Rosales Paintings

In early May 2005, Freedman and Knoedler asked Rosales to sign an "authorization form" that reads as follows:

> May 10, 2005
>
> Ann Freedman, President
> Knoedler & Company
> 19 East 70th St.
> New York, N.Y. 10021
>
> Dear Ann Freedman,
>
> I the undersigned, Mrs. Glafira Rosales, attest that I am the authorized agent, as well as a close family friend, of a private collector residing in Mexico and Switzerland. The owner requests that the family name remain private. The works of art described on the attached list were acquired by the current owner's father from the artists, with David Herbert as his advisor and agent. The works of art were passed by inheritance to his immediate heirs (son and daughter).
>
> I further attest that the owner has had absolute clear title to, the attached list of works of art, and that he has guaranteed their authenticity. I also affirm that I have had authorization to act as his agent in the handling of their consignments and/or sales to Knoedler & Company.

I assume all legal responsibility for these statements.

Rosales refused to sign the form, stating that she was "not comfortable about including the authenticity clause." Rosales explained that the purported owner "has been extremely clear that if we want to continue to do business, these are his terms, so [Rosales] does not want to jeopardize the relationship by pressing him," and the request would "raise his hackles." Accordingly, Knoedler revised the authorization form to omit the authenticity clause. Rosales did not identify the collector and his son.

* * *

H. The Dedalus Foundation's December 2007 Claim that the "Motherwells" Rosales had Brought to the Knoedler Gallery Were Forged

The Dedalus Foundation, Inc. is responsible for the Robert Motherwell catalogue raisonné. In three meetings with Freedman in December 2007 and January 2008, Foundation representatives told Freedman that they believed seven purported Motherwell works that Rosales had brought to Knoedler and the Weissman Gallery—owned by a former Knoedler employee—were forged. In January 2008, Freedman told Rosales about the Foundation's claims and the need to prepare a "bona[]fide defense" to these allegations.

As part of that effort, Freedman and Knoedler asked Rosales to complete a form in which she would disclose the identity of the original collector and his son. Freedman also gave Rosales (1) a confidentiality agreement requiring Knoedler not to disclose any information about the purported owner, and (2) a letter Rosales was to provide to the owner requesting an "emergency meeting," and informing him that the Dedalus Foundation had "strongly questioned the authenticity and legality of [the Motherwells]" that Rosales had brought to Knoedler, and "suggest[ed] that [Knoedler was] selling and trading in art that is counterfeit." Rosales did not identify the original collector or his son.

In March 2008, Knoedler retained James Martin of Orion Analytical, LLP, to conduct forensic tests of two of the alleged Motherwells Rosales had brought to Knoedler. In October 2008, Orion submitted a draft report indicating that the works were not authentic. Although the two paintings had allegedly been created in 1953 and 1955, the pigments used in the paintings did not exist until ten years later. Moreover, the same acrylic polymer emulsion paint had been used to create both works, and the use of such paint was "'remarkably inconsistent with what is known about Motherwell's use of acrylic paints,'" "'rais[ing] questions about when the works were actually painted.'" Finally, "'both paintings display[ed] patterns of circular abrasions, visible only with magnification, that point . . . to the use of an electric sander.'"

On November 7, 2008, Freedman, Andrade, and a Knoedler researcher met with Rosales. During that meeting, Rosales stated "that the transactions between Mr. X and the artists continued from the late 1940s through 1964." Rosales also stated that the current owner "remembers" travelling with his father to artists' studios and "remembers this ending in 1964." At the meeting, Andrade commented that "David Herbert and Ossorio were close friends," and both Andrade and Rosales then suggested that "Mr. X may have met David [Herbert] through Ossorio."

The next day—November 8, 2008—Rosales signed the following statement:

> I am a close friend (for over thirty years) to the family of and a liaison on behalf of a gentleman, currently residing in Mexico, with family homes in Switzerland. He prefers information about himself and his family to remain private and confidential. The artworks were acquired by the current owner's father directly from the various artists, and were passed by inheritance to his immediate heirs (son and daughter).
>
> It has recently been explained and clarified, in discussion with the owner, that his father, the original owner, was active in acquiring the works between the late 1940s and 1964. The works were acquired "off the record," directly from the artist's studios during trips made to New York related to the family business. It is interesting to note that the family had business in common with Alfonso Ossorio's family (the sugar business). In the early years of collecting activity Alfonso Ossorio was his primary advisor.
>
> Later (after 1951, during the Parsons and Janis years), David Herbert (a close friend of Ossorio's) gradually became the collector's primary advisor, in his role as dealer to the artists both in and outside of the gallery system, and he continued in that role through 1964. This was of significant financial support to the artists.
>
> The owner stopped travelling to New York due to a change in the family's business activities, and at the same time ceased purchasing works of art.
>
> The above information is accurate and true to the best of my knowledge.

I. The September 2009 Grand Jury Subpoena, the Termination of Freedman's Employment, and Hammer's Direction that No Additional Rosales Paintings be Sold

On August 31, 2009, [the] board of directors passed a resolution forming a Special Committee to investigate the purchases of artwork by Knoedler from Rosales and subsequent sales and attempted sales of this artwork. By August 2009, all Rosales Paintings in Knoedler's inventory were placed on a "not for sale" list. Knoedler had six unsold Rosales Paintings at that time....

On September 22, 2009, Knoedler was served with a grand jury subpoena. The subpoena related to the Rosales Paintings.... [Thereafter], Freedman resigned her position at Knoedler.

* * *

J. The Knoedler Gallery Closes

By July 2011, Knoedler was receiving numerous calls from customers expressing concerns about the authenticity of works they had purchased from Knoedler.

Hammer decided to close Knoedler on November 30, 2011, and announced the closing that same day. . . .

* * *

. . . On December 2, 2011, a *New York Times* article reported on the F.B.I.'s investigation of Knoedler and the abrupt closing of the Gallery. ("Possible Forging of Modern Art is Investigated," *New York Times.)*

Rosales has since admitted that all of the works she sold to Knoedler were "fakes created by an individual residing in Queens." Rosales has also admitted that she "agreed with others" to sell the forged works and "to make false representations as to the authenticity and provenance of those works."

II. Procedural History

* * *

On November 4, 2013, the De Sole Plaintiffs filed a Second Amended Complaint ("SAC"). The *De Sole* SAC pleads[, inter alia, fraud and fraudulent concealment claims against Knoedler and Freedman , and a breach of warranty claim against Knoedler].

* * *

Discussion

I. Summary Judgment Standard

Summary judgment is warranted when a moving party shows that "there is no genuine dispute as to any material fact" and that that party "is entitled to judgment as a matter of law."

* * *

Because Freedman's scienter or lack of scienter is at the heart of this case, the Court's analysis of Defendants' summary judgment motions begins with Freedman and Knoedler's motions directed at Plaintiffs' fraud and fraudulent concealment claims.

II. Fraud and Fraudulent Concealment

Freedman and Knoedler argue that they are entitled to summary judgment on Plaintiffs' fraud and fraudulent concealment claims because (1) there is no evidence that Freedman acted with scienter, and (2) Plaintiffs have not demonstrated that their reliance was justifiable.

* * *

B. Analysis

Freedman and Knoedler do not dispute that material misrepresentations and omissions were made and that Plaintiffs suffered damages. They contend, however, that Plaintiffs' fraud and fraudulent concealment claims fail because Plaintiffs have not put forth evidence demonstrating that (1) Freedman acted with scienter (*i.e.,* that her statements were made recklessly or with intent to deceive), and (2) that Plaintiffs' reliance was justifiable.

1. Scienter

Freedman argues that no reasonable jury could find by clear and convincing evidence that she acted with scienter. In this regard, Freedman cites her efforts to (1) exhibit the works "all over the world"; (2) hire a "celebrated art historian" to investigate the works' provenance; and (3) have the Rosales Paintings "validated by esteemed art experts of Abstract Expressionism." Freedman notes that she herself purchased several Rosales Paintings, and argues that all of her conduct is inconsistent with fraudulent intent. This Court disagrees.

Plaintiffs have offered ample circumstantial evidence demonstrating that Freedman acted with fraudulent intent and understood that the Rosales Paintings were not authentic. This evidence includes, *inter alia,* the fabricated stories of provenance, which shifted dramatically over time; the efforts to concoct a "cover story" with Rosales; Rosales' willingness to repeatedly sell purported "masterworks" to Knoedler for a fraction of their value on the open market; Rosales' refusal to share any meaningful information about the purported source of the paintings, and her unwillingness to sign a statement representing that the paintings were authentic; Rosales' inconsistent accounts of the size and scope of Mr. X's collection, which grew over time to include more than thirty hitherto undiscovered "masterworks"; the absence of any documentation concerning the paintings; the issues raised about the Diebenkorns Rosales brought to Knoedler early on; and the October 2003 IFAR Report—which Freedman reviewed—and which rejected the concocted provenance tale concerning Ossorio and raised serious concerns about the authenticity of the "Green Pollock" purchased by Jack Levy.

Moreover, in arguing that "many experts and scholars" "unambiguously conveyed that the [Rosales Paintings] were genuine, Freedman exaggerates the significance of these witnesses' testimony. For example, nearly all of the Rothko experts Freedman cited to the De Soles testified that they do not authenticate works of art. Moreover, many of the experts Freedman relies on testified that they were never asked by Freedman to authenticate works of art, and that they did not make a statement as to any work's authenticity. Plaintiffs have offered evidence that creates material issues of fact about (1) the amount and accuracy of information Freedman provided to the experts and galleries in which the Rosales Paintings were exhibited; (2) whether any of the experts were asked to authenticate the works; (3) the nature of the experts' reactions to and comments about the works they viewed; and (4) the impartiality and qualifications of certain experts.

The evidence concerning Freedman's efforts to show the Rosales Paintings at art exhibits likewise does not negate fraudulent intent. The public exhibitions had the effect of building a façade of credibility for the Rosales Paintings. Because Freedman and Knoedler had no documented provenance for any of the Rosales Paintings, the "viewing list" and exhibit history—together with Knoedler's endorsement—*was* the documentation Freedman and Knoedler used to sell these paintings.

Freedman's purchase of several Rosales Paintings likewise does not negate Defendants' evidence of fraudulent intent. In April 1997, Freedman swapped a Diebenkorn from her own collection for a Rosales "Rothko." No money changed hands. On August 1, 2000, Freedman and her husband purchased a "Motherwell" *Spanish Elegy* directly from Rosales for approximately $15,000. Finally, on September 1, 2000, Freedman and her husband purchased a "Pollock" directly from Rosales for $280,000.

Freedman's motives in swapping for and purchasing these Rosales Paintings will be determined by a jury. . . .

This Court concludes that there are material issues of fact as to whether Freedman and Knoedler acted with fraudulent intent in selling Rosales Paintings to Plaintiffs.

2. Reliance

Freedman contends that Plaintiffs are sophisticated art collectors who had the opportunity to investigate her alleged misrepresentations before purchasing the works. Freedman contends that had Plaintiffs performed "even minimal [due] diligence," they would have learned the facts that provide the basis for their fraud claims. Although it is true that Plaintiffs had purchased works of art before, this Court cannot conclude—as a matter of law—that Plaintiffs' alleged sophistication and experience rendered them unreasonable in relying on Freedman and Knoedler's representations concerning the paintings. An analysis of the factors cited in *Winnick* and other cases confirms this conclusion.

As an initial matter, . . . the De Soles . . . received "written confirmation of the truthfulness of the representations at issue." The De Soles requested and received a December 11, 2004 letter from Freedman in which she confirmed all of her earlier oral representations about the painting they later purchased, including its authenticity and provenance. . . .

The representations made by Freedman and Knoedler likewise contained no "hints of [] falsity"; to the contrary, Knoedler's sterling reputation lent credibility to Freedman's assertions.

Moreover, even assuming that "the truth theoretically might have been discovered," there is evidence in the record suggesting that any such discovery would be possible "only with extraordinary effort or great difficulty." The IFAR Report demonstrates the complexity of the task of ascertaining the authenticity and provenance of a work of art, particularly in the absence of any documentation concerning the painting. In preparing its report over a number of months, IFAR showed the "Green Pollock" to numerous Pollock experts; conducted "extensive archival and other research"; conducted materials and technical analysis; and closely examined the paint handling and style of the work, and the legitimacy of the purported Pollock signature. In sum, assuming that the forged nature of the paintings sold to Plaintiffs could have been discovered, there is evidence in the record suggesting that that discovery would have come "only with extraordinary effort or great difficulty."

As noted above, "reasonable reliance is . . . a question normally reserved for the finder of fact and [is] not usually amenable to summary judgment." Such is the case here.

Crediting Plaintiffs' evidence on this point, a reasonable jury could conclude that Plaintiffs justifiably relied on Freedman and Knoedler's representations. Accordingly, Freedman and Knoedler are not entitled to summary judgment on Plaintiffs' fraud and fraudulent concealment claims.

* * *

VI. Breach of Warranty

Knoedler has moved for summary judgment on the De Soles' breach of warranty claim. The De Soles allege that Knoedler and Freedman made the following representations directly to them:

(1) the Work was created by Mark Rothko;

(2) the Work was owned by the son of a Swiss private collector who obtained the Work from Rothko via David Herbert;

(3) the Work came directly to Knoedler from an individual, whom Knoedler and Freedman knew personally; and

(4) the Work had been authenticated by numerous experts, including David Anfam and Christopher Rothko.

The De Soles also allege that in a December 11, 2004 letter—provided at the request of the De Soles—Knoedler and Freedman state: "Knoedler warrants the authenticity and good title of [the purported Rothko painting sold to the De Soles]."

The De Soles claim that each of these representations constitutes an express warranty under N.Y. U.C.C. § 2–313(1).

* * *

B. Analysis

As an initial matter, Knoedler argues that neither Freedman's oral statements to the De Soles about the provenance and authenticity of the Rothko they purchased, nor Freedman's December 11, 2004 letter confirming her oral statements, are actionable warranties. According to Knoedler, any "'expressed opinion or judgment of the seller'" regarding the artist who created a piece of art is an opinion and does not create a warranty.

Knoedler's invoice for the Rothko definitively attributes the work to Rothko, however. Moreover, in Freedman's December 11, 2004 letter, she explicitly states that "Knoedler warrants the authenticity and good title of the painting, *Untitled, 1956*, and confirms its 'remarkably good condition.'" Freedman and Knoedler's statements go well beyond the expression of an opinion; they are statements of fact and clearly warrant the painting's authenticity.

Knoedler argues that the De Soles did not rely on Freedman's December 11, 2004 letter as the basis of the bargain they struck with Knoedler. At the time of the sale, however, the De Soles requested that Freedman put in writing her oral representations about the authenticity and provenance of the alleged Rothko. Moreover, Domenico De Sole testified that he "would not have sent the 8.4 million [on December 17, 2004] without a document that [Freedman] promised to me and was sent to me [on December 11, 2004]." In any event, the reliance element in a breach of warranty claim is not onerous: "the only reliance that is necessary is the buyer's belief that it was purchasing the seller's promise as to the truth of the matters stated in the warranty . . . [i.e.,] reliance is established if 'the express warranties are bargained-for terms of the seller.'" The evidence here is sufficient to demonstrate that the De Soles bargained for Freedman and Knoedler's warranties as to the authenticity and provenance of the alleged Rothko.

As to timeliness of the breach of warranty claim, it is undisputed that the De Soles purchased the Rothko from Knoedler and Freedman on December 17, 2004. Accordingly, the De Soles' breach of warranty cause of action accrued on that date, and the statute of limitations expired on December 17, 2008. Given that the De Soles filed this action on March 28, 2012, their breach of warranty claim is untimely unless the statute was extended for some reason. The De Soles have not pointed to any provision in the New York U.C.C. that extends the limitations period. Instead, the De Soles assert that the doctrine of equitable tolling applies to preserve their breach of warranty claim against Knoedler.

The factual premise for the De Soles' equitable tolling argument is a January 19, 2008 letter Freedman sent to the De Soles. In connection with arranging for insurance coverage for the alleged Rothko, the De Soles requested a written appraisal from Knoedler. In a January 19, 2008 letter, Freedman and Knoedler represent that "'the probable cost of replacing the [Rothko] with a similar work'" is $9 million. The De Soles contend that Freedman's January 19, 2008 letter constitutes an affirmative misrepresentation that triggers equitable tolling. The De Soles further argue that Knoedler and Freedman knew that the Rosales Paintings were forgeries at the time they provided the appraisal, but transmitted the false valuation of the "Rothko" in order to prevent the De Soles from becoming aware of a potential claim against Knoedler.

Knoedler contends that the January 19, 2008 letter provides no basis for applying equitable tolling, because it was provided "solely for insurance purposes." While the De Soles requested the letter for insurance purposes, there is a material issue of fact as to whether Freedman and Knoedler provided this letter solely for purposes of the De Soles' insurance needs. For the reasons discussed above, Plaintiffs have offered evidence demonstrating that well before January 2008 Freedman and Knoedler knew that the Rosales Paintings were forgeries. In representing to the De

Soles—more than three years after the sale of the purported Rothko—that the painting was worth $9 million, Knoedler was—in effect—reaffirming the authenticity of the Rothko and acting to conceal its prior fraudulent conduct. Finally, there is evidence that Eleanore De Sole read Freedman's letter at the time it was sent, thus providing a basis for reliance.

In sum, there are genuine issues of material fact concerning the De Soles' breach of warranty claim. Accordingly, Knoedler is not entitled to summary judgment on the De Soles' breach of warranty claim.

* * *

Conclusion

Defendants' motions for summary judgment are denied in part and granted in part as set forth above....

Notes and Questions

1. *Post-Purchase Due Diligence? Dawson* was decided under specific art legislation that explicitly referred to "the customs and usage of the trade" in determining "the degree of authenticity ... warranted," while *Balog* was governed by the UCC § 2-313 general warranty or opinion format. Judge Pence in *Balog* did not seem to think that difference was important in determining what a buyer must prove to establish that the warranty was inaccurate. Why? Similarly in *De Sole*, the general UCC provision and not New York's specialized statute was in play for the breach of warranty claim. This presumably was because the oral and written statements made by Freedman to the De Soles were so clearly warranties, and so found by the court.

On the statute of limitations issue, Judge Pence took care to distinguish the three cases (*Hammer Holdings*, *Rosen*, and *Firestone*) that did not toll the UCC's four-year statute of limitations for artwork purchased from a dealer. In each of those cases, the purchase was a painting for a significant sum of money. Do you think it was important to Judge Pence's reasoning that the good was an artwork and the art market is not like most commercial markets, or that the buyers were not high-end, sophisticated art buyers? In other words, was the exceptionality of the art market, or the ordinary nature of the purchasers, or both, a consideration?

Consider the *Rosen* case, where the court specifically determined that requiring a buyer to seek another expert's view on authenticity was not burdensome. "A person who spends a considerable sum of money for a painting understandably will, as the Rosens did here, obtain appraisals for insurance purposes. Requiring a purchaser to obtain that appraisal from an expert other than the seller is not an onerous burden." 894 F.2d 28, at 32. Moreover, the *Rosen* court believed that "[a] contrary holding would provide purchasers of art greater protection" than other purchasers and "would leave art dealers exposed ... indefinitely, a result that we do not believe was intended by the legislature." Like *Weisz I*, *Balog* is understandable from a consumer protection perspective, yet *Balog* is criticized because authenticity as a working standard in the art world is not necessarily a permanent condition.

De Sole raises the same questions more than 25 years later. The statute of limitations had clearly expired for the breach of warranty claim. The De Soles make the same argument that the Balogs made—the insurance appraisal for the artwork tolled the statute. The court agreed that this could serve to toll the statute. The question as to the sophistication of the buyers—and hence whether their reliance on Freedman's assertions was justified—was put in issue by the defendants. The De Soles were not first-time art buyers, nor was their purchase modest. Mr. De Sole was named chairman of Sotheby's in 2015. Nevertheless, the court determined for summary judgment purposes that there was a material question of fact. The sophistication argument was a tough one given the egregious fact pattern involving Freedman. The court summarily rejected Freedman's argument that her actions were without fraudulent intent: "This Court disagrees." Did you notice that one buyer in the Knoedler tale had included a rescission clause in the sales contract if IFAR did not deem the work authentic? Why didn't the De Soles do the same? Did they even have a sales contract? It is possible that they merely relied on the invoice and the reputation of Knoedler and Freedman. What is your transactional takeaway from *De Sole*? Although *De Sole* did go to trial in January 2016, the parties settled the case after two weeks. When Knoedler insisted the Rothko was authentic, Mr. De Sole said that's when he knew it wasn't. "My point of view was . . . give me my $8.3 million back and I'll walk away. Now you can sell this authentic Rothko for more. . . . When they absolutely refused to do that I knew that, one, the Rothko was definitely a fake, and two, they knew for sure that it was fake." More than 10 lawsuits were filed over the Knoedler forgeries. Eileen Kinsella, *Domenico De Sole Speaks about the Knoedler Fraud Trial*, ARTNETNEWS, Feb. 17, 2016, at news.artnet.com.

An ongoing issue in authenticity is the standard of care of a gallery. What due diligence should a gallery undertake when works are consigned to it for sale? At what point did the various red flags in *Knoedler* suggest something more was required? Why did Freedman try to have Rosales sign various statements regarding her clients?

2. *The Problem of Prints and Multiples.* Not all fine art is one of a kind; art multiples, such as lithographs, etchings and cast sculpture multiples, create exceptional opportunities for counterfeiting, as *Balog* demonstrated. Ever-improving technology assists the forger, as does the market ignorance and confusion resulting from the lack of industry-wide standards as to basic terminology and control of production processes, and lack of enforcement of general or art specific consumer protection laws. See Ralph E. Lerner & Judith Bresler, 1 ART LAW: THE GUIDE FOR COLLECTORS, INVESTORS, DEALERS & ARTISTS 451–491 (3d ed. 2005) for a thorough exposition of the issues involving multiples, including a listing of state statutes on art multiples, which overall "lack bite." Two of the next four cases arise from multiples. *SWCA Inc.* involves a question of authenticity for a surmoulage, a bronze cast not from the artist's original, but rather from a second or third generation bronze; while

Simon-Whelan involves a painting that was "one of several created . . . at Warhol's direction from an acetate personally created and chosen by Warhol."

D. Self-Regulation

In addition to ad hoc judicial determinations and legislative enactments, a third avenue, self-regulation, exists for the business reality posed by uncertain authenticity. That self-regulation takes transactional form in two ways, both of which are expressly provided for by contract. Christie's and Sotheby's, for example, provide guarantees of authenticity to their auction buyers for authenticity concerns within a specific time frame. They also reserve the discretionary right to rescind a sale in the consignment agreements with their owner-consignors, as the next two cases illustrate. See Chapter 9, *infra*, for additional perspective on rescission clauses in consignment agreements.

In addition to the Conditions of Sale, the Terms of Guarantee accompany each auction catalogue. The Terms of Guarantee reproduced below is from the Sotheby's Prints & Multiples Evening Sale in New York on October 22, 2020.

Sotheby's Terms of Guarantee*

As set forth below and in the Conditions of Sale, for all lots Sotheby's guarantees that the authorship, period, culture or origin (collectively, "Authorship") of each lot in this catalogue is as set out in the BOLD or CAPITALIZED type heading in the catalogue description of the lot, as amended by oral or written salesroom notes or announcements. Purchasers should refer to the Glossary of Terms, if any, for an explanation of the terminology used in the Bold or Capitalized type heading and the extent of the Guarantee. Sotheby's makes no warranties whatsoever, whether express or implied, with respect to any material in the catalogue other than that appearing in the Bold or Capitalized heading and subject to the exclusions below.

In the event Sotheby's in its reasonable opinion deems that the conditions of the Guarantee have been satisfied, it shall refund to the original purchaser of record the hammer price and applicable buyer's premium and overhead premium paid for the lot by the original purchaser of record.

This Guarantee is provided for a period of five (5) years from the date of the relevant auction, is solely for the benefit of the original purchaser of record at the auction and may not be transferred to any third party. To be able to claim under this Guarantee of Authorship, the original purchaser of record must: (i) notify Sotheby's in writing within three (3) months of receiving any information that causes the original purchaser of record to question the accuracy of the Bold or Capitalized type heading, specifying the lot number, date of the auction at which it was purchased and the reasons for such question; and (ii) return the Lot to Sotheby's at the

* Copyright Sotheby's; for the Conditions of Sale, see Chapter 3, *supra*.—Ed.

original selling location in the same condition as at the date of sale to the original purchaser of record and be able to transfer good title to the Lot, free from any third party claims arising after the date of such sale.

Sotheby's has discretion to waive any of the above requirements. Sotheby's may require the original purchaser of record to obtain at the original purchaser of record's cost the reports of two independent and recognized experts in the field, mutually acceptable to Sotheby's and the original purchaser of record. Sotheby's shall not be bound by any reports produced by the original purchaser of record, and reserves the right to seek additional expert advice at its own expense. It is specifically understood and agreed that the rescission of a sale and the refund of the original purchase price paid (the successful hammer price, plus the buyer's premium and overhead premium) is exclusive and in lieu of any other remedy which might otherwise be available as a matter of law, or in equity. Sotheby's and the Consignor shall not be liable for any special, punitive, incidental or consequential damages incurred or claimed, including without limitation, loss of profits or interest.

Sotheby's and Christie's guarantee authenticity to the original buyer for five years. The New York statute of limitations for a breach of contract is generally six years. N.Y. C.P.L.R. § 213. Consider UCC § 2-725(1), which provides that the statute of limitations can be reduced by agreement but not extended.

The next two cases, *Kohler* and *SWCA*, provide examples of the art market self-regulating for authenticity based on a contractual provision with the owner-consignor.

Kohler v. Leslie Hindman, Inc.

80 F.3d 1181 (7th Cir. 1996)

CUDAHY, J. An artist once produced a painting now called "The Plains of Meudon." For a while, the parties in this case thought that the artist was Theodore Rousseau, a prominent member of the Barbizon school, and that the painting was quite valuable. With this idea in mind, the Kohlers consigned the painting to Leslie Hindman, Inc., an auction house, and Richard Thune bought it at auction for $90,000 on the condition that it was, in fact, a Rousseau. It was not. The parties then pursued a lawsuit in the district court to determine who would get stuck with it. Upon a motion for summary judgment, the district court held that, as a matter of law, the contracts between the parties required that the Kohlers keep the painting. The Kohlers contend that the district court erred in its interpretation of the contracts, and they appeal. We affirm.

Background

The Kohlers inherited the painting from their mother, Dorothy Dings Kohler, in 1989. Two years later, they decided to sell it along with some other artwork from their mother's estate, and they contacted Leslie Hindman Auctioneers (Hindman,

Inc.). After arranging for the inspection of the artwork, Leslie Hindman, president of her eponymous auction house, met with the Kohlers and discussed the terms by which her company would sell it at auction. Hindman, Inc. and the Kohlers then entered into a consignment agreement which made the company the Kohlers' agent for the auction sale.

Among other things, the consignment agreement defined the scope of Hindman, Inc.'s authority as agent. Two aspects of that authority concern us here. First, Hindman, Inc. was obliged to sell the painting according to the conditions of sale spelled out in the auction catalog. Those conditions provided that neither the consignors nor Hindman, Inc. made any warranties of authenticity. Indeed, the conditions emphasized that "[a]ll lots are sold 'AS IS,'" and one provision of the conditions asserted that "[n]o statement anywhere, whether oral or written, shall be deemed" to be a warranty of authenticity. The conditions also provided that Hindman, Inc. would insure that title to all lots passed with the fall of the auctioneer's hammer. In addition to these prescriptions, another provision of the consignment agreement gave the company extensive and exclusive discretionary authority to cancel sales. In Paragraph 14 of the consignment agreement, Hindman, Inc. declared that

> We are authorized as your agent to accept the return and rescind the sale of any [p]roperty if we at any time in our sole discretion determine that the offering for sale of any [p]roperty has subjected us and/or you to any liability under a warranty of authenticity.

Along with the other artwork from the Dorothy Dings Kohler estate, Hindman, Inc. listed the painting in its auction catalog, noting that the painting was, in its best judgment, by Rousseau. Hindman, Inc. also displayed the painting at a pre-auction showing where Thune's agent, Simon Parkes, saw it and developed some doubts about its authenticity. He expressed those doubts to his principal and to Scot Campbell, an employee of Hindman, Inc. Campbell relayed Parkes' suspicions to Ms. Hindman, who was soon in touch with Thune. Thune was still interested in the painting, but he wanted to have it authenticated before committing to its purchase. Unable to obtain an authoritative opinion about its authenticity before the auction, Ms. Hindman and Thune made a verbal agreement that Thune could return the painting within approximately thirty days of the auction if he was the successful bidder and if an expert then determined that Rousseau had not painted it. Neither Ms. Hindman nor anyone else at Hindman, Inc. told the Kohlers about the questions concerning the painting or about the side agreement between Thune and Hindman, Inc.

At the auction on October 13, 1991, Thune prevailed in the bidding with a high bid of $90,000, and he took possession of the painting without paying. He then sent it to an expert in Paris who decided that it was not a Rousseau. Thune returned the painting to Hindman, Inc. in March 1992.

The Kohlers sued both Hindman, Inc. and Thune. They claimed that Hindman, Inc. had breached the consignment agreement with them and its fiduciary duty to them and had committed constructive fraud and conversion. They also claimed that they had a implied contract with Thune himself for the painting, and that Thune had breached that contract by failing to pay the $90,000. Hindman, Inc. and Thune each made various claims of their own.

After the district court dismissed the conversion claim, the parties made cross-motions for summary judgment on all of the remaining claims. The district court ruled that Hindman, Inc. and Thune were entitled to judgment on all of the Kohlers' claims against them. The Kohlers appeal that ruling.

Discussion

* * *

The parties here do not dispute the relevant facts; therefore our review focuses on the district court's application of the law to those facts. Because this is an action within the district court's diversity jurisdiction, Illinois' choice of law rules determine the applicable substantive law. In disputes such as this one that arise from a contract, Illinois law respects the contract's choice-of-law clause . . . and that agreement provides that their disputes should be governed by Illinois law. . . .

Indeed, all of the Kohlers' claims depend upon how the consignment agreement defined the scope of Hindman, Inc.'s authority as the Kohlers' agent. If Hindman, Inc. acted at all times within its authority, the Kohlers cannot prevail on any of their claims. Defining the scope of that authority requires an interpretation of the consignment agreement.

* * *

. . . [The Kohlers] proffer an interpretation of the consignment agreement that would put Hindman, Inc. in breach. They contend that the agreement made Hindman, Inc. powerless to do anything other than sell the painting "as is." They point out that the consignment agreement bound Hindman, Inc. to the terms of the auction catalog's conditions of sale, and those conditions informed prospective buyers that Hindman, Inc. sold every item "as is" and absolutely disclaimed all warranties of authenticity. The conditions also provided that high bidders would take title at the fall of the hammer. The Kohlers argue that the combination of these provisions clearly make the dealings of Hindman, Inc. with Thune unauthorized. The pre-auction side agreement with Thune was equivalent to a warranty of authenticity, which Hindman, Inc. promised not to make; and the rescission effected after the sale violated Hindman, Inc.'s duty to make the title to the painting pass with the fall of the hammer. The Kohlers acknowledge that Paragraph 14 of the consignment agreement did give Hindman, Inc. the authority to rescind sales in the face of a threat of liability under a warranty of authenticity, but they maintain that this authority could not have come into play here. Because the auction catalog contained such absolute disclaimers, the Kohlers believe that Hindman, Inc. could not possibly have faced any realistic threat of warranty liability. Consequently, they argue that Paragraph 14's authority had not been activated here.

The district court ruled that Hindman, Inc.'s authority to rescind was more expansive than the Kohlers thought and that Hindman, Inc. had acted within the scope of that authority. In its arguments, Hindman, Inc. unsurprisingly expresses complete agreement with this ruling and the reasoning behind it.

The district court focused on Paragraph 14 of the consignment agreement, which authorized Hindman, Inc. to rescind a sale when the company, in its "sole discretion," determined that it or its consignor was subject to liability under a warranty of authenticity. The district court concluded that this grant of discretion allowed Hindman, Inc. to rescind a sale whenever it perceived the threat of such liability, notwithstanding the auction catalog's emphatic disclaimers. In the district court's reading of the consignment agreement, once the questions about the authenticity of the painting arose, Hindman, Inc. had open-ended authority to avoid a lawsuit arising from a claim under a warranty of authenticity. Hindman, Inc. had the power to rescind or to make a conditional promise to rescind in side agreements with prospective buyers. The district court noted that such a side agreement was equivalent to a warranty of authenticity and would constitute a technical breach of Hindman, Inc.'s promise to adhere to the conditions of sale. But the district court reasoned that making a conditional promise to rescind was not a material breach because it was consistent with the exercise of the company's sole discretion to rescind.

The district court's decision emerged from the proper inquiry, and we must determine whether it correctly answered the questions it asked. Ultimately, we must determine the extent of Hindman, Inc.'s discretion to determine when it needed to exercise its authority to rescind a sale. If Hindman, Inc. had the sole discretion to decide to rescind a sale, then it had the authority to make a conditional promise to rescind. If Hindman, Inc. received this discretionary authority to rescind as a product of its bargain with the Kohlers, then its promise to rescind under certain conditions is not inconsistent with the bargained-for objectives of the consignment agreement. Under Illinois law, this means that the conditional promise to rescind would not breach the consignment agreement even if it has the same effect as a warranty of authenticity.

Determining the extent of Hindman, Inc.'s authority to rescind is difficult. The Kohlers' brief suggests a powerful argument: a holding that Hindman, Inc. had unlimited authority to rescind would undermine most of the specified limitations on the other aspects of the auctioneer's authority. Because Illinois law requires that contracts be interpreted so that all of their provisions be given effect, we cannot conclude that Paragraph 14 vitiates the rest of the consignment agreement. But neither can we ignore that paragraph's reference to "sole discretion." Therefore, we must determine the limits of the discretion that emerged from the consignment agreement.

Interpretation would be easier if we could find a customary meaning for "sole discretion" as used in auctioneers' consignment agreements. Unfortunately, our research has not revealed any Illinois case law on this point. But the ruling of a federal district court in New York can give us some guidance. In *Greenwood v. Koven,* 880 F.Supp. 186 (S.D.N.Y.1995), that court considered the extent of an auctioneer's authority under a consignment agreement with a provision like Paragraph 14. The district court there found that such a contract provision is highly analogous to a satisfaction clause (typically conditioning one party's performance on that party's satisfaction with the other party's performance). 880 F.Supp. at 198–99. Through a satisfaction clause, a party's exercise of judgment or discretion is a condition for its duty to perform. *See* 3A Arthur L. Corbin, Corbin on Contracts § 646 (1960); 2 E. Allen Farnsworth, Farnsworth on Contracts § 8.4 (1990). Because satisfaction clauses involve the same principles of contract law as apply here, we will treat Paragraph 14 as a satisfaction clause.

Illinois courts have developed rules for interpreting satisfaction clauses that require a classification. Thus, satisfaction clauses in Illinois come in two categories: those that make the exercise of discretion purely subjective and those that require the exercise of discretion according to objective factors. The first category includes satisfaction clauses invoking the feelings, taste or judgment of the party exercising discretion. When a satisfaction clause conveys this sort of subjective discretion, it does not, however, remove all limitations on the exercise of discretion. The party that has the right to act according to its personal judgment or within its sole discretion must still act in good faith.

On the other hand, a satisfaction clause may fall into the second category when it involves matters susceptible to objective evaluation; mechanical utility is a stereotype of such matters. When objective considerations control the exercise of discretion, the party to be satisfied must exercise its authority in a just and reasonable way.

These rules do not apply easily to Paragraph 14. By giving Hindman, Inc. "sole discretion," this provision suggests that the consignment agreement had defined Hindman, Inc.'s authority subjectively. The consignment agreement did not define any objective criteria that would control Hindman, Inc.'s exercise of judgment. Nevertheless, the object of Hindman, Inc.'s discretion was not a purely subjective phenomenon like taste or feeling. Rather, Hindman, Inc. had to evaluate risk, and demanding such an evaluation impliedly invoked rational analysis. The Kohlers were not giving Hindman, Inc. a contract right to emulate Chicken Little. Viewing all of these conditions together, the grant of "sole discretion" to assess risk is somewhat ambiguous as between objective and subjective satisfaction.

Ultimately, for lack of objective criteria, we must conclude that Hindman, Inc.'s exercise of its authority is bounded only by its satisfaction as limited, of course, by good faith. The principal factor leading us to this conclusion is the agreement's use of the phrase "sole discretion." This phrase denotes subjectivity. Moreover, this conclusion corresponds with the theoretical understanding of contract bargaining.

The consignment agreement made the interests of the Kohlers and Hindman, Inc. largely coincident. The Kohlers and Hindman, Inc. would each profit most from the same set of circumstances, namely the sale of the painting for the highest possible price. Given this identity of interests, the Kohlers could trust Hindman, Inc.'s subjective decision-making. For the purposes of analyzing the risk of liability, Hindman, Inc. and the Kohlers had the same perspective. Therefore, the Kohlers did not have to hold Hindman, Inc. to some external standard as a means of making the auctioneer's interests coincide with its own. At least in theory, it would be rational for the Kohlers to accept Hindman, Inc.'s good-faith subjective judgments as part of a bargain. Because the language of the contract clearly implies that the Kohlers did trust Hindman, Inc.'s subjective judgment, we conclude the consignment agreement held the auctioneer to a subjective standard.

Hindman, Inc.'s actions towards Thune, before and after the auction, meet the standard of good faith. The Kohlers contend that the side agreement and the subsequent rescission were entirely self-interested acts. In making this contention, they emphasize that no-one in the auction house informed them of the doubts about the painting's authenticity or about the negotiations with Thune. They seem to think that this lack of disclosure reflects a consciousness of guilt, or perhaps more precisely, a consciousness of pure self-interest. This contention, however, defies the logic of the consignment agreement. The consignment agreement created one overriding interest that was identical for both the Kohlers and Hindman, Inc. Therefore, anything that Hindman, Inc. did for itself, it apparently also did for the Kohlers.

It is true that the parties' interests were opposed in one respect: under Paragraph 10 of the consignment agreement, the Kohlers would have to pay Hindman, Inc. 20% of the auctioneer's most recent pre-sale estimate and the auctioneer's expenses if the Kohlers withdrew the painting from sale on account of doubts about its authenticity. Thus, Hindman, had some interest in promoting withdrawal because it could profit at the Kohlers' expense if doubts about the painting became so widespread that its sale at auction were no longer feasible. With respect to this interest, however, Hindman, Inc. apparently acted selflessly. Telling the Kohlers about Thune's doubts before the sale might have actually advanced Hindman, Inc.'s interests because the information might have given the Kohlers an incentive to withdraw. And even if the Kohlers had not decided to withdraw, the side agreement might still have been their best option. Under the side agreement, Hindman, Inc. maintained Thune's incentive to bid as if the painting were really a Rousseau; therefore it maximized the chances of a lucrative result for the auction. This was indeed an act of good faith, and it was made within the limits of Hindman, Inc.'s authority under the consignment agreement. The district court correctly ruled that Hindman, Inc. had not breached the consignment agreement.

This conclusion permits the easy resolution of the other issues that the Kohlers raise. Our conclusion that Hindman, Inc. acted in good faith means, of course, that the auctioneer did not breach its fiduciary duty. It also means that there was no constructive fraud. Under Illinois law, a breach of duty, especially fiduciary duty, is an essential element of a claim of constructive fraud. Because Hindman, Inc. breached no duty, the Kohlers cannot claim that it committed constructive fraud. Finally, the Kohlers cannot claim that they have a implied agreement with Thune for the sale of the painting at $90,000. Such a implied contract would exist only if the side agreement were invalid. Because Hindman, Inc. made the side agreement within the scope of its authority, that agreement is valid, and it protects Thune from the Kohlers' reach.

For these reasons, the judgment of the district court is

AFFIRMED.

Christie's Inc. v. SWCA, Inc.

867 N.Y.S.2d 650 (N.Y. Sup. Ct. 2008)

RAMOS, J. This is an action for damages arising out of the rescission of the sale of a bronze sculpture created by the artist Pablo Picasso, entitled *Tête Cubiste* (*Tête de Fernande*) (the Sculpture).

* * *

Background

In the spring of 2002, defendant SGA [Sculpture Guild of America] purchased the Sculpture from Universal Antiques for $30,000, and offered it to SWCA. SWCA contacted independent art dealer, Thomas Segal, to inquire if he knew of a potential buyer. Segal, in turn, contacted Christie's.

On June 27, 2002, Professor Werner Spies, author of the catalogue raisonné of Picasso sculptures, issued a certificate of authenticity (Spies Certificate) for the Sculpture, upon payment by SGA. In the Spies Certificate, he indicated that the Sculpture is a Picasso from the Vollard Edition.

On July 16, 2002, SWCA and Christie's signed a Letter Agreement (July 16 Letter Agreement), that authorized Christie's to sell the Sculpture on behalf of SWCA for $5,000,000. The July 16 Letter Agreement granted to Christie's the right to rescind the sale under certain circumstances. SWCA furnished to Christie's the Spies Certificate.

Thereafter, Christie's offered to sell the Sculpture to non-party art collector, Samuel I. Newhouse Jr. On July 19, 2002, Newhouse and Christie's signed a letter agreement (July 19 Letter Agreement). Pursuant to that agreement, Christie's agreed that Newhouse could rescind the sale if the Sculpture was found to be unauthentic.

Additionally, Christie's agreed to pay Segal 50% of the commission that it received for the sale of the Sculpture. After the sale to Newhouse, Christie's paid Segal $275,000.

A year and a half after the sale, Christie's unsuccessfully offered to re-sell the Sculpture on Newhouse's behalf. In September 2004, Christie's informed Newhouse that it recently developed concerns about the authenticity of the Sculpture, and sought to conduct additional research about its origins. Christie's sent the Sculpture to France for inspection by Pablo Picasso's son, Claude. Under French law, Claude Picasso retains the "droit moral" or moral right, to authenticate artwork created by his father. On October 19, 2004, Claude Picasso issued a certificate of authenticity for the Sculpture.

Nonetheless, Christie's persisted and continued its efforts to undermine the authenticity of the Sculpture. Christie's now contends that the Sculpture is a *surmoulage,* a bronze cast of a second or third generation bronze, rather than being from the Vollard Edition, a bronze cast from the original clay master created by Picasso. Most dealers consider *surmoulages* to be unauthentic.

After Christie's informed Newhouse of its doubts concerning the Sculpture's authenticity, Newhouse stated that it was "a legal problem." In June 2005, Christie's rescinded the sale to Newhouse. Thereafter, Christie's sought to rescind the sale from SWCA, and demanded a refund of the purchase price on the ground that it believed that the Sculpture was a *surmoulage;* SWCA refused.

* * *

Discussion

To prevail on a motion for summary judgment, the movant must establish entitlement to judgment as a matter of law, by producing sufficient evidence to demonstrate the absence of any trial issues of material fact. For the below stated reasons, SWCA's motion for summary judgment is denied, and Christie's cross-motion for summary judgment is denied, in part, and granted, in part.

I. Breach of Contract

The July 16 Letter Agreement entitles Christie's to rescind the sale of the Sculpture from SWCA "at any time" if it "reasonably determines that the sale may expose Christie's" to any liability, "including liability resulting from claims relating to title or authenticity."

SWCA moves for summary judgment as to the first cause of action for breach of contract on the ground that there are no triable issues of fact that the condition for rescission contained in the July 16 Letter Agreement was not met.

In contrast, Christie's contends that the July 16 Letter Agreement granted it a broad right to rescind the agreement. In addition, Christie's relies upon *Greenwood v. Koven,* 1993 WL 541181 [S.D.N.Y. 1993], for the principle that a subjective standard should apply to its exercise of the rescission provision and its belief that it was exposed to liability as to the Sculpture's authenticity.

The July 16 Letter Agreement explicitly gave Christie's the right to rescind the sale, but that right was conditioned upon Christie's "reasonable belief" that it would be exposed to liability. Under so-called "satisfaction clauses," where one party is granted a certain level of discretion to exercise a contract right to its satisfaction, courts must determine whether the parties intended that party to be reasonably satisfied, that is subject to the objective standard, or merely honestly, albeit unreasonably, satisfied, that is subject to a subjective standard (... *Greenwood v. Koven,* 880 F.Supp. 186, 199 [S.D.N.Y.1995]).

* * *

The contractual language at issue in *Greenwood,* 1993 WL 541181, upon which Christie's relies, is distinguishable. In *Greenwood,* the contract granted the purchaser the right to rescind the sale of a pastel by the painter Georges Braque based upon the purchaser's "sole discretion" as to whether it would be exposed to liability. Here, Christie's right to rescind is conditioned upon its "reasonable belief" that it would be exposed to liability, and thus, is subject to the objective standard.

In support of its contention that it reasonably believed that it may have been exposed to liability, Christie's argues that the consensus of opinions among "experts" at the time it conducted its investigation was that the Sculpture was a *surmoulage,* and thus, not an authentic work by Picasso. Christie's has little to support this contention....

* * *

Although Christie's decision to rescind based upon its fear of exposition to liability appears to have been motivated more by rumor and speculation, ultimately whether Christie's belief was reasonable is a question of fact for the fact-finder. Therefore, the court cannot determine as a matter of law whether the condition for rescission set forth in the September 16 Letter Agreement was met. SWCA's motion for summary judgment as to the first cause of action for breach of contract is denied.

II. Liability of Principal to Agent

SWCA moves for summary judgment as to the third cause of action for liability of principal to agent, that is premised upon the contention that Christie's was acting as SWCA's agent, and that it is liable for the breach of warranty of authenticity contained in the July 19 Letter Agreement.

SWCA acknowledges that SWCA and Christie's had an agency relationship, as memorialized in the July 16 Letter Agreement, and that SWCA was acting as Christie's' principal in the Newhouse transaction. Nonetheless, SWCA argues that Christie's went beyond its authority in furnishing an unqualified warranty of authenticity to Newhouse, and by selling the Sculpture to an undisclosed buyer, non-art merchant, Newhouse. Thus, SWCA contends that it cannot be bound as a principal to Christie's acts committed beyond the scope of authority.

Christie's contends that SWCA extended a warranty of authenticity for the Sculpture by providing Christie's with the Spies Certificate at the time of the sale. Alternatively, Christie's argues that an express warranty of authenticity is created under Article 2 of the Uniform Commercial Code (UCC), under section § 13.01 of the New York Arts and Cultural Affairs Law (NYACAL), and under customs and practices in the arts industry.

To establish that the unqualified warranty that Christie's included in the July 19 Letter Agreement with Newhouse was not authorized, SWCA points to the language of the July 16 Letter Agreement. It states,

> "You [SWCA] authorize us [Christie's] to *make the same representations and warranties* on your behalf to any purchaser with whom we conclude an agreement *pursuant to the terms of this letter*" (emphasis added).

The plain language of the July 16 Letter Agreement states that Christie's was only authorized to make, on SWCA's behalf, the same representations and warranties contained in the July 16 Letter Agreement.

SWCA made the following representations and warranties in the July 16 Letter Agreement:

> "You [SWCA] represent and warrant that . . . you have *no reason to believe* that the Property is not authentic or is counterfeit." (emphasis added).

The July 19 Letter Agreement with Newhouse obligates Christie's to "provide an original certificate by Werner Spies confirming the authenticity of the Property." SWCA contends that by including this phrase in the July 19 Letter Agreement, Christie's went beyond its authority, because it was authorized to provide only the representations and warranties to Newhouse that SWCA made in the July 16 Letter Agreement.

SWCA's argument is without merit. Although SWCA may have sought to limit the representations and warranties that Christie's was permitted to offer on its behalf, SWCA expressly authorized Christie's to furnish to the ultimate buyer the Spies Certificate, in addition to other documents in its possession relating to "the history and provenance" of the Sculpture. The July 16 Letter Agreement states,

> "You [SWCA] agree that you will *furnish to Christie's, for delivery to buyer,* all documents and records in your possession relating to the history and provenance of the Property, as well as *the original certificate of authenticity from Spies*" (emphasis added).

By authorizing Christie's to furnish to the buyer the Spies Certificate, the transaction to sell the Sculpture implicates the application of the New York's Arts and Cultural Affairs Law (NYACAL).

Under NYACAL, the furnishing of a certificate of authenticity by an art merchant to a non-art merchant creates an express warranty.

* * *

Nonetheless, the extent of what the express warranty of authenticity entails is not nearly as broad as Christie's contends. In the leading case interpreting the predecessor statute to NYACAL § 13.01, the court fashioned a standard for determining liability for breach of warranty, that is applicable here. The proper standard is whether the representations furnished by the seller with respect to the artwork can be said to have had a reasonable basis in fact at the time that the representations were made, as shown by testimony as a whole (*Dawson v. G. Malina, Inc.,* 463 F. Supp. 461, 467 [S.D.N.Y.1978]).

Ultimately, whether SWCA's description of the Sculpture contained in the Spies Certificate had a reasonable basis in fact at the time of the sale to Christie's is a question of fact, to be measured by the expert testimony provided at trial (*Dawson,* 463 F.Supp. at 467).

For these reasons, SWCA's motion for summary judgment as to the third cause of action for liability of principal to agent is denied.

* * *

Accordingly, it is

ORDERED that the summary judgment motion is denied; and it is further . . .

ORDERED that the remainder of the action shall continue.

Notes and Questions

1. *Aftermath. Christie's v. SWCA* was reportedly settled for an undisclosed amount.

2. *Identity of Interests?* In both *Kohler* and *SWCA*, the auction house on its own motion allowed the buyer to rescind the purchase because of an authenticity concern. At issue was the scope of the auction house's discretionary right to do so. Both courts determined that the right to rescind clause was a satisfaction clause. The next decision was whether the requisite satisfaction was to be determined objectively or subjectively. (Recall an analogous issue regarding a satisfaction clause in the portrait commission case of *Wolff v. Smith* from Chapter 1, *supra.*) Both *Kohler* and *SWCA* cited *Greenwood v. Koven* for guidance on the scope of discretion. Under the reasoning of that case, the *SWCA*'s "reasonably determines" clause was viewed objectively, while *Kohler*'s "sole discretion" was subjective and only limited by good faith.

This subjective standard in *Kohler* seemed to give the judge pause. The judge viewed the consignment agreement as creating an "identity of interests." Therefore, in theory at least, the owner could trust the auction house to exercise its discretion in a manner consistent with the owner's interest. The reality is that the auction house is an ongoing participant in the art market, while the owner may only intermittently participate. The auction house's interest in its ongoing reputation may trump a particular owner's express desire to sell "as is," without warranty.

In light of *Cristillana* and its confirmation of fiduciary responsibility owed to a consignor (Chapter 3, Part C, *supra*), what do you make of the Kohlers' charge that Hindman did not inform them of the "doubts about the painting's authenticity"?

There is a perception among some in the art industry that works sold at auction have a greater risk of being inauthentic than works sold through dealers. See, e.g., Part E, Note 5, *infra*. That perception coupled with the public function of auction houses previously noted may be reasons why auction houses require discretion to rescind even as that seems contrary to the fiduciary duty owed a consignor. See Chapter 9, *infra*.

E. Liability of Authenticators

Hahn v. Duveen

234 N.Y.S. 185 (N.Y. Sup. Ct. 1929)

BLACK, J. . . . Plaintiff, Hahn, claimed that her picture was an original by Leonardo da Vinci. Defendant said it was not painted by Leonardo, which was tantamount to saying that it was not an original by Leonardo and not a replica painted from the same model nor a duplicate painted from the original picture by Leonardo. There were two general contentions. Plaintiff claimed that her sacred rights of property had been invaded, in that defendant falsely and maliciously stated to a reporter of the *New York World* that the Hahn picture was not a genuine Leonardo da Vinci; that any expert who pronounced it genuine was not an expert; and that the genuine La Belle Ferroniere by Leonardo da Vinci was in the Louvre (No. 1600). Plaintiff said these statements by a man of defendant's position in the world of art, who had not seen the picture, had caused her special damage by causing the Kansas City Art Museum to call off negotiations then in progress regarding the purchase of the Hahn picture. Defendant, on the other hand, contended that the sacred right of free speech would be destroyed if such statements of opinion as he gave to the *New York World* could not be made in good faith regarding a picture that was before the public for sale and which had been the subject of newspaper articles in America and France. Thus there went to the jury the sharp issue between the rights of property and the rights of free speech. At the trial I charged the jury: 'If you believe defendant's statements about plaintiff's picture were false, there (was) is nothing in the occasion alone upon which defendant's statement was made, to rebut or negative (such) inference of malice, but it is for you to say whether or not the statement was made by defendant in good faith. In so deciding you will consider the actual language of the statement itself, as well as all the rest of the evidence before you.' Quoting Odgers on Libel and Slander, page 80, I further charged the jury that 'whenever a man unnecessarily intermeddles with the affairs of others, with which he is wholly unconcerned, such officious interference will be deemed malicious and he will be liable if special damage follow.' I, of course, coupled with this the qualification that the 'special damage must always be such as naturally or reasonably arises from the uttering of the slanderous words of the defendant.'

One of the first things the jury had to decide was whether or not Sir Joseph Duveen's statement that the Hahn picture was not by Leonardo da Vinci was made in good faith. Defendant, who had been put upon the stand by plaintiff as her first witness, sought to justify what he had said about the Hahn picture by stating that it could not be by Leonardo, because he knew that the genuine La Belle Ferroniere by Leonardo was in the Louvre (No. 1600). He further stated that he had 'always had my (his) own opinion about it. I told you that I have never changed my mind personally about the painter of the picture, about the authorship of the picture.' [Plaintiffs offered in evidence a letter signed by Duveen agreeing with "the most eminent connoisseurs" that the Louvre painting was "not by [Leonardo's] hand."—Ed.] Defendant put in evidence a Paris newspaper interview by Harry Hahn, the husband of plaintiff, disclaiming at that time any contention that the No. 1600 in the Louvre was not a genuine Leonardo. It will be seen, therefore, that there was ample evidence upon which to go to the jury upon the question of the good faith of both sides. In proceeding to consider whether there was sufficient evidence before the jury to warrant a verdict, the first and, indeed, the main point, is what sort of evidence the owner of a painting is required to present to a jury to prove that a painting is genuine. The law should be flexible enough to be just, and judicial methods and rules of evidence should in some measure conform to existing conditions. While we cannot take things for granted, less exactiture is sometimes required in proof now than before. A new situation exists in the world of art. Formerly the church, the state, and a few powerful men owned all the fine pictures and statuary. Their experts were men who created canvasses or marbles. [The court noted that as art moved out of this small market into a wider one, authenticity was often questioned.—Ed.] In cases where every witness, as well as the producer, was dead centuries before, the question of authenticity arose, some method of establishing authenticity other than the testimony of living witnesses was resorted to. This method was the reading of books by men who had studied the materials and methods of old painters, and taking the opinions of such experts. . . . In my charge to the jury I said upon the subject of experts: . . . 'There are two ways that experts in this case can help you with their opinions. One is by their study of the authentic history of a painting. The other by their study of the methods used or materials employed by the painters or schools of painting of the period in which it is claimed the pictures were painted.'

* * *

I have profound respect for critics whose conclusions rest upon facts. What they say should be carefully considered by a jury. The opinions of any other kinds of experts are as 'sounding brass and tinkling cymbals.' . . . There are also experts who admit that they have no formulas, rules, or ability to produce any artistic thing, but who claim to have a sixth sense which enables some of them after they have seen a picture even for five minutes to definitely determine whether it is genuine or not. I do not say that this faculty may not be possessed by some men, but it is not based upon enough objectiveness to convey definite meaning to a jury. It does happen, though, that some or all of these experts are to-day counseling the purchase or rejection of art objects of great value. The question therefore arises whether their testimony is competent, how competent it is, and what its probative value is. After carefully considering the really great arguments offered by counsel in this case, I am of the opinion that expert testimony of the proper sort, in connection with the other facts, is enough to have warranted a verdict in this case, and I therefore deny defendant's motion to dismiss.... The point I have to decide upon this motion to dismiss is not whether the Hahn picture or the Louvre picture No. 1600 is a genuine Leonardo. The only question I have to pass upon here is whether there was sufficient evidence before the jury at the end of the defendant's case to enable the jury to render a verdict for plaintiff or defendant. Concretely put, the real point is whether a dealer or an expert, however famous (and it is conceded that defendant is one of the greatest dealers in old paintings, although he modestly denies that he is an expert in the technical sense), can, without seeing a picture, declare that it is not the product of a certain master, and then, when damages are sought for the result of a statement that plaintiff must prove is false, malicious, and without probable cause, can contend that the proof of genuineness offered by plaintiff from the mouths of witnesses who have studied the admittedly genuine products of a certain master, familiarized themselves with the material upon which the picture is painted, the pigments used by the artist, his manner of treatment, and every characteristic that distinguishes that master's work, is not enough to enable a jury to reach a verdict. I do not believe a defendant in such circumstances can contend that the testimony of expert witnesses is not enough to enable the jury to reach a verdict. And this is especially true, because defendant had no way other than through the statements of expert witnesses to reach the conclusions that formed the basis of Mrs. Hahn's claim. I make these observations because defendant's memorandum refers to the case of Jendwine v. Slade, 2 Esp. 572, a case decided about 1799. While the court there said: 'There 'being no way of tracing the picture itself, it could only be matter of opinion whether the picture in question was the work of the artist whose name it bore, or not,' it did after its decision, for some reason, refer the cause to arbitration. I do not know upon what evidence the arbitrators gave their decision, but the learned chancellor said this 'opinion' evidence was all the evidence available.

The court's opinion quoted in the Jendwine Case was written over 100 years before Professor Laurie wrote on Pigments and Mr. Berensen wrote on Italian paintings, and nearly 100 years before the X-ray was developed by Professor Roentgen. I have no doubt about the competency of the proof given by expert witnesses as to the authenticity of the pictures they testified about. Its weight is another matter, and that was for the jury. The amount of importance to be attached to what the experts say depends entirely upon the factual basis for their conclusions.... The case thus resolved itself into a battle between experts.... Much as I regret that, I cannot write an opinion from which there can be an immediate appeal, so that the law may be at once finally fixed without the time and expense of another trial, I am constrained to hold that there was sufficient evidence before the jury to enable them to render a verdict. . . .

Motion to dismiss is denied, and case is restored to general calendar to be set for trial by stipulation, or upon motion of either party.

Notes and Questions

1. *Aftermath.* Duveen settled the lawsuit by paying $60,000 to Hahn for the painting. Given the court's repeated emphasis on expert opinion based on factual evidence, the settlement was prudent.

2. *Fair Comment.* The art world's reaction to *Duveen* was surprise that an art expert's opinion on authenticity, deemed fair comment, could be actionable. The fair comment defense requires that (1) the publication is an opinion, (2) that relates to the acts of an individual, and not the individual himself, (3) that is fair such that the reader can see the factual basis and come to her own conclusion, and (4) that the publication relates to a matter of public interest or to something available to the public. Actual malice or reckless disregard of the truth, however, invalidates the fair comment defense. As an internationally-known art dealer and critic, Duveen's categorical statement of inauthenticity to a newspaper reporter about a painting that he was not directly concerned with, and which was based solely on a photograph, can be seen as reckless and unprofessional. Viewed from this perspective, the concern of responsible and professional art experts over potential liability for their authenticity determinations may be misplaced. See, e.g., Travis v. Sotheby Parke Bernet Inc., Index No. 4290179 (N.Y. Sup. Ct., Nov. 11, 1982), where the professional conduct of Sotheby's art appraiser, who conducted in-depth research on the work as requested by the plaintiff resulting in an honest evaluation, absolved the appraiser from liability. There was a similar result in the English case of Luxmoore-May v. Messenger May Baverstock, 1 All E.R. 1067 (C.A. Eng. 1990). Plaintiffs selected a local auction house to research their two small paintings of foxhounds before offering them for sale. The paintings were sold at auction for £840. The court decided that the owners could not hold the local auction house to specialist standards when the owners learned shortly thereafter that the paintings were by George Stubbs and had sold at Sotheby's for £88,000. Similarly, Lariviere v. Thaw, 2000 WL 33965732 (N.Y. Sup. Ct. 2000), where members of the Pollock-Krasner Authentication Board were not liable for damages for the determination of inauthenticity of plaintiff's painting, as in accord with the submission agreement signed by plaintiff waiving his right to sue, where the plaintiff's case was "a laughable and clumsy attempt at fraud," a "childish plot." What if, however, it was Sotheby's or Christie's which missed the "sleeper" item? See James Marrone & Silvia Beltrametti, *"Sleeper" Antiquities: Misattribution in Sales of Ancient Art*, 27 Int'l J. Cult. Prop. 3 (2020) (describing concerns beyond monetary loss for misattributions of cultural property).

The concern among art experts for liability regarding their opinions remains. As the following note reveals, it is a concern that is not necessarily misplaced. Yet, it is not without recourse of its own.

3. *One Art Expert's Response.* Steve Seltzer, an authority on Western artist Charles M. Russell, was contacted by an Idaho auction house for his thoughts regarding a painting in advance of auction. The owner of the painting, Steve Morton, hoped to sell the painting for $650,000. Seltzer was familiar with the painting. He "knew instantly" that it was not a Russell, but rather a work of Seltzer's own grandfather, O.C. Seltzer, a contemporary and friend of Russell. Morton sued Seltzer for defamation, intentional interference with business relations, and negligence and sought a declaratory judgment of authenticity, an injunction against making statements regarding the work, and punitive damages. Morton's lawsuit was dismissed with prejudice "necessitated by Morton's and [his attorney] Gladwell's acknowledged awareness that they could not prevail on the merits" as Morton had no experts and Seltzer had many. Subsequently, Seltzer sued Morton, his attorney, and the law firm Gibson, Dunn & Crutcher, LLP for malicious prosecution and abuse of process. In a jury trial in Montana, Seltzer was awarded $21,350,000, which was reduced on appeal by the Montana Supreme Court to $11,250,000. Seltzer v. Morton, 154 P.3d 561 (Mont. 2007). Should Morton have proceeded in litigation without any expert?

4. *Experts' Commissions for Certification of Authenticity.* The *Duveen* court expressed skepticism of experts whose opinions were not based on articulable fact, likening their opinions to "sounding brass and tinkling cymbals." It also noted that "some or all of these experts are to-day counseling the purchase or rejection of art objects of a great value." As the next case illustrates, these two concerns—total subjectivity and pecuniary conflict—remain.

Ironically, one of Duveen's expert witnesses was Bernard Berenson, whose scholarly works were referenced by the court. As the preeminent Renaissance art expert of his time, Berenson became wealthy by furnishing certificates of authenticity to art collectors (including some of the most important American collectors, such as Isabella Stewart Gardner) for a commission based on a percentage of value. He also consulted for Duveen and allegedly received a confidential percentage of the sales proceeds. See Kenneth Clark, Another Part of the Wood (1974), for an insider's view of the workings at I Tatti, Berenson's villa in Florence. From the safe distance of time, Clark sharply perceives and portrays the corrupting impact of the then-prevailing practice of basing commissions for authenticating on the value of the authenticated work.

5. *From Artists, to Experts, to Boards.* The *Duveen* court noted that as the art market widened beyond the medieval and early Renaissance patrons of the church, the state, and wealthy aristocrats, questions of authenticity arose with greater frequency.

The earliest authenticators were artists themselves who sat as juries to settle art disputes and were often regarded as the only legitimate art authorities.

> Perhaps the most famous case of disputed pictures in the seventeenth century involved thirteen Italian paintings from the Reynst collection which were offered by Gerrit Uylenburgh (the son of Hendrick Uylenburgh, Rembrandt's business associate and in-law) to the elector of Brandenburg in 1671. When the attributions and quality of the pictures were challenged by the elector's adviser, the painter Hendrick de Fromantiou, the disputed works were submitted to successive juries of artists (including, among others . . . Johannes [Jan] Vermeer). The artist's opinions ranged wide, from one that deemed the paintings outright copies to another that saw them as weak originals, worth only one tenth of the asking price. The sale to the elector was never consummated, and the paintings went to public auction.

Peter C. Sutton, *Rembrandt and a Brief History of Connoisseurship*, in The Expert versus the Object 30–31 (Ronald D. Spencer ed., 2004).

An artist as the authenticator for his or her own work would seem to be ideal. One court, however, was presented with an artist (Balthazar Klossowski de Rola, aka Balthus) who disavowed the authenticity of a work previously owned by his ex-wife. The court noted that there may have been some prejudice in the disavowal. See Arnold Herstand & Co. v. Gallery: Gertrude Stein, Inc., 626 N.Y.S.2d 74 (App. Div. 1995). In 2016, a federal court, however, agreed with Scottish artist Peter Doig that he was not the author of a painting. The work had been offered for sale at auction by the plaintiff. After a well-publicized bench trial, the judge concluded there was "massive evidence" showing it was "impossible" for Doig to be the artist. Patrick O'Connell, *Ruling brushes off plaintiff in case of disputed Doig painting*, Chi. Trib., Aug. 24, 2016, at 6. The judge ruled this a case of mistaken identity as the presumed creator of the artwork was a teen-aged Peter Doige, a deceased Canadian carpenter. Fletcher v. Doig, 1:13-cv-03270 (N.D. Ill. 2016).

Lay connoisseurs were not completely unknown, although they were viewed with satirical derision. Rembrandt "delighted in ridiculing" art critics, and in one of his drawings, "a pompous lay connoisseur is sprouting ass's ears as a young man offers his own crude critique of the expert's judgment by defecating out of sight behind a panel." Peter C. Sutton, *Rembrandt and a Brief History of Connoisseurship*, in The Expert Versus the Object 30–31 (Ronald D. Spencer ed., 2004). Meanwhile, others worked to raise connoisseurship to a more intellectual level by developing logical and systematic approaches. For example, one important approach in developing the connoisseur's eye was the study of concrete details displayed by an artist in "material trifles," such as hands or ears, to reveal an artist's unique peculiarities. Scholarly works, including the catalogue raisonné, that sought to systemize knowledge began to appear regularly in the 19th century, and art history became a recognized and independent field of study. Reputable art experts today attain recognized status based on study and experience, but that does not mean certainty or uniformity of position for any particular work.

That the art world lacks "a formalized system for authenticating art that is perceived and acknowledged by all its denizens as rigorous, accountable, systemic, comprehensive and comprehensible" leads for calls that "no authentication decision be made by a single expert; both the appearance and reality of consensus are essential." Francis V. O'Connor, *Authenticating the Attribution of Art*, in The Expert versus the Object 20–23 (Ronald D. Spencer ed., 2004). Authentication boards emerged in the U.S. art market as a distinct provider of authentication services for the particular artist or artists represented. As the next case demonstrates, the de facto singular position of authority for authenticity given an authentication board can raise anticompetitive concerns. As a possible analogy, it is worth noting that under the French system of droit moral, the artist's family has the sole right to authenticate. See Chapter 7, *infra*.

Simon-Whelan v. Andy Warhol Foundation for the Visual Arts, Inc.

2009 WL 1457177 (S.D.N.Y. 2009)

SWAIN, J.

* * *

The Conspiracy

Plaintiff alleges that the Defendants have, for a period of twenty years, conspired to control the market for Andy Warhol artwork. . . . According to Plaintiff, Defendants have complete control over the authentication of Warhol artwork by virtue of the Board's status as sole recognized authentication authority for Warhol works and the Foundation's publication of an official catalogue of Warhol works. Defendants employ two methods for authenticating Warhol artwork. The first is a system of Board ratings of individual works as by Warhol, not by Warhol, or works as to which the Board expresses no opinion at the time. The second is informal authentication by virtue of inclusion in the Warhol Catalogue Raisonné (the "Catalogue"). The Catalogue, published by the Foundation, is an allegedly comprehensive listing of all authentic Warhol artwork in existence.

According to Plaintiff, the Board has denied the authenticity of works that were previously owned by the Estate and stamped with serial numbers from the Estate, routinely denies the authenticity of a certain percentage of Warhols, particularly when several from the same series are submitted, has denied authentication as a means of retaliation, has approached owners of Warhols to "lure" them into submitting their works for authentication, and changes its authentication policies when the change suits the Board's financial interests. Plaintiff alleges that Defendants use their control over the authentication methods to create a scarcity in the market for Warhol artwork and inflate the value of the Warhol works in the Foundation's possession.

At some time between 1988 and July 1990, the Estate implemented a policy requiring persons seeking authentication of works to sign a "Submission Agreement." The Board has continued the Estate's policy of requiring persons submitting works for authentication to sign the Submission Agreement. The Submission Agreement includes the following clause:

> By signing this letter Owner
>
> . . .
>
> (iii) hereby indemnifies the Authentication Board, the Foundation, the Estate of Andy Warhol (the "Estate"), and all members of and officers, directors, agents, representatives, employees and others at any time acting for the Authentication Board, the Foundation or the Estate (collectively, the "Indemnitees"), and agrees to defend and hold each Indemnitee harmless and releases, waives and covenants not to sue any Indemnitee, based upon any claim or liability asserted (a) by Owner or by any person or entity acquiring the Work, or any interest in the Work from Owner (a "Buyer") or any person or entity from whom Owner or any predecessor in interest acquired the Work which is based directly or indirectly on the legend or endorsement, if any, affixed to the Work, or on any letter herein referred to, or any other action by the Authentication Board or any other Indemnitee in connection herewith, including without limitation any claim that the opinion expressed therein is not correct, or (b) by any other person to whom Owner or the Buyer has made any statement or representation respecting the authenticity the Work or any action of the Authentication Board or any other Indemnitee in connection therewith, and hereby agrees to pay or reimburse each Indemnitee for all costs and expenses incurred by the Indemnitee in connection with any such asserted claim or liability, including without limitation the fees and expenses of legal counsel.

Double Denied

Plaintiff originally purchased a painting (referred to herein and in the Complaint as *Double Denied*) for $195,000 in 1989. According to Plaintiff, the painting is one of several created in August 1965 at Warhol's direction from an acetate personally created and chosen by Warhol. Plaintiff alleges that the painting had previously been authenticated by the Foundation and the Estate, including by [original executor] Hughes and [successor executor] Fremont, and had passed through several major dealers, each of whom had carefully vetted the painting's provenance.

Plaintiff offered to sell his painting in or about July 2001. Plaintiff alleges that, from July through December 2001, Fremont repeatedly urged Plaintiff, by telephone, email and in a face-to-face meeting in Los Angeles, to submit his painting to the Board. An interested buyer was also informed by the Board that it would not stand by the prior authentications; the painting would have to be submitted to the Board. Plaintiff submitted *Double Denied* for authentication on December 20, 2001, and signed a copy of the Submission Agreement dated December 21, 2001, in connection with the submission. The Board stamped the painting "Denied." After the Board's initial determination, Plaintiff was informed that he was welcome to resubmit the painting with additional documentation. Fremont urged him to resubmit the painting with additional documentation. Plaintiff spent more than a year documenting the painting's origin and history and resubmitted the painting with additional documentation in February 2003.

Plaintiff alleges that, on or about February 12, 2003, he was informed by Paul Morissey that Fremont had told Morissey that the painting had been denied again. By letter dated July 14, 2003, the Board notified plaintiff that it had rejected *Double Denied* a second time. The Board subsequently issued a letter, dated May 18, 2004, purporting to explain the basis of the Board's denial. Plaintiff alleges that the Board fraudulently denied the authenticity of *Double Denied* and that the denials were a foregone conclusion. Plaintiff alleges that, as a result of this second rejection, Plaintiff was unable to sell any of the Warhols that he owned without first submitting them to the Board and that he was ultimately forced to sell his Warhols through third-parties at a fraction of the price. Further, Plaintiff alleges that, by excluding *Double Denied* from the Catalogue, the Defendants have represented that the painting is a fake, thus depressing its market value.

Plaintiff brings this action requesting a declaratory judgment that the Submission Agreement is unenforceable, as well as injunctive, declaratory and monetary relief in respect of his claims under Section One and Two of the Sherman Act, the New York Donnelly Act, the Lanham Act, and for fraud and unjust enrichment. Defendants seek dismissal of Plaintiff's claims pursuant to Rule 12(b)(6) of the Federal Rules of Civil Procedure, arguing that the claims are barred by the release and covenant not to sue provisions of the Submission Agreements, that the allegations of the Complaint are insufficient to plead plausibly Plaintiff's antitrust claims because, *inter alia,* the claims are time barred and Plaintiff lacks standing to assert them, that the Complaint's Lanham Act and fraud allegations are likewise insufficient to meet the applicable pleading standards, and that the Complaint fails to state a claim for relief for unjust enrichment as against Fremont as "successor executor."

Discussion

* * *

Validity of the Submission Agreements

Defendants argue that Plaintiff has failed to state a claim for invalidation of the Submission Agreements he signed in connection with the Board's reviews of *Double Denied,* and that his entire Complaint should be dismissed, because the Submission Agreements include, *inter alia,* a provision in which Plaintiff "releases, waives and covenants not to sue any Indemnitee . . . based upon any claim or liability asserted (a) by [Plaintiff] or by any person or entity acquiring the Work, or any interest in the Work from [Plaintiff] . . . which is based directly or indirectly on the legend or endorsement, if any, affixed to the Work, or on any letter herein referred to, or any other action by the Authentication Board or any other Indemnitee in connection herewith, including without limitation any claim that the opinion is not correct."

The Complaint's allegations of fraud and wrongdoing in connection with the solicitation of the Submission Agreements are sufficient to state plausibly his claim for declaratory relief invalidating the exculpatory provisions of the agreements. A party may not invoke such an agreement to insulate itself from intentional wrongdoing, such as that alleged in this action. *See Kalisch-Jarcho, Inc. v. City of New York* 58 N.Y.2d 377, 384–85, 461 N.Y.S.2d 746, 448 N.E.2d 413 (N.Y.1983) ("[A]n exculpatory agreement, no matter how flat and unqualified its terms, will not exonerate a party from liability under all circumstances. Under announced public policy, it will not apply to exemption of willful or grossly negligent acts . . . [and] an exculpatory clause is unenforceable when, in contravention of acceptable notions of morality, the misconduct for which it would grant immunity smacks of intentional wrongdoing. This can be explicit, as when it is fraudulent, malicious or prompted by the sinister intention of one acting in bad faith." (internal citations omitted)). Plaintiff has sufficiently alleged that he was fraudulently induced into signing the submission agreements. The Complaint includes allegations that the Submission Agreements were utilized in an effort to conceal, and to protect Defendants from recriminations arising from, intentional, illegal action. Taking all inferences in Plaintiff's favor, he has sufficiently alleged facts in support of his claim for declaratory relief at this stage of the proceedings and Defendants' motion must be denied insofar as it seeks the dismissal of Plaintiff's declaratory judgment claim concerning the Submission Agreements.

Sherman Antitrust Act and New York Donnelly Act Claims

Plaintiff asserts claims under Section One of the Sherman Act, which prohibits combinations in restraint of trade, and under Section Two of that Act, which prohibits monopolization. Plaintiff also asserts a claim under New York State's antitrust statute-the Donnelly Act-which prohibits contracts or agreements in restraint of trade and monopolization. *See* N.Y. Gen. Bus. Law §§ 340 *et seq.* Defendants argue that Plaintiff has failed plausibly to plead a conspiracy and that the Complaint must therefore be dismissed under *Twombly* [*Bell Atlantic Corp. v. Twombly*, 550 U.S. 544 (2007)], and further argue that Plaintiff lacks standing, and that his antitrust claims are time-barred.

The New York Court of Appeals has held that the New York Donnelly Act should generally be construed in light of Sherman Act precedents. Accordingly, the Court analyzes Plaintiff's Sherman Act and New York Donnelly Act claims together.

Plausibility of Plaintiff's Antitrust Allegations

Defendants argue that Plaintiff has failed to plead plausibly his antitrust allegations. Having considered carefully all of Defendants' arguments, the Court disagrees. Plaintiff has alleged a conspiracy involving the only two entities authenticating Warhol works, the Foundation (through the Catalogue Raisonné) and the Board (through direct authentication), to restrict artificially competition in the market for authentic Warhols. This unreasonable restraint in violation of Section

One of the Sherman Act, it is alleged, raises the prices of the Foundation's Warhol works and ensures that galleries and museums choose Foundation works (so as to limit the risk that their authenticity will later be denied by the Board). Plaintiff has also alleged facts indicative of anticompetitive conduct with a specific intent to monopolize and a dangerous probability of achieving monopoly power in violation of Section Two of the Sherman Act.

Plaintiff asserts that the Board is completely dominated and controlled by the Foundation, and that the Foundation uses the Board to remove competing Warhols from the market in an attempt to monopolize the market. Plaintiff has alleged sufficient facts in support of the illegal restraint on trade and monopolization claims to satisfy the plausibility standard. For example, Plaintiff alleges that the Board has made unsolicited suggestions that owners of purported Warhol works submit their works for authentication; that the Board's authentication policies, to the extent that they exist, are applied inconsistently and allow the Board to reverse prior determinations when doing so would further the conspiracy; that the Board has refused to authenticate works that the Foundation previously attempted, unsuccessfully, to purchase; that the Board has denied the authenticity of works that others associated with the Estate and the Foundation have previously authenticated; and that, unlike other authentication boards, which are composed of well-qualified and well-known independent experts, the Board is populated by individuals who lack expertise in the authentication of Warhol works and who are not independent of the Foundation.

Plaintiff has also sufficiently identified a relevant geographic and product market in which trade was allegedly unreasonably restrained or monopolized, as required to state a claim under Sections One and Two of the Sherman Act. *See Kramer v. Pollock-Krasner Foundation,* 890 F.Supp. 250, 254 (S.D.N.Y.1995). "In determining the relevant market, the general rule is that commodities reasonably interchangeable by consumers for the same purposes make up that part of the trade or commerce monopolization of which may be illegal." *Vitale v. Marlborough Gallery,* No. 93 Civ. 6276, 1994 WL 654494, at *3 (S.D.N.Y. July 5, 1994) (internal quotations omitted). A narrowly defined submarket can be a relevant geographic product market. *Kramer,* 890 F.Supp. at 254. Plaintiff's allegations of a distinct submarket in the offering and sale, at auction or otherwise, of Andy Warhol works within the modern and contemporary art market are sufficient in this regard. *See Vitale,* 1994 WL 654494, at ("Examining plaintiff's assertion of a submarket in light of the above criteria, the Court finds, for the purposes of this motion to dismiss, that Jackson Pollock paintings may constitute a submarket, the monopolization of which may be unlawful under 15 U.S.C. § 1 or § 2.").

Plaintiff's Antitrust Injury

Defendants argue that Plaintiff does not have standing to assert his antitrust claims because he has not suffered an antitrust injury in connection with either his purchase of *Double Denied* or the Board's denial of the work. "An antitrust injury is an 'injury of the type the antitrust laws were intended to prevent and that flows from that which makes defendants' acts unlawful.'" *Paycom Billing Services, Inc. v. Mastercard Intern., Inc.*, 467 F.3d 283, 290 (2d Cir.2006), *quoting Brunswick Corp. v. Pueblo Bowl-O-Mat, Inc.*, 429 U.S. 477, 489, 97 S.Ct. 690, 50 L.Ed.2d 701 (1977).

Plaintiff's allegation that the double-stamping of "Denied" on his artwork in furtherance of the alleged antitrust conspiracy has prevented him from competing as a seller in the lucrative market for authentic Warhols is sufficient to frame an antitrust injury.

Plaintiff has not, however, alleged that he has suffered any injury arising from the alleged price-inflationary aspects of the conspiracy. Plaintiff did not purchase *Double Denied* from the Foundation, and nowhere in the Complaint does Plaintiff allege that *Double Denied* was ever sold by the Foundation or recognized by the Board as authentic. Plaintiff has thus failed to plead facts sufficient to demonstrate that he has standing to complain of any price-inflation aspect of the alleged antitrust conspiracy and the Complaint will be dismissed to the extent Plaintiff's claims are premised on allegations that Defendants' actions have artificially inflated prices for Warhol works. Those claims will be dismissed for the further reason that, as explained below, any claim that Plaintiff might possess for damages in connection with his purchase of *Double Denied* is time barred.

Statute of Limitations

The statute of limitations for federal antitrust claims is four years. *See* 15 U.S.C. § 15b. The statute of limitation for New York Donnelly Act claims is also four years. N.Y. Gen. Bus. Law §§ 340(5). Defendants argue that Plaintiff's antitrust claim must be dismissed in its entirety as time barred because, to the extent it is premised on his 1989 purchase of *Double Denied,* it was brought some 14 years too late and, to the extent it is premised on exclusion of *Double Denied* from the market for authentic Warhol works, it accrued in 2002 when the painting's authenticity was first denied.

As explained above, Plaintiff's allegations are insufficient to demonstrate that he has any claim against Defendants relating to the purchase price of his painting. Nor has he alleged facts that would warrant a finding of fraudulent concealment that would defeat the limitations bar even if he were able to articulate an antitrust claim premised on the price he paid for *Double Denied*. . . . Accordingly, this aspect of Plaintiff's antitrust claim will be dismissed.

However, the Court finds that Plaintiff's antitrust monopolization and market restraint allegations, insofar as they are based on the allegedly exclusionary impact of the Board's second denial of *Double Denied,* are not time-barred. Although the Board's original denial of Plaintiff's painting occurred more than five years before Plaintiff brought this action, Plaintiff has alleged facts sufficient, at this stage, to invoke the continuing conspiracy exception based on the Board's second denial. To come within the continuing conspiracy exception, "a plaintiff must allege that she has been injured by continued, separate antitrust violations within the limitations period." *Vitale v. Marlborough Gallery,* No. 93 Civ. 6276, 1994 WL 654494, at *5 (S.D.N.Y. July 5, 1994) (internal quotations omitted). The continuing conspiracy exception will start the statute of limitations anew if the plaintiff alleges "an overt act which (1) is a new and independent act that is not merely a reaffirmation of a previous act; and (2) inflicts new and accumulating injury on the plaintiff." (internal quotations omitted). Construing the allegations in the light most favorable to Plaintiff, the Court finds that Plaintiff has alleged sufficiently that the second denial was not a mere reaffirmation of the first. Plaintiff alleges that Defendants not only permitted, but encouraged, him to resubmit the painting with additional documentation and that he suffered additional, distinct injury as a result of the second denial.

Therefore, Plaintiff's individual Sherman Antitrust and New York Donnelly Act claims are dismissed with prejudice to the extent that they are based on his purchase of *Double Denied* because they are time barred, but Defendants' motion is denied to the extent that Plaintiff's federal and Donnelly Act monopolization and market restraint claims are based on the Board's rejection of *Double Denied* as an authentic Warhol.

Lanham Act Claim

Plaintiff asserts a violation of section 43(a) of the Lanham Act, which prohibits the use of false designation of origin, false or misleading description of fact or false or misleading representation of fact that is likely to cause confusion in commerce or in commercial advertising. In addition to arguing that Plaintiff is barred from bringing these claims insofar as they are based on Defendants' stamping of Plaintiff's painting "Denied" because the Submission Agreements included an acknowledgment that such a stamp could be affixed, Defendants argue that Plaintiff cannot assert a Lanham Act claim because the Act does not impose liability for statements of opinion, and that Plaintiff has not alleged a false statement in connection with commercial advertising as required by the "commercial advertising or promotion" prong of the Section 1125(a)(1).

As explained above, Plaintiff has alleged facts sufficient to state a claim for a declaration that the Submission Agreements are not enforceable. Thus, dismissal of Plaintiff's Lanham Act claims on the basis of the acknowledgment in those agreements is not appropriate at this stage.

Plaintiff has also alleged sufficient facts to state a claim under the Lanham Act in connection with Defendants' letters. Although it is well established that a "statement of opinion is not actionable under the Lanham Act if it could not reasonably be seen as stating or implying provable facts about a competitor's goods or services," *Boule v. Hutton,* 328 F.3d 84, 93 (2d Cir.2003), it is not clear, at this stage, that Defendants' letters were such mere statements of opinion. The Court cannot determine at this stage of the proceeding whether the Defendants' letters, although purporting to be opinions, could reasonably be seen as stating or implying provable facts about the authenticity of *Double Denied.* The Second Circuit's decision in

Boule, which involved the resolution of such issues based on factual findings after a bench trial, is not to the contrary.

* * *

Plaintiff has not, however, proffered allegations sufficient to frame a violation of the "commercial advertising or promotion" prong of the Lanham Act. "In this circuit, to constitute 'commercial advertising or promotion' under the Lanham Act, a statement must be: (1) commercial speech, (2) made for the purpose of influencing consumers to buy defendant's goods or services, and (3) although representations less formal than those made as part of a classic advertising campaign may suffice, they must be disseminated sufficiently to the relevant purchasing public." *Gmurzynska v. Hutton,* 355 F.3d 206, 210 (2d Cir.2004) (internal quotations omitted). Although Plaintiff alleges that the Catalogue, which is published by the Foundation, is the only recognized means of authentication other than direct authentication by the Board, the Complaint does not proffer allegations as to Defendants' use of the Catalogue in connection with the commercial offer of their goods and services.

Thus, the Court finds that Plaintiff has sufficiently alleged violations of Section 43(a) of the Lanham Act in connection with Defendants' letters, but has failed to allege sufficient facts to plead a Lanham Act claim in connection with the exclusion of *Double Denied* from the Catalogue.

* * *

Conclusion

For the foregoing reasons, Defendants' motion to dismiss the Complaint is granted in part and denied in part. Plaintiff's antitrust claims are dismissed for lack of standing to the extent that they are premised on inflation of the prices of Warhol artwork. Plaintiff's Lanham Act claim is dismissed insofar as it is premised on the exclusion of *Double Denied* from the Catalogue Raisonné. Defendant's motion is denied in all other respects....

SO ORDERED.

Notes and Questions

1. *Aftermath.* In October 2010, Joe Simon-Whelan announced that he would drop the lawsuit as he could no longer afford to proceed. The case was dismissed pursuant to a settlement agreement on November 15, 2010. The Warhol Foundation's press release called the dismissal a "complete vindication of both the Foundation and the Authentication Board." It also said its defense cost almost $7 million. Joe Simon-Whelan later issued a statement saying he ended the lawsuit with regret and he firmly stands by the facts of the red self-portraits.

On April 6, 2011, the Andy Warhol Foundation for the Visual Arts filed suit in New York state court against its insurance carrier seeking coverage for $6.6 million in legal expenses from the *Simon-Whelan* litigation. Six months later, the Board of Directors of the Andy Warhol Foundation announced the dissolution of the Andy Warhol Art Authentication Board, effective early 2012.

2. *Authentication Boards. Simon-Whelan* highlighted the role recognized authentication boards in the U.S. had in the art market. The case also played a pivotal role in artist-endowed foundations ultimately abandoning the authenticating role. Like *Duveen*, the case surprised the art world. Three issues deserve particular attention: the submission agreement, the antitrust claims, and the Lanham Act claims.

As a preliminary matter, to have a work authenticated by a board, the requesting party usually signs a submission agreement. That agreement generally contains an indemnification clause and perhaps a waiver of the right to sue. In Lariviere v. Thaw, 2000 WL 33965732 (N.Y. Sup. Ct. 2000), the court upheld the indemnification provision in a submission agreement, dismissed the lawsuit, and imposed monetary sanctions on the plaintiff's attorney. The difference between *Lariviere* and *Simon-Whelan* was not the words of the agreement but the actions of the parties. The *Lariviere* court noted that plaintiff's "childish plot" was "without any merit whatsoever, but constitutes a laughable and clumsy attempt at fraud." On the other hand, Simon-Whelan's allegation of fraud and wrongdoing against the defendants "in connection with the solicitation of the submission agreements" was sufficient to invalidate the exculpatory indemnity provisions. Basic public policy will not allow parties to claim the protection of an indemnity provision when there are allegations of intentional wrongdoing.

Note that the Submission Agreement allows the board to affix a legend or endorsement on the work. Unlike the scarlet letter, the denied stamp on the work is not easily removed and, some assert, can physically damage the work. Given that authenticity can be fluid, is stamping "denied" a wise policy? What is the alternative? There may be an issue under the Visual Artists Rights Act of 1990 (VARA) for the intentional mutilation or distortion of a work of visual art. See 17 U.S.C. § 106A(a)(3) and Chapter 7, *infra*.

Simon-Whelan asserted federal and state antitrust claims of conspiracy in restraint of trade and monopolization with sufficient particularity to survive the motion to dismiss. It was the first case to do so. Two previous cases making similar antitrust allegations against the Pollock-Krasner Foundation were dismissed. One (Vitale v. Marlborough Gallery, 1994 WL 654494 (S.D.N.Y. 1994)) was barred by the statute of limitations, the other (Kramer v. Pollock-Krasner Foundation, 890 F. Supp. 250 (S.D.N.Y. 1995)) failed to allege the relevant geographic and product market. In *Simon-Whelan*, some of the antitrust claims were allowed to proceed. The court drew a distinction between antitrust allegations that related to the purchase of the work and those that related to the denial. The court determined that the antitrust allegations arguably related to the purchase of the artwork in 1989 were time barred. With respect to the claims of monopolization and restraint of trade stemming from the double denial, the court found that the plaintiff plausibly pled the relevant market and antitrust injury. The dismissal of the case leaves the significant question of antitrust (monopolization and restraint of trade) for another day.

Notice how plaintiff's factual assertions (Board is not independent of the Foundation that owns many Warhol works and is populated by non-experts whose authentication policies are inconsistently applied) echo *Duveen*'s concerns of pecuniary conflict and total subjectivity.

The Lanham Act claim presents another setting for the authenticity as opinion-or-fact debate. As in *Duveen*, the defendant Board argued that its letters explaining the inauthentic determination were nonactionable opinion. The court however reserved judgment to determine if the letters, though couched as opinions, could "reasonably be seen as stating or implying provable facts." Is this the same issue presented in the *Jendwine* and *Power* cases?

Authentication cases are tough all around. It is not just the Andy Warhol Foundation that stopped authenticating. Many U.S. artist foundations have stopped authenticating works, including Pollack-Krasner, Roy Lichtenstein, Robert Rauschenberg, Keith Haring, Dedalus (Robert Motherwell), and Alexander Calder.

3. *Duty to Authenticate?* Simon-Whelan alleged the authenticating board acted improperly in denying authenticity to his painting. What if the board did nothing, taking a neither-confirm-nor-deny approach? Would that be actionable? Thome v. Alexander & Louisa Calder Foundation, 890 N.Y.S.2d 16 (N.Y. App. Div. 2009), posed that particular question. Thome sent the Foundation his submission seeking authentication for two theatrical stage sets as works of Alexander Calder. In the 1930s, Calder in fact created the stage sets for Erik Satie's musical composition, *Socrate*. Although that set was later destroyed, the original drawings were intact. In the 1970s, discussions about remounting the production began; Calder was contacted and responded favorably. The new plans were submitted to Calder in July 1976, and he verbally and in writing approved the plans. Calder died before being photographed with the set and before the production was performed in 1977.

In 1997, Thome decided to sell the stage sets and submitted his request to the Foundation for authentication and inclusion in the catalogue raisonné. The Foundation acknowledged receipt but has not otherwise confirmed or denied authenticity. A subsequent submission by a prospective buyer in 2005 also failed to elicit a formal response. In 2007, Thome filed the lawsuit seeking a judgment of authenticity, an injunction requiring inclusion in the catalogue raisonné, and damages for breach of contract, tortious interference with prospective business, and product disparagement.

The court dismissed the lawsuit, noting that the allegations "evoke our sympathy for plaintiff and some puzzlement at the lack of a response." *Id.* at 21. The court held that the Foundation owed no duty to the plaintiff and therefore plaintiff had no enforceable right to relief. With respect to a judicial determination of authenticity, the court noted its woeful lack of expertise in such a subjective matter, but most pointedly that a judicial determination is irrelevant in the marketplace:

> The point is that a declaration of authenticity would not resolve plaintiff's situation, because his inability to sell the sets is a function of the marketplace. If buyers will not buy works without the Foundation's listing them in its catalogue raisonné, then the problem lies in the art world's voluntary surrender of that ultimate authority to a single entity. If it is immaterial to the art world that plaintiff has proof that the sets were built to Calder's specifications, that Calder approved of their construction, then it will be immaterial to the art world that a court has pronounced the work "authentic." Plaintiff's problem can be solved only when buyers are willing to make their decisions based upon the Work and the unassailable facts about its creation, rather than allowing the Foundation's decisions as to what merits inclusion in its catalogue raisonné to dictate what is worthy of purchase.

The court drew a similar conclusion about injunctive relief compelling inclusion in the catalogue raisonné: "whether the art world accepts a catalogue raisonné as a definitive listing . . . is a function of the marketplace, rather than of any legal directive or requirements." *Id.* at 22. There is a noticeable link to Vasari's observations from 1568 about those who "concern themselves more with the name than the fact." See Part A, Note 3, following *Wright Hepburn, supra.*

With respect to the alleged contract claims, the court held that no contract existed—the Foundation's website inviting submissions was too vague to constitute a contractual undertaking. The product disparagement claim failed, because there was no affirmative assertion to a third party. Nevertheless, the court, in a nod to art exceptionalism, noted that in the art market, silence can be "indistinguishable from a direct assertion of inauthenticity." *Id.* at 28. It did not need to decide the particular point, however, because "the claim must in any event fail on statute of limitations grounds." *Id.* at 29.

The cultural questions raised by *Thome* can lead the would-be seller into a state of limbo. The art market demands proof of authenticity; there is a recognized authenticating body, but no requirement to respond.

4. *Irony in Authenticating Warhol. Simon-Whelan* revealed a particular fault line for the authentication of Warhol works. Warhol himself specifically challenged conventional ideas of originality and authorship. Warhol did not necessarily participate in the physical production of his works. Some works were made using industrial mass production techniques at his studio, the Factory. Warhol made a decision and left the execution of the silkscreen to his assistants. He did not directly participate in the physical creation of the artwork, and he used a rubber stamp signature. How does the traditional notion of the hand of the master embrace such a challenge? Authenticating Warhol is a particularly ironic inquiry when Warhol himself subverted conventional notions of authenticity. The typical authentication concerns for Old Masters reflect our distance of time from the creation of the art; today's authentication concerns for contemporary art may be based on the distance from production. How involved must the artist be in the conception, the execution, and

the production of an artwork for the work to be deemed authentic? Should it be artist specific? Artwork specific? Era specific? Where that line is drawn and by whom currently has significant economic consequences.

Malanga v. Chamberlain, 29 Misc. 3d 1235(A), 2010 WL 5105416 (N.Y. Sup. Ct. 2010), raises the authenticity claim from the other side. That decision, denying summary judgment and clearing the way for trial, begins:

> Is it, or it is not, a Warhol? The primary issue . . . is whether the artwork entitled the "315 Johns" was created in 1971 by the late Andy Warhol or by his studio assistant Gerard Malanga?

Gerard Malanga, widely acknowledged as one of Warhol's principal assistants at the Factory, claims the authorship and ownership of a work known as *315 Johns*. That work consists of 315 eight-by-eight inch square silkscreens depicting John Chamberlain's face. Chamberlain, a well-known artist, was a friend of Warhol's. The work was in Chamberlain's possession for a number of years. In 2000, at the request of Chamberlain, the Andy Warhol Authentication Board authenticated the work. Chamberlain allegedly sold it thereafter for $3.2 million. When Malanga met Chamberlain in 2004 and learned of the sale, Malanga demanded return of the work, claiming it as his own and asserting that Chamberlain knew it wasn't by Warhol. The case settled in 2011 on the eve of trial.

Chapter 5

Questions of Title: Stolen, Looted, and Encumbered Art

Good legal title for a newly acquired artwork is a basic requirement for the purchaser. Questions of title immediately suggest stolen property and the image of a thief in the night. Another image is that of art ambiguously transferred during times of war or conflict, most notably, art looted by the Nazis during World War II. These two set pieces create especially difficult legal and policy dilemmas for statute of limitations, conflict of laws, and sovereign immunity. If the item is deemed cultural property or national patrimony, an additional overlay of legal concerns arises, touched upon here and in the next chapter on Crossing Borders. The more mundane and vastly more commonplace topics of liens, encumbrances, and unauthorized transfers can also cloud title. Title disputes to artworks in a global marketplace have created a tangle of legal issues, with no promise of a universally satisfying solution.

A. Stolen and Looted Art

Three dominant factual contexts exist for stolen art in the U.S.—war-looted art, classic theft, and antiquities looting.

The central difficulty in all stolen art cases is the centuries-old impossible triangle: the innocent purchaser linked to the original owner by the thief. Virtually no legal system awards the thief good title; but between the original owner and the innocent purchaser, who should receive title to a unique indivisible artwork? The common law and civil law traditions have different initial responses based on different views of market integrity.

For the purchaser of an artwork, a moveable item of personal property whose possession is often private and not held open for public display, a challenge to title is like a bolt of lightning. For the original owner of art, the recovery is an answer to a prayer. As you read the cases, notice the varying importance given to the due diligence of owner and buyer. Is diligence a proxy for fairness? What does diligence do to certainty? Or stability of markets?

1. War-Looted Art

History is full of military victors carrying off the spoils of war. The Old Testament includes the siege of Jerusalem by the Babylonians under King Nebuchadnezzar in 586 B.C. and the plunder of Solomon's temple: "the sacrificial bowls which were of gold and silver these too the captain of the guard carried away. . . ." (Jeremiah 52:19). Those who have visited Rome may recall the Arch of Titus in the Roman Forum. It was erected in 81 A.D. to commemorate the victory of Titus in 70 A.D. in Jerusalem. One relief in particular shows rather vividly the victors displaying their plunder, including a menorah from Herod's Temple. From the Crusades comes another example of plunder: the exquisite four horses of the San Marco Basilica in Venice. These horses were taken from the Hippodrome during the sack of Constantinople in 1204. Six centuries later, Napoleon looted these same horses from San Marco and triumphantly paraded them in Paris in 1798. After Napoleon's military defeats in 1814 and 1815, the four horses were returned to San Marco through the Convention of Paris in 1815. During World War II, these horses were removed for safe keeping. Today, the original four horses are inside San Marco and copies stand in the façade.

There are many other examples but even from this brief sketch, the truth of the maxim, "To the victor go the spoils," is clear. "By the ancient law of nations, even what was *res sacrae* were not exempted from capture and confiscation." Henry Wheaton, Elements of International Law 395 (3d ed. 1845). And, yet, ancient norms and laws can be challenged. Against this background of military pillage and plunder, the discussion for an exception for certain property began to be heard. In 1758, Emheric de Vattel wrote in The Law of Nations 367 (Joseph Chitty ed., 1844):

> For whatever cause a country is ravaged, we ought to spare those edifices which do honor to human society, and do not contribute to increase the enemy's strength—such as temples, tombs, public buildings, and all works of remarkable beauty. It is declaring one's self an enemy to mankind, thus wantonly to deprive them of these monuments of art.

By the time of Napoleon's defeat and the Congress of Paris in 1815, this sentiment regarding cultural property began to take hold. The Duke of Wellington observed that Napoleon's well-organized looting of cultural property throughout Europe was "contrary to the principles of justice and the rules of modern war."

Almost 50 years later, Abraham Lincoln requested the promulgation of a military code for use during the Civil War. Professor Francis Lieber of Columbia College (now University) in New York drafted what is known as the Lieber Code (1863). It includes the following relevant sections:

Article XXXIV

> As a general rule, the property belonging to churches, to hospitals, or other establishments of an exclusively charitable character, to establishments of education, or foundations for the promotion of knowledge, whether public

> schools, universities, academies of learning or observatories, museums of the fine arts, or of a scientific character—such property is not to be considered public property in the sense of paragraph XXXI; but it may be taxed or used when the public service may require it.
>
> **Article XXXV**
>
> Classical works of art, libraries, scientific collections, or precious instruments, such as astronomical telescopes, as well as hospitals, must be secured against all avoidable injury, even when they are contained in fortified places whilst besieged or bombarded.
>
> **Article XXXVI**
>
> If such works of art, libraries, collections, or instruments belonging to a hostile nation or government can be removed without injury, the ruler of the conquering state or nation may order them to be seized and removed for the benefit of the said nation. The ultimate ownership is to be settled by the ensuing treaty of peace.
>
> In no case shall they be sold or given away, if captured by the armies of the United States, nor shall they ever be privately appropriated, or wantonly destroyed or injured.
>
> **Article XXXVII**
>
> The United States acknowledge and protect, in hostile countries occupied by them, religion and morality; strictly private property; the persons of the inhabitants, especially those of women; and the sacredness of domestic relations. Offenses to the contrary will be rigorously punished.
>
> This rule does not interfere with the right of the victorious invader to tax the people or their property, to levy forced loans, to billet soldiers, or to appropriate property, especially houses, lands, boats, or ships, and churches, for temporary and military uses.

The sentiments expressed in the Lieber Code were replicated in the Hague Convention Respecting the Laws and Customs of War on Land in 1907. It provided that "private property cannot be confiscated" (Art. 46) and that "pillage is formally forbidden" (Art. 47). Most pertinent is Article 56, which provides:

> The property of municipalities, that of institutions dedicated to religion, charity and education, the arts and sciences, even when State property, shall be treated as private property.
>
> All seizure of, destruction or wilful damage done to institutions of this character, historic monuments, works of art and science, is forbidden, and should be made the subject of legal proceedings.

These sentiments, however, did not stop the wanton destruction and looting of World War I or World War II. What was notable, however, was the enforcement of the Convention after World War I. The Treaty of Versailles of 1919 required the return of pillaged objects, compensation for destroyed works, and a "novel method of reparations—the replacement of lost objects with objects of a comparable nature and value." See Treaty of Versailles Arts. 245–247. More remarkable, however, may be the attempts to implement those policies during World War II.

In 1942, as plans for the Allied invasion of Europe developed, interested parties pressed for protective measures for cultural monuments and artworks. In 1943, President Roosevelt appointed the American Commission for the Protection and Salvage of Artistic and Historic Monuments in War Areas, chaired by Supreme Court Justice Owen Roberts (the "Roberts Commission"). See Report of the American Commission for the Protection and Salvage of Artistic and Historic Monuments, U.S. Gov't Printing Office, 1946. The goal of the Roberts Commission was two-fold: to provide the military with specialized people and strategic plans to protect cultural monuments during conflict, and to develop principles of restitution after the cessation of hostilities. For the first time in history, a small cadre of arts specialists (the Monuments, Fine Arts and Archives program) was assigned to military commanders in the field. After the armistice, the Monuments Men continued their work seeking, securing, and restituting looted works, consistent with the principles developed by the Roberts Commission and adopted by the Allies. The task was overwhelming and complex; three to five million objects were recovered and sent to official collecting points for sorting and cataloging. With respect to restitution, one operative principle was that restitution was made only to the country from which the property had been taken and not directly to the former owner. Each government, in turn, would develop its own protocol for returning the looted property.

Wartime restitution gradually ended by the 1970s as life moved on, but by the 1990s, a renewed interest in restitution for Holocaust victims and their families was evident. In 1998, the United States, in conjunction with the U.S. Holocaust Memorial Museum, hosted the Washington Conference on Holocaust-Era Assets, to which more than 40 governments and numerous international NGOs were invited. With respect to Nazi-confiscated art, the Washington Conference adopted eleven non-binding principles that emphasized researching provenance, publicizing the results of that research, and adopting standards to promote just and fair solutions for claims. Shortly thereafter, the American Association of Museums and the Association of Art Museum Directors adopted museum guidelines generally embracing the eleven principles. In 2009, at the Holocaust Era Assets Conference in Prague, the Terezin Declaration reaffirmed those principles, again in nonbinding fashion, for artworks "confiscated, sequestered and spoliated by the Nazis, the Fascists and their collaborators through various means including theft, coercion and confiscation, and on grounds of relinquishment as well as forced sales and sales under duress, during the Holocaust era between 1933–1945." The vague, nonbinding terms of the Washington Principles and Terezin Declaration, while morally appealing, created interpretative difficulties. See, e.g., *Reif v. Nagy* and *Orkin v. Taylor, infra*.

In 2016, Congress enacted the Holocaust Expropriated Art Recovery Act (HEAR), Pub. L. 114-308, 130 Stat. 1524 (2016), in an effort to promote the hearing of claims on the merits. HEAR's intent is to create a uniform federal statute of limitations for filing claims to recover artworks lost during the Nazi era (1933–1945). The Act sunsets on January 1, 2027.

The special case of World War II Nazi-looted art is an ongoing concern in the acquisition, ownership, and disposition of art that seems especially significant in the litigious, high stakes U.S. art market. *Menzel* is the beginning.

Menzel v. List

267 N.Y.S.2d 804 (N.Y. Sup. Ct. 1966)

KLEIN, J. This action in replevin was tried to the court and a jury. Plaintiff sought to recover a painting by Marc Chagall, which she and her husband had left in their apartment in Brussels when they fled in March, 1941, before the oncoming Nazis.

* * *

The Menzels . . . settled in the United States and lived here since 1941. Mr. Menzel died in 1960.

Search had been made by Mr. and Mrs. Menzel for the painting ever since the end of the war, but they were unable to locate it, until in 1962, it was discovered in the possession of defendant Albert A. List [who purchased it from Perls Galleries in 1955].

* * *

On or about March 31, 1941, the complaint alleges, the painting was "wrongfully and illegally looted and stolen from her former residence by the Nazi Goering-Rosenberg Group"; and "at no time has any compensation been paid for same by the German or Belgian governments or received by plaintiff from any other source".

* * *

. . . [T]he Menzels bought the painting in 1932 . . . in Brussels, and paid for it . . . the equivalent of $150. The painting remained in the Menzels' Brussels home until they fled in 1941.

The whereabouts of the painting between 1941 and 1955 are unknown.

Perls testified that he bought the painting in July 1955 . . . in Paris for $2800 in French francs.

He further stated that title was not warranted in writing or orally to third-party defendants; that . . . amongst such [reputable] galleries the offer of sale of any painting is in and of itself, in the custom of the trade as between galleries, warranty of title. Art galleries of such standing assume, without the necessity of inquiry, that an offer of sale constitutes a representation of authenticity and good title.

The defense also urged . . . that since the painting was described . . . as an oil, but in fact was a gouache, it was not the same painting. . . .

Likewise, the defendants maintained that the title of the painting having variously been referred to [by other names], it could not positively be identified as the same work....

The defendants also raised issues, as to Mrs. Menzel's right to bring this replevin action, in view of Mr. Menzel's death, since the original purchase was made by him.

The jury by its verdict for the plaintiff has established the identity of the painting, by whatever name, and whatever description; Mrs. Menzel's unqualified ownership of the painting; that the painting was looted and stolen from her apartment, as alleged in the complaint, and that the painting, or its value, which the jury fixed at $22,500, be awarded to Mrs. Menzel; and that List upon delivery of the painting to Mrs. Menzel recover the $22,500 from Perls Galleries.

The result reached is amply supported by the record, and the motion to set aside the verdict as contrary to the weight of the evidence is denied.

There remain for disposition ... numerous questions of law....

These include:

(I) the defense of the Statutes of Limitations of New York and Belgium;

(II) the plaintiff having fled Belgium, abandoned everything in her apartment;

(III) the painting was captured by occupying land forces on land and title accordingly passed to the nation prosecuting the war;

(IV) the painting was lawfully requisitioned by German authority, as an occupying power in the prosecution of the law and as confiscation of the property of its nationals;

(V) that the defendants are bona fide purchasers of the painting for value.

In their supplemental brief, the third-party defendants, planting themselves upon *Banco Nacional de Cuba v. Sabbatino*, 376 U.S. 398, 84 S.Ct. 923, 11 L.Ed.2d 804 (1964), urge with respect to IV, above, the applicability of the Act of State Doctrine; they assert that this Court should not 'assume jurisdiction to determine title as of 1941 to the property seized, requisitioned, confiscated or expropriated by duly authorized German officers from one of its own nationals, blacklisted as an enemy of the State' because of the "fortuitous" circumstance that the property was found here.

The court will treat these grounds *seriatim*. The resolution of these problems is made the more difficult in view of the fact that one of two innocent parties must bear the loss.

I

The defense of the Statute of Limitations appears to be based on the lapse of time since 1941 when the painting is asserted to have been stolen from the plaintiff, or since 1955 when List bought the painting from Perls.

This defense, however, has been held unavailable to the defendants in this action, by the decision of Streit, J., February 7, 1964, affd. 22 A.D.2d 647, 253 N.Y.S.2d 43 (October 6, 1964). In replevin, as well as in conversion, the cause of action against a person who lawfully comes by a chattel arises, not upon the stealing or the taking, but upon the defendant's refusal to convey the chattel upon demand.

II

Abandonment is defined as a voluntary relinquishment of a known right, . . . with no intent to reclaim.

* * *

The relinquishment here by the Menzels in order to flee for their lives was no more voluntary than the relinquishment of property during a holdup; and from the history of their search for the painting, there was obviously a continuing intent to reclaim.

The court finds, accordingly, as a matter of law, that there was here no abandonment.

III

Nor may this seizure be treated as lawful booty of war by conquering armies.

If the seizure is to be classified at all, it is to be classified as plunder and pillage, as those terms are understood in international and military law.

A.

Booty is defined as property necessary and indispensable for the conduct of war, such as food, means of transportation, and means of communication; and is lawfully taken.

Booty is described in the Annex to the Hague Convention of 1907 "between the United States and other Powers relative to the Opening of Hostilities", October 18, 1907, proclaimed February 28, 1910, 36 U.S. Stat. at L. 2259, Art. 53, at 2308:

> "An army of occupation can only take possession of cash, funds, and realizable securities which are strictly the property of the State, depots of arms, means of transport, stores and supplies, and, generally, all movable property belonging to the State which may be used for military operations."

The Hitler Government's definition was somewhat broader, but even that definition did not include works of art. . . .

B.

Pillage, or *plunder*, on the other hand, is the taking of private property not necessary for the immediate prosecution of war effort, and is unlawful.

Where pillage has taken place, the title of the original owner is not extinguished.

* * *

And in the first order issued by the 21st Army Group, July, 1944, upon the return of Allied Forces to the French beachhead, where the question arose what German property was booty ("butin de guerre"), under the general principles of the laws of war, it was provided:

> "The Germans have acquired no title to private movable property * * * which has been acquired by theft, looting, or pillage." . . .

IV.

We come now to the assertion that the Act of State Doctrine precludes any inquiry by this Court into the validity of the acts of the Nazis.

The Doctrine states, in terms of the most recent opinion on the subject by the Supreme Court of the United States, that "the Judicial Branch [of the government] will not examine the validity of a taking of property within its own territory by a foreign sovereign government, extant and recognized by this country at the time of suit, in the absence of a treaty or other unambiguous agreement regarding controlling legal principles, even if the complaint alleges that the taking violates customary international law". *Banco Nacional de Cuba v. Sabbatino*, supra, 376 U.S. 398 (1964), at 428, 84 S.Ct. 923, at 940.

In *Sabbatino*, the Supreme Court held that the United States District Court was without power to inquire into the validity of a decree of the Cuban [Castro] Government expropriating sugar which had belonged to a Cuban corporation whose stock was principally owned by United States residents, the effect being that the District Court was compelled to take the Cuban decree at face value.

Analysis of the Doctrine, as thus stated by the Supreme Court, indicates that invocation of the Doctrine rests upon the confluence of four factors:

> (A) the taking must be by a foreign sovereign government;
>
> (B) the taking must be within the territorial limitations of that government;
>
> (C) the foreign government must be extant and recognized by this country at the time of suit;
>
> (D) the taking must not be violative of a treaty obligation.

Analysis of the facts in the case at bar and the Court's own research into controlling principles lead inexorably to the conclusion that of these four factors, not one has been met.

A.

The taking was not by a foreign sovereign government.

The receipt in evidence, dated March 31, 1941, was given on the stationery of the "Militärbefehlshaber in Belgien und Nordfrankreich, Militärverwaltungschef, Einsatzstab der Dienststellen des Reichsleiters Rosenberg."

While the testimony and depositions before the Court are not clear as to the place of the Einsatzstab and the Reichsleiters Rosenberg as within or without the

German Government, the Court has, in the course of its own research, come upon the nub of the relationship.

In the opinion and judgment of the International Military Tribunal in *United States, French Republic, United Kingdom and U.S.S.R. v. Goering, Hess, Von Ribbentrop, Ley, Keitel, Kaltenbrunner, Rosenberg, et al.*, commonly called The Nurnberg Trial, International Military Trials, Nazi Conspiracy and Aggression, office of United States Chief Counsel for prosecution of Axis Criminality (United States Government Printing Office, 1947), likewise reported at 6 F.R.D. 69 (1946), the following lucid description of the activities of the "Einsatzstab * * * des Reichsleiters Rosenberg" is found (6 F.R.D. at 122–123):

> "The defendant Rosenberg was designated by Hitler on the 29th January 1940 Head of the Center for National Socialist Ideological and Educational Research, and thereafter the organization known as the 'Einsatzstab Rosenberg' conducted its operations on a very great scale. Originally designed for the establishment of a research library, it developed into a project for the seizure of cultural treasures. On the 1st March 1942, Hitler issued a further decree, authorizing Rosenberg to search libraries, lodges and cultural establishments, to seize material from these establishments, as well as cultural treasures owned by Jews. Similar directions were given where the ownership could not be clearly established. The decree directed the cooperation of the Wehrmacht High Command, and indicated that Rosenberg's activities in the West were to be conducted in his capacity as Reichsleiter, and in the East in his capacity as Reichsminister. Thereafter, Rosenberg's activities were extended to the occupied countries. The report of Robert Scholz, Chief of the special staff for Pictorial Art, stated:
>
> "During the period from March 1941 to July 1944 the special staff for Pictorial Art brought into the Reich 29 large shipments, including 137 freight cars with 4,174 cases of art works."
>
> "The report of Scholz refers to 25 portfolios of pictures of the most valuable works of the art collection seized in the West, which portfolios were presented to the Fuehrer. Thirty-nine volumes, prepared by the Einsatzstab, contained photographs of paintings, textiles, furniture, candelabra and numerous other objects of art, and illustrated the value and magnitude of the collection which had been made. In many of the occupied countries private collections were robbed, libraries were plundered, and private houses were pillaged.
>
> "Museums, palaces and libraries in the occupied territories of the USSR were systematically looted. Rosenberg's Einsatzstab, Ribbentrop's special 'Battalion,' the Reichscommissars and representatives of the Military Command seized objects of cultural and historical value belonging to the people of the Soviet Union, which were sent to Germany. Thus, the Reichscommissar of the Ukraine removed paintings and objects of art from Kiev and

> Kharkov and sent them to East Prussia. Rare volumes and objects of art from the palaces of Peterhof, Tsarskoye Selo, and Pavlovsk were shipped to Germany. In his letter to Rosenberg of the 3rd October 1941 Reichscommissar Kube stated that the value of the objects of art taken from Byelorussia ran into millions of rubles. The scale of this plundering can also be seen in the letter sent from Rosenberg's department to von Milde-Schreden in which it is stated that during the month of October 1943 alone, about 40 box-cars loaded with objects of cultural value were transported to the Reich."

* * *

In the circumstances, the Court finds that this painting was seized not by a foreign sovereign government but rather by "The Centre for National Socialist Ideological and Educational Research", an organ of the Nazi Party.

B.

The taking was not within the territory of the foreign government.

Since, as indicated, the taking was not by a foreign sovereign, the location of the property as within or without its jurisdiction is moot.

However, assuming, arguendo, that the taking had been by the German Government, it would nevertheless be invalid because not within its own territory.

Brussels, the site of the appropriation of the painting, was the territory of Belgium. The government of the Kingdom of Belgium in exile, in March 1941, was the recognized government of Belgium. The governments of Belgium and Holland "continue to exist as international entities".

"Military occupation, by itself, does not confer title, nor extinguish a nation."

* * *

C.

The Third Reich was neither extant nor recognized by the Government of the United States at the time of trial.

The Third Reich collapsed with the surrender in 1945.

D.

The seizure of this painting was in violation of specific treaty obligations to the United States.

The Constitution of the United States provides:

> "This Constitution, and the Laws of the United States which shall be made in Pursuance thereof; and all Treaties made, or which shall be made, under the Authority of the United States, shall be the supreme Law of the Land; and the Judges in every State shall be bound thereby, any Thing in the Constitution or Laws of any State to the Contrary notwithstanding."

Constitution of the United States, Art. VI.

* * *

[The court noted that the 1907 Hague Convention Relative to the Opening of Hostilities required previous and explicit warning before hostile actions commence and that the 1907 Hague Convention Respecting the Laws and Customs of War on Land specifically provided that private property was not to be confiscated and pillage was "formally forbidden." The U.S., Belgium, and Germany had signed both Hague Conventions.—Ed.]

1.

The very invasion of Belgium was a violation of these solemn treaty obligations. *United States v. Goering, supra*, 6 F.R.D. at 102, 108.

2.

The pillage so rampant during Nazi occupation was specifically held to be in violation of Article 56 of the Hague Convention of 1907. *United States v. Goering, supra*, 6 F.R.D. at 120–123.

Accordingly, in any view of the case, the Act of State Doctrine has no application.

* * *

V.

It is of no moment that Perls Galleries may have been a *bona fide* purchaser of the painting, in good faith and for value and without knowledge of the saga of the Menzels. No less is expected of an art gallery of distinction.

Throughout the course of human history, the perpetration of evil has inevitably resulted in the suffering of the innocent, and those who act in good faith. And the principle has been basic in the law that a thief conveys no title as against the true owner. *Silsbury v. McCoon*, 3 N.Y. 379, 383–384 (1850); II Kent Comm. 14th ed., per Holmes, 324–325.

"Provisions of law for the protection of purchasers in good faith which would defeat restitution [of Nazi confiscations] shall be disregarded." Law #59, U. S. Military Government for Germany, 10 Nov. 1947; Military Government Gazette, Amtsblatt der Militärregierung Deutschland, Amerikanisches Kontrollgebiet, Part I, Article 1, Para. 2. Cf. Re, Developments in Sovereign Immunity, 1 N.Y.L.F. 160, 201 (1955).

* * *

Conclusion

The jury has found plaintiff to be the sole and rightful owner of the painting. The court has found that she never abandoned it but that it was pillaged and plundered by the Nazis. No title could have been conveyed by them as against the rightful owners. The law stands as a bulwark against the handiwork of evil, to guard to rightful owners the fruits of their labors.

The motion to set aside the verdict is in all respects denied. Judgment may be entered accordingly.

Notes and Questions

1. *Menzel's Significance. Menzel* was the first Nazi-looted art restitution case in the U.S.; on that basis alone, it is a significant case. It is also a satisfying case in its return of the painting directly to Mrs. Menzel, the person from whom it was stolen and who searched for it. Legally, the case is a primer for subsequent art restitution cases, with *Menzel*'s holdings regarding statute of limitations and damages still influencing cases today.

The case is the recognized source for New York's demand-and-refusal rule as the governing statute of limitations for stolen art cases. See, e.g., Grosz v. Museum of Modern Art, 772 F. Supp. 2d 473, (S.D.N.Y. 2010), *aff'd*, 403 F. App'x 575 (2d Cir. 2010) (where the court dismissed the suit because it was not brought within three years of MoMA's refusal to return the artwork). *Menzel* was the first case to develop the Act of State doctrine in the context of the Nazi looting of art. In doing so, it provided the first domestic judicial glimpse into the systematic art plunder of the Third Reich. These two legal topics, statute of limitations and the Act of State doctrine, now joined by the issues of sovereign immunity and conflicts of law, are the primary issues in art title cases in the U.S. The following cases in this Part, in addition to cases in Chapters 6 and 8, are testaments to the ongoing importance of these two *Menzel* topics.

The question of damages sustained by the innocent buyer was also addressed in the *Menzel* litigation. Once defendant List returned the painting to Mrs. Menzel, the gallery from which List purchased the work was ordered to compensate List $22,500. List paid $4,000 for the painting in 1955. In a subsequent decision, New York's Court of Appeals determined that the painting's appreciation in value was properly an element of damages and was necessary to put List in the position he would have been in had the breach not occurred. Menzel v. List, 298 N.Y.S.2d 979 (N.Y. 1969). The gallery breached its implied warranty of good title under the UCC upon the sale to List. If List purchased the painting at auction instead of at a gallery, rescission and the return of his purchase price would have been his remedy. What justification is there for this difference in treatment?

Abandonment in *Menzel* has a very different factual appearance than the contract abandonment in *Brockhurst*, from Chapter One, but the underlying theory is the same. The defendant's allegation of abandonment in *Menzel* under the horrific circumstances of World War II seems a strategic blunder. In *Menzel*, the conflicts question (the defendant art gallery had purchased the Chagall from a reputable dealer in Paris in 1955 for $2,800) was not fully developed. Should French law have been consulted regarding the gallery's title? See discussion in A.4. Antiquities Looting, *infra*.

2. *Power of the Pen.* Nearly 30 years after *Menzel*, interest in the restitution of Nazi-looted art was reinvigorated. Three books may have played central roles. Lynn Nicholas's THE RAPE OF EUROPA (1994), a highly readable book, details the systematic looting of art carried out by the Nazi regime. The book became a documentary film, that was widely distributed, seen, and discussed. In 1997, Hector Feliciano published the equally riveting THE LOST MUSEUM (preceded by the original LE MUSÉE DISPARU in 1995), which revealed holdings of Nazi-looted art in French museums and elsewhere. In 1995, the Bard Graduate Center held an international academic symposium on the looting of art and cultural property during World War II. The symposium papers were published in 1997 as THE SPOILS OF WAR with Elizabeth Simpson as editor.

2. Classic Theft

Popular culture pictures an art thief as a high-tech, cosmopolitan, beautiful person, a nicely drawn parallel to the highly desirable artwork. The reality is far from the image. In the early hours of May 20, 2010, a lone, hooded, black-clad thief in the night cut away a padlock, broke a window, and stole five modern masterpieces (Picasso's *Dove with Green Peas*, Matisse's *Pastoral*, Georges Braque's *Olive Tree*, Amedeo Modigliani's *Woman with a Fan*, and Fernand Leger's *Still Life with Chandeliers*) from the Museum of Modern Art in Paris. The museum's security alarm system was broken for over a month, and the three night guards were apparently unaware of the theft, though a security camera recorded the thief's entrance. In 2017, Vjeran Tomic confessed to the theft and was sentenced to eight years in prison; two accomplices were also sentenced to prison. Benoit Morenne, *Paris's 'Spider-Man' Sentenced to 8 Years in Prison for Art Heist*, N.Y. TIMES, Feb. 21, 2017, at C2. The works remain missing.

Twenty years previously, in the early hours of March 18, 1990, two men wearing police uniforms entered the Isabella Stewart Gardner Museum in Boston, tied up the guards, turned off the functioning alarm system, and stole Vermeer's *The Concert*, Rembrandt's *Storm on the Sea of Galilee*, and other works. The FBI lists the Gardner theft as the biggest art theft in America (estimates range from $300–500 million). The works remain missing. Andrea Shea, *30 Years Later, the Gardner Heist's Emotional Toll Endures*, THE ARTERY (March 18, 2020), available at www.wbur.org/artery/2020/03/18/30-years-isabella-stewart-gardner-museum-heist-toll-endures.

Perhaps the most stunning art theft of all occurred over a century ago in August 1911: the theft of Leonardo da Vinci's *Mona Lisa* from the Louvre. It was such an unthinkable event that the initial report from a museum visitor noting its absence was dismissed by the guards, who assumed it had been removed for photographing. The police investigation was wide ranging, reportedly including questioning Picasso, but to no avail. Two years later in November 1913, Vincenzo Perugia, a former worker at the Louvre, tried to sell the *Mona Lisa* to the Uffizi Gallery (Florence's most famous museum) and was arrested.

Another brazen theft occurred on November 25, 2019, when thieves broke into the Green Vault at Dresden's Royal Palace. They stole 18th century jewelry valued by some at over $1 billion. Some experts fear that the collection may be destroyed. The "worst possible scenario would be professional robbers who just want the objects for their material value, the melted down gold or silver. . . . But as soon as the works are destroyed, they are of course lost forever." Kate Connolly, *Jewellery of 'immeasurable worth' stolen in dramatic Dresden museum heist*, The Guardian (Nov. 25, 2019), available at www.theguardian.com/world/2019/nov/25/thieves-steal-priceless-treasures-dresden-green-vault-museum, quoting Dutch art detective Arthur Brand. The jewelry remains missing.

Two questions emerge—who steals art and why steal high-profile, basically unsellable art? The first answer is relatively simple. According to Interpol, professional thieves steal art—sometimes on commission, but more often on their own initiative to fence the stolen property. Art is just a thing to steal. Nina Siegal, *What To Do with a Stolen van Gogh?*, N.Y. Times, May 28, 2020, at C1. Interpol also includes, to a much less degree, collectors as thieves for whom the art itself is the prize.

The answer to why depends on who is stealing. If it is a commissioned professional thief, many art theft experts today believe organized crime is behind the theft. The intent presumably is for the stolen art to be used as a type of currency or collateral in the underground economy. As greater international enforcement of anti-money laundering rules squeezes the illicit market, concern for art theft heightens. For thefts as collateral, the expectation is the artworks will be removed from viewers and the legitimate market for generations. An alternative theory is that an artwork stolen by a professional thief will be offered for ransom back to the owner or the insurer, "art-napping" as it were. A third theory—that a wealthy collector will commission a theft for a secret personal collection—is rejected by most art theft experts. For a person with the wealth to commission a theft, there is generally no reason to risk buying in the illicit market.

Artworks stolen by a professional thief for fencing may be the most vulnerable to loss or destruction as fencing a stolen high-profile artwork for anything approaching its true value is risky. It can also be risky for lawyers who come into possession of the artworks. See United States v. Mardirosian, 602 F.3d 1 (1st Cir. 2010), upholding the conviction of an experienced criminal defense attorney for possessing, concealing, and storing six paintings (including a $29 million Cezanne) stolen by a deceased client in 1978. Mardirosian secretly held the paintings for over two decades while concocting an elaborate plan involving a Swiss bank, a shell Panamanian corporation, and anonymous hiring of go-betweens to broker a deal for a finder's fee.

The French Museum of Modern Art, the Gardner and the Green Vault thefts seem to fit these two profiles for art theft by professional thieves. The *Mona Lisa* may be another story. Vicenzo Perugia reportedly stole the *Mona Lisa* to restore it to Italy and to avenge Napoleon's pillage of art. Never mind that the *Mona Lisa* was brought to France by da Vinci himself and purchased by Francois I after da Vinci's death. Others believe that Perugia was part of a bigger group hoping to sell multiple forgeries of the *Mona Lisa* to larcenous foreign collectors. Skeptics of that theory note that none of these forgeries was ever discovered. The Italian press embraced and seemingly celebrated Perugia's nationalistic motivation; nevertheless, he was convicted by an Italian jury. His sentence was reduced to time served. Recall the similar role nationalism played in Dutch art forger's van Meegeren's sentencing. See Chapter 4, *supra*.

The thefts in the next three cases seem to be crimes committed by thieves who had easy access to the artworks.

O'Keeffe v. Snyder

83 N.J. 478, 416 A.2d 862 (N.J. 1980)

POLLOCK, J.

* * *

I

The record . . . is fraught with factual conflict. Apart from the creation of the paintings by O'Keeffe and their discovery in Snyder's gallery in 1976, the parties agree on little else.

O'Keeffe contended the paintings were stolen in 1946 from a gallery, An American Place. The gallery was operated by her late husband, the famous photographer Alfred Stieglitz.

. . . In 1946, Stieglitz arranged an exhibit which included an O'Keeffe painting, identified as Cliffs. According to O'Keeffe, one day in March, 1946, she and Stieglitz discovered Cliffs was missing from the wall of the exhibit. O'Keeffe estimates the value of the painting at the time of the alleged theft to have been about $150.

About two weeks later, O'Keeffe noticed that two other paintings, Seaweed and Fragments, were missing from a storage room at An American Place. She did not tell anyone, even Stieglitz, about the missing paintings, since she did not want to upset him.

* * *

There was no evidence of a break and entry at An American Place. . . . Neither Stieglitz nor O'Keeffe reported them missing to the New York Police Department or any other law enforcement agency. Apparently the paintings were uninsured, and O'Keeffe did not seek reimbursement from an insurance company. Similarly, neither O'Keeffe nor Stieglitz advertised the loss of the paintings in Art News or any other publication. Nonetheless, they discussed it with associates in the art world and later O'Keeffe mentioned the loss to the director of the Art Institute of Chicago, but she did not ask him to do anything because "it wouldn't have been my way." O'Keeffe does not contend that Frank or Snyder had actual knowledge of the alleged theft.

Stieglitz died in the summer of 1946, and O'Keeffe explains she did not pursue her efforts to locate the paintings because she was settling his estate. In 1947, she retained the services of Doris Bry to help settle the estate. Bry urged O'Keeffe to report the loss of the paintings, but O'Keeffe declined because "they never got anything back by reporting it." Finally, in 1972, O'Keeffe authorized Bry to report the theft to the Art Dealers Association of America, Inc., which maintains for its members a registry of stolen paintings. The record does not indicate whether such a registry existed at the time the paintings disappeared.

... On February 11, 1976, O'Keeffe discovered that Ulrich A. Frank had sold the paintings to Barry Snyder, d/b/a Princeton Gallery of Fine Art. She demanded their return and, following Snyder's refusal, instituted this action for replevin.

Frank traces his possession of the paintings to his father, Dr. Frank, who died in 1968. ... Frank does not know how his father acquired the paintings, but he recalls seeing them in his father's apartment in New Hampshire as early as 1941–1943, a period that precedes the alleged theft. Consequently, Frank's factual contentions are inconsistent with O'Keeffe's allegation of theft. ... In 1965, Dr. and Mrs. Frank formally gave the paintings to Ulrich Frank, who kept them in his residences. ... In 1968, he exhibited anonymously Cliffs and Fragments in a one day art show in the Jewish Community Center in Trenton. All of these events precede O'Keeffe's listing of the paintings as stolen with the Art Dealers Association of America, Inc. in 1972.

Frank claims continuous possession of the paintings through his father for over thirty years and admits selling the paintings to Snyder. ...

As indicated, Snyder moved for summary judgment on the theory that O'Keeffe's action was barred by the statute of limitations and title had vested in Frank by adverse possession. ... On her cross motion, O'Keeffe urged that the paintings were stolen, the statute of limitations had not run, and title to the paintings remained in her.

* * *

III

* * *

... [T]he critical legal question is when O'Keeffe's cause of action accrued. The fulcrum on which the outcome turns is the statute of limitations in N.J.S.A. 2A:14-1, which provides that an action for replevin of goods or chattels must be commenced within six years after the accrual of the cause of action.

The trial court found that O'Keeffe's cause of action accrued on the date of the alleged theft, March, 1946, and concluded that her action was barred. The Appellate Division found that an action might have accrued more than six years before the date of suit if possession by the defendant or his predecessors satisfied the elements of adverse possession. ... [T]he Appellate Division concluded that Snyder had not established those elements and that the O'Keeffe action was not barred. ...

Since the alleged theft occurred in New York, a preliminary question is whether the statute of limitations of New York or New Jersey applies. The New York . . . statute of limitations on a cause of action for replevin does not begin to run until after refusal upon demand for the return of the goods. Menzel v. List (citation omitted). Here, O'Keeffe demanded return of the paintings in February, 1976. If the New York statute applied, her action would have been commenced within the period of limitations.

The traditional rule to determine which of two statutes of limitations is applicable is that the statute of the forum governs. . . . In the present case, none of the parties resides in New York and the paintings are located in New Jersey. On the facts before us, it would appear that the appropriate statute of limitations is the law of the forum. . . .

IV

On the assumption that New Jersey law will apply, we shall consider significant questions raised about the interpretation of N.J.S.A. 2A:14-1. The purpose of a statute of limitations is to "stimulate to activity and punish negligence" and "promote repose by giving security and stability to human affairs". Wood v. Carpenter, 101 U.S. 135, 139, 25 L.Ed. 807, 808 (1879). A statute of limitations achieves those purposes by barring a cause of action after the statutory period. In certain instances, this Court has ruled that the literal language of a statute of limitations should yield to other considerations.

To avoid harsh results from the mechanical application of the statute, the courts have developed a concept known as the discovery rule. The discovery rule provides that, in an appropriate case, a cause of action will not accrue until the injured party discovers, or by exercise of reasonable diligence and intelligence should have discovered, facts which form the basis of a cause of action. The rule is essentially a principle of equity, the purpose of which is to mitigate unjust results that otherwise might flow from strict adherence to a rule of law.

* * *

. . . [W]e conclude that the discovery rule applies to an action for replevin of a painting under N.J.S.A. 2A:14-1. O'Keeffe's cause of action accrued when she first knew, or reasonably should have known through the exercise of due diligence, of the cause of action, including the identity of the possessor of the paintings.

* * *

In determining whether O'Keeffe is entitled to the benefit of the discovery rule, the trial court should consider, among others, the following issues: (1) whether O'Keeffe used due diligence to recover the paintings at the time of the alleged theft and thereafter; (2) whether at the time of the alleged theft there was an effective method, other than talking to her colleagues, for O'Keeffe to alert the art world; and (3) whether registering paintings with the Art Dealers Association of America, Inc. or any other organization would put a reasonably prudent purchaser of art on constructive notice that someone other than the possessor was the true owner.

V

The acquisition of title to real and personal property by adverse possession is based on the expiration of a statute of limitations. Adverse possession does not create title by prescription apart from the statute of limitations.

To establish title by adverse possession to chattels, the rule of law has been that the possession must be hostile, actual, visible, exclusive, and continuous. Redmond v. New Jersey Historical Society, 132 N.J.Eq. 464, 474, 28A.2d 189 (E. & A. 1942). Redmond involved a portrait of Captain James Lawrence by Gilbert Stuart, which was bequeathed by its owner to her son with a provision that if he should die leaving no descendants, it should go to the New Jersey Historical Society. The owner died in 1887, when her son was 14, and her executors delivered the painting to the Historical Society. The painting remained in the possession of the Historical Society for over 50 years, until 1938, when the son died and his children, the legatees under his will, demanded its return. The Historical Society refused, and the legatees instituted a replevin action.

The Historical Society argued that the applicable statute of limitations, the predecessor of N.J.S.A. 2A:14-1, had run and that plaintiffs' action was barred. The Court of Errors and Appeals held that the doctrine of adverse possession applied to chattels as well as to real property, and that the statute of limitations would not begin to run against the true owner until possession became adverse. The Court found that the Historical Society had done nothing inconsistent with the theory that the painting was a "voluntary bailment or gratuitous loan" and had "utterly failed to prove that its possession of the portrait was 'adversary', 'hostile'." The Court found further that the Historical Society had not asserted ownership until 1938, when it refused to deliver the painting to plaintiff, and that the statute did not begin to run until that date. Consequently, the Court ordered the painting to be returned to plaintiffs.

* * *

Other problems with the requirement of visible, open, and notorious possession readily come to mind. . . .

The problem is even more acute with works of art. Like many kinds of personal property, works of art are readily moved and easily concealed. O'Keeffe argues that nothing short of public display should be sufficient to alert the true owner and start the statute running. Although there is merit in that contention from the perspective of the original owner, the effect is to impose a heavy burden on the purchasers of paintings who wish to enjoy the paintings in the privacy of their homes.

* * *

The limited record before us provides a brief glimpse into the arcane world of sales of art, where paintings worth vast sums of money sometimes are bought without inquiry about their provenance. There does not appear to be a reasonably available method for an owner of art to record the ownership or theft of paintings.

Similarly, there are no reasonable means readily available to a purchaser to ascertain the provenance of a painting. It may be time for the art world to establish a means by which a good faith purchaser may reasonably obtain the provenance of a painting. An efficient registry of original works of art might better serve the interests of artists, owners of art, and bona fide purchasers than the law of adverse possession with all of its uncertainties. Although we cannot mandate the initiation of a registration system, we can develop a rule for the commencement and running of the statute of limitations that is more responsive to the needs of the art world than the doctrine of adverse possession.

We are persuaded that the introduction of equitable considerations through the discovery rule provides a more satisfactory response than the doctrine of adverse possession. The discovery rule shifts the emphasis from the conduct of the possessor to the conduct of the owner. The focus of the inquiry will no longer be whether the possessor has met the tests of adverse possession, but whether the owner has acted with due diligence in pursuing his or her personal property.

* * *

Properly interpreted, the discovery rule becomes a vehicle for transporting equitable considerations into the statute of limitations for replevin. In determining whether the discovery rule should apply, a court should identify, evaluate, and weigh the equitable claims of all parties. If a chattel is concealed from the true owner, fairness compels tolling the statute during the period of concealment. . . .

* * *

The discovery rule will fulfill the purposes of a statute of limitations and accord greater protection to the innocent owner of personal property whose goods are lost or stolen. Accordingly, we overrule Redmond v. New Jersey Historical Society, . . . to the extent that [it holds] that the doctrine of adverse possession applies to chattels.

* * *

Our ruling not only changes the requirements for acquiring title to personal property after an alleged unlawful taking, but also shifts the burden of proof at trial. Under the doctrine of adverse possession, the burden is on the possessor to prove the elements of adverse possession. Under the discovery rule, the burden is on the owner as the one seeking the benefit of the rule to establish facts that would justify deferring the beginning of the period of limitations.

* * *

We reverse the judgment of the Appellate Division in favor of O'Keeffe and remand the matter for trial in accordance with this opinion.

Solomon R. Guggenheim Foundation v. Lubell

569 N.E.2d 426 (N.Y. 1991)

WACHTLER, J. The backdrop for this replevin action is the New York City art market, where masterpieces command extraordinary prices at auction and illicit dealing in stolen merchandise is an industry all its own. The Solomon R. Guggenheim Foundation, which operates the Guggenheim Museum in New York City, is seeking to recover a Chagall gouache worth an estimated $200,000. The Guggenheim believes that the gouache was stolen from its premises by a mailroom employee sometime in the late 1960s. The appellant Rachel Lubell and her husband, now deceased, bought the painting . . . in 1967 and have displayed it in their home for more than 20 years. Mrs. Lubell claims that before the Guggenheim's demand for its return in 1986, she had no reason to believe that the painting had been stolen.

On this appeal, we must decide if the museum's failure to take certain steps to locate the gouache is relevant to the appellant's Statute of Limitations defense. In effect, the appellant argues that the museum had a duty to use reasonable diligence to recover the gouache, that it did not do so, and that its cause of action in replevin is consequently barred by the Statute of Limitations. The Appellate Division rejected the appellant's argument. We agree with the Appellate Division that the timing of the museum's demand for the gouache and the appellant's refusal to return it are the only relevant factors in assessing the merits of the Statute of Limitations defense. We see no justification for undermining the clarity and predictability of this rule by carving out an exception where the chattel to be returned is a valuable piece of art. Appellant's affirmative defense of laches remains viable, however, and her claims that the museum did not undertake a reasonably diligent search for the missing painting will enter into the trial court's evaluation of the merits of that defense. . . .

* * *

The museum keeps track of its collection through the use of "accession cards," which indicate when individual pieces leave the museum on loan, when they are returned and when they are transferred between the museum and storage. The museum lent the painting to a number of other art museums over the years. The last such loan occurred in 1961–62. The accession card for the painting indicates that it was seen in the museum on April 2, 1965. The next notation on the accession card is undated and indicates that the painting could not be located.

Precisely when the museum first learned that the gouache had been stolen is a matter of some dispute. The museum acknowledges that it discovered that the painting was not where it should be sometime in the late 1960s, but claims that it did not know that the painting had in fact been stolen until it undertook a complete inventory of the museum collection beginning in 1969 and ending in 1970. According to the museum, such an inventory was typically taken about once every 10 years. The appellant, on the other hand, argues that the museum knew as early as 1965 that the painting had been stolen. It is undisputed, however, that the Guggenheim did not inform other museums, galleries or artistic organizations of the theft, and additionally, did not notify the New York City Police, the FBI, Interpol or any other law enforcement authorities. The museum asserts that this was a tactical decision based upon its belief that to publicize the theft would succeed only in driving the gouache further underground and greatly diminishing the possibility that it would ever be recovered. In 1974, having concluded that all efforts to recover the gouache had been exhausted, the museum's Board of Trustees voted to "deaccession" the gouache, thereby removing it from the museum's records.

Mr. and Mrs. Lubell had purchased the painting ... for $17,000 in May of 1967. The invoice and receipt indicated that the gouache had been in the collection of ... the museum mailroom employee suspected of the theft. They exhibited the painting twice, in 1967 and in 1981, both times at the Elkon Gallery. In 1985, a private art dealer brought a transparency of the painting to Sotheby's for an auction estimate. The person to whom the dealer showed the transparency had previously worked at the Guggenheim and recognized the gouache as a piece that was missing from the museum. She notified the museum, which traced the painting back to the defendant. On January 9, 1986, Thomas Messer, the museum's director, wrote a letter to the defendant demanding the return of the gouache. Mrs. Lubell refused ... and the instant action for recovery of the painting ... was commenced on September 28, 1987.

... In her summary judgment papers, the appellant argued that the replevin action to compel the return of the painting was barred by the three-year Statute of Limitations because the museum had done nothing to locate its property in the 20-year interval between the theft and the museum's fortuitous discovery that the painting was in Mrs. Lubell's possession. The trial court granted the appellant's cross motion for summary judgment, relying on *DeWeerth v. Baldinger,* 836 F.2d 103, an opinion from the United States Court of Appeals for the Second Circuit. ... The court reasoned ... that in order to avoid prejudice to a good-faith purchaser, demand cannot be unreasonably delayed and that a property owner has an obligation to use reasonable efforts to locate its missing property. ... Because the museum in this case had done nothing for 20 years but search its own premises, the court found that its conduct was unreasonable as a matter of law. Consequently, the court granted Mrs. Lubell's cross motion for summary judgment on the grounds that the museum's cause of action was time barred.

The Appellate Division ... held that the trial court had erred in concluding that "delay alone can make a replevin action untimely." The court stated that the appellant's lack of diligence argument was more in the nature of laches than the Statute of Limitations. ... The Appellate Division ... certif[ied] the following question: "Was the order of this Court, which modified the order of the Supreme Court, properly made?" We answer this certified question in the affirmative.

New York case law has long protected the right of the owner whose property has been stolen to recover that property, even if it is in the possession of a good-faith purchaser for value. ... The rule in this State is that a cause of action for replevin against the good-faith purchaser of a stolen chattel accrues when the true owner makes demand for return of the chattel and the person in possession of the chattel refuses to return it. Until demand is made and refused, possession of the stolen property by the good-faith purchaser for value is not considered wrongful....

In *DeWeerth v. Baldinger (supra)*..., the Second Circuit... impos[ed] a reasonable diligence requirement on the owners of stolen art. Although the court acknowledged that the question posed by the case was an open one, it declined to certify it to this Court.... We have reexamined the relevant New York case law and we conclude that the Second Circuit should not have imposed a duty of reasonable diligence on the owners of stolen art work for purposes of the Statute of Limitations.

While the demand and refusal rule is not the only possible method of measuring the accrual of replevin claims, it does appear to be the rule that affords the most protection to the true owners of stolen property. Less protective measures would include running the three-year statutory period from the time of the theft even where a good-faith purchaser is in possession of the stolen chattel, or, alternatively, calculating the statutory period from the time that the good-faith purchaser obtains possession of the chattel. Other States that have considered this issue have applied a discovery rule to these cases, with the Statute of Limitations running from the time that the owner discovered or reasonably should have discovered the whereabouts of the work of art that had been stolen (*see, e.g., O'Keeffe v. Snyder*).

New York has already considered—and rejected—adoption of a discovery rule. In 1986, both houses of the New York State Legislature passed [legislation that] would have modified the demand and refusal rule and instituted a discovery rule in actions for recovery of art objects brought against certain not-for-profit institutions.... Governor Cuomo vetoed the measure, however, on advice of the United States Department of State, the United States Department of Justice and the United States Information Agency....

The history of this bill..., together with the abundant case law spelling out the demand and refusal rule, convince us that that rule remains the law in New York and that there is no reason to obscure its straightforward protection of true owners by creating a duty of reasonable diligence. Our case law already recognizes that the true owner, having discovered the location of its lost property, cannot unreasonably delay making demand upon the person in possession of that property. Here, however, where the demand and refusal is a substantive and not a procedural element of the cause of action, it would not be prudent to extend that case law and impose the additional duty of diligence before the true owner has reason to know where its missing chattel is to be found.

Further, the facts of this case reveal how difficult it would be to specify the type of conduct that would be required for a showing of reasonable diligence. Here, the parties hotly contest whether publicizing the theft would have turned up the gouache.... In light of the fact that members of the art community have apparently not reached a consensus on the best way to retrieve stolen art, it would be particularly inappropriate for this Court to spell out arbitrary rules of conduct that all true owners of stolen art work would have to follow to the letter if they wanted to preserve their right to pursue a cause of action in replevin. All owners of stolen property should not be expected to behave in the same way and should not be held to a common standard. The value of the property stolen, the manner in which it was stolen, and the type of institution from which it was stolen will all necessarily affect the manner in which a true owner will search for missing property. We conclude that it would be difficult, if not impossible, to craft a reasonable diligence requirement that could take into account all of these variables and that would not unduly burden the true owner.

Further, our decision today is in part influenced by our recognition that New York enjoys a worldwide reputation as a preeminent cultural center. To place the burden of locating stolen artwork on the true owner and to foreclose the rights of that owner to recover its property if the burden is not met would, we believe, encourage illicit trafficking in stolen art. Three years after the theft, any purchaser, good faith or not, would be able to hold onto stolen art work unless the true owner was able to establish that it had undertaken a reasonable search for the missing art. This shifting of the burden onto the wronged owner is inappropriate. In our opinion, the better rule gives the owner relatively greater protection and places the burden of investigating the provenance of a work of art on the potential purchaser.

Despite our conclusion that the imposition of a reasonable diligence requirement on the museum would be inappropriate for purposes of the Statute of Limitations, our holding today should not be seen as either sanctioning the museum's conduct or suggesting that the museum's conduct is no longer an issue in this case. We agree ... that [appellant's] arguments ... are directed at the conscience of the court and its ability to bring equitable considerations to bear in the ultimate disposition of the painting.... [A]lthough appellant's Statute of Limitations argument fails, her contention that the museum did not exercise reasonable diligence in locating the painting will be considered by the Trial Judge in the context of her laches defense. The conduct of both the appellant and the museum will be relevant to any consideration of this defense at the trial level, and as the Appellate Division noted, prejudice will also need to be shown. On the limited record before us there is no indication that the equities favor either party. Mr. and Mrs. Lubell investigated the provenance of the gouache before the purchase by contacting the artist and his son-in-law directly. The Lubells displayed the painting in their home for more than 20 years with no reason to suspect that it was not legally theirs. These facts will doubtless have some impact on the final decision regarding appellant's laches defense. Because it is impossible to conclude from the facts of this case that the museum's conduct was unreasonable as a matter of law, however, Mrs. Lubell's cross motion for summary judgment was properly denied.

... [T]he order of the Appellate Division should be affirmed, with costs, and the certified question answered in the affirmative.

DeWeerth v. Baldinger

38 F. 3d 1266 (2d Cir. 1994)

WALKER, J. The appeal is the latest episode in a decade-long dispute over the ownership of an oil painting . . . by Claude Monet . . . previously owned by plaintiff Gerda Dorothea DeWeerth, a German citizen. It was discovered missing from DeWeerth's family castle after World War II, and was subsequently purchased by defendant, Edith Marks Baldinger, a New York resident, from third-party-defendant Wildenstein & Co., a New York art gallery. . . .

* * *

DeWeerth claims that her father purchased the Monet from a Berlin gallery in 1908 and that she inherited the painting after her father's death in 1922. She had the painting in her possession until 1943 when she transferred it to her sister's castle in southern Germany for safekeeping during World War II. DeWeerth's sister discovered that the painting was missing in 1945, after the departure of American soldiers who had been quartered in her home. The Monet resurfaced in 1956, at which time Wildenstein & Co. acquired it from a Swiss art dealer. Baldinger subsequently purchased the painting from Wildenstein in 1957 in undisputed good faith.

In 1982, DeWeerth discovered that Baldinger was in possession of the Monet and demanded its return. When Baldinger refused, DeWeerth promptly commenced a diversity action to recover it. . . . In April 1987, after a bench trial, Judge Broderick found that DeWeerth had established a superior right to possession of the Monet and issued a ruling in her favor. The district court specifically rejected Baldinger's two principal defenses of limitations and laches. . . .

In December 1987, another panel of this court reversed the district court's judgment on the ground that New York limitations law required a showing of reasonable diligence in locating stolen property and that DeWeerth had failed to make such a showing. . . . [O]n February 19, 1988, our mandate directing that the judgment in favor of DeWeerth be reversed was filed in the district court. . . .

On May 2, 1991, DeWeerth brought a motion before us to recall the prior mandate and vacate the judgment in light of *Solomon R. Guggenheim Foundation v. Lubell*, a decision by the New York Court of Appeals that held that the New York statute of limitations applicable to this action did not require a showing of reasonable diligence in locating stolen property. We denied the motion. . . .

On September 27, 1991, DeWeerth moved in the district court for relief pursuant to Fed.R.Civ.P. 60(b)(5) and (6) . . . . [On] October 16, 1992, Judge Broderick granted DeWeerth's motion . . . and this appeal followed.

* * *

II. Did the District Court Abuse its Discretion in Granting DeWeerth's Rule 60(b) Motion?

The district court granted DeWeerth's motion for relief from the final judgment under Rule 60(b)(6) and, alternatively, under Rule 60(b)(5). A "district court's grant or denial of relief under Rule 60(b), unless rooted in an error of law, may be reversed only for abuse of discretion." . . .

A. The Rule 60(b)(6) Determination

Rule 60(b) provides that the district court may relieve a party . . . from a final judgment . . . in five enumerated circumstances and, according to the sixth subpart, for "any other reason justifying relief from the operation of the judgment." Fed.R.Civ.P. 60(b)(6). We have held that subpart (6) is "properly invoked where there are extraordinary circumstances or where the judgment may work an extreme and undue hardship." . . .

Judge Broderick determined that the *Guggenheim* decision, and its import for this case, constituted an "extraordinary circumstance" justifying relief under Rule 60(b)(6). . . . In the first appeal in *DeWeerth,* we held that New York's applicable statute of limitations required the previous owner to demonstrate that she had acted with reasonable diligence in attempting to locate the stolen object, and that absent such a showing, the owner's otherwise timely suit would be barred. In *Guggenheim,* the New York Court of Appeals . . . expressly stated that the conception of New York law that we reached three years earlier in *DeWeerth* was wrong. In a unanimous decision, the Court of Appeals held that New York had a clearly established rule that the statute of limitations does not start to run until a *bona fide* purchaser refuses an owner's demand for return of a stolen art object, and that the Second Circuit should not have modified this rule by imposing a duty of reasonable diligence. . . .

Based on the New York Court of Appeals' opinion, the district court determined that DeWeerth would have prevailed . . . had she originally brought her suit in the New York state courts. It then held that *Erie Railroad Co. v. Tompkins,* 304 U.S. 64, 58 S.Ct. 817, 82 L.Ed. 1188 (1938), and its progeny entitled plaintiff to a modification of the final judgment. . . . It determined that the countervailing interest of both the parties and the courts in the finality of litigation was outweighed by the need "to prevent the working of an extreme and undue hardship upon plaintiff, to accomplish substantial justice and to act with appropriate regard for the principles of federalism which underlie our dual judicial system."

We have carefully considered the circumstances analyzed by the district court and conclude that they do not warrant relief under Rule 60(b)(6). . . . In our view, *Erie* simply does not stand for the proposition that a plaintiff is entitled to reopen a federal court case that has been closed for several years in order to gain the benefit of a newly-announced decision of a state court. The limited holding of *Erie* is that federal courts sitting in diversity are bound to follow state law on any matter of substantive law not "governed by the Federal Constitution or by Acts of Congress." 304 U.S. at 78, 58 S.Ct. at 822. However, the fact that federal courts must follow state law when deciding a diversity case does not mean that a subsequent change in the law of the state will provide grounds for relief under Rule 60(b)(6). . . .

DeWeerth argues that this case is distinguishable because the state court did not announce a "change in the law," but rather clarified that New York law is—and always was—contrary to what the federal court held it to be. While we agree that *Guggenheim* did not involve a "change in the law" . . . , we do not agree that *Guggenheim* stated that the question decided by the *DeWeerth* panel had long been settled in New York. The *Guggenheim* court stated only that New York's demand and refusal rule was well established; it did not state that the question of whether a due diligence requirement should be added to this rule was clearly settled. In fact, no earlier New York case had addressed this issue. . . .

When confronted with an unsettled issue of state law, a federal court sitting in diversity must make its best effort to predict how the state courts would decide the issue. The comprehensive opinion by now Chief Judge Jon O. Newman in *DeWeerth* accordingly surveyed New York caselaw and determined that a New York court called upon to decide the issue would be likely to impose a requirement of due diligence. . . .

It turned out that the *DeWeerth* panel's prediction was wrong.

* * *

We conclude that the prior *DeWeerth* panel conscientiously satisfied its duty to predict how New York courts would decide the due diligence question, and that *Erie* and its progeny require no more than this. The fact that the New York Court of Appeals subsequently reached a contrary conclusion in *Guggenheim* does not constitute an "extraordinary circumstance" that would justify reopening this case. . . . There is nothing in *Erie* that suggests that consistency must be achieved at the expense of finality. . . . Attempting to obtain such a result through Rule 60(b)(6) is simply an improvident course that would encourage countless attacks on federal judgments long since closed. . . .

* * *

We believe that the district court abused its discretion in ruling that the important interest in the finality of the judgment in this case, which was more than four years old at the time of that ruling, was outweighed by any injustice DeWeerth believes she has suffered by litigating her case in the federal as opposed to the state forum. Accordingly, we reverse the district court's decision granting her motion under Rule 60(b)(6).

* * *

Owen, District Judge. I respectfully dissent.

The majority recognizes that in dismissing Mrs. DeWeerth's action on New York statute of limitations grounds, the prior "*DeWeerth* panel's prediction was wrong." It was wrong in adding to New York's well-established demand and refusal rule a due diligence requirement, which the panel then found had not been met. Nevertheless, the majority leaves the dismissal standing, asserting first, that the prior panel was confronted with "an unsettled issue of state law," and second, that the doctrine of finality of judgments outweighs "any injustice DeWeerth believes she has suffered by litigating her case in the federal as opposed to the state forum."

I am unable to accept either of these conclusions. As to the majority's view that the pre-*DeWeerth* New York law was "unsettled", no prior New York statute of limitations ruling had any suggestion of a pre-demand due diligence requirement, or that the issue was ever raised, or even could have been considered. . . .

* * *

I am, of course, unhesitatingly one with the majority as to the "integrity of the [prior] *DeWeerth* decision [and] . . . the fairness of the process that was accorded DeWeerth." However, given the majority's acknowledgement "that the [prior] *DeWeerth* panel's prediction was wrong[,]" I cannot accept the result here that Mrs. DeWeerth, who sought our federal diversity jurisdiction, must now suffer the consequences not only of the said soon-corrected prediction, but also today's determination by the majority that for us to grant her Rule 60(b)(6) relief would have the Court embark on "simply an improvident course that would encourage countless attacks on federal judgments long since closed." Little more than two and one-half years elapsed from the denial of certiorari in the first *DeWeerth* appeal, and *Guggenheim's* authoritative pronouncement. Rule 60 exists as a remedy in an extraordinary case to accomplish justice. This I see as such a case. Should not the impact of *Guggenheim* rather be shouldered by us, notwithstanding the integrity of our error? While the doctrine of finality of judgments does address an important interest, it should not deter us from using Rule 60 today to do justice because we may have to deal hereafter with the Rule's invocation in unworthy cases.

Accordingly, contrary to the majority, I see no abuse of discretion by the District Court and would affirm on the scholarly and thorough opinion of Judge Broderick below.

Notes and Questions

1. *Statute of Limitations: Discovery or Demand-and-Refusal? O'Keeffe, Lubell,* and *DeWeerth* demonstrate the policy tension in applying statutes of limitations to stolen art in the possession of good faith buyers. All jurisdictions have statutes of limitations governing the owner's right to bring suit for recovery of stolen property or damages for its loss. The traditional reason for statutes of limitations is the uncertainty, and consequent systemic inefficiency, that would result in personal expectations, in the judicial system, and in markets, if stale assertions of a superior ownership right could be brought at any time. This seems especially applicable if the owner has slept on his rights while others innocently acquired stolen property. Statute of limitations are among the most basic of procedural rules governing the litigation of disputes. Inconvenient as a statute of limitations may be to one party or the other, the statute reflects important principles developed over centuries for the ordering of civil society. Wholesale rejection of statutes of limitations is a tactic, not a solution, for difficult cases. When faced with the concrete fact pattern of an

undisputed original owner seeking the recovery of long ago (21–37 years) stolen art, the two state court cases took very different approaches.

New Jersey's Supreme Court in *O'Keeffe* determined that the mechanical application of the six-year statute for replevin beginning on the date of the theft was not appropriate. The court also decided that the doctrine of adverse possession would not be available to the possessor of moveable chattels. Having rejected these two rules, the court held that the discovery rule (i.e., the statute of limitations would not begin to run until the owner discovers or should have discovered the facts giving rise to the cause of action) provided the appropriate balance for law and equity in stolen art cases. In remanding, the court specifically instructed the trial court to consider whether O'Keeffe was entitled to the discovery rule, by considering her due diligence over the 30-year period from the time of the theft.

A decade later, the New York Court of Appeals faced a similar scenario in *Lubell* where the museum admitted it took no steps to give notice of the theft over the 20-year period. Acknowledging the different approach taken by the New Jersey court, New York held firmly and unequivocally that the museum's lack of diligence did not change its long-standing demand-and-refusal rule. As previously held in *Menzel*, the three-year statute of limitations for replevin from a good faith purchaser began to run from the time of demand-and-refusal, and not from the time of the theft. In remanding, the court specifically noted, however that equitable concerns for due diligence would be appropriately considered in the context of the laches defense. On remand, the parties settled their case in 1993, with Mrs. Lubell keeping the painting following a payment to the museum.

Literally caught in between these two pivotal cases is *DeWeerth*, a most unfortunate resolution of a stolen art case. *DeWeerth* plainly exposed the policy divide in the two states' statute of limitations approaches. The reaction of many in the international art world to the whipsaw impact of the different statutes of limitations theories and the choice of forum was quite negative. How would you answer a European's charge of the U.S. court's pro-American litigant bias?

O'Keeffe and *Lubell* present two distinct procedural approaches, but it is important to note that both acknowledged a role for the owner's diligence. Under *O'Keeffe*, the owner's diligence will be a factor in determining if the discovery rule, instead of the mechanical rule, applies; whereas under *Lubell*, the owner's diligence can be an issue in the possessor's laches defense. While in quick readings, *O'Keeffe* can be seen as favoring the innocent possessor and *Lubell* the original owner, the acknowledgment in both cases of a role for equitable concerns creates a less sharp divide than first thought.

Note, however, a new federal statute of limitations (HEAR Act) enacted in 2016 adds another layer to the discussion. See A.3. Federal Statute of Limitations: HEAR Act, *infra*.

2. *Laches*. Laches is a doctrine in equity providing that an unreasonable delay will bar a claim if the delay prejudices the defendant. The doctrine developed

presumably because there was no statute of limitations for claims in equity. Equitable maxims, such as "equity aids the vigilant," suggest laches is equity's flexible statute of limitations. Dan B. Dobbs, 1 DOBBS LAW OF REMEDIES 104 (2d ed. 1993). As an affirmative equitable defense, laches applies to equitable actions, although a statute may extend the laches defense to other actions. Also, importantly, a judge in the exercise of her discretion, not a jury, decides whether laches is applicable. Laches is not a right; it rests within the judge's discretion, with the burden on the possessor to establish a basis for the laches defense. The possessor-proponent must establish three elements: a delay by the claimant in asserting the ownership claim, the unreasonableness of the delay, and prejudice to the possessor because of that delay.

Because facts and equitable discretion are critical to a claim of laches, any discussion, including the following, is presented merely as an overview.

a. Delay. Of the three elements, delay is the least independently developed. It often is folded into the unreasonableness or prejudice discussions. The central idea is notice and diligence. Why? Because equity, the source for laches, demands that parties not sleep on their rights. From the time of the theft until the assertion of the ownership claim, did the original owner act like an owner? Was the owner diligent in giving notice of the theft; did the owner seek the item out? See, e.g., Wertheimer v. Cirker's Hayes Storage Warehouse, 752 N.Y.S.2d 295 (2002) (plaintiffs failed to take any action for nearly a century); Sanchez v. Trustees of the University of Pennsylvania, 2005 WL 94847 (S.D.N.Y 2004) (70-year delay); Peters v. Sotheby's Inc., 821 N.Y.S.2d 61 (N.Y. Sup. Ct. 2006); In re Flamenbaum, 899 N.Y.S.2d 546 (N.Y. Sur. Ct. 2010) (51-year delay).

b. Unreasonable delay. Assuming there was a delay, was it unreasonable? This focuses on the reason for the delay, not its length. In Sotheby's Inc. v. Shene, 2009 WL 762697 (S.D.N.Y. 2009), the court held that a 60-year delay was not unreasonable, because the museum owner believed the 16th century book had been destroyed in a fire. Moreover, the museum had diligently pursued other objects it believed were stolen, and every page in the book was stamped with the museum's name. But in Greek Orthodox Patriarchate of Jerusalem v. Christie's, Inc., 1999 WL 673347 (S.D.N.Y 1999), a 70-year delay was not deemed reasonable where the order of monks was unaware that the book was even missing until it was offered for auction. Similarly, Stuart & Sons v. Curtis Publishing Co., 456 F. Supp. 2d 336 (D. Conn. 2006).

c. Prejudicial delay. If there was a delay and it was unreasonable, the possessor must show that she was prejudiced by that unreasonable delay. Proof of prejudice takes two primary forms, evidentiary and economic or expectations. Evidentiary prejudice usually involves the difficulty for the possessor in proving the bona fides of purchase transactions when witnesses or contracting parties are deceased or their memories have faded, and written records are no longer available. See Vineberg v. Bissonnette, 548 F.3d 50 (1st Cir. 2008) (defendant's laches defense failed because she did not show any evidence-based prejudice).

Economic or expectations prejudice arises when the possessor took actions or suffered consequences that she would otherwise not have taken or suffered if there had not been a delay. In non-art cases, a common example is the investment in a new business unknowingly based in part on another's patent. In art cases, economic prejudice might be found any time there is a division of property, such as during a divorce or upon death of a collector. If art was inherited by one child of the bona fide purchaser, would the child's receiving or choosing the art instead of another estate asset as the child's inheritance share suffice as economic prejudice? Would paying the estate tax on the full value of the property constitute economic prejudice?

3. *Transactional Takeaway.* The statute of limitations and laches defenses in disputed art ownership cases continue to evolve as litigants and courts become more familiar with stolen art cases, whether war-related or not. From a transactional perspective, one lesson is crystal clear: diligence on the part of the good faith purchaser requires more today than relying on the dealer or seller's assurances of good title. At a minimum for artworks of significance, the purchaser should have independent verification (preferably from multiple sources) that the work was not reported as stolen. Checking the various known databases, such as ALR, Artive, Interpol and the FBI, is an obvious step. See A.6. Law in Process, *infra*, for discussion on art registries.

3. Federal Statute of Limitations: HEAR Act

The policy tension between New York's demand-and-refusal rule and *O'Keeffe's* discovery rule may have hit a pause. In 2016, Congress enacted the Holocaust Expropriated Art Recovery Act, Pub. L. No. 114-308, 130 Stat. 1524 (2016) (HEAR Act). It applies a uniform 6-year statute of limitations for "a civil claim or cause of action . . . to recover any artwork or other property . . . lost " during the Nazi-era. HEAR sunsets on January 1, 2027. HEAR raises a number of questions. See Simon J. Frankel & Sari Sharoni, *Navigating the Ambiguities and Uncertainties of the Holocaust Expropriated Art Recovery Act*, 42 Colum. J. L. & Arts 157 (2019). One concern is the availability of the equitable defense of laches under HEAR. The next two cases, *Zuckerman* and *Nagy*, expose this new divide.

Zuckerman v. Metropolitan Museum of Art

928 F.3d 186 (2d Cir. 2019)

KATZMANN, Chief Judge:

* * *

Background

* * *

I. The Leffmanns

Paul Friedrich Leffmann, a German Jew from Cologne, purchased The Actor, a painting by Pablo Picasso, in 1912 (the "Painting") . . . .

* * *

By 1937, it became clear that life in Germany for Jews was . . . perilous. The Leffmanns decided to flee Germany for Italy. . . . Prior to fleeing Germany, the Leffmanns "arranged" for the Painting, one of their few remaining assets, "to be held in Switzerland by a non-Jewish German acquaintance."

But by early 1938, Italy was no longer a safe place for Jews. . . . The Leffmanns began to make plans to flee to Switzerland, which required money. On April 12, 1938, Paul Leffmann wrote to C.M. de Hauke, an art dealer whom the U.S. State Department later identified as dealing in Nazi-looted art, from whom Leffmann had previously rejected an offer to sell the Painting. Leffmann now sought to revive discussions about the possibility of a sale. As matters became more perilous for Jews in Italy, Leffmann "continued to try to sell the Painting through de Hauke." . . . Leffmann told de Hauke that he had rejected a $12,000 offer from another dealer.

Shortly after writing to de Hauke stating he had rejected an offer for $12,000 . . . , Leffmann sold the Painting in June 1938 for that very price to . . . Hugo Perls, and another art dealer, Paul Rosenberg.

Funded partially by their June 1938 sale of the Painting (the "Sale"), the Leffmanns fled to Switzerland in October 1938 [and then to Brazil].

* * *

. . . In 1947, after the war had ended, the Leffmanns returned to Europe . . . where they lived for the rest of their lives. Paul Leffmann died in 1956; Alice Leffmann died in 1966. While they were still alive, the Leffmanns brought a number of successful claims with the assistance of counsel for Nazi-era losses, but those claims were limited to property that was "taken in Germany" before the Leffmanns fled Germany. The Leffmanns made no demand to reclaim the Painting.

II. The Painting after the Leffmanns' Sale

In 1939, Paul Rosenberg loaned the Painting to the Museum of Modern Art ("MoMA") . . . ask[ing] MoMA to insure the Painting for $18,000. Sometime before October 28, 1940, Rosenberg consigned the Painting to the M. Knoedler & Co.

Gallery, [which] sold the painting to Thelma Chrysler Foy for $22,500. Thereafter, Foy . . . donated the Painting to the Met in 1952.

Since at least 1967, when the Painting appeared in the Met's published catalogue of French paintings, the Met's published provenance of the Painting listed Leffmann as a previous owner. Until recently, however, the provenance incorrectly suggested that Leffmann sold the Painting after 1912; it listed the provenance as "P. Leffmann, Cologne (in 1912); a German private collection (until 1938)."

III. Procedural History

On September 8, 2010, Plaintiff-Appellant, the Leffmanns' great-grandniece, demanded that the Met return the Painting. The museum refused. . . . On September 30, 2016, Zuckerman filed suit . . . asserting claims for conversion and replevin on the theory that the 1938 Sale was made under duress. On February 7, 2018, the district court dismissed Zuckerman's claims. . . . This appeal followed.

Discussion

On appeal, the Met argues, among other things, that Zuckerman's claims are barred by the doctrine of laches. We agree. Neither the Leffmanns nor their heirs made a demand for the Painting until 2010. This delay was unreasonable, and it prejudiced the Met. We further conclude that the HEAR Act, which creates a uniform, nationwide six-year statute of limitations for claims to recover art lost during the Holocaust era, does not preempt the Met's defense.

* * *

II. The Doctrine of Laches

. . . The doctrine of laches "protect[s] defendants against unreasonable, prejudicial delay in commencing suit." "A party asserting a laches defense must show that the plaintiff has inexcusably slept on its rights so as to make a decree against the defendant unfair." Laches . . . requires a showing by the defendant that it has been prejudiced by the plaintiff's unreasonable delay in bringing the action.

* * *

a. Unreasonable Delay

First, we conclude that the delay in this case was unreasonable. The Painting is an important and well-known work by an influential and celebrated artist. The Leffmanns sold it for a substantial sum to a French dealer. The Painting was then moved to the United States, where it was acquired by a major public institution. Meanwhile, the Leffmanns were in Brazil beginning in October 1938, and Switzerland from 1947 until Alice Leffmann died in 1966.

It is evident on the face of the complaint that the Leffmanns knew to whom they sold the Painting in 1938, and Zuckerman nowhere contends that the Leffmanns, despite making some post-war restitution claims, made any effort to recover the Painting. Indeed, over seventy years passed between the sale of the painting in 1938 and Zuckerman's demand that the Met return the Painting in 2010.

It is eminently understandable that the Leffmanns did not bring any claim for the Painting during the course of World War II and even, perhaps, for a few years thereafter.... However, it is simply not plausible that the Leffmanns and their heirs would not have been able to seek replevin of the Painting prior to 2010. As noted above, the Leffmanns, being a financially sophisticated couple, actively and successfully pursued other claims for Nazi-era losses. This is not a case where the identity of the buyer was unknown to the seller or the lost property was difficult to locate.... Nor is this a case where the plaintiff alleges that the buyers themselves exerted any undue or improper pressure on the sellers. The Leffmanns could have contacted ... MoMA, or the Met. Since at least 1967, "P. Leffmann" has been listed as a prior owner of the Painting. Although that—concededly incomplete—provenance was included in the Met's published catalogue, none of the Leffmanns' heirs demanded that the Painting be returned.

b. Prejudice

While the determination of prejudice is ordinarily fact-intensive ..., based on the unusual circumstances presented by the complaint, we conclude that the Met has been prejudiced by the more than six decades that have elapsed since the end of World War II. This time interval has resulted in "deceased witness[es], faded memories, ... and hearsay testimony of questionable value," as well as the likely disappearance of documentary evidence. Assuming *arguendo* that Plaintiff's central claim that the Sale is void because it was made under third-party duress is cognizable under New York law, resolution of that claim would be factually intensive and dependent on, among other things, the knowledge and intent of the relevant parties. No witnesses remain who could testify on behalf of the Met that the Sale was voluntary, or indeed on behalf of the Plaintiff that the Painting was sold "involuntar[ily]", because the Leffmanns "had absolutely no other alternative." Nor are there first-hand witnesses who could testify to facts relevant to the Met's possible affirmative defenses, including whether Foy purchased the Painting in good faith. On these facts, "the original owner[s'] lack of due diligence and prejudice to the party currently in possession are apparent," and the issue of laches can be decided as a matter of law.

c. The HEAR Act

Zuckerman argues in the alternative that, because her claims are timely pursuant to the applicable statute of limitations as codified by the HEAR Act, a laches defense is unavailable in this case.

The HEAR Act addresses the "unfair impediment" caused by "[s]tate statutes of limitations" that do not account for "the unique and horrific circumstances of World War II and the Holocaust" .... Specifically, the statute provides that "a civil claim or cause of action against a defendant to recover any artwork or other property that was lost during [the period between 1933 and 1945] because of Nazi persecution may be commenced not later than 6 years after the actual discovery by the claimant...." HEAR Act § 5(a).

Generally, "in [the] face of a statute of limitations enacted by Congress, laches cannot be invoked to bar legal relief."

This general rule does not apply to the HEAR Act. While the HEAR Act revives claims that would otherwise be untimely under state-based statutes of limitations, it allows defendants to assert equitable defenses like laches. The statute explicitly sets aside "defense[s] *at law* relating to the passage of time." HEAR Act § 5(a) (emphasis added). It makes no mention of defenses *at equity*. Moreover, a key Senate committee report accompanying the statute, discussed *infra*, unequivocally indicates that the Act does not preclude equitable defenses. S. Rep. No. 114-394, at 7.

Allowing defendants to assert a laches defense, despite the introduction of a nationwide statute of limitations . . . , comports with the overall legislative scheme advanced by the HEAR Act. One [purpose] of the HEAR Act is to ensure that claims to recover art lost in the Holocaust era are "resolved in a just and fair manner." HEAR Act § 3(2). But the HEAR Act does not allow potential claimants to wait indefinitely to bring a claim. To do so would be neither just nor fair. At the very core of a successful laches defense is prejudice to the defending party: even an unreasonable delay is not fatal to a claim if there has been no harm to the other party. Unlike a mechanical application of a statute of limitations, a laches defense requires a careful analysis of the respective positions of the parties in search of a just and fair solution.

Finally, the legislative history of the HEAR Act makes clear that Congress intended that laches remains a viable defense to otherwise covered claims. An early draft of the bill, introduced in the Senate Committee on the Judiciary on April 7, 2016, would have explicitly swept aside a laches defense. Holocaust Expropriated Art Recovery Act, S. 2763, 114th Cong. § 5(c)(2)(A) (as introduced in Senate, Apr. 7, 2016) (permitting recovery "[n]otwithstanding . . . any . . . defense at law *or equity* relating to the passage of time (*including the doctrine of laches*)" (emphasis added)). . . .

The final version of the bill, however, drops this language. . . . In addressing the amendment, which was in the nature of a substitute, the Senate Report explicitly noted that the new version "remove[d] the reference precluding the availability of equitable defenses and the doctrine of laches." *See* S. Rep. No. 114-394, at 7. Moreover, there is no mention of "other similar legal doctrines" in the purposes section of the final version of the statute. The final version notes that one of the purposes is to "ensure that claims to artwork and other property stolen or misappropriated by the Nazis are not unfairly barred by statutes of limitations but are resolved in a just and fair manner." HEAR Act § 3(2).; The HEAR act does not prevent defendants from asserting a laches defense. We emphasize that each case must be assessed on its own facts: while the laches defense succeeds here, in other cases it will fail and not impede recovery for claims brought pursuant to the HEAR Act.

Conclusion

For the reasons set forth above, we conclude that the HEAR Act does not preempt the Met's laches defense and that Zuckerman's claims are barred by laches. Accordingly, we AFFIRM the judgment of the district court.

Reif v. Nagy

80 N.Y.S.3d 629 (N.Y. Sup. Ct. 2018)

Charles E. Ramos, J.

* * *

Background

The plaintiffs are . . . heirs of Franz Friedrich ("Fritz") Grunbaum.

Mr. Grunbaum was a cabaret performer of Jewish Viennese descent living in Austria at the time of the *Anschluss*, and was a vocal critic of the Nazis. Mr. Grunbaum became a victim of Nazi persecution who was arrested in 1938 and murdered in the Dachau Concentration Camp in 1941. Prior to his arrest, Mr. Grunbaum was a prolific art collector who owned hundreds of works of art, including many by Schiele.

A series of Nazi-era documents reveal the gut-wrenching process by which Mr. Grunbaum's property was looted. . . . [T]he Nazis coerced Mr. Grunbaum to execute a Power of Attorney to his wife, enabling her to complete Jewish Property Declarations on his behalf while he was at the concentration camp.

. . . [A] Nazi official, appraised Mr. Grunbaum's property, revealing that it consisted of over four hundred works of art, eighty-one of which were Schiele works. . . . The authenticity of these documents is undisputed.

The defendants . . . are currently in possession of the Artworks [Egon Schiele's *Woman in a Black Pinafore* and *Woman Hiding Her Face*]. . . . Defendants assert that they have good title to the Artworks stemming from Mr. Grunbaum's sister-in-law, Mathilde Lukacs, who sold fifty-four works, including the Artworks, to a gallery in Switzerland. That gallery . . . subsequently advertised the works in a catalogue for sale in 1956. . . .

* * *

In an e-mail dated November 13, 2015, plaintiffs' attorney made a demand to defendants to return the Artworks to plaintiffs. The demand was refused, and this action followed. . . .

* * *

Discussion

This dispute is governed by New York law.

* * *

An action for replevin requires the plaintiff to show legal title or a superior right of possession. . . .

This case must be viewed in context. In 2016, Congress passed the Holocaust Expropriated Art Recovery Act of 2016 (HEAR Act). The two purposes of the HEAR Act are:

> (1) To ensure that laws governing claims to Nazi-confiscated art and other property further United States policy as set forth in the Washington Conference Principles on Nazi-Confiscated Art, the Holocaust Victims Redress Act, and the Terezin Declaration, and
>
> (2) To ensure that claims to artwork and other property stolen or misappropriated by the Nazis [during the Holocaust] are not unfairly barred by statutes of limitations but are resolved in a just and fair manner.

(HEAR Act, Pub L No 114-308, at § 3 [2016]). In pursuit of these aims, the HEAR Act extended the statute of limitations in which a claim may be brought to six years from the time that the artwork's identity and location, and the claimant's possessory interest, are discovered. Previously, CPLR 214 (3) limited the timeliness of actions for the return of Nazi-looted art to three years from the time that the true owner demanded the return of the chattel, and the good faith purchaser refused to return it. . . .

Before Congress adopted the Washington Conference Principles on Nazi-Confiscated Art (Principles) in the HEAR Act, the Principles, dated December 3, 1998, were endorsed by forty-four governments, including the United States, on December 3, 1998. Significantly, the Principles aim to assist in resolving issues surrounding Nazi-confiscated art:

> In establishing that a work of art had been confiscated by the Nazis and not subsequently restituted, consideration should be given to unavoidable gaps or ambiguities in the provenance in light of the passage of time and the circumstances of the Holocaust era (Washington Conference Principles on Nazi-Confiscated Art, at ¶ 4 [1998]).

The HEAR Act also adopts the Holocaust Victims Redress Act of 1997, which provides:

> [A]ll governments should undertake good faith efforts to facilitate the return of private and public property, such as works of art, to the rightful owners in cases where assets were confiscated from the claimant during the period of Nazi rule and there is reasonable proof that the claimant is the rightful owner (Holocaust Victims Redress Act, Pub L No 105-158, Title II, at § 202 [1997]).

The HEAR Act compels us to help return Nazi-looted art to its heirs. . . .

* * *

There is no triable issue of fact as to whether the Artworks belonged to Mr. Grunbaum before World War II. Although defendants attempt to dispute this, even the

Gallery on which defendants rely as the source of their provenance has confirmed that Mr. Grunbaum had owned the works. . . .

In the HEAR Act, the Principles, and the Holocaust Victims Redress Act, we are instructed to be mindful of the difficulty of tracing artwork provenance due to the atrocities of the Holocaust era, and to facilitate the return of property where there is reasonable proof that the rightful owner is before us. We accept that the Artworks were the property of Mr. Grunbaum, and that the entirety of Mr. Grunbaum's property was looted by the Nazis during World War II. As the heirs to Mr. Grunbaum, plaintiffs have made a threshold showing that they have an arguable claim of a superior right of possession to the Artworks, and that the Artworks are in the unauthorized possession of another who is acting to exclude plaintiffs' rights. Plaintiffs have therefore established to this Court's satisfaction that they have a *prima facie* case of both replevin and conversion.

Confronted with plaintiffs' *prima facie* case, the burden of proof shifts to defendants to establish they have a superior claim to the Artworks, or to at least raise a triable issue of fact. This they are unable to do.

Defendants have neither presented evidence nor raised a triable issue of fact to show that Mr. Grunbaum voluntarily transferred the subject artworks during his lifetime. Although the Nazis confiscated Mr. Grunbaum's artworks by forcing him to sign a power of attorney to his wife, who was herself later murdered by the Nazis, the act was involuntary (*Menzel v. List*, 49 Misc. 2d 300, at 305, 267 N.Y.S.2d 804) ("The relinquishment here by the Menzels in order to flee for their lives was no more voluntary than the relinquishment of property during a holdup . . . The court finds, accordingly, as a matter of law, that there was no abandonment."). A signature at gunpoint cannot lead to a valid conveyance.

. . . While defendants argue that they purchased the Artworks in good faith, title remains with the original owner or his heirs absent a valid conveyance of the works. As defendants have not shown that Mr. Grunbaum ever voluntarily transferred the Artworks to Ms. Lukacs, they cannot credibly allege that she owned them.

Moreover, any evidence to suggest that Ms. Lukacs possessed good title to the Artworks is absent from the record. . . .

* * *

Defendants' Answer presented eighteen defenses. . . .

The third [laches] and eighth [statute of limitations] defenses relate to the timeliness of plaintiffs' complaint. . . .

Moreover, the HEAR Act expanded the timeliness for actions to recover Nazi-looted artwork to six years from "the actual discovery by the claimant" of the "identity and location of the artwork" and of "a possessory interest of the claimant in the artwork" (HEAR Act, § 5[a]). Congress has also instructed that actions brought within six years will be timely, "[n]otwithstanding any defense at law relating to the passage of time" (*Id.*). Although defendants argue that the HEAR Act is inapplicable, this argument is absurd, as the act is intended to apply to cases precisely like this one, where Nazi-looted art is at issue. Since plaintiffs discovered the Artworks in November of 2015, their action is timely under the HEAR Act. The statute of limitations and laches defenses fail.

Defendants' laundry list of other defenses are also unsuccessful.

* * *

Accordingly, it is hereby

ORDERED that plaintiffs' motion for summary judgment on replevin and conversion claims is granted.

Notes and Questions

1. *Aftermath.* The Supreme Court denied the petition for a writ of certiorari in *Zuckerman.* 104 S. Ct. 1269 (Mar. 2, 2020). *Nagy* was affirmed on appeal. 106 N.Y.S.3d 5 (N.Y. App. Div. 2019). In affirming, the Appellate Division rejected Nagy's laches defense, noting "Nagy acquired both pieces in 2013. He suffered no change in position. Nor was any evidence lost between defendants' acquisition and plaintiffs' demand for the return of the Artworks." *Id.* at 22. In short, there was no prejudicial delay.

2. *HEAR and Laches. Zuckerman* and *Nagy* reveal a basic divide in the interpretation of the HEAR Act with respect to laches, with both cases exhibiting puzzling aspects.

The Second Circuit determined that HEAR does not bar a laches defense, because laches is a defense at equity, not a defense at law. For the Second Circuit, this was a straightforward decision based on the language of the statute and an examination of the legislative history.

Nagy reached the opposite result with the conclusory statement: "The statute of limitations and laches defenses fail." Judge Ramos used the purposes of the HEAR Act as determinative factors in interpreting the Act's scope. He fused the Washington Conference Principles on Nazi-Confiscated Art and the Holocaust Victims Redress into the operation of HEAR. "The HEAR Act compels us to help return Nazi-looted art to its heirs." A purposive interpretation is often used when there is statutory ambiguity and no pertinent legislative history. Yet HEAR is a statute of limitations; it does not address the merits of any recovery claim.

Procedurally, laches is "ordinarily fact-intensive" and rarely addressed at the pleadings level. Simon J. Frankel, *The HEAR Act and Laches After Three Years*, 45 N.C. J. Int'l L. 441, 447 (2020) (*HEAR Act and Laches*). Thus, ruling on a motion to dismiss is highly unusual. Was this an "active desire" by the Second Circuit to hold the laches defense compatible with the HEAR Act's purpose of resolving claims "in a just and fair manner"? Note, *Zuckerman v. the Metropolitan Museum of Art*, 133 Harv. L. Rev. 2196 (2020). Is it significant that *Zuckerman* was post-*Nagy*?

The conflicting determinations in *Zuckerman* and *Nagy* may presage uncertainty for the laches defense in HEAR cases in other circuits.

3. *Other HEAR Questions.* HEAR raises many other questions beyond laches. Some see constitutional issues, such as a possible violation of the Fifth Amendment's Takings Clause. See Herbert I. Lazerow, *Holocaust Art Disputes: The Holocaust Expropriated Art Recovery Act of 2016*, 51 Int'l Law. 195, 231 (2018).

Issues of scope abound. HEAR applies to claims "to recover any artwork or other property" but not to a damages claim. The term "artwork or other property" is defined expansively and includes, for example, applied art. That is a category that is expressly excluded from VARA's definition of a work of visual art and similarly excluded from Customs' categorization of art. The artwork must have been "lost ... because of Nazi persecution." One could argue that artworks stolen by American or Allied service personnel are not subject to HEAR, unless perhaps those works were previously looted by the Nazis. Can an argument be made that HEAR only covers artworks lost *to* the Nazis? As one commentator has said, HEAR is "not a model of clarity." See Frankel, *HEAR Act and Laches, supra*, at 442. Another concludes based on 25 years of experience in art restitution cases that "the outcome of future post-HEAR cases ... is surrounded by uncertainty." Donald S. Burris, *Restoration of Culture: A California Lawyer's Lengthy Quest to Restitute Nazi-Looted Art*, 45 N.C. J. Int'l L. 277, 330 (2020).

4. *Sunset and Finality.* HEAR will expire and no longer be available for claims filed after December 31, 2026. A sunset date recognizes that time is an important consideration in a legal system. Is December 31, 2026, a significant date? HEAR was enacted in December 2016, and ten years sounds straightforward enough. Is it also a signal from Congress that, as claimants become more attenuated in time from the Nazi era, the balance shifts to finality? Is this analogous to the *DeWerth* court refusing to allow Rule 60(b) relief because of the principle of finality of judgments?

4. Antiquities Looting

Qin Shi Huang (259–210 BC), the first Emperor of a unified China, is buried near Xian attended by thousands of terra cotta warriors. The site of his mausoleum was rediscovered accidentally in 1974 when farmers were digging for a well. The tomb remains unexcavated, but tantalizing insights as to its contents came from Shiji, or the Records of the Grand Historian, Sima Qian (145?–86 BC), a Han dynasty court historian. He writes of a vast underground mausoleum that is a replica of the above-ground imperial housing. It includes rivers made of mercury flowing through bronze mountains under a vault of a sky inlaid with pearls and gems. The Shiji tells of automatic shooting arrows strategically located in the tomb to deter tomb robbers. The terra cotta warriors and automatic shooting arrows have not deterred all thieves. In May 2010, four Chinese men were sentenced to death for robbing a tomb near Qin's; they used explosives and earth movers. See *Tomb Robbers Sentenced to Death in Central China*, China Daily, May 14, 2010, available at chinadaily.com.cn;

see also Amy Qin, *Tomb Robbing Makes a Comeback in China,* N.Y. Times, July 16, 2017, at A6.

Egyptian pyramids, the legendary tombs of the pharaohs, were similarly constructed in ways to deter looting of the royal treasures necessary for the pharaoh's use in the afterlife. Modern excavations revealed those measures were largely ineffective; tomb robbing occurred at the time of burial as well as thereafter, despite Old Kingdom inscriptions warning of severe punishment in the afterlife. Written records from the 20th Dynasty describe the trials of people accused of tomb robbing in the Valley of the Kings, including the mayor of western Thebes and other Theban officials.

A lesser known story of tomb robbing is that of Huaca de la Luna and Huaca del Sol, two flat-topped pyramids in Peru. The area was frequently looted over the centuries, including by Spanish conquistadores, but these two pyramids were relatively untouched. Built by the Moche people between the first and sixth centuries A.D., the pyramids were rediscovered in 1987 when police, on a tip, encountered a looter in possession of a gold death mask. The tip was furnished by a gang member upset by his share of the looted treasure. One gang member was killed when confronted by police. The site may be one of the most extraordinary finds in the Western Hemisphere. Bello, *Uncovering Peru's Neglected Splendors*, Economist, Feb. 28, 2019.

These three sketches present long-standing and seemingly universal concerns about antiquities looting and tomb robbing, with those concerns spanning centuries, civilizations, and socio-economic classes. The builders of these ancient tombs and pyramids incorporated some deterrent devices into the construction, yet officials involved in the ceremonial burials often took valuable artifacts, and pharaohs themselves used material from other tombs. Thieves therefore included not only the needy, but others if the opportunity arose.

Another type of antiquities taking involved a different opportunity, and it is the flashpoint for antiquities restitution today, the Elgin-Parthenon Marbles, located since 1816 in the British Museum in London. There is no escaping the dilemma posed by the demands for England to return the Marbles to Greece. It is one of today's most discussed and difficult example of cultural property restitution.

Scotsman Thomas Bruce, the 7th Earl of Elgin (1766–1841), was a member of the British House of Lords and a career diplomat. In 1800, Lord Elgin was the British ambassador to the Ottoman Empire, that then included most of Greece as it had for over three centuries. France and England were at war, and Napoleon's troops had invaded Egypt. Lord Elgin's task was to keep the Turks on good terms with the English as the English fought the French in Egypt. Lord Elgin also had a personal goal of advancing classical Greek art in England.

By 1800, the Parthenon on the Acropolis in Athens was largely in ruins. The interior had been stripped of treasure for centuries. In 1687, when the Parthenon functioned as a storage facility for Turkish gunpowder and the city was under siege, the roof and large parts of the long colonnades were destroyed by cannon shot from a

Venetian warship. The marble rubble was used as building material, as well as souvenirs for 18th century travelers. The ongoing degradation of the Parthenon was noted by many travelers to Athens.

With the French defeated, the Ottoman Empire again ruled Egypt, and the British ambassador was in a position of influence. In May 1801, Lord Elgin requested and received a firman issued by the Ottoman government. Its contents are unknown, but a second firman was issued in July 1801 granting Lord Elgin permission to freely enter the Parthenon, to draw and model the buildings, to erect scaffolding, to dig to discover the foundations, and to "take away any sculptures or inscriptions which do not interfere with the works or walls." Pursuant to this official firman, Lord Elgin did all of those things. He also removed some statues directly from the Parthenon itself. Before he left for England with the Marbles and drawings, he received letters from the Ottoman government confirming all that he had done.

Lord Elgin had funded this project on his own, and upon his return to England, he asked for compensation. In 1816, by a vote of 82 to 30, Parliament approved the purchase of the Marbles for the British Museum for £25,000. That sum was less than Elgin's expense, and went entirely to his creditors. Lord Elgin died penniless, a recluse in France in 1841. See William St. Clair, LORD ELGIN & THE MARBLES (3d ed. 1998), for a full account of the Marbles' removal by Lord Elgin, their impact on our understanding of Greek art and architecture, and the legal controversy that surrounds them.

In 1983, the Greek government formally requested the return of the Marbles. In 1984, the British government formally rejected the request. The calls for return of the Marbles continue today, with legal scholars and others actively debating the case. See, e.g., John Henry Merryman, *Thinking About the Elgin Marbles*, 83 MICH. L. REV. 1881 (1985); David Rudenstine, *Lord Elgin and the Ottomans; the Question of Permission*, 23 CARDOZO L. REV. 449 (2002); James Cuno, WHO OWNS ANTIQUITY? MUSEUMS AND THE BATTLE OVER OUR ANCIENT HERITAGE (2008).

Similar calls for repatriation come from other countries. For example, Egypt requested the return of the bust of Nefertiti from Germany, the Rosetta Stone from England, and the Zodiac Ceiling from France. None of these Egyptian requests has yet succeeded. On the other hand, after a plea made at the U.N. by the president of Zaire (now Democratic Republic of Congo) for restitution of African artworks, Belgium returned 144 pieces in 1973. Unfortunately, many of those pieces found their way back to markets in Europe, having been stolen. *Reflecting on past sins*, ECONOMIST, Mar. 30, 2019, at 61. More recently, in November 2018, France pledged to return 26 treasures taken from Benin during the colonial era by 2021. The decision to return the items stemmed from a report commissioned by French President Macron. That independent report authored by two academics recommends France permanently return objects removed during colonial times from African countries without their consent, if the country requests restitution. In November 2020, the necessary authorization from the French parliament was achieved, and 27 items are to be returned. While the French decision signals a shift in attitudes towards restitution, debate remains as to whether larger-scale restitution efforts will similarly succeed. Alternative options, such as long-term loans, remain possible. In November 2019, the Open Society Foundation announced a $15 million initiative to assist African nations seeking restitution of their cultural property. See Farah Nayeri, *France Lags on Return of Looted African Relics,* N.Y. Times, Nov. 26, 2019, at C2.

Autocephalous Greek-Orthodox Church of Cyprus v. Goldberg and Feldman Fine Arts, Inc.

917 F.2d 278 (7th Cir. 1990)

BAUER, C. J.

I. Background

In the early sixth century, A.D., a large mosaic was affixed to the apse of the ... Kanakaria Church in the village of Lythrankomi, Cyprus. The mosaic ... depicted Jesus Christ as a young boy in the lap of his mother, the Virgin Mary, who was seated on a throne [surrounded by] twelve apostles. The mosaic was displayed in the Kanakaria Church for centuries, where it became ... sanctified as a holy relic. ...

... [T]he Kanakaria mosaic was one of only a handful of such holy Byzantine relics to survive into the twentieth century. Sadly, however, war came to Cyprus in the 1970s, from which the mosaic could not be spared.

The Cypriot people have long been a divided people, approximately three-fourths being of Greek descent and Greek-Orthodox faith, the other quarter of Turkish descent and Muslem faith. No sooner had Cyprus gained independence from British rule in 1960 than ... [c]ivil disturbances erupted between Greek and Turkish Cypriots, necessitating the introduction of United Nations peacekeeping forces in 1964. (U.N. forces still remain in Cyprus). ...

The tensions erupted again in 1974, this time with more violent results. In July, 1974, the civil government of the Republic of Cyprus was replaced by a government controlled by the Greek Cypriot military. In apparent response, on July 20, 1974, Turkey invaded Cyprus from the north. ... The point at which the invading forces stopped is called the "Green Line." To this day, the heavily-guarded Green Line bisects Nicosia, the capital of the Republic, and splits the island from east to west.

* * *

Lythrankomi ... came under Turkish rule. Although the village and the Kanakaria Church were untouched by the invading forces in 1974, the villagers of Greek ancestry were soon thereafter "enclaved" by the Turkish military. Despite the hostile environment, the pastor and priests of the Kanakaria Church continued for two years [but] these clerics, and virtually all remaining Greek Cypriots, were forced to flee to southern Cyprus in the summer of 1976. ...

When the priests evacuated the Kanakaria Church in 1976, the mosaic was still intact. ... In November, 1979, a resident of northern Cyprus brought word ... [v]

andals had plundered the church, removing anything of value from its interior. The mosaic, or at least its most recognizable and valuable parts, had been forcibly ripped from the apse.... [T]he Kanakaria Church had been reduced to a stable for farm animals.

Upon learning of the looting ..., the Republic of Cyprus took immediate steps to recover them.... [T]hese efforts took the form of contacting and seeking assistance from many organizations and individuals, including the United Nations Educational, Scientific and Cultural Organization ("UNESCO"); the International Council of Museums; the International Council of Museums and Sites; Europa Nostra (an organization devoted to the conservation of the architectural heritage of Europe); the Council of Europe; international auction houses such as Christie's and Sotheby's; Harvard University's Dumbarton Oaks Institute for Byzantine Studies; and the foremost museums, curators and Byzantine scholars throughout the world. The Republic's United States Embassy also routinely disseminated information about lost cultural properties to journalists, U.S. officials and scores of scholars, architects and collectors in this country, asking for assistance in recovering the mosaics....

The Republic's efforts have paid off. In recent years, the Republic has recovered and returned to the Church of Cyprus several stolen relics and antiquities. The Republic has even located frescoes and other works taken from the Kanakaria Church, including the four mosaics at issue here....

To understand how these pieces of the Kanakaria mosaic resurfaced, we must trace the actions of appellant Peg Goldberg and the other principals through whose hands they passed in 1988.

Peg Goldberg is an art dealer and gallery operator ... in Carmel, Indiana. In the summer of 1988, Peg Goldberg went to Europe to shop for works for her gallery. Although her main interest is 20th century [works], Goldberg was enticed while in The Netherlands by Robert Fitzgerald, another Indiana art dealer and "casual friend" of hers, to consider the purchase of "four early Christian mosaics." In that connection, Fitzgerald arranged a meeting in Amsterdam for July 1st. At that meeting, Fitzgerald introduced Goldberg to Michel van Rijn, a Dutch art dealer, and Ronald Faulk, a California attorney. Van Rijn and Faulk were strangers to Goldberg. All she knew about them was what she learned in their few meetings, which included the fact that van Rijn, a published expert on Christian icons (she was given a copy of the book), had been convicted by a French court for art forgery; that he claimed to be a descendant of both Rembrandt and Rubens; and that Faulk was in Europe to represent Fitzgerald and van Rijn.

At that first meeting in Amsterdam on July 1, 1988, van Rijn showed Goldberg photographs of the four mosaics at issue in this case and told her that the seller wanted $3 million for them. Goldberg testified that she immediately "fell in love" with the mosaics. Van Rijn told her that the seller was a Turkish antiquities dealer who had "found" the mosaics in the rubble of an "extinct" church in northern Cyprus while working as an archaeologist "assigned (by Turkey) to northern Cyprus." (Goldberg knew of the Turkish invasion of Cyprus and of the subsequent division of the island.) As to the seller, Goldberg was also told that he had exported the mosaics to his home in Munich, Germany with the permission of the Turkish Cypriot government, and that he was now interested in selling the mosaics quickly because he had a "cash problem." Goldberg was not initially given the seller's identity. Goldberg also learned that Faulk, on behalf of Fitzgerald and van Rijn, had already met with this as-yet-unidentified seller to discuss the sale of these mosaics. Her interest quite piqued, Goldberg asked Faulk to return to Munich and tell the seller-whose identity, she would eventually learn, was Aydin Dikman-that she was interested.

Faulk dutifully took this message to Dikman in Munich, and returned to Amsterdam the following day. Faulk returned from that meeting with a contract he signed as agent for van Rijn to purchase the mosaics from Dikman for $350,000. When Goldberg met with Faulk on July 2, she was not told of this contract, however. Faulk merely informed her that Dikman still had the mosaics (though he was "actively negotiating with another buyer"), and that, in Faulk's opinion the export documents he had been shown by Dikman were in order. Faulk apparently showed Goldberg copies of a few of these documents, none of which, of course, were genuine. . . .

The next day (all of this happening rather fast), the principals gathered again in Amsterdam. Goldberg, van Rijn, Fitzgerald and Faulk agreed to "acquire the mosaics for their purchase price of $1,080,000 (U.S.)." The parties agreed to split the profits from any resale of the mosaics as follows: Goldberg 50%; Fitzgerald 22.5%; van Rijn 22.5%; and Faulk 5%. A document to this effect was executed on July 4, 1988, which document included a provision reading, "This agreement shall be governed by and any action commenced will be pursuant to the laws of the state of Indiana."

In those hectic early days of July, Goldberg contacted Otto N. Frenzel III, a friend and high-ranking officer at the Merchants National Bank of Indianapolis ("Merchants"), and requested a loan from Merchants of $1.2 million for the purchase of the mosaics. . . . Merchants assured her that financing could be arranged, if she could provide appraisals and other documents substantiating the transaction. With Fitzgerald's and van Rijn's help, Goldberg obtained the appraisals (all three of which valued the mosaics at between $3 and $6 million), and sent them to Merchants. That done, she and Fitzgerald hurried to Geneva, Switzerland, for the transfer of the mosaics, which was to take place on July 5. After arriving in Switzerland, Goldberg learned that her requested loan had been approved by Merchants and the money would be forthcoming, though a few days behind schedule. Her financing secured, Goldberg proceeded to the July 5 meeting as scheduled. She could not yet turn over the money, but she wanted to get a look at what she was buying.

The July 5 meeting was held in the "free port" area of the Geneva airport, an area reserved for items that have not passed through Swiss customs. Faulk and Dikman arrived from Munich with the mosaics, which were stored in crates. Dikman introduced himself to Goldberg and then left; this brief exchange was the only time the two would meet. Goldberg then inspected the four mosaics. She testified that she "was in awe," and that, despite some concern about the mosaics' deteriorating condition, she wanted them "more than ever."

During the few days that Goldberg waited in Switzerland for the money to arrive from Merchants, she placed several telephone calls concerning the mosaics. She testified that she wanted to make sure the mosaics had not been reported stolen, and that no treaties would prevent her from bringing the mosaics into the United States. She called UNESCO's office in Geneva and inquired as to whether any treaties prevented "the removal of items from northern Cyprus in the mid- to late-1970s to Germany," but did not mention the mosaics. She claims also to have called . . . the International Foundation for Art Research ("IFAR"), an organization that collects information concerning stolen art. She testified that she asked IFAR whether it had any record of a claim to the mosaics, and that, when she called back later as instructed, IFAR told her it did not. Judge Noland clearly doubted the credibility of this testimony, noting, among other things, that neither Goldberg nor IFAR have any record of any such search. (A formal IFAR search involves a fee and thus generates a bill that would serve as proof that a search was performed.) Judge Noland also questioned Goldberg's testimony that she telephoned customs officials in the United States, Switzerland, Germany and Turkey. The only things of which Judge Noland was sure was that Goldberg did *not* contact the Republic of Cyprus or the TRNC (from one of whose lands she knew the mosaics had come); the Church of Cyprus; "Interpol," a European information-sharing network for police forces; nor "a single disinterested expert on Byzantine art."

However Goldberg occupied her time from July 5 to July 7, on the latter date the money arrived. Goldberg took the $1.2 million reduced to $100 bills and stuffed into two satchels, and met with Faulk and Fitzgerald at the Geneva airport. As arranged, Goldberg kept $120,000 in cash and gave the remaining $1,080,000 to Faulk and Fitzgerald in return for the mosaics. . . . Along with the mosaics, Goldberg received a "General bill of sale" issued by Dikman to Goldberg and Feldman Fine Arts, Inc. The following day, July 8, 1988, Goldberg returned to the United States with her prize.

* * *

Peg Goldberg's efforts soon turned to . . . the resale of these valuable mosaics. She worked up sales brochures . . . and contacted several other dealers to help her find a buyer. Two of these dealers' searches led them both to Dr. Marion True of the Getty Museum in California. When told of these mosaics and their likely origin, the aptly-named Dr. True explained to the dealers that she had a working relationship with the Republic of Cyprus and that she was duty-bound to contact Cypriot officials about them. Dr. True called Dr. Vassos Karageorghis, the Director of the Republic's Department of Antiquities and one of the primary Cypriot officials involved in the worldwide search for the mosaics. Dr. Karageorghis verified that the Republic was in fact hunting for the mosaics that had been described to Dr. True, and he set in motion the investigative and legal machinery that ultimately resulted in the Republic learning that they were in Goldberg's possession in Indianapolis.

After their request for the return of the mosaics was refused by Goldberg, the Republic of Cyprus and the Church of Cyprus (collectively "Cyprus") brought this suit in the Southern District of Indiana for the recovery of the mosaics....

II. Analysis

* * *

B. Choice of Law

As a federal court sitting in diversity, the district court was obligated to (and did) apply the law of the state in which it sat—Indiana [including] Indiana's choice of law rules..... Judge Noland concluded that Indiana would choose to apply its own substantive law to this case. This ruling actually contained two parts. First, Judge Noland applied the two-step "most significant contacts" test used by Indiana courts for choice of law in Indiana tort cases. Second, ... Judge Noland looked to Swiss choice of law principles and determined that they, too, dictate that Indiana substantive law should control. On appeal, Goldberg claims ... these determinations were in error. Because we find Judge Noland's analysis under Indiana law to be free of error, we affirm his conclusion that Indiana law applies without reaching his discussion of Swiss law.

The district court properly considered Cyprus' suit ... a replevin action.... The district court could find no Indiana case dealing specifically with choice of law in replevin actions.... Thus, we will look (as did Judge Noland) to the choice of law principles Indiana generally applies in tort cases.

In *Hubbard* [*Mfg. Co. Inc. v. Greeson*], 515 N.E.2d 1071, the Indiana Supreme Court modified Indiana's traditional *lex loci delicti commissi* rule for choice of law in tort cases.... Citing the [rule's] often anomalous results ... as well as the recent trend away from it, the court in *Hubbard* ... established a two-step test, the first inquiry focusing on the contacts between the place of the wrong and the legal action. If these contacts are significant, the *lex loci* rule should be applied; if not, the court should move to the second inquiry, which focuses on which jurisdiction has the most significant contacts.

In this case, Judge Noland first determined that Switzerland—"the place of the wrong" because it was at the Geneva airport that Goldberg took possession and control of the mosaics—bears little connection to Cyprus' cause of action. He reached this conclusion based on ... the following facts: no Swiss citizen has or ever had an interest in this action, as none of the parties, actors in the transaction, or past or current interest-holders are Swiss citizens; and the temporal and geographical connection between the mosaics and Switzerland were "fortuitous and transitory," as the mosaics were on Swiss soil for only four days, never passed through Swiss customs (they remained in the "free port" area of the Geneva airport), and never otherwise entered the Swiss stream of commerce. Goldberg has failed to establish error in either these factual findings.... Thus, we agree that in this case an Indiana court would find Switzerland's contacts too attenuated to apply the *lex loci* rule, and thus would proceed to the second step of the analysis.

Moving to step two .., the contacts between the action and the two contending jurisdictions (Indiana and Switzerland) must be reviewed.... Judge Noland noted the following facts ... in favor of applying Indiana law: the defendants, those who financed and effected the transfer of the mosaics, and those who now hold the principal monetary interests in the mosaics are all Indiana citizens; the money used to purchase the mosaics came from an Indiana bank; the agreement among Goldberg, Fitzgerald, van Rijn and Faulk stipulates that Indiana law will apply, indicating Goldberg's reliance on the law of her home state; and the mosaics are presently being held in Indiana, where they have been stored since they entered the U.S. in July, 1988.... [W]e agree ... Indiana has the more significant contacts with and interest in this action. Thus, Indiana law and rules govern every aspect of this action, from the statute of limitations issues through the application of the substantive law of replevin.

C. Statute of Limitations

With great zeal, Goldberg has from the beginning of this action challenged the timeliness of Cyprus' complaint. Under Indiana's statute of limitations for replevin actions, Cyprus had six years from the time its cause of action accrued in which to sue for the recovery of the mosaics. Though the exact date of the looting of the Kanakaria Church is unknown, it is agreed that Cyprus first learned of the theft of their mosaics in November, 1979. It is also agreed that Cyprus first learned that the mosaics were in Goldberg's possession in late 1988. If Cyprus' cause of action accrued on the former date, their complaint, filed in March, 1989, was untimely. If, on the other hand, it accrued on the latter date (or at any other point after March, 1983), their complaint was timely. Thus, the dispositive determination is when did Cyprus' cause of action "accrue" within the meaning of Indiana's limitations statute.

* * *

... Indiana courts start with the following general rule: a cause of action accrues when the plaintiff ascertains, or by due diligence could ascertain, actionable damages....

* * *

Central to ... the discovery rule ... is the determination of the plaintiff's diligence in investigating the potential cause of action.

Applying these Indiana rules and principles ..., Judge Noland concluded that an Indiana court would find that Cyprus' action was timely filed. His primary ground for so concluding was his determination that, under a discovery rule, Cyprus' cause of action did not accrue until Cyprus learned from Dr. True that the mosaics were in Goldberg's possession in Indiana. In so holding, he looked not only to Indiana cases but also to general discovery rule principles, . . . and to *O'Keeffe v. Snyder*, a decision of the New Jersey Supreme Court addressing the accrual of a cause of action in the context of a replevin action involving a work of art. . . . Further, Judge Noland found, as a necessary precondition to the application of the discovery rule, that Cyprus exercised due diligence in searching for the mosaics. Thus, Judge Noland ruled that Cyprus was not, nor reasonably should have been, on notice as to the possessor or location of the mosaics until late 1988.

Goldberg attacks Judge Noland's discovery rule analysis on two grounds. First, she charges that . . . Judge Noland "announced a new rule of Indiana law in conflict with established Indiana limitations principles." Not so. Judge Noland applied legal principles set out in Indiana cases, and generally accepted elsewhere, to a new situation not yet addressed by the Indiana courts, exactly what a district court sitting in diversity is obligated to do when presented with a novel issue under state law. Further, his conclusion that in this case the operative "discovery" had to include the identity of the holder of the mosaics is eminently sound. In the context of a replevin action for particular, unique and concealed works of art, a plaintiff cannot be said to have "discovered" his cause of action until he learns enough facts to form its basis, which must include the fact that the works are being held by another and who, or at least where, that "other" is. Further, we note that any "laziness" this rule might at first blush invite on the part of plaintiffs is heavily tempered by the requirement that, all the while, the plaintiff must exercise due diligence to investigate the theft and recover the works.

Second, Goldberg attacks Judge Noland's due diligence finding. Specifically, she argues that Cyprus failed to contact several organizations it should have, particularly IFAR and Interpol. She also [argues] that events occurring before the end of 1983 should have started the clock ticking on Cyprus' cause of action, with particular emphasis on an article that appeared in a Turkish newspaper. We note first that the due diligence determination is . . . highly "fact-sensitive and must be decided on a case-by-case basis. . . . Further, in this case the assessment of Cyprus' diligence necessarily involves a contextual analysis of "a particular and nonrecurring set of historical events," as well as an assessment of the credibility of the various witnesses. . . . Thus, there is substantial support for a very deferential standard of review. Under any standard of review, however, Judge Noland's due diligence determination must be affirmed.

The record . . . makes it clear that . . . the Republic of Cyprus . . . took substantial and meaningful steps, from the time it first learned of the disappearance of the mosaics, to locate and recover them. The efforts by the Republic's officials, targeted at the likely points of sale of the mosaics, were sweeping and consistent with trade practices. . . . What's more, the record reveals that, upon learning of such Turkish press reports, Cyprus redoubled its efforts at notification and recovery. In sum, then, Judge Noland's conclusion that Cyprus was duly diligent and should not have discovered its cause of action before late 1988 stands on firm factual footing.

Goldberg's fervent attack on this conclusion at most establishes that an alternative view of the evidence was plausible, which is not enough to merit our disturbing it.

... [B]ecause we find no error in Judge Noland's determination that Cyprus was duly diligent and their action timely filed, we agree with his decision to reject without further discussion Goldberg's laches and estoppel arguments, and we follow the same prudent course.

D. The Merits of the Replevin Claim

Under Indiana law, replevin is an action at law "whereby the owner or person claiming the possession of personal goods may recover such personal goods where they have been wrongfully taken or unlawfully detained." ... To recover ... the plaintiff must establish three elements: "his title or right to possession, that the property is unlawfully detained, and that the defendant wrongfully holds possession." 25 I.L.E. *Replevin* § 42 (citations omitted).

Judge Noland applied these elements to the facts of this case and determined that Cyprus had met its burden as to each. Our review of this application of Indiana law to the facts convinces us that it is free of error: 1) the Kanakaria Church was and is owned by the Holy Archbishopric of the Church of Cyprus, a self-headed (hence "Autocephalous") church associated with the Greek-Orthodox faith; 2) the mosaics were removed from the Kanakaria Church without the authorization of the Church or the Republic (even the TRNC's [Turkish Republic of Northern Cyprus—a self-proclaimed government not recognized as legitimate by most nations—Ed.] unsuccessful motion to intervene claimed that the mosaics were improperly removed); and 3) Goldberg, as an ultimate purchaser from a thief, has no valid claim of title or right to possession of the mosaics.

We note that Judge Noland again backstopped his conclusion, this time conducting an alternative analysis under Swiss substantive law. Briefly, the court concluded that the Church had superior title under Swiss law as well, because Goldberg could not claim valid title under the Swiss "good faith purchasers" notion having only made a cursory inquiry into the suspicious circumstances surrounding the sale of the mosaics. As we state above, Indiana law controls every aspect of this action. Thus, Judge Noland's extensive (and quite interesting) discussion of Swiss law, as well as Goldberg's lengthy attack thereon, need not be reviewed. Cyprus adequately established the elements of replevin under Indiana law, on which ground alone we affirm the district court's decision to award the possession of the mosaics to the Church of Cyprus.

* * *

III. Conclusion

As [the poet Byron] laments, war can reduce our grandest and most sacred temples to mere "fragments of stone." Only the lowest of scoundrels attempt to reap personal gain from this collective loss. Those who plundered the churches and monuments of war-torn Cyprus, hoarded their relics away, and are now smuggling and selling them for large sums, are just such blackguards. The Republic of Cyprus, with diligent effort and the help of friends like Dr. True, has been able to locate several of these stolen antiquities; items of vast cultural, religious (and, as this case demonstrates, monetary) value. Among such finds are the pieces of the Kanakaria mosaic at issue in this case. Unfortunately, when these mosaics surfaced they were in the hands not of the most guilty parties, but of Peg Goldberg and her gallery. Correctly applying Indiana law, the district court determined that Goldberg must return the mosaics to their rightful owner: the Church of Cyprus. Goldberg's tireless attacks have not established reversible error in that determination, and thus, for the reasons discussed above, the district court's judgment is AFFIRMED.

Lest this result seem too harsh, we should note that those who wish to purchase art work on the international market, undoubtedly a ticklish business, are not without means by which to protect themselves. Especially when circumstances are as suspicious as those that faced Peg Goldberg, prospective purchasers would do best to do more than make a few last-minute phone calls. As testified to at trial, in a transaction like this, "All the red flags are up, all the red lights are on, all the sirens are blaring." In such cases, dealers can (and probably should) take steps such as a formal IFAR search; a documented authenticity check by disinterested experts; a full background search of the seller and his claim of title; insurance protection and a contingency sales contract; and the like. If Goldberg would have pursued such methods, perhaps she would have discovered in time what she has now discovered too late: the Church has a valid, superior and enforceable claim to these Byzantine treasures, which therefore must be returned to it.

[Judge Cudahy's concurring opinion is omitted.—Ed.]

Notes and Questions

1. *Aftermath.* The mosaics were returned to Cyprus in 1991, with nearly 50,000 people celebrating their return. Because of the damage to the mosaics during removal, shipment, and restoration, it is unlikely that the mosaics will ever be reinstalled in the church, regardless of the political situation. The Byzantine Museum of the Archbishop Makarios III Foundation houses the mosaics. Two of the four mosaics were determined to be fakes upon their return. See *A Lost Symbol of Cyprus is Found*, https://kanakariamosais.com.

Van Rijn cooperated with authorities in a sting operation against Dikman, who was convicted and sentenced to prison.

The Church of Cyprus continues recovery efforts. Singer Boy George returned an 18th century icon to the Church in January 2011, after a bishop spotted the icon in the singer's home during a television show. Boy George promptly returned it without payment, as he was unaware of its theft when he purchased it in 1985.

Most significantly, the Apostle Andrew mosaic, also looted from the Kanakaria Church, returned to Cyprus in 2018. The mosaic serves as the symbol of the Church's recovery efforts. It was returned "without a lengthy prosecution or a legal battle" but with private philanthropic assistance instead. *6th-Century Mosaic Depicting Apostle Andrew Repatriated to Cyprus*, THE NATIONAL HERALD, April 30, 2018, available at www.thenationalherald.com/199139/6th-century.

2. *Choice of Law: Lex Situs.* Goldberg argued strenuously for Swiss, and not Indiana, law to apply to the sales transaction. In general, Swiss law would use the principle of *lex situs*, meaning the applicable law is the law of the place where the tangible moveable property was located when the sale took place. If Swiss law did apply, the rule is the civil law norm that a purchaser of stolen property acquires title superior to the original owner *if* he purchases in good faith. This stands in direct contrast to the common law rule that a thief cannot convey good title. See Autocephalous Greek-Orthodox Church of Cyprus v. Goldberg, 717 F. Supp. 1374, 1400 (S.D. Ind. 1989). Under Swiss Law, a purchaser would need to prove good faith, and willful ignorance of red flags does not demonstrate good faith. As the court implied, Peg Goldberg's good faith was not a given.

More than two decades later, the Second Circuit resolved a similar conflicts question regarding the application of Swiss law or New York law. Bakalar v. Vavra, 619 F.3d 136 (2d Cir. 2010). In deciding that New York law was the appropriate choice of law, the Second Circuit observed that New York now resolves conflicts questions regarding personal property by using an interest analysis. The law of the jurisdiction that has the greatest interest in the litigation is to be applied, and the facts and contacts that have significance in making this determination are those that relate to the purpose of the law. One such purpose is the integrity of the New York art market, and not allowing it to become a center for stolen art, as had previously been observed in *Lubell.* In remanding the case, the Second Circuit specifically noted that New York law makes available the defense of laches.

The application of any jurisdiction's law can produce seemingly harsh results, and *lex situs* is no exception. Consider the case of Winkworth v. Christie Manson and Woods Ltd. [1980] Ch. 496, [1980] 1 All E.R. 1121, 1979 WL 68486. Winkworth was the owner of a collection of Japanese netsuke that were stolen from his home in England. The objects made their way to Italy, where they were sold to Marchese Paolo Da Pozzo, a good faith purchaser for value. Later Da Pozzo sent the collection to London for auction at Christie's. Winkworth learned of the auction and brought a lawsuit seeking return of his collection and an injunction prohibiting the sale.

The domestic law of each country was clear. If all events took place in England, Winkworth would prevail. Conversely, if all events took place in Italy, Da Pozzo would prevail. Which law should the English judge apply?

The judge adopted *lex situs*, acknowledging it as the pertinent conflicts rule of private international law, i.e., the validity of a transfer of movable property and its effect on the proprietary rights of anyone claiming thereunder are to be governed by the law of the country where the property is situated at the time of transfer.

Plaintiff conceded the general *lex situs* rule but argued that the exceptional facts of the case, "these English connecting factors," required a different rule. The court declined to alter firm precedent. "Intolerable uncertainty in the law would result if the court were to permit the introduction of a wholly fictional English situs when applying the principle . . . merely because the case happened to have a number of other English connecting factors." *Id.* at 509. In reaching this holding, the judge analogized to the traditional English rule of market overt.

3. *Market Overt.* That a thief cannot convey good title (*nemo dat quod non habet*) is a basic rule in U.S. jurisprudence, but not necessarily in common law jurisprudence. Until the enactment of the Sale of Goods (Amendment) Act of 1994, English common law recognized a 500-year exception for market overt. The special rule of market overt was that a bona fide purchaser of goods at a legally chartered market during daylight hours received good title, even if the seller did not have title to the goods. Like the UCC entrustment exception at the heart of the *Lindholm* case (Chapter 2, *supra*), the needs of a market economy prevailed over *nemo dat* and a strict *caveat emptor*:

> No doubt due to the degree of internationality inherent in their activities, merchants, it seems had from very early times known a special market law which attempted to protect those who engaged in trade, and though the usages of each individual market or fair might differ, their customary rules were aimed at regulating the commercial activities that went on there. As early as the ninth century, a German writer recorded a custom of merchants that a purchase made in an annual fair was to be valid, irrespective of whether it was "just or unjust."
>
> In England, markets and fairs became the centers in which most of the country's trade and commerce took place at all levels. As national and international trade developed, it must have been increasingly recognized that the good and effective regulation of such markets and fairs was essential for the commercial well-being of the nation, and the nascent common law did not attempt to interfere in the customary laws which had grown up around them.
>
> It is evident that English borough customs frequently went some way to protect the bona fide purchaser who bought in the local market. . . .
>
> Nor would the exercise of that customary protection given to a purchaser in the highly regulated forum of an open market have necessarily been unduly burdensome to owners who had lost their goods, for as the markets were the public places in which most goods were bought and sold, an owner might proclaim his loss in the local market and check the goods offered for sale there with some reasonable chance of finding that which had been stolen from him.

Peter M. Smith, *Valediction to Market Overt*, 41 Am. J. Legal Hist. 225, 227–228 (1997).

Despite the 1995 abolition of market overt in England, "the doctrine, however, continues to exert an influence internationally, particularly with respect to the antiquities and art market, where questions of title to be determined in the courts of one country concern stolen goods purchased in another which allows a bona fide purchaser to acquire a good title following a sale in market overt." *Id.* at 226. In addition, market overt may exist in other nations. See, e.g., Ji Lian Yap, *Appraising the Market Overt Exception*, 3 J. Int'l Comm. L & Tech. 254 (2008), discussing Hong Kong's market overt exception.

In *Menzel*, the court noted that Law #59 of the U.S. Military Government for Germany would "disregard" provisions of law that protected good-faith purchasers, if those provisions would defeat restitution of Nazi-looted property. Would this have applied to the English rule of market overt?

4. *Dr. True and Rule of No Provenance.* As Judge Bauer noted, Marion True was the curator of antiquities at the J. Paul Getty Museum in Los Angeles. It was a position she held for many years until she resigned in 2005. In 2000, Dr. True was formally investigated by Italian authorities for criminal activity in receiving stolen property and conspiracy to traffic in stolen property. In 2005, she was officially charged. It was the first time a museum official was criminally so charged with respect to works held in the museum, some acquired before her arrival.

While the Italian prosecutor presented the government's case against Dr. True off and on over a five-year period (2005–2010), other Italian officials began negotiations with U.S. museums to return works the Italian government deemed stolen. With the backdrop of the well-publicized charges against Dr. True, agreements were reached with New York's Metropolitan Museum of Art, Boston's Museum of Fine Arts, Los Angeles's Getty, and others, to return certain works in exchange for loans and cultural cooperation. During that same time frame, U.S. museums adopted a strict rule for new antiquities acquisitions. If there is no provenance, there will be no purchase.

In October 2010, without ever having had to defend herself or call witnesses, the case against Dr. True was bureaucratically over, dismissed on statute of limitations grounds. Dr. True believes the case was politically motivated. The Italian prosecutor Paolo Ferri never imagined Dr. True going to jail. "She was on trial for one reason, to show an example of what Italy could do." Geoff Edgers, *One of the world's most respected curators vanished from the art world. Now she wants to tell her story*, Wash. Post (Aug. 22, 2015). See also Randy Kennedy, *Ex-Curator for Getty Speaks Out About Trial*, N.Y. Times, Movies, Performing Arts/Weekend Desk at 2 (Jan. 6, 2011); Hugh Eakin, *Marion True on her Trial and Ordeal*, The New Yorker, Blog: News-Desk (Oct. 14, 2010).

5. *Lydian Hoard: Repatriation, Re-Loss and Return.* The Republic of Turkey sued the Metropolitan Museum of Art for replevin to recover a collection of 6th century B.C. artifacts, known as the Lydian Hoard. The works were illegally excavated from burial sites in southern Turkey in the 1960s and illegally exported to the United

States. Between 1966 and 1970, the Met purchased the artifacts from dealers for $1.5 million, and thereafter kept the works generally in storage until 1984, when some were publicly displayed as "East Greek treasure."

A Turkish journalist noted similarities to looted Turkish artifacts and alerted Turkish authorities. In 1986, Turkey demanded return of the Lydian Hoard; the Met refused; and a lawsuit was filed in 1987. The Met's motion for summary judgment was denied in 1990. Republic of Turkey v. Metropolitan Museum of Art, 762 F. Supp. 44 (S.D.N.Y. 1990). After three additional years of discovery and negotiations, the parties settled the case with the Met returning the Lydian Hoard to Turkey in 1993.

After the return of the Lydian Hoard, the collection was first placed on display in Ankara's Museum of Anatolian Civilizations. In 1995, the treasure was relocated to a remote town near the site of the illegal excavations and placed in a museum without an alarm system. Between 2001 and 2006, a total of 769 visitors came to the one-story museum to see the treasure on display in a glass case secured by a rudimentary lock. In April 2006, alerted by an anonymous tip, Turkish authorities announced the theft of a prized piece of the Lydian Hoard, a priceless gold hippocampus (sea horse) brooch. The piece on display was a fake. Most shocking was the arrest of the museum's director. In 2009, he was convicted and sentenced to prison for the theft. See Sharon Waxman, Loot: The Battle over the Stolen Treasures of the Ancient World (2008), for a compelling account of the Lydian Hoard story. The brooch was rediscovered in Germany and returned to Turkey in 2013. See Leila Amineddoleh, *The Politicizing of Cultural Heritage*, 45 N.C. J. Int'l L. 333 (2020), rejecting the concern about security of repatriated objects as a defense to repatriation.

5. War-Looted Art — Again

Republic of Austria v. Altmann

541 U.S. 677 (2004)

Justice Stevens delivered the opinion of the Court.

* * *

I

Because this case comes to us from the denial of a motion to dismiss on the pleadings, we assume the truth of the following facts alleged in respondent's complaint.

Born in Austria in 1916, respondent Maria V. Altmann escaped the country after it was annexed by Nazi Germany in 1938. She settled in California in 1942 and became an American citizen in 1945. She is a niece, and the sole surviving named heir, of Ferdinand Bloch-Bauer, who died in Zurich, Switzerland, on November 13, 1945.

Prior to 1938 Ferdinand, then a wealthy sugar magnate, maintained his principal residence in Vienna, Austria, where the six Klimt paintings and other valuable works of art were housed. His wife, Adele, was the subject of two of the paintings. She died in 1925, leaving a will in which she "ask[ed]" her husband "after his death" to bequeath the paintings to the Gallery. The attorney for her estate advised the Gallery that Ferdinand intended to comply with his wife's request, but that he was not legally obligated to do so because he, not Adele, owned the paintings. Ferdinand never executed any document transferring ownership of any of the paintings at issue to the Gallery. He remained their sole legitimate owner until his death. His will bequeathed his entire estate to respondent, another niece, and a nephew.

On March 12, 1938, in what became known as the "Anschluss," the Nazis invaded and claimed to annex Austria. Ferdinand, who was Jewish and had supported efforts to resist annexation, fled the country ahead of the Nazis, ultimately settling in Zurich. In his absence, according to the complaint, the Nazis "Aryanized" the sugar company he had directed, took over his Vienna home, and divided up his artworks, which included the Klimts at issue here, many other valuable paintings, and a 400-piece porcelain collection. A Nazi lawyer, Dr. Erich Führer, took possession of the six Klimts. He sold two to the Gallery in 1941 and a third in 1943, kept one for himself, and sold another to the Museum of the City of Vienna. The immediate fate of the sixth is not known. 142 F.Supp.2d, at 1193.

In 1946 Austria enacted a law declaring all transactions motivated by Nazi ideology null and void. This did not result in the immediate return of looted artwork to exiled Austrians, however, because a different provision of Austrian law proscribed export of "artworks . . . deemed to be important to [the country's] cultural heritage" and required anyone wishing to export art to obtain the permission of the Austrian Federal Monument Agency. "Seeking to profit from this requirement," the Gallery and the Federal Monument Agency allegedly adopted a practice of "forc[ing] Jews to donate or trade valuable artworks to the [Gallery] in exchange for export permits for other works."

The next year Robert Bentley, respondent's brother and fellow heir, retained a Viennese lawyer, Dr. Gustav Rinesch, to locate and recover property stolen from Ferdinand during the war. In January 1948 Dr. Rinesch wrote to the Gallery requesting return of the three Klimts purchased from Dr. Führer. A Gallery representative responded, asserting-falsely, according to the complaint—that Adele had bequeathed the paintings to the Gallery, and the Gallery had merely permitted Ferdinand to retain them during his lifetime.

Later the same year Dr. Rinesch enlisted the support of Gallery officials to obtain export permits for many of Ferdinand's remaining works of art. In exchange, Dr. Rinesch, purporting to represent respondent and her fellow heirs, signed a document "acknowledg[ing] and accept[ing] Ferdinand's declaration that in the event of his death he wished to follow the wishes of his deceased wife to donate" the Klimt paintings to the Gallery. In addition, Dr. Rinesch assisted the Gallery in obtaining both the painting Dr. Führer had kept for himself and the one he had sold to the Museum of the City of Vienna. At no time during these transactions, however, did

Dr. Rinesch have respondent's permission either "to negotiate on her behalf or to allow the [Gallery] to obtain the Klimt paintings."

In 1998 a journalist examining the Gallery's files discovered documents revealing that at all relevant times Gallery officials knew that neither Adele nor Ferdinand had, in fact, donated the six Klimts to the Gallery. The journalist published a series of articles reporting his findings, and specifically noting that Klimt's first portrait of Adele, "which all the [Gallery] publications represented as having been donated to the museum in 1936," had actually been received in 1941, accompanied by a letter from Dr. Führer signed "'Heil Hitler.'"

In response to these revelations, Austria enacted a new restitution law under which individuals who had been coerced into donating artworks to state museums in exchange for export permits could reclaim their property. Respondent—who had believed, prior to the journalist's investigation, that Adele and Ferdinand had "freely donated" the Klimt paintings to the Gallery before the war—immediately sought recovery of the paintings and other artworks under the new law. A committee of Austrian Government officials and art historians agreed to return certain Klimt drawings and porcelain settings that the family had donated in 1948. After what the complaint terms a "sham" proceeding, however, the committee declined to return the six paintings, concluding, based on an allegedly purposeful misreading of Adele's will, that her precatory request had created a binding legal obligation that required her husband to donate the paintings to the Gallery on his death.

Respondent then announced that she would file a lawsuit in Austria to recover the paintings. Because Austrian court costs are proportional to the value of the recovery sought (and in this case would total several million dollars, an amount far beyond respondent's means), she requested a waiver. The court granted this request in part but still would have required respondent to pay approximately $350,000 to proceed. When the Austrian Government appealed even this partial waiver, respondent voluntarily dismissed her suit and filed this action in the United States District Court for the Central District of California.

II

Respondent's complaint advances eight causes of action and . . . asserts jurisdiction under § 2 of the [Foreign Sovereign Immunities Act of 1976, 28 U.S.C. § 1602 *et seq.* (FSIA)] . . . . The complaint further asserts that petitioners are not entitled to immunity under the FSIA because the Act's "expropriation exception," § 1605(a)(3), expressly exempts from immunity all cases involving "rights in property taken in violation of international law," provided the property has a commercial connection to the United States or the agency or instrumentality that owns the property is engaged in commercial activity here.

Petitioners filed a motion to dismiss. . . . Their immunity argument proceeded in two steps. First, they claimed that as of 1948, when much of their alleged wrongdoing took place, they would have enjoyed absolute immunity from suit in United

States courts. Proceeding from this premise, petitioners next contended that nothing in the FSIA should be understood to divest them of that immunity retroactively.

The District Court rejected this argument, concluding both that the FSIA applies retroactively to pre-1976 actions and that the Act's expropriation exception extends to respondent's specific claims. Only the former conclusion concerns us here.... [T]he court noted that the FSIA itself provides that "'[c]laims of foreign states to immunity should *henceforth be decided* by courts of the United States ... *in conformity with the principles set forth in this chapter.*'" In the court's view, this language suggests the Act "is to be applied to all cases decided after its enactment regardless of when the plaintiff's cause of action may have accrued."

The Court of Appeals agreed that the FSIA applies to this case ... however, the panel reasoned that applying the FSIA to Austria's alleged wrongdoing was not impermissibly retroactive because Austria could not legitimately have expected to receive immunity for that wrongdoing even in 1948 when it occurred....

We granted certiorari, 539 U.S. 987, 124 S.Ct. 46 (2003), and now affirm the judgment of the Court of Appeals, though on different reasoning.

III

Chief Justice Marshall's opinion in *Schooner Exchange v. McFaddon*, 7 Cranch 116, 3 L.Ed. 287 (1812), is generally viewed as the source of our foreign sovereign immunity jurisprudence. In that case, the libellants claimed to be the rightful owners of a French ship that had taken refuge in the port of Philadelphia. The Court first emphasized that the jurisdiction of the United States over persons and property within its territory "is susceptible of no limitation not imposed by itself," and thus foreign sovereigns have no right to immunity in our courts. *Id.*, at 136. Chief Justice Marshall went on to explain, however, that as a matter of comity, members of the international community had implicitly agreed to waive the exercise of jurisdiction over other sovereigns in certain classes of cases, such as those involving foreign ministers or the person of the sovereign. Accepting a suggestion advanced by the Executive Branch, see *id.*, at 134, the Chief Justice concluded that the implied waiver theory also served to exempt the *Schooner Exchange*—"a national armed vessel ... of the emperor of France"—from United States courts' jurisdiction. *Id.*, at 145–146.

In accordance with Chief Justice Marshall's observation that foreign sovereign immunity is a matter of grace and comity rather than a constitutional requirement, this Court has "consistently ... deferred to the decisions of the political branches—in particular, those of the Executive Branch—on whether to take jurisdiction" over particular actions against foreign sovereigns and their instrumentalities. Until 1952 the Executive Branch followed a policy of requesting immunity in all actions against friendly sovereigns. In that year, however, the State Department concluded that "immunity should no longer be granted in certain types of cases." In a letter to the Acting Attorney General, the Acting Legal Adviser for the Secretary of State, Jack B. Tate, explained that the Department would thereafter apply the "restrictive theory" of sovereign immunity:

> "A study of the law of sovereign immunity reveals the existence of two conflicting concepts of sovereign immunity, each widely held and firmly established. According to the classical or absolute theory of sovereign immunity, a sovereign cannot, without his consent, be made a respondent in the courts of another sovereign. According to the newer or restrictive theory of sovereign immunity, the immunity of the sovereign is recognized with regard to sovereign or public acts *(jure imperii)* of a state, but not with respect to private acts (*jure gestionis*).... [I]t will hereafter be the Department's policy to follow the restrictive theory ... in the consideration of requests of foreign governments for a grant of sovereign immunity."

As we explained in our unanimous opinion in *Verlinden [B.V. v. Central Bank of Nigeria*, 461 U.S. 480 (1988)], the change in State Department policy wrought by the "Tate Letter" had little, if any, impact on federal courts' approach to immunity analyses: "As in the past, initial responsibility for deciding questions of sovereign immunity fell primarily upon the Executive acting through the State Department," and courts continued to "abid[e] by" that Department's "'suggestions of immunity.'" 461 U.S., at 487, 103 S.Ct. 1962. The change did, however, throw immunity determinations into some disarray, as "foreign nations often placed diplomatic pressure on the State Department," and political considerations sometimes led the Department to file "suggestions of immunity in cases where immunity would not have been available under the restrictive theory." *Id.*, at 487–488, 103 S.Ct. 1962. Complicating matters further, when foreign nations failed to request immunity from the State Department:

> "[T]he responsibility fell to the courts to determine whether sovereign immunity existed, generally by reference to prior State Department decisions.... Thus, sovereign immunity determinations were made in two different branches, subject to a variety of factors, sometimes including diplomatic considerations. Not surprisingly, the governing standards were neither clear nor uniformly applied." *Ibid.*

In 1976 Congress sought to remedy these problems by enacting the FSIA, a comprehensive statute containing a "set of legal standards governing claims of immunity in every civil action against a foreign state or its political subdivisions, agencies, or instrumentalities." *Id.*, at 488, 103 S.Ct. 1962. The Act "codifies, as a matter of federal law, the restrictive theory of sovereign immunity," *ibid.*, and transfers primary responsibility for immunity determinations from the Executive to the Judicial Branch. The preamble states that "henceforth" both federal and state courts should decide claims of sovereign immunity in conformity with the Act's principles.

The Act itself grants federal courts jurisdiction over civil actions against foreign states, § 1330(a), and over diversity actions in which a foreign state is the plaintiff, § 1332(a)(4); it contains venue and removal provisions, §§ 1391(f), 1441(d); it prescribes the procedures for obtaining personal jurisdiction over a foreign state, § 1330(b); and it governs the extent to which a state's property may be subject to attachment or execution, §§ 1609–1611. Finally, the Act carves out certain exceptions to its general grant of immunity, including the expropriation exception on which respondent's complaint relies. See *supra,* at 2245–2246, and n. 5. These exceptions are central to the Act's functioning: "At the threshold of every action in a district court against a foreign state, . . . the court must satisfy itself that one of the exceptions applies," as "subject-matter jurisdiction in any such action depends" on that application. *Verlinden,* 461 U.S., at 493–494, 103 S.Ct. 1962.

IV

The District Court [held] that the FSIA's expropriation exception covers petitioners' alleged wrongdoing, and the Court of Appeals affirmed that holding. As noted above, however, we declined to review this aspect of the courts' opinions, confining our grant of certiorari to the issue of the FSIA's general applicability to conduct that occurred prior to the Act's 1976 enactment, and more specifically, prior to the State Department's 1952 adoption of the restrictive theory of sovereign immunity. We begin our analysis of that issue by explaining why, contrary to the assumption of the District Court and Court of Appeals, the default rule announced in our opinion in *Landgraf* [*v. USI Film Products,* 511 U.S. 244 (1994)] does not control the outcome in this case.

* * *

. . . In our view . . . *Landgraf's* antiretroactivity presumption, while not strictly confined to cases involving private rights, is most helpful in that context. ("[T]he great majority of our decisions relying upon the antiretroactivity presumption have involved intervening statutes burdening private parties"). The aim of the presumption is to avoid unnecessary *post hoc* changes to legal rules on which parties relied in shaping their primary conduct. But the principal purpose of foreign sovereign immunity has never been to permit foreign states and their instrumentalities to shape their conduct in reliance on the promise of future immunity from suit in United States courts. Rather, such immunity reflects current political realities and relationships, and aims to give foreign states and their instrumentalities some *present* "protection from the inconvenience of suit as a gesture of comity." Throughout history, courts have resolved questions of foreign sovereign immunity by deferring to the "decisions of the political branches . . . on whether to take jurisdiction." *Verlinden,* 461 U.S., at 486, 103 S.Ct. 1962. In this *sui generis* context, we think it more appropriate, absent contraindications, to defer to the most recent such decision—namely, the FSIA—than to presume that decision *inapplicable* merely because it postdates the conduct in question.

V

This leaves only the question whether anything in the FSIA or the circumstances surrounding its enactment suggests that we should not apply it to petitioners' 1948 actions. Not only do we answer this question in the negative, but we find clear evidence that Congress intended the Act to apply to preenactment conduct.

To begin with, the preamble of the FSIA expresses Congress' understanding that the Act would apply to all postenactment claims of sovereign immunity. That section provides:

> "*Claims* of foreign states to immunity should *henceforth* be decided by courts of the United States and of the States in conformity with the principles set forth in this chapter." 28 U.S.C. § 1602 (emphasis added).

Though perhaps not sufficient to satisfy *Landgraf's* "express command" requirement, this language is unambiguous: Immunity "claims"—not actions protected by immunity, but assertions of immunity to suits arising from those actions—are the relevant conduct regulated by the Act; those claims are "henceforth" to be decided by the courts. As the District Court observed, this language suggests Congress intended courts to resolve *all* such claims "in conformity with the principles set forth" in the Act, regardless of when the underlying conduct occurred.

The FSIA's overall structure strongly supports this conclusion. Many of the Act's provisions unquestionably apply to cases arising out of conduct that occurred before 1976. . . . And there has never been any doubt that the Act's procedural provisions relating to venue, removal, execution, and attachment apply to all pending cases. Thus, the FSIA's preamble indicates that it applies "henceforth," and its body includes numerous provisions that unquestionably apply to claims based on pre-1976 conduct. In this context, it would be anomalous to presume that an isolated provision (such as the expropriation exception on which respondent relies) is of purely prospective application absent any statutory language to that effect.

Finally, applying the FSIA to all pending cases regardless of when the underlying conduct occurred is most consistent with two of the Act's principal purposes: clarifying the rules that judges should apply in resolving sovereign immunity claims and eliminating political participation in the resolution of such claims. We have recognized that, to accomplish these purposes, Congress established a comprehensive framework for resolving any claim of sovereign immunity:

> "We think that the text and structure of the FSIA demonstrate Congress' intention that the FSIA be the sole basis for obtaining jurisdiction over a foreign state in our courts. Sections 1604 and 1330(a) work in tandem: § 1604 bars federal and state courts from exercising jurisdiction when a foreign state *is* entitled to immunity, and § 1330(a) confers jurisdiction on district courts to hear suits brought by United States citizens and by aliens when a foreign state is *not* entitled to immunity. As we said in *Verlinden,* the FSIA 'must be applied by the district courts in every action against a foreign sovereign, since subject-matter jurisdiction in any such action depends on the existence of one of the specified exceptions to foreign sovereign immunity.'" *Argentine Republic v. Amerada Hess Shipping Corp.,* 488 U.S. 428, 434–435, 109 S.Ct. 683, 102 L.Ed.2d 818 (1989) (quoting *Verlinden,* 461 U.S., at 493, 103 S.Ct. 1962).

The *Amerada Hess* respondents' claims concerned conduct that postdated the FSIA, so we had no occasion to consider the Act's retroactivity. Nevertheless, our observations about the FSIA's inclusiveness are relevant in this case: Quite obviously, Congress' purposes in enacting such a comprehensive jurisdictional scheme would be frustrated if, in postenactment cases concerning preenactment conduct, courts were to continue to follow the same ambiguous and politically charged "'standards'" that the FSIA replaced.

We do not endorse the reasoning of the Court of Appeals. Indeed, we think it engaged in precisely the kind of detailed historical inquiry that the FSIA's clear guidelines were intended to obviate. Nevertheless, we affirm the panel's judgment because the Act, freed from *Landgraf's* antiretroactivity presumption, clearly applies to conduct, like petitioners' alleged wrongdoing, that occurred prior to 1976 and, for that matter, prior to 1952 when the State Department adopted the restrictive theory of sovereign immunity.

VI

We conclude by emphasizing the narrowness of this holding. To begin with, although the District Court and Court of Appeals determined that § 1605(a)(3) covers this case, we declined to review that determination. Nor do we have occasion to comment on the application of the so-called "act of state" doctrine to petitioners' alleged wrongdoing. Unlike a claim of sovereign immunity, which merely raises a jurisdictional defense, the act of state doctrine provides foreign states with a substantive defense on the merits. Under that doctrine, the courts of one state will not question the validity of public acts (acts *jure imperii*) performed by other sovereigns within their own borders, even when such courts have jurisdiction over a controversy in which one of the litigants has standing to challenge those acts. Petitioners principally rely on the act of state doctrine to support their assertion that foreign expropriations are public acts for which, prior to the enactment of the FSIA, sovereigns expected immunity. Applying the FSIA in this case would upset that settled expectation, petitioners argue, and thus the Act "would operate retroactively" under *Landgraf.* But because the FSIA in no way affects application of the act of state doctrine, our determination that the Act applies in this case in no way affects any argument petitioners may have that the doctrine shields their alleged wrongdoing.

Finally, while we reject the United States' recommendation to bar application of the FSIA to claims based on pre-enactment conduct, nothing in our holding prevents the State Department from filing statements of interest suggesting that courts decline to exercise jurisdiction in particular cases implicating foreign sovereign immunity. The issue now before us concerns interpretation of the FSIA's reach—a "pure question of statutory construction . . . well within the province of the Judiciary." While the United States' views on such an issue are of considerable interest to the Court, they merit no special deference. In contrast, should the State Department choose to express its opinion on the implications of exercising jurisdiction over *particular* petitioners in connection with *their* alleged conduct, that opinion might well be entitled to deference as the considered judgment of the Executive on a particular question of foreign policy. We express no opinion on the question whether such deference should be granted in cases covered by the FSIA.

The judgment of the Court of Appeals is affirmed.

It is so ordered.

[Concurring opinions of Justice Scalia and Justice Breyer are omitted.]

* * *

Justice KENNEDY, with whom THE CHIEF JUSTICE and Justice THOMAS join, dissenting.

This is an important decision for interpreting the Foreign Sovereign Immunities Act of 1976 (FSIA or Act), 28 U.S.C. § 1602 *et seq.* As the Court's careful opinion illustrates, the case is difficult. In my respectful view, however, its decision is incorrect.

At the outset, here is a summary of my primary concerns with the majority opinion: To reach its conclusion the Court must weaken the reasoning and diminish the force of the rule against the retroactivity of statutes, a rule of fairness based on respect for expectations; the Court abruptly tells foreign nations this important principle of American law is unavailable to them in our courts; this is so despite the fact that treaties and agreements on the subject of expropriation have been reached against a background of the immunity principles the Court now rejects; as if to mitigate its harsh result, the Court adds that the Executive Branch has inherent power to intervene in cases like this; this, however, is inconsistent with the congressional purpose and design of the FSIA; the suggestion reintroduces, to an even greater degree than before, the same influences the FSIA sought to eliminate from sovereign immunity determinations; the Court's reasoning also implies a problematic answer to a separation-of-powers question that the case does not present and that should be avoided; the ultimate effect of the Court's inviting foreign nations to pressure the Executive is to risk inconsistent results for private citizens who sue, based on changes and nuances in foreign affairs, and to add prospective instability to the most sensitive area of foreign relations.

The majority's treatment of our retroactivity principles, its rejection of the considered congressional and Executive judgment behind the FSIA, and its questionable constitutional implications require this respectful dissent.

* * *

The court's approach further leads to the unprecedented conclusion that Congress' Article I power might well be insufficient to accomplish the central objective of the FSIA. The Court, in addition, injects great prospective uncertainty into our relations with foreign sovereigns. Application of our usual presumption against imposing retroactive effect would leave powerful precedent intact and avoid these difficulties.

With respect, I dissent.

Orkin v. Taylor

487 F.3d 734 (9th Cir. 2007)

THOMAS J.

* * *

I

* * *

As the Nazis' persecution accelerated, [Jewish art collector Margarete] Mauthner fled Germany to South Africa in 1939, leaving her possessions behind. She remained there until her death in 1947, at the age of 84. What happened to [Vincent van Gogh's] *Vue de l'Asile et de la Chapelle de Saint-Rémy* during that time is not clear from the record. . . .

Notably, the Orkins do not contend that the painting was confiscated by the Nazis. Rather, they allege economic coercion, contending that Mauthner sold the painting "under duress." They note that laws promulgated by the Allied Forces after the conclusion of World War II established a presumption that any transfer or relinquishment of property by a persecuted person within the period January 30, 1933 to May 8, 1945 was an act of confiscation. Military Government Law No. 59 § 375(b).

Taylor contends that, at best, the record shows that the painting was sold through two Jewish art dealers to a Jewish art collector, with no evidence of any Nazi coercion or participation in the transactions.

In short, the parties agree that Mauthner once owned the painting and that it was later possessed by Alfred Wolf. . . . Sometime in the early 1960s, the Estate of Alfred Wolf commissioned Sotheby's to sell [the painting] . . . .

. . . Elizabeth Taylor began collecting art in the 1950s. . . . Taylor learned [the painting] would be offered at a Sotheby's auction in April 1963. She . . . was successful in purchasing the painting . . . for £92,000.

Taylor's acquisition was publicized at the time. Subsequently, the 1970 *catalogue raisonné* referenced Taylor's ownership. From November 1986 until March 1987, the painting was exhibited publicly at the Metropolitan Museum of Art in New York, in an exhibition entitled *Van Gogh in Saint Rémy and Auvers.*

In 1990, Taylor offered the painting for sale through Christie's auction house in London. The provenance for the sale lists Taylor as the current owner, with the prior owners being Alfred Wolf (of Stuttgart and Buenos Aires), Marcel Goldschmidt & Co. (of Frankfurt), Margarete Mauthner (of Berlin), Paul Cassirer (of Berlin), and Johanna van Gogh-Bonger (of Amsterdam). The work did not sell at the auction.

In 1998, Congress enacted three statutes pertaining to victims of Nazi persecution: the Holocaust Victims Redress Act ("Act"), the Nazi War Crimes Disclosure Act of 1998, and the United States Holocaust Assets Commission Act of 1998. The Orkins allege that their inquiry into whether their ancestor, Mauthner, may have lost her art collection due to Nazi persecution began upon the passage of these acts. They retained a law firm in 2001 and claim that, until their attorneys completed their investigation, they did not discover the basis of their current claim. The Orkins allege that, before they began that investigation, they did not know that Mauthner had owned *Vue de l'Asile et de la Chapelle de Saint-Rémy,* that she had lost the painting as a result of Nazi persecution, that Taylor had bought the painting, or that there was a legal basis for recovering the painting. They also claim that they first learned of Taylor's ownership in 2002, through a rumor on the internet that Taylor was interested in selling the painting.

In December 2003, the Orkins wrote a letter to Taylor, demanding that she return the painting to them. After some discussion of settlement, Taylor wrote a response letter declining settlement and asserting that the Orkins' claim to the painting was untimely. Taylor then filed a complaint for declaratory relief to establish her title.

In 2005, the Orkins filed their First Amended Complaint for recovery of the painting....

* * *

II

The district court properly dismissed the Orkins' federal claims on the ground that the Holocaust Victims Redress Act did not create a private right of action against private art owners. In determining whether a federal statute creates a private right of action, congressional intent is the cornerstone of the analysis. The Supreme Court has established a four-factor test for discerning whether a statute creates a private right of action. *Cort v. Ash,* 422 U.S. 66, 95 S.Ct. 2080, 45 L.Ed.2d 26 (1975). Under that test, we must ask: (1) whether the plaintiff is a member of a class that the statute especially intended to benefit, (2) whether the legislature explicitly or implicitly intended to create a private cause of action, (3) whether the general purpose of the statutory scheme would be served by creation of a private right of action, and (4) whether the cause of action is traditionally relegated to state law such that implication of a federal remedy would be inappropriate.

The most important inquiry under *Cort* is the second factor: whether there is "any indication of legislative intent, explicit or implicit, either to create such a remedy or to deny one." ...

The plain text of the Holocaust Victims Redress Act leaves little doubt that Congress did not intend to create a private right of action. The Orkins rely on § 202 of the Act, entitled "Sense of the Congress Regarding Restitution of Private Property, Such as Works of Art." That section reads in its entirety as follows:

> It is the sense of the Congress that consistent with the 1907 Hague Convention, all governments should undertake good faith efforts to facilitate the return of private and public property, such as works of art, to the rightful owners in cases where assets were confiscated from the claimant during the

period of Nazi rule and there is reasonable proof that the claimant is the rightful owner.

Act § 202, 112 Stat. at 17–18.

"Sense of the Congress" provisions are precatory provisions, which do not in themselves create individual rights or, for that matter, any enforceable law. . . .

Additionally, the Act's legislative history indicates that even its most ardent supporter did not intend for the bill to create a private right of action. Rather, the legislative intent was to encourage state and foreign governments to enforce existing rights for the protection of Holocaust victims. . . .

* * *

With respect to the third *Cort* factor, the text and history of the legislation reveal that its overarching purpose was not to provide for private litigation. Rather, the general purpose of the statutory scheme was to fund research efforts and to declassify records, while simultaneously encouraging foreign governments, as well as public and private institutions, to do likewise. In other words, the motivating concern was *not* access to courts; it was access to information. In fact, throughout the committee hearings, witnesses testified that courts would likely do a poor job of resolving Holocaust victims' claims. Specifically, the committee heard testimony that the difficulties of tracing information would likely preclude effective judicial resolution of discrete claims, and several museum directors testified that alternative fora such as mediation and arbitration were preferable to litigation. The general purposes of the statute, therefore, do not support the conclusion that Congress intended to provide a private right of action in this case.

* * *

In short, the Act does not satisfy any of the *Cort* factors. . . . Given the absence of congressional intent to create a private right of action, the Orkins' assertion of a federal right of action must fail.

III

The district court also properly concluded that the Orkins' state-law claims were time-barred. California provides a three-year statute of limitations for any action arising from the "taking, detaining, or injuring" of any "goods or chattels." Cal.Civ .Proc.Code § 338(c). In 1983, the statute of limitations was amended to specify that a "discovery rule" governs accrual of causes of action for recovery of "any article of historical, interpretive, scientific, or artistic significance." *Id.* In other words, under the new law, an action for recovery of artwork accrues when the rightful owner discovers the whereabouts of the artwork. Before 1983, the statute did not specify when a cause of action for theft would accrue.

The Orkins do not argue that the 1983 amendment applies retroactively to their allegations of a 1939 theft and a 1963 conversion. Rather, they contend that the discovery rule applies even under pre-1983 law. . . .

* * *

The California Supreme Court has never confronted the question of what rule governs accrual of pre-1983 causes of action for theft and conversion. The California Supreme Court has, however, specifically held that the discovery rule, whenever it applies, incorporates the principle of constructive notice. [*Jolly v. Eli Lilly & Co.*, 44 Cal.3d 1103, 1109, 245 Cal.Rptr. 658, 751 P.2d 923 (1988)]. . . .

Under *Jolly*, the latest possible accrual date of the Orkins' cause of action was the date on which they first reasonably could have discovered, through investigation of sources open to them, their claim to and the whereabouts of the van Gogh painting. From the face of the Orkins' complaint, it is apparent that Taylor's acquisition of the painting was certainly discoverable at least by 1990, when she held it out for sale in an international auction, and most probably as early as 1963, when she acquired the painting in a highly publicized international auction. In fact, the complaint alleges—and demonstrates by attachment—that Taylor bought the painting at a publicized auction in 1963, that Taylor was listed as the owner of the painting in a publicly available 1970 *catalogue raisonné*, and that Taylor publicly offered the painting for sale in 1990. Had the Orkins investigated any of those publicly-available sources, they could have discovered both their claim to the painting and the painting's whereabouts long before the 2002 internet rumor was posted.

We therefore affirm the district court's conclusion that the Orkins' state-law claims are time-barred. Even under the most generous possible rule for accrual of the causes of action, the claims expired in or before 1993-three years after the last public announcement of Taylor's ownership. The district court correctly held that the Orkins' state law claims were untimely filed.

Congress did not create a private right of action in passing the Holocaust Victims Redress Act, which merely reflected the sense of Congress. The Orkins' state law claims are time-barred. The district court was entirely correct in dismissing the complaint. We need not, and do not, reach any of the other issues urged by the parties.

AFFIRMED.

Von Saher v. Norton Simon Museum of Art at Pasadena

897 F.3d 1141 (9th Cir. 2018)

McKeown, Circuit Judge:

* * *

Background

The Paintings

At the center of this controversy are two Renaissance masterworks—"Adam" and "Eve"—painted by Lucas Cranach the Elder ("the paintings" or "the Cranachs"). In 1931, Dutch art dealer Jacques Goudstikker purchased the Cranachs from the Soviet Union at an auction in Berlin called "the Stroganoff Collection." The paintings became the property of the art dealership in which Goudstikker was principal shareholder ("the Goudstikker Firm" or "the Firm").

In May 1940, as the Nazis invaded the Netherlands, Goudstikker and his family fled to South America. . . . Goudstikker died on the boat trip. . . .

After Goudstikker's death, Nazi Reichsmarschall Hermann Göring and his cohort Alois Miedl "bought" the Goudstikker Firm and its assets through a series of involuntary written agreements. . . . These "forced sales" proceeded in two parts: Miedl acquired the Firm, its showroom, some of its paintings, and the family's villa and castle for 550,000 guilders ("the Miedl transaction"). Göring purchased other artworks, including the Cranachs, for two million guilders—the equivalent of over 20 million current U.S. dollars ("the Göring transaction").

After World War II, the Allied Forces in Germany recovered . . . the Cranachs. The Allies turned the paintings over to the Dutch government in 1946.

The Dutch Restitution System

During and after the war, the Dutch government created systems of restitution and reparations for losses incurred by its citizens at the hands of the Nazis. The pillars of those systems were established in a series of royal decrees. . . .

* * *

Royal Decree E100

The Dutch government enacted Royal Decree E100 in 1944. The decree established a Council for Restoration of Rights ("the Council"), with broad and exclusive authority to declare null and void, modify, or revive "any legal relations that originated or were modified during enemy occupation of the [Netherlands]."

The Council had the exclusive power to order the return of property and to restore property rights to the original Dutch owners. . . .

The Dutch government set a July 1, 1951 deadline for claimants to file E100 restoration-of-rights petitions with the Council. After that deadline, the Council could still order restoration of rights of its own accord, but claimants were no longer entitled to demand restitution. Usually, if an original owner received money or other consideration in exchange for property taken by the Nazis, the original owner was required to return the sale price to the Dutch government in order to obtain restitution.

Decree E100 also authorized the Council to dispose of property of "unknown owners": "If the owner has not come forward within a period to be further determined by Us, items that have not yet been sold shall be sold. . . ." The Dutch government set the deadline for owners "com[ing] forward" at September 30, 1950.

Royal Decree E133

The Dutch government enacted Royal Decree E133 in 1944 to expropriate enemy assets in order to compensate the Netherlands for losses it suffered during World War II. Article 3 of E133 provided that within the Netherlands, all "[p]roperty, belonging to an enemy state or to an enemy national, automatically passes in ownership to the State with the entering into force of this decree. . . ." The expropriation of enemy property was automatic and continued until July 1951, when the Netherlands ceased hostilities with Germany.

Von Saher's Family Declined to Seek Restoration of Rights in the Cranachs

After the war, the Dutch government seized what previously had been the Goudstikker Firm (now the Miedl Firm) as an enemy asset and appointed new administrators. Goudstikker's widow (and von Saher's mother-in-law) Desi returned to the Netherlands to pursue restitution.

With Desi and new leadership in place, on the strategic advice of its business advisers and legal counsel, the Goudstikker Firm decided not to pursue restitution for the Göring transaction. Specifically, the Firm believed that seeking restitution would have "left [the business] with a large number of works of art that are difficult to sell"; "led to the revival of an art dealership with all pertinent negative consequences," including "find[ing] a suitable person to run such a business"; and "led to a considerable reduction in the [business's] liquid assets." The Firm's attorney Max Meyer laid out his advice in a memorandum to the Firm. . . .

In 1949, Meyer wrote to the Dutch agency holding the Göring artworks to express that the Firm was releasing any claim it had to those pieces: "I would also like to take this opportunity to confirm that the Art Trade J. Goudstikker LLC waives the right to file for restoration of rights regarding goods acquired by Goering. . . ." The memorandum accompanying that letter showed that Meyer was aware that he could have filed a claim to restore rights in both the Göring and Miedl transactions, because they would have been voidable under E100. In proceedings before the modern Dutch Restitution Committee, Marei von Saher conceded that "Goudstikker made a deliberate and well-considered decision not to seek restoration of rights with respect to the goods that had been acquired by Göring."

By contrast, the Firm decided to pursue restitution for the Miedl transaction, including other artworks and real estate. Just shy of the July 1, 1951 E100 deadline, the Firm filed with the Council a petition for restoration of rights concerning the Miedl transaction only. In August 1952, the Firm and the Dutch government settled the Firm's restitution claims.

The Dutch Government Sold the Cranachs to Stroganoff, Who Sold Them to the Museum

In the 1960s, Stroganoff petitioned the Dutch government, asserting that he was the rightful owner of the Cranachs because the Soviet government had stolen them from him. In 1966, the parties reached an amicable settlement in which Stroganoff bought "back" the paintings from the Netherlands in exchange for dropping his restitution claims.

Through his agent, in 1971 Stroganoff sold the Cranachs to the Museum for $800,000. The Cranachs have been on public display since that time.

Von Saher Pursued Restitution from the Dutch Government

In the 1990s, Marei von Saher—the only living heir of Jacques and Desi Goudstikker—began seeking restitution for artworks that the Firm "sold" to Göring. As part of those efforts, von Saher filed an E100 petition for restoration of rights in the Dutch Court of Appeals (the legal successor to the Council for Restoration of Rights) for all paintings acquired by Göring, including the Cranachs. The Court of Appeals denied the petition, concluding that the Firm "made a conscious and well considered decision to refrain from asking for restoration of rights with respect to the Göring transaction." Von Saher appeared to be at a dead end.

But in 2001, the Netherlands reevaluated its "bureaucratic" restitution process, transforming its mission from a "purely legal approach" to "a more moral policy approach." In doing so, the Dutch government created a new Restitution Committee, to advise . . . on restitution claims for property that was still in the possession of the Dutch government. Embracing the change in forum, von Saher petitioned the State Secretary for over 200 artworks that the Firm "sold" to Göring and that were still held by the Dutch government. Her claim did not include the Cranachs.

After receiving a non-binding recommendation from the Restitution Committee, the State Secretary ruled that von Saher's claim for the artworks . . . had already been 'settled" in the 1950s and in the 1999 Dutch Court of Appeals decision. The State Secretary nonetheless decided to return to von Saher all the paintings . . . still in the possession of the Dutch government. The State Secretary expressly stated that the decision to return the other paintings did not include the Cranachs.

Von Saher I

Out of options with the Dutch government, in 2007 von Saher filed a federal diversity action against the Museum. . . . The action alleged timeliness under a California civil-procedure statute that allowed the rightful owners of confiscated Holocaust-era artwork to recover their items from museums or galleries and set a filing deadline of December 31, 2010. The district court dismissed the action, finding von Saher's claims untimely and . . . California's special statute . . .

unconstitutional. We affirmed . . . provid[ing] von Saher leave to amend her complaint in case she could allege that she lacked notice such that her claims were timely under California's generic statute of limitations for property actions. . . .

Von Saher II

Soon after our decision in *Von Saher I*, the California legislature amended its statute of limitations for actions "for the specific recovery of a work of fine art brought against a museum, . . . in the case of an unlawful taking or theft . . . within six years of the actual discovery by the claimant or his or her agent." Cal. Civ. Proc. Code § 338. The legislature made the amendment retroactive and von Saher amended her complaint accordingly.

The Museum again moved to dismiss, this time arguing that von Saher's claims conflicted with federal foreign policy. The district court granted the motion. On appeal, we reversed and remanded, over a dissent from Judge Wardlaw.

* * *

Although the panel posited that this was "a dispute between private parties," it was "mindful that the litigation of this case may implicate the act of state doctrine." The case was remanded for further factual development and to determine whether the doctrine applies to von Saher's claims.

* * *

Summary Judgment to the Museum on Remand

On remand . . . the district court conducted over a year of discovery and considered the parties' cross-motions for summary judgment. Applying Dutch law, the district court granted summary judgment to the Museum, concluding . . . the Dutch government possessed good title to the paintings when it sold them to Stroganoff, who then conveyed good title to the Museum.

Analysis

* * *

The act of state doctrine is a "rule of decision" requiring that "the acts of foreign sovereigns taken within their own jurisdictions shall be deemed valid." . . . We apply the doctrine only when we are "require[d] . . . to declare invalid, and thus ineffective . . . , the official act of a foreign sovereign." Hence, we apply the doctrine here, because "the relief sought" by von Saher would necessitate our "declar[ing] invalid" at least three "official act[s] of" the Dutch government "performed within its own territory."

I. Von Saher's Theory Would Require the Court to Invalidate Official Acts of the Dutch Government

Von Saher's recovery hinges on whether she — not the Museum — holds good title to the paintings. The Museum's defense, in turn, depends on its having received good title from Stroganoff, who forfeited his own restitution claim to the paintings when he bought them from the Netherlands in 1966. It is therefore a necessary condition of von Saher's success that the Dutch government's conveyance of the paintings to Stroganoff be deemed legally inoperative. For von Saher to succeed, we would also need to disregard both the Dutch government's 1999 decision not to restore von Saher's rights in the Cranachs and its later statement that her claim to the Cranachs had been "settled." Because it is "essential to" von Saher's cause of action that these three official actions of the Dutch government be held invalid, the act of state doctrine applies. We examine these three acts in turn.

A. The Dutch Government's Conveyance to Stroganoff

... [T]he act of state doctrine may apply to quiet title actions like von Saher's that would require a court to nullify a foreign nation's conveyances. What matters is "whether the conveyance ... constituted an official act of [the] sovereign." There is little doubt that the Dutch government's conveyance to Stroganoff qualifies as an official act of the Netherlands.

We view the conveyance not as a one-off commercial sale, but as the product of the Dutch government's sovereign internal restitution process. Under that process, the Netherlands passed Royal Decrees E133, to expropriate enemy property, and E100, to administer a system through which Dutch nationals filed claims to restore title to lost or looted artworks. Whatever the exact legal effect of those decrees ... we cannot avoid the conclusion that the post-war Dutch system adjudicated property rights by expropriating certain items from the Nazis and restoring rights to dispossessed Dutch citizens. No one disputes, for example, that the Firm successfully availed itself of the post-war system by petitioning for restoration of rights in the artworks it had sold to Miedl.

Expropriation of private property is a uniquely sovereign act. ...

In *Von Saher II*, we reasoned that if "the Museum can show that the Netherlands returned the [paintings] to Stroganoff to satisfy some sort of restitution claim, that act could 'constitute a considered policy decision by a government. ...'"

But we see no reason why the Museum cannot likewise show that the Netherlands transferred the paintings to Stroganoff as part of a decades-long "considered policy decision" that was inextricably linked to its rights-restoration proceedings under the royal decrees. In order to sell to Stroganoff, the Dutch government must have concluded that its proceedings with respect to the Cranachs and von Saher's family were final. That interpretation is consistent with the position of von Saher's predecessors, who wrote to the Dutch government that they "waive[d] the right to file for restoration of rights regarding [thc Cranachs]," and made a strategic, counseled decision not to file a claim on the Göring transaction in order to keep the substantial sale price. The Dutch government clearly understood the Firm to mean what it said; the government began selling unclaimed artworks shortly after the E100 filing deadline, including other works from the Göring transaction. The record on remand is clear.

* * *

After years of negotiations, the Netherlands and Stroganoff decided to "settle the case by means of an amicable arrangement": Stroganoff offered to "buy back" the paintings in exchange for dropping his restitution claims for both the Cranachs and the Rembrandt. The Dutch government entered into the agreement only after carefully considering the public policy ramifications of doing so—the Dutch Minister of Culture initially opposed the proposal because "the two Cranachs are especially important for the Dutch cultural collection." Ultimately, however, the Dutch Minister of Culture considered the settlement to be in "the interest[s] of the country." The Dutch Minister of Finance likewise signed off on the settlement, reinforcing our understanding that the Netherlands entered into the agreement with the careful consideration of high-ranking officials.

Considered holistically, the administration of E100 and E133, the settlement with von Saher's family, and the conveyance of the Cranachs to Stroganoff in consideration of his restitution claim constitute an official act of state that gives effect to the Dutch government's "public interests."

B. The Dutch Court of Appeals Decision not to Restore Von Saher's rights to the Paintings

Von Saher's theory also would require us to disregard the 1999 Dutch Court of Appeals decision denying the restoration of von Saher's rights in the paintings. This ruling is a second act of state authorizing the transfer of the Cranachs to Stroganoff.

In 1998, von Saher petitioned the Dutch government to surrender all property from the "Goudstikker collection" over which the State had gained control. The Dutch State Secretary rejected the request, advising that "[i]n my opinion, directly after the war—even under present standards—the restoration of rights was conducted carefully."

Von Saher then filed an E100 petition for restoration of rights in the Dutch Court of Appeals . . . for all artworks involved in the Göring transaction, including the Cranachs. The Court of Appeals denied the restoration of von Saher's rights in the paintings, noting that "[f]rom the documents submitted it appears that [the Firm] at the time made a conscious and well considered decision to refrain from asking for restoration of rights with respect to the Goring transaction." . . . The Court of Appeals also offered an opinion on the process, concluding that "[t]he Netherlands created an adequately guaranteed procedure for handling applications for the restoration of rights," which was not "in conflict with international law."

Under E100, the Dutch Court of Appeals . . . was the only venue through which von Saher could have received restitution for, and restoration of rights in, the Cranachs. By administering the exclusive postwar remedial scheme for artwork taken by the Nazis, and refusing von Saher's restoration of rights in the paintings, the Dutch Court of Appeals carried out an official action that is particular to sovereigns. . . . The Dutch ruling provides an additional act of state that deems valid the transfer to Stroganoff.

C. The Dutch Government's Decision that the Rights to the Cranachs had been "Settled"

Based on government activities after the 1999 Dutch Court of Appeals decision, von Saher contends that the act of state doctrine either does not apply or should operate on her behalf. But rather than aid von Saher, those later activities provide a third official act supporting the legality of the Stroganoff transfer.

Inspired by the 1998 Washington Conference Principles on Nazi-Confiscated Art, the Netherlands departed in 2001 from a "purely legal approach" to restitution in favor of "a more moral policy approach." ...

The new restitution policy was not an official pronouncement that the previous Dutch policy was invalid, however. Nor was the new policy established to re-examine old cases. Far from it, the new policy categorically did not apply to "settled case[s]," defined as those in which "either the claim for restitution resulted in a conscious and deliberate settlement or the claimant expressly renounced his claim for restitution."

To help administer the new policy, in 2001 the Dutch ... established a "Restitution Committee" [whose main task] was to advise the State Secretary on "applications for the restitution of items of cultural value of which the original owners involuntarily lost possession due to circumstances directly related to the Nazi regime *and which are currently in the possession of the State of the Netherlands.*" (Emphasis added).

With a new system in place, in 2004 von Saher filed a claim for 267 artworks ... still in the possession of the Dutch government. Crucially, the claim did not include the Cranachs. ... [T]he Restitution Committee ... issued a non-binding recommendation to the Secretary that the Dutch government return certain of the works to von Saher.

Von Saher asserts that the Restitution Committee's nonbinding recommendation to the Secretary was itself an act of state. ... But that interpretation is incorrect. Advisory recommendations that cannot bind the sovereign are not acts of state. ...

The Dutch State Secretary then issued a *binding* decision on von Saher's restitution claim. ... Importantly, the Secretary disavowed the Committee's findings. ... "Unlike the Restitution Committee I am of the opinion that in this case it is a matter of restoration of rights which has been settled." The Secretary concluded that the von Saher claim was "settled" by the 1999 "final decision" of the Court of Appeals. ... Because von Saher's case was "settled," her claim was "not included in the current restitution policy."

Although von Saher's was a settled claim that fell outside the new policy, the Secretary nonetheless decided, *ex gratia*, to return to von Saher the over 200 paintings ... that were still in Dutch possession. ...

The Dutch government's decision to return the paintings still in its possession did not disrupt the government's prior, binding acts of state concerning the

Cranachs. The State Secretary . . . explicitly stated that the Cranachs were "not a part of the claim for which [she] decided on February 6[, 2006] to make the return." Accordingly, she "refrain[ed] from an opinion regarding the two pieces of art under the restitution policy," and refused to "reverse[]" the prior decisions of the State Secretary . . . and the Dutch Court of Appeals. The Secretary's final determination that rights to the Cranachs had been fully "settled" marks the third act of the Dutch state counseling our application of the doctrine.

II. Exceptions to The Act of State Doctrine do not Apply

Having concluded that the Dutch government's transfer of the paintings and its later decisions about the conveyance were "sovereign acts," we still "must determine whether any exception to the act of state doctrine applies." None does.

A. "Purely Commercial Acts"

A plurality of the Supreme Court has recognized a potential exception to the act of state doctrine for "purely commercial acts"—*i.e.* where "foreign governments do not exercise powers peculiar to sovereigns," but rather "exercise only those powers that can also be exercised by private citizens." The Supreme Court and our court have never decided whether such an exception exists.

Nor must we decide in this case whether such an exception exists. Expropriation, claims processing, and government restitution schemes are not the province of private citizens. Those are "sovereign policy decision[s]" befitting sovereign acts. Because the Dutch government's administration of E100 and E133 and its settlement of Stroganoff's restitution claim are not "purely commercial acts," we do not decide whether such an exception exists.

B. The "Second Hickenlooper Amendment"

The eponymous "Second Hickenlooper Amendment" restricts application of the act of state doctrine, "but only in respect to 'a confiscation or other taking after January 1, 1959.' . . . [T]he Dutch government did not transfer the paintings to Stroganoff until 1966, a conveyance that "may constitute a taking or confiscation." Yet as the record illustrates, the Dutch government did not take or confiscate anything from von Saher's family in 1966; the family had long since "waive[d] the right to file for restoration of rights" in order to keep the substantial sale price. . . .

Further, the Amendment bars application of the act of state doctrine only when the governmental action violates "principles of international law." As von Saher's expert recognized, "international law respects the law as it stood at the time when the decisions were taken."

When the Dutch government administered E133 and E100, the . . . Allies imposed claims-filing deadlines for property taken by the Nazis. . . . [P]rospective owners who opted not to file a claim before the deadline were treated as having forfeited their rights to the property. For example, the Court of Restitution Appeals noted that a deadline set in Military Law 59 recognized that "it was imperative to fix a date with finality on which the legal rights of all parties, whether they be individual claimants or successor organizations could be ascertained." . . . The Dutch system clearly aligned with contemporaneous restitution schemes. . . .

Because the Dutch government did not "confiscate" the paintings from von Saher's family after 1959, and because the conveyance to Stroganoff did not violate international law, the Second Hickenlooper Amendment poses no obstacle to the application of the act of state doctrine.

III. The Policies Underlying the Act of State Doctrine Support its Application Here

Even where "the validity of the act of a foreign sovereign within its own territory is called into question, the policies underlying the act of state doctrine may not justify its application." The Supreme Court laid out three such policies in [*Banco Nacional de Cuba v.] Sabbatino*:

> [1] [T]he greater the degree of codification or consensus concerning a particular area of international law, the more appropriate it is for the judiciary to render decisions regarding it. . . . [2] [T]he less important the implications of an issue are for our foreign relations, the weaker the justification for exclusivity in the political branches. [3] The balance of relevant considerations may also be shifted if the government which perpetrated the challenged act of state is no longer in existence.

376 U.S. at 428, 84 S.Ct. 923.

All three of these policies support invocation of the doctrine here. Notably, no one has identified an international consensus regarding the *invalidity* of the Dutch post-war restitution procedures. If anything, the U.S. State Department and Office of the Solicitor General expressed in their amicus brief in *Von Saher I* that post-war restitution proceedings in the Netherlands were "bona fide." Second, the State Department and Solicitor General's Office confirmed in their brief that upholding the Dutch government's actions is important for U.S. foreign policy:

> When a foreign nation, like the Netherlands here, has conducted bona fide post-war internal restitution proceedings following the return of Nazi-confiscated art to that nation under the external restitution policy, *the United States has a substantial interest in respecting the outcome of the nation's proceedings.*

(Emphasis added). This position makes practical sense. Reaching into the Dutch government's post-war restitution system would require making sensitive political judgments that would undermine international comity. . . . Finally, we are dealing with a government that has been in continuous existence since the relevant acts of state. As noted, the decisions of the Dutch Court of Appeals and the State Secretary that deemed the Cranachs a "settled" question are quite recent. Von Saher asks us to do what the Dutch government refused to do in the 1999 Court of Appeals decision — restore her rights to the Cranachs. Second-guessing the Dutch government would violate our "commitment to respect the finality of 'appropriate actions' taken by foreign nations to facilitate the internal restitution of plundered art."

Our judiciary created the act of state doctrine for cases like this one. In applying it, we presume the validity of the Dutch government's sensitive policy judgments and avoid embroiling our domestic courts in re-litigating long-resolved matters entangled with foreign affairs. Without question, the Nazi plunder of artwork was a moral atrocity that compels an appropriate governmental response. But the record on remand reveals an official conveyance from the Dutch government to Stroganoff thrice "settled" by Dutch authorities. For all the reasons the doctrine exists, we decline the invitation to invalidate the official actions of the Netherlands.

AFFIRMED.

Concurring opinion omitted.

Federal Republic of Germany v. Philipp

171 S. Ct. 703, 2021 WL 357254 (Feb. 3, 2021)

Chief Justice Roberts delivered the opinion of the Court.

I

This case concerns several dozen medieval relics and devotional objects known as the Welfenschatz. . . .

. . . (During the late 1920s,) a consortium of three art firms owned by Jewish residents of Frankfurt purchased the Welfenschatz. . . . By 1931, the consortium had sold about half of the collection's pieces. . . .

Conditions facing the consortium changed dramatically after the collapse of the German economy and the rise of the Nazi government. . . . The complaint alleges . . . a combination of political persecution and physical threats [coerced] the consortium into selling the remaining pieces to Prussia in 1935 for approximately one-third of their value. . . .

. . . For nearly 60 years, the treasure has been maintained by Stiftung Preussischer Kulturbesitz (SPK) . . . and it is now displayed at a museum in Berlin. SPK is an instrumentality of the Federal Republic.

Respondents . . . trace their lineages back to the three members of the consortium. The heirs [claim the sale to Prussia was unlawful].

In 2014, the parties agreed to submit the claim to the German Advisory Commission. . . . After hearing from expert witnesses and reviewing documentary evidence, the Commission . . . concluded that the sale had occurred at a fair price without duress.

Disappointed by the proceedings in Germany, the heirs filed suit in Federal District Court in Washington, D.C. . . . seeking $250 million in compensation. Petitioners . . . moved to dismiss the case . . . because the heirs' claims did not fall within the FSIA's exception to immunity for "property taken in violation of international law." Germany reasoned that the purchase of the Welfenschatz could not have violated international law because a sovereign's taking of its own nationals' property is not unlawful under the international law of expropriation. The heirs responded that the exception did apply because Germany's purchase of the Welfenschatz was an act of genocide and the taking therefore violated the international law of genocide.

The District Court denied Germany's motion and a panel of the D.C. Circuit affirmed. The panel agreed . . . the exception for property taken in violation of international law was satisfied because "genocide perpetrated by a state even against its own nationals is a violation of international law." The D.C. Circuit declined Germany's request for en banc review.

* * *

We granted certiorari.

II

Enacted in 1976, the Foreign Sovereign Immunities Act supplies the ground rules for "obtaining jurisdiction over a foreign state in the courts of this country." The Act creates a baseline presumption of immunity from suit. "[U]nless a specified exception applies, a federal court lacks subject-matter jurisdiction over a claim against a foreign state."

The heirs contend that their claims fall within the exception for "property taken in violation of international law" because the coerced sale of the Welfenschatz, their property, constituted an act of genocide, and genocide is a violation of international human rights law. Germany argues that the exception is inapplicable because the relevant international law is the international law of property—not the law of genocide—and under the international law of property a foreign sovereign's taking of its own nationals' property remains a domestic affair. This "domestic takings rule" assumes that what a country does to property belonging to its own citizens within its own borders is not the subject of international law.

A

Known at the founding as the "law of nations," what we now refer to as international law customarily concerns relations among sovereign states, not relations between states and individuals.

The domestic takings rule invoked by Germany derives from this premise. Historically, a sovereign's taking of a foreigner's property, like any injury of a foreign national, implicated the international legal system because it "constituted an injury to the state of the alien's nationality." Such mistreatment was an affront to the sovereign, and "therefore the alien's state alone, and not the individual, could invoke the remedies of international law." A domestic taking by contrast did not interfere with relations among states.

The domestic takings rule has deep roots not only in international law but also in United States foreign policy. Secretary of State Cordell Hull most famously expressed the principle in a 1938 letter to the Mexican Ambassador following that country's nationalization of American oil fields. The Secretary conceded "the right of a foreign government to treat its own nationals in this fashion if it so desires. This is a matter of domestic concern." The United States, however, could not "accept the idea" that "these plans can be carried forward at the expense of our citizens."

The domestic takings rule endured even as international law increasingly came to be seen as constraining how states interacted not just with other states but also with individuals, including their own citizens. The United Nations Universal Declaration of Human Rights and Convention on the Prevention of Genocide became part of a growing body of human rights law that made "how a state treats individual human beings . . . a matter of international concern." These human rights documents were silent, however, on the subject of property rights. International tribunals therefore continued to maintain that international law governed "confiscation of the property of foreigners," but "measures taken by a State with respect to the property of its own nationals are not subject to these principles."

* * *

We confronted this dispute over the existence of international law constraints on sovereign takings in [*Banco Nacional de Cuba v. Sabbatino*, 376 U.S. 398 (1964),] where we were asked to decide claims arising out of Cuba's nationalization of American sugar interests in 1960. . . . Hesitant to delve into this controversy, we instead invoked the act of state doctrine, which prevents United States courts from determining the validity of the public acts of a foreign sovereign.

Congress did not applaud the Court's reticence. Within months of *Sabbatino*, it passed the Second Hickenlooper Amendment. . . . The Amendment prohibits United States courts from applying the act of state doctrine where a "right[] to property is asserted" based upon a "taking . . . by an act of that state in violation of the principles of international law." Courts and commentators understood the Amendment to permit adjudication of claims . . . against foreign nations for expropriation of American-owned property. But nothing in the Amendment purported to alter any rule of international law, including the domestic takings rule.

Congress used language nearly identical to that of the Second Hickenlooper Amendment 12 years later in crafting the FSIA's expropriation exception. . . .

Based on this historical and legal background, courts arrived at a "consensus" that the expropriation exception's "reference to 'violation of international law' does not cover expropriations of property belonging to a country's own nationals." *Republic of Austria v. Altmann*, 541 U.S. 677, 713 (2004) (Breyer, J., concurring).

B

The heirs urge us to change course. They read "rights in property taken in violation of international law" . . . as a broad incorporation of any international norm. Focusing on human rights law, the heirs rely on the United Nations Convention on Genocide. . . . According to the heirs, the forced sale of their ancestors' art constituted an act of genocide because the confiscation of property was one of the conditions the Third Reich inflicted on the Jewish population to bring about their destruction.

We need not decide whether the sale of the consortium's property was an act of genocide, because the expropriation exception is best read as referencing the international law of expropriation rather than of human rights. We do not look to the law of genocide to determine if we have jurisdiction over the heirs' common law property claims. We look to the law of property.

And in 1976, the state of that body of law was clear: A "taking of property" could be "wrongful under international law" only where a state deprived "an alien" of property....

The heirs concede that at the time of the FSIA's enactment the international law of expropriation retained the domestic takings rule. But they argue that Congress captured all of international law in the exception.... In support of that assertion, they note that the exception concerns "property *taken* in violation of international law"—not "property *takings* in violation of international law." This distinction between "takings" and "taken," they say, is the difference between incorporating the specific international law governing takings of property and incorporating international law writ large.

We would not place so much weight on a gerund. The text of the expropriation exception as a whole supports Germany's reading. In its entirety the clause provides that United States courts may exercise jurisdiction over a foreign sovereign in any case

> "in which rights in property taken in violation of international law are in issue and that property or any property exchanged for such property is present in the United States in connection with a commercial activity carried on in the United States by the foreign state; or that property or any property exchanged for such property is owned or operated by an agency or instrumentality of the foreign state and that agency or instrumentality is engaged in a commercial activity in the United States." 28 U.S.C. § 1605(a)(3).

The exception places repeated emphasis on property and property-related rights, while injuries and acts we might associate with genocide are notably lacking. That would be remarkable if the provision were intended to provide relief for atrocities such as the Holocaust. A statutory phrase concerning property rights most sensibly references the international law governing property rights, rather than the law of genocide.

* * *

Germany's interpretation of the exception is also more consistent with the FSIA's express goal of codifying the restrictive theory of sovereign immunity.... Under the restrictive view... immunity extends to a sovereign's public but not its private acts. Most of the FSIA's exceptions, such as the exception for "commercial activity carried on in the United States," comport with the overarching framework of the restrictive theory.

It is true that the expropriation exception, because it permits the exercise of jurisdiction over some public acts of expropriation, goes beyond even the restrictive view. In this way, the exception is unique; no other country has adopted a comparable limitation on sovereign immunity.

History and context explain this nonconformity. As events such as Secretary Hull's letter and the Second Hickenlooper Amendment demonstrate, the United States has long sought to protect the property of its citizens abroad as part of a defense of America's free enterprise system.

Given that the FSIA "largely codifies" the restrictive theory, however, we take seriously the Act's general effort to preserve a dichotomy between private and public acts. It would destroy that distinction were we to subject all manner of sovereign public acts to judicial scrutiny under the FSIA by transforming the expropriation exception into an all-purpose jurisdictional hook for adjudicating human rights violations.

C

Other provisions of the FSIA confirm Germany's position. The heirs' approach, for example, would circumvent the reticulated boundaries Congress placed in the FSIA with regard to human rights violations. Where Congress did target injuries associated with such acts, including torture or death, it did so explicitly and with precision. . . .

These restrictions would be of little consequence if human rights abuses could be packaged as violations of property rights and thereby brought within the expropriation exception to sovereign immunity. And there is no reason to suppose Congress thought acts of genocide or other human rights violations to be especially deserving of redress only when accompanied by infringement of property rights. We have previously rejected efforts to insert modern human rights law into FSIA exceptions ill suited to the task. We do so again today.

We have recognized that "'United States law governs domestically but does not rule the world.'" We interpret the FSIA as we do other statutes affecting international relations: to avoid, where possible, "producing friction in our relations with [other] nations and leading some to reciprocate by granting their courts permission to embroil the United States in expensive and difficult litigation."

As a Nation, we would be surprised—and might even initiate reciprocal action—if a court in Germany adjudicated claims by Americans that they were entitled to hundreds of millions of dollars because of human rights violations committed by the United States Government years ago. There is no reason to anticipate that Germany's reaction would be any different were American courts to exercise the jurisdiction claimed in this case.

III

The heirs offer several counterarguments, but none can overcome the text, context, and history of the expropriation exception.

First, the heirs rely on the 2016 Foreign Cultural Exchange Jurisdictional Immunity Clarification Act. The Act amends the FSIA to explain that participation in specified "art exhibition activities" does not qualify as "commercial activity" within the meaning of the expropriation exception. . . . The provision, however, does not apply to claims brought against Germany arising out of the period from January 1933 through May 1945. According to the heirs, this clarification of the expropriation exception shows that Congress anticipated Nazi-era claims could be adjudicated by way of that exception.

We agree with the heirs, but only to a limited extent. Claims concerning Nazi-era art takings could be brought under the expropriation exception where the claims involve the taking of a *foreign* national's property. As for the heirs' suggestion that the Clarification Act demonstrates that Congress meant to abrogate immunity for any Nazi-era claim, however, we do not interpret Congress's effort to *preserve* sovereign immunity in a narrow, particularized context—art shows—as supporting the broad *elimination* of sovereign immunity across all areas of law. The Clarification Act did not purport to amend the critical phrase here—"taken in violation of international law"—and we will not construe it to do so.

The heirs also rely on other statutes aimed at promoting restitution to the victims of the Holocaust. The Acts include the Holocaust Victims Redress Act of 1998; the Holocaust Expropriated Art Recovery Act of 2016 (HEAR Act; and the Justice for Uncompensated Survivors Today (JUST) Act of 2017. . . .

* * *

These laws do not speak to sovereign immunity. That is the province of the FSIA, which provides the carefully constructed framework necessary for addressing an issue of such international concern. The heirs have not shown that the FSIA allows them to bring their claims against Germany. We cannot permit them to bypass its design.

IV

We hold that the phrase "rights in property taken in violation of international law," as used in the FSIA's expropriation exception, refers to violations of the international law of expropriation and thereby incorporates the domestic takings rule.

We do not address Germany's argument that the District Court was obligated to abstain from deciding the case on international comity grounds. Nor do we consider an alternative argument noted by the heirs: that the sale . . . is not subject to the domestic takings rule because the consortium members were not German nationals at the time of the transaction. The Court of Appeals should direct the District Court to consider this argument, including whether it was adequately preserved below.

The judgment of the Court of Appeals for the D.C. Circuit is vacated, and the case is remanded for further proceedings consistent with this opinion.

It is so ordered.

Notes and Questions

1. *Aftermath*. Following the Supreme Court's decision in *Altmann*, the plaintiffs and the Austrian government agreed to end all litigation and submitted to final binding arbitration. In 2006, the ownership of five Klimts was awarded to the plaintiffs. The stunning *Adele Bloch-Bauer I* was privately sold for a reported $135 million to Ronald S. Lauder. It is on display at the Neue Galerie in New York, a museum founded in part by Mr. Lauder. The remaining recovered works were sold at Christie's November 2006 auction for $192.7 million. Maria Altmann died on February 7, 2011, at the age of 94. See Anne-Marie O'Connor, The Lady in Gold: The Extraordinary Tale of Gustav Klimt's Masterpiece, Portrait of Adele Bloch-Bauer (2015).

Elizabeth Taylor's title to the Van Gogh was established when the petition for writ of certiorari was denied. 552 U.S. 990 (2007). Elizabeth Taylor died on March 23, 2011 at the age of 79. Her van Gogh was sold in 2012 at a Christie's auction in London for $16 million, and it was later sold in Australia in 2018 for $40 million. Australian Associated Press, *Elizabeth Taylor's Van Gogh Fetches $US40 million,* May 16, 2018.

The Norton Simon Museum's title was similarly established when the petition for writ of certiorari was denied. 587 U.S.—, 139 S. Ct. 2616 (May 20, 2019). Perhaps not conclusively established, however. On October 27, 2020, reports suggest Ukraine is seeking to present its claim to the Cranachs. Marina Baranovskaya, *Ukraine seeks to bring home Renaissance artwork sold under false pretenses,* Oct. 27, 2020, at www.dw.com/en/ukraine-seeks-to-bring-home-renaissance-artwork-sold-under-false-pretenses/a-55407860.

2. *Impact of Altmann*. Despite the Court's conclusion "emphasizing the narrowness" of the holding, *Altmann* was extremely important for Nazi-era art cases. It removed the traditional jurisdictional bar of sovereign immunity, thereby allowing private U.S. litigants to bring cases in U.S. courts directly against foreign governments. Many private litigants welcomed the Court's decision. From the perspective of international law and relations, the *Altmann* decision raised serious issues that persist.

The U.S. government had filed an amicus brief on behalf of Austria in the Supreme Court arguing against the retroactivity of the FSIA. The government's position was that non-retroactivity was particularly important in this type of case where the conduct was extensively addressed in treaties, agreements, and separate legislation on the assumption that claims could not be litigated in the U.S. courts. Additionally, retroactively denying immunity was against international law norms and could jeopardize U.S. foreign interests going forward. Some academic commentators agree. See, e.g., Mary Ellen O'Connell, *Beyond Wealth: Stories of Art, War and Greed*, 59 Ala. L. Rev. 1075 (2008). *Altmann* sidestepped considering the "'so-called' act of state doctrine." If the parties had not agreed to final binding arbitration, could Austria have argued the Act of State doctrine? In light of *Von Saher*, the answer seems to be yes; however, the significant factual differences between the two cases do not suggest the doctrine would necessarily be deemed dispositive.

3. *Impact of Orkin. Altmann* successfully removed the jurisdictional bar and thereby greatly increased the pool of potential defendants and the visibility and viability of Nazi-era claims. *Orkin* attempted to have an equally dramatic impact: the creation of a new federal claim based on the Sense of Congress statement. That attempt was unsuccessful. Short of a private cause of action, what "good faith efforts to facilitate the return of private property" would you suggest? Is there a due process concern? How would you resolve it? See Marie Cornu & Marc-André Renold, *New Developments in the Restitution of Cultural Property: Alternative Means of Dispute Resolution*, 17 Int'l J. Cult. Prop. 1 (2010), for a presentation of successful approaches that have been used in different locations throughout the world.

Factually, the Orkins' claim was premised on a sale under economic duress, not art confiscated by the Nazis. This was a significant and intentional departure from many prior Nazi-era art cases. Because the case was dismissed on statute of limitations grounds and lack of a private federal cause of action, this factual aspect of the case was not fully developed. Should sales under duress or economic coercion be viewed the same as confiscated art? From whose perspective should we consider that question? Does the HEAR Act offer any insight on this question? See Zuckerman v. Metropolitan Museum of Art, 928 F.3d 186 (2d Cir. 2019), *supra*.

4. *Impact of Von Saher.* The Ninth Circuit's opinion, after ten years of litigation, was a signal that the Act of State doctrine retains vitality as a defense for private litigants. Also noteworthy was the concurring opinion's observation that the case should not have proceeded past the district court's dismissal on preemption grounds in March 2012. The impact of *Von Saher* is uncertain, although its careful presentation of the Act of State doctrine within the facts of the case suggests attention to foreign policy implications is not misplaced.

5. *Impact of Philipp.* Less than two months after hearing oral arguments on December 7, 2020, the Supreme Court issued its unanimous decision in *Philipp*. The Court held that FSIA's expropriation exception is to be interpreted in light of the international law governing property rights and not the international law of genocide. "We do not look to the law of genocide.... We look to the law of property." 2021 WL 357254 at *6. In doing so, the Court confirmed the long-established domestic takings rule—expropriations of property belonging to a country's own nationals are not covered by FSIA's expropriation exception. The Court reasoned from the history, text, and context of the FSIA. It is hard to miss the Court's pragmatic understanding of sovereignty: "As a Nation, we would be surprised... if a court in Germany adjudicated claims by Americans that they were entitled to hundreds of millions of dollars because of human rights violations committed by the United States years ago." *Id.* at *9. *Philipp* is a significant case and deserves more attention and consideration than these preliminary remarks written within a day of the Court's opinion can reasonably provide. That said, *Philipp* may not be over. The Court vacated and remanded the case. The question of whether the members

of the consortium were German nationals at the time of the sale may need to be determined.

6. *Ongoing Discoveries.* World War II ended in 1945, yet over the subsequent 75 years, looted artworks have continued to surface. Often, the artworks come to the market because the owner dies and the beneficiaries decide to sell the artworks. Sometimes, however, artworks re-appear in surprising situations. For example, in September 2010, an elderly gentleman was traveling by train from Zurich to Munich as he had done many, many times in the past. Cornelius Gurlitt was asked a routine question by a customs official, why was he traveling that day? He responded that he had just sold an artwork and he was returning home. He appeared nervous as he showed the man his 9,000 Euros sales proceeds. Further investigation into a possible tax issue led the authorities to search his home. That search revealed over 1,500 artworks, including works by Picasso, Chagall, Matisse, and Delacroix. The art trove was complicated, because his father Hildebrand Gurlitt was a noted art dealer with ties to the Third Reich. Extensive provenance research on 1,039 of the artworks over a five-year period confirmed that 12 were looted or likely looted works, and 297 were considered degenerate art. It is hoped that with technology and increasing cooperation across national boundaries, provenance research will identify more artworks. It is worth noting that provenance research is intensely time-consuming and requires highly specialized art historians and others to complete. It is not an easy task. See Sophie Gilbert, *The Persistent Crime of Nazi-Looted Art*, The Atlantic, March 11, 2018, available at www.theatlantic.com/entertainment/archive/2018/03/cornelius-gurlitt-nazi-looted-art/554936/; Nicholas M. O'Donnell, A Tragic Fate: Law and Ethics in the Battle Over Nazi-Looted Art (2017).

6. Antiquities Looting—Again

Barnet v. Ministry of Culture and Sports of the Hellenic Republic

961 F.3d 193 (2d Cir. 2020)

Menashi, Circuit Judge:

In this appeal, we decide whether Greece's assertion of ownership over an ancient horse figurine was "in connection with a commercial activity" by Greece within the meaning of the Foreign Sovereign Immunities Act. We conclude that the assertion of ownership was in connection with Greece's enactment and enforcement of patrimony laws that declare the figurine to be the property of Greece and that these are sovereign rather than commercial activities. Accordingly, the FSIA does not authorize jurisdiction over this dispute, and we reverse and remand with instructions to dismiss for lack of jurisdiction.

* * *

Background

I

In 1932, Greece enacted the Antiquities Act, which states that "[a]ll antiquities movable or immovable found in Greece and in any State land, in rivers, lakes and at the bottom of the sea, and in municipal, monasterial and private estates from ancient times onwards, are the property of the State." Diatagma (1932:5351) [hereinafter Antiquities Act] . . . .

* * *

In 2002, Greece enacted the On the Protection of Antiquities and Cultural Heritage in General Act, which states that "the Greek State shall care for the protection of cultural objects originating from Greek territory whenever they may have been removed from it" and "wherever they are located." Nomos (2002:3028) [hereinafter Cultural Heritage Act]. The 2002 Act further provides that "[m]ovable ancient monuments dating up to 1453 belong to the State in terms of ownership and possession, are imprescriptible and *extra commercium*." *Id.*, Art. 21(1). The holder of such an object "may transfer his possession, after notifying the [Ministry of Culture] of his intention and the personal data of the candidate holder, who shall submit an application for a permit of possession," but "[a]ny transfer effected without this permit shall be null and void and the movable monuments shall be taken without formalities by the State." *Id.*, Art. 28(1).

* * *

II

The bronze horse figurine at the center of this case is "of Corinthian type, 14 cm tall, [and] from the Geometric Period." It was sold at a public auction in Switzerland in 1967. Thereafter, the figurine was acquired by antiquities dealer Robin Symes, who then sold it to [the Barnets] in 1973. [Mr. Barnet passed away in 1992, and Mrs. Barnet in 2017. Thereafter, her] Trust consigned the figurine for auction at Sotheby's.

Sotheby's planned to auction the figurine on May 14, 2018, in New York City. On April 25, 2018, Sotheby's published an auction catalogue online that included the figurine as "Lot 4, Greek Figure of a Horse of Corinthian type, of stylized attenuated form standing on an openwork rectangular base, with crested mane with fine notches at the edge, cylindrical muzzle nearly encircled by grooved markings, long striated ears, and fragmentary tail, Bronze, Height 5 ½ in (14 cm), Geometric Period, circa 8th Century BC, Greek," with an estimated auction price of $150,000 to $250,000.

On May 11, 2018, the Friday prior to the Monday auction date, the Greek Ministry of Culture emailed a letter to Sotheby's marked "URGENT." The letter made the following points:

- Greece "has become aware of your intention to auction, among other items, a bronze figurine of a horse, dated in the end of the Geometric era, in a session that will take place in New York in 14/05/2018."

> • "[T]hree photos of this specific figurine are included in the Symes-Michailides photo archive," and the "specific figurine, which you intend to auction, is of Greek origin."
>
> • "There are no records in the archives of our Service (i.e. an export permit from Greece) to prove that this figurine has left the country in a legal way."
>
> • "The Greek National Law 5351/1932 on Antiquities and the one following it, Law 3028/2002, on the Protection of Antiquities and Cultural Heritage in General state that all movable ancient monuments belong to the State in terms of ownership and possession, are imprescriptible and *extra commercium*. Additionally, according to the Greek Criminal Law (Act 3028/2002, article 55) the illegal acquisition and trading of cultural property of great value . . . constitutes a serious criminal offence, irrespective of where it takes place."
>
> * * *
>
> • "For all above reasons and reserving all our rights, WE ASK YOU TO:— immediately withdraw the ancient Greek figurine of the list from the items to be auctioned on 14/05/2018[;] refrain, from today on, from any activity related to any type of delivery of the figurine to any third party[; and] contact us immediately in order to confirm your intention to conform to the above and subsequently cooperate for the repatriation of the coin [sic] and its return to the Greek state." *Id.* at 133–34.

After receiving the letter, Sotheby's withdrew the figurine from its auction and responded to Greece in writing, disputing Greece's claim to ownership but inviting Greece to provide any evidence in support of its claim. Greece did not respond.

On June 5, 2018, Sotheby's and the trustees of the Trust sued Greece in the Southern District of New York. Plaintiffs seek no damages or injunctive relief. The sole count for relief is for a "Declaration of Ownership."

Greece filed a motion to dismiss for lack of jurisdiction, arguing that Greece was immune from suit by reason of sovereign immunity and that Plaintiffs had not satisfied any FSIA exception. On June 21, 2019, the district court denied that motion. . . .

Greece filed an interlocutory appeal of that order. . . .

Discussion

I

"The FSIA provides the sole basis for obtaining jurisdiction over a foreign state in the courts of this country. . . ." Sovereign immunity from suit is the default rule, subject only to specific exceptions.

The parties agree that the only exception at issue in this case is the "commercial-activity exception," which contains three separate clauses:

> A foreign state shall not be immune from the jurisdiction of courts of the United States . . . in any case . . . in which the action is based [1] upon a

> commercial activity carried on in the United States by the foreign state; or [2] upon an act performed in the United States in connection with a commercial activity of the foreign state elsewhere; or [3] upon an act outside the territory of the United States in connection with a commercial activity of the foreign state elsewhere and that act causes a direct effect in the United States[.]

28 U.S.C. § 1605(a)(2).

Plaintiffs focus on clause 3, also known as the "direct-effect clause," and accordingly our analysis is limited to that provision. To satisfy the clause, the suit must be "(1) based upon an act outside the territory of the United States; (2) that was taken in connection with a commercial activity of [Greece] outside this country; and (3) that caused a direct effect in the United States."

* * *

II

We first must identify Greece's predicate "act" that "serves as the basis for plaintiffs' claims." We look for the "core" action taken by Greece outside the United States for which relief is sought as defined by the "elements of [the] claim that, if proven, would entitle [Plaintiffs] to relief under [their] theory of the case."

The district court correctly concluded that "sending the Demand Letter" from Greece to Sotheby's in May 2018 was the predicate act. The letter "assert[ed] an ownership interest in the Bronze Horse when demanding that Sotheby's withdraw the figure from the auction." The complaint confirms that sending the letter claiming ownership was the "core" act that Plaintiffs challenge.

Having identified the core predicate act—sending a letter asserting ownership of the figurine—we next determine whether that act was taken "in connection with a commercial activity" by Greece outside the United States. It was not.

The district court analyzed whether sending a letter claiming ownership was an act that a private party may typically undertake in the marketplace and, concluding that it was, the court found that act to be commercial and therefore not sovereign. The error in this analysis was treating Greece's act of sending the letter as *both* the predicate "act" *and* the related "commercial activity" required by § 1605(a)(2). The direct-effect clause applies when a suit seeks relief for an "act" that a foreign state undertakes "in connection with a commercial activity," and a single act cannot be undertaken in connection with itself....

But we think the parties have properly focused on the direct-effect clause because the letter was not a single, self-contained activity.... It is apparent that Greece undertook the act of sending the letter in connection with its claim of ownership over the figurine pursuant to its patrimony laws. Identifying the activity in connection with which the letter was sent, as the statute requires, reveals its sovereign nature: Greece has claimed ownership over the figurine by adopting legislation that nationalizes historical artifacts and by enforcing those patrimony laws.

In its letter to Sotheby's, Greece expressly invoked the "Greek National Law 5351/1932 on Antiquities and the one following it, Law 3028/2002, on the Protection of Antiquities and Cultural Heritage in General," which "state that all movable ancient monuments belong to the State in terms of ownership and possession, are imprescriptible and *extra commercium*." Those laws declare artifacts such as the figurine to be the property of Greece. Those laws also regulate the export of artifacts such as the figurine and impose criminal liability in certain circumstances, as Greece noted in its letter.

Nationalizing property is a distinctly sovereign act. Just as nationalization or expropriation of property is considered a sovereign activity rather than a commercial "claim of ownership" by the foreign state, so too here Greece is acting in a sovereign capacity by enforcing laws that regulate ownership and export of nationalized artifacts. A "foreign state's exercise of the power of its police has long been understood ... as peculiarly sovereign in nature," as has "the sovereign's right to regulate its exports" through a permitting process.

The FSIA directs that the commercial or sovereign character of an activity be determined by reference to the "nature" of the activity rather than its "purpose." Here, the "outward form" of Greece's "activity" was the enactment and enforcement of laws declaring the figurine to be state property. Its insistence on recognition of and obedience to its patrimony laws are not "the *type* of actions by which a private party engages in 'trade and traffic or commerce,'" nor is that activity "analogous to a private commercial transaction." Plaintiffs contend that because Greece has not physically seized the figurine it has not undertaken the sovereign acts of nationalization or law enforcement. But we think that adopting its patrimony laws and insisting on compliance with those laws is enough to establish that its activity was sovereign rather than commercial.... Even though a private party might be able to send a letter disputing ownership of an object, no private party could nationalize historical artifacts and regulate the export and ownership of those nationalized artifacts—and that is the activity in connection with which Greece sent its letter.

* * *

Plaintiffs contend in response that the patrimony laws may not even apply to this particular figurine because it is unclear whether it left Greece before the patrimony laws went into effect or because the laws may be unenforceable here because of due process concerns about applying Greek law to property in the United States. But these arguments confirm that the issue in this case—ownership of the figurine—is inextricably bound up with sovereign activity. Litigation of Plaintiffs' claims would require the district court to evaluate the validity, scope, and application of Greece's patrimony laws—putting at issue precisely those sorts of sovereign acts for which Greece enjoys sovereign immunity. "[P]ermitting the cause of action here would appear to undermine the immunity Congress intended to confer on [Greece] under the FSIA."

Conclusion

Greece's act of sending the letter was not in connection with a commercial activity outside of the United States. Because the direct-effect clause of the commercial-activity exception in 28 U.S.C. § 1605(a)(2) is not satisfied, the district court erred in concluding that it had jurisdiction. We therefore . . . REVERSE. . . .

Notes and Questions

1. *FSIA and the Direct-Effect Clause. Barnet* raises another exception to sovereign immunity, that of the direct-effect clause. In order for that exception to apply, two requirements must be met. First, there must be a predicate act taken by the sovereign outside of the U.S. Second, that predicate act must be "in connection with a commercial activity." The predicate act was the sending of the letter to Sotheby's asserting its ownership claim, and it was also alleged to be the "in connection with" activity. The Second Circuit rejected the one act serving both requirements. Beyond that jurisdictional determination, the Second Circuit also made clear that the substance of Greece's actions was inherently sovereign in nature. It was defining and protecting its cultural property, not merely acting like an owner of private property.

2. *Transactional Takeaway. Barnet* creates another ownership dilemma for the art market. A nation can give notice of a patrimony-type ownership claim against a property without fear of being embroiled in litigation. That is undoubtedly a powerful tool for combating antiquities looting. On the other hand, the U.S. possessor now has property under a cloud of title and cannot require that nation to defend its claim in court. What does *Barnet* suggest for sales going forward?

7. Law in Process

With the opening of government records, especially Eastern European, in the 1990s, increasing ease of access to international databases, shifting public attitudes to art title disputes, and the record high values for artworks, litigation or the threat of litigation over title to art has intensified. Newton's third law of motion holds true: for every action, there is an equal and opposite reaction. The reactions in the art world to the heightened concerns over questions of title include transactional safeguards, pre-emptive litigation, self-regulation, and specific legislation.

1. *Transactional Responses.* In *O'Keeffe*, *Lubell* and *Autocephalous Church*, there was a common thread of notice—whether giving notice of the theft (as in *O'Keeffe* and *Lubell*) or checking for that notice (as in *Autocephalous Church*). Giving notice in medieval market days was relatively easy to accomplish. An owner would go to the local market to search for his goods while loudly and widely proclaiming the theft of his property. This had two consequences—the loud and public giving of notice decreased the likelihood of there being a good faith buyer, and searching the

local market had a reasonable likelihood of success. See Peter M. Smith, *Valediction to Market Overt*, 41 AM. J. LEGAL HIST. at 228 (1997). Global art markets changed the simple paradigm of the owner's local and vocal notice. Not surprisingly, technology became the new town crier, serving the function of global and digitally-accessible notice.

The legitimate art market has two primary transactional responses for title concerns: art registries for notice and diligence, and title insurance for economic protection.

a. Art registries. The Art Loss Register (ALR, www.artloss.com) is a for-profit company in London created in 1990 by major businesses in the insurance and art industries. ALR's primary business functions are to offer and maintain private item registration for stolen art, antiques and collectables and to assist in search and recovery services. ALR also provides registration for items "pre-loss." The databases are maintained on a confidential basis and are not publicly searchable. There is a fee for item registration and a fee upon the successful recovery of the item. See Eileen Kinsella, *The Art Loss Register Is Entangled in Three Major International Art Disputes*, ARTNETNEWS, June 5, 2015, available at https://news-artnet.com/art-world/art-loss-register-embroiled-least-three-international-art-disputes-305134.

Artive, an art registry, is a not-for-profit company headquartered in the United States since 2016 (www.artive.org). Its stated mission is to help protect and preserve the world's cultural heritage by recording and indexing data for present and future generations. It intends to do so through the use of technology, including blockchain. Consistent with its mission to reduce the information gap that exists in the art market, Artive's item registration is free and its database is freely accessible. Due diligence reports are also available for a fee and based on Artive's own database as well as other relevant external databases.

Interpol (www.interpol.int) has been involved in investigating cultural property thefts since 1947. Its database has over 50,000 items reported as stolen by authorized law enforcement agencies. Anyone can apply to check the database in real time. Interpol also maintains an active art section that disseminates information about stolen or forged works in international commerce. Domestically, since 2004, the FBI has an Art Crime Team of 20 specialists throughout the country. In 2010, the Bureau started the National Stolen Art File (NSAF), a free online searchable database of works stolen primarily in the U.S., with some international pieces included (www.fbi.gov/investigate/violent-crime-art-theft). To be included in the NSAF, the item stolen must be uniquely identifiable, have historic or artistic significance, and have a value of $2,000 or more (less, if associated with a major crime). While only law enforcement can add items to the database, the site itself is publicly searchable (other than investigative information), underscoring a welcome public-private cooperation.

The Nazi-Era Provenance Internet Portal is a searchable database of objects held in U.S. museums that changed hands in Continental Europe during the Nazi-era (1933–1945). (www.nepip.org). Other databases and websites include Central Registry of Information on Looted Cultural Property, 1933–1945, www.lootedart.com; Commission for Art Recovery, www.commartrecovery.org; Holocaust Art Restitution Project, plundered-art.blogspot.com; and New York's Holocaust Claims Processing Office, www.dfs.ny.gov/consumers/holocaust_claims.

b. Art title insurance. Despite criticism, *Lubell* supports the general proposition that an owner does not need to give notice of an art theft. Lack of diligence can be considered, however, as part of a laches defense. Transactionally, this gap means that searching the art registries and obtaining a clean search result, while showing due diligence for the purchaser, does not equate to clear title for the purchaser. A second protective step, one that is the norm for real estate transactions, is title insurance.

Art title insurance is a relatively new product for art transactions. Similar in concept to title insurance for real estate, the owner of the artwork would pay a one-time fee, averaging about 2–3% of appraised value, for title coverage. Coverage is for the present owner and extends to his heirs. The policies are not an off-the-shelf insurance product; they must be individually researched.

The relative newness of this type of policy and the small market of insurers means that a cost-benefit analysis for a potential insured is hard to reliably construct. Because of a general climate of increasing litigation and third-party claims, a consumer's peace of mind, which is probably the factual heart of all insurance, may be the most important factor. In reviewing any such title policy, carefully consider the exclusions and who is responsible for supplying provenance detail.

The art market could be becoming more receptive to art title insurance. The Salander bankruptcy auction at Christie's in June 2010 provided art title insurance to all purchasers. See Chapter 9, A.2 Recovering for Errant Dealer's Actions: Lawsuits and Insurance Claims, Note 2, following *Frigon v. Pacific Indemnity Company, infra*. ARIS, the pioneer in the U.S. offering art title insurance, is part of the Argo Group, a major publicly traded insurance group. See Kate Taylor, *Title Insurance Spreads to Art Sales*, N.Y. Times, Nov. 11, 2010, at C1.

2. *Quiet Title Actions: The Best Defense?* In March 2009, Yale University filed a complaint in federal district court seeking "to quiet its good title" to its masterpiece *The Night Café* by Vincent Van Gogh. *The Night Café* v. Konowaloff, 5 F. Supp. 3d 237 (D. Conn. 2009), *aff'd*, 620 F. App'x 60 (2015), *cert. denied*, 136 S. Ct. 1494 (2016) (upholding Yale's title). It was a preemptive strike by Yale to litigation threatened by the defendant, Pierre Konowaloff. Recall that Elizabeth Taylor took a similar approach in *Orkin v. Taylor, supra*.

The not-for-profit status and quasi-public function of a museum may be a double-edged sword. Assets held by a not-for-profit are held in trust, subject to a fiduciary duty to protect those assets for the public. See Toledo Museum of Art v.

Ullin, 477 F. Supp. 2d 802 (N.D. Ohio 2006), where TMA sought a declaratory judgment to quiet title for Paul Gauguin's *Street Scene in Tahiti* purchased by TMA in 1939 against heirs of Martha Nathan, a Jewish woman born in Germany, who after the war, vigorously pursued her rights to many works of art but specifically not this Gauguin; and Detroit Institute of Arts v. Ullin, No. 06-10333, 2007 U.S. Dist. Lexis (E.D. Mich. March 31, 2007), a similar action regarding van Gogh's *The Diggers*. In 2010, Konowaloff also sued the Metropolitan Museum of Art demanding the return of *Mme. Cezanne in the Conservatory*, on a similar theory. Konowaloff v. The Metropolitan Museum of Art, 2011 WL 4430856 (S.D.N.Y. 2011), *aff'd*, 702 F.3d 140 (2d Cir. 2012), *cert. denied*, 570 U.S. 906 (2013) (upholding the Met's title based on Act of State defense).

3. *A Word from Museums.* In December 2002, the directors of leading museums in Europe and North America signed the following:

Declaration on the Importance and Value of Universal Museums.

The international museum community shares the conviction that illegal traffic in archaeological, artistic, and ethnic objects must be firmly discouraged. We should, however, recognize that objects acquired in earlier times must be viewed in the light of different sensitivities and values, reflective of that earlier era. The objects and monumental works that were installed decades and even centuries ago in museums throughout Europe and America were acquired under conditions that are not comparable with current ones.

Over time, objects so acquired—whether by purchase, gift, or partage—have become part of the museums that have cared for them, and by extension part of the heritage of the nations which house them. Today we are especially sensitive to the subject of a work's original context, but we should not lose sight of the fact that museums too provide a valid and valuable context for objects that were long ago displaced from their original source. The universal admiration for ancient civilizations would not be so deeply established today were it not for the influence exercised by the artifacts of these cultures, widely available to an international public in major museums. Indeed, the sculpture of classical Greece, to take but one example, is an excellent illustration of this point and of the importance of public collecting. The centuries-long history of appreciation of Greek art began in antiquity, was renewed in Renaissance Italy, and subsequently spread through the rest of Europe and to the Americas. Its accession into the collections of public museums throughout the world marked the significance of Greek sculpture for mankind as a whole and its enduring value for the contemporary world. Moreover, the distinctly Greek aesthetic of these works appears all the more strongly as the result of their being seen and studied in direct proximity to products of other great civilizations.

Calls to repatriate objects that have belonged to museum collections for many years have become an important issue for museums. Although each case has to be judged individually, we should acknowledge that museums serve not just the citizens of one nation but the people of every nation. Museums are agents in the development of culture, whose mission is to foster knowledge by a continuous process of reinterpretation. Each object contributes to that process. To narrow the focus of museums whose collections are diverse and multifaceted would therefore be a disservice to all visitors.

Retrieved at: http://icom.museum/pdf/E_news2004/p4_2004-1.pdf. See also James Cuno, WHO OWNS ANTIQUITY? (2008), for a museum director's view of the importance of the encyclopedic museum for all people.

The concept of a universal museum is controversial and not universally accepted. One commentator notes that James Cuno did not include the term in his book and has, as head of the Getty, in fact repatriated works. See Kwame Opoku, *Declaration on the Importance and Value of Universal Museums: Singular Failure of an Arrogant Imperialistic Project,* ModernGhana (Jan. 27, 2013), available at www.modernghana.com/news/441891/declaration-on-the-importance-and-value-of univers.html; Tristram Hunt, *Should Museums return their colonial artefacts?,* The Guardian (June 29, 2019), available at https://www.theguardian.com/culture/2019/jun/29/should-museums-return-their-colonial-artefacts.

4. *Special Statute of Limitations.* When there is a recurring problem, it is common to seek a legislative solution. Recall the special art legislation regarding the opinion-or-warranty debate for authenticity disputes in Chapter 4, *supra*. A similar legislative approach occurred when California enacted a special statute of limitations for the recovery of Holocaust-era artwork in 2002. Cal. Code Civ. Pro. § 354.3 (since repealed). The Ninth Circuit declared the statute unconstitutional as being preempted under the foreign affairs doctrine. Von Saher v. The Norton Simon Museum of Art at Pasadena, 592 F.3d 954 (9th Cir. 2010).

Ultimately, and in partial response to that decision, Congress stepped in at the federal level to address the concern with the enactment of the HEAR Act in 2016. It imposes a uniform six-year statute of limitations for claims to recover artworks lost due to Nazi persecution "[n]otwithstanding any other provision of Federal or State law." HEAR will sunset for claims filed after December 31, 2026. See A.3. Federal Statute of Limitations: HEAR Act, *supra*.

Other countries face the same dilemma. See, e.g., Leila Amineddoleh, *The Extension of Statutes of Limitations for the Restitution of Nazi-Looted Art,* 31 Ent. & Sports L. 23 (May 2014); Louise Carron, *On Law, Museums, and Nazi-Era Looted Art in France and the United States,* Center for Art Law (April 16, 2018), available at itsartlaw.org/2018/04/16/restitution-at-last/ (describing France's National Recoveries Registry (MNR—Musees Nationaux Recuperation) that lists the orphan works that France is safeguarding for the true owners; for these works, there is no statute of limitations).

5. *Tax Solutions?* In practice, tax can play an important role in structuring or finetuning a transaction. The following commentary suggests using two income tax deductions, the charitable and theft loss deductions, as another approach to reconciling some stolen art cases between individual claimants. (Please note the theft loss deduction is not available to individuals for tax years 2018–2025.) The use of a tax approach may diffuse some of the zero-sum game approach of litigation and avoid a determination of wrongdoing by either of the two current claimants.

On Art Theft, Tax, And Time: Triangulating Ownership Disputes Through the Tax Code

Anne M. Rhodes, 43 San Diego L. Rev. 495 (2006)

III. Charitable Deduction

The charitable deduction has been a part of the federal income tax system since 1917. While there have been periodic reforms to Section 170 over time, the basic outline has remained fairly constant for most taxpayers: donations to qualified charities by taxpayers can qualify for an income tax deduction. Once, however, the charitable gift moves from a monetary one to a work of art, statutory and regulatory requirements, qualitative as well as quantitative, become extremely demanding. Despite the complexity, there are two variations where buyers in disputed art cases have successfully used the charitable deduction in fashioning a settlement. One involved stolen antiquities returned to the Greek government using a U. S. charity as a conduit; the other involved the transfer of a Nazi-looted work of art to a U.S. museum.

A. Greece v. Ward: Mycenaean Treasure from Aidonia

In April 1993, the Michael Ward Gallery, a prominent antiquities gallery in New York, announced a show, "Gold of the Mycenaeans," featuring a rare collection of Greek antiquities dating from the 15th century BC. The exhibition catalogue showed a collection of gold jewelry and artifacts, with the collection's price set at $1,500,000. The collection was stunning, not only for its obvious aesthetic value, but, to some antiquities experts, for its obvious similarity to looted Mycenaean cemetery treasures from Aidonia. The government of Greece, having reviewed the catalogue, contacted the Ward Gallery to demand the return of its cultural property. The demand was unsuccessful. Within two weeks of the rejection, Greece files a lawsuit in the Southern District of New York requesting that the sale be enjoined and that Greece be declared the owner of the collection. For seven months, negotiations continued on the case.

Michael Ward, the Director of the Ward Gallery, was a prominent scholar-dealer and a member of a US presidential panel concerning art smuggling. He was determined to end the controversy without further litigation. A direct transfer of the disputed collection to Greece would certainly have done so, but instead a triangulation of ownership interests was created.

The Society for the Preservation of the Greek Heritage, a Washington-based 501(c)(3) charity, agreed to accept the donation of the collection from the Ward Gallery, and the Greek government simultaneously agreed to drop its claim against the Ward Gallery. The charitable deduction under the Internal Revenue Code was the critical link. For a transfer of property to a recognized public charity, the Ward Gallery could deduct the donation of the tangible personal property as long as the use of the tangible property was related to the charity's purposes. The Gallery would need to ascertain that the charity did not intend to sell the property or put it to an unrelated use. What was that intended use? It was to transfer the property back to Greece. By triangulating the transfer, through a conduit charity, Mr. Ward and the Greek government were able to settle their controversy.

B. Goodman v. Searle: Landscape with Smokestacks

Daniel C. Searle purchased a Degas pastel-over-monotype, Landscape with Smokestacks, for $850,000 in July 1987. A member of the Art Institute of Chicago's Board of Trustees, Mr. Searle was informed by the Art Institute of the availability of the Degas, as well as its desirability. But for a lack of acquisition funds, the Art Institute would itself have purchased the Degas. The Art Institute made the arrangements for Mr. Searle to view the Degas at the apartment of its then current owner in New York; and at Mr. Searle's request, the landscape was sent to the Art Institute for inspection. It was given a "clean bill of health." Seven years after his purchase, Mr. Searle loaned the Degas to the Metropolitan Museum of Art in New York for an exhibition. Grandsons of Friedrich and Louise Gutmann, who were killed in the Holocaust, saw the catalogue for the exhibition and recognized the work as one that had belonged to their grandparents. With their aunt Lili Gutmann, Nick and Simon Goodman sued Daniel Searle in July, 1996 for the return of the Degas. The controversy was highly publicized, by both print and broadcast media. The value of the Degas was estimated to be $1,100,000. On the eve of trial in summer 1998, the parties settled their litigation. The charitable deduction played a role.

The settlement agreement provided that each of Lili Gutmann, Nick Goodman, Simon Goodman and Daniel Searle would transfer her or his ownership interest in the Degas to the Art Institute of Chicago. Daniel Searle's transfer would be a gift of his interest; the Gutmann family transfers would be sales. The total sales price would be one-half of the then fair market value of the Degas.

By each side recognizing at some level an ownership interest of the other, and then by both triangulating their interests to create ownership in a new third party, the dispute was resolved. Today Landscape with Smokestacks hangs in the Art Institute with a plaque reflecting its prior dual ownership, a "purchase from the collection of Fritz and Louise Gutmann and a gift of Daniel C. Searle."

Mr. Searle paid $850,000 for the Degas in 1987 and received a $243,750 charitable deduction for the transfer of his ownership interests in 1998 to the Art Institute. Mr. Searle clearly suffered an economic loss. Was there another tax approach to explore?

IV. Theft Loss Deduction

Section 165(a) provides a general deduction for losses sustained in a taxable year, with subsection (c)(3) restricting individual taxpayers' personal, non-business losses to those arising from "fire, storm, shipwreck, or other casualty, or from theft." There is no statutory definition of theft; and the Regulations provide merely that theft is "deemed to include, but shall not necessarily be limited to, larceny, embezzlement, and robbery." Cases and rulings under Section 165(c)(3) nevertheless have drawn a tight line as to what constitutes a theft, and routinely distinguish theft losses from other losses, with the two elements of criminality and timing having particular prominence and relevance.

In order to claim a theft loss, a taxpayer first needs to prove an illegal, wrongful taking, not just that the property is missing.

Second, the taking must be illegal and done with criminal intent, with illegality being determined under the law of the state where the taking occurred. For thefts of a routine nature, say auto thefts, this is not a particularly stringent standard. In the context of a foreign country's expropriation or nationalization of a taxpayer's personal property, however, using the internal law of that country to determine illegality seldom yields a deduction for the taxpayer.

The Act of State doctrine may not necessarily foreclose a theft deduction when Nazi-looted art is returned to the original owner. First, one may argue the doctrine itself was inappropriately incorporated into the tax system. Simply put, a deduction by a taxpayer under the Internal Revenue Code does not interfere with the President's ability to set foreign policy, involve the United States Government in the internal affairs of a sovereign state, or pose a threat to that sovereign's assets. The realm of the doctrine is international diplomacy, not the Form 1040. Second, even if the Act of State doctrine is relevant to the Code, the facts of a particular case may negate its application. [Menzel v. List, 267 N.Y.S.2d 804 (1966)—Ed.]

Can an innocent buyer of Nazi-looted art legitimately now claim a theft loss deduction when that work of art is required to be returned to the heirs? Resolving the Section 165(c)(3) issue of timing will be critical to the decision.

Virtually all theft loss cases pose the situation of the taxpayer as the direct victim of the thief and the consequent theft; there are no intermediary transfers. The question of a time delay in a theft scenario was addressed early in the statute and was easily resolved in favor of the taxpayer: a theft was deemed to be sustained for purposes of the deduction when it was discovered. The lapse of time is not, therefore, by statutory pronouncement, fatal to the deduction. Yet when presented with a theft loss deduction claimed by an innocent purchaser one or more sales transactions removed from the thief, there is a split in the Circuits.

1. Boothe v. Commissioner, [82 T.C. 804 (1984), rev'd, 768 F.2d 1140 (9th Cir. 1985)]

In 1960, Mr. Boothe sold his interest in certain Soldier's Additional Homestead Rights, which he had purchased in 1959. These rights originally had been granted to certain soldiers who served in the Civil War, and allowed them to apply and receive a fee interest in certain federal lands. These rights were freely assignable. Mr. Boothe's rights were traceable to William H. Dooley, Jr., the original grantee, who perfected his claim in 1873. [I]n 1898, Mr. Dooley assigned all his rights to Mr. Black. Thereafter, in 1916, Mr. Dooley again sold all his rights to B.A. Mason. Thirty-five years after his purchase, Mr. Mason sold to Mr. Davis in 1951. It was from Mr. Davis's estate in 1959 that Mr. Boothe purchased the disputed rights for $4,400. Fourteen months later, Mr. Boothe then sells his interest to R. L. Spoo. When (an) attempt to exercise was made (by Spoo) with respect to land in Oregon, the Bureau held the rights invalid due to the 1898 assignment to Mr. Black.

Mr. Spoo then sues Mr. Boothe for breach of warranty of title and recovers a judgment of $20,792 in damages. Mr. Boothe pays the judgment in 1977 and claims a theft loss deduction on his income tax return. The Commissioner denies the theft loss deduction since Mr. Boothe was not the victim of a theft.

The sole issue before the Tax Court was the characterization of the $20,792 judgment paid by Mr. Boothe as either a theft loss under § 165(c) or a capital loss under § 162(f). It was unnecessary for the majority to determine if a taxpayer "who is not the direct victim" can claim the deduction as a theft loss. Two dissenting opinions supported by eight judges were filed.

On appeal, the Ninth Circuit, in a per curiam opinion, noted that the "unusual facts in this case created sharp differences of opinion. ... We agree and adopt the dissenting opinion of Judge Korner." Kosner viewed the case as involving two separate and distinct events. The first was a theft "even though (Boothe) was not the immediate purchaser from the fraudulent vendor." This theft occurred in 1959 when Mr. Boothe purchased his interest, but it was discovered by the taxpayer only when litigation was concluded in 1977, and thus deductible in 1977.

The Ninth Circuit in *Boothe* removed the perceived obstacle of direct connection between the thief and victim; and did so when the theft spanned 43–61 years (from the fraudulent sale by Mr. Dooley in 1916 to Mr. Boothe's innocent purchase in 1959 to discovery in 1977), multiple purchasers (Mr. Mason to Mr. Davis, to Mr. Boothe), and apparent judicial and administrative acceptance of validity (inclusion in Mr. Davis's estate, and Bureau of Land Management holding). These attributes of time, multiple sales and apparent title/acceptance will often be present in the Nazi-looted art cases. This makes *Boothe* very citable, but the sharp differences in opinion noted by the Ninth Circuit persist.

2. Krahmer v. U.S., [9 Ct. Cl. 49 (Claims Court 1985), aff'd in part and rev'd in part, 810 F. 2d 1145 (Fed. Cir. 1987)].

In 1985, the same year as the Ninth Circuit opinion in *Boothe*, the Claims Court decided *Krahmer v. United States*, another theft loss deduction case. In *Krahmer* not only was the timing of the alleged theft an issue, but another issue, particularly pertinent in art cases, emerged as well. The distinction between losses attributable to thefts involving art and those to misattribution or authenticity raised concerns about the scope and meaning of theft involving art for tax purposes.

The *Krahmer* trial court denied a theft loss deduction for misattribution of (a) Poussin painting. The Court determined that since there was no forgery but only "an erroneous statement by the seller as to the likely artist," it would be necessary for the taxpayer to establish that the seller defrauded the taxpayer by "knowingly and intentionally misattributing" the work.

The trial court allowed the deduction, for the second painting with the forged Chase signature, as ipso facto fraudulent:

> Unlike the "Poussin", the "Chase" painting was signed, and that signature was a forgery. Thus, anyone who sustained a loss on purchase in the belief that the painting was by William Merritt Chase was the victim of a theft by false pretenses or swindle.

As to the government's contention that the taxpayer must be the direct victim of the forger, the trial court was unpersuaded:

> It is apparent that Congress' concern was not to punish the wrongdoer but to provide tax relief to the *victim* of the loss. . . . The intended connection is between the taxpayer and the loss, or more specifically in this case, between the taxpayer and the theft, not between the taxpayer and the thief. Thus, it should make no difference in the application of this relief statute whether the taxpayer dealt directly with the forger or was the victim once or several steps removed.
>
> * * *
>
> Here, plaintiff has suffered a loss at the hands of a forger, however distant in time or privity was the forger's act. Plaintiff need not know the identity of the forger. He need only prove that the forgery was the cause of the loss. By his discovery of the forgery, perpetrated by persons unknown, plaintiff has satisfied his burden.

On appeal in 1987, the Federal Circuit Court of Appeals held the lower court's determination that the "mere existence of the forged signature . . . was sufficient to prove a theft by false pretenses is incorrect as a matter of law, and we reverse it." Significantly the Federal Circuit held that the taxpayer was required to show that the art dealer, from whom the taxpayer had purchased the painting, knowingly and intentionally defrauded him by the misattribution. The court required an active deception at the time of the taxpayer's purchase, reasserting a direct link between the thief and the taxpayer.

Conclusion

Six decades after the end of World War II, controversies over the ownership of Nazi-looted art continue to emerge. Time has worked a shift in perceptions and expectations for those controversies; time is no longer an ally for the repose of title. This unsettling of bona fide expectations of title for an innocent buyer raises claims in law and in equity that are equally meritorious to those of the original owners. For a legal system that adjudicates on a case by case basis, a claim over ownership of a unique work of art is a zero-sum game; one winner, one loser. This harsh reality of uniqueness, set against the competing interests of legitimate market concerns and demands of restorative justice, requires fresh and open inquiry into workable solutions.

Tax is an eminently practical system that affords two possible strategies for those ownership disputes. Using the charitable deduction would generally resolve the dispute by creating an outright public ownership, and hence public benefit and oversight. Using the theft loss deduction, ownership would generally remain private, but the public would nevertheless bear some of the direct financial costs in the ownership shift from one party to the other. The public benefit is admittedly less direct: assistance in dispute resolution, and support for private ownership of property as well as protection of legitimate market expectations. Perhaps because of this imbalance in public costs and benefits, the availability of the theft loss deduction may not be as straightforward as the charitable deduction. Time, manifested by the Service's apparent requirement of direct nexus between the thief and the taxpayer, should not be a stumbling block for the theft loss deduction strategy in the limited context of Nazi-looted art. The language of the Code does not require the nexus and perhaps even recognizes a different timeframe for theft. There is case law support for tracing the theft back in time through multiple purchases. Finally, general tax policy concerns do not and should not outweigh the stated U.S. policy to assist in the restoration of Nazi-looted art.

B. Liens, Claims, and Encumbrances

1. In General

Liens, claims, and encumbrances are indirect challenges to title. They proceed generally from disputed or unsatisfied economic obligations of the title holder or possessor. As the *Whitcraft* case demonstrates, there is risk to advisors in underestimating the reach of liens, claims, and encumbrances.

Whitcraft v. Brown

570 F.3d 268 (5th Cir. 2009)

BENAVIDES, J. Lois Whitcraft and Phillip Offill appeal from a civil contempt order issued by the district court in the underlying proceeding. We affirm in part and vacate in part the district court's contempt order.

I.

On July 2, 2007, the Securities and Exchange Commission ("SEC") sued certain individual and entities, including Jeffrey Bruteyn, son of Appellant Whitcraft and client of Appellant Offill, an attorney, for securities fraud. The SEC also joined ... [Hess Financial corporation, which was partially owned or controlled by Bruteyn]. The same day, the district court issued a temporary restraining order freezing Bruteyn's assets ("freeze order"). The freeze order provided in pertinent part that:

> Defendant and Relief Defendants, their officers, agents, employees, servants, attorneys and all persons in active concert or participation with them, who receive actual notice of this order by personal service or otherwise, are

> restrained and enjoined from, directly or indirectly, making any payment or expenditure of funds . . . and from assigning[,] conveying, transferring, encumbering, disbursing, dissipating, selling, hypothecating, or concealing any assets, monies, or other property owned by or in the actual or constructive possession of defendants or Relief Defendants.

SEC v. Amerifirst Funding, Inc., 2008 WL 282275, *1 (N.D.Tex. February 1, 2008). The court also filed an order appointing William D. Brown as temporary receiver, and granting him exclusive jurisdiction over all assets of the named defendants and relief defendants ("receivership order"). In relevant part, the receivership order directs:

> [a]ll persons, including defendants and Relief Defendants, and their officers, agents, servants, employees, brokers, facilitators, attorneys, and all persons in active concert or participation with them who receive actual notice of [the] order by personal service or otherwise [to] . . . promptly deliver to the Receiver all Receivership Assets in the possession or under the control of any one or more of them[.] No separate subpoena shall be required.

Id.

On July 5, 2007, Bruteyn and several of his business associates and personal friends met at the office of Offill, Bruteyn's lawyer, to discuss how Bruteyn would access funds for his living expenses and legal fees. . . . Bruteyn suggested that the money in [related corporation] United Financial's account be transferred to Hess Financial and be made available for his expenses. Offill informed Bruteyn that, because Hess Financial was subject to the freeze order, such a maneuver would violate the order.

Bruteyn then proposed selling a Picasso painting hanging in his bedroom to United Financial in exchange for $500,000. Offill initially expressed concern that the Picasso was covered by the freeze order but eventually opined that the transaction would be legal as Bruteyn maintained that the painting was owned by his mother, Lois Whitcraft ("Whitcraft"). Bruteyn phoned his mother and obtained her permission to sell the painting. That same day, United Financial purchased the Picasso for $431,161. The money was wired into Whitcraft's account and placed at Bruteyn's disposal.

* * *

On September 24, 2007, the receiver and the SEC filed a motion to show cause seeking to hold Bruteyn, Whitcraft . . . , and Offill in civil contempt for violating the receivership and freeze order through the transaction engineered on July 5, 2007. . . . Following the evidentiary hearing, on February 1, 2008, the district court found Bruteyn, Whitcraft, and Offill in contempt. The court held that there was clear and convincing evidence that Whitcraft and Offill knowingly aided and abetted Bruteyn in violating the freeze order. . . . Whitcraft and Offill alone appeal.

II.

We review contempt orders and sanctions imposed thereunder for an abuse of discretion. We review the district court's underlying findings of fact for clear error and its underlying conclusions of law de novo.

As the district court noted, "[a] movant in a civil contempt proceeding bears the burden of establishing by clear and convincing evidence 1) that a court order was in effect, 2) that the order required certain conduct by the respondent, and 3) that the respondent failed to comply with the court's order." A court order binds not only the parties subject thereto, but also non-parties who act with the enjoined party. Although good faith is not a defense to a civil contempt order, good faith is relevant to whether a non-party knowingly aided or abetted another in violating a court order.

III.

The district court held that Offill had violated the freeze order, which prohibited Bruteyn (and his officers, agents, servants, employees, and attorneys or other persons who were in active concert or participation with him) from "directly or indirectly[] making any payment or expenditure of funds" and "from assigning[,] conveying, transferring, encumbering, disbursing, dissipating, selling, hypothecating, or concealing any assets, monies, or other property owned by or in the actual or constructive possession" of Bruteyn or the relief defendants. Offill challenges the district court's holding that the receiver proved by "clear and convincing evidence" that (1) that a court order was in effect, (2) that the order required certain conduct by Offill, and (3) that the Offill failed to comply with the court's order.

The district court did not abuse its discretion in finding Offill in civil contempt. As to the first element of contempt, the parties do not dispute that at the time the Picasso was sold to United Financial on July 5, 2007, the freeze order was in effect. As to the second element, the order, by its terms, required certain conduct by Offill, who was Bruteyn's lawyer at the time of the transaction. The freeze order clearly states that it binds persons who "receive actual notice of this order by personal service or otherwise" including the defendant Bruteyn's "attorneys." On July 3, 2007, Offill accepted service of the SEC's complaint, which included the freeze order, on behalf of Bruteyn. Offill therefore had actual notice of the freeze order. Beyond being bound by the order by virtue of his role as Bruteyn's attorney, the district court also found that Offill was also a person in "active concert or participation" with Bruteyn. Offill—with full knowledge of the freeze order's terms—was an active participant in discussions about how to get funds to Bruteyn, approved of the sale of the Picasso, and Offill's office served as the place to consummate the sale. The final element of civil contempt—that the respondent failed to comply with the freeze order—was also satisfied. Offill failed to comply with court order by assisting Bruteyn in conveying and transferring "assets" and "monies" that were in Bruteyn's "actual or constructive possession." The Picasso was in Bruteyn's actual possession at the time of the sale—it hung in his bedroom in the home he used as his residence. Thus, the Picasso was an asset in the actual possession of Bruteyn, and was prohibited from being transferred under the freeze order. Offill's actions facilitating the sale of the Picasso "aided or abetted [Bruteyn] . . . with knowledge that [Bruteyn] was violating the court's orders." *Waffenschmidt* [*v. MacKay*], 763 F.2d at 726. The district court did not abuse its discretion in holding Offill in contempt of the freeze order.

* * *

IV.

For the foregoing reasons, the district court's order holding Offill . . . in civil contempt is AFFIRMED IN PART with regard to Phillip Offill. . . .

Notes and Questions

1. *Lawyer's Duties.* Offill knew that the suggested transaction with Hess Financial violated the freeze order; but he had a different opinion on the Picasso. One fact apparently influenced him: the Picasso hung in Bruteyn's bedroom, "in the home he used as his residence." The home was owned by Bruteyn's stepfather, and the Picasso was owned by Bruteyn's mother. Offill may have believed that another's true ownership trumped the freeze order. While another's true ownership may be the basis for a release or discharge of the freeze order for a particular piece of property, Offill's response to his client's request should have been framed by the words of the freeze order: "in the actual or constructive possession."

The Picasso was apparently only a "reproduction print of relatively modest value," and not an original, as Whitcraft asserted. Does this question of authenticity complicate the case? The sales transaction occurred on the same day, July 5th, that it was proposed, a rather tight time frame for the seller to gather, and the buyer to review, the documentation. Dispensing with documentation and moving too quickly can raise questions of breach of fiduciary duties for the corporate officers. What is Offill's professional responsibility? Who was his client?

2. *Scope.* ARIS, a company specializing in art title insurance, estimates that 25% of art title questions proceed from theft, and 75% proceed from liens, claims, and encumbrances. These latter questions may not technically dispute title but instead affect one's economic position with respect to the artwork. As a practical matter, that may be a distinction without a difference; an artwork that is subject to a lien, claim, or encumbrance may be seized and sold.

When dealing with liens, claims, and encumbrances in real property, a prospective buyer can check the pertinent recorder of deeds or title registration office. For artworks, there is no equivalent place or registry. Because of their economic focus, there are some traditional sources of liens, claims, and encumbrances that echo the 3Ds for selling art: debt, death and divorce.

Courts issue freeze orders, as in *Whitcraft*, to prevent property transfers pending resolution of the parties' dispute. Commonly, the filing of a bankruptcy suit involves a freeze order. A divorce court may issue an order freezing marital assets, which the court in Lindholm v. Brant, 925 A.2d 1048 (Conn. 2007), Chapter 2, *supra,* deemed a red flag, requiring some degree of inquiry in order for the buyer to be in good faith.

Art may be pledged as collateral for loans, and the borrowers are often allowed to continue their personal possession of the art. Transfers of the art, including merely moving from one location to another, may violate the terms of the loan. For example, in 2009, three large banks, ABN AMRO, JP Morgan Chase + Co, and Credit Suisse, all asserted creditor interests in art works owned, directly or indirectly, by a Dutch businessman. The art collection located in various places around the world had allegedly been double pledged as collateral. *ABN Amro secures Reijtenbagh art collection*, NRC HANDELSBLAD (April 27, 2009), http://vorige.nrc.nl/international/article2225388.ece/ABN_Amro_secures_Reijtenbagh_art_collection.

If litigation went to judgment, a judgment creditor may seek enforcement of the judgment through seizure of art. For example, federal marshals seized over $6 million of art from the booth of Galerie Gmurzynska, a Swiss art gallery at the 2009 Art Basel Miami Beach art fair to satisfy a private judgment for $750,000. The underlying suit was an insurance matter allegedly involving damage that occurred to a painting while on consignment at the defendant gallery. Works seized from Gmurzynska stand returned, THE ART NEWSPAPER at 1 (Art Basel Miami Beach Weekend Ed. Dec. 5–6, 2009), http://www.theartnewspaper.com/fairs/Art-Basel-Miami-Beach/2009/4.pdf. A judgment creditor need not, however, have any causal connection to the art.

Some liens have particular common law histories that might not at first blush seem relevant for art, for example, warehouse and transportation liens. Economic conditions may cause businesses to downsize, with some businesses moving art off site to specifically-designed warehouses. The art handlers and warehouses have a right to liens for repayment of fees under UCC or state law.

Another type of claim can center on conditions imposed in a prior transfer. If an artwork was donated to a charity, a donor may have imposed a restriction that can affect subsequent transfers. See, e.g., Georgia O'Keeffe Museum v. Fisk University, 312 S.W.3d 1 (Tenn. Ct. Ap. 2009); also Chapter 10, *infra*. In noncharitable transfers, restrictive conditions are less common and usually do not defeat title; nevertheless, disputes can arise.

Marguerite Hoffman privately sold a Rothko painting, *Untitled (1961)*, through a dealer, L&M Arts, to an undisclosed buyer in 2007. Because of a strong desire to keep her 2007 sale private and quiet, the contract had a confidentiality provision, with the buyer agreeing to "make maximum effort to keep all aspects of this transaction confidential" "indefinitely." When Hoffman learned that the Rothko was to be publicly auctioned at Sotheby's in May 2010, she filed suit the week of the auction, alleging breach of contract and various torts. Hoffman v. L&M Arts, No.3:10-cv-953 (N.D. Tex. 2010). The Rothko *Untitled (1961)* sold for over $31 million at the

Sotheby's auction, outperforming its $18-$25 million estimate. If you were representing the buyer, what would your advice have been in advance of the auction?

In a sales or consignment agreement, the seller warrants that she is able to transfer good title and that there are no liens, claims, or encumbrances. For a buyer, this warranty is non-negotiable. The strength of a seller's warranty for liens, claims, and encumbrances depends on the seller's continued existence and economic strength, both of which are non-constants. A buyer should not rely solely on the seller's warranty. As the value of the work increases, so too the economic risk, and title insurance may be a mechanism to manage some or all of that economic risk.

2. Art-Secured Loans

Art-secured lending is of growing interest. Estimates suggest that in 2019 there was $21–24 billion in outstanding loans against art, approximately $18–20 billion of which represents loans to collectors and private individuals and $1.7–2.4 billion of which represents loans to galleries and dealers. The U.S. likely accounts for more than 90% of the underwriting market. Several reasons exist for this dominance. Americans are used to borrowing. There is less cultural bias in the U.S. to debt. Americans may be more open to viewing their art as a strategic asset class, i.e., another form of investment that can be monetized. Most importantly from a transactional perspective, the U.C.C. provides a uniform and recognized legal framework for recording the lender's security interest in the encumbered property. Conversely, in Europe, each nation provides its own system. See Deloitte & ArtTactic, ART & FINANCE REPORT 2019 107–123 (6th ed. 2019); Georgina Adam, *In debt we trust: the rise of art-secured lending*, ARTNEWSPAPER (Dec. 6, 2018), available at www.theartnewspaper.com/analysis/in-debt-we-trust-the-rise-of-srt-secured-lending; but cf., Marcos Costa Leite & Pierre Naquin, *Art Loans: already in decline?*, GAZETTE DROUOT, June 26, 2019, available at www.gazette-drouot.com/article/art-loans%253A-already-in-decline%253F/8783.

Whether to individuals or galleries, art-secured lending poses significant hurdles because of the nature of art and the art market. For lenders, the difficulty of risk assessment is often of prime concern. Valuation and good legal title are basic elements for secured lending. Loans backed by collateral depend on the value of the collateralized property. Authenticity is a prime component of value, and, as previously discussed, authenticity for any particular artwork is not a permanent condition. Additionally, for secured loans, the debtor must have an interest in the property to transfer a security interest in the property to the lender. A debtor's presumed good marketable title can be challenged on multiple grounds, such as stolen or looted property, use of endangered materials, or violations of import/export regulations (all topics discussed in this chapter and the next). Because valuation and good legal title to artworks can be so fluid, the risk of such loans may be greater than in other contexts. See Kevin Ray, *(In)Security—Secured Transactions in Art and Cultural Property*, 25 DEPAUL J. ART, TECH. & INTELL. PROP. L. 501, 505 (2015).

These concerns may affect the terms of the loans. Many lenders will lend up to 40–50% of the appraised value of the art. Because values can change quickly, lenders may lend only against a collection and not merely one artwork. Minimum amounts for the loans as well as time periods may apply; interest rates can vary. Some lenders may require a personal guarantee (recourse loan as opposed to nonrecourse). Most significantly, some lenders will take possession of the artwork. For individuals, this may not be palatable, as the artwork is part of their daily life and personal residence; they would miss it. See Wildenstein & Co. v. Wallis, 756 F. Supp. 158 (S.D.N.Y. 1991) (where wife borrowed against artworks without husband's knowledge and made copies to replace the originals of which lender took possession).

In addition to these concerns, lenders must assess the integrity of the debtor. One recurring concern for dealer or gallery loans is the debtor's double-pledging or selling the collateral without the permission of the lender. A recent example involved the auction sale of *Untitled* by Rudolf Stingel, a photorealist portrait of Pablo Picasso, sold at Christie's in May 2019 for $6.5 million. The only problem was there were multiple claims of ownership and encumbering interests in the work. In June 2020, fugitive art dealer Inigo Philbrick was captured on the Pacific island of Vanuatu and returned to U.S. jurisdiction to face criminal charges relating to fraudulent practices in art sales and loans. He lengthens the list of accused criminal art dealers. The following is from the unsealed complaint in United States v. Inigo Philbrick, 20 MAG 4507, ¶4.c (S.D.N.Y April 30, 2020):

> From in or about 2016, up to and including in or about 2019, in order to maintain and finance his art business, PHILBRICK engaged in a scheme to defraud multiple individuals and entities involved in the art market. As part of and in furtherance of the fraudulent scheme, PHILBRICK made material misrepresentations and omissions to art collectors, investors, and lenders in order to procure access to valuable fine art and to obtain sales proceeds, funding, and loans premised on his alleged ownership of fine art. In particular, PHILBRICK knowingly and willfully misrepresented the ownership of certain artworks, for example, by selling a total of more than 100 percent ownership in an artwork to multiple individuals and entities without the knowledge or permission of co-owners, and without disclosing the ownership interests of third parties to buyers and lenders. As part of the fraudulent scheme, PHILBRICK also furnished false and fraudulent sales and consignment contracts in order to artificially inflate the value of artworks and to conceal the discovery of his scheme.

In addition to the criminal charges, multiple parties filed civil lawsuits against Philbrick related to the criminal charges. See Judd Tully, *New Court Filing Reveals Further Details in Case of Embattled Dealer Inigo Philbrick*, ARTNews, Dec. 13, 2019, available at https://artnews.com/art-news/news/inigo-philbrick-rudolf-stingel-memorandum-1202672509/.

Part Two

Ownership

Enjoying art is the reason collectors collect, and they wish to do so free of legal concerns. Three aspects of ownership can raise legal issues. For artworks acquired abroad, one immediate concern is bringing the artwork home. Chapter 6 explores the movement of art across international borders, with its attendant concerns of customs and import and export restrictions on the free flow of art. Chapter 7 introduces moral rights, a concept imported from abroad that gives an artist ongoing rights in an artwork even after its sale. The artist's moral rights and the collector's ownership rights are being recalibrated. By lending artworks to museums, collectors allow a wider audience to enjoy those artworks. Chapter 8 develops the template for documenting art loans to museums.

Chapter 6

Crossing Borders

Art is a highly desirable good across international markets. As art moves through those markets, considerations beyond the immediate buyer and seller come into play. Crossing borders means leaving one legal jurisdiction to enter another, with the possibility of multiple and diverse approaches to legal questions. When importing artworks, two types of concerns can arise. First are questions of symbolic importance, such as cultural property and national identity. Second are revenue and security concerns, such as tax avoidance and money laundering. This chapter will focus primarily on the legal aspects of importing art into the U.S. It is a two-tier approach. All imported artwork will go through the normal customs process. Some may be subject to an overlay of import restrictions for certain works considered cultural property or patrimony by other nations.

A. Customs Process

1. Classification as Art

Is it art? That wonderful, tantalizing, philosophical question presents itself. The general mien of a transactional lawyer leaves the qualitative artistic judgment to the client. Nevertheless, sometimes no matter how assiduously avoided, the basic art question requires an unavoidable yes-no answer. See Christine Haught Farley, *Judging Art*, 79 Tul. L. Rev. 805 (2005); Brian Soucek, *Aesthetic Judgment in Law*, 69 Ala. L. Rev. 381 (2017).

Any object imported into the U.S. must be classified for customs purposes. For decades, artworks have received favored customs treatment. The monetary impact of an imported item claiming status as art can be significant.

Brancusi v. United States

T.D. 43063, 54 Treas. Dec. 428 (U.S. Cust. Ct. 1928)

WAITE, J. The importation in this case is invoiced as a bronze bird and mentioned in the record as "Bird in flight." It was entered as a work of art in the form of a sculpture and claimed to be entitled to entry free of duty under paragraph 1704 of the tariff act of 1922. It was assessed by the collector of customs at 40 per cent ad valorem as a manufacture of metal under paragraph 399 of the same law. The respective paragraphs are as follows:

> Par. 399. Articles or wares not specially provided for . . . if composed wholly or in chief value of iron, steel, lead, copper, brass, nickel, pewter, zinc, aluminum, or other metal, but not plated with platinum, gold, or silver, or colored with gold lacquer; whether partly or wholly manufactured, 40 per centum ad valorem.
>
> Par. 1704. Original paintings . . . [o]riginal sculptures or statuary, including not more than two replicas or reproductions of the same; but the terms "sculpture" and "statuary" as used in this paragraph shall be understood to include professional productions of sculptors only, whether in round or in relief, in bronze, marble, stone, terra cotta, ivory, wood, or metal, or whether cut, carved, or otherwise wrought by hand from the solid block or mass of marble, stone or alabaster, or from metal, or cast in bronze or other metal or substance, or from wax or plaster, made as the professional productions of sculptors only; and the words "painting" and "sculpture" and "statuary" as used in this paragraph shall not be understood to include any articles of utility, nor such as are made wholly or in part by stenciling or any other mechanical process. . . .

The importation appears to be a production in bronze about 4 1/2 feet high supported by a cylindrical base about 6 inches in diameter and 6 inches high. It is highly polished and burnished brass or bronze, symmetrically constructed with a top between 1 and 2 inches in diameter. It terminates at the top in a point which might be caused by the cutting of the piece diagonally across and upward until it terminates in an edge. It increases in size as it descends with a slight curve to the middle, from which point it decreases and terminates about 10 inches from the pedestal, where it is cylindrical, and from that point it increases in size in a conical shaped base which rests upon the pedestal.

* * *

The piece is characterized, as stated above, as a bird. Without the exercise of a rather vivid imagination it bears no resemblance to a bird except, perchance, with such imagination it may be likened to the shape of the body of a bird. It has neither head nor feet nor feathers portrayed in the piece. As stated above, it is entirely smooth on its exterior, which is a polished and burnished surface.

Considerable testimony was produced on both sides. On the part of the plaintiff the testimony of the sculptor was taken and of one other who claimed to be and probably was a professional artist. Other witnesses were produced who have been familiar with art and art works in their study and in museums and as artists and writers upon art. All of these declared the production to be a piece of sculpture and a work of art, the work of a professional artist and sculptor, Brancusi.

Two witnesses were produced on the part of the Government who have had experience in art or sculpture, who were, in fact, under the accepted definition, sculptors. These pronounced the importation to be neither a work of art nor sculpture.

There is no question in the mind of the court but that the man who produced the importation is a professional sculptor, as is shown by his reputation and works and the manner in which he is considered by those competent to judge upon that subject. We also find it is an original production.

The requirements of the paragraph under which this is claimed to be entitled to free entry provide for original sculptures, the works of a professional sculptor, with the further proviso that the term shall not be understood to include any articles of utility. The term "works of art," which originally appeared as the heading of the predecessor of this paragraph (par. 717 of the act of 1909), was dropped therefrom in the enactment of the 1913 law (par. 652), and the latter was reenacted, practically without change, as paragraph 1704 of the present tariff law. Nevertheless, this court has held that to be entitled to free entry under said paragraph 1704, articles must be works of art. . . .

Having found that this is the work of a professional sculptor, and that it is original, the question then for us to determine is as to whether it conforms to the definition given under the law for works of art. It must be conceded that what have been determined to be works of art under the decisions of recent years, would, under the more remote decisions of the courts, not only the customs courts but the United States Supreme Court, have been rejected as not falling within that term. We think that under the earlier decisions this importation would have been rejected as a work of art, or, to be more accurate, as a work within the classification of high art. Under the influence of the modern schools of art the opinion previously held has been modified with reference to what is necessary to constitute art within the meaning of the statute, and it has been held by the Court of Customs Appeals that drawings or sketches, designs for wallpaper and textiles, are works of art, although they were intended for a utilitarian purpose.

Government counsel in support of the contention that this importation is not sculpture, cites the case of *United States v. Olivotti* (7 Ct. Cust. Appls. 46; T.D. 36309). In defining the term "sculpture" the court there said:

> Sculpture as an art is that branch of the free fine arts which chisels or carves out of stone or other solid material or models in clay or other plastic substance for subsequent reproduction by carving or casting, imitations of natural objects, chiefly the human form, and represents such objects in their true proportions of length, breadth, and thickness, or of length and breadth only.

This decision was handed down in 1916. In the meanwhile there has been developing a so-called new school of art, whose exponents attempt to portray abstract ideas rather than to imitate natural objects. Whether or not we are in sympathy with these newer ideas and the schools which represent them, we think the fact of their existence and their influence upon the art world as recognized by the courts must be considered.

The object now under consideration is shown to be for purely ornamental purposes, its use being the same as that of any piece of sculpture of the old masters. It is beautiful and symmetrical in outline, and while some difficulty might be encountered in associating it with a bird, it is nevertheless pleasing to look at and highly ornamental, and as we hold under evidence that it is the original production of a professional sculptor and is in fact a piece of sculpture and a work of art according to the authorities above referred to, we sustain the protest and find that it is entitled to free entry under paragraph 1704, supra. Let judgment be entered accordingly.

Notes and Questions

1. *Impact of Brancusi.* The decision in *Brancusi* was hailed as a win for modern art as well as for Brancusi. Unfortunately, that may be an overstatement. The court's opinion seemed to have been heavily influenced by the beauty of the sculpture, which was sitting daily in the court room. The judge described the sculpture as "beautiful," "pleasing to look at," and "highly ornamental." Beauty would be a narrow and slippery base on which to judge something as art for legal purposes. Stephanie Giry, *An Odd Bird*, available at www.legalaffairs.org/issues/September-October-2000/story_giry_sepoct2002.msp.

2. *Brief History of Customs and Art.* The *Brancusi* rule generally remains true today—artworks are duty free in the U.S. It was not always the case.

Customs was the first substantive law passed by the new Congress of the United States (Act of July 4, 1789, Ch. 2, 1 Stat., An Act for laying a Duty on Goods, Wares, and Merchandise imported into the United States), befitting the economic needs of running a new government. There was no specific mention of artworks. "Pictures and prints" were first mentioned in § 1 of the Tariff Act of August 10, 1790, as being specifically subject to a 10% ad valorum duty. In § 2 of the Act of April 27, 1816, "statues, busts, casts, paintings, drawings, engravings" imported by any society incorporated for philosophical, literary, education, or the encouragement of the fine arts were specifically exempted from duty. A century later, that template was little changed. The Tariff Act of 1909 imposed a 15% ad valorum duty on paintings and sculpture (§ 470), but similarly exempted imports by not-for-profit societies, as well as certain artworks which are proved to be more than 20 years old, and other works if more than 100 years old (§ 717). This brief synopsis attests to the blunt revenue raising focus of customs. Nonetheless, within a generation of the nation's founding, the exemption for paintings and sculpture manifested a new nation's desire to encourage cultural institutions. Throughout customs history, there has been a recognized line of demarcation in favor of the free fine arts, in contrast to works of artisans or craftsmen, works of utility, or works employing mechanical processes. See Chapter 7, *infra*, for a similar approach underlying moral rights.

The Tariff Act of 1913, the first meaningful customs revision since the Civil War, introduced the federal income tax. The net effect was to shift the brunt of federal revenue raising away from customs to the new income tax. It accomplished this by significantly increasing the duty-free list, specifically including therein "original paintings . . . , original drawings . . . , original sculptures or statuary." For those artworks, their importation now became duty free and the importer's identity also became irrelevant. (§652) Does this shift provide an argument for an expansive customs interpretation of a work of art?

More recently, however, the United States has reimposed tariffs against some imports into the United States. In 2019, the World Trade Organization allowed the U.S. to tax $7.5 billion of European exports to the U.S. An import duty of 25% on printed matter may impact the import of certain lithographs and photographs from the U.K. and Germany. Trade relations with China may also result in tariffs on certain imports of artworks into the U.S. Trade disputes that could result in the imposition of tariffs provide another reminder to doublecheck current laws and regulations before giving advice.

3. *EU Perspective.* In 2006, Haunch of Venison, a London gallery, imported *Six Alternating Cool White/Warm White Fluorescent Lights Vertical and Centered*, a 1973 light sculpture by Dan Flavin, and *Hall of Whispers*, a 1995 video installation by Bill Viola from the U.S. The gallery classified the works as art on the customs declarations. Under the U.K. version of Chapter 97 of the Common Customs Tariff, works of art would be assessed a reduced Value Added Tax (VAT) rate of 5% and no customs duties. U.K. customs rejected the classification of the works as art and assessed a full VAT of 17.5% and a customs duty of 3.7%. On appeal to the U.K. VAT and Duties Tribunal in 2008, the initial customs decision was rejected, and the works were deemed properly classified as works of art. This was not, however, the end of the matter.

In August 2010, the European Commission ruled that pioneering light sculptor Dan Flavin's "so-called light installation" is not art but "wall light fittings." Similarly, Bill Viola's video installation is not art but a "projector," having been "modified by [the] artist with a view to appear as a work of 'modern art.'" Commission Regulation (EU) No. 731/2010 (Aug. 11, 2010). One consequence of this classification is that all such installations entering any EU member state from outside of the EU will likely be subject to the standard VAT rate and customs duty. For purposes of assessing the tax, it seems as if the authorities determined value on the artwork's market value as art, not the wall fittings or used projecter value. See Maev Kennedy, *Call that art? No, Dan Flavin's work is just simple light fittings, say EU experts*, The Guardian 3 (Dec. 21, 2010). The U.K.'s exit from the EU in 2021 could restore the 2008 decision of the U.K. VAT and Duties Tribunal categorizing the work as art. The is-it-art debate famously at the center of *Brancusi* continues for customs purposes.

4. *Customs Process—Classification of Imported Items.* To import an artwork into the U.S. requires a familiarity with the basic import rules of U.S. Customs and Border Protection ("CBP"), under the authority of the Department of Homeland Security. As in the acquisition process, proper documentation based on a proper factual determination is essential to moving an artwork across borders. Three

determinations are critical in the importing process: classification of the item (as in *Brancusi*), its country of origin, and value. It is only when all three determinations have been made that a decision as to whether the item may enter the U.S. and its rate of duty, if any, can be made. See CBP, What Every Member of the Trade Community Should Know About: Works of Art, Collector's Pieces, Antiques, and Other Cultural Property (2006), available at www.cbp.gov. Country of origin and value, important elements in the next two cases, *One Tintoretto Painting* and *An Antique Platter of Gold*, will be discussed in the notes thereafter. See A.2. Regulatory Documentation and Forfeiture, *infra*.

Since 1989, the classification of any import into the U.S. is based on the International Harmonized Tariff Schedule (HTS), currently consisting of 22 sections and 99 chapters. Classification of goods in the HTS is the key to determining correct duty rates (usually *ad valorem*) and the ultimate payment due for the goods on entry. Accurate classification of goods is a legal matter. For legal purposes, navigating through the 99 chapters of the HTS to find the proper classification of a good requires analysis dictated by the General Rules of Interpretation (GRI), which are the same for all importers in all trading countries using the HTS. The United States and other countries frequently have additional notes, on a per Chapter basis, that are particular to the classification of imported goods crossing their borders, subject to the GRIs. As shown below, Chapters may have additional notes that exclude or include goods for classification in that Chapter. Chapter 97, Works of Art, Collectors' Pieces and Antiques, is the most relevant for our purposes. In 2018, Statistical Notes were added to that chapter that requires importers to categorize items of cultural property more precisely. Chapter 97 is as follows:

Harmonized Tariff Schedule of the United States (2020) Revision 26
Annotated for Statistical Reporting Purposes

CHAPTER 97

WORKS OF ART, COLLECTORS' PIECES AND ANTIQUES

XXI
97 - 1

Notes

1. This chapter does not cover:

(a) Unused postage or revenue stamps, postal stationery (stamped paper) or the like, of heading 4907;

(b) Theatrical scenery, studio backdrops or the like, of painted canvas (heading 5907) except if they may be classified in heading 9706; or

(c) Pearls, natural or cultured, or precious or semiprecious stones (headings 7101 to 7103).

2. For the purposes of heading 9702, the expression "original engravings, prints and lithographs" means impressions produced directly, in black and white or in color, of one or of several plates wholly executed by hand by the artist, irrespective of the process or of the material employed by him, but not including any mechanical or photomechanical process.

3. Heading 9703 does not apply to mass-produced reproductions or works of conventional craftsmanship of a commercial character, even if these articles are designed or created by artists.

4. (a) Subject to notes 1 through 3 above, articles of this chapter are to be classified in this chapter and not in any other chapter of the tariff schedule.

(b) Heading 9706 does not apply to articles of the preceding headings of this chapter.

5. Frames around paintings, drawings, pastels, collages or similar decorative plaques, engravings, prints or lithographs are to be classified with those articles, provided they are of a kind and of a value normal to those articles. Frames which are not of a kind or of avalue normal to the articles referred to in this note are to be classified separately.

Additional U.S. Notes

1. Heading 9703 covers not only original sculpture made by the sculptor, but also the first 12 castings, replicas or reproductions made from a sculptor's original work or model, by the sculptor himself or by another artist, with or without a change in scale and whether or not the sculptor is alive at the time the castings, replicas or reproductions are completed.

2. Whenever an article is entered for sale under heading 9706, and thereafter determined to be not over 100 years of age, a duty of 6.6 percent ad valorem for articles subject to column 1-general treatment, free of duty for goods originating in the territory of Canada or a duty of 25 percent ad valorem for articles subject to column 2 treatment shall be assessed thereon in addition to any other duty or penalty imposed on such article under the tariff schedule.

Statistical Notes:

1 For the purposes of statistical reporting number 9705.00.0075, "Archaeological pieces" are objects of cultural significance that are at least 250 years old and are of a kind normally discovered as a result of scientific excavation, clandestine or accidental digging or exploration on land or under water. For the purposes of statistical reporting number 9705.00.0080, "Ethnographic pieces", which may also be called "ethnological pieces" are objects that are the product of a tribal or nonindustrial society and are important to the cultural heritage of a people because of their distinctive characteristics, comparative rarity or their contribution to the knowledge of the origins, development or history of that people. See Customs and Border Protection (CBP) Informed Compliance Publication on "Works of Art, Collector's Pieces, Antiques, and Other Cultural Property".

2. For statistical reporting of merchandise provided for in subheading 9705.00.00, collections made up of articles of more than one type of cultural property, i.e., zoological, biological, paleontological, archaeological, anatomical, etc., shall be reported by their separate components in the appropriate statistical reference numbers, as if separately entered.

Harmonized Tariff Schedule of the United States (2020) Revision 26
Annotated for Statistical Reporting Purposes

XXI
97-2

Heading/ Subheading	Stat. Suf-fix	Article Description	Unit of Quantity	Rates of Duty 1 General	Rates of Duty 1 Special	Rates of Duty 2
9701		Paintings, drawings and pastels, executed entirely by hand, other than drawings of heading 4906 and other than hand-painted or hand-decorated manufactured articles; collages and similar decorative plaques; all the foregoing framed or not framed:				
9701.10.00	00	Paintings, drawings and pastels[1/]	No.	Free[2/]		Free
9701.90.00	00	Other[3/]	No.	Free[2/]		Free
9702.00.00	00	Original engravings, prints and lithographs, framed or not framed[4/]	No.	Free[2/]		Free
9703.00.00	00	Original sculptures and statuary, in any material[4/]	No.	Free[2/]		Free
9704.00.00	00	Postage or revenue stamps, stamp-postmarks, first-day covers, postal stationery (stamped paper) and the like, used or unused, other than those of heading 4907[5/]	No.	Free[2/]		Free
9705.00.00		Collections and collectors' pieces of zoological, botanical, mineralogical, anatomical, historical, archeological, paleontological, ethnographic or numismatic interest		Free[2/]		Free
		Numismatic (collector's) coins, other than archaeological pieces:				
	01	Coins made prior to the 14th century and not known to be thedirect products of excavations, finds or archaeological sites	g			
		Other:				
		250 years or more in age:				
	10	Gold[6/]	g			
	40	Other[6/]	g			
		Other:				
	50	Gold[6/]	g			
	65	Other[6/]	g			
	79	Archaeological pieces of a kind described in statistical note 1 to this chapter	kg			
	80	Ethnographic pieces of a kind described in statistical note 1 to this chapter	kg			
	85	Other[7/]	kg			
9706.00.00		Antiques of an age exceeding one hundred years		Free[2/]		Free
	20	Silverware[4/]	kg			
	40	Furniture[4/]	kg			
	60	Other[6/]	kg			

5. *Quantitative Limits for Sculpture.* Many artworks are easily classified under Chapter 97 as artworks, some works are expressly excluded, and some works are not so easily classified. Sculpture seems to generate more Customs attention than any of the other Chapter 97 subheadings. The two Chapter 97 U.S. notes dealing with sculpture share a notion that original sculpture, as a duty-free work of art, is meant

to be limited. Too many multiples of the work, even if done by the artist, refute the fine art status and smack of commercial (as opposed to artistic?) appeal.

Two quantitative benchmarks have emerged from this that should be considered for U.S. imports. First, only the original sculpture plus the first 12 castings are duty free. Thus, for a Degas sculpture in an edition of say 46, only the original plus #1–12 will qualify as original sculpture; #13–46 will not.* The second quantitative limitation is the so-called rule of 50: "when an artist . . . produces more than 50 in an edition, it is no longer fine art and none will be allowed duty-free." CBP, What Every Member of the Trade Community Should Know About: Works of Art, Collector's Pieces, Antiques, and Other Cultural Property (2006), available at www.cbp.gov. Why is there no similar quantitative disallowance for large editions of original engravings, prints, and lithographs? Cf. Visual Artists Rights Act of 1990 for works in editions of 200 or fewer, Chapter 7, *infra*.

6. *Two or More Possible Classifications.* Some artistic creations present difficulties in import classification because their intrinsic nature is mixed and therefore the *Brancusi* question—is it art?—returns. Internal Advice HQ 963158, 2000 WL 459246 (Customs, January 14, 2000), reproduced below, deals with the question of utilitarian articles as possible artworks. It was requested by Sotheby's, which had imported articles for auction classifying them as original sculptures. The objects by the recognized artists, brothers Diego and Alberto Giacometti, consisted of tables, lamps, chairs, and armchairs, cast in bronze at a foundry. Customs determined that Sotheby's import documents did not comply with Customs Regulations 19 C.F.R. § 10.48 (reproduced in A.2. Regulatory Documentation and Forfeiture, *infra*). Importantly, however, the Internal Advice also rejected Sotheby's claim that certain utilitarian articles *could* be covered by heading 9703.00. As you read this, consider if this is analogous to the new EU regulation on light sculptures and video installations discussed in Note 2, *supra*.

* For a cautionary note on Degas sculpture, see William D. Cohan, *A Controversy over Degas*, ARTNEWS 87–97 (April 2010), concerning the authenticity of 46 bronzes produced in 1997 and 1998 from a plaster cast of *Little Dancer Aged 14,* recently discovered and purportedly by Degas.

United States Customs Service
Department of the Treasury
RE: Internal Advice; Sotheby's Inc.'s; Diego Giacometti; Criteria for Sculptures

HQ963158, 2000 WL 459246 (Customs)

* * *

ISSUE: Whether utilitarian articles created by professional sculptors may qualify as original sculptures and statutory, in any material, in heading 9703.00.00, HTSUS?

LAW AND ANALYSIS:

* * *

The predecessor of the HTSUS, the Tariff Schedules of the United States (TSUS), contained a similar provision as contained in heading 9703.00.00, HTSUS. Item 765.15, TSUS, which provided for original sculptures and statuary (including the first 10 castings, replicas, or reproductions made from a sculptor's original work or model with or without a change in scale and whether or not the sculptor is alive at the time the castings, replicas, or reproductions are completed) all the foregoing made in any form from any material as the professional productions of sculptors only, whether in round or in relief, and whether cut, carved or otherwise wrought by hand or cast. Essentially, with the exception of the increase from 10 to 12 copies, heading 9703.00.00, HTSUS, with the Chapter notes and applicable regulations, conforms to item 765.15, TSUS. However, the headnotes for item 765.15, TSUS, specifically excluded from coverage, "any articles of utility or for industrial use". This specific wording of the exclusion of articles of utility is not found in heading 9703.00.00, HTSUS.

Accordingly, counsel is of the opinion that articles of utility are not excluded from heading 9703.00.00, HTSUS, and/or, that even under interpretations of the courts and Customs for item 765.15, TSUS, articles of utility were not excluded if the artistic character became "so compelling that the utilitarian achievement of the artisan is lost in the realized sentiment of the artist", quoting *U.S. v. Olivotti*, 7 Ct of Cust. Appls. 46, T.D. 36309, (1916).

Olivotti, supra, concerned a marble font, found not to be a work of art, and marble seats. The marble seats or chairs were copies of a Grecian original found in a Vatican museum that were made by a sculptor. The end of the arm rests contained carved lions' heads and paws. Paragraph 653 of the Tariff Act of 1913, a predecessor of heading 9703.00.00, HTSUS, provided for free entry of original sculpture and two reproductions that were not articles of utility. Sculptures that qualified for classification in paragraph 653 but exceeded the limitation for reproductions may be classified as statuary, sculptures or copies, in paragraph 376 of the Act of 1913. Paragraph 376 did not contain the "articles of utility" exclusion and did not require "originality". The marble seats concerned classification under paragraph 376, not paragraph 653. Notwithstanding the absence of the utility exclusion, the court applied the utilitarian exclusion for sculptured articles. The reasoning of the court concerning utilitarian use follows:

> "These carvings, even if they could be regarded as demanding the exercise of sculptural art, were evidently designed as an embellishment of the seats, and it would be going far to say that of themselves they were sufficient to give the character of sculptures to the entirely of which they are a minor, not a predominating, part. It may be conceded for the purposes of this case that because of the sculptural work upon them, the articles under consideration have an artistic beauty which otherwise they would not possess. Nevertheless, no one gazing upon them can forget that they are seats or chairs, and that they are not the expression of the sculptor's impulse to imitate some object in nature as he conceived it to be, but a conception brought to material form primarily and principally to serve a useful purpose, and not to please. The making of seats and chairs is strictly industrial, not sculptural, art; and when the sculptor's hand is called upon to make such conveniences artistic and beautiful, his work reaches no higher plane than the purely decorative, unless it be so compelling that the utilitarian achievement of the artisan is lost in the realized sentiment of the artist.... The seats here involved were not designed to serve as mere settings for whatever of sculptural work there may be upon them, but as seats to which such sculptural work clearly bears the relation of adornment and nothing more. They must, therefore, be classed as articles of utility produced by industrial art because of a sense of need or usefulness and not as sculptures or examples of fine art the activities of which are chiefly, if not wholly, called into play by sentiment and for the purpose of appealing to the emotions."

Downing v. U.S., 66 Cust. Ct. 33 (1971), supports the position that articles of utility were excluded under item 765.15, TSUS. This decision sums up the history of the utilitarian exclusion in the tariff acts prior to the HTSUS. Six oak door panels were removed from the doors of a church, shipped to England, used by a sculptor to carve bas-relief of sheep, and returned. The court held that the panels, as parts of doors before being carved and subsequently, were articles of utility and excluded under item 765.15, TSUS. The court noted the exception in *U.S. v. Baumgarten*, 2 Ct. Cust. Appls 32 (1911), in which the court found that the form of a vase was used by the artist merely as a support for the real work, of human figures surrounding the bowl of the vase and that the sculptor's work was "so compelling that the utilitarian achievement of the artisan is lost in the realized sentiment of the artist," and therefor it was not an article of utility. The court also noted that in *Olivotti, supra*, the utility exclusion was applied notwithstanding that an expressed exclusion was not contained in the applicable statutory provision. The panels, as parts of doors, were articles of utility.

Notwithstanding the court decisions under TSUS and the prior tariff acts, counsel is of the opinion since there is no specific exclusion under heading 9703.00.00, HTSUS, articles of utility may be classified therein.

Note 3, Chapter 97, HTSUS, states that "heading 9703 does not apply to mass-produced reproductions or works of conventional craftsmanship of a commercial character, even if these articles are designed or created by artists". In addition, the Explanatory Notes (EN's) to the Harmonized Commodity Description and Coding System, which represent the official interpretation of the tariff at the international level, facilitate classification under the HTSUS by offering guidance in understanding the scope of the headings and General Rules of Interpretation of the HTSUS, states that heading 9703 excludes the following articles, even if they are designed or created by artists:

(a) Ornamental sculptures of a commercial character.

(b) Articles of personal adornment and other works of conventional craftsmanship of a commercial character (ornaments, religious effigies, etc.).

(c) Mass-produced reproductions in plaster, staff, cement, papier maché, etc.

The exclusions stated in Note 3, Chapter 97, HTSUS, and as enumerated by the EN's, of "works of conventional craftsmanship" and/or "ornamental sculptures of a commercial character", even if the articles are designed or created by artists (sculptors), equates to the exclusion of articles of utility.

New York Ruling Letter 889119, dated August 17, 1993, cited by counsel, limited the sculptures to furniture "that are not capable of any functional use", that is to say, articles of utility are not covered under heading 9703.00.00, HTSUS.

We do not have a full description of all of the articles covered by the consumption entry and some of them may not be articles of utility. Sculptures created by Diego Giacometti that are not utilitarian articles may be classified in heading 9703.00.00, HTSUS, upon compliance with the requirements of Note 3, and additional U.S. Note 1, Chapter 97, HTSUS, and 19 CFR 10.48. The burden is upon the importer to show compliance with the requirements on a case by case basis.

HOLDING: The articles in question, ornamental chairs, lamps, etc., created by professional sculptors and designed to be used as furniture, are excluded from heading 9703.00.00, HTSUS. This position is in harmony with the decisions of the courts, as discussed above, Note 3, Chapter 97, HTSUS, and our decisions under the HTSUS. See recent Headquarters Ruling Letter 960924, dated September 15, 1999, and cases cited therein.

The articles are also precluded from heading 9703.00.00, HTSUS, by virtue of Additional U.S. Note 1, Chapter 97, HTSUS, and applicable regulations.

* * *

2. Regulatory Documentation and Forfeiture

Whether duty free or dutiable, artworks entering the U.S. are subject to formal documentation and procedural requirements, violations of which can result in fines and, as the next two cases show, possible forfeiture. Customs brokers (some specializing in fine art) are licensed to handle goods through the importing and exporting process. See Racine Berkow, *Import and Export*, in MUSEUM REGISTRATION METHODS 338–341 (Rebecca A. Buck & Jean Allman Gilmore eds., 5th ed. 2010).

Each artwork must have a commercial invoice for formal entry into the U.S. that contains the following information: shipper's name and contact information; recipient's name and contact information; artist's name, title, quantity, medium, size of each work; component materials; if a multiple, size of the edition and number of the work in that edition; declared value (transaction value, otherwise fair market value). 19 C.F.R. § 143.3(a)(3). A bond is required for formal entry. 19 C.F.R. § 113.61.

In addition, for works under headings 9702 (engravings) or 9703 (sculpture), the applicable Customs Regulation, 19 C.F.R. § 10.48 (as of Oct. 13, 2015), provides:

> (a) Invoices covering works of art claimed to be free of duty under subheadings 9702.00.00 and 9703.00.00, HTSUS, shall show whether they are originals, replicas, reproductions, or copies, and also the name of the artist who produced them, unless upon examination the Customs officer is satisfied that such statement is not necessary to a proper determination of the facts.
>
> (b) The following evidence shall be filed in connection with the entry: A declaration, or its electronic equivalent, in the following form by the artist who produced the article, or by the seller, shipper or importer, showing whether it is original, or in the case of sculpture, the original work or model, or one of the first twelve castings, replicas, or reproductions made from the original work or model; and in the case of etchings, engravings, woodcuts, lithographs, or prints made by other hand-transfer processes, that they were printed by hand from hand-etched, hand-drawn, or hand-engraved plates, stones, or blocks:
>
>> I , ____, do hereby declare that I am the producer, seller, shipper or importer of certain works of art, namely ____ covered by the annexed invoice dated ____; that any sculptures or statuary included in that invoice are the original works or models or one of the first twelve castings, replicas, or reproductions made from the sculptor's original work or model; and that any etchings, engravings, woodcuts, lithographs, or prints made by other hand-transfer processes included in that invoice were printed by hand from hand-etched, hand-drawn, or hand-engraved plates, stones, or blocks.

Neither of the next two cases presents a customs classification question; instead each focuses on the veracity of the prepared customs documentation. Each case has background music that unquestionably played a significant role in the government's decision to bring a forfeiture proceeding.

United States v. One Tintoretto Painting

691 F.2d 603 (2d Cir. 1982)

CARDAMONE, J. We are called upon to decide a forfeiture case commenced by the United States of America against a painting entitled "The Holy Family with Saint Catherine and Honored Donor," as defendant in rem. Two hundred years or so before the plaintiff United States came into being, the defendant in rem was painted by the tempestuous Italian Renaissance painter Tintoretto.[1] Claiming that this valuable masterpiece was smuggled into the United States, the government instituted the instant forfeiture proceeding as a civil action in rem for failure to pay customs duties.... The government sought to enforce the forfeiture in a proceeding which afforded the owner an opportunity to appear and be heard.

... Issac Silberberg (claimant) asserted ownership of the Tintoretto painting and filed a verified answer. The government then moved ... for summary judgment.... Judge Lasker granted the motion. We believe, however, that the claimant raised a genuine issue of fact regarding the purported forfeiture which precludes summary judgment and entitles claimant to his day in court.

Claimant Silberberg, an Israeli national ... purchased the painting without being aware of its authorship in a second-hand shop in Moscow in 1948 after his discharge from duty as an officer in the Soviet Army. Suspecting that the painting was valuable, he paid the equivalent of $20,000 in rubles. Upon moving to Vienna in 1975 and then to Tel Aviv in 1978, he openly displayed the painting in his home.... Silberberg decided to sell it in 1979.... Finding there was no market in Israel, he entrusted the painting to Raymond Vinokur, a long-term social and business acquaintance [who] told Silberberg that he was knowledgeable in the field of art. An arrangement was made between them for Vinokur to sell the picture in the United States on a commission basis.

Vinokur then engaged in the shady maneuvers that led to the arrest of the Tintoretto painting. Vinokur flew to New York on December 5, 1979 and falsely stated on his entry permit that he would be staying at the Barbizon Plaza Hotel in New York City, when in fact he intended to and did stay at the home of one Efin Nezhinsky in Queens, New York. On December 10, 1979 a package containing the Tintoretto arrived in the United States from Germany aboard a KLM flight which landed at John F. Kennedy International Airport (JFK) in New York.

---

1. Tintoretto's name was Jacopo Robusti. Because his father was a dyer or "tintore," he was called "Tintoretto" or little dyer. He lived his entire life (1518–1594) in Venice, Italy. He was, along with Titian and Veronese, one of the masters of the Venetian School during the period of the High Italian Renaissance. H. Tietze, Tintoretto (1948). There is some suggestion that the painting is not by Tintoretto, but by his son, Domenico. R. Palluchini and P. Rossi, Le Opere Tintoretto Sacre e Profane 378 Cat. 142 (Tomo Secondo 1982).

During the preceding month of November 1979 the Federal Bureau of Investigation (FBI) . . . had begun an investigation regarding this painting. An FBI agent confirmed . . . the masterpiece's authenticity and . . . that it had been stolen from . . . East Germany at the close of World War II. The painting was thereafter reputed to have been taken to the Soviet Union in the possession of a Soviet General and later transported to Israel. On December 10 the agent was informed that Nezhinsky had picked up a package containing the Tintoretto at JFK. The customs forms which Nezhinsky completed and signed falsely stated that the Tintoretto was his personal property, for his own use, not for resale, and had a value of $500. Posing as an art dealer, the FBI agent subsequently met with Vinokur at a Madison Avenue Hotel, offered to purchase the painting, and asked Vinokur whether it could be resold. Upon informing the agent that the painting was marketable and that he would sell it to the agent for $250,000, Vinokur was arrested.

On January 22, 1980, Vinokur pled guilty to making false statements in a Customs Bureau document in violation of 18 U.S.C. § 542. As a result of Vinokur's conviction, the government obtained possession of the picture and, later in 1980, instituted this action.

II

Forfeiture statutes, which derive from English common law principles, embody the concept that a forfeiture is absolute. Thus, an owner's interest in the article may be forfeited even though the owner was not a participant in and had no knowledge of the illegal acts which brought about the forfeiture. . . . The underlying rationale for this principle is a legal fiction dating back several thousand years based on the apocryphal notion that "it" is the inanimate object, not its possessor or owner, which offends against the law. While this action may be one that is quasi-criminal, it is a separate and distinct proceeding from the criminal proceeding against the offending person (here Vinokur) and forfeiture is "no part of the punishment for the criminal offense," *Various Items of Personal Property*, 282 U.S. at 581, 51 S.Ct. at 283 (citation omitted).

III

The sole issue before us is whether there was a proper award of summary judgment for the government based upon its complaint seeking a forfeiture of the subject painting.

The standard under which a summary judgment motion is tested requires a showing "that there is no genuine issue as to any material fact and that the moving party is entitled to a judgment as a matter of law." Fed.R.Civ.P. 56(c). . . .

* * *

IV

The government argues that it has long been the rule that the owner's innocence is no defense to a claim of forfeiture. An exception may exist—the only exception says the government—where the object is stolen or taken from the owner without his consent. Thus, the government contends that since this painting was freely transferred from claimant Silberberg to Vinokur, a forfeiture works no deprivation of Silberberg's due process rights under the Fifth Amendment. We disagree.

In our view the claimant arguably fits within a second exception which the Supreme Court voiced in dicta in *Calero-Toledo v. Pearson Yacht Leasing Company*, 416 U.S. 663, 94 S.Ct. 2080, 40 L.Ed.2d 452. In *Calero* police found marijuana aboard a yacht that had been leased by its owners. Although the owners had no involvement in or knowledge of the lessee's wrongful use of the boat, the vessel was forfeited. In sustaining that determination the Supreme Court noted the one exception upon which all parties agree: "it would be difficult to reject the constitutional claim of an owner whose property subjected to forfeiture had been taken from him without his privity or consent." *Id.* at 689, 94 S.Ct. at 2094 (citations omitted). Immediately thereafter, the Court continued by stating:

> Similarly, the same might be said of an owner who proved not only that he was uninvolved in and unaware of the wrongful activity, but also that he had done all that reasonably could be expected to prevent the proscribed use of his property; for, in that circumstance, it would be difficult to conclude that forfeiture served legitimate purposes and was not unduly oppressive.

Id. at 689–90, 94 S.Ct. at 2094–95 (footnote and citation omitted).

Although merely dicta, the second exception suggested in *Calero* is in accord with the policy and history of civil forfeiture in this country. Recognizing the broad sweep of the forfeiture statutes, the Supreme Court has stated that when "viewed in their entirety, it is manifest that they are intended to impose a penalty only upon those who are significantly involved in a criminal enterprise." The history of forfeiture clearly demonstrates that its principal purpose was to protect government revenues, not to impose punishment without fault on those who are acting "in good faith and without negligence" . . . .

Given the existence of the second exception, we must next determine whether Silberberg has raised a sufficient issue of fact as to whether he falls within its purview. The affidavits from Vinokur, Silberberg and others at least raise an arguable claim that Silberberg was not involved in or aware of the smuggling of his painting into the United States. . . .

In support of his contention that he met this requirement, Silberberg states in an affidavit that he first met Vinokur socially in Tel Aviv in 1975 and thereafter dealt with him in business. He entrusted Vinokur with the sale of the painting because he knew Vinokur personally and because Vinokur enjoyed a good reputation in the Tel Aviv business community. Vinokur had, to the best of Silberberg's knowledge, never been charged with any crime. Silberberg swears that he was assured by Vinokur that all precautions would be taken with the painting including conforming to customs regulations, paying any duties if required, and properly packing the painting to prevent damage. All of this was at Vinokur's expense to be reimbursed by Silberberg when the picture was sold. In fact Silberberg contracted to reimburse Vinokur for any duties that had to be paid. By entering into this reimbursement agreement, Silberberg arguably did all that reasonably could be expected of him to avoid the proscribed use of his property....

We think that claimant Silberberg is entitled to his day in court because the recitation in these affidavits raises sufficient factual issues to preclude the granting of summary judgment for the government....

* * *

Accordingly, we reverse the order granting summary judgment and remand the case for trial on the issue of forfeiture of the Tintoretto painting.

United States v. An Antique Platter of Gold

184 F.3d 131 (2d Cir. 1999)

WINTER, J. Michael H. Steinhardt appeals from Judge Jones's ordering of the forfeiture of a "Phiale," an antique gold platter. The district court held that false statements on the customs entry forms and the Phiale's status as stolen property under Italian law rendered its importation illegal. As such, the Phiale was subject to forfeiture.

* * *

Background

At issue is a Phiale of Sicilian origin that dates from the 4th Century B.C. Its provenance since then is largely unknown, other than its possession by Vincenzo Pappalardo, a private antique collector living in Sicily, who traded it in 1980 to Vincenzo Cammarata, a Sicilian coin dealer and art collector, for art works worth about $20,000. Cammarata sold it in 1991 to William Veres, the owner of Stedron, a Zurich art dealership, for objects worth about $90,000.

Veres brought the Phiale to the attention of Robert Haber, an art dealer from New York....

On December 4, 1991, Haber, acting for Steinhardt, finalized an agreement to purchase the Phiale for slightly more than $1 million-plus a 15% commission, making the total price paid by Steinhardt approximately $1.2 million. Haber and Veres also agreed to a "Terms of Sale," which stated, *inter alia*, that "[i]f the object is confiscated or impounded by customs agents or a claim is made by any country or governmental agency whatsoever, full compensation will be made immediately to the purchaser."...

On December 10, 1991, Haber flew from New York to Zurich, Switzerland, and then proceeded to Lugano, near the Italian border, where he took possession of the

Phiale on December 12. The transfer was confirmed by a commercial invoice issued by Stedron, describing the object as "ONE GOLD BOWL-CLASSICAL . . . DATE-C. 450 B.C. . . . . VALUE U.S. $250,000." The next day, Haber sent a fax to Jet Air Service, Inc. ("Jet Air"), Haber's customs broker at John F. Kennedy International Airport. . . . Jet Air prepared an Entry Summary form (Customs Form 7501), which also listed the country of origin as [Switzerland] and stated the Phiale's value at $250,000, as Haber's fax had indicated. . . .

On December 15, Haber returned to the United States from Zurich with the Phiale and later gave it to Steinhardt. Before completing the purchase, Steinhardt had the piece authenticated through a detailed examination by the Metropolitan Museum of Art. Thereafter, the Phiale was displayed in his home from 1992 until 1995.

Under Article 44 of Italy's law of June 1, 1939, an archaeological item is presumed to belong to the state unless its possessor can show private ownership prior to 1902. On February 16, 1995, the Italian government submitted a Letters Rogatory Request to the United States seeking assistance in investigating the circumstances of the Phiale's exportation and asking our government to confiscate it so that it could be returned to Italy. In November 1995, the Phiale was seized from Steinhardt pursuant to a warrant. . . .

* * *

Discussion

We review the grant of summary judgment *de novo*. . . .

As noted, the district court found that summary judgment was proper on either of two independent statutory bases. We hold that importation of the Phiale violated 18 U.S.C. § 545 because of the false statements on the customs forms. We need not, therefore, address whether the NSPA [National Stolen Property Act] incorporates concepts of property such as those contained in the Italian patrimony laws. Cf *United States v. McClain*, 545 F.2d 988, 994–97 (5th Cir. 1977) (adopting broad definition of property under NSPA).

Section 545 prohibits the importation of merchandise into the United States "contrary to law" and states that material imported in such a manner "shall be forfeited." 18 U.S.C. § 545. The government claims that the importation of the Phiale was illegal because it violated 18 U.S.C. § 542, which prohibits the making of false statements in the course of importing merchandise into the United States. Steinhardt claims, however, that an element of a Section 542 violation is that such a false statement must be material and that the government has failed to show materiality in the instant case, at least for purposes of summary judgment. He further contends that Section 545 provides him with an innocent owner defense and that forfeiture would violate the Excessive Fines Clause of the Eighth Amendment in light of the Supreme Court's recent decision in *United States v. Bajakajian,* 524 U.S. 321, 118 S. Ct. 2028, 141 L.Ed.2d 314 (1998).

A. Materiality Under Section 542

Section 542 states in pertinent part:

> Whoever enters or introduces . . . into the commerce of the United States any imported merchandise by means of any fraudulent or false invoice, declaration, affidavit, letter, paper, or by means of any false statement, written or verbal . . . or makes any false statement in any declaration without reasonable cause to believe the truth of such statement, or procures the making of any such false statement as to any matter material thereto without reasonable cause to believe the truth of such statement [shall be guilty of a crime].

18 U.S.C. § 542. There can be no dispute that the designation of Switzerland as the Phiale's country of origin and the listing of its value of $250,000 were false. . . .

* * *

The dispute pertinent to this appeal concerns the proper test for materiality. Steinhardt argues for a "but for" test of materiality, *i.e.*, a false statement is material only if a truthful answer on a customs form would have actually prevented the item from entering the United States. The district court, however, employed a "natural tendency" test, asking whether the false statement would have a natural tendency to influence customs officials. The circuits are divided as to the proper test. . . . We adopt the natural tendency test.

The statutory language, caselaw, and the statutory purpose lead us to this conclusion. First, the statute prohibits importations "by means of" a false statement. Although there is overlap, this language is not synonymous with "because of," and ought not be read so narrowly. Instead, the ordinary meaning of the statutory language requires only that the false statements be an integral part of the importation process. In this case, the false statements were on custom forms and thus easily meet the by means of requirement.

Second, the Supreme Court has noted that "[t]he most common formulation of [materiality] . . . is that a concealment or misrepresentation is material if it 'has a natural tendency to influence or was capable of influencing, the decision of' the decision making body to which it was addressed." . . .

Finally, the natural tendency approach is far more consistent with the purpose of the statute—to ensure truthfulness of representations made during importation—than is a but for test. Under a but for test, lying would be more productive because the government would bear the difficult burden of proving what would have happened if a truthful statement had been made. . . . The statutory purpose would thus be frustrated by the narrow reading suggested by appellant.

We therefore hold that "a false statement is material under [S]ection 542 if it has the potential significantly to affect the integrity or operation of the importation process as a whole, and that neither actual causation nor harm to the government need be demonstrated." For a trier of fact to determine whether a statement can significantly affect the importation process, it need ask only whether a reasonable customs official would consider the statements to be significant to the exercise of his or her official duties. . . . With this test in mind, we turn to the misstatements on the Phiale's entry form.

Steinhardt contends that even under a natural tendency test, the misstatements are immaterial.

* * *

Customs Directive No. 5230-15, regarding the detention and seizure of cultural property, fatally undermines Steinhardt's contention that listing Switzerland as the country of origin was irrelevant to the Phiale's importation. The Directive advised customs officials to determine whether property was subject to a claim of foreign ownership and to seize that property. Customs Directive No. 5230-15 (Apr. 18, 1991) [hereinafter "Directive"]. An item's country of origin is clearly relevant to that inquiry.

Steinhardt contends, however, that the Directive does not cover the Phiale and, therefore, the misstatements could not have been material because there was no legal basis for the Phiale's seizure. We disagree. The Directive provides a basis for seizing cultural property under the NSPA in the seizure provisions of 19 U.S.C. § 1595a(c). Seizure of the Phiale would clearly be authorized by this provision under *United States v. McClain,* 545 F.2d 988 (5th Cir.1977), which held that violations of a nation's patrimony laws are covered by the NSPA. Because Steinhardt asserts that *McClain* was improperly decided, he claims that the customs officials lacked a statutory basis to seize the Phiale.

This argument, however, misperceives the test of materiality. Regardless of whether *McClain*'s reasoning is ultimately followed as a proper interpretation of the NSPA, a reasonable customs official would certainly consider the fact that *McClain* supports a colorable claim to seize the Phiale as having possibly been exported in violation of Italian patrimony laws. Indeed, the Directive explicitly references the *McClain* decision and informs officials that if they are unsure of the status of a nation's patrimony laws, they should notify the Office of Enforcement. Knowing that the Phiale was from Italy would, therefore, be of critical importance.

Even if such a seizure might ultimately fail in court—an issue we need not address—the misstatement was still material because it had the "potential significantly to affect the integrity or operation of the importation process"—the manner in which Customs handles the assessment of duties and passage of goods into the United States. To decide otherwise would give an importer license and incentive to mislead customs officials whenever the legal basis of a seizure was somewhat unclear. . . .

* * *

B. Innocent Owner Defense

Steinhardt next contends that even if the statements were material, Section 545 affords him an innocent owner defense. Our discussion will assume for purposes of analysis that Steinhardt is such an innocent owner. While numerous statutes contain an explicit innocent owner defense, Section 545 does not, and there is no reason to believe that the omission in Section 545 was anything but deliberate. Steinhardt argues, however, that the Due Process Clause entitles him to such a defense.

This argument has been rejected by the Supreme Court. In *Bennis v. Michigan*, 516 U.S. 442, 116 S.Ct. 994, 134 L.Ed.2d 68 (1996), Court upheld a Michigan statute that permitted the forfeiture of an automobile co-owned by an innocent owner.... Against this long line of precedent, Steinhardt relies principally ... our decision in *United States v. One Tintoretto Painting*, which also relied on the *Calero-Toledo* dicta. However, the *Bennis* Court explicitly rejected this language, *see Bennis*, 516 U.S. at 449–450, 116 S. Ct. 994, and we must follow suit.

C. Eighth Amendment

While Steinhardt raised an Eighth Amendment claim in the district court, he did not raise it on appeal. Nonetheless, he now contends that under the Supreme Court's recent decision in *United States v. Bajakajian*, 524 U.S. 321, 118 S.Ct. 2028, 141 L.Ed.2d 314 (1998), handed down after the briefs were filed in this case, the forfeiture violates the Excessive Fines Clause of the Eighth Amendment. We disagree.

Bajakajian involved a criminal prosecution for failing to report the transporting of more than $10,000 out of the United States. The Court held that this proceeding triggered the Excessive Fines Clause and that the seizure of the entire amount, in excess of $357,000, would violate this constitutional safeguard. Critical to the Court's analysis, however, was that the forfeiture ... which Mr. Bajakajian pleaded guilty to violating, constituted a punishment....

* * *

... [I]mportant to the inquiry is the nature of the statute that authorizes forfeiture. As opposed to ... the provisions at issue in *Bajakajian*, Section 545 is a customs law, traditionally viewed as non-punitive.... The Phiale is thus classic contraband, an item imported into the United States in violation of law....

We therefore affirm.

Notes and Questions

1. *Aftermath*. The Supreme Court denied the petition for a writ of certiorari in *Antique Platter* in January 2000 (Steinhardt v. United States, 528 U.S. 1136 (2000)), and the Phiale was ceremoniously returned to Italy in February. Steinhardt, Haber, and Veres were tried in an Italian Court in Palermo for illegally exporting the Phiale. In 2004, Steinhardt was acquitted, while Haber and Veres were convicted and received suspended sentences of one year and three months.

Although Veres contractually agreed to indemnify Steinhardt if the Phiale was confiscated by CBP, he reportedly lacked the resources to do so. Think how you would address this practical problem in the sales contract. Is the risk similar to that of authenticity?

2. *False Statements: Country of Origin and Value.* In *Tintoretto* and *Antique Platter (Steinhardt),* the forfeiture proceedings under 18 U.S.C. § 545 were based on making false statements on customs forms, which is prohibited under 18 U.S.C. § 542. *Tintoretto* was a FBI sting operation in real time. The actionable statements in *Tintoretto* were unequivocally false: the painting was the agent's personal property, for his own use, not for resale, and was worth $500. If true, the painting would have been exempt from duty. From the time of the painting's entry into the U.S. to the time of the guilty plea was less than two months. In contrast, the false statements in *Antique Platter* concerned the Phiale's country of origin and its value. The Phiale passed through customs and was in Steinhardt's possession for almost four years before seizure.

Country of origin and value are two of the more common mistakes in customs declarations with the burden on the importer to show reasonable care. See Leslie Alan Glick, Guide to United States Customs and Trade Laws (3d ed. 2008).

For CBP purposes, country of origin generally means where the article was manufactured or substantially transformed, reflecting the day-to-day trade focus of customs. When dealing with older artworks or cultural property, determining the country of origin can be a challenge, as the upcoming *Peru v. Johnson* case shows. Tintoretto presumably created his painting in 16th century Venice (which was not yet Italy). The painting was thereafter removed from Dresden in East Germany (now Germany), taken to the Soviet Union (now Russia), thence to Austria and Israel. The Phiale dates from 450 B.C. and was illegally excavated from Sicily (which, in 450 B.C., was then the territory of ancient Greece) with its place of creation uncertain. If Steinhardt's documentation had listed Greece as the country of origin, would that have changed the result?

In the general context of customs, country of origin was historically important, because the tariff rates were based on whether goods came from countries with the preferential most favored nation status or elsewhere. Today, in the context of items properly classified as artworks or antiquities, the U.S. tariff rate is generally meaningless, except for imports from those countries with which tariffs may now be in force. The primary significance of country of origin for works of art or antiquities is not revenue, but whether the item is cultural property "subject to a claim of foreign ownership" covered by a treaty or domestic legislation. Consequently, the country of origin for customs purposes should have a purposive interpretation. In the context of *Antique Platter,* therefore, country of origin should be listed as Italy.

Country of origin thus triggers the second tier of CBP import analysis, the consideration of special rules for the protection of cultural property. CBP specifically notes that regardless of foreign law, "if a violation of US law occurs [e.g., a false statement—Ed.] the articles may be subject to seizure and forfeiture under U.S. law." CBP, What Every Member of the Trade Community Should Know About: Works of Art, Collector's Pieces, Antiques, and Other Cultural Property 14 (2006), available at www.cbp.gov.

The third basic determination for imports is value, and the preferred method of valuing is transaction value. See Leslie Alan Glick, Guide to United States Customs and Trade Laws 36 (3d ed. 2008) ("[W]hen importation results from a sale where the buyer and seller are unrelated parties, the dutiable value is determined by the selling price. This method, known as transaction value in the US, is the most frequently used. . . ."). Neither *Tintoretto*'s $500 nor *Antique Platter*'s $250,000 valuation met the standard of transaction value; each was clearly false.

If there has not yet been a sale of a work being imported for auction, what method of valuation is appropriate for customs? In HQ 547381, 2000 WL 552651 (U.S. Customs Service, March 14, 2000) (another Sotheby's request related to the imported Giacometti furniture, see Note 6, following *Brancusi, supra*), CBP noted that in the absence of the preferred transaction value, the alternative methods (in order) are transaction value of identical or similar merchandise, deductive value, computed value, and finally the "fallback" method. As the items were unique and to be auctioned more than 90 days after import, neither the transaction value of identical or similar merchandise or the deductive value was appropriate. As the computed value involves determining the value of the materials and fabrication process, it was also not appropriate. The fallback method is to make a valuation from one of the above methods, reasonably adjusted for the situation. Based on the fallback method, CBP determined that the appropriate value was the auction reserve amount, as that was the "only mutually accepted value that reflects both a seller's and Sotheby's assessment of the item's current market value."

3. *Forfeiture.* Forfeiture is an extreme and seemingly heavy-handed remedy in U.S. jurisprudence. The *Tintoretto* court's openness in 1982 to an additional innocent owner defense was foreclosed by the Supreme Court's 1996 decision in *Bennis,* as the 1999 *Antique Platter* court pointedly noted. The legislative reaction to *Bennis* was relatively direct, if not swift. In 2000, Congress enacted the Civil Asset Forfeiture Reform Act, 18 U.S.C. §983, creating a uniform innocent owner defense for most civil forfeiture cases. Forfeitures pursuant to the "Tariff Act 1930 or any other provision of law codified in title 19" are, however, specifically exempted from the act's provisions. See United States v. Eighteenth Century Peruvian Oil on Canvas Painting of the "Doble Trinidad," 597 F. Supp. 2d 618 (E.D. Va. 2009).

Stripped down, Steinhardt's forfeiture was triggered solely by his agent's false statements on the customs forms, primarily the country of origin designation. Although the underlying facts certainly give pause, technically, the illegal excavation in Italy, the smuggling into Switzerland, and subsequent sale were irrelevant to the CBP forfeiture. Both *Tintoretto* and *Antique Platter* are powerful reminders that crossing borders requires an awareness and strong sensitivity to the procedural requirements of CBP.

4. *Use Tax.* Bringing an artwork purchased abroad into the U.S. can also have domestic tax consequences. It is common knowledge that many states and localities impose sales taxes on the purchase of goods within their jurisdictions. See Chapter 1, *supra*. What may be surprising is a state's use tax. When a resident purchases goods outside the state's jurisdictional boundaries and then brings those goods into the jurisdiction, the state may impose a use tax on these goods in an effort to protect state tax revenues and in-state businesses from lower out-of-state sales tax rates. This is an effort to neutralize competition among the states for sales transactions. See also Chapter 1, *supra*, for discussion of use and sales taxes and international freeports.

In complex regulatory areas like customs and taxation, the devil is in the details. Consider the rules for who is a resident for purposes of New York's use tax. See generally N.Y. Dep't Taxation and Finance, Form ST-140-I, available http://www.tax.nygov/pdf/current_forms/st/st140i.pdf. Any individual who maintains a permanent place of abode in New York is a resident for use tax purposes. A permanent place of abode is a dwelling maintained by the person, or by another for that person to use (without regard to ownership), on other than a temporary or transient basis, specifically including second homes, apartments, dorm rooms, and military housing. A person can easily be a resident of more than one state for sales and use tax purposes. Under these rules, someone who is not a New York resident for personal income tax purposes may be surprised to learn that she is or was a resident for sales and use tax purposes. A later move into New York with an artwork purchased when the individual was a deemed resident for use tax purposes will require the payment of New York use tax. An example can illustrate the reach of use taxes. A senior executive with a multinational company from Brazil spends ten days a month in New York at an apartment maintained by her employer for her exclusive use. Two years later, she accepts a job in New York with another company and moves her household (including artworks purchased within the two years) from Rio to New York. How would anyone know? CBP can provide information from customs declarations to New York taxing authorities.

B. Import and Export Restrictions

If the CBP documentation for an artwork is correct, the artwork will normally clear customs and be allowed entry into the U.S. As the *Antique Platter* case indicated, the designated country of origin may trigger CBP's consideration of import restrictions placed on certain items of cultural property by the U.S. This section develops this second area of customs—that of import and export restrictions, especially the interplay of U.S. import restrictions related to failures of other nations' export restrictions on cultural property.

The term cultural property does not have one exclusive meaning in U.S. law, in other countries' laws, or in international law, in part reflecting the conflicting views on which items should be subject to import and export restrictions and other protective measures. Unless otherwise noted, the term cultural property as used herein shall be its most expansive interpretation, but a close reading of the pertinent legislation is required for true analysis.

Notes

1. *Cultural Property Implementation Act.* The 1970 UNESCO Convention on the Means of Prohibiting and Preventing the Illicit Import, Export and Transfer of Ownership of Cultural Property provides the essential backdrop to the import and export restrictions that have developed with respect to artworks or antiquities as cultural property. The unsavory facts of *Antique Platter* and the next two cases, *Peru* and *Schultz*, provide a concrete context for understanding the 1970 Convention.

Broader concerns over the destruction of archaeological sites by clandestine excavations, and the plunder and pillage of public and private artworks during times of war and conflict, stretch back centuries. The founding of the UN and UNESCO post-World War II provided the intellectual moment and diplomatic venue for sustained, collective discussion on protecting cultural property, ultimately resulting in the adoption of the 1970 Convention.

The U.S. Senate consented to the 1970 Convention in 1972. That consent was specifically accompanied by one reservation and six understandings. The 1970 Convention was not self-executing. Each state party to the 1970 Convention needed to adopt domestic legislation to implement the Convention. In this sense, the U.S. accepted the 1970 Convention with its adoption of the Convention on Cultural Property Implementation Act (CPIA), 19 U.S.C. §§ 2601–2613 in 1983. That decade-long delay and the U.S.'s consent with its specific reservation and understandings reflect the deep, sharp, sometimes bitter, divides in the art world over the movement of items of cultural property in international trade, as well as governmental concerns on the shift in enforcement responsibility from the export to the import side. See Paul Bator, *An Essay on the International Trade in Art*, 34 Stan. L. Rev. 275 (1982); John Henry Merryman, *Two Ways of Thinking About Cultural Property*, 80 Am. J. Int'l L. 831 (1986); *Art Systems and Cultural Property*, 15 Art Antiquities & Law 99 (2010). Despite the uneven history of the 1970 Convention for the U.S. and other nations, the 1970 Convention continues to be implemented, and its importance as an agent of soft change in societal attitudes and in hard-edged enforcement mechanisms has never been greater. See Patrick J. O'Keefe, Commentary on the 1970 UNESCO Convention 107–123 (2d ed. 2007).

CPIA has two import restrictions for the U.S. Section 308 is a one-sentence straightforward prohibition on the U.S. import of any "article of cultural property, documented as appertaining to the inventory of a museum or religious or secular public monument or similar institution in any State Party which is stolen from such institution after the effective date." Section 308 generally mirrors Article 7(b)(i) of the 1970 Convention. It is a section of limited applicability largely due to the date restriction and documentation as part of inventory requirement;

it is not, however, without impact. See United States v. An Original Manuscript Dated November 19, 1778, 1999 WL 97894 (S.D.N.Y. 1999), concerning the CBP seizure and forfeiture of a Father Junipero Serra manuscript stolen from the Mexican National Archives after 1983, where the individual (non-dealer) purchaser was not entitled to reasonable compensation for the article, as the purchaser did not establish he was an innocent purchaser, despite his inquiries as to provenance, his hiring of an attorney, and paying fair market value. See also Autocephalous Greek-Orthodox Church of Cyprus v. Goldberg & Feldman Fine Arts, Inc., 917 F.2d 279, 297 (7th Cir. 1990) (Cudahy, J., concurring: "This section is not directly applicable here . . . , because the mosaics were [not—Ed.] stolen after the effective date of the statute"), Chapter 5, *supra*.

The import restrictions under Section 307 covering archaeological or ethnological materials are significantly more complex, underscoring the political difficulties in framing the scope of the domestic legislation and enforcement responsibility. The Section 307 import restrictions are only activated by another country's request to the U.S. for such import restrictions. The request must show that (i) the country's cultural patrimony is in jeopardy from pillage, (ii) the country has taken protective measures to address that concern, (iii) the import restrictions would be of substantial benefit in deterring the pillage and less drastic remedies are not available, and (iv) the import restrictions would be consistent with the intercultural interests of the international community. The Cultural Property Advisory Committee will review the request and make a recommendation to the President. Under the CPIA, the President is authorized to enter into bilateral or a multinational agreement with the country or countries for a maximum of five years, subject to renewal. 19 U.S.C. §2602.

Archaeological and ethnological items subject to this provision due to a bilateral or multinational agreement may not be imported into the U.S., unless accompanied by a "certification or other documentation . . . that such exportation was not in violation of the laws of the State Party." CBP is the front-line enforcer of the CPIA and enforces the import restrictions of the countries with which the U.S. has entered into bilateral agreements. As of November 2020, there were 23 listed countries (Algeria, Belize, Bolivia, Bulgaria, Cambodia, China, Chile, Colombia, Cyprus, Ecuador, Egypt, El Salvador, Greece, Guatemala, Honduras, Iraq, Italy, Jordan, Libya, Mali, Peru, Syria and Yemen).

Perceived shortcomings in the CPIA led to the use of other legal theories and statutes in cases concerning foreign cultural property in the U.S., causing some confusion as to the role of the CPIA. Judge Cudahy's concurrence in *Autocephalous Greek-Orthodox Church* noted the technical irrelevance of CPIA ("the statute is directed at import controls rather than replevin suits"), but urged judicial recognition of CPIA's policy ("the policy that the Act embodies is clear: at the very least, we should not sanction illegal traffic in stolen cultural property that is clearly documented as belonging to a public or religious institution."). Autocephalous Greek-Orthodox Church of Cyprus v. Goldberg & Feldman Fine Arts, Inc., 917 F.2d 279,

297 (7th Cir. 1990). The next two cases, *Peru* and *Schulz*, represent two divergent legal approaches to the problem of illegally exported cultural property.

2. *Other Import Restrictions.* CBP enforces other import restrictions that can affect artworks or cultural property on entry into the U.S. Some predate CPIA and reflect similar concerns, such as the Pre-Colombian Monumental, Architectural Sculpture or Murals Act of 1972 (19 U.S.C. §§2091–2095), and a bilateral Treaty with Mexico signed March 24, 1971, covering certain states' archaeological, historical and cultural property.

Some restrictions proceed directly from political concerns, such as the Cuban Assets Control Regulations, 31 C.F.R. Part 515, dating from July 8, 1963, and restrictions imposed at various times on imports from Iraq, Iran, Sudan, and Burma. Another type of import restriction focuses on materials used, e.g., the Endangered Species Act of 1973, 16 U.S.C. §§1531–1544, which would restrict imports of works incorporating ivory or bird feathers, for example. See Kirk Wallace Johnson, The Feather Thief (2018), for a fascinating account of the theft of historic bird feathers and skins from the British Museum of Natural History by an American champion fly-tier for use in salmon fishing. It is worth noting that absent a domestically accepted obligation, the illegal export of property from another country is not, in and of itself, a violation of U.S. import laws. See CBP, What Every Member of the Trade Community Should Know About: Works of Art, Collector's Pieces, Antiques, and Other Cultural Property 14 (May 2006); see also Jeanneret v. Vichy, 693 F.2d 259 (2d Cir. 1982); but cf., United States v. Schultz, 333 F.3d 393 (2d Cir. 2003).

Government of Peru v. Johnson

720 F. Supp. 810 (C.D. Cal. 1989)

GRAY, J. The Government of Peru . . . contends that it is the legal owner of eighty-nine artifacts that have been seized by the United States Customs Service from defendant Benjamin Johnson. The plaintiff charges the defendant with conversion of these articles and seeks an order for their return. Judgment will be rendered for the defendant.

Irrespective of the decision in this matter, the court has considerable sympathy for Peru with respect to the problems that it confronts as manifested by this litigation. It is evident that many priceless and beautiful Pre-Columbian artifacts excavated from historical monuments in that country have been and are being smuggled abroad and sold to museums and other collectors of art. Such conduct is destructive of a major segment of the cultural heritage of Peru, and the plaintiff is entitled to the support of the courts of the United States in its determination to prevent further looting of its patrimony.

However, there is substantial evidence that Mr. Johnson purchased the subject items in good faith over the years, and the plaintiff must overcome legal and factual burdens that are heavy indeed before the court can justly order the subject items to be removed from the defendant's possession and turned over to the plaintiff. The trial of this action has shown that the plaintiff simply cannot meet these burdens.

1. The Plaintiff Cannot Establish that the Subject Artifacts were Excavated in Modern Day Peru.

The plaintiff has no direct evidence that any of the subject items came from Peru. It alleges, on information and belief, that they were taken from Peru or excavated from archeological sites in that country. The plaintiff's principal witness was Dr. Francisco Iriarte . . . Peru's foremost archeologist in Pre-Columbian artifacts. Dr. Iriarte examined each of the eighty-nine artifacts . . . and he usually asserted the belief that it came from a particular excavation site or specific area in Peru. I have no doubt that Dr. Iriarte has seen artifacts taken from those respective locations. . . . However, Dr. Iriarte admitted that Peruvian Pre-Columbian culture spanned not only modern day Peru, but also areas that now are within the borders of Bolivia and Ecuador, and many of the population centers that were part of the Peruvian Pre-Columbian civilization, and from which artifacts have been taken, are within those countries. The fact that the subject items are identifiable with excavation sites in modern Peru does not exclude the possibility that they are equally similar to artifacts found in archeological monuments in Bolivia and Ecuador. . . .

Moreover, Columbia also borders Peru, and customs documents that appear to pertain to some of the subject items assert Columbia to be the country of origin. . . . However, they do further point up the difficulty that the court has in concluding that any specific one of the items concerned in this action originated within the present boundaries of Peru.

I was impressed by Dr. Iriarte's testimony. He doubtless is knowledgeable. . . . In some instances, he admitted that an item may have come from Ecuador or Columbia or Mexico or even Polynesia, but nonetheless retained the opinion that it had been found in a particular area of Peru, due to its similarity to other objects taken from that site. Because of the many other possibilities, this court cannot base a finding of ownership upon such subjective conclusions. We are far from certain as to the country of origin of any of the artifacts here concerned. This unfortunate circumstance precludes an adjudication that they came from Peru.

2. The Plaintiff Cannot Establish Its Ownership at the Time of Exportation.

Even if it were to be assumed that the artifacts came from Peru, in order for the plaintiff to recover them, it must prove that the Government of Peru was the legal owner at the time of their removal from that country. Such ownership depends upon the laws of Peru, which are far from precise and have changed several times over the years.

(a) *1822–1929.* The plaintiff, in its Second Post Trial Brief, submitted . . . copies of the statutes upon which it relies to establish that, from 1822 to the present time, Peru owned the artifacts located in that country. However, in its pleadings . . . the plaintiff identified Law No. 6634 of June 13, 1929, as the earliest enactment that formed the legal basis for its ownership claims. Federal Rule of Civil Procedure 44.1 provides that "[a] party who intends to raise an issue concerning the law of a foreign country shall give notice by pleadings or other reasonable written notice." I find that initial presentation of these purported pre-1929 enactments after the case has been tried cannot constitute "reasonable notice", and I decline to consider them in rendering this decision.

* * *

The defendant's expert, Professor Alan Sawyer . . . testified that it is impossible to determine from examination of the items here concerned when they were excavated or left the country of origin, and that many Peruvian artifacts were brought into the United States before 1929. It follows that if any of the subject items left Peru before 1929, the plaintiff cannot claim ownership of them.

(b) *1929–1985.* A written opinion by Professor MacLean asserts that what Law No. 6634 means "is that if a person found an archeological object before June of 1929 this object belongs to him; but if that person found the object after June 1929 it belongs to the State." Article 11 of Law No. 6634 provides that privately owned Pre-Columbian artifacts must be registered in a special book "which shall be opened at the National Museum of History", and that any "[o]bjects which, after one year beginning on the day the book is opened, have not been registered, shall be considered the property of the State."

From the record at the trial, I cannot determine when the "special book" called for by Article 11 was opened or whether it ever has been opened. . . .

On January 5, 1985, Law No. 6634 was repealed and replaced by Law No. 24047. According to Professor MacLean's written opinion, "[a]fter that date there is also the obligation for private persons to register their archeological objects and if they do not comply with this obligation that *could* mean that the objects belong to the State." (Emphasis added.)

In . . . this confusing situation, I am assuming that none of the artifacts have been duly registered. However, I do not know whether the repeal of Law No. 6634 nullifies the registration requirement therein contained. If it does, a private owner could have retained an unregistered item through January 1985 without losing his title. . . .

(c) *From January 1985 to the Present.* . . . Professor MacLean's written opinion states . . . "if a person finds after 5th January of 1985 an archeological object it can belong to him." . . . However, on June 22, 1985, a new statute provided specifically that all archeological sites belong to the state. "So if a private person digs a site and excavates its objects [he] is taking somebody else's property", according to Professor MacLean's written opinion. Thus, it would appear that if any artifacts here concerned were privately excavated between January 5 and June 22, 1985, they would constitute private property, rather than being owned by Peru.

3. Michael Kelly's Testimony Does Not Establish Peru's Ownership.

Mr. Michael Kelly testified that in August 1987 he brought to Mr. Johnson's home in California certain artifacts that he believed to have come from Peru. But all of his information as to the country of origin of these items was strictly hearsay. . . .

Despite Mr. Kelly's testimony, which was designed to show that Mr. Johnson was implicated in, or at least was aware of, the smuggling activities . . . , I am not satisfied that Mr. Johnson received any of the items here concerned with the knowledge that they were illegally removed from Peru.

4. The Uncertainty of the Domestic Application of Peru's Ownership Laws.

Official documents of Peru long have asserted, in one way or another, the interest of the state in preserving its artistic objects as "part of the national cultural wealth," that they are "untouchable, inalienable and inprescriptable," and that their removal from the country is "categorically forbidden." Such declarations are concerned with protection and do not imply ownership. However, the law of June 13, 1929, does proclaim that artifacts in historical monuments are "the property of the State" and that unregistered artifacts "shall be considered to be the property of the State." Nonetheless, the domestic effect of such a pronouncement appears to be extremely limited. Possession of the artifacts is allowed to remain in private hands, and such objects may be transferred by gift or bequest or intestate succession. There is no indication in the record that Peru ever has sought to exercise its ownership rights in such property, so long as there is no removal from that country. The laws of Peru concerning its artifacts could reasonably be considered to have no more effect than export restrictions, and, as was pointed out in *United States v. McClain,* 545 F.2d 988, 1002 (5th Cir.1977), export restrictions constitute an exercise of the police power of a state; "[t]hey do not create 'ownership' in the state. The state comes to own property only when it acquires such property in the general manner by which private persons come to own property, or when it declares itself the owner."

The second time that the case of *United States v. McClain* came before the Fifth Circuit, the opinion stated: "It may well be, as testified so emphatically by most of the Mexican witnesses, that Mexico has considered itself the owner of all pre-Columbian artifacts for almost 100 years. If so, however, it has not expressed that view with sufficient clarity to survive translation into terms understandable by and binding upon American citizens." 593 F.2d 658, 670 (5th Cir.1979). Under all of the above discussed circumstances, I find the same comment to be applicable here.

5. Conclusion.

Peru may not prevail in this action to recover the artifacts here concerned because:

(a) We do not know in what country they were found and from which they were exported.

(b) If they were found in Peru, we do not know when.

(c) We do not know if they were in private possession in Peru more than one year after the official registry book was opened.

(d) The extent of Peru's claim of ownership as part of its domestic law is uncertain.

United States v. Schultz

333 F.3d 393 (2d Cir. 2003)

MESKILL, J.

* * *

Schultz was a successful art dealer in New York City. On July 16, 2001, he was indicted on one count of conspiring to receive stolen Egyptian antiquities that had been transported in interstate and foreign commerce, in violation of 18 U.S.C. § 371. The underlying substantive offense was a violation of 18 U.S.C. § 2315, the National Stolen Property Act (NSPA).

Schultz moved to dismiss the indictment, asserting that the items he was charged with conspiring to receive were not stolen within the meaning of the NSPA. Specifically, Schultz contended that the Egyptian antiquities he allegedly conspired to receive were not owned by anyone, and therefore could not be stolen. The prosecution asserted that the antiquities were owned by the Egyptian government pursuant to a patrimony law known as "Law 117" which declared all antiquities found in Egypt after 1983 to be the property of the Egyptian government. After an evidentiary hearing, the district court denied the motion to dismiss in a written memorandum and order. Schultz was tried before a jury in January and February 2002.

The following facts were adduced at trial.

In 1991, Schultz met Jonathan Tokeley Parry (Parry), a British national.... Parry showed Schultz a photograph of an ancient sculpture of the head of Pharaoh Amenhotep III, and told Schultz that he had obtained the sculpture in Egypt earlier that year from a ... a building contractor. Parry had used an Egyptian middle-man named Ali Farag (Farag) to facilitate the deal. Parry had smuggled the sculpture out of Egypt by coating it with plastic so that it would look like a cheap souvenir, then removed the plastic coating once the sculpture was in England.

Schultz offered Parry a substantial fee to serve as the agent for the sale of the Amenhotep sculpture, which Parry accepted. Parry and Schultz discussed the problems that might arise if they were discovered to have the piece, and set out to create a false provenance for the sculpture, so that they could sell it.... Parry and Schultz invented a fictional collection, the "Thomas Alcock Collection," and represented to potential buyers that the sculpture came from this collection. With Schultz's knowledge, Parry prepared fake labels, designed to look as though they had been printed in the 1920s, and affixed the labels to the sculpture. Parry also restored the sculpture using a method popular in the 1920s.

Acting as Parry's agent, Schultz attempted to sell the Amenhotep sculpture ... but was unsuccessful. Eventually, Parry sold the sculpture to Schultz for $800,000, and Schultz sold it to a private collector in 1992 for $1.2 million. . . .

Parry and Schultz became partners [bringing] more Egyptian antiquities into America for resale, smuggling them out of Egypt disguised as cheap souvenirs, assigning a false provenance to them, and restoring them with 1920s techniques. . . .

* * *

In 1992, Parry and Farag learned that someone had reported them to the Egyptian authorities for dealing in antiquities. Due in part to the assistance of Farag's father, who was a powerful Egyptian government official, Parry and Farag were able to get their names removed from police records by paying a bribe to certain corrupt members of the Egyptian antiquities police. These same corrupt police officers then entered into a deal with Parry and Farag, offering them a variety of antiquities in police possession in exchange for Parry and Farag paying off some debts owed by the police officers. . . .

* * *

In June 1994, Parry was arrested in Great Britain, and Farag was arrested in Egypt. Each was charged with dealing in stolen antiquities. Schultz was aware of the arrests and communicated extensively with Parry after his arrest about Parry's legal situation. Parry and Schultz also continued to correspond regarding plans for new acquisitions.

* * *

Discussion

I. Application of the NSPA to Cases Involving Patrimony Laws

In order to preserve its cultural heritage, Egypt in 1983 enacted a "patrimony law" which declares all antiquities discovered after the enactment of the statute to be the property of the Egyptian government. The law provides for all antiquities privately owned prior to 1983 to be registered and recorded, and prohibits the removal of registered items from Egypt. The law makes private ownership or possession of antiquities found after 1983 illegal. Schultz's primary argument is that the NSPA does not apply to cases in which an object was "stolen" only in the sense that it was possessed or disposed of by an individual in violation of a national patrimony law. . . . The government contends . . . the NSPA applies to *any* stolen property, regardless of the source of the true owner's title in the property. The question, in other words, is whether an object is "stolen" within the meaning of the NSPA if it is an antiquity which was found in Egypt after 1983 and retained by an individual (and, in this case, removed from Egypt) without the Egyptian government's consent.

The NSPA reads, in pertinent part, as follows:

> Whoever receives, possesses, conceals, stores, barters, sells, or disposes of any goods, wares, or merchandise, securities, or money of the value of

> $5,000 or more . . . which have crossed a State or United States boundary after being stolen, unlawfully converted, or taken, knowing the same to have been stolen, unlawfully converted, or taken . . . [s]hall be fined under this title or imprisoned not more than ten years, or both.

18 U.S.C. § 2315 (2000).

This statute is unambiguous. It applies to goods that are "stolen, unlawfully converted, or taken." Goods that belong to a person or entity and are taken from that person or entity without its consent are "stolen" in every sense of that word. . . . Accordingly, Schultz's actions violated the NSPA if the antiquities he conspired to receive in the United States belonged to someone who did not give consent for Schultz (or his agent) to take them. That "someone" is the nation of Egypt.

In 1983, Egypt enacted Law 117. The law, which is entitled "The Law on the Protection of Antiquities," reads, in pertinent part, as follows:

> *Article 1*
>
> An "Antiquity" is any movable or immovable property that is a product of any of the various civilizations or any of the arts, sciences, humanities and religions of the successive historical periods extending from prehistoric times down to a point one hundred years before the present, so long as it has either a value or importance archaeologically or historically that symbolizes one of the various civilizations that have been established in the land of Egypt or that has a historical relation to it, as well as human and animal remains from any such period.
>
> *Article 6*
>
> All antiquities are considered to be public property-except for charitable and religious endowments. . . . It is impermissible to own, possess or dispose of antiquities except pursuant to the conditions set forth in this law and its implementing regulations.
>
> *Article 7*
>
> As of [1983], it is prohibited to trade in antiquities.
>
> *Article 8*
>
> With the exception of antiquities whose ownership or possession was already established [in 1983] or is established pursuant to [this law's] provisions, the possession of antiquities shall be prohibited as from [1983].

* * *

Schultz contends that in spite of its plain language, Law 117 is not a "real" ownership law, and that Egypt . . . merely seeks to restrict their export. The district court disagreed, finding . . . that the plain language of Law 117 accurately reflects its purpose and effect: to vest absolute and true ownership of all antiquities found in Egypt after 1983 in the Egyptian government.

* * *

... Law 117 makes it clear that the Egyptian government claims ownership of all antiquities found in Egypt after 1983, and the government's active enforcement of its ownership rights confirms the intent of the Law. Accordingly, we conclude ... the antiquities that were the subject of the conspiracy in this case were owned by the Egyptian government.

The question thus becomes whether Schultz's actions in conspiring to take antiquities owned by the Egyptian government pursuant to Law 117 out of Egypt violate the NSPA. Schultz argues that even if Law 117 does intend to vest true ownership of all antiquities with the Egyptian government, that sort of "ownership" should not be recognized by the United States for purposes of prosecution under the NSPA.

Schultz urges us to adopt a narrow reading of the NSPA. However, the Supreme Court and this Court have acknowledged that the NSPA has a "broad purpose," and that "the statute should be broadly construed." We have held that the language of the NSPA "is broad enough to justify the federal courts in applying the statute whenever they determine that the [property was] stolen in another country. Accordingly, there can be no doubt that if the antiquities involved in the conspiracy were stolen in Egypt and then shipped to the United States, the NSPA would be violated.

* * *

Notwithstanding all of the above, Schultz insists that the antiquities are not "stolen" within the meaning of the NSPA because they were never truly owned by the Egyptian government. The leading opinion addressing this question was issued by the Fifth Circuit, over 25 years ago, in *United States v. McClain,* 545 F.2d 988 (5th Cir.1977). The parties frame the question on appeal as whether the Second Circuit should adopt the reasoning set forth by the Fifth Circuit in *McClain.*

Schultz asserts that we should reject the holding in *McClain* based on existing Second Circuit precedent, which he reads as being hostile to *McClain*. Schultz then raises several additional arguments in support of his position, namely: (1) that *McClain* 's approach conflicts with United States policy, (2) that the enactment of the Convention on Cultural Property Implementation Act of 1983, 19 U.S.C. §§ 2601–2613 (CPIA), "confirms that Congress never intended [the] NSPA to reach ownership claims based upon national vesting laws when the property has not been reduced to the possession of the foreign state," and (3) that the common law definition of "stolen" would not reach the property at issue here. We address each of these arguments in turn.

A. McClain in the Second Circuit

The *McClain* defendants were convicted of conspiring to violate the NSPA by importing artifacts from Mexico that were covered by a Mexican law declaring all such artifacts to be owned by the Mexican government. The defendants claimed, as

Schultz does here, that the NSPA did not apply to "stolen" objects that were taken in violation of patrimony laws. The Fifth Circuit concluded that the NSPA did apply to such objects.

* * *

Summarizing its decision in *McClain,* the Fifth Circuit stated:

> This conclusion is a result of our attempt to reconcile the doctrine of strict construction of criminal statutes with the broad significance attached to the word "stolen" in the NSPA. Were the word to be so narrowly construed as to exclude coverage, for example, with respect to pre-Columbian artifacts illegally exported from Mexico after the effective date of the 1972 [patrimony] law, the Mexican government would be denied protection of the [NSPA] after it had done all it reasonably could do [to vest] itself with ownership to protect its interest in the artifacts. This would violate the apparent objective of Congress: the protection of owners of stolen property. If, on the other hand, an object were considered "stolen" merely because it was illegally exported, the meaning of the term "stolen" would be stretched beyond its conventional meaning. Although "stealing" is not a term of art, it is also not a word bereft of meaning. It should not be expanded at the government's will beyond the connotation depriving an owner of its rights in property conventionally called to mind.

McClain, 545 F.2d at 1001–02 (footnotes omitted). We agree that the Fifth Circuit reached the proper balance between these competing concerns in *McClain.*

* * *

iii. Steinhardt

Schultz also contends that our decision in *Steinhardt* indicates that we have rejected the holding of *McClain.* In *Steinhardt,* [*United States v. An Antique Platter of Gold,* 184 F.3d 131, 134 (2d Cir. 1999) (*Steinhardt*),] the district court had found that an Italian antiquity should be forfeited by Steinhardt, who had imported it into the United States, because (1) Steinhardt had made material misrepresentations on a customs form or, (2) in the alternative, the antiquity was properly owned by the Italian government pursuant to a patrimony law and was therefore stolen property within the meaning of the NSPA and subject to forfeiture. On appeal, we concluded that Steinhardt had made a material misstatement on a customs form.... Accordingly, the Court concluded that the antiquity was subject to forfeiture. The Court declined to reach the alternative ground ... stating: "We need not ... address whether the NSPA incorporates concepts of property such as those contained in the Italian patrimony laws."

It is irrelevant that we previously reviewed a case in which it was not necessary to reach the question now before us.... We find Schultz's reliance on *Steinhardt* unpersuasive.

B. United States Policy

Schultz contends that it is United States policy not to enforce the export restrictions of foreign nations. Schultz offers no evidence in support of this assertion, but even if his assessment of United States policy is accurate, the outcome of this case is unaffected. We have already concluded . . . that Law 117 is an ownership law, not an export-restriction law. . . .

C. The CPIA

Schultz contends that the adoption of the CPIA shows that Congress did not intend the NSPA to apply to objects such as the ones he conspired to bring to the United States. The CPIA implements a United Nations convention that was ratified by the United States in 1982, the purpose of which was to achieve "greater international cooperation towards preserving cultural treasures that not only are of importance to the nations whence they originate, but also to greater international understanding of our common heritage."

* * *

Schultz argues that the CPIA was intended to be the only mechanism by which the United States government would deal with antiquities and other "cultural property" imported into the United States. However, nothing in the language of the CPIA supports that interpretation, and the legislative history shows that exactly the converse is true. . . .

* * *

The CPIA is an import law, not a criminal law; it is not codified in Title 18 ("Crimes and Criminal Procedure"), with the NSPA, but in Title 19 ("Customs Duties"). It may be true that there are cases in which a person will be violating both the CPIA and the NSPA when he imports an object into the United States. But it is not inappropriate for the same conduct to result in a person being subject to both civil penalties and criminal prosecution, and the potential overlap between the CPIA and the NSPA is no reason to limit the reach of the NSPA.

For the reasons set forth above, we conclude that the passage of the CPIA does not limit the NSPA's application to antiquities stolen in foreign nations.

* * *

E. Summary

In light of our own precedents and the plain language of the NSPA, we conclude that the NSPA applies to property that is stolen in violation of a foreign patrimony law. The CPIA is not the exclusive means of dealing with stolen artifacts and antiquities, and reading the NSPA to extend to such property does not conflict with United States policy. We believe that, when necessary, our courts are capable of evaluating foreign patrimony laws to determine whether their language and enforcement indicate that they are intended to assert true ownership of certain property, or merely to restrict the export of that property. . . .

Although we recognize the concerns raised by Schultz and the *amici* about the risks that this holding poses to dealers in foreign antiquities, we cannot imagine that it "creates an insurmountable barrier to the lawful importation of cultural property into the United States." Our holding does assuredly create a barrier to the importation of cultural property owned by a foreign government. We see no reason that property stolen from a foreign sovereign should be treated any differently from property stolen from a foreign museum or private home. The *mens rea* requirement of the NSPA will protect innocent art dealers who unwittingly receive stolen goods, while our appropriately broad reading of the NSPA will protect the property of sovereign nations.

II. Defense of Mistake of United States Law

Schultz argues on appeal that the district court erred in refusing to allow him to present a defense of mistake of law. Specifically, Schultz sought to argue to the jury that he did not know that importing antiquities owned by the Egyptian government pursuant to Law 117 violated the NSPA. The government contends that the district court was correct to bar this defense, relying on "the venerable principle that ignorance of the law generally is no defense to a criminal charge."

Schultz concedes that this is the general rule, but asserts that certain exceptions exist. Schultz cites three cases in which he contends that the Supreme Court found a defense of mistake of law was proper. . . .

* * *

. . . Each of the cases relied on by Schultz is inapposite, for two reasons.

First, these decisions involve specific intent statutes. For instance, the statute at issue in [*United States v.*] *Lizarraga-Lizarraga* [541 F.2d 826 (9th Cir. 1976)] (now repealed) made it unlawful "willfully" to export certain items to Mexico. The inclusion of the term "willfully," the court found, made it clear that Congress intended to punish only those who exported ammunition knowing it was unlawful to do so. . . .

The NSPA does not include the term "willfully." The section of the NSPA applicable to Schultz reads as follows:

> Whoever receives, possesses, conceals, stores, barters, sells, or disposes of any goods, wares, or merchandise, securities, or money of the value of $5,000 or more . . . which have crossed a State or United States boundary after being stolen, unlawfully converted, or taken, *knowing the same to have been stolen, unlawfully converted, or taken* . . . [s]hall be fined under this title or imprisoned not more than ten years, or both.

18 U.S.C. § 2315 (2000) (emphasis added). The *only* knowledge requirement in the NSPA is knowledge that the goods were "stolen, unlawfully converted, or taken." . . .

Second, the cases cited by Schultz are inapposite because each concerns conduct that normally might not be considered unlawful. The *Lizarraga-Lizarraga* Court, for instance, emphasized that in enacting the statute of conviction, Congress "did not intend to criminally penalize innocent or negligent errors."

In addition, the record demonstrates that Schultz's actions were not "innocent" or merely "negligent." This is not a case in which the defendant believed that he was doing something lawful, and was surprised to find that his conduct could result in criminal sanctions. To the contrary, Schultz was conspiring to *smuggle* antiquities out of Egypt and into the United States. He was defrauding (or attempting to defraud) potential buyers.... Furthermore, Schultz and Parry demonstrated a keen awareness of the illegality of their actions by communicating in "code," forging documents, and even explicitly discussing the possibility that one or more of them might end up in prison.

We conclude that the district court did not err in denying Schultz's request to present a defense of mistake of American law. The jury did not have to find that Schultz knew what he was doing was illegal. As long as the jury found beyond a reasonable doubt that Schultz knew the antiquities were "stolen," the jury, following the law, would have been required to convict Schultz even if it believed he had misunderstood American law.

* * *

Conclusion

We conclude that the NSPA applies to property that is stolen from a foreign government, where that government asserts actual ownership of the property pursuant to a valid patrimony law. We find the remainder of Schultz's claims to be without merit. Accordingly, the judgment of the district court is hereby affirmed.

Notes and Questions

1. *Aftermath. Peru* was affirmed on appeal. Government of Peru v. Wendt, 933 F.2d 1013 (9th Cir. 1991).

The Supreme Court denied Schultz's petition for a writ of certiorari. 540 U.S. 1106 (2004). Frederick Schultz was one of America's top antiquities dealers in the 1990s. He was a politically astute Princeton graduate, president of the National Association of Dealers in Ancient, Oriental, and Primitive Art, and a member of the Cultural Property Advisory Committee during the Clinton administration. Following his conviction, Schultz was sentenced to 33 months in federal prison at Fort Dix, New Jersey and ordered to pay a $50,000 fine. See Barry Meier & Martin Gottlieb, *Loot: Along the Antiquities Trail; An Illicit Journey Out of Egypt, Only a Few Questions Asked*, N.Y. Times, Feb. 23, 2004, at A1, for a fascinating account of the smuggling of an Egyptian stele that was a critical piece in unraveling the smugglers' scheme.

2. *Some Legal Prehistory: McClain and Hollinshead.* In *Peru* and *Schultz*, the courts cited United States v. McClain, 593 F.2d 658 (5th Cir. 1979), approvingly, but to very different end results. *McClain* involved pre-Columbian artifacts smuggled from Mexico. Following an FBI sting operation, the defendants were convicted twice at

trial of violating NSPA in receiving, concealing, or selling stolen property in interstate and foreign commerce and also of conspiracy to do the same. The Fifth Circuit struck the NSPA convictions but upheld the conspiracy conviction. In striking the NSPA convictions, the Fifth Circuit determined (similar to the *Peru* court) that certain of the foreign laws arguably claiming ownership of all unexcavated artifacts were too unclear and uncertain, especially for criminal conviction, under U.S. law. The Fifth Circuit was clear (like the *Schultz* court), however, that the NSPA *could* apply to foreign cultural property cases. It rejected defendants' argument that the NSPA was superceded in this type of cultural property case by the Pre-Columbian Monumental, Architectural Sculpture or Murals Act of 1972.

The Fifth Circuit noted in *McClain* that the Ninth Circuit upheld the application of the NSPA to the illegal export of a stela from Guatemala in United States v. Hollinshead, 495 F.2d 1154 (9th Cir. 1974). Clive Hollinshead was the first defendant to be convicted under the NSPA for dealing in cultural property. The *Hollinshead* facts were quite blatant—the defendant arranged for a Mayan stela to be cut into pieces, transported out of the Guatemalan jungle, and eventually brought to the U.S. The Ninth Circuit determined that because Hollinshead's admissions evidenced knowledge that the stela was stolen, it was not necessary for the U.S. to prove that Hollinshead knew Guatemala law vested title in itself. As it happens, Hollinshead may have been peripherally involved in the *McClain* case. While Hollinshead was on probation for his conviction, the *McClain* court noted that he may have supplied several of the artifacts involved in the *McClain* case.

These two pre-CPIA cases from the 1970s, *McClain* and *Hollinshead*, were seen as weak precedents for a vigorous application of the NSPA to cultural property litigation. Nevertheless, the theory of *McClain*, as *Schultz* ultimately showed, had long term traction.

3. *From Peru to Schultz.* The shift in theory and result from *Peru* to *Schultz* represents a significant advancement in the protection afforded by U.S. policy and laws against the illicit trade in antiquities. This shift was not necessarily inevitable and reflects the larger shifts in societal attitudes and law enforcement mechanisms on illicit trade. See Patty Gerstenblith, *Schultz* and *Barakat*: *Universal Recognition of National Ownership of Antiquities*, 14 ART ANTIQUITY & LAW 21 (2009), for a comparative view of U.S. and U.K. enforcement of foreign nations' vesting laws. *Peru* was an unsuccessful civil action for conversion, brought by the foreign government, against the purchaser of the artifacts. *Schultz* was a successful criminal action for conspiracy to receive stolen property, brought by the U.S., against the art dealer-importer.

The 14 years between the two cases was marked by an increasing appreciation of the negative impact of archaeological pillage on our understanding of the cultures from which the objects are stolen. That appreciation was also accompanied by increasing global cooperation, often via bilateral treaties or emergency declarations between the U.S. and requesting countries under the CPIA. That cooperation similarly increased in the almost two decades from the time of the *Schultz* decision. For example, in 2017, the Hobby Lobby Corporation forfeited over 400 ancient cuneiform tablets imported from Iraq. See United States v. Approximately Four Hundred Fifty Ancient Cuneiform Tablets, et al., Verified Complaint *in Rem*, 17-CV-398 (N.Y.E.D. 2017). In its settlement with the U.S., Hobby Lobby also paid a $3 million fee, in part due to its compliance failures with its importations. The owners of Hobby Lobby were the primary funders of the Museum of the Bible in Washington D.C. Many items in the museum's collection were subject to controversy, including most recently, the Gilgamesh Dream Tablet. See, e.g., United States v. One Cuneiform Tablet Known as the "Gilgamesh Dream Tablet," Verified Complaint *in Rem*, #20-CV-2222 (E.D.N.Y. May 18, 2020).

The strength of CPIA is primarily executive and not judicial. CPIA sets the domestic framework for U.S. diplomacy in bilateral treaties on cultural property. The soft diplomacy of the CPIA is significant. CPIA is also the enforcement device that triggers CBP's second level review for import and provides the mechanism for subsequent seizures. As the cause of action for a specific case involving the illicit trade of cultural property, the CPIA may be a less powerful tool than the NSPA, but CPIA's forfeiture potential is quite real.

4. *Bilateral Agreements.* CPIA attempts to balance the two divergent positions on the movement of cultural property—internationalists in favor of free trade and nationalists in favor of restricted trade—along an axis of international cooperation. That axis is itself balanced between the responsibility of the art-exporting country to protect its cultural property through education, research, and border export enforcement, and the responsibility of the art-importing country to honor the import restrictions. The 2016 extension of the original 2001 agreement between the U.S. and Italy is illustrative of that balance. The agreement is captioned a Memorandum of Understanding (MOU) and not a treaty. A MOU is generally viewed in international law as not legally binding. The intent of the signatories controls whether the agreement is binding. Given the multiple extensions of the U.S. and Italian agreement, it seems the intent to have a binding agreement is clear. Article II is the heart of the 2016 extension of the U.S. and Italian MOU:

Article II

Public Awareness / Outreach

A. Representatives of the Government of the United States of America and representatives of the Government of the Italian Republic shall take appropriate steps to publicize all matters concerning this Memorandum of Understanding, and to inform their respective law enforcement and public citizenry about the legal effects and limitations, including the non-retroactive nature, of this Memorandum of Understanding.

B. The Government of the Italian Republic shall endeavor to use the opportunity of exhibitions of returned objects to educate the Italian and international public about the damage caused by archaeological site looting and the loss of knowledge wrought from such looting.

Protection / Conservation

C. The Government of the Italian Republic agrees to continue its strong support of scientific archaeological research, protection of archaeological heritage, and protective measures for archaeological sites, particularly in areas at greatest risk from looters.

D. The Government of the United States recognizes the outstanding work of the Government of the Italian Republic to protect its cultural heritage with respect to the 1970 UNESCO Convention. The Government of the Italian Republic shall continue its efforts to:

1. ensure the prompt prosecution of looters,
2. strengthen, in whatever way necessary, the Carabinieri Special Unit for the Protection of Artistic Heritage and facilitate the exchange of information with competent agencies, and
3. create and pursue innovative and effective ways to detect and stop the looting of archaeological sites.

Collaboration / Interchange

E. The Government of the United States of America recognizes that the Government of the Italian Republic permits the interchange of archaeological materials for cultural, exhibition, educational and scientific purposes to enable widespread public appreciation of and legitimate access to Italy's rich cultural heritage. The Government of the Italian Republic and the Government of the United States of America agree to support further interchange by:

1. entering into discussions about how to increase the number and overall length of long-term loans of objects of archaeological or artistic interest for knowledge, research and educational and exhibition purposes, agreed upon, on a case-by-case basis, by American and Italian museums or similar institutions, recognizing the spirit of goodwill that exists between cultural institutions in both countries;
2. encouraging American museums and universities to propose and participate in joint excavation projects authorized by the Ministry of Cultural Heritage and Activities and Tourism, with the understanding that certain of the scientifically excavated objects from such projects could be given as a loan to the American participants through specific agreements with the Ministry of Cultural Heritage and Activities and Tourism; and
3. promoting agreements for academic exchanges and specific study programs agreed upon by Italian and American museums and universities.

F. The Government of the Italian Republic, in advancing the broadest possible participation in and exchanges between American and Italian museums, shall use its best efforts to:

1. adopt uniform and transparent procedures regarding international loan requests, including by providing a central point of information in order to facilitate loan procedures nationwide;
2. remove impediments that may exist in facilitating loans from the United States to Italy and from Italy to the United States and facilitate as much as possible subsequent loan operations:
   - by establishing reasonable courier and other related loan fees;

- by further exploring opportunities for reciprocity such as loans of objects, technical expertise, and educational programs.

3. continue to explore the feasibility of promoting a legislative initiative on the application of immunity from seizure for certain objects of cultural significance imported into the Italian Republic for temporary display or exhibition.

G. Noting that the law of the Italian Republic, as it currently stands, allows the purchase of archaeological objects of verified legal provenance, the Government of the Italian Republic and the Government of the United States will continue to discuss and explore ways to facilitate further the final legal export of such objects.

Law Enforcement

H. The Government of the Italian Republic shall continue to use its best efforts to stop the illicit use of metal detectors in archaeological areas.

I. The Government of the Italian Republic and the Government of the United States of America agree to encourage greater collaboration among law enforcement and members of the antiquities trade through increased information sharing for due diligence and research purposes in ways that do not jeopardize active criminal investigations.

J. The Government of the Italian Republic shall endeavor to engage proactively with the countries that have a demonstrable market or serve as transit points for archaeological objects from Italy to prevent the illicit trafficking of this material.

Reporting

K. Each Government shall keep the other informed of the effectiveness of the measures agreed to in this MOU; reports shall be exchanged to coincide with an interim review and if there should be a proposal to extend the MOU.

5. *U.K. and EU Export Restrictions.* The export restrictions placed on artworks or cultural property vary by nations. Some nations lack export restrictions, some have selective restrictions, and others have de facto prohibitions. Whenever the purchase of an artwork located in a foreign jurisdiction is contemplated, it is imperative to ascertain the relevant export restrictions, if any, and to plan the purchase agreement accordingly. Conditioning the sale on the existence of a valid export license, or its procurement within a certain period of time, and documentation would be a basic provision.

Exports of artworks from member nations of the European Union present a linked approach, consisting of pertinent national legislation and EU legislation. The original EU legislative foundation proceeds from the 1957 Treaty of Rome, which established the European Economic Community (EEC). A primary objective of the EEC was to establish a common market and promote the free movement of goods among its member nations. Nevertheless, Article 36 of the Treaty of Rome specifically allowed members to prohibit or restrict exports for "the protection of national treasures possessing artistic, historic or archaeological value," provided, however, that such restrictions were not a "means of arbitrary discrimination or a disguised restriction on trade" among the members.

At the time of the 1957 Treaty of Rome, many European nations already had enacted national legislation restricting the export of their cultural property. The U.K., for example, enacted wartime export restrictions in 1939 that were later seen, and then deemed, to cover export of certain artworks on grounds of national interest. After the war, the Waverley Committee made recommendations that led to the creation of the Reviewing Committee on the Export of Works of Art and Objects of Cultural Interest in 1952. The Reviewing Committee assesses an application for an export license based on the following criteria (known as the "Waverley Criteria") for items of national artistic heritage (of at least 50 years of age and certain minimum value):

1. Is the item closely associated with our history and national life?
2. Is the item of outstanding aesthetic importance?
3. Is the item of outstanding significance for the study of some particular branch of art, learning or history?

The philosophical linchpin of the U.K. export licensing process is a recognition of, and a balance among, the four competing interests: protection of national heritage, rights of the individual owning the item, the exporter or overseas purchaser, and the position and reputation of the U.K. art industry. The process is open, transparent, and participatory. The pragmatic key is economic. A determination of the Reviewing Committee (after soliciting written submission from the applicant) can be to defer the export decision, thereby allowing time for a U.K. public institution to raise funds to purchase the item at a recommended fair market price. If funds cannot be raised, the export license generally is issued. See Museums, Libraries and Archives, Council Notice: UK Export Licensing for Cultural Goods (2010), available at www.culture.gov.uk; see also Michael Polonsky & Jean-Francois Canat, *The British and French Systems of Control of the Export of Works of Art*, 45 Int'l & Comp. L.Q. 557 (1996).

What would have happened to individually owned U.K. art collections and the London auction market if the denial of an export license was not generally accompanied by a substitute fair market value offer to purchase?

In 1992, the EU for the first time required an export license for the "export of cultural goods outside the customs territory of the Community." See Council Regulation (EEC) No. 3911/92 of December 9, 1992, repealed in 2008 and replaced by Council Regulation (EC) No. 116-2009 of 18 December 2008. The cultural goods covered by the Regulation cover 15 categories (somewhat paralleling tariff headings), with age (over 50, 75, or 100 years, with limited exceptions) being the decisive criterion combined with a minimum threshold value (between 0 and 150,000 Euros). Any export, whether temporary or permanent, requires a license. This EU export license may be refused if the cultural good is covered by national treasures legislation. Recall in Faggionato v. Lerner, 500 F. Supp. 2d 237 (S.D.N.Y. 2007), Chapter 2, *supra*, the concern regarding the French export license for the Monet.

While the U.K. was a member of the EU, there was a dual system in place for the export licensing. With the departure of the U.K. from the EU in 2021, artworks purchased in the U.K. that are exported to a EU country as well as artworks imported into the U.K. from a EU country will face fundamentally different documentation and tax consequences. Uncertainty remains on the contours of those differences.

Third Drafting Exercise: Customs

To: Junior Associate

From: Senior Partner

Our client Mr. Smith was approached by the Hong Kong owner of a car, the exterior of which has been painted by an internationally acclaimed American artist. The car was manufactured in Germany, the painting occurred in Beijing, and it was later exhibited at the Hong Kong Museum of Art as part of a special exhibit on newer visions of artists on art and commerce. Before the painting, the car was valued at $100X, after the painting it was appraised at $500X, which is the Hong Kong owner's asking price. Mr. Smith believes that is high and thinks its value is probably more in the $300–350X range. Mr. Smith respects this artist and owns several more conventional works by the artist.

Mr. Smith, a previous purchaser of artworks from abroad, wants our input as to the customs status of this art car. He's aware it is an unusual artwork; that's part of its appeal. One customs broker he contacted said it was almost certainly not an artwork for customs purposes, but maybe, if only the body of the car came in, it could be sculpture. Mr. Smith filled me in on two pieces of history that might give additional context to our advice. The first is the BMW Art Cars and the second concerns the *Brancusi* case.

In 1975, a French race car driver and art dealer asked his friend Alexander Calder to paint the BMW that he would drive in the 1975 Le Mans endurance race. Calder obliged. Since that time, BMW has commissioned various artists, including Andy Warhol, Roy Lichtenstein, Frank Stella, David Hockney, Jenny Holzer, Jeff Koons and Cao Fei, to paint a BMW Art Car. The BMW Art Cars have been exhibited at museums in the United States and abroad.

Constantin Brancusi did not primarily participate in the *Brancusi* case. Photographer Edward Steichen and artist Marcel Duchamp (of ready-made fame) championed the case in order to establish formal acceptance for a wider view of art, with art patron Gertrude Vanderbilt Whitney providing financial support. A central element of the *Brancusi* holding was the recognition that art evolves and that this newer school of art enjoyed legitimacy among professional artists. Mr. Smith tells me that for many artists today (think Takashi Murakami, Jeff Koons, and Damien Hirst), the merging of art with technology and commerce is part and parcel of their artistic expression. Customs has also evolved since *Brancusi*. Its function historically was revenue raising, today, its more significant functions are the enforcement of the country's international trade policies and the security of the county's borders.

Please draft a memo for my review detailing the pertinent CBP issues if Mr. Smith were to import this art car. By the way, would it matter if a museum (Mr. Smith sits on two boards) were the importer?

Chapter 7

Moral Rights

Moral rights are a creation of the civil law tradition. For American lawyers trained in a tradition of private property ownership as powerful and absolute, it is an unusual concept. The American adoption of moral rights in 1990 for works of visual art creates a new challenging paradigm of ownership. Not quite a shadow co-ownership, moral rights can nevertheless affect the use, possession, and disposition of the artwork. This chapter explores the origins of moral rights in the U.S. and its evolving application to artists and owners. The lesson is clear: artwork is exceptional; it is not a commodity like any other.

A. Background of Moral Rights

1. Origins of Droit Moral

Moral rights are the special, noneconomic rights that artists have over their creations, that persist even after an artwork is sold. Moral rights, a relatively new concept for the U.S., are directly traceable to le droit moral, a concept of the civil law tradition, primarily of French origin.

The civil law emphasizes positive law and does not generally consider the judiciary as a source of law. Somewhat uncharacteristically, therefore, the roots of droit moral in the 19th century are judicial. See John Henry Merryman, *The Refrigerator of Bernard Buffet*, 27 Hastings L. Rev. 1023 (1976). At least as early as 1845, a French court recognized an artist's particular interest in maintaining a work's integrity. "Independent of the pecuniary interest, there exists for the artist an interest more precious, that of reputation." Martin A. Roeder, *The Doctrine of Moral Rights: A Study in the Law of Artists, Authors and Creators*, 53 Harv. L. Rev. 554, 555 (1940). A series of 19th century French cases sketched the contours of droit moral. One such well-recognized case involved American artist James McNeill Whistler (1834–1903).

Whistler spent most of his professional life in France and England. No shrinking violet, he "has a particularly sensitive personality, as everyone knows."* When one of his works was criticized by the English art critic, John Ruskin ("I . . . never expected to hear a coxcomb ask two hundred guineas for flinging a pot of paint in

* *Whistler's Paris Suit Ends*, N.Y. Times at BRIZ (Dec. 18, 1897).

the public's face"), Whistler sued Ruskin for libel in 1878. Whistler won the case, but was awarded only one farthing (less than a penny) in damages.* A decade later, in 1890, Whistler wrote the well-named THE GENTLE ART OF MAKING ENEMIES. Soon thereafter, he was engaged in another lawsuit, this time in Paris.

The lower court held in 1895 in favor of the plaintiff Lord Eden, and Whistler appealed.** After the 1897 appellate verdict in Whistler's favor, Whistler picked up his writing pen and wrote another book, EDEN V. WHISTLER, THE BARONET & THE BUTTERFLY, A VALENTINE WITH A VERDICT (1899). The following case excerpts from that appeal are from his book.

Whistler versus Eden

Court of Appeal. Paris.
First Chamber, before Monsieur Le Premier President, DEC. 1897

[Whistler was highly prized as a portraitist, and Lord Eden desired a portrait of his wife. When the initial price for a full portrait was quoted at over 500 guineas, Lord Eden balked and, through an intermediary, asked the price for a head portrait instead. The quoted price was between 100–150. Lady Eden dutifully sat for the portrait, which evolved over time into a whole figure, not just a head. Lord Eden was very pleased by this and anxious to take possession of the portrait. Eden went to Whistler's studio in Paris on February 14, 1894. The painting of Lady Eden was virtually, but not wholly, complete. Eden left an envelope, calling it a valentine, and told Whistler to open it after he left. The envelope contained a check for the minimum amount of 100 guineas; Whistler was not pleased. While Eden was away in India, Whistler included the painting, "Brown and Gold: Portrait of Lady E," in an exhibition.

Upon Eden's return from India, he demanded the painting. Whistler refused, indicating he was not yet fully finished with the portrait. When Lord Eden brought suit in Paris, Whistler made changes to the work, including painting out Lady Eden's face.—Ed.]

THE PRESIDENT: Will you explain the object of your suit?

MR. BEURDELEY: It is this. The Civil Tribunal of the Seine gave judgment against an artist for not having delivered a picture ordered from him. The Tribunal ruled that the artist was to refund the price of the picture, to hand over the picture itself and to pay damages with interests thereupon. We appeal against this triple penalty as excessive....

THE PRESIDENT: Do you offer to give up the picture?

---

* Elizabeth Pennell & Joseph Pennell, THE WHISTLER JOURNAL 316–17 (1921); *Current Topics Abroad*, N.Y. TIMES at 5 (Nov. 27, 1878).

** See Whistler v. Eden, [1898] Recueil Periodique et Critique [D.P.] II 465 (Cour d'appel, Paris): agreed Eden v. Whistler, [1900] [D.P.] I, 497 [1900] Recueil Sirey [S. Jur.] I 490 (Cass. civ.).

MR. BEURDELEY: On the contrary, we protest against the decision by which we are condemned to refund the price and give up the picture—a picture which has been modified, and which is at present an incomplete expression of the artist's idea, cannot, under the conditions, be assigned to the person who originally commissioned it.

* * *

There is another reason why Sir William should not have the portrait. It is no longer a portrait of his wife. . . .

Now what, in fact was the contract? Not that Mr. Whistler should paint a portrait of some sort, but that he should paint a portrait of Lady Eden. As Lady Eden's portrait no longer exists, there can be no reason why another portrait or sketch should be handed over to Sir William Eden.

There is yet a third reason, gentlemen, why this picture should not be given up. . . . The picture as it now stands is not finished. It is a mere sketch, a design: you cannot oblige the artist to give up an unfinished work, and allow the incomplete creations of his heart and brain to circulate in the world. As present, gentlemen, we have a preparation, a harmony in brown and gold; something is eventually to dominate those harmonious tints-a new face; but as yet it is in the stage of conception, not in that of birth. Hence it is absolutely impossible to both to obey the ruling of the lower Court and to satisfy Sir William Eden.

JUDGEMENT

THE COURT, Having heard the counsels for plaintiff and defendant, and the summing-up of the Advocat-General, and being called upon to pronounce judgment against the decision of the Civil Tribunal of the Seine, given March 20, 1895,

* * *

HEREBY

confirms the judgment against which appeal is made in so far as it is set forth the material facts, And confirms it in ordering the appealant to refund the 2625 francs (100 guineas) paid him by William Eden, with five per cent interest thereon from February 14, 1894, and to pay 1000 francs (£40) damages with interest.

But rules that the judgment was at fault in declaring that William Eden became the owner of the picture as soon as the contracting parties had agreed as to the thing and the price.

Amending this clause of the judgment, and pronouncing afresh, the Court declares the contract between the parties to have been merely an agreement to execute, resolving itself, in the event of non-execution, into a question of damages; it therefore leaves the artist master and proprietor of his work till such time as it shall please him to deliver it, and give up the holding thereof.

It discharges Whistler from all obligation to give up the portrait to William Eden laid upon him by the lower Court, but declares, on the other hand, that so long as the work remains incomplete and unfit to deliver, Whistler can make no sort of use of it, public or private.

It orders Whistler to pay the costs of the first suit, and William Eden to pay costs of appeal.

The fine to be refunded.

---

2. Droit Moral and the Berne Convention

By the early 20th century, droit moral was a well-established doctrine of European intellectual property law. The primary French conception of droit moral is a natural right of the artist as creator; and specifically not as a right bestowed by a sovereign. As such, it transcends mere property or economic rights. Its hallmarks are that it is personal, perpetual, inalienable, and unassignable. It is also in description singular (le droit moral), evincing an almost theological one-ness of artist and creation, even though in practice it includes multiple rights pertinent for artists. The moral rights adopted by any particular country will vary, as will the judicial interpretations and applications of those rights, but the following are some familiar ones:

- Right of authorship or attribution—Droit á la paternité. The artist has the right to be acknowledged by name or pseudonym as the creator, or to put forth the work anonymously. The right includes the right to prevent the artist's work from being attributed to someone else, or using the artist's name on works not created by her.
- Right of disclosure—Droit de divulgation. The artist has the sole right to decide if and when a work shall be published. See *Whistler, supra*.
- Right to withdraw or modify—Droit de retrait ou de repentir. The artist has the right to prevent publication or to withdraw published works from circulation. To do this, however, the artist must pay those who have been assigned the property rights.
- Right of integrity—Droit au respect de l'oeuvre. Most crucially, the artist has the right to preserve her work from alteration, modification, mutilation or distortion, and at times, destruction.
- Right of resale proceeds—Droit de suite. An artist may have the economic right to participate in the proceeds of subsequent sales. While this is often discussed under moral rights, this is clearly a direct ongoing economic right in the artist.

Inspired by the 18th–19th century age of political revolutions, the intellectual currents among authors and artists led to the first multilateral copyright treaty in 1886, the Berne Convention for the Protection of Literary and Artistic Works. Moral rights were not a part of the Berne Convention in its original form; however, in 1928, the Rome revisions added Article 6*bis*:

> (1) Independently of the author's economic rights, and even after . . . transfer of said rights, the author shall have the right to claim authorship (attribution) and to object to any distortion, mutilation or other modification (integrity) of or other derogatory action in relation to, the said work, which would be prejudicial to his honor or reputation.

The U.S. did not sign the Berne Convention until 1988, largely due to the different views of copyright and the presence of moral rights. When Congress enacted the Berne Convention Implementation Act of 1988, it emphasized the trade benefits, beneficial harmonization aspects, and a minimalist approach to change: only changes clearly required by the Berne Convention would be made. Specifically with respect to Article 6*bis*, Congress reported the U.S. met its treaty obligations for moral rights through existing federal and state statutes and common law principles. Consequently, it was unnecessary to adopt moral rights. The existing balance between authors and proprietors was maintained; but not for long. Within two years, the Visual Artists Rights Act of 1990 (VARA) was enacted, providing the first federal statute on moral rights.

Why did the U.S. resist moral rights? And what factors prompted the U.S. to change? Speaking very broadly, one traditional response for U.S. resistance stems from the different conceptions of intellectual property law. In the civil law system (at least from the French perspective), droit moral is a natural right based on the artist's creative spirit, a distinctive right of personality. In the U.S., copyright is a creation of the Constitution. It is a utilitarian construct borne of the English common law system that balances economic and proprietary rights among the author, the publisher, the public, and the sovereign. Our legal starting points and assumptions were different enough to cause concern.

Two cultural aspects may have played supporting roles in the U.S. resistance to moral rights. First, in the 19th century, the center of the art world was Europe, not the U.S. Consequently, there was not a strong domestic base to support change. Second, the singularity and supremacy of the artist's right could be seen as conflicting with the very American right of free speech. See Geri J. Yonover, *The "Dissing" of DaVinci: The Imaginary Case of Leonardo v. Duchamp: Moral Rights, Parody, and Fair Use*, 29 Val. U. L. Rev. 935, 952–54 (1995). The first obstacle receded in the latter half of the 20th century. The second obstacle remains, with some asserting that VARA is, ironically, destructive of the modern artistic impulse. See, e.g., Amy Adler, *Against Moral Rights*, 97 Cal. L. Rev. 263 (2009).

As for what prompted the change, three steps helped to develop receptivity to moral rights in the U.S. As is often the case in the U.S., those three steps came from different parts of the common law laboratory. Those steps were important case law decisions, state moral rights statutes, and a federal initiative. See Thomas Cotter, *Pragmatism, Economics, and the Droit Moral*, 76 N.C. L. Rev. 1 (1997).

a. Case law approach. Gilliam v. American Broadcasting Companies, 538 F.2d 14 (2d Cir. 1976), was the first judicial recognition of the concept of moral rights, albeit in a functional rather than explicit guise. ABC had contracted with Time Life, the U.S. distributor for certain BBC programs, to broadcast two 90 minute specials. Each comprised three 30-minute Monty Python's Flying Circus programs. In order to provide time for commercials, ABC edited the programs without the knowledge or consent of the Monty Python group of writers and performers. Twenty-four minutes of the 90 minutes were eliminated. Once they saw the tapes, Monty Python brought an injunction action against ABC under copyright infringement, arguing that the truncated and garbled versions of their programs were derivative works in violation of their copyright and licensing agreements. They also argued a violation of §43(a) of the Lanham Act because the televising of the "mutilation" of the work constituted a false description or false representation. The Second Circuit granted the injunction, specifically noting that while American copyright law "as presently written, does not recognize moral rights," the economic foundation of U.S. copyright law was nevertheless hospitable to addressing artists' claims of misrepresentation or mutilation of their works through other avenues, such as contract.

The Monty Python case was exceptional as a judicial adoption by-any-other-name of the moral right of integrity for an artist. The norm for litigated cases was closer to Crimi v. Rutgers Presbyterian Church, 89 N.Y.S.2d 813 (N.Y. Sup. Ct. 1949). In *Crimi*, the plaintiff had won a commission to paint a church mural. Eight years after its unveiling and with eight years of increasing criticism from members, the church had the mural painted over. Crimi sued, alleging the obliteration of the mural violated his continued proprietary interest in the mural and damaged his reputation. The court examined the doctrine of moral rights and determined that it was not a part of U.S. law. The court noted that Crimi should have acted prospectively by addressing the issue in his commission contract. See Merryman, Elsen & Urice, LAW, ETHICS AND THE VISUAL ARTS 436–438 (5th ed. 2007), for a full discussion of the evolutionary steps toward moral rights and the practical problems of U.S. equivalents.

b. State moral rights legislation. In 1979, California enacted the California Art Preservation Act (CAL. CIV. CODE §987), the first such statute in the U.S. Apparently, the unthinking bureaucratic alteration of Alexander Calder's mobile *Pittsburgh* was one prompt for the legislation. *Pittsburgh*, a monumental 30-foot-tall black and white mobile, was donated in 1958 to Allegheny County to be hung in the Pittsburgh airport. At the airport, the officials painted it green and gold (the county's colors), reoriented the sculpture, and made it rigid. Calder vigorously protested to no avail until his death in 1976; the county finally relented two years after he died. See Richard Mayer, *California Arts Legislation Goes Federal*, 15 HASTINGS COMM/ENT. L.J. 981 (1993). The California statute declared that the alteration or destruction of fine art implicated two interests: the artist's interest in his reputation and the public's interest in protecting and preserving cultural and artistic creation. The artist, and for 50 years after his death, his heir, legatee or personal representative, may file suit to enforce the rights granted by the statute. By subsequent legislation, California recognized the public's interest by extending standing to art organizations to bring suit to preserve or restore the integrity of works of fine art.

New York's version of moral rights took a different approach to the right of integrity. Its focus is on the damage to an artist's reputation from the public display of an altered, defaced, or mutilated work. N.Y. ARTS & CULT. AFF. L. § 14.03 (McKinney 2020) (preempted by VARA). Under both the California and the New York statutes, the artist has the right of paternity, that is, to claim or disclaim authorship.

Following the leadership of California and New York, other states also enacted moral rights statutes.* The significant question today is the pre-emption of a given state's statute because of VARA. While VARA and its legislative history gives Congress's specific intent with respect to preemption, preemption is not necessarily preordained. 17 U.S.C. § 301(f). It requires a determination on a case-by-case basis, and in the context of the particular work of art and the alleged violation. Cf., e.g., Phillips v. Pembroke Real Estate, 288 F. Supp. 2d 89 (D. Mass. 2003) (not preempted); Board of Managers of Soho International Arts Condo. v. City of New York, 2003 WL 21403333 (S.D.N.Y. 2003) (preempted). A broader preemption argument was at issue in Close v. Sotheby's, 894 F. 3d 1061 (9th Cir. 2018), discussed *infra.*

c. Berne Convention Implementation Act. In 1988, after 102 years, the U.S. signed the Berne Convention, the premier international copyright treaty. The U.S. specifically declined to adopt the moral rights provision, Article 6*bis*, asserting that its treaty obligations with respect to artists' rights were sufficiently addressed by existing state and federal statutes and common law doctrines. House and Senate Reports detail the specific, focused attention paid to Article 6*bis* in legislative hearings, and in congressional fact-finding trips to Geneva and Paris. The final House Bill, H.R. 4262, replaced H.R. 1623 by eliminating the sections on moral rights. The House's legislative intent was crystal clear. The Senate's action was equally unambiguous: "Consequently, the moral rights' doctrine is not incorporated into the U.S. law by this statute."

Within two years, the supporters of moral rights prevailed, and the Visual Artists Rights Act of 1990 was enacted. Public Law No. 101-650, No. 101-650, 104 Stat. 5089 (1990). On the last legislative day of the 101st Congress, a bill authorizing new federal judgeships passed. To ensure its passage, other bills were appended. One of them was VARA. "Without so much as a word of debate or discussion, the Artists' Act became law." Geri J. Yonover, *The "Dissing" of DaVinci: The Imaginary Case of Leonardo v. Duchamp: Moral Rights, Parody, and Fair Use*, 29 VAL. U. L. REV. 935, 965 (1995), citing George C. Smith, *Let the Buyer of Art Beware; Artists Moral Rights Trump Owners Property Rights under the Visual Artists Rights Act*, RECORDER, Jan. 10, 1991, at 4.

* States include, e.g., CONN. GEN. STAT. § 42-116t (West 2020); LA. REV. STAT. ANN. §§ 51:2151 to 51:2156 (West 2020); 27 ME. R.S.A. § 303 (West 2020); MASS. GEN. LAWS ANN. ch. 231, § 85S (West 2020); N.J. STAT. ANN. § 2A:24A-1 to 2A:24A-8; N.M. STAT. ANN. §§ 13-4B-1 to 14-4B-3 (West 2020); R.I. GEN. LAWS §§ 5-62-2 to 5-62-12 (West 2020).

B. U.S. Moral Rights: Visual Artists Rights Act of 1990 (VARA)

After resisting moral rights for decades, the United States adopted its first federal legislation incorporating moral rights in 1990. Visual Artists Rights Act of 1990, Pub. L. No. 101-650 (tit. VI), 104 Stat. 5089 (1990). VARA is not free-standing; it is situated within Title 17 Copyright. Placement within copyright creates a recognized framework within which the courts are developing the rules for VARA. Those frameworks, however, are not co-terminus. Copyright is broader than VARA and recognition of that is important for the development of moral rights in the U.S. Some urge caution in using copyright law's increasing expansiveness as the leitmotif for VARA. See, e.g., Roberta Rosenthal Kwall, *Inspiration and Innovation: The Intrinsic Dimension of the Artistic Soul*, 81 Notre Dame L. Rev. 1945 (2006). Others argue the incompatibility of VARA and copyright law. See, e.g., Amy Adler, *Why Art Does Not Need Copyright*, 86 Geo. Wash. L. Rev. 313 (2018). In 2019, after hearings and study, the Copyright Office concluded "that the many diverse aspects of the current moral rights patchwork—including copyright law's derivative work right, state moral rights statutes and contract law—are generally working well and should not be changed," although certain narrow changes should be considered. Karyn A. Temple, U.S. Copyright Office, *Authors, Attribution, and Integrity: Examining Moral Rights in the United States*, 4, Apr. 2019.

VARA's statutory definition of a work of visual art (17 U.S.C. § 101) and the statutory rights of attribution and integrity (17 U.S.C. § 106A) are provided here:

17 U.S.C. § 101

* * *

A "work of visual art" is—

(1) a painting, drawing, print, or sculpture, existing in a single copy, in a limited edition of 200 copies or fewer that are signed and consecutively numbered by the author, or in the case of sculpture, in multiple cast, carved, or fabricated sculptures of 200 or fewer that are consecutively numbered by the author and bear the signature or other identifying mark of the author, or

(2) a still photographic image produced for exhibition purposes only, existing in a single copy that is signed by the author, or in a limited edition of 200 copies or fewer that are signed and consecutively numbered by the author.

A work of visual art does not include—

(A)(i) any poster, map, globe, chart, technical drawing, diagram, model, applied art, motion picture or other audiovisual work, book, magazine, newspaper, periodical, data base, electronic information service, electronic publication, or similar publication;

(ii) any merchandising item or advertising, promotional, descriptive, covering, or packaging material or container;

(iii) any portion or part of any item described in clause (i) or (ii);

(B) any work made for hire; or

(C) any work not subject to copyright protection under this title.

* * *

§ 106A. Rights of certain authors to attribution and integrity

(a) Rights of attribution and integrity.—Subject to section 107 and independent of the exclusive rights provided in section 106, the author of a work of visual art—

(1) shall have the right—

(A) to claim authorship of that work, and

(B) to prevent the use of his or her name as the author of any work of visual art which he or she did not create;

(2) shall have the right to prevent the use of his or her name as the author of the work of visual art in the event of a distortion, mutilation, or other modification of the work which would be prejudicial to his or her honor or reputation; and

(3) subject to the limitations set forth in section 113(d), shall have the right—

(A) to prevent any intentional distortion, mutilation, or other modification of that work which would be prejudicial to his or her honor or reputation, and any intentional distortion, mutilation, or modification of that work is a violation of that right, and

(B) to prevent any destruction of a work of recognized stature, and any intentional or grossly negligent destruction of that work is a violation of that right.

(b) Scope and exercise of rights.—Only the author of a work of visual art has the rights conferred by subsection (a) in that work, whether or not the author is the copyright owner. The authors of a joint work of visual art are coowners of the rights conferred by subsection (a) in that work.

(c) Exceptions.—

(1) The modification of a work of visual art which is a result of the passage of time or the inherent nature of the materials is not a distortion, mutilation, or other modification described in subsection (a)(3)(A).

(2) The modification of a work of visual art which is the result of conservation, or of the public presentation, including lighting and placement, of the work is not a destruction, distortion, mutilation, or other modification described in subsection (a)(3) unless the modification is caused by gross negligence.

(3) The rights described in paragraphs (1) and (2) of subsection (a) shall not apply to any reproduction, depiction, portrayal, or other use of a work in, upon, or in any connection with any item described in subparagraph (A) or (B) of the definition of "work of visual art" in section 101, and any such reproduction, depiction, portrayal, or other use of a work is not a destruction, distortion, mutilation, or other modification described in paragraph (3) of subsection (a).

(d) Duration of rights.—

(1) With respect to works of visual art created on or after the effective date set forth in section 610(a) of the Visual Artists Rights Act of 1990, the rights conferred by subsection (a) shall endure for a term consisting of the life of the author.

(2) With respect to works of visual art created before the effective date set forth in section 610(a) of the Visual Artists Rights Act of 1990, but title to which has not, as of such effective date, been transferred from the author, the rights conferred by subsection (a) shall be coextensive with, and shall expire at the same time as, the rights conferred by section 106.

(3) In the case of a joint work prepared by two or more authors, the rights conferred by subsection (a) shall endure for a term consisting of the life of the last surviving author.

(4) All terms of the rights conferred by subsection (a) run to the end of the calendar year in which they would otherwise expire.

(e) Transfer and waiver.—

(1) The rights conferred by subsection (a) may not be transferred, but those rights may be waived if the author expressly agrees to such waiver in a written instrument signed by the author. Such instrument shall specifically identify the work, and uses of that work, to which the waiver applies, and the waiver shall apply only to the work and uses so identified. In the case of a joint work prepared by two or more authors, a waiver of rights under this paragraph made by one such author waives such rights for all such authors.

(2) Ownership of the rights conferred by subsection (a) with respect to a work of visual art is distinct from ownership of any copy of that work, or of a copyright or any exclusive right under a copyright in that work. Transfer of ownership of any copy of a work of visual art, or of a copyright or any exclusive right under a copyright, shall not constitute a waiver of the rights conferred by subsection (a). Except as may otherwise be agreed by the author in a written instrument signed by the author, a waiver of the rights conferred by subsection (a) with respect to a work of visual art shall not constitute a transfer of ownership of any copy of that work, or of ownership of a copyright or of any exclusive right under a copyright in that work.

Notes and Questions

1. *Work of Visual Art Defined.* In order for VARA to apply, there must first be a "work of visual art." Section 101's definition has two parts: a positive statement (an original painting, drawing, print or sculpture, existing in an edition of 200 or fewer copies, signed and numbered by the artist, and a still photographic image produced for exhibition purposes only in an edition of 200 or fewer copies, signed and numbered by the artist) and a list of exclusions. Taken together, the overall sense is that of fine art, similar to customs descriptions. There is the added requirement of numbering and signing by the artist. Look again at VARA's exclusions. Is this too narrow a description of visual art for artists today? Artworks that are second generation reproductions or computer art are not covered, nor are applied art, motion pictures or other audio-visual works. Recall Bill Viola's *Hall of Whispers*, the video installation that was not deemed art for EU customs purposes. Chapter 6, *supra*. Is it similarly not art for VARA purposes?

The line of demarcation for VARA protection may be based on the distinction between fine art and commercial art, which in turn may be based somewhat on reasonable expectations of the buyer or public. For example, in Pollara v. Seymour, 344 F.3d 265 (2d Cir. 2003), plaintiff claimed a large banner painted by her for a nonprofit's information table was protected by VARA. The court disagreed, noting that Congress chose "only a narrow subset" of what could be art and specifically excluded promotional or advertising works.

Classification problems similar to those in customs have inevitably arisen as VARA becomes more widely known. The principal cases of *Carter*, *Mass MoCA*, *Kelley*, and *Cheffins*, *infra*, deal with the statutory definition of a work of visual art.

2. *Rights of Attribution and Integrity.* Of the various rights that moral rights could include, VARA adopted two—the rights of attribution and integrity. From the perspective of a collector, VARA's protection for the artist primarily concerns the "distortion, mutilation, or other modification" to the work of visual art that would be "prejudicial" to the artist's "honor or reputation." In addition, subject to limitations, an artist may prevent any destruction of a work of "recognized stature." Cf., Martin v. City of Indianapolis, 192 F.3d 608 (7th Cir. 1999) (work deemed of recognized stature); Scott v. Dixon, 309 F. Supp. 2d 395 (E.D.N.Y. 2004) (work not deemed of recognized stature). See also Castillo v. G & M Realty L.P., 950 F. 3d 155 (2d Cir. 2020), *infra*, where aerosol artwork deemed of recognized stature.

The historic reputational concern is clear. For lawyers and collectors in the American legal tradition, VARA presents a new lens through which to view ownership of an artwork. Three scenarios address common moral rights concerns for the owner of a work of visual art. First is the provocatively expressed throwing darts at art, that is, the intentional mutilation of works of art; the second involves issues in conservation of the work; and the third is the curating of art loans.

a. Throwing darts at art. Art collectors, like artists and critics, can have contradictory public images. They may be esteemed for their perceptive eye, their stewardship, and their generosity in ultimately sharing their collections with the public. They may also be criticized for their eccentric tastes, their elitism, and their conspicuous consumption. Whichever view one held, it was undeniable that the art collection was the collector's property to do with as she pleased. If throwing darts at art was her desire, it was also her prerogative as owner. VARA ended that approach. See Joseph L. Sax, PLAYING DARTS WITH A REMBRANDT (1999). But there was little to suggest that such decadent game playing was real. To the contrary, a private collector has every incentive to maintain the physical integrity of artworks in her collection. Many cases brought under VARA show that disputes tend to occur with art that is in or has entered the public or commercial space or sphere, and not with art privately held by an individual collector. Like the rhetorical "if a tree falls in the forest" question, one might even question if throwing darts at art in the privacy of one's home can be prejudicial to the artist's honor or reputation. Must there be a public component?

There are, however, two somewhat more commonplace activities for a private art collector that realistically could create VARA integrity concerns: conservation efforts and museum art loans. Both issues are specifically addressed by VARA in the exclusions section.

b. Conservation. Section 106A(c)(1) explicitly excludes from VARA's integrity protection modifications due to the passage of time or the inherent nature of the materials used. No one is required to stop or reverse the ravages of time; moreover, modifications that result from conservation are also exempt, unless that modification was caused by gross negligence. Consequently, conservation (or restoration) is not precluded by VARA, and, in that sense, conservation efforts are encouraged. The line VARA draws to protect the artist's integrity right in conservation cases is gross negligence. If there is such gross negligence, the artist has the right to prevent the use of her name with that object if it would be prejudicial to her honor or reputation. How would this issue present?

In the 1980s, Yaacov Agam was commissioned to create an outdoor sculpture for a commercial building in Chicago. His *Communication X9* is a 43-foot-tall colorful kinetic sculpture, an "op-art totem pole," located at a very busy and windy Chicago intersection. By the 1990s, the work was beginning to fade and peel. Agam suggested a restorer who had worked on his pieces before; the owner, however, chose another restorer. That restorer contacted Agam for guidance on the 1,410 different colors used in the work. Agam supplied information but apparently not in a format usable by the restorer. Communications broke down, the restorer proceeded to complete the job. Agam, not having had communications in a while, contacted the owner who arranged for a viewing at the warehouse. Upon seeing the work, Agam was shocked. He felt his creation was erased and replaced with an inferior work. Nevertheless, the piece was re-installed but has since been removed. Because the work was created in the early 1980s, VARA was not applicable. No legal proceeding was brought, and Agam has publicly renounced that piece. See Deanna Isaacs, *Restored or Wrecked*?, CHICAGO READER (Nov. 22, 2007).

Artist David Ascalon did file a lawsuit alleging VARA violations stemming from the restoration of his 1994 Holocaust memorial sculpture in Harrisburg, Pennsylvania. After learning of some deterioration, Ascalon offered to restore the work. The non-profit owner chose another to restore the piece. After seeing the restored work, which had, inter alia, removed his name, Ascalon deemed the work drastically altered. See Daniel Grant, *When Creator and Owner Clash*, WALL ST. J., August 31, 2010, at D5. The case settled.

In these two situations, the artist was alive and was consulted in some fashion. If after consultation, the owner had taken no conservation efforts and let time and the elements take their toll, would a VARA integrity action be available? Note that the conservation exception applies for purposes of § 106A(a)(3). It does not specify its applicability to § 106A(a)(1) or (2). Because the consequence of a conservation modification can be de-attribution, if conservation is planned, the prudent approach would be to contact the artist if alive regarding the details of conservation. But see Noland v. Janssen, 2020 WL 2836464 (S.D.N.Y. Jun. 1, 2020), *infra*.

If conservation is required due to a cause covered by insurance (e.g., smoke or water damage due to a fire), carriers and the insured should be aware of additional potential claims if conservation is not properly completed. Even proper restoration can lead to a claim for monetary damages due to "reputational" damage. Picasso's *Le Marin* was damaged while at Christie's awaiting auction in 2018. Christie's paid $487,625 to restore the work and paid $18.74 million to compensate for the loss in value. See Steadfast v. T.C. Nugent, 1:20-CV-03959 (S.D.N.Y. 2020). On the other hand, sometimes the monetary damages can reverse themselves. Picasso's *Le Reve,* damaged in 2006, reportedly decreased in value from $135 million to $85 million. It sold in 2013 for $155 million.

c. Curating art loans. Special museum exhibitions are important in the cultural life of a community, and curators will often seek art loans to fully realize an exhibition's potential. Being included in an exhibition is generally a positive and noteworthy event for an artist and the artwork's owner. What if the artist is disappointed by the public exhibition and presentation? VARA specifically excludes the "modification of visual art which is the result of . . . the public presentation, including lighting and placement" from an integrity violation, unless the modification is caused by gross negligence. 17 U.S.C. § 106A(c)(2). This is a most interesting section for two related reasons. First is the idea that curating can rise to the level of an integrity violation. Second is understanding how to apply the standard of gross negligence for curating that would result in prejudice to the artist's honor or reputation. While no reported cases deal with such issues, one can readily imagine hypothetical scenarios that might create questions for VARA. An example, perhaps, would be an exhibition of "Tasteless and Really Bad Art." An alternative scenario could be if an artist decides the location of his works in room 2 or next to another artist is unworthy, or the matting and frames are inappropriate, or the work being suffused with a blue light or accompanied by an insufficiently praiseworthy curatorial description is prejudicial to his honor or reputation. Would any of those assertions be actionable under VARA? From the perspective of the collector, should an art loan agreement include an indemnity from the museum for gross negligence in curating?

Many museums are, and want to be, active participants in their communities. How would you advise a museum curator who wants to add a football helmet, baseball hat, or basketball jersey of the local city's team to an outdoor sculpture during a championship run? Caution would dictate contacting the artist for a VARA waiver. 17 U.S.C. § 106A(e)(1).

3. *Transferability and Waiver.* Section 106A(e)(1) explicitly provides that VARA rights may be waived but may not be transferred. This differs significantly from the French construct, which views moral rights as personal, perpetual, inalienable, and unassignable. Each approach is consistent with the country's underlying conception of moral rights. In the U.S., the view is a balancing of rights within an economic context. Consequently, the artist can bargain and waive the rights in a particular transaction, but interestingly cannot wholly transfer the right. What accounts for this deviation from the American tradition of free alienability? The French view

le droit moral as civil rights of the individual or personality rights. Viewed as an intrinsic element of an individual's civil rights, their inalienability and unassignability are conceptually understandable, even if not economically robust. See Jean-Luc Piotraut, *An Authors' Right-Based Copyright Law: The Fairness and Morality of French and American Law Compared*, 24 CARDOZO ARTS & ENT. L.J. 549 (2006). Think how you would draft a contract provision contemplating the issue of moral rights.

4. *Copyright Basics.* VARA is a small part of the copyright domain. While copyright is a separate and intricate course in its own right, a few broad brushstrokes are provided here for general guidance. Copyright is a form of protection for the author of "original works of authorship" recognized in the Constitution and provided for by Congress in Title 17 of the U.S. Code. The owner of the copyright for an original work has the exclusive right during the duration of the copyright to make copies, to prepare derivative works, to distribute copies to the public (by sale or other transfer, or by rental, lease, or lending), and to perform or display the work publicly. 17 U.S.C. § 106. Limitations on these rights are provided for in sections 107 through 121, including the constantly evolving "fair use" exception of § 107 and the public display exception of § 109(c) for the owner of a particular copy, lawfully made. The copyright owner can grant a license to the owner of an artwork or to others to any of the rights of the copyright owner.

Copyright, and the entirety of intellectual property law, is a dynamic field, played out against constantly developing technology, law, and cases. It is best to proceed cautiously and to consult with those who are expert in the field. See Jane C. Ginsburg, *Overview of Copyright Law*, in OXFORD HANDBOOK OF INTELLECTUAL PROPERTY LAW (Rochelle Dreyfuss & Justine Pila eds., Oxford University Press 2018).

C. Case Law Interpreting Works of Visual Art

Carter v. Helmsley-Spear, Inc.

71 F.3d 77 (2d Cir. 1995)

CARDAMONE, J.

* * *

Plaintiffs John Carter, John Swing and John Veronis (artists or plaintiffs) are professional sculptors who work together and are known collectively as the "Three-J's" or "Jx3." On December 16, 1991 [the building's then-managing company] SIG entered into a one-year agreement with the plaintiffs . . . "to design, create and install sculpture and other permanent installations" in the building, primarily the lobby. Under the agreement plaintiffs had "full authority in design, color and style," and SIG retained authority to direct the location and installation of the artwork within the building. The artists were to retain copyrights to their work and SIG was to receive 50 percent of any proceeds from its exploitation. On January 20, 1993 SIG and the artists signed an agreement extending the duration of their commission for an additional year. [In mid-June 1993, new managing entity] Limited Partnership assumed the agreement with plaintiffs and in December 1993 again extended the agreement.

The artwork . . . is a very large "walk-through sculpture" occupying most, but not all, of the building's lobby. The artwork consists of a variety of sculptural elements constructed from recycled materials, much of it metal, affixed to the walls and ceiling, and a vast mosaic made from pieces of recycled glass embedded in the floor and walls. . . .

. . . [O]n April 6, 1994 defendant Helmsley-Spear, Inc. took over management of the property [and] informed the artists that they could no longer continue to install artwork at the property, and instead had to vacate the building. These representatives also made statements indicating that defendants intended to remove the artwork already in place in the building's lobby.

As a result of defendants' actions, artists commenced this litigation. . . .

A bench trial was subsequently held in June and July 1994, at the conclusion of which the trial court granted the artists the permanent injunction prohibiting defendants from distorting, mutilating, modifying, destroying and removing plaintiffs' artwork. . . . This appeal and cross-appeal followed.

Discussion

I. Artists' Moral Rights

A. History of Artists' Moral Rights

* * *

The term "moral rights" has its origins in the civil law and is a translation of the French *le droit moral,* which is meant to capture those rights of a spiritual, non-economic and personal nature. The rights spring from a belief that an artist in the process of creation injects his spirit into the work and that the artist's personality, as well as the integrity of the work, should therefore be protected and preserved. *See* Ralph E. Lerner & Judith Bresler, *Art Law* 417 (1989) (*Art Law*). Because they are personal to the artist, moral rights exist independently of an artist's copyright in his or her work. *See, e.g.,* 2 *Nimmer on Copyright* 8D-4 & n. 2 (1994) (*Nimmer*).

While the rubric of moral rights encompasses many varieties of rights, two are protected in nearly every jurisdiction recognizing their existence: attribution and integrity. The right of attribution generally consists of the right of an artist to be recognized by name as the author of his work or to publish anonymously or pseudonymously, the right to prevent the author's work from being attributed to someone else, and to prevent the use of the author's name on works created by others, including distorted editions of the author's original work. The right of integrity allows the author to prevent any deforming or mutilating changes to his work, even after title in the work has been transferred.

In some jurisdictions the integrity right also protects artwork from destruction. Whether or not a work of art is protected from destruction represents a fundamentally different perception of the purpose of moral rights. If integrity is meant to stress the public interest in preserving a nation's culture, destruction is prohibited; if the right is meant to emphasize the author's personality, destruction is seen as less harmful than the continued display of deformed or mutilated work that misrepresents the artist and destruction may proceed.

Although moral rights are well established in the civil law, they are of recent vintage in American jurisprudence. Federal and state courts typically recognized the existence of such rights in other nations, but rejected artists' attempts to inject them into U.S. law. Nonetheless, American courts have in varying degrees acknowledged the idea of moral rights, cloaking the concept in the guise of other legal theories, such as copyright, unfair competition, invasion of privacy, defamation, and breach of contract.

* * *

Artists fared better in state legislatures than they generally had in courts. California was the first to take up the task of protecting artists with the passage in 1979 of the California Art Preservation Act, Cal.Civ.Code § 987 *et seq.* (West 1982 & Supp.1995), followed in 1983 by New York's enactment of the Artist's Authorship Rights Act, N.Y.Arts & Cult. Aff. Law § 14.03 (McKinney Supp.1995). Nine other states have also passed moral rights statutes, generally following either the California or New York models.

B. Visual Artists Rights Act of 1990

Although bills protecting artists' moral rights had first been introduced in Congress in 1979, they had drawn little support. The issue of federal protection of moral rights was a prominent hurdle in the debate over whether the United States should join the Berne Convention, the international agreement protecting literary and artistic works. Article 6*bis* of the Berne Convention protects attribution and integrity. . . .

* * *

Congress passed the Berne Convention Implementation Act of 1988, Pub.L. No. 100-568, 102 Stat. 2853 (1988), and side-stepped the difficult question of protecting moral rights. It declared that the Berne Convention is not self-executing, existing law satisfied the United States' obligations in adhering to the Convention, its provisions are not enforceable through any action brought pursuant to the Convention itself, and neither adherence to the Convention nor the implementing legislation expands or reduces any rights under federal, state, or common law to claim authorship of a work or to object to any distortion, mutilation, or other modification of a work.

Two years later Congress enacted the Visual Artists Rights Act of 1990 (VARA or Act), Pub.L. No. 101-650 (tit. VI), 104 Stat. 5089, 5128–33 (1990). Construing this Act constitutes the subject of the present appeal. . . .

Its principal provisions afford protection only to authors of works of visual art—a narrow class of art defined to include paintings, drawings, prints, sculptures, or photographs produced for exhibition purposes, existing in a single copy or limited edition of 200 copies or fewer. With numerous exceptions, VARA grants three rights: the right of attribution, the right of integrity and, in the case of works of visual art of "recognized stature," the right to prevent destruction. For works created on or after June 1, 1991—the effective date of the Act—the rights provided for endure for the life of the author or, in the case of a joint work, the life of the last surviving author. The rights cannot be transferred, but may be waived by a writing signed by the author. Copyright registration is not required to bring an action for infringement of the rights granted under VARA, or to secure statutory damages and attorney's fees. All remedies available under copyright law, other than criminal remedies, are available in an action for infringement of moral rights. With this historical background in hand, we pass to the merits of the present litigation.

II. Work of Visual Art

* * *

A. Singleness of the Work

As a preliminary matter, we must determine whether the trial court correctly found that the work is a single piece of art, to be analyzed under VARA as a whole, rather than separate works to be considered individually. This finding was a factual one.... [T]he parties entered into a joint stipulation relating to numerous facts, including a definition of "the Work." This stipulated definition contained a long, detailed list of all the sculptural elements contained in the building's lobby. The district court found that, with a few precise exceptions determined to be separate works of art, the artwork created by plaintiffs in the lobby was a single work....

The trial court found further support for its conclusion in the method by which the artists created the work-each additional element of the sculpture was based on the element preceding it so that they would mesh together. The result was a thematically consistent, inter-related work whose elements could not be separated without losing continuity and meaning....

* * *

B. The Statutory Definition

A "work of visual art" is defined by the Act in terms both positive (what it is) and negative (what it is not). In relevant part VARA defines a work of visual art as "a painting, drawing, print, or sculpture, existing in a single copy" or in a limited edition of 200 copies or fewer.... Concededly, considered as a whole, the work is a sculpture and exists only in a single copy. Therefore, the work satisfies the Act's positive definition of a work of visual art. We next turn to the second part of the statutory definition—what is not a work of visual art.

* * *

III. Work Made for Hire

Also excluded from the definition of a work of visual art is any work made for hire. 17 U.S.C. § 1012(B). A "work made for hire" is defined in the Copyright Act, in relevant part, as "a work prepared by an employee within the scope of his or her employment." *Id.* § 101(1). Appellants maintain the work was made for hire and therefore is not a work of visual art under VARA. The district court held otherwise, finding that the plaintiffs were hired as independent contractors.

A. Reid Tests

The Copyright Act does not define the terms "employee" or "scope of employment." In *Community for Creative Non-Violence v. Reid,* 490 U.S. 730, 109 S.Ct. 2166, 104 L.Ed.2d 811 (1989), the Supreme Court looked to the general common law of agency for guidance. It held that a multi-factor balancing test was required to determine if a work was produced for hire (by an employee) or was produced by an independent contractor. The Court elaborated 13 specific factors:

> the hiring party's right to control the manner and means by which the product is accomplished . . . the skill required; the source of the instrumentalities and tools; the location of the work; the duration of the relationship between the parties; whether the hiring party has the right to assign additional projects to the hired party; the extent of the hired party's discretion over when and how long to work; the method of payment; the hired party's role in hiring and paying assistants; whether the work is part of the regular business of the hiring party; whether the hiring party is in business; the provision of employee benefits; and the tax treatment of the hired party.

Reid, 490 U.S. at 751–52, 109 S.Ct. at 2178–79. While all of these factors are relevant, no single factor is determinative. Instead, the factors are weighed by referring to the facts of a given case.

The district court determined that the sculpture was not "work for hire" and therefore not excluded from the definition of visual art. The *Reid* test is a list of factors not all of which may come into play in a given case. The *Reid* test is therefore easily misapplied. We are usually reluctant to reverse a district court's factual findings as to the presence or absence of any of the *Reid* factors and do so only when the district court's findings are clearly erroneous. By contrast, the ultimate legal conclusion as to whether or not the sculpture is "work for hire" is reviewed *de novo.* The district court correctly stated the legal test. But some of its factual findings, we think, were clearly erroneous.

B. Factors Applied

The district court properly noted . . . five factors which would be relevant in nearly all cases: the right to control the manner and means of production; requisite skill; provision of employee benefits; tax treatment of the hired party; whether the hired party may be assigned additional projects. Analysis begins with a discussion of these factors.

First, plaintiffs had complete artistic freedom with respect to every aspect of the sculpture's creation. Although the artists heeded advice or accepted suggestions from building engineers, architects, and others, such actions were not a relinquishment of their artistic freedom. The evidence strongly supports the finding that plaintiffs controlled the work's "manner and means" ....

The district court also correctly found the artists' conception and execution of the work required great skill in execution. Appellants' contention that the plaintiffs' reliance on assistants in some way mitigates the skill required for this work is meritless.... The right to control the manner and means and the requisite skill needed for execution of this project were both properly found by the district court to weigh against "work for hire" status.

The trial court erred, however, when it ruled that the defendants could not assign the artists additional projects. First, the employment agreement between SIG Management Company and the artists clearly states that the artists agreed not only to install the sculpture but also to "render such other related services and duties as may be assigned to [them] from time to time by the Company." By the very terms of the contract the defendants and their predecessors in interest had the right to assign other related projects to the artists. The district court incorrectly decided that this language supported the artists' claim to be independent contractors. While the artists' obligations were limited to related services and duties, the defendants nonetheless did have the right to assign to plaintiffs work other than the principal sculpture.

Further, the defendants did, in fact, assign such other projects.... On at least three different occasions the plaintiffs were assigned additional projects, which they completed without further compensation.... The point is that the performance of other assigned work not of the artists' choosing supports a conclusion that the artists were not independent contractors but employees.

We must also consider factors the district court correctly found to favor finding the sculpture to be work for hire. Specifically, the provision of employee benefits and the tax treatment of the plaintiffs weigh strongly in favor of employee status. The defendants paid payroll and social security taxes, provided employee benefits such as life, health, and liability insurance and paid vacations, and contributed to unemployment insurance and workers' compensation funds on plaintiffs' behalf.... All of these facts strongly suggest the artists were employees.

* * *

Conclusion

Accordingly, the district court's order insofar as it held the work was one not made for hire is reversed and the injunction vacated. In all other respects, the order of the district court is affirmed. Each party to bear its own costs.

Massachusetts Museum of Contemporary Art Foundation v. Büchel

593 F.3d 38 (1st Cir. 2010)

LIPEZ, J. As one observer has noted, this case, which raises important and unsettled legal issues under the Visual Artists Rights Act ("VARA"), may well serve as "the ultimate how-not-to guide in the complicated world of installation art." Geoff Edgers, *Dismantled,* The Boston Globe, Oct. 21, 2007, at 1N. Artist Christoph Büchel conceived of an ambitious, football-field-sized art installation entitled "Training Ground for Democracy," which was to be exhibited at the Massachusetts Museum of Contemporary Art ("MASS MoCA," or "the Museum"). Unfortunately, the parties never memorialized the terms of their relationship or their understanding of the intellectual property issues involved in the installation in a written agreement.

* * *

I.

[MASS MoCA was interested in pursuing a large installation with Büchel. Over a period of months, beginning in October 2005, the parties entered into discussions, culminating in MASS MoCA's acceptance of Büchel's project *Training Ground for Democracy.* It was set to open on December 16, 2006. Although each side provided the other with a written agreement, no agreement was formally signed by both parties. In August 2006, Büchel spent ten days at MASS MoCA developing a basic schematic model of the installation, and MASS MoCA agreed to fund and purchase the items indicated by Büchel. During the fall 2006, tensions developed between the parties. MASS MoCA thought the artist's demands were increasingly unreasonable and expensive; and Büchel thought the museum was undermining his artistic vision and not following instructions.

As conflicts continued, the installation lagged behind schedule and the December opening was postponed. A March 2007 date was the new target. Once Büchel left in December 2006 for the holidays, the parties' working relationship deteriorated substantially. MASS MoCA continued to work on the installation during spring 2007. By May 2007, it was clear, through increasingly vitriolic exchanges, that Büchel would not complete the installation. MASS MoCA filed this lawsuit. The next day, MASS MoCA announced the cancellation of *Training Ground* and the opening of a new exhibit, "Made at MASS MoCA," a documentary on the complex issues that can arise in the context of collaborative projects between artists and museums. The district court granted the museum's motion for summary judgment, rejecting Büchel's claims under VARA and the Copyright Act.—Ed.]

II.

* * *

A. The Copyright Act

Under the Copyright Act, "[c]opyright protection subsists . . . in original works of authorship fixed in any tangible medium of expression." 17 U.S.C. § 102(a). A copyright owner has certain exclusive rights to the work, which are enumerated in 17 U.S.C. § 106. . . . Of particular relevance to this litigation, the copyright holder has the exclusive right to publicly display the copyrighted work and to prepare derivative works based upon it. 17 U.S.C. § 106(5), (2). . . . The remedies provided by the Copyright Act include injunctive relief and actual or statutory damages. *See* 17 U.S.C. §§ 502, 504.

* * *

C. Does VARA Apply to Unfinished Works of Art?

Büchel argues that the district court erred by failing to recognize that VARA applies with equal force to incomplete artistic endeavors that would otherwise be subject to VARA protection. He asserts that the Act's plain language compels such a conclusion, which he claims is confirmed by the legislative history and sparse case law interpreting the statute. The Museum, for its part, does not argue that unfinished works are excluded from VARA's scope. . . .

We do not read the district court's ruling to conclude categorically that VARA does not apply to unfinished works. Rather, the court held that, if the statute applied, "display of th[e] unfinished installation would have violated neither Büchel's right of attribution nor his right of integrity." Nonetheless, the court repeatedly expressed skepticism about Büchel's claim . . . observing at one point in its opinion that "unfinished art may not be covered by VARA at all."

* * *

The definition of a "work of visual art" for VARA purposes is stated "in terms both positive (what it is) and negative (what it is not)." *Carter,* 71 F.3d at 84. An unfinished sculptural installation such as "Training Ground for Democracy" is not one of the items specifically excluded from VARA protection, and MASS MoCA wisely does not attempt to argue otherwise. Instead, we must determine whether the "positive" aspect of the definition of "work of visual art" includes an *unfinished* version of a "sculpture[] existing in a single copy." 17 U.S.C. § 101.

The text of VARA itself does not state when an artistic project becomes a work of visual art subject to its protections. However, VARA is part of the Copyright Act, and that Act's definition section . . . specifies that its definitions, unless otherwise provided, control throughout Title 17. That general definitional section of the Copyright Act states that a work is "created" when it "is fixed in a copy . . . for the first time." Further, "where a work is prepared over a period of time, *the portion of it that has been fixed at any particular time constitutes the work as of that time.*" A work is "fixed" when it has been formed, "by or under the authority of the author," in a way that is "sufficiently permanent or stable to permit it to be perceived, reproduced, or otherwise communicated for a period of more than transitory duration."

Not surprisingly, based on section 101's general definitions, courts have held that the Copyright Act's protections extend to unfinished works.

Reading VARA in accordance with the definitions in section 101, it too must be read to protect unfinished, but "fixed," works of art that, if completed, would qualify for protection under the statute. . . . At least one circuit has previously assumed VARA's applicability to unfinished works. *See Carter,* 71 F.3d at 83–88 (discussing VARA claims stemming from an unfinished, walk-through sculpture being installed in the lobby of a building).

* * *

We thus hold that VARA protects the moral rights of artists who have "created" works of art within the meaning of the Copyright Act even if those works are not yet complete.

* * *

V.

We summarize our holdings:

1. VARA's protection of an artist's moral rights extends to unfinished creations that are "works of art" within the meaning of the Copyright Act;

* * *

Affirmed in part, vacated in part, and remanded for further proceedings consistent with this decision. Each party is to bear its own costs.

[Opinion continues in D. Case Law Interpreting Rights of Attribution and Integrity, *infra*.]

Kelley v. Chicago Park District

635 F.3d 290 (7th Cir. 2011)

SYKES, J. Chapman Kelley is a nationally recognized artist known for his representational paintings of landscapes and flowers—in particular, romantic floral and woodland interpretations set within ellipses. In 1984 he received permission from the Chicago Park District to install an ambitious wildflower display at the north end of Grant Park, a prominent public space in the heart of downtown Chicago. "Wildflower Works" was thereafter planted: two enormous elliptical flower beds, each nearly as big as a football field, featuring a variety of native wildflowers and edged with borders of gravel and steel.

Promoted as "living art," Wildflower Works received critical and popular acclaim, and for a while Kelley and a group of volunteers tended the vast garden, pruning and replanting as needed. But by 2004 Wildflower Works had deteriorated, and the City's goals for Grant Park had changed. So the Park District dramatically modified the garden, substantially reducing its size, reconfiguring the oval flower beds into rectangles, and changing some of the planting material.

Kelley sued the Park District for violating his "right of integrity" under the Visual Artists Rights Act of 1990 ("VARA"), and also for breach of contract. The contract claim is insubstantial; the main event here is the VARA claim, which is novel and tests the boundaries of copyright law. . . .

The district court held a bench trial and entered a split judgment. . . . The court then held for Kelley on the contract claim, but found his evidence of damages uncertain and entered a nominal award of $1. Both sides appealed.

We affirm in part and reverse in part. . . .

* * *

II. Discussion

* * *

A. Kelley's Moral-Rights Claim Under the Visual Artists Rights Act of 1990

* * *

2. Vara's scope

VARA amended the Copyright Act and provides a measure of protection for a limited set of moral rights falling under the rubric of "rights of attribution" and "rights of integrity"—but only for artists who create specific types of visual art. 17 U.S.C. § 106A(a). The statutory coverage is limited to paintings, drawings, prints, sculptures, and photographs created for exhibition existing in a single copy or a limited edition of 200 or less. . . .

* * *

This definition also contains a number of specific exclusions: e.g., posters, maps, and globes; books, newspapers, magazines, and other periodicals; "motion picture[s] or other audiovisual work[s]"; merchandising and promotional materials; "any work made for hire"; and "any work not subject to copyright protection under this title."

This last exclusion simply reinforces the point that VARA supplements general copyright protection; to qualify for moral rights under VARA, a work must first satisfy basic copyright standards. Under the Copyright Act of 1976, copyright subsists in "original works of authorship fixed in any tangible medium of expression, now known or later developed, from which they can be perceived, reproduced, or otherwise communicated." "Works of authorship" include "pictorial, graphic, and sculptural works." VARA's definition of "work of visual art" is limited to a narrow subset of this broader universe of "pictorial, graphic, and sculptural works" that are otherwise eligible for copyright; only a select few categories of art get the extra protection provided by the moral-rights concept.

Several exceptions limit the scope of the rights granted under the statute:

* * *

> (2) *The modification of a work of visual art which is the result of conservation, or of the public presentation, including lighting and placement,* of the work *is not a destruction, distortion, mutilation, or other modification* described in subsection (a)(3) *unless the modification is caused by gross negligence.*

17 U.S.C. § 106A(c) (emphasis added). The second of these—the "public presentation" exception—is at issue here. . . .

* * *

3. Is Wildflower Works a painting or sculpture?

The district court held that Wildflower Works was both a painting and a sculpture but was insufficiently original to qualify for copyright. Alternatively, the court concluded that it was site-specific art and held that all site-specific art is implicitly excluded from VARA. Other arguments . . . were not reached.

On appeal Kelley contests the district court's conclusions regarding originality and site-specific art. The Park District defends these holdings and also reiterates the other arguments it made in the district court, except one: The Park District has not challenged the district court's conclusion that Wildflower Works is a painting and a sculpture.

This is an astonishing omission. VARA's definition of "work of visual art" operates to narrow and focus the statute's coverage; only a "painting, drawing, print, or sculpture," or an exhibition photograph will qualify. These terms are not further defined, but the overall structure of the statutory scheme clearly illuminates the limiting effect of this definition. Copyright's broad general coverage extends to "original works of authorship," and this includes "pictorial, graphic, and sculptural works." 17 U.S.C. § 102(a)(5). The use of the adjectives "pictorial" and "sculptural" suggests flexibility and breadth in application. In contrast VARA uses the specific nouns "painting" and "sculpture." To qualify for moral-rights protection under VARA, Wildflower Works cannot just be "pictorial" or "sculptural" in some aspect or effect, it must actually *be* a "painting" or a "sculpture." Not metaphorically or by analogy, but *really.*

That Kelley considered the garden to be both a painting and a sculpture—only rendered in living material—is not dispositive. . . .

* * *

The district judge worried about taking "too literalist an approach to determining whether a given object qualifies as a sculpture or painting." His concern was the "tension between the law and the evolution of ideas in modern or avant garden (*sic*) art; the former requires legislatures to taxonomize artistic creations, whereas the latter is occupied with expanding the definition of what we accept to be art." We agree with this important insight. But there's a big difference between avoiding a literalistic approach and embracing one that is infinitely malleable. The judge appears to have come down too close to the latter extreme.

In short, this case raises serious questions about the meaning and application of VARA's definition of qualifying works of visual art—questions with potentially decisive consequences for this and other moral-rights claims. But the Park District has not challenged this aspect of the district court's decision, so we move directly to the question of copyrightability, which is actually where the analysis should start in the first place.

4. Is Wildflower Works copyrightable?

To merit copyright protection, Wildflower Works must be an "original work [] of authorship fixed in a[] tangible medium of expression . . . from which [it] can be perceived, reproduced, or otherwise communicated." The district court held that although Wildflower Works was both a painting and a sculpture, it was ineligible for copyright because it lacked originality. . . .

* * *

The district court took the position that Wildflower Works was not original because Kelley was not "the first person to ever conceive of and express an arrangement of growing wildflowers in ellipse-shaped enclosed area[s]." This mistakenly equates originality with novelty; the law is clear that a work can be original even if it is not novel. No one argues that Wildflower Works was copied; it plainly possesses more than a little creative spark.

* * *

The real impediment to copyright here is . . . that a living garden lacks the kind of authorship and stable fixation normally required to support copyright. Unlike originality, authorship and fixation are *explicit* constitutional requirements; the Copyright Clause empowers Congress to secure for "authors" exclusive rights in their "writings." U.S. Const. art 1, § 8, cl. 8. The originality requirement is implicit in these express limitations on the congressional copyright power. The Supreme Court has "repeatedly construed all three terms in relation to one another [or] perhaps has collapsed them into a single concept"; therefore, "[w]ritings are what authors create, but for one to be an author, the writing has to be original."

"Without fixation," moreover, "there cannot be a 'writing.'" . . .

A work is "fixed" in a tangible medium of expression "when its embodiment in a copy or phonorecord . . . is sufficiently permanent or stable to permit it to be perceived, reproduced, or otherwise communicated for a period of more than transitory duration." 17 U.S.C. § 101. . . . .

Finally, "authorship is an entirely human endeavor." Authors of copyrightable works must be human; works owing their form to the forces of nature cannot be copyrighted. [S]*ee also* U.S. COPYRIGHT OFFICE, COMPENDIUM II: COPYRIGHT OFFICE PRACTICES § 503.03(a) ("[A] work must be the product of human authorship" and not the forces of nature.) (1984); *id.* § 202.02(b).

Recognizing copyright in Wildflower Works presses too hard on these basic principles. We fully accept that the artistic community might classify Kelley's garden as a work of postmodern conceptual art. We acknowledge as well that copyright's prerequisites of authorship and fixation are broadly defined. But the law must have some limits; not all conceptual art may be copyrighted. In the ordinary copyright case, authorship and fixation are not contested. . . . But this is not an ordinary case. A living garden like Wildflower Works is neither "authored" nor "fixed" in the senses required for copyright.

Simply put, gardens are planted and cultivated, not authored. A garden's constituent elements are alive and inherently changeable, not fixed. Most of what we see and experience in a garden—the colors, shapes, textures, and scents of the plants—originates in nature, not in the mind of the gardener. At any given moment in time, a garden owes most of its form and appearance to natural forces, though the gardener who plants and tends it obviously assists. All this is true of Wildflower Works, even though it was designed and planted by an artist.

. . . If a garden can qualify as a "work of authorship" sufficiently "embodied in a copy," at what point has fixation occurred? When the garden is newly planted? When its first blossoms appear? When it is in full bloom? How—and at what point in time—is a court to determine whether infringing copying has occurred?

In contrast, when a landscape designer conceives of a plan for a garden and puts it in writing—records it in text, diagrams, or drawings on paper or on a digital-storage device—we can say that his intangible intellectual property has been embodied in a fixed and tangible "copy." . . . The same cannot be said of a garden, which is not a fixed copy of the gardener's intellectual property. Although the planting material is tangible and can be perceived for more than a transitory duration, it is not stable or permanent enough to be called "fixed." Seeds and plants in a garden are naturally in a state of perpetual change; they germinate, grow, bloom, become dormant, and eventually die. This life cycle moves gradually, over days, weeks, and season to season, but the real barrier to copyright here is not *temporal* but *essential.* The essence of a garden is its vitality, not its fixedness. It may endure from season to season, but its nature is one of dynamic change.

* * *

In short, Wildflower Works presents serious problems of authorship and fixation that . . . other examples of conceptual or kinetic art do not. Because Kelley's garden is neither "authored" nor "fixed" in the senses required for basic copyright, it cannot qualify for moral-rights protection under VARA.

5. Site-specific art, and the public-presentation and building exceptions

This case also raises some important questions about the application of VARA to site-specific art, as well as the statute's public-presentation and building exceptions. Though we need not decide these questions, we do have a few words of caution about the district court's treatment of the issue of VARA and site-specific art. The court classified Wildflower Works as a form of site-specific art; we see no reason to upset this factual finding. The court then adopted the First Circuit's holding in *Phillips* [*v. Pembroke Real Estate, Inc.*, 459 F.3d 128 (1st Cir. 2006),] that site-specific art is categorically excluded from VARA. This legal conclusion is open to question.

* * *

There are a couple of reasons to question this interpretation of VARA. First, the term "site-specific art" appears nowhere in the statute. Nothing in the definition of a "work of visual art" either explicitly or by implication excludes this form of art from moral-rights protection. . . .

Second, *Phillips*'s all-or-nothing approach to site-specific art may be unwarranted. Site-specific art is not *necessarily* destroyed if moved; modified, yes, but not always utterly destroyed. . . .

Then there is the matter of the building exception, which applies to works "incorporated in or made part of a building in such a way that removing the work from the building will cause the destruction, distortion, mutilation, or other modification of the work." 17 U.S.C. § 113(d)(1)(A). . . . On its face this exception covers a particular kind of site-specific art. Its presence in the statute suggests that site-specific art is not categorically excluded from VARA.

These observations are of course general and not dispositive. Because we are resolving the VARA claim on other grounds, we need not decide whether VARA is inapplicable to site-specific art.

* * *

For the foregoing reasons, we AFFIRM the judgment in favor of the Park District on the VARA claim; . . . and REMAND with instructions to enter judgment for the Park District.

Cheffins v. Stewart

825 F.3d 588 (9th Cir. 2016)

O'Scannlain, Circuit Judge:

We must decide whether the Visual Artists Rights Act applies to a used school bus transformed into a mobile replica of a 16th-century Spanish galleon.

I

A

Plaintiffs Simon Cheffins and Gregory Jones, along with a number of volunteers, built the *La Contessa*, a replica of a 16th-century Spanish galleon for use at the Burning Man Festival. [It was built on the base of] a used school bus. . . . When completed, the *La Contessa* was approximately sixty feet wide and sixteen feet long with a mast over fifty feet tall.

. . . Festival participants took rides on the *La Contessa*, and at least two weddings were performed on its deck. . . . [I]t was used as part of a marching band performance, and, in 2005, it was the centerpiece of a children's treasure hunt, among other things.

After . . . the 2005 Festival[], Cheffins and Jones stored the *La Contessa* on land . . . [with the pertinent legal] permission to do so. In late 2005, . . . defendant Michael Stewart took possession of the land in fee simple through a limited liability company.

Cheffins and Jones did not relocate the *La Contessa* after the change of property ownership. Rather, it sat unmoved on Stewart's land until December 2006. Sometime during that month, Stewart intentionally burned the wooden structure of the *La Contessa* so that a scrap metal dealer could remove the underlying school bus from his property.

B

Cheffins and Jones filed this suit . . . alleging that Stewart violated the Visual Artists Rights Act, and committed common law conversion when he destroyed the *La Contessa*. . . .

II

* * *

A

* * *

As the text of the statute shows, the VARA only applies to "works of visual art." It does not define the term "work of visual art," but the VARA is part of the Copyright Act, which defines "work of visual art" in the affirmative and in the negative. . . .

. . . [A] "work of visual art" is not:

(A)(i) any poster, map, globe, chart, technical drawing, diagram, model, *applied art*, motion picture or other audiovisual work, book, magazine, newspaper, periodical, data base, electronic information service, electronic publication, or similar publication;

(ii) any merchandising item or advertising, promotional, descriptive, covering, or packaging material or container;

(iii) any portion or part of any item described in clause (i) or (ii).

Id. (emphasis added).

B

On summary judgment, Stewart asserted, and the trial court subsequently concluded, that the *La Contessa* was not a "work of visual art" because it was "applied art."

III

A

The VARA does not define the term "applied art," and federal courts have rarely had occasion to interpret its meaning. In *Carter v. Helmsley-Spear, Inc.*, 71 F.3d 77 (2d Cir. 1995), the Second Circuit held that a sculpture constructed of portions of a school bus and affixed to a wall in a building lobby was not "applied art." It explained that the term "applied art" means "two-and three-dimensional ornamentation or decoration that is affixed to otherwise utilitarian objects." The court further explained that the sculpture was not "applied art" simply because it was affixed to "the lobby's floor, walls, and ceiling" because "[i]nterpreting applied art to include such works would render meaningless VARA's protection for works of visual art installed in buildings."

The Second Circuit provided an additional gloss on what constitutes a "work of visual art," and by extension what constitutes "applied art," in *Pollara v. Seymour*, 344 F.3d 265 (2d Cir. 2003), where it explained that the "VARA may protect a sculpture that looks like a piece of furniture, but it does not protect a piece of utilitarian furniture, whether or not it could arguably be called a sculpture." ...

We agree in large part with the Second Circuit's analysis. As the Second Circuit suggested, the focus of our inquiry should be on whether the object in question originally was—and continues to be—utilitarian in nature. Such a focus comports with dictionary definitions of the term "applied art." For example, *Webster's Dictionary* defines "applied art" as "employed in the decoration, design or execution of *useful* objects." ... These definitions suggest that, in its ordinary meaning, applied art consists of an object with a utilitarian function that also has some artistic or aesthetic merit.

Further, this approach makes sense in the statutory context in which "applied art" is used in 17 U.S.C. § 101. "Applied art" is enumerated in a list that also contains, *inter alia*, maps, globes, charts, technical drawings, diagrams, models, newspapers, periodicals, data bases, and electronic information services. The fact that the other items in the list are utilitarian objects leads us to conclude that the listed items are related by their practical purposes and utilitarian functions, requiring a focus on utility when construing the term "applied art."

We therefore hold that an object constitutes a piece of "applied art"—as opposed to a "work of visual art"—where the object initially served a utilitarian function and the object continues to serve such a function after the artist made embellishments or alterations to it. This test embraces the circumstances both where a functional object incorporates a decorative design in its initial formulation, and where a functional object is decorated after manufacture but continues to serve a practical purpose. Conversely, "applied art" would not include a piece of art whose function is purely aesthetic or a utilitarian object which is so transformed through the addition of artistic elements that its utilitarian functions cease.

B

We respond briefly to the concern expressed in the concurrence that the standard we adopt today may not be workable—that it raises difficult questions regarding where exactly the line defining "applied art" will be drawn. The analysis we adopt today directs the court's attention away from assessments of an object's artistic merit and instead toward the object's practical utility. The standard is relatively simple: where a functional object, despite claims of artistic merit, continues to serve a utilitarian purpose, it is applied art. Although the answers to some of the questions regarding this standard may be clear, resolution of the case before us does not require us to provide a comprehensive inventory of all the objects that will or will not meet the definition of "applied art."

Indeed, the call for a "more textured and flexible definition of applied art," raises even greater concerns of line drawing. The concurrence would have judges "evaluate [a] work as a whole," to determine "whether the artistic creation is subservient" to its "useful function." Such an analysis necessarily requires courts to express judgments regarding the importance of an object's artistic qualities, and to determine whether those qualities predominate over the object's non-artistic utility. Even approached from the perspective of a "reasonable observer," the question for a court remains whether an objectively reasonable person would conclude that a creation is more "art" than useful object. How different judges could answer such a question on a consistent basis is anything but clear.

Any attempt to guide judicial determinations of an amorphous concept like "applied art" is unlikely to be completely satisfying to all. But the approach we adopt today instructs courts to focus precisely on an object's continuing utility—and not to ask whether that utility is somehow subservient to an artistic creation. Difficult cases may still arise, but our standard aims to limit the situations in which they do.

C

We now apply this standard to the facts of this case.

The *La Contessa* began as a simple school bus—an object which unquestionably served the utilitarian function of transportation. To transform the bus into the *La Contessa*, Cheffins and Jones adorned it with the visual trappings of a 16th-century Spanish galleon. While the *La Contessa*'s elaborate decorative elements may have had many artistic qualities, the *La Contessa* retained a largely practical function even after it had been completed. At Burning Man, the *La Contessa* was used for transportation, providing rides to festival-goers, hosting musical performances and weddings, and serving as a stage for poetry and acrobatics shows. Indeed, the *La Contessa* often was driven about the Festival grounds and was banned from the Festival in 2004 because "its unsafe driving practices far exceeded community tolerance and out-weighed the visual contribution" it made.

Under the definition we adopt today, the *La Contessa* plainly was "applied art." It began as a rudimentary utilitarian object, and despite being visually transformed through elaborate artistry, it continued to serve a significant utilitarian function upon its completion. As "applied art," the *La Contessa* was not a work of visual art under the VARA and therefore not eligible for its protection. Therefore, the trial court properly granted summary judgment to Stewart on Cheffins and Jones's VARA claim.

* * *

AFFIRMED.

McKeown, Circuit Judge, concurring:

I write separately to express my concern with the majority's definition of applied art, which centers on whether an object has or retains a utilitarian function. This focus runs the risk of unduly narrowing the protections of artists under the Visual Artist Right's Act of 1990, 17 U.S.C. § 106A ("VARA"), and not focusing on the work as a whole. Although the majority's formulation may protect the clearest cases—those works that are "purely aesthetic" or "so transformed through the addition of artistic elements that [their] utilitarian functions cease"—it leaves other cases—such as works of art that incorporate utilitarian elements, or that could be put to practical purposes—out in the cold. To better effectuate the purpose of VARA, we need a more nuanced definition of "applied art" .... In determining whether a work is "applied art," the right question to ask is whether the primary purpose of the work as a whole is to serve a practical, useful function, and whether the aesthetic elements are subservient to that utilitarian purpose. Because the bus/Spanish galleon *La Contessa* is applied art under either standard, I concur in the judgment....

* * *

Notes and Questions

1. *Classifying Protected Works of Visual Art.* The issue in these four cases was whether the particular work was covered by VARA. That fundamental question was posed and determined after each of the courts presented the background of VARA,

often noting that VARA did not fit within traditional common law doctrines of property. Judicial recognition that VARA is a departure from common law suggests the development of VARA's caselaw will be aided by thoughtful, balanced advocacy. Let us consider each of the four cases from the perspective of classification.

a. Work made for hire. *Carter* is the easiest of these classification cases because there was a judicially recognized test to employ. Aside from the limited question of divisibility or singleness of the work, the artwork easily met the positive part of the statutory definition. As for the definition's negative part, for the sculpture to receive VARA protection, it must escape being deemed a work made for hire. The artwork, therefore, needed to be viewed in the context of the artist's economic relationship to the building's owner, and not in the context of art. For that determination, the trial court applied the test developed by the Supreme Court in *Reid* to the facts of *Carter*. Did the Second Circuit persuade you that the trial court's factual determination was clearly erroneous? A normal commission agreement (like Mr. Smith's from the First Drafting Exercise) is not a work made for hire, even though the buyer might believe otherwise. Think if you want to revise the commission agreement you drafted to take into account VARA rights. If so, what revisions would you make?

b. Unfinished works. *Mass MoCA* specifically addressed the question of VARA's applicability to unfinished works of art, in particular, a sculpture. Like the Second Circuit in *Carter*, the First Circuit answered its question within the statute's copyright framework, here examining the rubric of being "fixed." Under the general definition and case law precedent, "fixed" does not require completion. VARA, therefore, can apply to unfinished works. The question of VARA's applicability to unfinished works was not entirely new. *Carter* also involved an unfinished sculpture, although the issue was not directly discussed. Is it so clear that VARA should apply to unfinished works of an artist who is alive and competent? Assume you represent one of the parties in this case, if there was a written agreement, how would you draft the agreement to deal with the question of completion? Were you surprised that Mass MoCA did not have a written contract with Büchel? Governance structures and commissioning protocols may not have been as fully developed then as they are today.

c. Is it art at all? *Kelley* delved into this definitional question with gusto, deeming the defendant's concession that the garden was a painting or sculpture "astonishing." Judge Sykes employed a careful statutory analysis to highlight the differences in language used in VARA from that of the copyright provisions. She sent a clear message that an "infinitely malleable" interpretation is not consistent with statutory language. Like Gertrude Stein's "a rose is a rose is a rose," Judge Sykes tells us that a garden is a garden, and not a painting or a sculpture. Judge Sykes concluded the opinion with a discussion of VARA's application to site-specific art, which she also acknowledges is not necessary to the holding. It was clear Judge Sykes wants to dispel errant interpretations by nipping them in the bud.

The actual holding however presented between these two discussions is pure copyright. It proceeds from the negative part of the statutory definition of a work of visual art. Interestingly, as in *Mass MoCA*, the holding focused on the "fixedness" of the work. While Büchel's *Training Ground for Democracy* was not artistically complete, it was sufficiently fixed for copyright, whereas Kelley's garden was artistically complete, but not sufficiently fixed.

d. Applied art. Two decades after *Carter*, the Ninth Circuit addressed VARA's applied art exception in *Cheffins*. The majority and concurring opinions used *Carter*'s discussion of applied art as utilitarian in nature as their starting points. The majority and concurring opinions agreed that *La Contessa* was applied art and therefore not protected by VARA. Where the opinions diverged was the role an art analysis would play in that determination. Judge O'Scannlain's opinion held to a bright line non-art approach ("where a functional object . . . serves a utilitarian purpose, it is applied art"). Judge McKeown's concurring opinion preferred a more nuanced approach that incorporates an art perspective. Consequently, a judge should consider "whether the primary purpose of the work as a whole is to serve" a utilitarian purpose and, if so, whether the "aesthetic elements are subservient to that utilitarian purpose." Both opinions acknowledged that VARA did not provide a definition for applied art. Each opinion therefore cited dictionaries, while Judge O'Scannlian used traditional ones, Judge McKeown used art dictionaries.

In her concurrence, Judge McKeown cited VARA's legislative history that downplayed the difficulties inherent in the definitions, deeming the exclusions "self-explanatory." Courts should use "common-sense" and "generally accepted standards of the artistic community." *Cheffins*, at 600, citing H.R. Rep. No. 101-514, at 11, 13. A lingering problem is the perception that judges are loath to make aesthetic judgments. This "doctrine of avoidance" is generally traced to Justice Holmes. "It would be a dangerous undertaking for persons trained only to the law to constitute themselves final judges of the worth of pictorial illustrations." Bleistein v. Donaldson Lithographing Co., 188 U.S. 239, 251 (1903). See also Christine Haight Farley, *Judging Art*, 79 Tul. L. Rev. 805 (2005); but cf. Brian Soucek, *Aesthetic Judgment in Law*, 69 Ala. L. Rev. 381 (2018).

2. *Site-Specific Art.* In Phillips v. Pembroke Real Estate, Inc., 459 F.3d 128 (1st Cir. 2006), the First Circuit held that VARA did not apply to site-specific art. In site-specific art, the artist incorporates the environment as one of the media with which he works. David Phillips was a sculptor whose 27 sculptures were specifically commissioned in 1999 by Pembroke for Eastport Park in Boston. In 2001, Pembroke decided to alter the design of the park, and it hired another artist to conduct the redesign. That new plan required the removal and relocation of much of Phillips's work; after discussions, Pembroke reconfigured again, this time retaining most of Phillips's works but relocating some. Thereafter, Pembroke reverted to the original redesign plan. Phillips sued on VARA right of integrity grounds. The question on appeal to the First Circuit was whether VARA prohibits the removal of site-specific works. That court answered that "VARA does not apply to site-specific art at all." The argument that persuaded the court was the public presentation exception in § 106A(c)(2). That exception excludes from VARA integrity protection modifications that result from public presentation, including placement. The court

determined that Congress did not intend to create a dual regime for that exception, having it apply only to free-standing or moveable art. Moreover, statutes in derogation of the common law are to be read with a presumption favoring retention of long-established principles, unless the statutory purpose is clearly to the contrary. The First Circuit was clear—VARA is not applicable to site-specific art.

Judge Sykes in the Seventh Circuit's *Kelley* opinion was not willing to let the First Circuit's blanket statement go unchallenged. Though unnecessary for the *Kelley* decision, it was clear that Judge Sykes questions the *Phillips* interpretation based primarily on the language of VARA.

D. Case Law Interpreting Rights of Attribution and Integrity

Massachusetts Museum of Contemporary Art Foundation v. Büchel

593 F.3d 38 (1st Cir. 2010)

[For facts of case, see C. Case Law Interpreting Works of Visual Art, *supra*.]

III.

Given Büchel's right to protection under VARA . . . , we must now assess the district court's ruling that Büchel failed to raise a genuine issue of material fact with respect to any of his claims. . . .

We first consider Büchel's claims asserting violations of his attribution and integrity rights under VARA and then address his claims under other provisions of the Copyright Act, which assert violations of his rights to control the display of the installation and to create derivative works based on it.

A. The Scope of Vara's Integrity and Attribution Rights

1. The Right of Integrity

VARA's right of integrity . . . provides that an artist shall have the right "to prevent any intentional distortion, mutilation, or other modification of [his or her] work which would be prejudicial to his or her honor or reputation, and [that] any intentional distortion, mutilation, or modification of that work is a violation of that right." It thus allows artists to protect their works against intentional modifications that would be prejudicial to their honor or reputations.

There is arguably some uncertainty about the plaintiff's burden of proof in a case such as this because the second part of section (a)(3)(A)—stating that "any intentional distortion, mutilation, or modification of th[e] work is a violation" of the right of integrity—does not explicitly require a showing of prejudice when the alteration already has occurred and damages, rather than injunctive relief, would be the appropriate remedy. . . . We have found no case law discussing a possible difference in the showing required for injunctive relief and damages for right-of-integrity claims.

Some courts, however, have assumed without analysis that the prejudice showing is necessary for both injunctive relief and damages. At least one commentator likewise accepts, without discussion, that the damages remedy requires a showing of prejudice. *See* Melville B. Nimmer, 3-8D *Nimmer on Copyright* § 8D.06[C][1] . . . .

* * *

We agree with Nimmer's view of the provision, including the application of the prejudice requirement to a claim for damages. . . .

* * *

2. The Right of Attribution

VARA's right of attribution grants the author of a work of visual art the right, in part, (1) "to claim authorship of that work"; (2) "to prevent the use of his or her name as the author of any work of visual art which he or she did not create"; and (3) "to prevent the use of his or her name as the author of the work of visual art in the event of a distortion, mutilation, or other modification of the work which would be prejudicial to his or her honor or reputation." 17 U.S.C. § 106A(a)(1), (2). . . .

The right of attribution under VARA thus gives an artist a claim for injunctive relief. . . . Whether VARA entitles an artist to damages for violation of the right of attribution is a separate question. We find the answer in the difference between the statutory language. . . . Subsection (a)(3) of section 106A, which codifies the right of integrity, . . . [has] an additional clause stating "any intentional distortion, mutilation, or modification of that work is a violation of that right." . . .

No such "violation" clause is included in the sections codifying the right of attribution. The legislative history sheds no light on this difference, but Nimmer speculates as follows:

> Perhaps the implication is that whereas an integrity violation could give rise to a monetary recovery, failure to attribute is remediable solely through injunction. If that conclusion were intended, Congress certainly could have expressed its intent less obliquely.

We agree with Nimmer's surmise that VARA does not provide a damages remedy for an attribution violation. Where the statutory language is framed as a right "to prevent" conduct, it does not necessarily follow that a plaintiff is entitled to damages once the conduct occurs. . . .

* * *

B. Büchel's Vara Claims

With this legal framework in mind, we turn to the record before the district court. By dismantling "Training Ground," the Museum prevented the further use of Büchel's name in connection with the work, eliminating any basis for injunctive relief, and we therefore do not address the attribution claim in our VARA analysis.

We thus consider the evidence in the light most favorable to Büchel in determining whether there are genuine issues of material fact regarding the alleged violations of his right of integrity.

As noted above, the district court concluded that Büchel's right of integrity was not implicated by MASS MoCA's conduct.... The court stated that "[t]o suggest that the display of an unfinished and abandoned work somehow constitutes a distortion, mutilation, or modification of that non-existent work is simply inconsistent with the ordinary usage of those terms." Having concluded that VARA applies with full force to unfinished works, however, we cannot accept the district court's reliance on the unfinished state of "Training Ground" to minimize the rights of its creator.

It cannot be disputed that, at least by the time Büchel left North Adams in December 2006, "Training Ground" was "fixed" within the meaning of the Copyright Act.... Although far from complete..., the sculpture had an established presence in Building 5. Büchel thus had rights in the work that were protected under VARA, notwithstanding its unfinished state.

Büchel alleges that MASS MoCA violated his right to integrity in three distinct ways: first, by continuing to work on the installation without his authorization...; second, by using tarpaulins to "partially cover"... the installation, and allowing Museum visitors to see it in that condition; and third, merely by showing Büchel's work in its unfinished state.... Büchel asserts that these actions caused prejudice to his honor or reputation.

* * *

1. Continuing Work on "Training Ground"

Büchel asserts that, in the months following his departure..., the Museum encroached on his artistic vision by making modifications to the installation that in some instances were directly contrary to his instructions. In rejecting Büchel's VARA claims, the district court... found that these "[f]umbled efforts to assist in creating, or failing to create, a work of art are not equivalent to distortion, modification, or mutilation of the art."

Although a jury might agree with the court's assessment, the evidence viewed in the light most favorable to Büchel would allow a finding that at least some of the Museum's actions violated VARA. The record permits the inference that, even during his time as an artist-in-residence at MASS MoCA, Museum staff members were disregarding his instructions and intentionally modifying "Training Ground" in a manner that he did not approve....

* * *

[By early February 2007], direct communication between Büchel and the Museum became sparse. It was during this time, Büchel alleges, that the Museum developed a "Plan B" to be implemented in the event-which was looking increasingly likely-that he did not return to finish the exhibit. Plan B, which involved publicly exhibiting the unfinished installation without the artist's permission, called for completing various elements of the installation in a way the Museum knew might differ from Büchel's artistic concept. . . .

At least some Museum staff members recognized that continuing to work on the installation without Büchel's input might be problematic. Later in the February 14 email chain, [employee] Dante Birch noted that he was "interested in protecting the museum from intellectual property issues." . . . [Museum Director] Thompson's plans also raised concern among other MASS MoCA employees, including curator Susan Cross, who cautioned Thompson in a January 31 email that "we tend to forget that whether we're doing the welding or not, there is an 'author'—an artist for whom we shouldn't make decisions. . . . At what point, if at all, does an artist lose his right to owning the idea and his/her 'intellectual property?' . . . I think it is still art and still belongs to Buchel."

* * *

MASS MoCA argues that the evidence, taken in its entirety, does not add up to a triable issue with respect to a violation of Büchel's right of integrity, but shows only that Museum personnel were attempting to carry out Büchel's vision based on his instructions. Indeed, the Museum notes that the work slowed as Büchel's instructions became unavailable. . . . Other communications in the record also could be interpreted as showing the Museum doing its best to carry out Büchel's concept for the art work.

As we have noted, a jury may well accept the Museum's depiction of its intention and its actions. At this juncture, however, the record must be viewed in the light most favorable to Büchel. The evidence we have described would permit a jury to find that the Museum forged ahead with the installation in the first half of 2007 knowing that the continuing construction in Büchel's absence would frustrate-and likely contradict-Büchel's artistic vision. We thus conclude that a jury issue exists as to whether these actions effected an intentional distortion or other modification of "Training Ground" that subjected MASS MoCA to liability under VARA.

* * *

2. Showing "Training Ground" Covered with Tarpaulins

Büchel also claims that MASS MoCA improperly modified and distorted "Training Ground" when it partially covered it with the yellow tarpaulins and displayed it in that condition. He asserts . . . that visitors looked behind the tarps, that the tarp-adorned installation was "judged by others to be Büchel's work, and that his honor and reputation were harmed by it." In response, the Museum argues that the yellow tarpaulins were merely functional—a way of keeping people "out" of the installation—rather than an aesthetic modification of the artwork. . . .

* * *

. . . [A]lthough the installation unquestionably looked different with the tarpaulins partially covering it, we agree . . . the mere covering of the artwork by the

Museum, its host, cannot reasonably be deemed an intentional act of distortion or modification of Büchel's creation. To conclude otherwise would be to say that, even if all had gone well, the Museum would have been subject to a right-of-integrity claim if it had partially covered the work before its formal opening to prevent visitors from seeing it prematurely.

... In our view, a finding that the Museum's covering of the installation constituted an intentional act of distortion or modification of Büchel's artistic creation would stretch VARA beyond sensible boundaries.

3. Exhibiting "Training Ground" in Its Unfinished State

Büchel maintains ... merely exhibiting the work of art in its unfinished state, without the artist's consent, constitutes a distortion. We reject this claim. A separate moral right of disclosure (also known as the right of divulgation) protects an author's authority to "prevent third parties from disclosing [his or her] work to the public without the author's consent," and is not covered by VARA.

... [W]e decline to interpret VARA to include such a claim where a separate moral right of disclosure is widely recognized in other jurisdictions and Congress explicitly limited the statute's coverage to the rights of attribution and integrity. *See* Amy M. Adler, *Against Moral Rights,* 97 Cal. L.Rev. 263, 268 (2009) (noting that most European countries "recognize a right of divulgation, giving the artist the right to decide when (and whether) the work is complete and can be shown"). ... Any right Büchel possesses to withhold display of his artwork must be found outside VARA. We consider below his claim to such a right under section 106(5) of the Copyright Act.

* * *

IV.

* * *

A. Public Display

The owner of a copyrighted work has the exclusive right to "display the copyrighted work publicly." 17 U.S.C. § 106(5). Displaying a work is defined as "show[ing] a copy of it, either directly or by means of a film, slide, television image, or any other device or process." 17 U.S.C. § 101. A "copy" includes the original. Büchel argued ... that the Museum's repeated public exhibitions of "Training Ground for Democracy" constituted a public display of his work in violation of his exclusive right under section 106(5). The district court gave no explicit reason for its dismissal of this claim. ...

The court also remarked, however, that since Büchel "would have suffered a violation of no right recognized by this statute, this messy situation simply fell outside the boundary of VARA and, a fortiori, outside the more general provisions of the Copyright Act." This statement reflects a misreading of the Copyright Act. As we have explained, the moral rights granted to specific artists under VARA are separate and independent from the economic rights guaranteed by section 106. Thus, the inadequacy of claims under VARA does not, on its own, signify the inadequacy of more traditional copyright claims.

We thus turn specifically to this claim. The Museum argues . . . the unfinished work was never publicly displayed. However . . . there is significant record evidence suggesting that the work was repeatedly and deliberately exhibited to numerous individuals.

MASS MoCA also asserts an affirmative defense under section 109(c), which provides that "the owner of a particular copy lawfully made under this title, or any person authorized by such owner, is entitled, without the authority of the copyright owner, to display that copy publicly." The Museum argues that it owned the physical copy of "Training Ground," and that section 109(c) therefore permitted it to display the unfinished work. Here again, however, the record reveals disputed issues of fact with respect to whether the Museum's copy was "lawfully made," as it may have been created in violation of the artist's rights under VARA. Moreover, Büchel introduced evidence to rebut the Museum's assertion that "the installation's various components" all belonged to, or were purchased by, MASS MoCA. Finally, Büchel presented evidence that the Museum understood that the physical copy of the installation belonged to him. Accordingly . . . we cannot say that a reasonable jury could not conclude that the Museum violated his exclusive right to publicly display "Training Ground for Democracy."

* * *

V.

We summarize our holdings:

1. VARA's protection of an artist's moral rights extends to unfinished creations that are "works of art" within the meaning of the Copyright Act;

2. The right of integrity under VARA protects artists from distortions, mutilations or modifications of their works that are prejudicial to their reputation or honor, and prejudice must be shown for both injunctive relief and damages;

3. Büchel has adduced sufficient evidence to raise a genuine issue of material fact as to whether MASS MoCA violated his right of integrity . . . by modifying "Training Ground" over his objections in a manner that harmed his honor or reputation . . . ;

4. Büchel's right-of-attribution claim is moot, as VARA provides only injunctive relief to protect the right of attribution and the installation no longer exists;

5. The record reveals a genuine issue of material fact as to whether MASS MoCA violated Büchel's exclusive right under section 106(5) of the Copyright Act to display his work publicly; . . .

We thus remand the case for further proceedings on Büchel's remaining right-of-integrity claim under VARA and his public display claim under section 106 of the Copyright Act.

Affirmed in part, vacated in part, and remanded for further proceedings consistent with this decision. Each party is to bear its own costs.

Noland v. Janssen

2020 WL 2836464 (S.D.N.Y. Jun. 1, 2020)

J. Paul Oetken, District Judge:

In 1990, Defendant Wilhelm Schürmann, a German art collector, purchased a wooden sculpture by renowned visual artist Cady Noland. The sculpture, which resembles the façade of a log cabin and is aptly titled "Log Cabin Façade," was displayed outdoors in Germany for several years on the bare ground. The elements took their toll, and in December 2010, at the direction of Defendant Schürmann and Defendant KOW, a conservator replaced the sculpture's original, then-rotted wooden components with new parts fabricated by the same Montana manufacturer as the original logs. Noland claims that the refurbishment and later attempt to sell the refurbished work infringed her copyright in the work and violated her moral rights under the Visual Artists Rights Act ("VARA"), 17 U.S.C. § 106A.

* * *

I. Background

A. Factual Background

* * *

Log Cabin Façade, the artwork at the center of this case, is a sculpture composed mainly of wooden logs, arranged to resemble the front façade of a log cabin in size and structure. . . .

In or around 1990, an art gallery in Cologne, Germany, sold Log Cabin Façade to Defendant Wilhelm Schürmann. Sometime after June 1, 1991, Schürmann contacted Noland and asked her for permission to stain the work and to exhibit it outdoors, which Noland authorized.

From approximately 1995 to 2005, the stained work resided at a museum in Aachen, Germany, where it was displayed outdoors without a protective foundation, leading to the serious deterioration of the structure. Eventually, Schürmann had the sculpture removed from the museum and hired KOW, a German art gallery, to evaluate the work. KOW, in turn, hired a conservator, who concluded that all of the wooden components of the work—including all of the logs—would need to be replaced.

Using copies of Noland's original specifications and plans, KOW and Schürmann ordered precut logs and other wooden parts from Master Log Homes, the Montana-based company that had supplied the original parts to Noland in 1990. The replacement logs, though similar to those initially used by Noland, differ in some subtle respects, namely, in their natural imperfections and variations. The logs were shipped to Germany where they were assembled into a "refurbished" Log Cabin Façade.

. . . After the reconstitution of Log Cabin Façade, Schürmann hired Janssen Gallery [located in Berlin] to act as his agent in reselling the work. Janssen enlisted help [to] market and sell the reconstituted Log Cabin Façade in the United States [and] eventually succeeded in finding an Ohio-based buyer. But as this Court's prior opinion recounts in greater detail, the sale ultimately fell through after Noland renounced the refurbished work. *See Noland*, 2019 WL 1099805, at *2.

B. Procedural Background

Noland initiated this action on July 18, 2017. On March 8, 2019, this Court granted Defendants' motion to dismiss the then-operative Second Amended Complaint. Noland's complaint, the Court held, failed to allege a basis for the extraterritorial application of the U.S. copyright laws to Defendants' conduct in Germany. . . . Accordingly, the Court dismissed the copyright and VARA claims and then declined to exercise pendent jurisdiction over the remaining German and state law claims.

Noland was granted leave to amend the complaint "one final time," and she filed the now-operative Third Amended Complaint on April 2, 2019. . . .

* * *

III. Discussion

[Court's discussion of extraterritoriality and domestic allegations are omitted.]

C. Vara Claims

Finally, the Third Amended Complaint alleges that the marketing of Log Cabin Façade using Noland's name, as well as the related dissemination of the photographs and plans, violated Noland's rights under VARA. Noland faces an uphill battle in defending her VARA claims: the creation of the original Log Cabin Façade concededly predates VARA's effective date, and the original work as sold in 1990 does not qualify for that statute's protection.

Noland does not contest that the sculpture did not initially qualify for protection under VARA. Rather, she argues that she authored a derivative work when she permitted Schürmann to stain the sculpture sometime after the effective date of the statute, and that derivative work is entitled to VARA protection. Even if the Court were to make many of the leaps required by Noland's line of reasoning—that the staining created a copyrightable derivative work, that the derivative work qualifies for protection under VARA, and that the marketing of the refurbished stained work violated those rights—Noland *still* would not prevail on her claim. That is because the author of the derivative work—and therefore the holder of any VARA rights vis-à-vis the staining—would be Schürmann, *not* Noland. According to Noland's own allegations, the idea and request to stain the work originated with Schürmann and it was Schürmann who effectuated the staining. He would therefore be the author of the stained derivative work. That Noland gave him permission to do so when asked is of no moment; a copyright holder's licensing of a derivative work by a secondary author is a routine feature of copyright law. And though Noland now argues that her role in the staining of the work was more substantial, including choosing the stain color, she "cannot supplement [her] fourth attempt at pleading with new facts asserted in [her] opposition brief." The Court therefore has no occasion to consider the relevance of these new, belated allegations.

Of course, the creation of the derivative work would not terminate any preexisting copyright in the underlying work that Noland held as the author of the pre-staining sculpture. But she is not able to grandfather in her preexisting sculpture to VARA's coverage simply by virtue of the later derivative work, of which she is not the author. The remaining VARA claims must be dismissed.

IV. Conclusion

For the foregoing reasons, Defendants' motion to dismiss is GRANTED.

Castillo v. G & M Realty L.P.

950 F.3d 155 (2d Cir. 2020),
cert. denied, 141 S. Ct. 363 (Oct. 5, 2020)

Barrington D. Parker, Circuit Judge:

* * *

. . . Wolkoff [a principal in G&M, owned] a series of dilapidated warehouse buildings. . . . Jonathan Cohen, a distinguished aerosol artist, . . . and other artists rented studio spaces in the warehouses and [with Wolkoff's consent] filled the walls with aerosol art, with Cohen serving as curator. Under Cohen's leadership, the site, known as 5Pointz, evolved into a major global center for aerosol art. It attracted thousands of daily visitors, numerous celebrities, and extensive media coverage.

"Creative destruction" was an important feature of the 5Pointz site. Some art . . . achieved permanence, but other art . . . was repeatedly painted over. An elaborate system of norms—including Cohen's permission and often consent of the artist whose work was overpainted—governed the painting process. . . . During its lifespan, 5Pointz was home to a total of approximately 10,650 works of art.

In May 2013, . . . Wolkoff . . . sought municipal approvals looking to demolish 5Pointz. . . . Cohen applied to the New York City Landmark Preservation Commission to have 5Pointz designated a site of cultural significance. The application was unsuccessful. . . .

At that point, Cohen, joined by numerous 5Pointz artists, sued under VARA to prevent destruction of the site. . . .

Early in the litigation, Plaintiffs applied for a temporary restraining order to prevent the demolition of the site, which the district court granted. As the TRO expired, Plaintiffs applied for a preliminary injunction. On November 12, 2013, the court denied the application in a minute order but told the parties that a written opinion would soon follow.

That night, Wolkoff began to destroy the artwork. He banned the artists from the site and refused them permission to recover any work that could be removed. Several nights later (and before the district court's written opinion could issue), Wolkoff deployed a group of workmen who, at his instruction, whitewashed the art.

* * *

On February 12, 2018, the district court . . . found that 45 of the works had achieved recognized stature, that Wolkoff had violated VARA by destroying them, and that the violation was willful. . . .

Where a violation of VARA is established, the statute permits the injured party to recover either actual damages and profits or statutory damages. . . . Ultimately, the district court concluded that it could not reliably fix the market value of the destroyed paintings and, for that reason, declined to award actual damages. . . .

Nonetheless, the court did award statutory damages. It determined that statutory damages would serve to sanction Wolkoff's conduct and to vindicate the policies behind VARA. . . . Judge Block awarded the maximum amount of statutory damages: $150,000 for each of the 45 works, for a total of $6.75 million.

* * *

Discussion

I.

* * *

. . . VARA gives "the author of a work of visual art" the right "to prevent any destruction of a work of recognized stature" and provides that "any intentional or grossly negligent destruction of that work is a violation of that right." VARA further permits the artist "to prevent any intentional distortion, mutilation, or other modification of [his or her work] which would be prejudicial to his or her honor or reputation," and provides that "any intentional distortion, mutilation, or modification of that work is a violation of that right." 17 U.S.C. § 106A(a)(3)(A). The latter provision applies regardless of a work's stature. These rights may not be transferred, but they "may be waived if the author expressly agrees to such waiver in a written instrument signed by the author."

Additionally, the statute contains specific provisions governing artwork incorporated into a building. If the artwork is incorporated "in such a way that removing the work from the building will cause the destruction, distortion, mutilation, or other modification of the work," then the artist's rights may be waived if and only if he "consented to the installation of the work in the building . . . in a written instrument." *Id.* § 113(d)(1). This instrument must be "signed by the owner of the building and the author" and must "specif[y] that the installation of the work may subject the work to destruction, distortion, mutilation, or other modification, by reason of its removal." *Id.* However, "[i]f the owner of a building wishes to remove a work of visual art which is a part of such building and which can be removed from the building without the destruction, distortion, mutilation, or other modification of the work," then the artist's rights prevail unless one of two things has occurred. *Id.* § 113(d)(2). First, the building's owner "has made a diligent, good faith attempt without success to notify the author of the owner's intended action affecting the work of visual art." *Id.* Or second, the owner has "provide[d] such notice in writing and the person so notified failed, within 90 days after receiving such notice, either to remove the work or to pay for its removal." *Id.*

Damages for violations of VARA's rights of attribution and integrity are governed by general copyright law and include both actual and statutory damages. Statutory damages may range from $750 to $30,000 per work "as the court considers just." *Id.* § 504(c)(1). However, if "the [artist] sustains the burden of proving, and the court finds, that [a violation of VARA] was committed willfully, the court in its discretion may increase the award of statutory damages to a sum of not more than $150,000 [per work]." *Id.* § 504(c)(2).

II.

The crux of the parties' dispute on this appeal is whether the works at 5Pointz were works of "recognized stature," thereby protected from destruction under § 106A(a)(3)(B). We conclude that a work is of recognized stature when it is one of high quality, status, or caliber that has been acknowledged as such by a relevant community....

The most important component of stature will generally be artistic quality. The relevant community will typically be the artistic community.... This approach helps to ensure that VARA protects "the public interest in preserving [the] nation's culture" [and] ensures that the personal judgment of the court is not the determinative factor in the court's analysis.

* * *

[III.]

Accordingly..., the artists were required to demonstrate that their work had achieved recognized stature. Judge Block found... "the plaintiffs adduced such a plethora of exhibits and credible testimony,... that even under the most restrictive of evidentiary standards almost all of the plaintiffs' works easily qualify as works of recognized stature."...

... [O]n this appeal, Wolkoff must demonstrate that Judge Block abused his discretion or that findings of fact he made were clearly erroneous, not simply debatable.

Initially, Wolkoff contends that the great majority of the works in question were temporary ones which, for that reason, could not meet the recognized stature requirement. We disagree. We see nothing in VARA that excludes temporary artwork from attaining recognized stature. . . .

The statute does not adopt categories of "permanent" and "temporary" artwork, much less include a definition of these terms. VARA is distinctive in that "[a] work of visual art is defined by the Act in terms both positive (what it is) and negative (what it is not)." In narrowing the scope of the statute, Congress adopted a highly specific definition of visual art. In light of this specificity, we see no justification for adopting an additional requirement not included by Congress. . . .

Additionally, at least as recently as 2005, New York City saw a clear instance where temporary artwork achieved recognized stature. That winter, artists Christo Vladimirov Javacheff and Jeanne-Claude Denat, known collectively as "Christo," installed 7,503 orange draped gates in Central Park. This work, known as "The Gates," lasted only two weeks but was the subject of significant critical acclaim and attention, not just from the art world but also from the general public. As Wolkoff concedes, "The Gates" achieved recognized stature and would have been protected under VARA.

In recent years, "street art," much of which is "temporary," has emerged as a major category of contemporary art. . . . For example, noted street artist Banksy has appeared . . . on *Time* magazine's list of the world's 100 most influential people. . . . Banksy's work is . . . acknowledged, both by the art community and the general public, as of significant artistic merit and cultural importance. Famously, Banksy's *Girl with a Balloon* self-destructed after selling for $1.4 million at Sotheby's, but, as with Banksy's street art, the temporary quality of this work has only added to its recognition.

. . . Although a work's short lifespan means that there will be fewer opportunities for the work to be viewed and evaluated, the temporary nature of the art is not a bar to recognized stature.

The district court correctly observed that when Congress wanted to impose durational limits on work subject to VARA, it knew how to do so. For example, the statute provides that "[t]he modification of a work of visual art which is a result of the passage of time or the inherent nature of the materials is not a distortion, mutilation, or other modification described in subsection (a)(3)(A)." 17 U.S.C. § 106A(c)(1). . . . Congress also imposed a durational limit insofar as the statute protects only works that are "fixed"—"sufficiently permanent . . . to be perceived . . . for a period of more than transitory duration." *Id.* §§ 101, 102(a). We have held that a work that exists for only 1.2 seconds is of merely transitory duration but have noted with approval cases holding that a work "embodied . . . for at least several minutes" is of more than transitory duration. It is undisputed that the 5Pointz works survived far longer than this and therefore satisfied the statute's minimal durational requirement.

. . . Wolkoff [also] contends that because the artists were aware that the 5Pointz buildings might eventually be torn down, they should have expected their work to be destroyed.... VARA accounts for this possibility. Under § 113(d), if the art at 5Pointz was incorporated into the site such that it could not be removed without being destroyed, then Wolkoff was required to obtain "a written instrument ... that [was] signed by the owner of the building and the [artist] and that specifie[d] that installation of the work may subject the work to destruction, distortion, mutilation, or other modification, by reason of its removal." 17 U.S.C. § 113(d)(1)(B). It is undisputed that no such instrument was executed. If, on the other hand, the 5Pointz art could have been safely removed, then Wolkoff was required to provide written notice of the planned demolition and to allow the artists 90 days to remove the work or to pay for its removal. *See id.* § 113(d)(2)(B). Again, it is undisputed that Wolkoff did none of this.

IV.

* * *

Finally, Wolkoff contends that the district court erroneously focused on the stature of the 5Pointz site rather than the individual 5Pointz works.... The district court did not focus exclusively on the stature of the site.... [W]e easily conclude that the site of a work is relevant to its recognition and stature and may, in certain cases, render the recognition and stature of a work beyond question. Appearance at a major site—*e.g.*, the Louvre or the Prado—ensures that a work will be recognized, that is, seen and appreciated by the public and the art community.... Consequently, we see no error when the district court considered the 5Pointz site itself as some evidence of the works' recognized stature.

* * *

V.

Appellants next challenge the district court's award of damages. The court did not award actual damages because it could not quantify the market value of the 5Pointz art. However, the court found that Appellants' violation of VARA was willful.... A violation is willful when a defendant had knowledge that its conduct was unlawful or recklessly disregarded that possibility.

... Wolkoff admitted his awareness, prior to destroying 5Pointz, that the artists were pressing VARA claims. Additionally ... Wolkoff testified that, although he was advised by counsel both before and after the destruction, he chose "to hire people to whitewash[] it in one shot instead of *waiting for three months*" .... Wolkoff did not help his cause when he later reminded the district court that he "would make the same decision today."

Most troubling ... is Wolkoff's decision to whitewash the artwork at all.... Wolkoff could have allowed the artwork to remain visible until demolition began, giving the artists time to photograph or to recover their work....

... The district court was entitled to conclude, based on this record, that Wolkoff acted willfully and was liable for enhanced statutory damages.

VI.

Finally, we address Wolkoff's challenge to the amount of the statutory damages awarded—$6,750,000—the maximum amount allowed. . . .

The district court carefully considered the six factors relevant to a determination of statutory damages and concluded that "Wolkoff rings the bell on each relevant factor." Those six, drawn from copyright law, are "(1) the infringer's state of mind; (2) the expenses saved, and profits earned, by the infringer; (3) the revenue lost by the copyright holder; (4) the deterrent effect on the infringer and third parties; (5) the infringer's cooperation in providing evidence concerning the value of the infringing material; and (6) the conduct and attitude of the parties."

First, Wolkoff's state of mind is documented in the district court's extensive finding on willfulness. . . . Wolkoff, a sophisticated real estate developer, was "willing to run the risk of being held liable for substantial statutory damages rather than to jeopardize his multimillion dollar luxury condo project." Moreover, Wolkoff whitewashed the artworks without any genuine business need to do so. It was simply, as the district court found, an "act of pure pique and revenge" toward the artists who had sued him. . . .

The lost revenue prong is not as straightforward. . . . The district court declined to award actual damages . . . based on the difficulty of quantifying Appellees' loss. . . . Unlike actual damages, statutory damages do not require the precise monetary quantification of injury. Consequently, the district court was within its discretion in determining that Appellees' loss was significant, for purposes of statutory damages, but not compensable through actual damages. As the district court expressly recognized, "[t]he value of 5Pointz to the artists' careers was significant, and its loss, though difficult to quantify, precluded future opportunities and acclaim."

The deterrent effect . . . also supports the amount of statutory damages imposed by the court. Wolkoff admitted that he had no remorse for his actions. To the contrary he confessed that he "would make the same decision today." In these circumstances, a maximum statutory award could serve to deter Wolkoff from future violations of VARA. It could further encourage other building owners to negotiate in good faith with artists whose works are incorporated into structures and to abide by the 90-day notice provision set forth in VARA when incorporated art can be removed without destruction or other modification.

The final factor—the conduct and attitude of the parties—also cuts in favor of the maximum statutory award. During the preliminary injunction phase, Wolkoff testified that it was critical that demolition of the site occur within a few months at most because otherwise he stood to lose millions of dollars in credits and possibly the entire project. Wolkoff later changed his testimony and stated that at the time of the preliminary injunction hearing, there was at most a "possibility" that a delay would have caused him financial loss. Subsequently, the evidence at trial established that Wolkoff had not even applied for a demolition permit until four months after the whitewashing, and he admitted that he suffered no loss for the delay. The district court described these statements as "conscious material misrepresentation[s]" and noted that had they not been made, it would have granted the preliminary injunction.

In contrast, throughout the proceedings below, the artists complied with what the law required.... Judge Block noted that the artists "conducted themselves with dignity, maturity, respect, and at all times within the law." In sum, we conclude that the district court appropriately analyzed each relevant factor and see no abuse of discretion. We have considered Wolkoff's other contentions and conclude that they lack merit.

Conclusion

For the foregoing reasons, the judgment of the district court is AFFIRMED.

Notes and Questions

1. *Timeframes and Permission.* In these three cases, artists ask the courts to protect their VARA interests but they do so at three different stages in the artwork's timespan. For Büchel, the violations occurred during his creation process; for Noland, during the owner's conservation process; and for the 5Pointz artists, after the artworks' destruction by the owner. Does the point in time matter? VARA rights are not specifically organized along a neat timeline, yet VARA inherently recognizes timeline distinctions. For example, conservation and public presentation in § 106A(c)(1) and (2) and the destruction of a work of visual art in § 106A(a)(3)(B) are statutory time markers that generally involve the owner. The creation process is not statutorily delineated but is embedded in the definition of a work of visual art and copyright's concept of fixedness and, consequently, centers on the artist.

Whether the artist gave permission or authorization was an issue in the cases as well. Does permission matter for VARA? Yes. VARA allows an artist to waive the rights of attribution and integrity in writing (§ 106A(e)) and provides a degree of contractual freedom in the buildings exception (§ 113(d)).

a. Creation. *Mass MoCA* provides a window into the practical workings of a major art installation. Without a strong collaborative impulse and a clear contractual limit on the museum's independent actions, the process disintegrated. Notice that Büchel alleged the museum did not follow his instructions. In other words, Büchel did not waive his VARA rights, and the museum did not have the requisite permission to overrule the artist's vision. No final artwork was actually created, but the unfinished artwork would be accorded VARA protection. Because attribution provides injunctive relief only, the museum's dismantling of *Training Ground* terminated Büchel's attribution claim. His integrity claim was allowed to proceed, as he made a sufficient showing that the museum's actions disregarded his VARA rights. There are echoes from *Whistler v. Eden* here. The artist's right in the creation process—even if the artwork is never fully realized—"leaves the artist master and proprietor of his work till such time as it shall please him to deliver it." No other voice matters.

b. Conservation. Cady Noland delivered *Log Cabin* into the marketplace as a fully finished artwork. While in the owner's hands, time, the inherent nature of the materials, and outdoors public presentation damaged the artwork. The owner contacted the artist and received permission to stain the artwork. Thereafter, additional conservation measures were taken in accordance with the artist's original plan and specifications. VARA excepts from an artist's integrity right modifications due to passage of time and nature of materials (§ 106A(c)(1)) and for modifications and destruction due to conservation or public presentation unless caused by gross negligence (§ 106A(c)(2)). Hence, VARA favors conservation by owners but does not mandate it. Unfortunately, *Log Cabin* was outside of VARA protection as a preexisting artwork. Moreover, the court rejected Noland's bootstrap argument that her grant of permission for the post-June 1, 1991, staining resulted in the creation of a new artwork by the artist. That permission was deemed "of no moment" to the court. Consequently, the court avoided the central and important question of whether the owner's restoration resulted in an unauthorized copy and a violation of the artist's integrity rights.

c. Destruction. Under VARA, the author's integrity right extends to prevent the "destruction of a work of recognized stature," with any intentional destruction being a violation of that right (§ 106A(a)(3)(B)). That integrity right is specifically made subject to § 113(d)'s special rules governing artworks incorporated into buildings. If works are not of recognized stature, the protection does not apply. The 5Pointz artists therefore had to establish the recognized stature of the artworks and to do so without the benefit of a statutory definition. The Second Circuit determined the standard would be met upon a showing that the artwork was "of high quality, status, or caliber that has been acknowledged as such by a relevant community." That the artworks were often of a temporary nature was not relevant. On the other hand, evidence of the recognized stature of the location was relevant as it could be viewed as some evidence of the recognized stature of the artwork. From the inception of the artworks in 2002 until the 2013 destruction, oral permissions between the 5Pointz artists and the owner were not unusual. In that sense, the artworks at 5Pointz had a legal foothold that much aerosol art does not. Unfortunately, in breaking with the decade-long pattern of permission requests and doing so in the midst of litigation, the owner subjected himself to the maximum statutory damages and the payment of $2 million for plaintiffs' attorneys fees. There is no doubt that VARA violations have enforcement bite.

2. *Buildings Exception*. Section 106A(a)(3)'s right of integrity is "subject to the limitations set forth in section 113(d)." That section, known as the buildings exception, creates a matrix that attempts to balance the rights of building owners and artists who have works of visual art "incorporated in or made part of a building." If an artist consented to the installation of a work in a building pre-VARA and its removal would cause a destruction or other modification, then the artist's attribution and

integrity rights shall not apply upon that removal. Similarly, if post-VARA, the artist and the owner agree in a writing that specifically states the work may be subject to destruction or other modification if removed, the artist's attribution and integrity rights do not apply upon removal. However, if the artwork could be removed from the building without destruction or modification, then the artist shall have the attribution and integrity rights unless the owner (1) makes a good faith effort to notify the artist about the proposed action by registered mail, or (2) actually gives written notice and the artist does not act within 90 days after receiving the notice to remove the work at her own expense.

Odd as it may seem, murals incorporated into buildings are often removable without damage. Removability is a factual inquiry that would be determined on a case-by-case basis. See e.g., Botello v. Shell Oil Co., 280 Cal. Rptr. 535 (1991); Board of Managers of Soho International Arts Condominium v. City of New York, 2005 WL 1153752 (S.D.N.Y. 2005).

What rights does an aerosol artist have in works created on a building without the owner's permission? As written, the buildings exception is premised on owner-and-artist discussion and therefore does not specifically address this issue. It is an issue that creates confusion in the U.S. and elsewhere. See Sara Rosano & Birgit Kurtz, *Tear Down This Wall? The Destruction of Sanctioned Street Art under U.S. and Italian Law*, 30 FORDHAM INTELL. PROP. MEDIA & ENT. L.J. 767 (2020).

3. *Assessing Artists' De-Attributions.* Conceptual artist Cady Noland is vigilant in enforcing her attribution and integrity rights. On November 7, 2011, Noland inspected three of her works that were up for auction at Sotheby's on November 10, 2011. She disavowed *Cowboys Milking*, because in her estimation, its condition was materially different from the time of its creation. Sotheby's withdrew the work from its planned auction. The consignor thereafter sued Sotheby's and the artist for breach of contract and tortious interference with contractual relations. The case was ultimately dismissed. Sotheby's actions were consistent with Sotheby's rights under the consignment agreement to withdraw any work at any time if "there is doubt as to its authenticity or attribution." The propriety of Noland's disavowal was not addressed. Marc Jancou Fine Art Ltd v. Sotheby's, 2012 WL 7964120 (N.Y. Sup. Ct. 2012), *aff'd*, 107 A.D.3d 637 (N.Y. App. Div. 2013).

Before Noland's lawsuit against Janssen over *Log Cabin*, the Ohio buyer of *Log Cabin* brought a lawsuit against Janssen and others. Scott Mueller was seeking to enforce the buyback provision under the *Log Cabin* sales contract. Under that contract, Mueller was entitled to the return of his $1.4 million purchase price if the artist disavowed the work. Before the work was shipped, Noland disavowed the work when she learned that logs were replaced without her permission. Mueller v. Janssen, 225 F. Supp. 3d 201 (S.D.N.Y. 2016). Her disavowal was a handwritten, all caps fax in which she wrote "THIS IS NOT AN ARTWORK" and "FROM NOW ON, THE PROVENANCE MUST INCLUDE THE FACT THAT THE PIECE WAS 'REPAIRED' BY A CONSERVATOR BUT THE ARTIST WASN'T CONSULTED."

Beyond any particular case, is the artist's attribution right under VARA sacrosanct? Can there be such a thing as an invalid disavowal by an artist? Is there an objective reasonableness standard that comes into play when an owner's private property rights are affected by that disavowal? In *Whistler*, the court accorded the artist sole power to determine when a work was fully created, but there was a time constraint. The artist was "master and proprietor of his work *till* such time as it shall please him to deliver it." (Emphasis added.) How we are to balance the rights of artists and those of owners under VARA remains a work in progress. See Sinclair Marber, *They Can't Take that Away from Me: An Indemnification Solution to Unmerited VARA Claims*, 41 Colum. J. L. & Arts 319 (2017–18).

4. *Time to Reconceptualize VARA?* In the thirty years since VARA's passage, doubts continue to be expressed about the scope and operation of VARA. One notable concern is VARA's compatibility with copyright law. By placing VARA within the Copyright Act, the rules for copyright provide the default framework for judicial textual analysis for unanswered VARA questions. In terms of statutory construction, this is unremarkable. At times, however, the inadequacy of that approach has disserved the protective goals of VARA. In *Kelley*, Judge Sykes determined that an artwork must be copyrightable in order to constitute a work of visual art for VARA purposes. Achieving this standard may be especially acute for works of postmodern art. For example, Cady Noland applied more than once for a copyright on *Log Cabin*, and the applications were rejected. The Copyright Office was "placed in the odd position of asking, 'This work may be art, but is it copyrightable?'" Regan A. Smith, *Curious Cases of Copyrightability Before the Copyright Office*, 43 Colum. J. L. & Arts 343 (2020). Questions of artistic merit are to be avoided by the copyright bureaucracy, yet art is at the core of VARA. Some therefore suggest it is time to free VARA from copyright. See Amy Adler, *Why Art Does Not Need Copyright*, 86 Geo. Wash. L. Rev. 313 (2018); Megan E. Noh, *U.S. Law's Artificial Cabining of Moral Rights: The Copyrightability Prerequisite and Cady Noland's Log Cabin*, 43 Colum. J. L. & Arts 353 (2020).

E. Droit de Suite

Close v. Sotheby's, Inc

894 F.3d 1061 (9th Cir. 2018)

Bybee, Circuit Judge:

* * *

I. Legal and Factual Background

A. The Droit de Suite

Many nations recognize the *droit de suite,* under which artists receive a royalty each time the original, tangible embodiment of their work is resold. The practice was first recognized in France in 1920 . . . . In those countries that recognize it, the *droit de suite* is considered a moral right, albeit one with economic value. *See generally* U.S. Copyright Office, Droit de Suite: *The Artist's Resale Royalty* (Dec. 1992) ("1992 Copyright Report"); U.S. Copyright Office, *Resale Royalties: An Updated Analysis* (Dec. 2013) ("2013 Copyright Report") . . . .

* * *

The *droit de suite* also appears in international copyright law. Since 1948, the Berne Convention has recognized that artists possess an "inalienable right to an interest in any sale of the work subsequent to the first transfer by the author of the work." Berne Convention for the Protection of Literary and Artistic Works art. 14*ter*(1), Sept. 9, 1886, as amended Sept. 28, 1979, S. Treaty Doc. No. 99-27 (1986). . . . [T]he Berne Convention makes the recognition of such rights optional, but rewards such recognition with reciprocity: countries recognizing the right will protect the right of each others' artists.

The United States became a signatory to the Berne Convention in 1989, but . . . it has not adopted the *droit de suite*. . . . A *droit de suite* provision made its way into an early version of the Visual Artists Rights Act of 1990 ("VARA") but was removed. . . . Instead, VARA directed the Copyright Office to conduct a study on the feasibility of implementing such a right in the United States.

In 1992, the Copyright Office issued an extensive report concluding that there was insufficient economic or copyright-policy justification to adopt the *droit de suite* in the United States. *See generally* 1992 Copyright Report. . . . Two decades later . . . the Copyright Office revisit[ed] the issue, and the Copyright Office issued a second report. *See generally* 2013 Copyright Report. This time, in light of "the adoption of resale royalty laws by more than thirty additional countries since the Office's prior report," the Copyright Office endorsed "implementation of a resale royalty right in the United States . . . as one alternative to address the disparity in treatment of artists under the copyright law." Congress has not acted on the Copyright Office's recommendation.

B. The California Resale Royalties Act of 1976 ("CRRA")

The CRRA is "the first, and thus far only, American recognition of the *droit de suite*." Under the CRRA, the seller of "a work of fine art" or the seller's agent must withhold 5% of the sale price and pay it to the artist.... Notably, the artist's right to the 5% royalty may not be waived or reduced by contract.

As originally enacted, the CRRA applied to sales of fine art in California *or* by a California seller (whether inside California or not). But ... we have since limited the statute to regulate only sales in California. Other conditions to the CRRA's application include, inter alia, that the artist must be a citizen of the United States or resident of California; the sale must occur after the initial sale by the artist (i.e., it must be a resale); the sale must be for $1,000 or more; the sale cannot be for less than the purchase price paid by the seller; and the sale must occur during the artist's life or within 20 years of his death.

* * *

C. First Proceedings before the District Court and First Appeal

In 2011, plaintiffs filed putative class-action complaints ... alleging claims under the CRRA.... The statute of limitations ... is three years after the date of the relevant sale or one year after discovery of that sale, whichever is longer. Plaintiffs accordingly sought to represent two classes: (1) a class of artists or their estates purportedly owed CRRA royalties on sales that took place within three years of when the actions were filed; and (2) a class of artists or their estates purportedly owed CRRA royalties on sales that were never disclosed to the artists and that took place more than three years before the actions were filed—all the way back to the CRRA's effective date of January 1, 1977.

The district court dismissed plaintiffs' complaints with prejudice, holding that the CRRA's regulation of sales outside California violated the dormant Commerce Clause.... Sitting en banc, we agreed ... but held that ... plaintiffs still had potentially viable claims respecting in-state sales. We remanded....

D. Second Proceedings before the District Court

... In 2016, the district court granted defendants' motions and dismissed the actions with prejudice, holding that the CRRA was preempted by federal copyright law, as a matter of both conflict and express preemption.

* * *

II. Analysis

"It is well-established that Congress has the power to preempt state law." In general, there are three forms of preemption: express preemption, conflict preemption, and field preemption. Because Congress has not preempted the field in copyright law, only two forms of preemption are at issue here: express and conflict....

A. Express Preemption

The 1976 Copyright Act adopted, for the first time, an express preemption provision in § 301(a) and thereby accomplished a sea change in the relative powers of the states vis-à-vis the federal government over copyright protection.... Section 301(a) states:

> On and after January 1, 1978, all legal or equitable rights that are equivalent to any of the exclusive rights within the general scope of copyright as specified by section 106 in works of authorship that are fixed in a tangible medium of expression and come within the subject matter of copyright as specified by sections 102 and 103, whether created before or after that date and whether published or unpublished, are governed exclusively by this title. Thereafter, no person is entitled to any such right or equivalent right in any such work under the common law or statutes of any State.

17 U.S.C. § 301(a). In accordance with § 301(a), we have adopted a two-pronged test to determine whether a state law claim is preempted by the 1976 Act. "First, we decide whether the subject matter of the state law claim falls within the subject matter of copyright as described in 17 U.S.C. §§ 102 and 103." "Second, assuming it does, we determine whether the rights asserted under state law are equivalent to the rights contained in 17 U.S.C. § 106, which articulates the exclusive rights of copyright holders."

With respect to the first prong, the subject matter of copyright encompasses "original works of authorship fixed in any tangible medium of expression. . . ." This includes, for example, "pictorial, graphic, and sculptural works." There is no doubt that plaintiffs' claims under the CRRA for resale royalties on works of "fine art" . . . fall within the subject matter of copyright. Plaintiffs do not dispute this prong of the test.

The second prong is also satisfied—that is, plaintiffs' state law claims assert rights "equivalent to rights within the general scope of copyright as specified by section 106 of the Copyright Act." To explain why this is so, we begin with a short history of the first sale doctrine. The Copyright Act of 1891 provided that the copyright owner had "the sole liberty of printing, reprinting, publishing, completing, copying, executing, finishing, and vending" the copyrighted work. In *Bobbs-Merrill Co. v. Straus*, the Supreme Court construed the right to "vend" as being limited to the first sale, 210 U.S. 339 (1908). . . .

Congress codified the first sale doctrine in the 1909 Copyright Act and later retained it in the 1976 Act. Today, § 109(a) provides that "the owner of a particular copy or phonorecord lawfully made under this title, or any person authorized by such owner, is entitled, without the authority of the copyright owner, to sell or otherwise dispose of the possession of that copy or phonorecord." 17 U.S.C. § 109(a). "The practical effect of this language is to significantly circumscribe a copyright owner's exclusive distribution right 'only to the first sale of the copyrighted work' because 'once the copyright owner places a copyrighted item in the stream of commerce by selling it, he has exhausted his exclusive statutory right to control its distribution.'" One purpose of the first sale doctrine is to effect the "common law's refusal to permit restraints on the alienation of chattels. Another purpose is to "free[] courts from the administrative burden of trying to enforce restrictions upon difficult-to-trace, readily movable goods" and "avoid[] the selective enforcement inherent in any such effort."

. . . Section 106(3) grants copyright holders the exclusive right "to distribute copies or phonorecords of the copyrighted work to the public by sale or other transfer of ownership, or by rental, lease, or lending," while the first sale doctrine circumscribes that right by limiting it to the first sale of a copyrighted work.

Although the CRRA's resale royalty right and § 106(3)'s distribution right are not coextensive, they are equivalent. . . . [B]oth concern the distribution of copies of artwork and define artists' right (or lack thereof) to payment on downstream sales of those copies.

The equivalence of the two rights is further underscored by the manner in which the CRRA both expands and restricts the federal distribution right. The CRRA *expands* the federal distribution right because, whereas the first sale doctrine limits artists' right to payment to the first sale, the CRRA grants artists an unwaivable right to a 5% royalty on all downstream sales. Indeed, the CRRA is designed precisely to alter the first sale doctrine by affording artists a right to at least some measure of payment on every sale after the first. At the same time, the CRRA also *restricts* the federal distribution right by forbidding artists from fully alienating copies of their artwork. In effect, the CRRA creates an inalienable restraint on alienation.

In short, the CRRA does not merely grant an additional right beyond what federal copyright law already provides but fundamentally reshapes the contours of federal copyright law's existing distribution right. This runs counter to § 301(a), which precludes "all legal or equitable rights that are equivalent to any of the exclusive rights within the general scope of copyright," even if they are not precisely within the contemplation of the Copyright Act.

Plaintiffs raise a number of arguments in response. First, they argue that the CRRA cannot be expressly preempted because it creates a monetary, not a distribution, right. According to plaintiffs, the CRRA governs proceeds on the sale of art, not the distribution of art itself; a seller need only pay the artist a royalty, not obtain the artist's permission to make a sale. But plaintiffs' attempted distinction between monetary and distribution rights takes an unduly narrow view of § 106(3). That provision . . . represents copyright holders' ability to receive payment for selling copies of their work. Even though there are differences in how the CRRA and § 106(3) affect artists' right to payment—one requires a royalty on all sales after the first, and the other contemplates full alienation upon the first sale—there is significant overlap between the two for the reasons explained above.

Second, plaintiffs argue that the CRRA's resale royalty right cannot be expressly preempted because artists can create a similar right by contract. Plaintiffs have misunderstood the difference between a law that permits an act and a law that compels an act. . . . The CRRA . . . is a restraint on contract because the artist and the purchaser cannot contract around the *droit de suite*. The artist cannot agree to waive the 5% royalty. . . .

* * *

Finally, plaintiffs point to the legislative history of VARA [but VARA] . . . post-dates the 1976 Copyright Act by over a decade. . . . It is not legislative history of the preemption clause adopted in the 1976 Act. . . .

In short, the CRRA . . . is therefore expressly preempted by § 301(a). Plaintiffs' CRRA claims arising after the effective date of the 1976 Act—January 1, 1978—are barred.

B. Conflict Preemption

Unlike the 1976 Act, the 1909 Act contained no express preemption provision. Our holding on express preemption therefore does not account for plaintiffs' claims, if any actually exist, that arose between the CRRA's effective date of January 1, 1977, and the 1976 Act's effective date of January 1, 1978. This remaining sliver of claims is preempted only if it conflicts with the 1909 Act. Our decision in *Morseburg* . . . is squarely on point . . . holding that the CRRA does *not* conflict with the 1909 Act. *Morseburg*, 621 F.2d at 977–78.

* * *

III. Conclusion

Our decision today means that the CRRA had a short effective life. California's statute permissibly coexisted for exactly one year alongside the 1909 Act. Once the 1976 Act took effect, however, the balance of state versus federal copyright protection shifted and the CRRA was preempted by § 301(a). Thus, plaintiffs at most can only state claims for the period between the CRRA's effective date of January 1, 1977, and the 1976 Act's effective date of January 1, 1978. We express no opinion as to the merits of plaintiffs' remaining claims, if any exist.

Notes and Questions

1. *Artist's Resale Rights—Droit de Suite.* The artist's resale right gives an artist a percentage interest in the proceeds from the resale of his work. VARA did not adopt this right. Unlike other moral rights of a nonpecuniary nature, this is clearly an ongoing economic interest of the artist in his work. The resale right began in France in 1920 and was adopted over time by other civil law countries. California adopted it in 1976. Its enforcement domestically and internationally was, however, modest. Article 14 of the Berne Convention made explicit provision for the resale royalty beginning in 1948, but only to the extent a country's internal law required.

In 2001, there was a major change when the European Union issued Directive 2001/841 EC requiring member nations to adopt the artist resale right "in a harmonized, consistent basis." The U.K. was quite vocal in its opposition, fearing the impact of a "tax" would compromise its well-established auction market. Its greatest concern was that owners looking to sell at auction would bypass London and the U.K. in favor of countries like the U.S. without resale rights, as had happened in Paris when France adopted and enforced the right. The U.K. argued for additional time to phase in the adoption of its resale rights. As originally implemented in the U.K., the resale royalty only applied to living artists but was extended in 2012 to deceased artists who died within 70 years of the sale. Quantitatively, the rate for the artist resale right in the EU is a declining graduated rate, ranging from 4% to 0.25%, with a maximum resale right of 12,500 Euros. The charge is imposed on a sale, including those at a loss. What justification is there for charging a resale royalty for sales at a loss? Would a work that was "bought-in" at auction be subject to the resale royalty? Sales solely between private individuals are excluded from the EU right. With the U.K.'s departure from the EU in 2021, the artist resale royalty in the U.K. may—or may not—be affected.

The artist resale right remains controversial. See Merryman, Elsen & Urice, LAW, ETHICS AND THE VISUAL ARTS 579–612 (5th ed. 2007), for a thorough presentation of the arguments for and against the resale right. See also Guy A. Rub, *The Unconvincing Case for Resale Royalties*, 124 YALE L.J.F. 1 (2014), http://yalelawjournal.org/forum/the-unconvincing-case-for-resale-royalties. Nevertheless, at least 60 countries adopted it. For example, Australia enacted the Resale Royalty Right for Visual Artists Act 2009, effective June 9, 2010. It provides a flat 5% royalty to Australian artists who are citizens or permanent residents (or their heirs for 70 years post-death) with respect to works acquired after the effective date and resold for more than AU$1,000 in a commercial resale. It continues to generate controversy, generally along economic lines. Early critics noted that in its first months of operation, it raised AU$90,000 for artists against a government cost of AU$1,500,000 for a 3-year period. In a 2019 report, the Australian government noted that "stakeholders are polarized" over the resale royalty scheme. In general, artists and arts organizations support the scheme, while art market professionals do not. With 10 years of experience, "the art market appears to be adjusting." Whether the scheme can be self-supporting, however, is not certain. It took until April 2014 for the revenue raised (AU$2.2 million) to equal the governmental costs of the scheme. As of September 30, 2019, cumulative receipts were AU$7.5 million from 19,964 resales. See Australian/Department of Communications and the Arts, *Post-Implementation Review—"Resale Royalty Right for Visual Artists Act 2009" and the Resale Royalty Scheme* (2019), at arts.gov.au.

For the owner who sells an artwork, the possible imposition of the artist resale right adds another consideration to the decision-making process.

2. *Contractual Alternative.* One reason given by Congress against the adoption of moral rights was that U.S. law provided for equivalent protection. In 1971, for example, an art dealer promoted a three-page Artist's Agreement. It obligated the first buyer to pay the artist a 15% royalty on the subsequent sale of the work, among other rights given or retained by the artist. Some artists continue to incorporate similar provisions in their sales agreements. See Daniel Grant, *Fine Art Sales Often Come with Strings Attached*, WALL ST. J., Apr. 12, 2015. Recall Jeff Koons's similar

provision in MAFG Art Fund LLC v. Gagosian, 2014 WL 359341 (N.Y. Sup. Ct. 2014), Chapter 2, *supra*.

Which is the better choice: legislation or contract? Consider the following:

> I would argue that the contract is preferable by far. In contrast to the legislative option, which pits artists and collectors against each other in antagonistic positions, contracts that collectors agree to strengthen their relationships with artists and encourage collectors to be stewards of artists' works. Legislation only grants monetary royalties and does not cover exhibition-related rights, which, for some artists, are more important. The resale royalty being calculated off the profit made from a sale . . . makes it a more agreeable proposition for collectors (and is more fair) than legislative proposals, which call for royalties to be calculated off the sale price, meaning a collector would be liable even if she sells at a loss. Current proposed legislation would also paternalistically prohibit the artist from selling the rights, so that an artist could not sell future potential royalties for a lump sum. . . . And generally, as a flexible document, the artist can modify the terms of a contract.

Kibum Kim, *Could a Long-Forgotten Contract Settle the Artist Resale Royalties Debate?*, HYPERALLERGIC, Jan. 5, 2015.

As a practical matter, the ability to contract may be dependent on the artist's reputation and the artwork's desirability and price-point. Nevertheless, it is worth remembering that even if legislation is enacted, it does not necessarily terminate an artist's ability to make private arrangements. And to do so at the time the artist's rights are most protected: "*till* such time as it shall please him to deliver it." *Whistler v. Eden, supra.*

Chapter 8

Art Loans

Public exhibition of artworks or cultural property can significantly impact the civic, cultural, and educational life of a community. Many artworks on display at museums, universities, and other venues are loaned for exhibition purposes by their owners.

This chapter explores the difficult factual and legal issues that arise when artwork is merely loaned instead of given outright to the recipient. Lending artworks or cultural property requires familiarity with the common law of bailments, loan agreements, and, especially in the context of international loans, an awareness of the possibility of legal process, including seizure.

A. Old Loans

The traditional informality of art transactions included the realm of art loans. For centuries, owners of artworks lent those works to a wider world, often through a museum, a university, or a church. Proving the nature of the art transfer when documentary evidence is, at best, negligible and personal memories have dimmed is difficult. This legal history of old loans remains important for institutions possessing artworks with old loan status and for the lending families. Both must contend with the legal and factual uncertainty that such old loans involve.

The legal construct developed in the old loan context, as shown in the following two cases from both sides of the Atlantic, sets the stage for new art loans. Today's art loan documentation builds upon this legal history; much like Shakespeare's observation, the past is prologue.

In re Escot Church
Exeter Consistory Court, 1979

[1979] 3 W.L.R. 339

* * *

Cur. adv. vult. May 31. CALCUTT Ch. read the following judgment. Escot House, near Honiton, is the family seat of Sir John Kennaway. In about 1838 his forbears built Escot Church. . . . Over the years the Kennaway family have, with others, furnished and adorned the church. Sir John is patron of the living, and he was until very recently one of the churchwardens.

For a number of years prior to 1977 there hung in the church an oil painting of the Holy Mother and Child. Prior to 1977 the painting was apparently in a poor state of repair and [i]n 1977 it was . . . restored. . . . There was at this time some talk of sale, but this came to nothing. . . .

In October 1977, however, Sir John asserted that the painting had come to the church in the first place from Escot House, and that it had merely been loaned to the church; and he asked for it back.

* * *

The principal question which I have to determine is title. Who now owns the painting? Does it belong to the Kennaway family or does it belong to the church? If the painting came from Escot House and was merely loaned to the church, then it remains Kennaway property. . . .

* * *

If the painting once belonged to the Kennaway family, but was given by the family to the church, there can be no doubt that the property in the painting passed to the churchwardens. Property could also have passed to them if the Kennaways, without any specific intention of giving the painting to the church, intended to dedicate the painting to God's service and delivered the painting into the custody of the churchwardens.

> "A person may give or dedicate goods to God's service in such a church, and deliver them into the custody of the churchwardens, and thereby the property is immediately changed. And if a man erect a pew in the church, or hang up a bell in the steeple, they do thereby become church goods (though they are not expressly given to the church), and he may not afterwards remove them; if he does, the churchwardens may sue him:"

See Burn's Ecclesiastical Law, 6th ed. (1797), vol. 1, title "Church," para. 24, p. 377. The first volume of Degge's Parson's Counsellor (1685) is cited as authority for the first part of this proposition; but, as it seems to me, greater authority probably is to be derived from the constant repetition of the passage which I have cited in successive editions of *Burn.*

The evidence as a whole persuades me that the painting did in fact come from Escot House. [The court further determined that the painting came into the church about 1950.—Ed]

* * *

Mrs. Hilda Feather gave evidence which I found impressive. . . . Mrs. Feather told me (and I accept it) that Lady Kennaway had told her that because the painting had been considered unsuited to a bathroom in Escot House, it had been given to the church.

Lady Kennaway nevertheless asserted at the hearing that her intention at the time when the painting was introduced into the church was simply to loan the painting to the church, and that she never intended to make a gift of it. She said that she did not think that it would stay so long in the church.

If a mere loan of the painting had been intended, then it is accepted on Sir John's behalf that it stands alone amongst the many items which his family have introduced into the church over the years: all the others have been gifts. It is common ground that nothing was said at the time to indicate that it was intended as a mere loan. In my view, if a loan had been intended, something would have been said to someone at the time. . . . It is common ground that when Mr. E.H. Brown, the treasurer of the parochial church council, was considering having the painting restored, and so incurring expenditure, he spoke to Sir John about the painting but Sir John said nothing to him to indicate that the painting belonged to the Kennaway family and that it was merely on loan. . . . In my view, if the painting had been a mere loan, Sir John would have said so.

My only anxiety in this matter stems from a report of a parochial church council meeting of September 6, 1977, and noted in "Newsletter" for October 1977, when it was recorded "The picture now restored, and ownership declared." This suggested to me that the parochial church council might have been something less than sure that the church did in fact own the painting. Mr. Tennant told me, however, that there was never any doubt in his mind and that there was no dispute at the parochial church council meeting as to ownership: the declaration which was made and recorded was simply made because the possibility of sale was then in mind, so that it became important to make a positive assertion of ownership. Not without some hesitation, I accept this explanation.

* * *

On a consideration of the whole of the evidence, I am satisfied that in or about 1950 Lady Kennaway intended to give and did in fact give the painting to the church, so that title passed to the churchwardens. I am also satisfied that Lady Kennaway intended at the time that the painting should be dedicated to God's service, and that she caused the painting to be delivered into the custody of the churchwardens; so that title also passed to the churchwardens in this way.

It was not until there was talk of sale that it was ever suggested that the painting still belonged to the Kennaway family. Perhaps the Kennaway family resented the suggestion that their gift might be converted into mere cash: such a reaction would not be very surprising. Perhaps the painting was believed to be of great value. Whatever the motive, Sir John took the unfortunate and untenable course of asserting that title to the painting remained in his family. This I cannot accept, and accordingly I have no alternative but to dismiss this petition. Petition dismissed. (C.N.)

In re Estate of McCagg

450 A.2d 414 (D.C. Ct. App. 1982)

NEWMAN, C.J.

* * *

I

In 1917, Therese Davis McCagg loaned two oil paintings, *South American Landscape*, by Frederic Church, and *Mountain Scene*, by Francois Diday, to the National Gallery of Art, now known as the National Museum of American Art [Smithsonian Institution—Ed.], without charge, so that they could be enjoyed by the public. The loan agreement is evidenced only by correspondence between Mrs. McCagg and the Museum. It contains no limit on the duration of the loan, nor any indication that the loan would terminate upon Mrs. McCagg's death. Nor is there evidence of an oral agreement between the parties imposing any time limit.

Mrs. McCagg died in 1932. Her will made no specific bequest of the paintings, but contained a residuary clause giving all property not otherwise distributed to her four siblings, on whose descendants' behalf the present suit is brought. Since Mrs. McCagg's executor did not collect those assets, as he did the remainder of her estate, it is fair to infer that neither he nor the residuary legatees were aware of the existence of the paintings. The accounting of the estate was judicially approved in 1933.

The descendants of the legatees did not learn of the paintings until late 1979, when an art dealer who had inquired about the Church painting at the Museum brought it to their attention. On June 17, 1980, appellee . . . petitioned to reopen the estate on the basis of newly discovered assets. The petition was granted. . . . A formal written demand was presented to the Museum's registrar . . . which was . . . refused. . . . The trial court . . . issued an order directing appellant to deliver the paintings to the estate so that they could be distributed to their owners. The Museum now appeals that order.

II

The loan of the paintings, without any limit on the time for demanding their return, constituted a bailment for an indefinite term, which neither party disputes. The law regarding the accrual of a cause of action for the return of the bailed property is longstanding and clear. The bailee is under no duty to return the property to the owner until demand is made, and thus cannot be in breach of that duty before such demand. Accordingly, a cause of action for return of the property does not arise until demand has been made and refused, or the bailee takes some action inconsistent with the bailment. . . .

At no time before 1980 did Mrs. McCagg or the Museum terminate the bailment, or take any action inconsistent with it. At Mrs. McCagg's death, the paintings were estate assets. At that time title rightfully lay in her siblings, the residuary legatees, a fact which the Museum does not dispute. Demand for delivery was not made and refused until January 1981. A cause of action for the return of the paintings to the estate, and through it to the descendants of the legatees, arose at that time and not before. The motion seeking relinquishment of the paintings was filed less than three weeks after the first refusal to deliver them, well within the applicable three year statute of limitations. D.C.Code 1981, § 12-301(2).

The Museum, however, contends that Mrs. McCagg's successors in interest were required to demand return of the paintings, or otherwise affirmatively assert their continued ownership, at some time in the past, at the risk of forfeiture to the Museum. In other words, their right to demand delivery could only be exercised for a limited time, notwithstanding the lack of any temporal limit in the loan agreement. The Museum asserts that the demand should have been made by the closing of the estate in 1933, or at least within a "reasonable time" thereafter. Accordingly, the clock would begin to run on a cause of action to recover the paintings at that time. Given that starting point, the Museum concludes that, whatever time period is used, time ran out well before the reopening of the estate in 1980. At that time, according to this theory, the paintings became the property of the Museum. While the theory places a burden on the bailor to take affirmative steps in order to *retain* that which is hers to begin with, the bailee had no comparable responsibility to take action in order to *acquire* title.

The Museum raises several interrelated legal and factual arguments in support of its theory. First, appellant argues that where no time for making demand is specified, a court must define a finite "reasonable time." ... If one substitutes the word "may" for "must," the principle is sound. However, one must understand its proper function and limitations, which the Museum tends to ignore. The so-called reasonable time "rule" is, or should be, merely a particular application of familiar principles of implied contractual terms. The basic premise is simple: the lack of an explicit provision is not necessarily dispositive as to the parties' intent. A party may show that an implied term can be inferred from explicit provisions, or from the circumstances surrounding the formation of the agreement. ... But while an implied finite time for demand is appropriate where intended by the parties, one is not to be automatically imposed notwithstanding the apparent lack of such intent. ...

* * *

In sum, we decline to adopt a rule that a limited time for making demand must be imposed regardless of the parties' intent. To put the same conclusion in a somewhat different way, an unlimited period may be reasonable, depending on the circumstances.

With this understanding in mind, there is no basis for reversal. The trial court's refusal to impose a finite reasonable time rule was correct as a matter of law. Nor can we disturb the finding that the bailment was to continue for an indefinite term. On its face, the bailment agreement neither specifies a limited time for demand, nor otherwise suggests that any was contemplated. ... The nature of the loaned property indicates that a loan spanning several decades would not be unreasonable, since, with appropriate storage or display, oil paintings can last for centuries. These circumstances establishing the reasonableness of a very long term loan distinguish this case from those in which a finite reasonable time standard was applied.... Thus, in light of the parties' explicit agreement and the surrounding circumstances, there was adequate support for the conclusion that there was no implicit limitation on the time for reclaiming the paintings. In other words, an indefinite delay was entirely reasonable under the circumstances.

Similarly, we find no support for the conclusion that the death of the bailor triggered a duty to demand delivery....

The Museum also argues that it was forced to undergo certain unbargained-for hardships stemming from the delay in making demand, or the failure to notify it of the owner's death. [Costs of conservation and potential liability for doing so without consultation with owners.—Ed.] This contention falls wide of the mark. It cannot reasonably be said that the failure to notify the Museum forced it to do anything it did not want to do. If at any time it found the benefits of holding the paintings outweighed by the costs, it could have terminated the bailment by notifying Mrs. McCagg, or, after her death, her successors. Alternatively, the Museum could have sought negotiations to modify the terms of the bailment. If reasonably diligent, bona fide efforts to locate Mrs. McCagg or her successors failed, then constructive notice by publication might suffice. The clock would begin to run on a cause of action for return of the paintings at that time.... When the applicable statute of limitations had run out, title would be settled in the Museum. But the Museum never made any attempt, reasonably diligent or otherwise, to end the bailment or assert title to the paintings. To the contrary, every indication suggests that the Museum desired to retain the paintings in its possession, notwithstanding the alleged hardships it endured as a result, rather than prompt the owners to recover them. Under these circumstances, the successive owners were not required to continually reassert ownership at the peril of losing their title.

Finally, appellant invokes the discovery rule, which marks a partial departure from the general rule that the statute of limitations begins to run when the facts giving rise to a cause of action occur....

The leading case applying the discovery rule in a dispute involving title to works of art is *O'Keeffe v. Snyder*, [83 N.J. 478, 491, 416 A.2d 862 (1980)]....

However, the discovery rule is of no help to appellant. As one commentator has observed,

> The *O'Keeffe* decision should not have a great impact on the "permanent loan" problem. As previously demonstrated, it is well established that a bailee for an indefinite time must take some action inconsistent with the terms of the bailment in order to gain title by adverse possession or to bar return of an art object by the running of the statute of limitations. This action must either be communicated to the bailor or be such that a

> reasonable person would understand that the bailee is claiming title or otherwise committing an act of conversion. Because the statute of limitations does not start to run on the making of a permanent loan, it makes no difference if the discovery rule is substituted for the doctrine of adverse possession. Quite simply, there is nothing to discover. [Ward, *The Georgia Grind: Can the Common Law Accommodate the Problems of Title in the Art World, Observations on a Recent Case,* 8 J.C. & U.L. 533, 548 (1982) (footnote omitted).]

In this case, events giving rise to the estate's cause of action did not occur until 1980, when Mrs. McCagg's successors were well aware of their rights and promptly took legal action to enforce them. By contrast, the Museum's theory ignores the fact that the cause of action did not accrue until demand was made. This theory would hold that, by the exercise of reasonable diligence, the executor or legatees should have discovered the existence of the *paintings*—not the accrual of a cause of action—at some earlier time. However, that proposition, if true, would be relevant only on the basis of a premise that we have rejected: that Mrs. McCagg's successors were under a duty to demand return within some limited time. Indeed, if the Museum's theory that the clock should be deemed to have begun running at Mrs. McCagg's death were valid, application of the discovery rule might well defeat its claim.[6]

In sum, we find no persuasive reason for converting an indefinite gratuitous loan into a de facto gift. When demand for delivery was made and refused, legal steps to enforce the right of possession were taken promptly. Neither the original bailor nor her successors were required, at the risk of forfeiting title, to demand the paintings at any earlier time. Accordingly, the trial court's order directing delivery of the paintings to the estate was proper.

Affirmed.

Notes and Questions

1. *Art Loans as Bailments.* An art loan is not strictly speaking a loan. Museums developed and used this colloquial term to describe the transfer of the temporal possession of an artwork to a museum, generally for exhibition purposes. As such, art loans fall within the law of bailments. A bailment is created when one (the

---

6. The record suggests that neither the legatees nor their successors learned of the accrual of their right to require delivery of the paintings until late 1979. If so, it cannot be contended that they failed to discover their rights at an earlier time due to their own lack of reasonable investigation, since they were apparently unaware that there was anything to search for. This situation thus stands in sharp contrast to *O'Keeffe,* where the owner was well aware of the existence of the paintings and the fact that they had been stolen, and thus could be expected to take steps to find them. Accordingly, the discovery rule arguably could be invoked to toll the statute of limitations until 1979, and the present suit would still be timely.

bailor) voluntarily delivers possession of personal property to another (the bailee) with the agreement, express or implied, that the property shall be returned (i) when the bailment's special purpose is accomplished, or (ii) otherwise upon the demand of the bailor.

Three questions frame the art loan-bailment discussion. First, is the transfer properly classified as a bailment, or is it something else, such as a gift? If it is a bailment, a subsidiary question arises—can the passage of time change the classification? Second, what is the bailee's duty of care and liability for the property in its possession? Third, are there any modifications—contractual or statutory—that apply?

Classifying an art loan as a bailment, instead of a gift, generally depends on the intent of the parties at the time of the transfer. See Mac'Avoy v. Smithsonian Institution, 757 F. Supp. 60 (D.D.C. 1991). Written documentation of a contractual undertaking would be the norm today for any significant art loan. See Parts B and C, *infra*. For old loans, as in *Escot Church* and *McCagg*, it was commonplace to dispense with such formalities, although notably, McCagg's letter correspondence was sufficient to establish a loan. As *Escot Church* shows, absent clear written documentation, classification is a factual inquiry dependent on the facts and circumstances properly presented to the court. In the classification inquiry, the parties' actions may be determinative. Sir John's actions over a 20-plus-year involvement with the church without any mention of the painting's status as a loan did not corroborate his position. In fact, his actions and silence were consistent with a gift. In contrast, McCagg's family as the successor bailor had no interactions with the Smithsonian and that, paradoxically, was a good thing for the McCaggs. For many old loans, this lack of contact and interaction with the museum bailee is extremely common and creates considerable practical uncertainty for the museum. Once in litigation, museums as bailees of indeterminate or indefinite art loans (sometimes also referred to as "permanent loans") argue the passage of time as a defense, with mixed results.

A portrait of Captain James Lawrence, known for his dying command during the War of 1812 ("Don't give up the ship"), was at issue in Redmond v. New Jersey Historical Society, 28 A.2d 189 (N.J. 1942). The portrait by early American artist Gilbert Stuart (who also painted the iconic portrait of George Washington) was transferred to the Society in 1888 by the executor of the claimants' grandmother's estate. The grandmother's will gave all her property to her son Preston, who was a minor at her death. She specifically provided that if Preston died "leaving no descendants," then the portrait "shall go" to the Society. Shortly after the death of Preston in 1938, his children demanded the return of the portrait, which was refused.

The Society did not dispute the Redmond descendants' original title and claim to the Stuart portrait; it straightforwardly argued statute of limitations and laches given its 50-year possession, of the portrait. The court rejected the Society's assertions of title by adverse possession because there was "nothing in the stated acts of . . . the Society to justify a 'repudiation' by the Society of Preston's right to the portrait or to justify the conclusion that the Society exercised dominion over the portrait 'inconsistent' with Preston's right . . . or that the Society did 'some act' which had the 'effect of destroying or changing the quality of the portrait.'" *Id.* at 194–95.

Exhibiting the portrait and taking care of it was not a sufficient assertion of ownership where legal title was clearly elsewhere. Similarly, laches was inappropriate because there was no proof that anyone in the family knew or had reason to know of the Society's claim of ownership. It must be noted that *O'Keeffe*, Chapter 5, *supra*, expressly overruled *Redmond*'s application of the adverse possession doctrine for tangible personal property in favor of the discovery rule. As there was no proof in *Redmond* that anyone in the family knew of the Society's arguable assertion of ownership, this change in legal approach may not have the desired effect, as the *McCagg* court pointedly observed in footnote 6.

More recent cases, however, are less forgiving of the bailor's inaction, and the defense of statute of limitations is gaining some traction. Lackawanna Chapter of Railway & Locomotive Historical Society, Inc. v. St. Louis County, 606 F.3d 886 (8th Cir. 2010) (*Lackawanna II*), involved the 1953 loan of a historic steam locomotive, No. 952, from Lackawanna to St. Louis County's Museum of Transportation. The loan was not formalized, but there was written correspondence using the word "loan." In *Lackawanna I*, 497 F.3d 832 (8th Cir. 2007), the Eighth Circuit held that the 1953 transfer was, at a minimum, an implied bailment for an indefinite period outside the reach of the statute of frauds, and remanded for consideration of the statute of limitations in the old loan context.

On remand, the trial court held that Lackawanna's 2002 replevin action accrued in 1995 or 1996 (when the Museum, in response to a request from Lackawanna for a temporary return of No. 952 for display in Pennsylvania, wrote that it "is committed to retaining this engine in its collection"), and not in 2002 (when Lackawanna formally demanded return of the engine). Missouri's five-year statute of limitations for replevin therefore barred the action. In *Lackawanna II*, the Eighth Circuit affirmed, noting that the Museum's actions in 1995 and 1996 were "inconsistent with the bailment 'and in defiance of bailor's rights.'" *Lackawanna II* is a reminder that while an indefinite loan may generally fall outside an absolute statute of limitations, demand for return cannot be unreasonably delayed by the bailor when there is any possible assertion of ownership by the bailee. Similarly, see Pagliai v. Del Re, 2001 WL 220013 (S.D.N.Y. 2001), where the court deemed 14 years from the time of the painting's delivery to the demand for its return an unreasonable period of time for a conversion cause of action, but, nevertheless, held the defendant a constructive trustee.

In addition to statute of limitations, a jurisdiction may have a specific statute of frauds for bailments. See, e.g., Eisen v. Eisen, 1992 WL 25211 (D. Kan. 1992).

2. *Bailee's Duty of Care.* In *Escot Church* and *McCagg*, the bailees undertook the conservation and restoration of the paintings during their time of possession. For the Church, there was no legal consequence to this action, because the Church was

deemed the owner. For the Smithsonian as a bailee and not as an owner, there could have been liability for acting to conserve, and, conversely, there could also have been liability if it did not act to conserve. The duty of care by the bailee at common law depends on the status of the bailment from a benefits perspective. If the bailment is for the sole benefit of the bailor (a gratuitous bailment), the bailee's standard of care is slight with liability only for gross negligence. If the bailment is for the parties' mutual benefit, the bailee's standard of care is ordinary and reasonable care with liability imposed for ordinary negligence. Finally, if the bailment is for the sole benefit of the bailee, the standard of care is high with liability for slight negligence. How would you characterize an art loan for exhibition?

In Prince v. Alabama State Fair, 17 So. 449 (Ala. 1895), an artist, in response to an invitation to participate in an art fair, prepared and sent a painting on the understanding that the painting would be returned when the art fair closed. The painting was lost and consequently not returned. The defendant introduced evidence that it had a sufficient number of watchmen during the fair and a sufficient number of art handlers thereafter. The lower court held the transaction to be a gratuitous bailment (that is, solely for the artist's benefit) and that the art fair was not liable. On appeal, the Alabama Supreme Court reversed and held the transaction to be a mutual benefit bailment and that actual pecuniary benefit was not necessary. From the court's perspective, the art fair-bailee hoped to benefit from the pecuniary receipts from visitors, "and the artist bailor hoped to benefit from winning recognition" and "the gratification thereby offered her."

Consequently the art fair-bailee needed to establish its ordinary care, which is "materially dependent upon the nature and value of the thing bailed, and its liability to loss or injury." Thus, "a man would not be expected to take the same care of . . . a load of wood as of a box of rare paintings; of a nude block of marble as of an exquisitely sculptured statue." The court determined that the art fair's negligence "occurred after the close of the fair, when the policemen had been withdrawn," and those who were packing and shipping were "unknown . . . and of their skill or integrity there is a want of evidence."

In *McCagg*, Judge Newman implies that the loan was a gratuitous bailment, describing the loan as "without charge," and an "indefinite gratuitous loan." Do you think that characterization would hold if the McCaggs were suing the Smithsonian for damage to the painting from its conservation or restoration efforts, with its attendant liability for slight negligence? Alternatively, if the Smithsonian did not take affirmative steps to conserve or restore the work, would liability attach to its inaction?

Perhaps one can draw a distinction between a pure exhibition loan and an indefinite loan. Is there a benefit to the McCaggs from the paintings just being at the Smithsonian? In Lindholm v. Brant, 925 A.2d 1048 (Conn. 2007), Chapter 2, *supra*, plaintiff loaned Warhol's *Red Elvis* for two exhibitions in part because she believed the exhibitions would increase the work's value or desirability.

3. *Contractual and Statutory Modifications.* The legal and practical uncertainties generated by old loans led to two distinct responses. On the intake side today, formal procedures and documentation requirements for art loans are common in major museums. See discussion in Part C. Art Loans in Practice, *infra*. Today, contracts mitigate much of the uncertainty inherent in common law bailment for old loans. Old loans should now be just that—old and cold. Although many, if not most, museums still have some old loans on their books, no new ones should appear. The second response was legislation at the state level, prompted by the professional museum community's desire to regularize museum collections records. Old loan legislation has four primary purposes: to create a method for determining ownership for old loans that appear to be abandoned, to establish a procedure for terminating old loans by museums, to deal with issues of conservation, and to limit actions for recovery. The vast majority of states enacted some type of old loan legislation, some with a very limited applicability. See Association of Registrars and Collection Specialists, List of Old Loan Legislation, at https://www.arcsinfo.org/content/documents/arcsmuseumpropertyandoldloanlegislationjune2018.pdf.

Old loan legislation is not generally well known, and its scope remains uncertain. See Lackawanna Chapter of Railway & Locomotive Historical Society v. St. Louis County, 606 F.3d 886 (8th Cir. 2010). Some question the constitutionality of such legislation. See Linden Havemeyer Wise, *Old Loans: A Collections Management Problem*, ALI-ABA Course of Study, LEGAL PROBLEMS OF MUSEUM ADMINISTRATION, March 28, 1990.

4. *Other Art Bailment Situations.* The law of bailment is not limited in the art context to old loans or even new loans for exhibition. Any time the physical possession of an artwork is transferred, a bailment may be created. The conservation or appraisal of an artwork, for example, may involve three separate bailments—the outgoing transportation, the conservator's or appraiser's office, and the return transportation. Consigning a work for auction or sale by a dealer, lending artwork to family or friends, a court-ordered deposit of an artwork pending resolution of a dispute, are all common examples of bailments throughout the transactional arc of acquisition, ownership, and disposition of art. See Steven Mark Levy, *Storage and Transportation of Artwork*, ART LAW HANDBOOK 119–188 (Roy S. Kaufman, ed. 2004 Supp.).

B. New Loans

In deciding whether to lend an artwork, that is, to part with physical possession and control for a period of time, three primary concerns arise—damage, theft, and threat of legal process. Concerns about damage and theft are personal or business, not necessarily legal, judgments. Concerns regarding damage can be specific, such as the fragile or compromised condition of a particular work, or general, such as the rigors of transportation and extra handling. Theft is always a possibility for artworks regardless of their location or context, but theft concerns may be reduced if the loan is to a major museum whose institutional security system may be superior to that of an individual collector. From a practical perspective, the financial downside of damage and theft is addressed by insurance, which occupies a central position in the loan agreement.

The next cases demonstrate the newest concern in art loans—whether the lender is an individual or a museum—the threat of legal process. As an external risk, it is a difficult issue to address satisfactorily in the loan agreement. See Norman Palmer, *Adrift on a Sea of Troubles: Cross-Border Art Loans and the Specter of Ulterior Title*, 38 VAND. J. TRANSNAT'L L. 947 (2005).

In the Matter of the Grand Jury Subpoena Duces Tecum Served on the Museum of Modern Art

93 N.Y.2d 729 (N.Y. 1999)

WESLEY, J.

* * *

In this case we must determine whether Arts and Cultural Affairs Law § 12.03, which protects the artwork of nonresident lenders from "any kind of seizure" while on exhibit in New York State, encompasses a subpoena duces tecum requiring production of two paintings by Egon Schiele on loan to the Museum of Modern Art in New York from the Leopold Foundation in Vienna. The subpoena was issued by the New York County District Attorney's office pursuant to a Grand Jury investigation into the theft of those paintings during the German annexation of Austria. The statute's language and history lead us to conclude that the protection of section 12.03—which in the past has been used in the context of civil actions—applies under the circumstances of this case.

I.

In October 1997, the Leopold Foundation in Vienna loaned more than 150 works by Egon Schiele, the renowned Austrian expressionist, to the Museum of Modern Art for a three-month exhibit. "Portrait of Wally" and "Dead City III" were among the paintings exhibited. For three years prior to the exhibit in New York City, the collection was on a worldwide tour. . . . After the Museum's exhibit ended, the collection was scheduled for exhibition in Spain.

On December 31, 1997, five days before the exhibition was to close, the Museum received two letters from persons claiming that "Portrait of Wally" and "Dead City III" were stolen from their rightful owners during the Nazi annexation of Austria.

* * *

In response, the Museum sent [a] letter, dated December 31, 1997, the Museum indicat[ing] that, while it was sympathetic . . . it had a contractual obligation to return the entire Leopold collection to the lender after the exhibition closed. . . .

* * *

On January 7, 1998 the New York County District Attorney's office served the Museum with a Grand Jury subpoena duces tecum and demanded the production of "Portrait of Wally" and "Dead City III."

* * *

II.

The issue before us has two distinct facets. We must determine whether section 12.03 of New York's Arts and Cultural Affairs Law is limited to civil proceedings. If not, we must then determine whether the subpoena issued in this case effectuates a seizure of the paintings and is thus prohibited by the statute.

Section 12.03 provides:

> "§ 12.03. Exemption from seizure
>
> "*No process* of attachment, execution, sequestration, replevin, distress *or any kind of seizure* shall be served or levied upon any work of fine art while the same is enroute to or from, or while on exhibition or deposited by a nonresident exhibitor at any exhibition held under the auspices or supervision of any museum, college, university or other nonprofit art gallery, institution or organization within any city or county of this state for any cultural, educational, charitable or other purpose not conducted for profit to the exhibitor, nor shall such work of fine art be subject to attachment, seizure, levy or sale, for any cause whatever in the hands of the authorities of such exhibition or otherwise" (emphasis added).

While section 12.03 delineates certain types of civil process, the unconditional language preceding and following this clause—"[*n*]*o* process" and "*or any* kind of seizure"—in no way suggests that the Legislature meant the delineated terms to be either exclusive or exhaustive. Indeed, there is no limiting language in section 12.03; the words are unqualified. Hence, on a facial reading of the statute, we are confident that the words—unrestricted as they are—are not limited to civil processes.

The legislative history of section 12.03 amply supports our interpretation. While the impetus for this statute was a civil lawsuit involving the civil seizure of artwork on display at a Buffalo museum, a comprehensive reading of the history reveals a consistent, unyielding legislative intent to promote artistic and cultural exchanges by creating a climate in New York free from the threat of seizure by judicial process and by encouraging nonresidents to share their works of art with the public. The essence of this legislation is perhaps best captured in Governor Rockefeller's Memorandum of Approval, which states that many exhibitions in New York State:

> "rely in most instances on loans of works of art for their success. The promotion and continuation of these events is necessary to maintain New York's status as the art center of the Nation and is beneficial to the general cultural atmosphere of the State.
>
> "Works of art lent by non-resident exhibitors are currently subject to seizure by legal process in the State. . . .

> "The bill, by exempting such works of art from legal process where their presence in the State of New York is solely by the generosity of the exhibitor and not for any commercial purpose, will go far to allay the fears of potential exhibitors and enable the State of New York to maintain its pre-eminent position in the arts" (Governor's Mem approving L 1968, ch 1065, 1968 NY Legis Ann, at 495).

The statute's intent is twofold: to insulate nonresident lenders from seizures via legal process and, concomitantly, to protect State cultural institutions that depend upon the free flow of art for the benefit of the people of the State of New York. These purposes are also reflected in the Attorney General's Memorandum of Support that the increased fear of harassment of nonresident artists and collectors regarding seizures could reap "incalculable harm" for New York's cultural institutions if the bill did not become law (Attorney General's Mem, Bill Jacket, L 1968, ch 1065).

* * *

In response [to a concern that the bill would prevent a rightful owner from recovering stolen property—Ed.], the Attorney General questioned the wisdom of creating any loopholes in the statute, reasoning that such exemptions would force potential good-faith lenders to seek legal advice before lending artwork to museums, thus defeating the bill's purpose:

> "To puncture the exemption sought by this bill with a single major loophole . . . thus forcing 'potential-lenders-in-good-faith' to seek legal advice before lending their works to museums of this State would be self-defeating, since non-resident artists and patrons of the arts can exercise their free alternative to stay out of trouble by keeping their possessions safely at home. The proverb that 'half a loaf is better than nothing' is exceedingly inapposite in this instance. . . .
>
> "The primary policy concern of this bill is . . . with the museums and other cultural institutions of this State which are completely and thoroughly dependent upon the free flow of works of art into the State for the purpose of conducting exhibitions of major public interest. The exemption conferred by this bill upon the lenders of works of art is a small favor for the other risks involved in crating, shipping and exposing these works, often of fragile construction, to large New York audiences. Considering the alternatives open to potential lenders—to keep their works at home—it would seem that the State of New York is in no morally tenable position to bargain and equivocate over the *scope* of this bill if the cultural welfare of the People and their cultural institutions is of any real significance to its lawmakers and if this bill serves that welfare" (Attorney General's Supplemental Mem, Bill Jacket, L 1968, ch 1065 [emphasis in original]).

. . . Thus, this history, coupled with the language of the statute, demonstrate a clear mandate from the Legislature. The statute's "no loopholes" approach compels our holding that Arts and Cultural Affairs Law § 12.03 is not limited to civil process.

III.

This determination does not end our inquiry. According to the language of the statute, before the legal process in question runs afoul of the statute, it must constitute or effectuate a "seizure." We interpret "seizure" according to its commonly understood meaning. . . .

* * *

"Seizure," as used in everyday parlance, is understood to mean "the action or an act of seizing, or the fact of being seized; confiscation or forcible taking possession" (Oxford English Dictionary [2d ed 1989]). . . . While this Court has not had occasion to comment upon the meaning of "seizure" in a property context, the commonly understood meaning comports with the United States Supreme Court's definition of "seizure" as "some meaningful interference with an individual's possessory interests in . . . property" (*United States v Jacobsen,* 466 US 109, 113).

Given the facts of this case, we reject the Museum's argument that there are no conceivable circumstances in which a judicial process may abide the statute. In order to afford artwork the protective cloak of section 12.03, the process at issue—whether civil or criminal—must constitute or effectuate meaningful interference with a lender's possessory interest in that property. The statutory language is unequivocal.

What then is the effect of the subpoena in this case? Clearly, a subpoena duces tecum is a process of a court. . . . While a subpoena of this kind generally does not authorize the seizure, impoundment or other disruption in possession of property, and is not intended to deprive its custodian of control . . . , nonetheless in the context of this case the subpoena rises to the level of "meaningful interference with [the lender's] possessory interest" for purposes of section 12.03. In the absence of a court ruling limiting the issuer's right to retain the evidence, "the prosecutor may lawfully exercise dominion and control over the evidence" . . . . No ruling limiting the People's right to retain the paintings has been issued here. The paintings, which were scheduled to leave New York well over a year and a half ago, are still present in this State and an indictment has not been forthcoming. As a practical consequence of the subpoena, the Museum has been and would continue to be precluded indefinitely from returning the paintings to the Leopold Foundation. We conclude that the subpoena here has interfered significantly with the Leopold Foundation's possessory interests in the paintings by compelling their indefinite detention in New York, and thus effectuating a seizure.

IV.

* * *

We fully appreciate the profound and opposing interests presented by this case. The District Attorney has a constitutional responsibility to identify and prosecute criminal activity, while the Museum seeks to make works of art from all over the world available to New Yorkers. These two significant interests have come into conflict as a result of Nazi atrocities. The Legislature of this State made a significant policy decision 30 years ago when it enacted the predecessor to section 12.03. As a court of law, we cannot alter that policy under the guise of legislative interpretation. The language of the statute is clear, the intent of the Legislature manifest.

The People's remaining argument is without merit.

Accordingly, the order of the Appellate Division should be reversed, with costs, and the Museum's motion to quash the Grand Jury subpoena duces tecum should be granted.

Notes and Questions

1. *Aftermath.* Hours after this decision, the U.S. Attorney for the Southern District of New York obtained a federal seizure warrant for *Wally.* The U.S. Attorney acted at the request of Customs (CBP), which deemed *Wally* stolen property. Consequently, its import and potential export could violate the National Stolen Property Act. See discussion of CBP's forfeiture authority in Chapter 6, *supra.* While there is also a federal anti-seizure statute for international art loans (discussed in detail below), its protection requires an application that MoMA failed to file. A federal forfeiture suit therefore was initiated. United States v. Portrait of Wally, 105 F. Supp. 2d 288 (S.D.N.Y. 2000) ("*Wally I*"). For ten years after the federal seizure ("the ensuing years have seen a steady stream of motion practice"), *Wally* remained in a secret hiding place in the U.S. as the contentious litigation slowly continued to unfold. United States v. Portrait of Wally, 663 F. Supp. 2d 232, 246 (S.D.N.Y. 2009) ("*Wally IV*"). The 2009 opinion determined that *Wally* had in fact been stolen from the Viennese Jewish art dealer and collector Lea Bondi Jaray during the Nazi occupation of Austria. The judge denied both parties' motions for summary judgment, however, and held that a trial was warranted to determine whether *Wally* was knowingly imported as stolen property. A trial date of July 26, 2010, was set. On July 20, 2010, however, the litigation was settled by a $19 million payment from the Leopold Museum to the Bondi Estate. Mr. Leopold died on June 29, 2010.

The 1999 Court of Appeals decision also prompted legislative action. The New York legislature amended its Arts and Cultural Affairs Law § 12.03 to limit its scope to civil seizures only, effective as of May 24, 2000. That enactment, however, was repealed as of June 1, 2002, because the necessary subsequent legislative action did not occur. Lerner & Bresler, 2 Art Law 736 (3d ed. 2005). The amendment and repeal mirrors the difficult push and pull of the competing policies. Think about how, as a transactional lawyer, this back-and-forth approach would affect your advice to a foreign lender or a New York museum. What is the transactional consequence of such legal uncertainty?

2. *Federal Immunity from Seizure Act.* In 1965, the United States became the first country to enact a national anti-seizure law for art loans. 22 U.S.C. § 2459.

The legislation was apparently in response to a Cold War-era request from the Soviet Union regarding artworks to be loaned to the University of Richmond. The legislation's basic goal is to encourage foreign lenders to allow art loans to U.S. educational or cultural institutions. Since then, more countries (or political subdivisions) have enacted some version of immunity, exemption from forfeiture, or anti-seizure laws. The nations include Australia, Austria, Belgium, Canada (five provinces), France, Germany, Ireland, Israel, Switzerland, and the United Kingdom. Stephen J. Knerly, Jr. & Kristen L. Gest, *International Loans: State Immunity and Anti-Seizure Laws*, in ALI-ABA LEGAL ISSUES IN MUSEUM ADMINISTRATION, April 1--3, 2009.

Exemption from Judicial Seizure of Cultural Objects Imported for Temporary Exhibition United States Code Title 22. Foreign Relations and Intercourse

Chapter 33. Mutual Educational and Cultural Exchange Program

§ 2459. Immunity from seizure under judicial process of cultural objects imported for temporary exhibition or display

(a) Agreements; Presidential determination; publication in Federal Register

Whenever any work of art or other object of cultural significance is imported into the United States from any foreign country, pursuant to an agreement entered into between the foreign owner or custodian thereof and the United States or one or more cultural or educational institutions within the United States providing for the temporary exhibition or display thereof within the United States at any cultural exhibition, assembly, activity, or festival administered, operated, or sponsored, without profit, by any such cultural or educational institution, no court of the United States, any State, the District of Columbia, or any territory or possession of the United States may issue or enforce any judicial process, or enter any judgment, decree, or order, for the purpose or having the effect of depriving such institution, or any carrier engaged in transporting such work or object within the United States, of custody or control of such object if before the importation of such object the President or his designee has determined that such object is of cultural significance and that the temporary exhibition or display thereof within the United States is in the national interest, and a notice to that effect has been published in the Federal Register.

(b) Intervention of United States attorney in pending judicial proceedings

If in any judicial proceeding in any such court any such process, judgment, decree, or order is sought, issued, or entered, the United States attorney for the judicial district within which such proceeding is pending shall be entitled as of right to intervene as a party to that proceeding, and upon request made by either the institution adversely affected, or upon direction by the Attorney General if the United States is adversely affected, shall apply to such court for the denial, quashing, or vacating thereof.

(c) Enforcement of agreements and obligations of carriers under transportation contracts

Nothing contained in this section shall preclude (1) any judicial action for or in aid of the enforcement of the terms of any such agreement or the enforcement of the obligation of any carrier under any contract for the transportation of any such object of cultural significance; or (2) the institution or prosecution by or on behalf of any such institution or the United States of any action for or in aid of the fulfillment of any obligation assumed by such institution or the United States pursuant to any such agreement.

Given the existence of federal immunity, why did MoMA fail to request it for *Wally*? Some believe that MoMA and other New York museums relied on the automatic nature of New York's anti-seizure statute and only applied for federal immunity if the foreign lender specifically requested it. Would MoMA have any liability to the Leopold Museum for not seeking federal immunity? What impact would federal immunity have on *Wally*, assuming it was granted? Remember, *Wally* was before Republic of Austria v. Altmann, 541 U.S. 677 (2004), Chapter 5, *supra*; a different outcome would have been highly likely (and undoubtedly so for the seizure aspect of the case), but not necessarily so.

Requesting immunity is now routine for international art loans, thanks to the cautionary tale of *Wally*. In the years since the passage of the federal Immunity from Seizure Act, there have been only a handful of cases involving it, and most of them were dismissed. *See* Stephen J. Knerly, Jr. & Kristen L. Gest, *International Loans: State Immunity and Anti-Seizure Laws*, in ALI-ABA Legal Issues in Museum Administration, April 1–3, 2009. The *Malewicz* case below is the headline-making exception.

3. *Applying for Federal Immunity.* Three broad elements define the U.S. anti-seizure legislation: eligible property, an application process, and court grant of immunity. Only loaned property that is (i) "of cultural significance" and imported into the U.S. from a foreign country, (ii) subject to an agreement between a foreign owner and the U.S. or "one or more cultural or educational institutions" in the U.S., and (iii) for a temporary exhibition in the U.S. at a cultural exhibition "administered, operated, or sponsored, without profit by any such cultural or educational organization," can qualify under the Immunity from Seizure Act. To qualify, however, prior to the importation, the President through his designee (now the Department of State, formerly USIA) must make two determinations (that the property is of "cultural significance" and the temporary exhibition is in the "national interest") and then publish a notice to that effect in the Federal Register. In order to accomplish this, the borrowing institution must make application to the U.S. Department

of State in accordance with its current protocols. Changes in administrations can result in changes in those protocols. For example, in 2020, the State Department's sample request format is a three-paragraph application letter (available at https: /www.state.gov/sample-application-and-contract-language/). On the other hand, from 2009–2017, the State Department's published checklist had nine items, mostly of a routine documentary nature, such as a schedule of property, copies of loan agreements and related commercial agreements, dates and venues for importation and exhibition, verifying statements regarding the non-profit nature of the exhibit and the institution, and contact person information. In addition, that application had to contain a scholarly statement concerning the cultural significance of the object and, most significantly, a statement certifying that the applicant has conducted professional, independent, multi-source provenance research and either (i) does not know or have reason to know of any competing claims of ownership, or (ii) discloses and describes any such concern. See Application Procedure and Checklist (Revised January 2017), available at https://2009-2017.state.gov/s/l/3196.htm. What would the impact be if such research raises an unsettling provenance concern? Should the borrowing institution inform the lender? The other potential owners? Should the immunity request go forward? Consider that under the Freedom of Information Act, the immunity application may be available to third parties, subject to the deletion of proprietary information.

The final element—court grant of immunity—protects the borrowing institutions and any carriers (but not lenders) from any action that would deprive them of custody or control of the objects. Note that it is a court, a federal court independent of the executive branch, that grants immunity, not the U.S. Department of State; hence, for foreign lenders who seek a governmental guarantee, the Immunity from Seizure Act does not provide the comfort they seek. *Malewicz* raises an additional question as to the scope of immunity.

Malewicz v. City of Amsterdam

362 F. Supp. 2d 298 (D.D.C. 2005)

[Heirs of Kazimir Malevich, a 20th century Russian artist who was a pioneer of geometric abstractionism, sued the City of Amsterdam for allegedly misappropriating certain of his paintings. Suit was filed two days before the close of a Malevich exhibition at the Menil Collection in Houston; the paintings were previously on exhibition loan to the Guggenheim in New York. The works on loan for the exhibition at the U.S. museums had received immunity from court process under the federal Immunity from Seizure Act. The court was confronted, inter alia, with the interplay of that Act with the Foreign Sovereign Immunities Act (FSIA), previously discussed in *Altmann* and *Philipp*, Chapter 5, *supra*—Ed.]

COLLYER, J.

* * *

B. Present in the United States

The 14 Malewicz works at issue here were temporarily present in the United States for exhibition at the Guggenheim and the Menil Collection. They were shipped back to Amsterdam when the second exhibition closed and actually left this country before the City was served with the complaint. . . . The City argues that the artwork was not "present in the United States" as a matter of fact when the City was served and was not "present in the United States" as a matter of law during the course of the exhibitions.

It is undisputed that the 14 works were physically present in the United States when the Malewicz Heirs filed the first complaint in this matter. The City understandably likens FSIA § 1605(a)(3) [the expropriation exception] to an *in rem* action and points out that jurisdiction in an *in rem* action vests only upon assertion of judicial authority over the *res* and not upon the filing of opening papers. . . . [T]he assertion of authority over the *res* is ordinarily accomplished by seizure. . . . "Seizure" in this instance would be unavailable because of the Immunity from Seizure Act. The problem with the City's argument is that it ignores the salient history and purpose of FSIA.

* * *

. . . Congress passed FSIA in 1976 to codify the restrictive theory of sovereign immunity and to place primary responsibility for interpreting and applying FSIA standards in the Judiciary. . . . Critically for this point, FSIA intentionally overrode the common-law requirement that a plaintiff obtain *in rem* jurisdiction over property before suit could be filed against a foreign sovereign. . . . It would be anomalous to re-insert the jurisdictional requirements of an *in rem* action when Congress so clearly intended to remove them from consideration. The Court concludes that Plaintiffs' filing of the complaint while the artworks were physically present in this country was sufficient to meet the "present in the United States" factor of FSIA without regard to later service of the complaint.

Whether the artworks were present in the United States for purposes of legal process raises a different question and is one of the points on which the United States has indicated its interest.

The Department of State . . . pursuant to 22 U.S.C. § 2459 ("§ 2459"), . . . protects imported artworks and cultural objects by making them immune from seizure and other forms of judicial process. It is undisputed that the Malewicz Heirs could not seek to seize the artwork while it was in this country under a grant of such § 2459 immunity. . . . As described by the United States, "Plaintiffs are therefore using the window of opportunity afforded by the Malewicz exhibition[s] as the jurisdictional hook for their claims." . . . Plaintiffs do not disagree.

. . . The United States informs the Court that § 2459 was enacted . . . because the Second Hickenlooper Amendment, 22 U.S.C. § 2370(e)(2), adopted one year before § 2459 . . . "sharply restricted application of the Act of State doctrine as a bar to jurisdiction over claims to property allegedly taken in violation of international law." . . . Section 2459 was passed to address this "threat to cultural exchange" and specifically to address situations in which "[a]s a condition to the loan, [a foreign nation] insisted on a grant of immunity from seizure as protection against [its] former . . . citizens who had valid claims to the title of the work." *Id.* at 6 (*quoting* Rodney M. Zerbe, *Immunity from Seizure for Artworks on Loan to United States Museums,* 6 NW. J. Int'l L. & Bus. 1121 n 21 (1985)).

The United States argues that § 1605(a)(3) of FSIA "requires a sufficient nexus with the United States to provide fair notice to foreign states that they are submitting themselves to U.S. jurisdiction and abrogating their sovereign immunity." . . . The connection under § 1605(a)(3) is, of course, that the foreign state is carrying on a commercial activity in this country and not conducting itself as a sovereign. According to the United States, "[f]oreign states are unlikely to expect that this standard is satisfied by a loan of artwork for a U.S. Government-immunized exhibit that must be carried out by a borrower on a non-profit basis. . . ." The United States urges the Court to give its concerns "great weight 'as the considered judgment of the Executive on a particular question of foreign policy.'" *Id.* (*quoting Altmann,* 124 S. Ct. at 2255). . . .

* * *

The U.S. Statement presents the Court with something of a dilemma. The opinions of the United States are entitled to "great weight," especially when speaking in the realm of foreign policy as the Statement does with respect to cultural exchanges and interpreting the statutory terms that affect the Mutual Educational and Cultural Exchange Program. However, the Court concludes that § 2459 granting immunity and § 1605(a)(3) establishing jurisdiction for certain claims against a foreign sovereign are both clear and not inconsistent. The Court is bound to the plain meaning of these statutes. . . . The relationship between the two statutory provisions is more clearly perceived by the Malewicz Heirs: in fact, they are unrelated except that a cultural exchange might provide the basis for contested property to be present in the United States and susceptible, in the right fact pattern, to a FSIA suit.

Clearly, as the United States and the City argue, § 2459 protects loaned artworks and cultural items from seizure or judicial process. . . . A litigant with a claim against a foreign sovereign may *not* seize that sovereign's property that is in this country on a cultural exchange and the litigant may *not* serve the receiving museum with judicial process to interfere in any way with the physical custody or control of the artworks. The Malewicz Heirs have tried to do neither. They have sued the City of Amsterdam, not the Guggenheim or the Menil Collection. Had this lawsuit begun and concluded before the Malewicz Collection left this country, no order of this Court would have, or could have, affected the custody or control that the museums (and carriers) exercised over the artworks. The Immunity from Seizure Act deprives all U.S. courts from taking any action to obtain physical custody of the Malewicz Collection or other cultural icons granted immunity while in this country.

Instead, the happenstantial presence in this country of 14 pieces by Kazimir Malewicz fulfilled one requirement for FSIA jurisdiction: that the contested property be "present" in this country at the time of suit. The current absence of the artworks from the United States might make a court order to return the works to the Malewicz Heirs only as valuable as their ability to persuade a Dutch court to enforce it but, because of § 2459, the presence or absence of the property makes no difference during the litigation, as long as it was "present" when suit was filed.

Because the Malewicz Heirs are not seeking judicial *seizure* of the artworks, the City's and the United States' reliance on § 2459 is misplaced. Immunity from seizure is not immunity from suit for a declaration of rights or for damages arising from an alleged conversion if the other terms for FSIA jurisdiction exist. . . .

* * *

The Court concludes that the 14 Malewicz artworks were "present in the United States" for purposes of FSIA jurisdiction.

C. Commercial Activity by the Foreign State

Plaintiff's amended complaint states without elaboration that the 14 Malewicz pieces were "in the United States in connection with a commercial activity carried on in the United States by Amsterdam, namely loaning the 14 works for exhibitions in the United States starting in May 2003." . . . The United States advises that "[t]he possibility that such a minimal level of contact will necessarily suffice to provide jurisdiction threatens to chill the willingness of sovereign lenders to participate in the section 2459 program." The City of Amsterdam agrees and states that it would not have loaned the Malewicz artworks if it had known that it could face litigation. It also protests that it was merely a lender from a distance and not engaged in commercial activity here.

In determining whether a foreign state has engaged in "commercial activity" in the United States, the Congress has done us no favors by its choice of words.

* * *

At 28 U.S.C. § 1605(a)(3), FSIA allows suits against foreign states over "rights in property taken in violation of international law . . . [when] that property . . . is present in the United States in connection with a commercial activity carried on in the United States by the foreign state." At 28 U.S.C. § 1603(e), we are instructed that "commercial activity carried on in the United States by a foreign state" means "commercial activity carried on by such state and having substantial contact with the United States." [The court determined that the City of Amsterdam engaged in "commercial activities" because, under the relevant test, the nature — as opposed to the purpose — of the activity (here an art loan) is not limited to sovereigns: a private person or entity could engage in the same action. — Ed.]

* * *

There is one further critical point. The City of Amsterdam and the United States argue that the City's contacts with this country are insubstantial and insufficient to expose it to FSIA jurisdiction. This is not an insubstantial point and it requires a detailed factual analysis of the nature and extent of such contacts. . . .

The existing record does not permit the Court to ascertain the substantiality of the City's contacts or activities with or in the United States in connection with the loan of the Malewicz artworks. . . . The extent and the nature of the City of Amsterdam's contacts with this country must be identified and addressed before the Court can determine its own jurisdiction, or lack thereof, over Plaintiff's amended complaint.

[The court denied the City's motion to dismiss.—Ed.]

Malewicz v. City of Amsterdam

517 F. Supp. 2d 322 (D.D.C. 2007)

[The City of Amsterdam submitted additional evidence to the court on the question of the insubstantiality of its contacts with the U.S. and renewed its motion to dismiss for lack of jurisdiction.—Ed.]

COLLYER, J.

* * *

III. Analysis

A. Jurisdiction Under The FSIA—The Expropriation Exception.

The FSIA provides the "sole basis for obtaining jurisdiction over a foreign state in [American] courts." . . .

Here, Plaintiffs argue that the Court has jurisdiction over this suit against the City under the expropriation exception. *See* 28 U.S.C. § 1605(a)(3). Four elements must be present in order for the FSIA's expropriation exception to apply: (1) "rights in property" are at issue; (2) the property was "taken in violation of international law"; (3) the "property is present in the United States"; and (4) the property is present in the United States "in connection with a commercial activity carried on in the United States by the foreign state."

1. Commercial Activity in the United States-Substantial Contact.

. . . It is the fourth element of the expropriation exception that is at issue in the instant motion. With respect to that element, the phrase "commercial activity carried on in the United States by a foreign state" means "commercial activity carried on by such state and having substantial contact with the United States." *See* 28 U.S.C. § 1603(e).

* * *

In support of its renewed motion, the City submits the Second Supplemental Declaration of Geurt Imanse, who is the Stedelijk Museum's Chief Curator for Painting and Sculpture. . . .

a. Terms of the Loan Agreement.

According to Mr. Imanse, the American Museums solicited the loan of the paintings from the City in June 2002.... There were no face-to-face negotiations; all discussions about the terms and conditions of the loan were by telephone and written correspondence.... By letter dated August 13, 2002, the Stedelijk agreed to loan the Malewicz paintings to the American Museums and to the Deutsche Guggenheim Berlin.... The letter outlined the terms and conditions under which the Stedelijk would loan the paintings.... This letter, together with three "loan-agreement forms," comprised the entire loan agreement between the Stedelijk and the American Museums.... The letter and all three forms were signed in the Netherlands by W.S. van Heusden on behalf of the Stedelijk. *Id.* The forms were signed by Elissa Myerowitz on behalf of the Guggenheim Foundation on October 2, 2002, although the record does not indicate where she executed those documents....

Initially, the Stedelijk insisted on procuring its own insurance for the paintings to be paid by the American Museums.... Ultimately, however, the American Museums provided insurance through a combination of federal indemnity coverage and private fine-arts insurance.... Thus, the American Museums paid the entire cost of insurance. *Id.* The Stedelijk also required the American Museums to obtain immunity from seizure for the paintings while they were in the United States.... Pursuant to that request, the Guggenheim Foundation obtained a grant of immunity from the U.S. Department of State....

Under the terms of the loan agreement, the Stedelijk transferred possession of the paintings to the American Museums in Amsterdam.... Once the American Museums had completed their exhibits, they shipped the paintings to Amsterdam at which point the Stedelijk took them back into its possession....

The City argues that no substantial contact with the United States can be found based on the negotiation and execution of the loan agreement because the City did not solicit the loan and no Stedelijk representative traveled to the United States during this process.... The City further argues that because the American Museums were solely responsible for paying the costs of insuring and shipping the Malewicz paintings from Europe to the United States and for obtaining immunity from seizure for the paintings, the American Museums shouldered most of the responsibility for the paintings.... And because the American Museums' conduct cannot be imputed to the City... the terms and conditions of the loan agreement do not establish substantial contact.

b. Did the City send representatives to the United States in connection with the loan?

As an additional term of the loan agreement, the City insisted that expert artwork handlers escort the paintings while they were in transit and when they were unpacked for display in the American Museums in order to ensure their safety and proper handling.... The City also insisted that the escorts oversee the repackaging of the paintings once they were finished being displayed.... At the hearing on the City's renewed motion, counsel stated that the City did not insist that the escorts be employees of the Stedelijk, but the American Museums nonetheless chose to have Stedelijk employees—including Mr. Imanse—act as the escorts for the paintings. . . . Thus, Mr. Imanse and other curators from the Stedelijk accompanied the paintings from the Netherlands to Berlin, and later from Berlin to New York, then to Houston, and ultimately back to the Netherlands. . . . In total, five Stedelijk escorts were in the United States for 34 days in connection with the loan. . . . The American Museums paid all costs (travel, accommodation, and so on) associated with the Stedelijk couriers who accompanied the art and oversaw its handling. . . .

The City downplays the role played by the Stedelijk's escorts and seeks to characterize their presence in the United States as "isolated and transitory." . . . Plaintiffs, on the other hand, place load-bearing importance on the presence of these escorts in the United States. . . . Plaintiffs emphasize that it was the Stedelijk that insisted upon the escorts' presence in the United States and that the escorts maintained a degree of control over the paintings while they were in the United States.

c. What consideration did the American Museums offer for the loan?

The Stedelijk demanded an administrative fee of $300 per painting from each museum in consideration for lending the art. . . . The Stedelijk also charged the Menil €1,750 for 19 color transparencies of the Malewicz paintings. . . . Thus, both American Museums paid administrative fees of €10,662 for 36 paintings, and the Menil paid an additional €1,750 for the transparencies. . . . In addition, the Stedelijk required the American Museums to pay the cost of transporting the paintings from the Stedelijk to their various destinations. . . . This included €21,324 in "crating" costs—*i.e.*, the costs of packaging the paintings for shipment from the Stedelijk to the American Museums. The Stedelijk received the funds from the American Museums by wire transfer; it did not receive the funds through an American bank. . . .

The City contends that the "nominal" fee of $300 per painting was merely to offset a fraction of the administrative costs that the Stedelijk incurred in loaning the artworks. . . . The actual costs incurred by the Stedelijk were much greater than the amount it received from the American Museums. . . . Thus, the loan was not a profit-making venture for the Stedelijk nor was it a *quid pro quo* for future loans of American art; it was an effort to make an "international cultural exchange. . . ."

Plaintiffs take a much different view. . . . Plaintiffs describe the $300 per painting fee as "exorbitant" and stress the American Museums' efforts to dissuade the Stedelijk from charging any fee. . . . Plaintiffs also emphasize the other costs incurred by the American Museums, such as shipping costs and the charges for the transparencies paid by the Menil. . . . In addition, Plaintiffs offer a letter written by the Stedelijk's Director, Rudi Fuchs, in which he stated that the Stedelijk "need[s] the money" in connection with an exhibition of Malewicz's paintings in Paris which, Plaintiffs argue, shows that the City's motive was to make a profit, not to make a "cultural exchange. . . ."

The City offers persuasive arguments as to each separate element of the transaction: the American Museums solicited the loan, and the City negotiated and executed the loan documents in the Netherlands; the American Museums were responsible for obtaining insurance and indemnity; the American Museums took possession of the paintings in the Netherlands and returned possession to the City in the Netherlands; the Stedelijk escorts were only in the United States for a total of 34 days, and their expenses were paid by the American Museums; and the City charged only a nominal fee for loaning the artwork. The problem with the City's position, however, is that it treats each of these facts in isolation rather than collectively. When the facts are taken together, the City's contact with the United States in connection with this transaction is more significant than it contends.

* * *

The contacts here are more extensive than in [two prior D.C. Circuit Court cases.—Ed.]. The City contracted with the American Museums knowing that the paintings would be displayed in the United States—and knowing of the heirs' claim that the City had unlawfully taken the paintings without just compensation. The City received nearly €25,000 as consideration for the contract with the American Museums, a substantial sum. More critically, it agreed to send several employees, including its Chief Curator for Paintings and Sculptures, to the United States to oversee the safety of the paintings while they were on loan. And while the contract did not require that the overseers be Stedelijk employees, it was the Stedelijk that insisted that the contract include the requirement that expert couriers accompany the artwork, and the Stedelijk knowingly agreed to send its employees pursuant to that provision of the contract. These Stedelijk employees spent, collectively, 34 days in the United States—hardly insubstantial. In short, the City contracted with the American Museums to send its Malewicz artworks to the United States, and a major portion of that contract was performed in the United States with the ready assistance of Stedelijk employees to help ensure its success. Thus, while the City may have technically performed its obligations in the Netherlands, the American Museums performed a significant part of the contract in the United States with the help and participation of Stedelijk employees, which strongly militates in favor of finding substantial contact.... The Court therefore finds that the City's contact with the United States in connection with the loan of the Malewicz artwork was substantial.

* * *

[The court proceeds to discuss Statute of Limitations, Act of State doctrine, and *Forum Non Conveniens.*—Ed.]

IV. Conclusion

Whether the City's contact with the United States in connection with the loan of the Malewicz paintings was "substantial" is a close question, but the record contains sufficient contacts to establish jurisdiction under the FSIA's expropriation exception.

The City's other arguments fall short. . . . Accordingly, the City's Renewed Motion to Dismiss will be denied.

Notes and Questions

1. *Aftermath.* The *Malewicz II* decision was immediately appealed, but the parties settled prior to any decision, and the case was dismissed. 2008 WL 2223219 (D.C. Cir. 2008). The settlement included all Malewicz works in the Stedelijk Museum, not just the 14 artworks on loan, and resulted in five works being transferred to the plaintiffs. One of those paintings, Malewicz/Malevich's *Suprematist Composition*, 1916, was sold for $60,002,500 at a Sotheby's auction in November 2008.

The court's determinations were chilling for museums. That the Immunity from Seizure Act did not immunize the lender from suit and that the relatively normal lending process resulted in substantial contacts of a commercial nature for the FSIA expropriation exception were unexpected results. Many feared a negative impact on incoming international loans. Consequently, after *Malewicz,* interest was expressed in amending the FSIA to protect a foreign owner from any suit based on the presence in the U.S. of an artwork protected under the Immunity from Seizure Act. Craig Blackwell, *Legislative Update* 356, ALI-ABA Legal Issues in Museum Administration, March 24–26, 2010.

The Foreign Cultural Exchange Jurisdictional Immunity Clarification Act, Pub. L. 114-319 (2016), attempts to address these issues by adding a new section to the FSIA, Section 1605(h), Jurisdictional Immunity for Certain Art Exhibition Activities. It provides that for works covered by immunity, "any activity in the United States of such foreign state . . . that is associated with the temporary exhibition . . . shall not be considered to be commercial activity. . . ." There are, however, two important exceptions. The first is for Nazi-era claims (§ 1603(h)(2)(A)). The second provides an exception for takings based on claims of "acts of a foreign government as part of a systemic campaign of coercive confiscation or misappropriation of works from members of a targeted and vulnerable group . . . after 1900" (§ 1603(h)(2)(B)(ii)–(iii)). In a nod to the "fair notice" argument of the U.S. State Department in *Malewicz,* the Act requires that the Secretary of State "shall ensure that foreign states that apply for immunity . . . are appropriately notified" of the Act. Pub. L. 114-319 § 3. The impact of this new legislation on international art loans remains uncertain. Would the result in *Malewicz* change under this new legislation?

2. *An Art Loan Ban.* As a result of litigation over ownership of the Schneerson Library and Archive (an invaluable collection of Jewish religious books and manuscripts) housed in Russia, Russia announced a ban on art loans to the U.S. In July 2010, a default judgment against Russia and in favor of the plantiff's rights to the Schneerson collection was granted. Agudas Chasidei Chabad of U.S. v. Russian Federation, 729 F. Supp. 2d 141 (D.D.C. 2010). Russia participated in the litigation

until the D.C. Court of Appeals paved the way for all claims of the plaintiff to proceed, finding that Russian reliance on sovereign immunity was misplaced. 528 F.3d 934 (D.C. Cir. 2008). Subsequent diplomatic efforts to assure the Russian government that their previously agreed to art loans would be protected from seizure were not persuasive. As a spokesperson for the Hermitage said: "The United States will not give us absolute guarantees that our works are going to be returned. So for now we are refraining from sending them." Those works included paintings by Gauguin, Cezanne, and others originally headed for exhibitions at the Metropolitan Museum of Art in New York and the National Gallery of Art in Washington. See Carol Vogel & Clifford J. Levy, *Dispute Derails Art Loans from Russia*, N.Y. Times, The Arts at 1 (Feb. 2, 2011).

If you advised a foreign owner, how would you assess the risk? Recall the straightforward analysis offered in the *Wally*-MoMA litigation concerning the legislative history for the New York anti-seizure statute. To force potential lenders "to seek legal advice before lending their works to museums ... would be self-defeating, since non-resident artists and patrons ... can exercise their free alternative" and keep their works "safely at home." Times and best practices have changed in the art world significantly since 1968. Merely seeking legal advice is not the problem today for international art loans that it was perceived to be in the 1960s. Sophisticated lenders recognize the complexities involved in cross border transactions, and for them, it is the gaps in law, policy, practice, and perceptions that pose the unsettling concerns.

3. *FSIA Exception for State-Sponsored Terrorism*. In 2008, Congress amended FSIA to add an exception from sovereign immunity for state sponsors of terrorism, thus broadening "the rights of individuals seeking to obtain and enforce judgments against foreign sovereigns arising out of terrorist acts." Rubin v. Iran, 270 F.R.D. 7, at *9, 2010 WL 3501554, at *9 (D.C. Cir. 2010). See also Aryeh S. Portnoy et al., *The Foreign Sovereign Immunities Act: 2008 Year in Review*, 16 L. & Bus. Rev. Am. 179 (2010). The scope of that amendment was at issue when *Rubin* went before the Supreme Court.

Rubin v. Islamic Republic of Iran

538 U.S.—, 138 S. Ct. 816 (2018)

Justice Sotomayor delivered the opinion of the Court.

The Foreign Sovereign Immunities Act of 1976 (FSIA) grants foreign states and their agencies and instrumentalities immunity from suit in the United States (called jurisdictional immunity) and grants their property immunity from attachment and execution in satisfaction of judgments against them. See 28 U.S.C. §§ 1604, 1609. But those grants of immunity are subject to exception.

Petitioners hold a judgment against respondent Islamic Republic of Iran pursuant to one such exception to jurisdictional immunity, which applies where the foreign state is designated as a state sponsor of terrorism and the claims arise out of acts of terrorism. The issue presented in this case is whether certain property of

Iran, specifically, a collection of antiquities owned by Iran but in the possession of respondent University of Chicago, is subject to attachment and execution by petitioners in satisfaction of that judgment. . . .

* * *

I

A

On September 4, 1997, Hamas carried out three suicide bombings. . . . [P]etitioners sued Iran . . . alleging that Iran was responsible for the bombing because it provided material support and training to Hamas. At the time of that action, Iran was subject to the jurisdiction of the federal courts pursuant to [the precursor to § 1605A], which rescinded the immunity of foreign states designated as state sponsors of terrorism with respect to claims arising out of acts of terrorism. Iran did not appear in the action, and the District Court entered a default judgment in favor of petitioners in the amount of $71.5 million.

When Iran did not pay the judgment, petitioners brought this action . . . to attach and execute against certain Iranian assets located in the United States in satisfaction of their judgment. Those assets—a collection of approximately 30,000 clay tablets and fragments containing ancient writings, known as the Persepolis Collection—are in the possession of the University of Chicago, housed at its Oriental Institute. University archeologists recovered the artifacts during an excavation of the old city of Persepolis in the 1930's. In 1937, Iran loaned the collection to the Oriental Institute for research, translation, and cataloging.

* * *

B

. . . This Court consistently has recognized that foreign sovereign immunity "is a matter of grace and comity on the part of the United States." . . .

Prior to 1952, the State Department generally held the position that foreign states enjoyed absolute immunity from all actions in the United States. But, as foreign states became more involved in commercial activity in the United States, the State Department . . . began to follow the "restrictive" theory of foreign sovereign immunity. . . . Immunity typically was afforded in cases involving a foreign sovereign's public acts, but not in "cases arising out of a foreign state's strictly commercial acts."

In 1976, Congress enacted the FSIA in an effort to codify this careful balance. . . . As a default, foreign states enjoy immunity . . . subject to certain express exceptions [including exceptions for commercial activity and state-sponsored terrorism] . . . .

With respect to the immunity of property, the FSIA similarly provides as a default that "the property in the United States of a foreign state shall be immune from attachment arrest and execution." § 1609. But, again, there are exceptions, and § 1610 . . . subsection (a) expressly provides that property "shall not be immune" from attachment and execution where, *inter alia*, it is "used for a commercial activity in the United States" and the "judgment relates to a claim for which the foreign state is not immune under section 1605A . . . regardless of whether the property is or was involved with the act upon which the claim is based."

Prior to 2008, the FSIA did not address expressly under what circumstances, if any, the agencies or instrumentalities of a foreign state could be held liable for judgments against the state. Faced with that question in *First Nat. City Bank v. Banco Para El Comercio Exterior de Cuba,* 462 U.S. 611, 103 S.Ct. 2591, 77 L.Ed.2d 46 (1983) (*Bancec*), this Court held that "government instrumentalities established as juridical entities distinct and independent from their sovereign should normally be treated as such." Thus, as a default, those agencies and instrumentalities of a foreign state . . . cannot be held liable for acts of the foreign state.

Nevertheless, the Court recognized that such a stringent rule should not be without exceptions. . . . But the Court declined to develop a [formula for determining the exceptions], leaving lower courts with the task. . . . Over time, the Courts of Appeals coalesced around . . . five factors (referred to as the *Bancec* factors) . . . .

In 2008, Congress amended the FSIA and added § 1610(g). Section 1610(g)(1) provides:

> "(g) Property in Certain Actions.—
>
> "(1) In general. [T]he property of a foreign state against which a judgment is entered under section 1605A, and the property of an agency or instrumentality of such a state, including property that is a separate juridical entity or is an interest held directly or indirectly in a separate juridical entity, is subject to attachment in aid of execution, and execution, upon that judgment as provided in this section, regardless of [the *Bancec* factors]." . . .

[There is] no dispute that, at a minimum, § 1610(g) serves to abrogate *Bancec*. . . . The issue at hand is whether § 1610(g) does something more; whether . . . it provides an independent exception to immunity so that it allows a § 1605A judgment holder to attach and execute against *any* property of the foreign state, regardless of whether the property is deprived of immunity elsewhere in § 1610.

II

We turn first to the text of the statute. Section 1610(g)(1) provides that certain property will be "subject to attachment in aid of execution, and execution, upon [a § 1605A] judgment *as provided in this section*." (Emphasis added.) The most natural reading is that "this section" refers to § 1610 as a whole, so that § 1610(g)(1) will govern the attachment and execution of property that is exempted from the grant of immunity as provided elsewhere in § 1610.

Other provisions of § 1610 unambiguously revoke the immunity of property of a foreign state, including specifically where a plaintiff holds a judgment under § 1605A, provided certain express conditions are satisfied. For example, subsection (a) provides that "property in the United States . . . used for a commercial activity in the United States . . . shall not be immune" from attachment and execution in seven enumerated circumstances, including when "the judgment relates to a claim for which the foreign state is not immune under section 1605A. . . ." § 1610(a)(7). . . . And two other provisions within § 1610 specifically allow § 1605A judgment holders to attach and execute against property of a foreign state, "[n]otwithstanding any other provision of law" . . . .

Section 1610(g) conspicuously lacks the textual markers, "shall not be immune" or "notwithstanding any other provision of law," that would have shown that it serves as an independent avenue for abrogation of immunity. In fact, its use of the phrase "as provided in this section" signals the opposite: A judgment holder seeking to take advantage of § 1610(g)(1) must identify a basis under one of § 1610's express immunity-abrogating provisions to attach and execute against a relevant property.

* * *

Moreover, our reading of § 1610(g)(1) is consistent "with one of the most basic interpretive canons, that [a] statute should be construed so that effect is given to all its provisions, so that no part will be inoperative or superfluous, void or insignificant." Section 1610 expressly references § 1605A judgments in its immunity-abrogating provisions. . . . If the Court were to conclude that § 1610(g) establishes a basis for the withdrawal of property immunity any time a plaintiff holds a judgment under § 1605A, each of those provisions would be rendered superfluous because a judgment holder could always turn to § 1610(g), regardless of whether the conditions of any other provision were met.

* * *

Throughout the FSIA, special avenues of relief to victims of terrorism exist, even absent a nexus to commercial activity. Where the FSIA goes so far as to divest a foreign state or property of immunity in relation to terrorism-related judgments, however, it does so expressly. Out of respect for the delicate balance that Congress struck in enacting the FSIA, we decline to read into the statute a blanket abrogation of attachment and execution immunity for § 1605A judgment holders absent a clearer indication of Congress' intent.

III

* * *

C

All else aside, petitioners contend that any uncertainty in § 1610(g) should be resolved by giving full effect to the legislative purpose behind its enactment. Petitioners posit that Congress enacted § 1610(g) "with the specific purpose of removing the remaining obstacles to terrorism judgment enforcement." In support of that position, they reference . . . a footnote . . . in *Bank Markazi* [*v. Peterson*], 578 U.S. ———, 136 S.Ct. 1310, 194 L.Ed.2d 463 that notes that Congress "expand[ed] the availability of assets for postjudgment execution" when it added § 1610(g) by making "available for execution the property (whether or not blocked) of a foreign state sponsor of terrorism, or its agency or instrumentality, to satisfy a judgment against that state." But *Bank Markazi*'s characterization of § 1610(g) simply mirrors the text of § 1610(g) and is entirely consistent with the Court's holding today that § 1610(g) expands the assets available for attachment and execution by abrogating this Court's decision in *Bancec* with respect to judgments held under § 1605A. . . .

IV

For the foregoing reasons, we conclude that 28 U.S.C. § 1610(g) does not provide a freestanding basis for parties holding a judgment under § 1605A to attach and execute against the property of a foreign state, where the immunity of the property is not otherwise rescinded under a separate provision within § 1610. The judgment of the Seventh Circuit is affirmed.

It is so ordered.

Justice KAGAN took no part in the consideration or decision of this case.

Notes and Questions

1. *Importance of Cultural Property? Rubin* exemplifies the difference between receiving a judgment for millions of dollars and actually receiving the millions of dollars. Many litigants face the prospect of unsatisfied judgments. In *Rubin*, however, the overlay of sovereign immunity added an extra dimension. The Supreme Court took a tight and technical approach in construing the language of § 1610(g)(1) of the FSIA. It unanimously determined that § 1610(g)(1) did not create a new exception to the norm of immunity for property of a sovereign or an agency or instrumentality of the sovereign. The Court construed § 1610(g)(1)'s "in this section" language to serve a limiting function. One must therefore find—elsewhere within § 1610—a specific exception to the norm of immunity for property from execution and attachment. The Rubins were unable to do this. Their request to interpret the statute in light of Congress's evident purpose was unavailing. The Court noted "the delicate balance that Congress struck" in the FSIA, and without a "clearer indication" of Congressional intent, the Court would not upset that balance by reading into the statute a "blanket abrogation of attachment and execution immunity."

With its reference to FSIA's delicate balance, the Court signals awareness that sovereign immunity has significant and serious consequences beyond the immediate case. Less clear in the opinion is whether the nature of the property that was the subject matter of the attachment made a difference to the Court. In its amicus brief, the United States made that point:

> The property here at issue consists of ancient Persian artifacts, documenting a unique aspect of Iran's cultural heritage, that were lent to a U.S. institution in the 1930s for academic study. . . . Executing against such unique cultural artifacts could cause affront and reciprocity problems that are different in kind from execution under any other provision.

Brief for the United States as Amicus Curiae Supporting Respondents, Rubin v. Islamic Republic of Iran, at 31–3, 538 U. S.—(2018). See also James A.R. Nafziger, *Enforcement of Judgments: Rubin v. Islamic Republic of Iran, Foreign Sovereign Immunity and the Protection of Cultural Property*, 55 Willamette L. Rev. 475 (2019); Jeffrey A. Van Detta, *Suing Sponsors of Terrorism in U.S. Courts: Rubin v. Islamic Republic of Iran and Jesner v. Arab Bank PLC*, 29 Ind. Int'l & Comp. L. Rev. 303 (2019).

Rubin was a difficult loss for the victims and their families. They were not alone. As of August 2008 when many of the attachment suits were underway, there were $28 million of nonblocked assets of Iran in the U.S. and $16 million of blocked assets against $9.6 billion in outstanding judgments against Iran. *Id.* at 314.

2. *Impact on Long-Term Loans for Study.* As noted in the Court's opinion, the University of Chicago's Oriental Institute holds the Persepolis Collection. The federal district court in Illinois had previously determined that the Persepolis Collection was in fact the property of Iran. Rubin v. Iran, 2008 WL 2501996 (N.D. Ill. 2008), modified, 2008 WL 2502039 (N.D. Ill. 2008).

The Persepolis Fortification Tablets are part of a collection of ancient Persian cuneiform administrative texts written between 506 and 497 B.C. The tablets were discovered in Iran in the 1930s by archeologists from the Oriental Institute and loaned by Iran to the Institute in 1936 for long-term study. That study remains ongoing. *Rubin* is a collection matter; it differs from the ownership disputes in *Wally* and *Malewicz.* Does this suggest that the borrowing institution of any qualifying art loan from a foreign owner, even a loan from a national government of cultural property clearly owned by it, can file for immunity under the federal Immunity from Seizure Act? Note that the tablets were lent to the Oriental Institute for long-term study, not exhibition. How does that affect a grant of immunity? Should Congress consider amending the federal Immunity from Seizure Act to broaden its scope to any loan of art or cultural objects to U.S. cultural or educational institutions, regardless of the loan's purpose? Or revising the FSIA once again to specifically exempt art loans from the reach of judgments? See Danica Curavic, *Compensating Victims of Terrorism or Frustrating Cultural Diplomacy? The Unintended Consequences of the Foreign Sovereign Immunities Act's Terrorism Provisions*, 43 Cornell Int'l. L.J. 381 (2010).

C. Art Loans in Practice

1. *To Loan or Not to Loan.* There are two contexts in which an art loan to a museum comes up for a collector—either the collector is solicited by the borrower (say for a particular special exhibition) or the collector solicits the borrower (perhaps as a precursor to a permanent gift). Regardless of context, an art loan needs to be documented, with major museums having a standard form for incoming loans, and a lender having the ability to custom draft a separate agreement. The next two

sections provide examples of each. Before the loan agreement is signed, the lender needs to address the basic question—does she lend the work at all? Shakespeare's "neither a lender nor a borrower be" is routinely ignored, but the undercurrents of the concern need to be addressed.

In deciding whether to lend, the three general concerns (damage, theft, and legal process) are weighed against the various reasons for lending. Some lend for personal reasons (e.g., to share the work with a larger audience, to advance scholarship, or out of a sense of civic pride or duty), others for economic reasons (e.g., to support or increase the work's value through visibility or by reducing provenance or authenticity concerns, or to have temporary relief from costs of ownership, such as insurance). It is worth noting that sometimes a willing lender may be frustrated in her ability to lend. For example, the relevant government may not approve an export license, or the work of art may be subject to an ongoing restriction from a will or trust. See Norman Palmer, Art Loans 37–88 (Kluwer 1997), for a discussion of incentives and constraints.

While the motivations for a loan, for the most part, are not legal judgments, understanding the lender's motivation can be important in drafting the loan agreement or fine-tuning the loan conditions.

2. *Museum's Conditions for Art Loans.* The following is a generic example of the general loan conditions for an exhibition loan at a U.S. museum. As you read the Conditions for Art Loans, notice how the conditions address many of the practical problems associated with old loans. A museum's pre-printed loan agreement may contain two parts. The first part is specific to the particular loan and provides a record of basic descriptive materials (identity of parties, specific dates for the loan, and identification of the loaned work), an acknowledgement that the lender has read and consents to the attached loan conditions, and signatures of the parties. It can also include factual references to whose insurance is operative, who has the copyright or photograph reproduction rights, and shipping and display information. This basic information is necessary for maintaining the museum's registry. See Sally Freitag et al., *Loans*, in Museum Registration Methods 120 (Rebecca A. Buck & Jean Allman Gilmore eds., 5th ed. 2010), and The Metropolitan Museum of Art, Collections Management Policy 15–17 (Sept. 8, 2020), at www.metmuseum.org, for a description of the process from a museum's perspective. The second part of the loan agreement is the pre-printed loan conditions, the lawyer's domain. For many art loans, a form similar to this will be the operative document due to ease, convenience, costs, and perhaps inertia; and for many, many art loans, it works.

Conditions for Art Loans

1. **Care, Preservation & Exhibition.** The Museum will provide the object lent with the same care it provides for comparable property of its own. Objects will be protected from fire, theft, mishandling, and extremes of light, temperature and humidity while in the Museum's custody, subject to the limitations stated in Article 3. It is understood by the Lender and the Museum that all tangible objects are subject to gradual inherent deterioration for which neither party is responsible.

Evidence of damage not described in Lender's Condition Report at the time of receipt or while in the Museum's custody will be reported immediately to Lender.

The Lender will be requested to provide written authorization for any alteration, restoration, or repair, including framing or reframing.

The Museum retains the right to determine when, if, and for how long objects borrowed will be exhibited.

2. **Transportation & Packing.** The Lender certifies that the object lent is in such condition as to withstand ordinary strains of packing, transportation, and handling. A written Condition Report of objects prior to shipment must be sent by the Lender to the Museum; otherwise, it will be assumed that the objects lent are received in the same condition as when leaving the Lender's possession. Condition Reports will be made at the Museum on arrival and departure.

Costs of transportation and packing will be borne by the Museum unless the loan is at the Lender's request. The method of shipment must be agreed upon by both parties. If the object is to be returned at Lender's request (without prior written agreement), to any address other than that from which it was collected, the Lender shall pay any additional costs necessitated by such a change, if so directed by the Museum.

Costs of customs formalities will be borne by the Museum. Government Regulations will be adhered to in international shipments.

The Lender will provide that the object lent is adequately and securely packed for the type of shipment agreed upon, including any special instruction for unpacking and repacking. The object will be returned packed in the same or similar materials as received unless otherwise authorized by the Lender.

3. **Insurance.** Unless Lender provides insurance, the object will be insured for the amount specified herein under U.S. Government indemnity or under the Museum's "all risk" wall-to-wall policy but subject to the exclusions in the fine arts policy. By way of general illustration and not limitation, the Museum's policy excludes: wear and tear, gradual deterioration, moths, vermin, inherent vice or loss or damage from any repairing, restoration or retouching process; hostile or warlike action or weapons in time of peace or war, seizure or destruction under quarantine or customs regulations, confiscation by order of any public authority, and risks of contraband or illegal transportation or trade; and loss or damage to property shipped under "on deck" bills of lading. Where the Museum provides insurance, this loan agreement when signed and delivered by the Museum shall act as a certificate of insurance naming Lender as an additional insured.

4. **Reproduction & Credit.** Unless otherwise notified in writing by the Lender, the Museum may photograph, telecast, or reproduce the object lent for educational, catalogue and publicity purposes.

The Museum will give credit to the Lender as specified on the face of this agreement in any publications. Whether individual labels are provided for objects on exhibition is at the discretion of the Museum.

5. **Changes In Ownership, Address, Or Both.** It is the responsibility of the Lender or his or her agent to notify the Museum promptly in writing if there is a change in ownership of the object lent (whether through *inter vivos* transfer or death) or if there is a change in the identity or address of the Lender. The Museum assumes no responsibility to search for a Lender of record who cannot be reached at the address of record.

6. **Return Of Loans.** The Museum's right to return the loan shall accrue absolutely at the termination date of the loan. If reasonable efforts to return the work fail, then the Museum shall have the right to place the work in storage at Lender's expense for storage fees and the cost of insurance, and to have and enforce a lien for such fees and costs. If the work is not claimed

after three years from the date of commencement of this loan, Lender hereby gives all right, title and interest in the work as an unrestricted and unredeemable absolute charitable gift to the Museum.

When the loan is returned by the Museum, Lender shall have 30 days to examine and make any claims for damages. If claim is not made within the 30 days, then Lender hereby waives such claim.

Lender waives any claim for damages owing to delays in returning the work for reason beyond the reasonable control of the Museum. Lender exonerates and releases the Museum from liability exceeding the fine arts policy limits and from causes beyond the scope of its fine arts policy, and waives any right of subrogation against the Museum for losses paid under Lender's fine arts insurance.

7. **Applicable Law.** This agreement shall be constructed in accordance with the laws of ____________.

3. *A Lender's Agreement.* The following is an art loan agreement drafted from the perspective of a lender of an artwork that is of significance to him and of great interest to the borrowing museum. As you read this hand-drafted agreement, you will notice that perspective creates a very different tone for this agreement compared to the generic Conditions for Art Loans. You should also observe, however, that both contain the same basic elements.

Art Loan Agreement

This Art Loan Agreement is made and entered into as of the ________ day of ________, 20XX, by and between ________ (the "Lender") and Known Museum (the "Museum") by its Director ________.

WHEREAS, Lender is the owner of the work of art (the "Work") listed in Schedule A attached hereto;

WHEREAS, the Director of the Museum has the necessary authority to enter into this Art Loan Agreement and to commit Museum to all of the duties, commitments and obligations under this Art Loan Agreement;

WHEREAS, Museum wishes to borrow the Work from Lender for purposes of a special exhibition; and

WHEREAS, Lender wishes to lend the Work to Museum for its special exhibition;

NOW THEREFORE, Lender and Museum in consideration of the representations and promises made herein agree as follows:

1. **Term, Purpose and Location.** The term of the loan shall be from ________, 20XX to ________, 20XX, for the purpose of a special exhibition to be organized by the Museum. The sole venue of the special exhibition is the Museum.

Lender and Museum agree that if for any reason the special exhibition is not so organized or undertaken by Museum, or if Museum determines not to exhibit the Work in the special exhibition, then Lender's obligation hereunder to lend the Work to Museum shall forthwith terminate and the Work, if in the possession or control of Museum, shall be returned promptly to Lender, notwithstanding the stated term of this Art Loan Agreement. Absent such circumstance, Museum shall have the right to possess the Work during the term of the loan.

2. **Credit Line.** For purposes of exhibition, catalogue, and publicity, the credit line shall read: Anonymous. Museum agrees to honor Lender's desire for confidentiality.

3. **Copyright, Reproduction, and Artist's Rights.** The copyright to the Work is currently owned by ________, not Lender. Museum agrees not to reproduce the Work without the written consent of the copyright holder. The Work was created by ________, an American

artist who is now deceased. Museum agrees to indemnify and hold Lender harmless from any and all demands, claims, suits, judgments, damages, and losses (including attorney and other professional fees, and costs), incurred or asserted against Lender by reason of Museum's unauthorized use of any photograph or reproduction of the Work, or by its failure to use reasonable efforts to prevent such unauthorized reproduction.

4. **Insurance.** Museum shall provide all risk, wall to wall, fine arts insurance coverage for the Work, for the value stated in Schedule A, specifically including coverage for acts of terrorism. Museum agrees to provide Lender with a Certificate of Insurance or Certificate of Indemnity, or both, as the case may be. Museum agrees to accept total responsibility for the Work wall to wall for the value stated in Schedule A, and accepts responsibility for any error or deficiency in any such insurance or indemnity coverage, specifically including coverage for acts of terrorism.

In the event of partial loss or damage, Lender and Museum shall agree as to the reasonable cost of repair to the Work and the amount of any diminished value of the Work after such repair. In the event that Lender and Museum can not so agree, then each of them shall appoint an appraiser, and those two appraisers together shall select a third appraiser to determine the reasonable cost of repair and loss in value. Museum shall bear all costs in connection with the appraiser's determination.

5. **Transportation, Packing and Handling.** Museum, in consultation and agreement with Lender, shall arrange for the packing, handling and shipping of the Work from Lender's premises to Museum and for its return to Lender, at mutually convenient times. In no event shall the pick up time from Lender's premises be earlier than ________, 20XX for transport to Museum and no later than 10 days after the close of the special exhibit for the Work's return. All costs of packing (including construction of a crate, if any and the storage and disposal of all packing materials), handling, and shipping shall be borne by Museum.

[Museum agrees to arrange and pay for a professional courier (whether from its staff or otherwise) to accompany the Work at all times during transport.]

6. **Care, Preservation and Exhibition.** Museum agrees to exercise the same degree of care for the Work as it does for comparable property of its own. The Work will be protected from fire, theft, mishandling, dirt, insects and vermin, and extremes of light, temperature, and humidity while in Museum's custody.

Museum agrees that prior to packing the Work for transport to Museum, Museum (by a Museum conservator or other qualified professional staff) shall prepare a Condition Report, and shall make a copy of such Condition Report available to Lender. The Condition Report shall be updated by Museum upon (i) the arrival and unpacking of the Work at Museum; (ii) any change in condition of the Work during the special exhibition; (iii) the repacking of the Work for return to Lender; and (iv) the return and unpacking of the Work at Lender's premises. All costs associated with the Condition Report shall be borne by Museum. Museum will not perform any conservation on the Work, or frame or reframe the Work, without the Lender's written consent.

The Work shall be exhibited subject to the following special conditions: [insert any special requirement].

7. **Return of the Work.** Subject to Article 1 or unless otherwise mutually agreed in writing, the loan terminates at the date specified in Article 1, and Museum shall return the Work to Lender within 10 days of termination.

In the event that ownership of the Work changes during the term of the loan (whether due to inter vivos transfer or death), Lender or an authorized representative shall promptly notify Museum in writing of such ownership change and of the name and address of the new owner.

The Work will only be returned to the premises of the lender of record, or to a mutually agreed upon location; provided that if there is a change of ownership and the delivery location is of much greater distance than the original location, the lender of record shall bear any additional shipping, packing, and handling costs, if so requested by Museum.

8. **Integration and Governing Law.** This agreement contains all the representations, promises, agreements and conditions, either written or oral, between Lender and Museum, and may not be changed or modified except in writing signed by Lender and Museum (or their authorized representatives). The law of State A shall govern this Art Loan Agreement. This Art Loan Agreement shall inure to the benefit of, and shall be binding on, the successors, heirs, executors and administrators of Lender and Museum.

IN WITNESS WHEREOF, Lender and Museum have executed this Art Loan Agreement as of the date first set forth above.

Known Museum

____________________	By: ____________________
Lender 123 Main Street Anytown, State A	Its Director 456 Museum Way Anytown, State A

Schedule A

This Schedule A is attached to and forms a part of that certain Art Loan Agreement executed by Lender and Museum as of the ________ day of ________, 20XX, and identifies the Work which is the subject matter of such Art Loan Agreement, namely:

Artist: Value For Insurance:

Title:

Medium:

Date:

Dimensions:

4. *Discussion Points for Art Loan Agreements.* The following are some, but by no means all, points that merit additional attention in drafting art loan agreements. As in prior exercises, a careful comparison of the two sample agreements remains instructive.

a. Care, preservation, and exhibition. The "same care" standard is commonly used. Some museums will add a clause specifically negating any obligation to exercise a duty of care for loaned property higher than what it provides for its own property. What is the utility of such a statement? Is it merely repetitive at best, or ambiguous at worst? Or is it an attempt to deal with the common law of bailment and its history of varying duties?

Consider the museum's preferred right to determine when, if, and for how long the work will be exhibited. For many lenders, on the other hand, the point of the loan is to exhibit the work. The lender prefers an express duty to exhibit, and if the work is not to be exhibited, the lender desires the work to be returned. How would you draft the clause to balance these competing views? In drafting the clause, you may want to keep in mind these two similarly competing anecdotes. Consider a lender who withdraws a featured object from exhibit because it has been sold at a price that the lender cheerfully acknowledges was enhanced due to the object's inclusion in the exhibit. Conversely, consider a lender who arranges for an intercontinental trip with family and friends to view the exhibit only to find the loaned object was excluded. If there is a duty to exhibit (expressed or implied), what are the damages for the breach? Does the action sound in tort or contract?

Both the Museum's Conditions for Art Loans and the Lender's Art Loan Agreement presuppose a single venue for the exhibit. Care must be taken throughout the agreement if the exhibit will involve more than one venue.

b. Transportation and packing. The mere movement of museum quality artworks or cultural property risks damage to the objects. It is perhaps the most significant jointly shared concern in an art loan. Establishing the pre-loan condition of the object is critical for two reasons: first, for making the basic knowing determination of whether or not to lend the object, and second, as the baseline physical measure in the assessment of any (further) damage. For private collectors, the representation of the work's condition as suitable for packing, traveling, and handling as provided in the Museum's Conditions for Art Loans is somewhat problematic, as most individuals are not qualified to make such an assessment nor are many transportation carriers. In the Lender's Agreement, the borrowing museum prepares the pre-arrival condition report.

Transportation costs, including for couriers and art experts, are generally borne by the borrowing museum, although surprisingly some forms are silent on this. Recall how the *Malewicz* court characterized this relatively common protocol.

With respect to transportation and packing costs, should it matter who requested the loan? For a sense of the technical complexity that can accompany the movement of a work of art, see David Ryan, *Moving and Rigging Safety* 315–321, and Brent Powell, *Packing and Crating* 322–331, both in Museum Registration Methods (Rebecca A. Buck & Jean Allman Gilmore eds., 5th ed. 2010). See also Andrew Dickson, *How to move a masterpiece: the secret business of shipping priceless artworks*, The Guardian (Mar. 21, 2019).

c. Insurance. This is the most pressing issue for art loans, with the default rule in the Museum Conditions for Art Loans being the museum provides wall to wall coverage under its all risk, fine arts insurance policy. Notice the educational function of providing examples of some standard exceptions to "all risk." (See *Frigon*, Chapter 9, *infra*, for further consideration of "all risk.") Because art loans are so common for many museums, museums prefer their own insurance coverage for certainty and administrative ease, and many lenders agree. Some lenders, however, will prefer to keep their own coverage and have the borrower pay the allocable premium. If so, the borrower should either be specifically included as an additional assured or subrogation against the borrower should be waived. Why? Either of these actions will generally protect the borrowing museum from being sued by the lender's insurance carrier in the event that the carrier pays out on a claim. Additionally if a lender kept her own insurance coverage, it is important to determine if her coverage includes art loans or if there is a geographic limitation on the coverage. Notice that the Lender's Agreement requires the museum to bind itself for coverage, regardless of whether its insurance carrier does or does not pay for the damage. Does deeming the signed loan agreement a certificate of insurance, as provided for in the Museum's Conditions for Art Loans, sufficiently protect the lender? Consider the questions that could arise if there was damage to multiple loaned works on display in a special exhibit. For example, what if there is a cap in the insurance policy on the total amount paid?

Valuation, for insurance purposes, can create issues at the inception of the loan and during the time of the loan. The lender includes the object's fair market value in the loan agreement; museums do not and should not provide the valuation for works on loan. The lender may be asked for an appraisal if the fair market value seems off, whether high or low. When might a value be unrealistically low?

Major exhibits (especially those involving more than one venue) can require significant advance planning with loan agreements being signed a year or more before the exhibition. See, e.g., Kelly Crow, *The Louvre's Leonardo Loan Hunt*, WALL ST. J., Oct. 23, 2019, at A11 ("The loans were our biggest nightmare," quoting Vincent Delieuvin, the curator in charge of the Louvre exhibition for the 500th anniversary of Leonardo da Vinci's death, the largest ever-mounted). What if an item's value increases from the time of the agreement to the date of the exhibit? Or, during the time of the exhibit? Art values can be quite volatile, even when general market conditions are relatively calm. It is not unheard of to request and receive additional coverage for appreciated works, especially when supported by an independent appraisal. How would you revise the form to specifically provide for, or to exclude, such adjustment in coverage? Might the length of the loan affect this provision? Adjusting insurance values is generally an exercise in who pays and not an exercise in availability of coverage. If the lender has kept her own insurance coverage, increasing the coverage should be a relatively straightforward transaction, followed by a determination as to who pays for such extra insurance. If the museum provides coverage and does not allow for adjustment, the lender may still be able to increase coverage under her own policy, although issues of secondary coverage can come into play.

Did you notice that the Museum Conditions for Art Loans mentions U.S. Government indemnity as a possible source of coverage for loss? See The Arts and Artifacts Indemnity Act, 20 U.S.C. §§ 971–977; recall *Malewicz*, noting insurance coverage, in part, by federal indemnity.

Wall to wall (also sometimes referred to as "nail to nail") generally means coverage from the time the work is removed from its place of hanging or display at the lender's premises to its return to the same place. For individual collectors, the assumed time frame for coverage usually presents no problem, but for institutional lenders, it can. Museums sometimes lend because a gallery may be undergoing renovation or expansion. How does wall to wall work if the original location no longer exists? Or, if the renovation is significantly behind schedule? The stated dates for the loan may provide evidence as to the time frame for coverage. The parties may find it best to clarify the time frame for wall to wall coverage in the loan agreement in such circumstances.

A word of caution: Insurance is highly specialized and coverage can vary markedly, e.g., hurricane insurance is more common in Florida than in Illinois. It is necessary to consult the policy, and it is always prudent to contact the insurance carrier to give notice about the loan, to ascertain coverage, and to address any particular concerns that arise.

d. Reproduction and credit. The public exhibition of an artwork involves a consideration of intellectual property law, in particular the rights of the copyright owner and the moral rights of the work's author, if any. From a transactional perspective, the first determination is to ascertain the identity of the copyright owner and if the work is subject to the artist's moral rights. If the lender of the work also owns its copyright, then the lender can authorize the reproduction of the work for all of the exhibition's purposes. If the lender does not own the copyright, the lender (or any person authorized by the lender) nevertheless does have the right under U.S. law to publicly display the actual work, assuming the work was lawfully made. See 17 U.S.C. § 109(c); Massachusetts Museum of Contemporary Art Foundation v. Büchel, 593 F.3d 38 (1st Cir. 2010), Chapter 7, *supra*. This right to exhibit does not extend to reproduction; however, under copyright law's fair use doctrine, it is generally understood that a museum can photograph or copy the work for registration and archival purposes, and for internal scholarship and research. Notice how the two agreements diverge over the allocation of responsibility in making these determinations: in the Museum's Conditions for Art Loans, the museum asserts the right to reproduce unless notified in writing by the lender, while in the Lender's Agreement, the museum agrees not to reproduce unless it secures the permission from the copyright owner.

Art loans may similarly involve moral rights of the artist. For example, moving a work that is arguably site-specific, or displaying the work with other artists or in an exhibit that the artist feels is prejudicial to his reputation, could give rise to VARA violations. If the artwork is subject to moral rights, the loan agreement should clearly provide who bears responsibility for seeking the permission of the artist (or other holder of the moral rights), and for any violation of such rights.

A related aspect of an art loan for public exhibition can come from the subject matter of the work. If the work is, say, a portrait of an individual, the subject's right of privacy may also need to be addressed.

Intellectual property law is highly complex, dynamic, and for international loans or works of international artists, multi-jurisdictional. For situations where the identity of the copyright holder is cloudy or uncertain, or where an artist's moral rights may exist, it is basic lawyering to first ascertain the facts and to engage special counsel (foreign or domestic) to assist, if appropriate. In all cases, the loan agreements should spell out the parties' obligations and responsibilities to these potential third party stakeholders. See Lionel Bently & Brad Sherman, *Copyright Aspects of Art Loans*, in ART LOANS 239–318 (Norman Palmer ed, 1997), for an overview of intellectual property concerns in six nations, including the U.S.

For those lenders who wish to be identified (as opposed to an anonymous or private collection listing), care needs to be taken as to the proper title holder. For example, if the artwork was previously transferred by an individual owner into a family trust or partnership, then the use of the individual name would technically be incorrect. More importantly, it could raise an estate or a gift tax question as to the bona fides of the individual's prior transfer.

e. Change in ownership or address. This mundane provision can provide interesting practical questions. If ownership does change, what is the museum's duty of inquiry as to the new owner? For example, if the lender dies during the term of the loan, the lender's spouse may request the return of the work. What proof of ownership or authority should the museum request from the spouse? Would a court order appointing the spouse as executor suffice? What about a certified copy of the bequest of the work to the spouse? Before answering, remember a decedent's will may be subject to challenge in a will contest suit. Similarly, if the owner's address changes, say from Illinois to Arizona, how does that impact the museum's transportation, handling, and insurance obligations?

Some agreements provide that if ownership changes due to a sale, the borrowing institution is entitled to a certain percentage of the sales proceeds. Under what circumstance would this make sense to the lender? Does this provision raise any concern regarding the institution's non-profit status?

f. Return of loans. This contractual provision un-does the problematic indefinite time feature of old loans, by setting a definite period of time within which the loan ends and the artwork returns to the owner. Notice that the return provision in the Museum's Conditions for Art Loans goes further and operates to transfer ownership of the work as an "unrestricted and unredeemable absolute charitable gift" to the Museum after three years. Other museum forms that adopt a similar approach have time frames as short as one year. What would constitute "reasonable efforts" to return an artwork that is subject to an ownership dispute?

5. *Taxes Briefly.* Most museums in the U.S. are organized and operated as entities exempt from federal income taxation and, as a general corollary, donations to them can provide federal income, estate, and gift tax deductions for a donor. Speaking very broadly, when the donation is not cash but tangible personal property, such as an artwork, the rules for the federal tax deductions become inordinately complex. See Chapters 10 and 11, *infra*, for an overview of tax considerations. An art loan does not qualify for a federal income tax charitable deduction because it is a split interest gift. 26 U.S.C. § 170(f)(3). But as the making of the art loan is generally not

seen as giving rise to income for the lender, the practical consequence is that while there is no income tax benefit, neither is there an income tax detriment. Could one argue on a theoretical level that a museum's reimbursement to the lender for insurance costs is income to the lender?

It is a different scenario for federal gift tax purposes. The making of an art loan is a transfer of property by gift, which would subject the art loan to federal gift tax. 26 U.S.C. § 2501. The normal gift tax charitable deduction does not apply because of the split interest rules—the same reason the income tax charitable deduction was denied. 26 U.S.C. § 2522(c)(2). Congress however addressed this taxable dilemma for donors of art loans by enacting a special exclusion from gift tax for certain loans of artwork. If the loan is of "any archeological, historic or creative tangible personal property" to an entity exempt from federal taxation and the use of the loaned property is related to the entity's purpose or function (such as a museum), then the loan shall not be treated as a transfer subject to federal gift tax. 26 U.S.C. § 2503(g). Thus, this exclusion from gift tax for certain art loans effectively means there is no gift tax liability for qualifying art loans.

For a foreign lender (nonresident, not a U.S. citizen) of artworks on loan to a public gallery or U.S. museum for exhibition purposes, there is an estate tax provision exempting such property from the U.S. estate tax should the foreign lender die during the course of the loan. 26 U.S.C. § 2105(c). See Priv. Ltr. Rul. 9141014 (Oct. 11, 1991) for a determination by the I.R.S. that a foreign lender of 65 artworks to a U.S. public museum can qualify for the exemption even though (i) the works rotate so that only 40% of the works are on display at any one time ("we consider the whole collection to be on exhibition for purposes of section 2105(c)") and (ii) two of the works were purchased in the U.S. and immediately loaned to the museum ("section 2105(i) does not depend upon the fulfillment of a useless act such as exporting the 2 items and then importing them back into the U.S."). Compare this approach with the federal Immunity from Seizure Act, which does seem to require the "useless" act. Context matters.

Fourth Drafting Exercise: Art Loan Agreement

To: Junior Associate

From: Senior Partner

Our client Mr. Smith was approached by the President of his alma mater to participate in a special exhibition to be organized by the University's Museum. The exhibition will coincide with the University Museum's 100th anniversary next year, and is intended to highlight the artistic works of its students and faculty over that 100 years.

As it happens, Mr. Smith's personal art collection includes three works that might be of interest to the Museum, and his company's art collection has one significant work that would presumably be of great interest. The total value of those works in his private collection is about $50X and for the one work in the Smith Co. collection the value is $200X. He and the company carry fine arts coverage in those full amounts.

Mr. Smith is inclined to participate—he has great appreciation for his University education and is a loyal financial supporter of his University. He has no concern about the Museum's facility. It has a state-of-the-art gallery in terms of lighting, temperature and humidity controls. He is somewhat concerned about the Museum's ability to provide beefed-up security for this special exhibit, and he has spoken directly and frankly to the President and Museum Director. They assured him that during the 100th anniversary exhibition, the museum will hire experienced, professional security guards, and not rely primarily on work study students.

All of the works are in good condition and travel worthy. The special exhibit is scheduled for a full academic year, September 1st through May 31st. The President and Museum Director indicated that most of the special events will take place in the fall, so a loan for the fall only would definitely be acceptable. Mr. Smith prefers this option, perhaps with the possibility to extend at his discretion.

The three works (two drawings, and one small sculpture) in Mr. Smith's personal collection were all by a well-known professor/artist who died in the early 1960s. The relevant work in the Smith Co. collection is an 8-foot tall metal sculpture from the mid-1990s by a well-known, living American artist.

The University Museum does not have a useable art loan agreement for this purpose. Please draft for my review an art loan agreement that protects Mr. Smith, but is not overly onerous in terms of the University Museum's obligations. Knowing my client, he'll probably end up also making a significant contribution to the Museum's 100th anniversary campaign . . . which hasn't been announced, but I'm sure it's coming!

Mr. Smith will probably just continue his own insurance coverage, but better doublecheck his natural disaster type coverage, because the University Museum is in an earthquake prone area, far from Mr. Smith's home and Smith Co.'s operations in State X, which is more susceptible to hurricanes. Again, please give me a heads up on any non-obvious assumptions you make and on anything you think we should particularly alert Mr. Smith (or Smith Co.) to for this art loan.

Part Three

Disposition

Ownership is not forever. At some point, a collector's ownership of an artwork will end. The disposition of that artwork has two primary parameters for the owner—the time of disposition (during life or at death) and whether the owner will receive consideration for the artwork (a sale or exchange as opposed to a gift or bequest). The disposition of an artwork is, of course, the flip side of its acquisition. Like artistic perspective, the legal landscape can appear quite different depending on where you are standing.

Chapter 9 concerns dispositions involving consideration, generally sales through dealers and auction houses. Chapter 10 focuses on dispositions without consideration, introducing gratuitous transfers to charitable and non-charitable beneficiaries, during life and at death. Chapter 11 concludes with the important topic of valuation.

Chapter 9

Sales and Exchanges

Once the decision to dispose of an artwork is made, the next decision is whether to use a dealer or to sell at auction. Personal and business judgment and experience normally guide the seller in choosing the venue the seller deems most appropriate for the artwork at the time.

The chapter begins with the dealer transaction, highlighting its distinctive legal need for the seller to plan for protecting the artwork from the possible claims of the dealer's creditors or from the dealer's misdeeds. Consignment agreements, the documentary evidence of the seller and dealer or auction house, are next considered. The chapter concludes with a brief overview of exchanges involving art as an alternative to a traditional sale.

A. Disposition through a Dealer

1. The Problem of a Dealer's Creditors

After deciding to sell, the owner must decide where—through a dealer or at auction? In either case, the owner should sign a consignment agreement with the dealer or auction house. A consignment occurs when a seller (the "consignor") delivers goods to another (the "consignee") to hold for sale to a third party. This should sound familiar, as a consignment is a bailment that creates a specialized agency relationship.

Using a dealer is considered by many collectors to be private, discrete, more lucrative, faster, and subject to more control by the seller than an auction. There is no hard-and-fast rule governing the choice of marketing venue. Dealer and auction houses are both recognized as legitimate and viable venues. The decision is based on many facts and circumstances that a seller will weigh with due diligence. Regardless of the decision, a consignment agreement will document the terms and conditions of the arrangement. The consignment agreement is often a form agreement provided by the dealer or auction house. For many sellers, their focus is on the most basic of terms: the sales price on the one hand, and the expenses and commission on the other.

There is, however, an extra factor that needs to be considered if the decision is made to sell through a dealer. It is the potential, but very serious, problem of a dealer's creditors or others laying claim to the consigned artwork while in the dealer's possession. *Haley & Steele* and *Kraken* are cautionary tales of what can go wrong in a dealer consignment. They serve as reminders that a lawyer needs to think beyond the client's immediate transaction and protect the client's interests and property from the claims of third parties.

In the Matter of Haley & Steele, Inc.

20 Mass. L. Rptr. 204, 2005 WL 3489869 (Super. Ct. 2005)

Van Gestel, J.

* * *

Background

... [T]he issue ... involves the sorting out of rights between and among individuals ensnared in the fraud flowing from the failure of Haley & Steele, Inc. ("Haley & Steele"), a Newbury Street art dealership. A substantial amount of valuable artwork ... was seized by Century Bank & Trust Co. (the "Bank") as a primary secured creditor of Haley & Steele.

... [T]he Court appointed Camille F. Sarrouf, Esquire, as a Special Master.... In [his] report, Mr. Sarrouf ... established and identified five categories of claimants: (1) bailors; (2) bona fide purchasers; (3) consumer consignors; (4) commercial consignors; and (5) parties who did not fall within any of the foregoing categories. It is the rights of those individuals characterized as consumer consignors, as opposed to general creditors, of Haley & Steele that are in issue here.

Individual customers of Haley & Steele delivered artwork, called "consigned goods," for purposes of sale pursuant to documents entitled "consignment agreements." Generally, these consignment agreements gave Haley & Steele the right to keep the artwork for various periods of time and to sell the artwork at usually agreed-upon amounts for agreed-upon commissions. Haley & Steele also undertook and was obliged under the consignment agreements to care for, insure and handle the artwork.

Discussion

* * *

In the 1999 amendments to the Uniform Commercial Code, G.L.c. 106, sec. 2-326 was rewritten, as were parts of Article 9 .... [Section] 2-326 now reads as follows:

> (1) Unless otherwise agreed, if delivered goods may be returned by the buyer even though they conform to the contract, the transaction is
>
> (a) a "sale on approval" if the goods are delivered primarily for use, and
>
> (b) a "sale or return" if the goods are delivered primarily for resale.
>
> (2) Goods held on approval are not subject to the claims of the buyer's creditors until acceptance; goods held on sale or return are subject to such claims while in the buyer's possession.

(3) Any "or return" term of a contract for sale is to be treated as a separate contract for sale within the statute of frauds section of this Article (Section 2-201) and as contradicting the sale aspect of the contract within the provisions of this Article on parole or extrinsic evidence (Section 2-202).

Some of the creditors of Haley & Steele advocate for the application of sec. 2-326 to that artwork that was delivered to Haley & Steele which falls outside the definition of "consignment" contained in Article 9 of the Uniform Commercial Code. Others . . . contend that consignments of consumer goods are not considered Article 9 consignments, citing to the definitions in sec. 9-102(20). Sec. 9-102(20) reads as follows:

(20) "Consignment" means a transaction, regardless of its form, in which a person delivers goods to a merchant for the purpose of sale and:

(A) The merchant:

(i) deals in goods of that kind under a name other than the name of the person making delivery;

(ii) is not an auctioneer; and

(iii) is not generally known by its creditors to be substantially engaged in selling the goods of others;

(B) with respect to each delivery, the aggregate value of the goods is $1,000 or more at the time of delivery;

(C) the goods are not consumer goods immediately before delivery; and

(D) the transaction does not create a security interest that secures an obligation.

Sec. 9-102(23) defines "consumer goods" to mean "goods that are used or bought for use primarily for personal, family, or household purposes."

This Court concludes, and rules, that to the extent that those persons listed in the Special Master's Fifth Report as "consumer consignors"-as opposed to "commercial consignors"-are persons whose goods consisted of artwork that was used or bought for use primarily for personal, family, or household purposes immediately before delivery to Haley & Steele, then their artwork falls outside of the "consignment" defined in sec. 9-102(20).

This conclusion results from a reading of the plain language of the statute, which is, of course, the Court's obligation. . . .

This Court is persuaded by the logic of the argument that a typical consumer depositor of artwork with a consignee like Haley & Steele should not be required to comply with the complexities of secured lending under Article 9 of the Uniform Commercial Code in order to have protection from Haley & Steele's general creditors. That being said, however, do the mandates of sec. 2-326 come into play when there is a consumer consignment that is not covered by Article 9? In other words, are these consumer consignments a "sale or return" as defined in sec. 2.326(1)(b), and, if so, do they become subject to the claims of Haley & Steele's general creditors while in Haley & Steele's possession?

Certainly, prior to the 2001 amendments, sec. 2-326 appears to have reached consignments of the kind here discussed. See subsection (3) of the former sec. 2-326.

However, any comparison of the statutory language before and after the 2001 amendments make clear that subsection (3) has been significantly rewritten, and any reference to consignments has been wholly removed. This Court considers that something that it cannot ignore and should not presume was unintentional on the part of the Legislature.

In this context, it does not pass unnoticed that Article 2 covers "Sales." The Article is "limited to those [agreements] relating to the present or future sale of goods." "A 'sale' consists in the passing of title from the seller to the buyer for a price (section 2.401)." Sec. 2-106(1). Sec. 2-401 makes it clear that title to goods passes from the seller to the buyer in any manner and on any conditions explicitly agreed upon by the parties.

In the typical Haley & Steele "Art Consignment Agreement," there is specific language to the effect that "title to each of the Artworks remains in the Consignor until the Consignor has been paid," or there is reference "to the following item of *your* property" (emphasis added), the latter implying that title will not pass until a certain designated "Minimum Retail Price" is obtained. Under either arrangement, it is clear that title is not expected to pass from the consignor to Haley & Steele, but rather, with the assistance of Haley & Steele, title will pass from the consignor to the ultimate purchaser upon payment of an appropriate retail price to the consignor and a commission to Haley & Steele.

To characterize a consignment as a sale or return, the Court must be able to conclude that there was a "present sale" of the consigned goods. Sec. 2-326 requires a sale. Title must be delivered to a buyer, which is not what happens when goods pass from a consignor to a consignee. See, e.g., *Goss v. Morgansen's Ltd. (In re Morgansen's Ltd.)*, 2005 WL 2370856 at *9.

In Comment 4 to the amended sec. 2-326, it is said that "[c]ertain true consignment transactions were dealt with in the former Sections 2-326(3) and 9-114. These provisions have been deleted and have been replaced by new provisions of Article 9." Respected commentators James J. White and Robert S. Summers, in 4 Uniform Commercial Code at 38 (5th ed.), posit that "[i]t is unlikely that the drafters wished to leave the consumer consignor worse off than a commercial consignor, yet that would be the outcome if consumer consignments (now excluded from Article 9) are governed by 2-326."

In the present absence of any Uniform Commercial Code regulation, consumer consignments are now governed, once again, by the common law. This, then, is essentially the law of bailments. . . .

> The law of bailment is a special branch of jurisprudence under the common law. It is founded upon express or implied contract between the parties.

> The delivery of a chattel in bailment, apart from specific stipulation, confers on the bailee the right to use and enjoy possession free from control by the bailor, subject to the obligation to do so with care, with due regard to its nature and characteristics and its preservation in safety, and to return it in good order barring unavoidable casualties at the expiration of the bailment. *The general title remains with the bailor; the bailee maintains a special interest for the purposes of the bailment.* (Emphasis added.) *Nash v. Lang*, 268 Mass. 407, 414 (1929). See also *King v. Trustees of Boston University*, 420 Mass. 52, 59–60 (1995).

Conclusion

Based upon the law as discussed and interpreted above, this Court rules that evidentiary findings by the Special Master, as included in his Fifth Report, that certain consignors are "consumer consignors" are adequate, without more, if grounded upon the fact that the artwork in issue was, immediately before its delivery to Haley & Steele, consumer goods.

Kraken Investments Limited v. Jacobs (In re Salander-O'Reilly Galleries, LLC, Debtor)

2014 WL 7389901 (S.D.N.Y. 2014)

BRICCETTI, District Judge.

* * *

Background

On March 17, 2010, Lawrence Salander, owner and manager of Salander–O'Reilly Galleries, LLC ("SOG" or "Debtor"), an art gallery in New York City, pleaded guilty to scheming to defraud SOG's investors and consignors. Prior to Salander's plea . . . creditors commenced an involuntary Chapter 7 bankruptcy proceeding against SOG . . . later converted to a voluntary Chapter 11 case (the "Bankruptcy Case").

Prior to the bankruptcy petition, two events relevant to the instant appeal occurred. First, SOG borrowed approximately $29 million from First Republic Bank (the "Bank"), secured by SOG's assets, pursuant to a loan agreement (the "Loan Agreement"). Second, Kraken, owner of a painting by Sandro Botticelli entitled *Madonna and Child* (the "Botticelli"), consigned the Botticelli to SOG, with an asking price of $9.5 million. . . . If successful, SOG would receive a commission of $1 million. The painting was not sold, and the consignment expired in or about June 2007, prior to the commencement of the Bankruptcy Case.

After Salander's fraudulent scheme was uncovered and it became apparent SOG would be unable to meet its obligations, numerous parties asserted claims of ownership to thousands of pieces of art in SOG's possession. Kraken was one such party. . . .

To resolve disputed claims to artwork in a fair and efficient manner, the Bankruptcy Court established a protocol to determine which works were property of SOG's estate (the "Protocol"). . . . The Protocol required parties asserting ownership in artwork to file an "Art Claim" . . . . On May 28, 2014, Kraken filed an Art Claim asserting its ownership interest in the Botticelli. Kraken also filed a Proof of Claim for $9.5 million, assigned Claim No. 289, on July 17, 2008.

* * *

Upon evaluating Kraken's Art Claim and Claim No. 289, the working group determined the Botticelli was not a "non-estate asset." Kraken promptly requested non-binding mediation—the only remedy available to it under the Protocol—disputing the working group's finding. After several mediation sessions, the discussions reached an impasse. . . . [T]he Bankruptcy Court ordered the claims dispute to proceed as an adversary proceeding. . . .

* * *

On March 21, 2014, the Bankruptcy Court denied both [parties' summary judgment] motions, and Kraken now appeals from the denial of its motion. . . .

Discussion

* * *

II. Interpretation of the Loan Agreement

Sections 6.1 and 6.2 of the Loan Agreement are those pertinent to the instant appeal. Section 6.1 states:

> *Security Interest.* (a) To secure the payment and performance of all Obligations of the Borrower to the Bank, the Borrower hereby grants to the Bank a continuing security interest in the following properties, assets and rights of the Borrower, wherever located, whether now owned or hereafter acquired or arising, and all proceeds and products thereof (all of the same being hereinafter called the "Collateral"): all personal and fixture property of every kind and nature including without limitation all goods (including inventory, equipment and any accessions thereto). . . .

Section 6.2 states:

> *Status of the Collateral.* With respect to Collateral at the time the Collateral becomes subject to the Bank's security interest, the Borrower represents, warrants and covenants that:
>
> (a) The Borrower shall be the sole owner, free and clear of all liens, claims, security interests and encumbrances. . . .
>
> The failure of any Collateral to fully comply with the provisions of this Section 6.2 shall not affect, terminate, modify, or otherwise limit the Bank's lien or security interest in the Collateral.

The Bankruptcy Court found Section 6.1 "unambiguously grants the Bank a lien" on consigned goods because the security interest provided to the Bank under the Loan Agreement was for "'all personal property . . . of every kind and nature.'" Further, the Bankruptcy Court reasoned Section 6.2 functions as a representations and warranties guarantee that cannot limit "whether or not the Bank's lien attaches to the collateral."

The Court disagrees with the Bankruptcy Court's interpretation of the Loan Agreement. Although the Court agrees the Loan Agreement can mean only one thing, what it plainly means is that the Bank was given a broad security interest in inventory *owned* by the Debtor. As such, the Loan Agreement unambiguously does *not* grant the Bank a lien on consigned artwork.

* * *

The Bankruptcy Court read Section 6.1's grant of a security interest unambiguously to include consigned goods because they are "'personal property . . . of every kind and nature.'" At first glance, this broad grant of interest appears to be just that—broad—and expansive enough to subsume non-owned property, like consigned artwork. However, the Bankruptcy Court failed to consider the language preceding the "all personal and fixture property" clause, which states the security interest is for property "whether now owned or hereafter acquired or arising." The plain meaning of this language demonstrates the Bank was given a lien in all personal property, "of every kind and nature," *owned* or thereafter *owned* by SOG. If the property is not *owned* by SOG, it cannot be Collateral for the loan.

It is undisputed Kraken owns the Botticelli. It is undisputed the consignment agreement did not alter Kraken's ownership interest. It is undisputed the Botticelli was never "owned" or "acquired" by SOG. Thus, while the Bank was given an ample security interest in order to secure its loan, the Botticelli was not included in the definition of Collateral by the contract's terms. Section 6.1 unambiguously defines Collateral as property owned by SOG, and consigned artwork, by its very nature, is owned by its owner, not the consignee.

Additionally, the Bankruptcy Court found Section 6.2 supports its conclusion that Collateral includes consigned artwork because any other reading would be a limitation of Section 6.1 and in clear contravention of the last paragraph of Section 6.2. Although the Bankruptcy Court's interpretation of Section 6.2's function was correct, Section 6.2's required representations and warranties actually reinforces the exclusion of consigned artwork from the definition of Collateral. To read Section 6.2 any other way would ignore the intent of the parties.

The Bankruptcy Court correctly found Section 6.2 "imposes a requirement on the Debtor to make certain representations and warranties to the Bank without limiting whether or not the Bank's lien attaches to the collateral." Section 6.2 serves an important function, and allows the Bank to pursue a breach of warranty claim against the Debtor while maintaining the broad grant of security interest established in Section 6.1. But, Section 6.2 only requires SOG to make representations and warranties regarding Collateral, which, as already established by the clear and plain language of Section 6.1, does not include consigned artwork.

Further, Section 6.2 would make no sense if, as the Bankruptcy Court suggested, the definition of Collateral included consigned artwork. It would be illogical to require SOG to make ownership representations if the Bank's security interest attached to all property, indiscriminate of actual ownership, because while representing it was the "sole owner," SOG would be fully aware that was not true. The parties did not intend to impose a lien on property that did not meet the definition of Collateral under Section 6.1, and therefore, Section 6.2 functions to deter false representations and needless disputes in which a lien would ultimately be found to be invalid because, for example, it attached to un-owned property. Thus, while the Court agrees Section 6.2 serves the function the Bankruptcy Court identified, that function only makes sense if the definition of Collateral does not include consigned artwork.

The last paragraph of Section 6.2 does not nullify this analysis. The Bank's security interest in un-owned property cannot be irrefutably established merely because SOG failed to "fully comply" with the representation requirements of Section 6.2. That reading suggests SOG's simple statement it is the "sole owner" transforms un-owned property into Collateral under the Loan Agreement. Rather, the Bank's security interest in *Collateral* is irrefutably established even if SOG does not comply fully with Section 6.2's requirements.

* * *

The Court need not address the parties' arguments regarding the Protocol, as a correct interpretation of the Loan Agreement serves as a basis for the reversal of the Order below.... Kraken's ownership right to the Botticelli is unambiguous under the Loan Agreement, and the Protocol does not infringe on this right.

Conclusion

The Order of the Bankruptcy Court is REVERSED.

Notes and Questions

1. *Aftermath.* Haley & Steele was an arts institution in Boston for more than a century. Its abrupt closing surprised the arts community. Because the Commonwealth of Massachusetts consigned certain valuable Paul Revere prints to Haley & Steele, greater attention and publicity ensued. One consequence was the amendment of Massachusetts' Consignment of Fine Art Law to extend its protection to non-artist consignors. MASS. GEN. LAW, Ch. 104A, § 1. See Brenda Ulrich & Shannon Jamieson, *Muddled Waters: An Addendum on the Consignment of Fine Art Law in Massachusetts*, 37 J. ARTS MGMT, L. & SOC. 301 (2008). See Note 6, Artist Consignment Statutes, *infra*.

The Botticelli painting at issue in *Kraken* was returned shortly after the court's decision. The owners hoped this "landmark case" would help future art consignors "who cannot spend $2 million on litigation and seven years in court." Eileen

Kinsella, *7 Year Legal Battle Returns Seized $10 Million Botticelli Painting*, ARTNET-NEWS, Dec. 9, 2014, at https://news.artnet.com/market/7-year-legal-battle-returns-seized-10-million-botticelli-painting-193092. Their hope may not be realized. See Note 2, *infra*.

2. *Rewriting Loan Agreements.* Commercial lenders and their lawyers viewed *Kraken* very differently from those in the art world. From their perspective, the decision was "surprising" given that the language in the loan agreement was "fairly common." Drafting Matters, 51 No. 10 U.C.C. Law Letter NL3 (2017). Consequently, loan agreements should be "updated in response to [the decision] . . . interpreting a blanket security agreement as limited to property owned by the Debtor." For example, one suggestion is to add language specifically concerning consignments, such as, "including any such collateral hereafter consigned to the Debtor or in which the Debtor acquires rights or the power to convey rights." *After-Acquired Property Clause, §9.2.2.1 Form 2*, Unif. Laws Anno. U.C.C. Forms and Materials (2015). See also Stephen L. Sepinuck, *Collateralizing What the Debtor Does Not Own*, TRANSACTIONAL L., Feb. 2015, at 2.

The transactional takeaway remains the same: consignors should file the UCC-1 Financing Statement to perfect their security interest—in their own property—for bankruptcy purposes of the dealer-consignee.

3. *UCC and Consignments—A Brief History.* In *Haley & Steele*, the judge noted the significant changes to consignment law brought about by the 1999 amendments to Article 9 of the UCC. He concluded a true consignment of consumer goods was now outside the scope of the UCC for purposes of protecting the consignor's property from the claims of the consignee's creditors. The proverbial page of history will be instructive in understanding the interplay of consignments with the UCC and common law.

Prior to the 1999 amendments, consignments were governed under both Article 9 Secured Transactions and Article 2 Sales. This duality caused confusion and uncertainty to consignors (who wished to protect their ownership in the consigned property) and to the consignee's creditors (who wished to satisfy their claims from the consignee and property in its possession). Pre-revision §2-326 provided most of the UCC law on consignments. In general, pre-revision §2-326 subordinated the consignor's interest to the rights of the consignee's creditors, unless the consignor could satisfy one of three exceptions. The first and most important was to prove the consignee was "generally known by his creditors to be substantially engaged in selling the goods of others." The second was to show compliance with signage requirements. The third was to have formally filed a financing statement under Article 9. The second and third exceptions were not especially helpful to consumers. Signage requirements under local law were generally nonexistent, effectively negating §2-326's second exception. As for the third exception, because most consumers do not know about, let alone file, an Article 9 financing statement, the exception rang hollow for consumers. Consequently, in the event the consignee became insolvent, filed for bankruptcy, or pledged the consigned property as collateral for a loan, the consumer consignor was left to prove the "generally known" exception in order to fully retain his property. Consumers were overwhelmingly unsuccessful in their attempts to do so. For example, establishing the art industry norm that most art dealers include works on consignment in their galleries was not sufficient. One needs to particularize the proof to that dealer's creditors, and do so by number of creditors, not by the size of their claims. Moreover, the consumer consignor also had to establish the substantiality of the dealer's consignments in comparison to other sources of the dealer's inventory. Not many individual art consignors would have the resources or persistence to uncover the necessary facts to identify the consignee's creditors, to formally establish how many of them knew the consignee sold goods belonging to others, and then to prove that the consignments were a substantial portion of the consignee's business. Notice there was no incentive for the consignee or its creditors to cooperate with the consignor in proving the "generally known" exception. The individual consignor faced a daunting uphill battle under pre-revision § 2-326 to protect her consigned property from the seemingly preferred claims of the consignee's creditors. This practical, if not structural, unevenness of consumers' and creditors' positions under § 2-326 helps explain the climate for the 1999 revisions.

In the 1999 revisions to Article 9 and Article 2, the drafters removed mention of consignments from UCC § 2-326 and provided a new definition of "consignment" in UCC § 9-102(a)(20) as set forth in *Haley & Steele*. For consignments covered by § 9-102(a)(20), the legal consequences follow the UCC. The consignment is deemed a security interest, the consignor is treated as a secured party, the consignee as a debtor, and the consigned property as collateral. If the consignor does *not* perfect the consignor's security interest, then Article 9 treats the consignee as having sufficient rights in the consigned property to allow the consignee to give a security interest to a third party. That third party may perfect the security interest, which in turn gives the third party rights superior to the consignor-owner. Steve Weise & Stephen L. Sepinuck, *Personal Property Secured Transactions*, 70 Bus. Law. 1243, 1245–46 (2015). See also In re TSAWD Holdings, 565 B.R. 292, 303–04 (Bkrtcy. D. Del. 2017), declining to extend *Kraken* because the decision rested on contract law and not the UCC.

The most common form of perfecting a security interest is by filing a standardized Form UCC-1 Financing Statement in the state in which the consignee-dealer is located. The two other methods of perfecting one's interest are by taking possession and perfecting an attachment. UCC § 9-308(a). Thus, if the consignment of the artwork falls within the definitional ambit of UCC § 9-102(a)(20) (for example, artwork held as investment property), it is clear that the consignor must take the additional step of perfecting its interest. Filing a Form UCC-1 Financing Statement will protect the property from the consignee's creditors. There is no longer a requirement that the consignee sign the Form UCC-1 as long as the consignee agrees to the filing, which can be provided for in the consignment agreement. Similarly, the consignee should be required to notify its secured creditors.

4. *The Puzzle of Non-Article 9 Consignments.* If a consignment does not fall within the revised UCC § 9-102(a)(20)'s definition of a consignment, there is some confusion regarding the consignor's and consignee's recourse in the event of a consignee's failure. "Exactly where consignees of this (non-Article 9 consignment) stand is not entirely clear." See James J. White & Robert S. Summers, 4 UNIFORM COMMERCIAL CODE 37 (5th ed. 2002). Some suggest revising the UCC to create separate treatment of consignment law to reduce the uncertainty. See Willa Gibson, *Untangling the Web of Consignment Law: The Journey from the Common Law & Article 2 to Revised Article 9*, 10 WM. & MARY BUS. L. REV. 413 (2019).

If the consignment is not an Article 9 consignment, does revised UCC § 2-326 retain any relevance? Or are such consignments completely removed from the UCC? *Kraken* sidestepped this issue by holding the Lender's Agreement definition of collateral did not include consigned artwork. *Haley & Steele*, however, clearly answered this question. It held that the common law, not UCC, governs. Other courts agreed. See In re Music City RV, LLC, 304 S.W.3d 806 (Tenn. 2010), where the Tennessee Supreme Court unanimously held (in response to a certified question from the U.S. Bankruptcy Court) that the consignment of an RV by a consumer to an auto dealership, for the purpose of selling to a third party, is not a transaction covered by Tennessee's UCC § 2-326. Also Mackela v. Bentley, 614 S.E.2d 648 (S.C. App. 2005), which found that a minivan was a consumer good not a consignment item under § 9-102(a)(20) and therefore not collateral for the auto dealership's creditor. But In re Morgansen's Ltd., 302 B.R. 784 (E.D.N.Y. 2003), aff'd in part, remanded in part, 2005 WL 2370856 (E.D.N.Y. 2005), took a different approach to these so-called orphan consignments.

Morgansen's was in the business of selling various expensive items, including artworks, at its shop in Southampton, New York, to retail customers, interior designers, and other dealers. Approximately 70% of the items in its shop were on consignment. From time to time, Morgansen's would conduct auction sales of its inventory, and there was signage to that effect. Unfortunately, the business was not successful, and Morgansen's eventually filed for bankruptcy. The trustee in bankruptcy proposed that an auction sale be conducted of all items in Morgansen's possession, and various "alleged consignors" protested. None, apparently, had filed any UCC financing statements. The Bankruptcy Court approved the sale over the consignors' objections.

The Bankruptcy Court deemed its approach "standard":

> The law of consignments is governed by the Uniform Commercial Code (UCC) especially sections UCC 9-102(a)(20) and next UCC 2-326, as amended.... The standard approach is first to go to Section 9-102(a)(20), and if the transaction does not fit under this section, then to go next to Section 2-326; if the transaction does not fit under Section 2-326, then the transaction falls entirely outside the Uniform Commercial Code, and the Court must then fall back on the common law of bailments and other traditional practices.

302 B.R. 784, 787.

While the approach may be standard (see James J. White & Robert S. Summers, 4 Uniform Commercial Code 37 (5th ed. 2002); G. Ray Warner, *Consigned to Confusion: Consignments under Revised Article 9*, 20-Jan Am. Bankr. Inst. J. 30 (2002); Raymond W. Dusch, *Court Negates UCC Article 9 Consignment Law Improvements* (2004) (available at http://www.allbusiness.com/finance/941245-1.html), the court's application of these revised sections to the facts is confusing and unsatisfactory. The consumer consignors argued that Morgansen's was an auctioneer and thus not a merchant for purposes of § 9-102(20)'s consignment definition. The court rejected the argument, because the consignors did not present evidence as to the size or frequency of auctions held by Morgansen's nor cite any authority as to the meaning of "auctioneer" when an entity does both sales and auctions. The court also rejected the "generally known" argument determining that the outside sign indicating auctions and the "personal knowledge of a few protesting consignors does not satisfy their burden of proof." The court decided that no further analysis of § 9-102(a)(20) was required (there was *no* discussion regarding the status of the property as consumer goods) and it moved to § 2-326. It deemed that section dispositive: "The law is painfully clear—anybody who delivers goods with a 'right of return' to a merchant who sells them under its own name is at risk that the merchant may file for bankruptcy relief, and the trustee will liquidate the goods for the benefit of the creditors." Finally, the court determined that the relationship between Morgansen's and its consignors "was clearly not a bailment."

Two years later and after the auction had occurred, the case was appealed. On appeal, the District Court agreed with the Bankruptcy Court's decision that this was not an Article 9 consignment. With respect to § 2-326, the District Court noted that non-Article 9 consignments may be covered by Article 2; but ultimately remanded to determine if Morgansen's was a "buyer" for purposes of UCC § 2-326. Under UCC § 1-103, a "buyer" is a "person who buys or contracts to buy goods." See In re Morgansen's Ltd., 2005 W.L. 2370856 (E.D.N.Y. 2005). See also G. Ray Warner, *Consigned to Confusion: Consignments Under Revised Article 9*, 20—Jan. Am. Bankr. Ints. J. 30, 31, n. 7 ("This change may cause confusion for two reasons. First, many attorneys are used to thinking of consignments as sale-or-return transactions. Second, the correct reading of revised § 2-326 requires that great emphasis be placed on its use of the term 'buyer,' and a casual reader may not realize that the term excludes a 'consignee.'").

5. *Consignment of Art—Developing a Matrix.* The confusion generated by the 1999 revisions to the UCC consignment provisions and the divergent court interpretations as to their scope increases the need for a lawyer's measured response in planning for the consignment of an artwork. In order to determine when the filing of a UCC-1 Financing Statement is necessary or merely advisable, a matrix approach can be helpful. Revised UCC § 9-102(a)(20) defines consignment for our purposes with two main variables: the merchant and the property. The consignor is a modest third variable.

To be a merchant under § 9-102(a)(20) requires three things. First, the merchant must deal in goods of that kind under a name other than the consignor's name. Second, the merchant must not be an auctioneer. Third, the merchant is not generally known by its creditors to be substantially engaged in selling other people's goods. Taking all three together, one sees the glimmer of a UCC position: protecting the merchant's creditors who apparently could be misled into advancing funds by the appearance of a full "inventory." If the merchant is an auctioneer, on the other hand, its creditors should automatically be on notice because of the inherent nature of an auction and an auctioneer's "inventory." The auctioneer requirement would seem to be objective, and with slightly more than half of states licensing auctioneers, and some cities (e.g., New York) also having licensing requirements, presumably, one's license would be de facto evidence of status. For jurisdictions without a licensing requirement, when the Bankruptcy Judge was faced with a dual functioning entity, the judge determined that it was not sufficiently proven to be an auctioneer. These three merchant requirements, therefore, create a clear divide for the art consignment agreement—dealers or galleries will most likely be deemed merchants, while recognized auction houses are clearly not merchants.

There are also three property requirements. First, the property delivered by the consignor to the merchant must be of like kind to the property in which the merchant deals. Second, the aggregate value per delivery must be $1,000 or more. Third, the goods cannot be consumer goods "immediately before delivery." The property's like kind requirement overlaps with the merchant requirement, thereby sharing the apparent creditor notice concern. A Picasso for sale at an art gallery would not raise a concern for gallery creditors, while a Picasso for sale at an auto dealership should naturally raise a question for the auto dealership's creditors. The $1,000 is a de minimus line, and consumer goods are excepted. Taking these three attributes together, the focus on the commercial and business nature of the goods is unmistakable, with small amounts and consumer goods falling outside its scope.

The consumer goods exception appears to be pro-consignor, but caution is necessary in the art context. UCC § 9-102(a)(23) defines consumer goods as "goods that are used or bought for use primarily for personal, family, or household purposes." Is an artwork per se a consumer good? That answer is clearly no. Who the owner is and how the work was used "immediately before delivery" are critical questions. The answers may be hazy.

If the owner-consignor is a business entity, perhaps a family limited partnership (even if the artwork is on display at family member's home), it would be hard to argue consistent with the partnership's documentation that the artwork is a consumer good. On the other hand, the mere status of an owner-consignor as an individual collector does not resolve the inquiry. What if the individual collector is collecting for investment purposes, his personal investment purposes? What if the artwork was originally bought primarily for personal use, but over time, the collector began to value its investment potential? What if the artwork was on loan at a museum "immediately before delivery" to the dealer? What if the owner-consignor is a guardian or fiduciary for an adult with dementia who is now moving to a nursing facility? As a transactional lawyer, you should assume the merchant's creditors will resist attempts to categorize valuable artwork as a consumer good "immediately before delivery." This creates the second divide for art consignments. Consignments by individual owners of artworks from their homes that they have never categorized as investment or portfolio property for any purpose (e.g., tax or financing) are most likely consumer goods; anything short of that raises definitional questions.

With these two divides established, a matrix for art consignment under UCC § 9-102(a)(20) emerges:

	Consumer Good	Not a Consumer Good
On Consignment with Dealer	Non-Article 9 Consignment	Article 9 Consignment
With Auction House	Non-Article 9 Consignment	Non-Article 9 Consignment

The consequence here for Article 9 consignments is clear and straightforward—file a UCC-1 financing statement so that the dealer's creditors have notice and the client's artwork is protected from the dealer's creditors. The consequence for the Non-Article 9 consignment is uncertain, as it places us squarely within the confusion over the applicability of the particular state's UCC § 2-326. In those jurisdictions that apply UCC § 2-326 to the Non-Article 9 consignments (e.g., apparently New York under *Morgansen's*), the answer is file a financing statement. In those jurisdictions that do not apply UCC § 2-326 (e.g., Massachusetts under *Haley & Steele*), the state's common law of bailment or agency is most likely applicable and filing is generally not required. The hard question is what to do in the majority of states that have not addressed the question. Until a state answers that question, a protective filing may be the most cautious approach.

6. *Artist Consignment Statutes.* More than 30 states have enacted special statutes concerning artists consigning their work to dealers for sale.* The thrust of these statutes is to protect artist consignors, generally by categorizing the artist-dealer

---

* Alaska Stat. § 45.65.200 (2020); Ariz. Rev. Stat. Ann. § 44-1772 (2021); Ark. Code Ann. § 4-73-207 (2020); Cal. Civ. Code § 1738.6 (2021); Colo. Rev. Stat. § 6-15-102 (2021); Conn. Gen. Stat. Ann. § 42-116K (2020); Fla. Stat. Ann. § 686.503 (2020); Ga. Code Ann. §§ 10-1-520 to -529 (2020); Idaho Code Ann. § 28-11-102 (2021); 815 ILCS 320/0.01 (2020); Iowa Code Ann. §§ 556D.2-.5 (2021); Ky. Rev. Stat. Ann. §§ 365.855-.860 (2021); La. Rev. Stat. Ann. § 51:2151 (2020); Md. Code Ann., Com. Law §§ 11-8a-01 to -04 (2021); Mass. Ann. Laws ch. 104A, §§ 1-6 (2021); Mich. Comp. Laws Ann. §§ 442.311-.315 (2021); Minn. Stat. Ann. §§ 324.01-.10 (2021); Mo. Ann. Stat. §§ 407.900-.910 (2020); Mont. Code Ann. §§ 22-2-501 to -503 (2020); N.H. Rev. Stat. Ann. §§ 352:3-:12 (2020); N.J. Stat. Ann. §§ 12A:2-329 to -336 (2021); N.M. Stat. Ann. §§ 56-11-1 to -3 (2021); McKinney's Arts & Cult. Aff. Law § 12.01 (2020); N.C. Gen. Stat. Ann. §§ 25C-1 to -4, 25c-12 (2020); Or. Rev. Stat. §§ 359.200-.255 (2020); Pa. Cons. Stat. Ann. Tit. 73§§ 2121-30 (2021); R. I. Laws §§5-62-2 (2020); Tenn. Code Ann. §§ 47-25-1001 to -1006 (2021); Tex.

relationship as a fiduciary one, with the artworks and sales proceeds being deemed trust property. This categorization has legal significance in two respects: it protects the artist in her relationship with the dealer by establishing the legal parameters of that relationship, and by virtue of those parameters, it may serve to protect the artist's works from the dealer's creditors. The equivocation on the second point comes from the failure of many of those statutes to expressly exempt these consignments from the UCC. Section 1–104 of the UCC states no section "shall be deemed to be impliedly repealed by subsequent legislation." As artwork in the hands of the creating artist is not a consumer good "immediately before" its transfer to the dealer, the consignment is most likely an Article 9 consignment. This creates the worst type of whipsaw scenario—an artist relies on the specialized artist consignment statute, and therefore does not file a Form UCC-1 believing it to be unnecessary. There is also an aspect of doctrinal confusion in these statutes as a trust is a fiduciary relationship with a split of title—legal title in the trustee and equitable title in the beneficiary. In a consignment, a fiduciary relationship of principal and agent is created but there is no transfer of legal title. See Lerner & Bresler, 1 ART LAW 39–43 (3d ed. 2005); Tad Crawford & Susan Mellon, THE ARTIST-GALLERY PARTNERSHIP: A PRACTICAL GUIDEBOOK TO CONSIGNING ART 65 (1998). In response to the Salander-O'Reilly Galleries collapse (see Note 2 after *Frigon, infra*), New York amended its artist consignment statute. It strengthens the protection of the trust by requiring creation of trust accounts for sales proceeds, and by providing penalties for violations and a private cause of action with attorney fees. Significantly, the New York law now states that the trust property and trust funds are held in a statutory trust and that no such property shall become the property of the consignee or "be subject or subordinate to any claims, liens or security interest of any kind or nature whatsoever of the consignee's creditors." N.Y. ARTS & CULT. AFF. L. § 12.01-1(a)(v).

2. Recovering for Errant Dealer's Actions: Lawsuits and Insurance Claims

Filing a UCC-1 Financing Statement may protect the consignor's artwork from the claims of the dealer's creditors, but if the dealer sells the work and misappropriates the proceeds, or exchanges the work for another, the consignor's work may be irretrievably gone. See Lindholm v. Brant, 925 A.2d 1048 (Conn. 2007), Chapter 2, *supra*, for the rights of a good faith purchaser for value from an errant dealer under the UCC's entrustment exception. How does one minimize the financial fallout from a dealer's malfeasance? The most direct approach is proceeding against the dealer in contract, tort, or for breach of a fiduciary duty. *Schulhof* took this approach. But suing the dealer may be ineffective as a practical matter. *Frigon* involved another

---

OCC. CODE ANN. §§ 2101.001-.003 (2019); WASH. REV. CODE §§ 18.110.010-.030, 18.110.900 (2021); WIS. STAT. ANN. §§ 129.01-.08 (2020).

approach: filing an insurance claim. It is a novel assertion vigorously contested by the insurance company.

Schulhof v. Jacobs

54 N.Y.S. 3d 613 (N.Y. Sup. Ct. 2017)

Charles E. Ramos, J.

Background

... Mr. Schulhof, a resident of the State of New York, is the executor of the estate of his deceased mother, Mrs. Schulhof....

From 1998 until Mrs. Schulhof's passing on February 23, 2012, Jacobs has worked as a curator and advisor for the art collection owned by Mrs. Schulhof (the "Schulhof Collection"). During this time, Jacobs also ran her own business, Lisa Jacobs Fine Art ("LJFA"), where she bought and sold art and worked as a curator and advisor.

On October 25, 2011, Mr. Schulhof and Jacobs entered into a written agreement ("October Agreement"), wherein Jacobs was to locate a buyer for a painting in the Schulhof Collection entitled "Future Sciences Versus the Man" by Jean-Michel Basquiat (the "Work") for a minimum purchase price of $6 million in exchange for a $50,000 fee....

Pursuant to the October Agreement, Jacobs would receive a $50,000 fee upon commission of a final sale. The October Agreement provided that Jacobs was "*not to accept any fee from the purchaser, in cash or in kind.*" The October Agreement also provided that Defendant was to contact Mr. Schulhof prior to approaching any prospective purchaser. Further, according to the October 2011 Agreement, Jacobs was prohibited from presenting or seeking purchase offers below $6 million without written confirmation of a lower price.

Jacobs alleges that prior to the October Agreement, she and Mrs. Schulhof had entered into a separate agreement that entitled her to receive a "buyers premium." However, Jacobs has not set forth any admissible concrete evidence supporting the existence of this agreement.

On November 1, 2011, Jacobs met with Amy Wolf ("Wolf"), an art dealer, to discuss the sale of the Work. Jacobs informed Wolf that the asking price for the Work was $6.5 million. By November 2, 2011, Jacobs and Wolf reached an agreement for the sale of the Work for $6.5 million....

* * *

On November 7, 2011, Jacobs informed Mr. Schulhof by email that she "was able to get the [buyer] up to 5.5 million. We have a firm deal" ("November Email"). As a result, Mr. Schulhof agreed to accept $5.5 million as the purchase price for the Work. Jacobs suggested that the transaction be structured as a two-step process, stating that the buyer wanted to remain anonymous. Honoring such request,

Mr. Schulhof sold the Work to Jacobs for $5,450,000, and Jacobs was to immediately resell it to Wolf for a purported $5.5 million.

On November 11, 2011, Jacobs executed a contract with Wolf, to sell Wolf the Work for $6,500,000 ("November Agreement"). . . .

After receiving the $6.5 million purchase price from Wolf, Jacobs wired $5,450,000 to Mr. Schulhof on November 16, 2011. It is undisputed that Mr. Schulhof was never informed that Jacobs received a profit of $1 million in connection with the sale of the Work or that the buyer had accepted the $6.5 million offer.

Approximately one year later, Mr. Schulhof discovered that the purchase price for the Work was actually $6.5 million and that Jacobs kept not only her agreed $50,000 but also an additional $1 million from the sale of the Work.

On August 26, 2013, Mr. Schulhof commenced the instant action asserting causes of action for breach of fiduciary duty, fraud, breach of contract, restitution, and unjust enrichment. . . .

* * *

Discussion

* * *

In an action to recover damages for fraud, a plaintiff must establish "a misrepresentation or a material omission of fact which was false and known to be false by defendant, made for the purpose of inducing the other party to rely upon it, justifiable reliance of the other party on the misrepresentation or material omission, and injury.

The record is clear that Jacobs misrepresented that the buyer was only willing to pay $5.5 million for the Work with knowledge that the buyer was actually willing and ready to pay $6.5 million. Mr. Schulhof has sufficiently established that Jacobs made such representations to induce him into accepting the $5.5 million purchase price, and Mr. Schulhof reasonably relied on such representation in deciding to sell the Work. This Court also finds that there is no triable issue of fact as to the damages, as it is clear that Mr. Schulhof was damaged in the amount of approximately $1 million due to Jacobs' fraud. As such, Jacobs's failure to disclose said fact constitutes actionable fraud, entitling Mr. Schulhof to summary judgment in his favor.

The Court also finds that Jacobs misrepresented that the purchase price was for $5.5 million and that she had gotten the confidential buyer "up to" $5.5 million, thereby leading Mr. Schulhof to reasonably believe that Jacobs had pushed the undisclosed buyer as high as she could. Given Jacobs and Mrs. Schulhof's longstanding business relationship combined with the terms of the October Agreement, Jacobs owed a fiduciary duty to Mr. Schulhof as executor, thereby obligating her to disclose the $6.5 million offer prior to entering into the November Agreement.

Furthermore, Jacob's actions and misrepresentations were in direct breach of the October Agreement, which obligated Jacobs to notify Mr. Schulhof of all purchase offers above $6 million and prohibited Jacobs from receiving a fee of any kind from the purchaser, which would include the additional $1 million in commission she fraudulently obtained. Jacobs' failure to abide by the terms of the October Agreement and the resulting damages of $1 million warrants the conclusion that Mr. Schulhof has sufficiently established his breach of contract claim, in the event that it would be necessary for this Court to rule on the contract formation issues. Given our decision on the other causes of action, such determination need not be made.

As to Mr. Schulhof's restitution claim, Jacobs, as a faithless servant, must account to Mr. Schulhof for the $1 million of secret profits earned for the sale of the Work. Additionally, Jacobs' disloyalty to Mr. Schulhof causes her to forfeit the $50,000 in compensation earned for the sale of the Work.

* * *

Accordingly, it is . . .

ORDERED that the clerk of this Court is hereby directed to enter judgment in favor of the plaintiff in the sum of $1,050,000 . . . together with interest from November 16, 2011, costs and disbursements.

Frigon v. Pacific Indemnity Company

2007 WL 756384 (N.D. IL 2007)

GETTLEMAN, J.

* * *

Facts

. . . The Frigons are connoisseurs of fine art and have bought and sold fine art for a number of years. At the heart of this case are eleven paintings owned by the Frigons and insured by defendant under a "Masterpiece Policy". The Policy covered "*all risk* of physical loss to valuable articles [including the eleven paintings] unless stated otherwise or an exclusion applies." (Emphasis in original).

The Frigons purchased the eleven paintings from R.H. Love Galleries in Chicago (the "Gallery"). They had formed a close business and personal relationship with Richard H. Love. . . . As a result of that relationship, the Frigons purchased most of their collection . . . from the Gallery, including the eleven paintings at issue. Periodically, the Frigons would place a painting back with the Gallery for resale under a consignment agreement. Between 1997 and 2002 each of the eleven paintings at issue were placed with the Gallery for sale on consignment pursuant to either a written form consignment agreement provided by the Gallery, or an oral agreement between plaintiffs and the Gallery. Plaintiffs have paid over $1 million for the eleven paintings, which have been consigned for a minimum sale price aggregating $1,600,000.

Unbeknownst to plaintiffs, the Gallery was insolvent and [] to stay afloat the Gallery had begun selling consigned items for less than the minimum agreed price and keeping the proceeds rather than remitting them to the consignors. Among those items "unlawfully" sold by the Gallery were plaintiffs' eleven paintings.... Plaintiffs were not informed of these "sales" and received no payments from the Gallery. Finally, in January 2003, Richard Love told plaintiffs that the highest priced painting, which had been consigned for a minimum sale price of $300,000 in mid-November 2002, had been sold.... In a letter, Love stated that the paintings had been sold on an installment basis with plaintiffs to receive twelve equal installments payments of $36,250 for a total of $435,000. In fact, the painting had been "sold" for a one-time cash payment of $150,000 and a trade for another painting. At the time that Love wrote to plaintiffs, the Gallery had already deposited the $150,000 into its own bank account.

Plaintiffs received two installment payments of $36,250. In the Spring of 2003, after the payments stopped, Henry Frigon became concerned and demanded that all his paintings be returned. [O]n April 8, 2003, Richard Love admitted that all the paintings had been sold, and that the Gallery had spent the proceeds and could not pay plaintiffs the minimum sales price.

On May 2, 2003, plaintiffs made a loss report to defendant. Defendant has denied coverage....

Discussion

The Policy at issue is an "All-Risk" policy which ... means that it covers all causes of physical loss of the insured property, unless specifically excluded. There is no dispute that the paintings at issue are all covered under the Policy and that plaintiffs are no longer in possession of ten of the paintings....

Plaintiffs, as the insureds, have the initial burden of showing the existence of a covered loss. The burden then shifts to the insurer to show an exception to coverage....

Defendant argues initially that plaintiffs cannot establish a covered loss. Specifically, defendant argues that plaintiffs can establish only that the paintings were sold on consignment and that the Gallery has not remitted payment to plaintiffs. Thus, according defendant, all that plaintiffs establish is a business debt which is not covered by the Policy. Defendant argues that plaintiff admits that all of the paintings "were sold under the Consignment Agreements entered with Love Galleries," and that they are simply disappointed in the (zero) return on their investment.

This rather simplistic argument falters on many levels, the most obvious of which is that plaintiffs do not in any way admit that the paintings were sold "under the Consignment Agreements." In fact, plaintiffs allege, and it appears to be undisputed, that each and every painting was sold in violation of the terms of the applicable Consignment Agreement. Moreover, it is also undisputed that little, if any of the proceeds from the "sales" went to plaintiffs. According to the undisputed facts, the Gallery simply took the paintings, sold them or traded them for whatever it could get and kept the proceeds, not revealing to plaintiffs that the paintings were gone.

In *Metalexpert Co. v. Gen-O-Ral Processing Corp.*, 365 F.2d 178, 180 (7th Cir.1966), the court held that when the consignee sold the consigned item and failed to turn over the proceeds, his rightful possession became a wrongful conversion. In *Metalexpert,* the consignee was authorized to sell the item and, thus, converted the funds received. In the instant case, the Gallery sold the paintings without authority and then failed to remit the proceeds, thereby converting both the paintings and the money received. . . . As defendant admits, in Illinois a conversion is "any unauthorized act, which deprives a man of his property permanently or for an indefinite time. . . ."

There can be no doubt that the Gallery's unauthorized sales deprived plaintiffs of their property. . . . As far as plaintiffs are concerned . . . the conduct of the Gallery toward their paintings is no different than had the Gallery taken the paintings on consignment and destroyed them. The fact that the Gallery may owe plaintiffs the value of the lost paintings is no more significant than the fact that a thief would owe the victim of his theft the value of the stolen property. Accordingly, the court concludes that plaintiffs have met their burden of showing a covered loss, and defendant has failed to meet its burden of showing an exception to coverage. Consequently, for purposes of this insurance coverage dispute, the court finds that the loss of the paintings is covered by the Masterpiece Policy.

Finally, defendant also argues that because the Gallery was plaintiffs' agent when it converted the paintings, plaintiffs "put the Galleries' in motion" by entering the consignment agreements. Thus, defendant argues for application of the exclusion for loss occurring as a result of an intentional act by the insured, which provides:

> We do not cover any loss caused intentionally by you or a family member, or by a person directed by you or a family member to cause a loss. An intentional act is one whose consequences could have been foreseen by a reasonable person.

According to defendant, plaintiffs cannot claim a loss for an intentional act by the Gallery taken pursuant to the consignment agreement. Of course, the Gallery's actions were not taken pursuant to the consignment agreement but in contravention of it. Therefore, the exclusion does not apply. Additionally, no reasonable person could foresee the Gallery converting the paintings for its own profit. Accordingly, the court concludes that the loss of the paintings sustained by the plaintiffs as a result of the Gallery's conduct is covered by the Policy. . . .

Conclusion

For the reasons set forth above, the court . . . declares that plaintiffs' loss is covered by the Policy. . . .

Memorandum Opinion and Order on Motion for Reconsideration

* * *

Defendant argues that this court's opinion "misunderstood certain facts and misapplied the law of conversion." Defendant is wrong.

In its January 16, 2007, opinion the court stated that all of the paintings at issue had been improperly sold by the Gallery by the end of 2002. Defendant now argues that the court held that the Gallery had "converted" the paintings by that time, which predates the period of insurance in the instant policy. Defendant's position is incorrect. Although the Gallery may have breached the consignment agreements at that point in time, the conversion occurred when plaintiffs demanded the return of their property and the Gallery refused. That occurred in March 2003, within the instant policy period. It was the Gallery's failure to return the property on demand that was the final element of the conversion.... Until plaintiffs demanded the paintings, the Gallery could have reacquired them and then returned them to plaintiffs. When it ultimately failed to do so it committed the conversion. Defendant's argument that the Gallery did not "retain" the paintings after plaintiffs' demand because it had already transferred title is specious....

Finally, the court rejects defendant's arguments that there is an issue of fact as to whether certain of the paintings were "sold" in compliance with the assignment agreement because Mr. Love testified that he "believed" he had a right to "trade" the paintings. Love's belief is irrelevant. The consignment agreements are unambiguous. The Gallery was to sell for a minimum price. The contracts gave the Gallery some discretion as to payment terms, such as whether to extend credit or demand cash up front, but nothing in the contracts allowed the Gallery to barter the items. In any event, the Gallery did not remit payment and thus was required to return the paintings upon demand. Its failure to do so constitutes conversion.

Accordingly, defendant's motion to reconsider is denied.

Notes and Questions

1. *Aftermath. Schulhof* was affirmed on appeal. 70 N.Y.S.3d 462 (N.Y. App. Div. 2018). The court upheld the determination of a fiduciary relationship between the decedent and the art consultant-defendant. Consequently, the faithless servant doctrine was applicable. It is important to note that not all art consultants are deemed fiduciaries. Merely providing advice upon which another relies is not sufficient to establish a fiduciary relationship. See Mueller v. Michael Janssen Gallery, 225 F. Supp. 3d 201 (S.D.N.Y. 2016).

Pacific Indemnity settled the case with the Frigons reportedly for a "handsome payment." Richard Love closed his Chicago gallery in 2010; but legal issues continued. In September 2010, the F.B.I. seized his files over ongoing lawsuits from disappointed consignors. If you advised an insurance company regarding its policy contracts for "all risk" fine arts coverage, is it time to rewrite the policies, charge a higher premium, or require pre-notification of any consignment? Maybe yes, maybe no. "[I]t would cost too much money to re-file in all the states [they] operate in ... and they're willing just to leave the policy language the way it is." Rebecca Woan, *What Can Be Covered*, 25 DePaul J. Art, Tech. & Intell. Prop. 479, 488 (2015).

Frigon may be an outlier and not represent a trend in all risk coverage. See, e.g., Dae Assoc. v. AXA Art Ins. Co., 158 A.D.3d 493 (N.Y. App. Div. 2018) (policy did not cover defects in title when stolen artwork returned to owner); Flaum v. Great Northern Ins. Co., 904 N.Y.S.2d 647 (Sup. Ct. 2010) (policy did not cover purchase of forged Renoir). In short, all risk coverage may not cover all risks in the art market. See Robert L. Tucker, *Stolen Art, Looted Antiquities, and the Insurable Interest Requirement*, 29 Quinnipiac L. Rev. 611 (2011).

2. *Salander Saga*. Richard Love's conduct was not novel; many similar stories can be told. The Kraken *Botticelli* was caught in the spectacular failure of New York's Salander-O'Reilly Galleries. Larry Salander pled guilty in March 2010 to 29 felony counts relating to art fraud, primarily by selling works not owned by him and pocketing the proceeds and also by luring investors into fraudulent art investments, some of which were Ponzi-type schemes. Salander-O'Reilly Galleries was once deemed the world's best art gallery. Its list of clients was glittering and included museums, movie stars, world class athletes, artists, estates, and foundations, among others. Many of them fell victim to Salander's fraud. On August 3, 2010, Salander was sentenced to 6–18 years in prison and ordered to pay $120 million in restitution to his victims. Those victims are unlikely to fully recover their losses from him. Eileen Kinsella, *Untangling the Salander Mess*, ARTnews 110 (Summer 2010); Eileen Kinsella, *Supreme Court Declines Investor Claim for $21.6 Million from Salander-O'Reilly Swindle*, Artnetnews (Mar. 24, 2015).

The unraveling of Salander-O'Reilly Galleries was a shock to the art market because of the scope and size of the fraud as well as the celebrity status of Salander and his clientele. It was seen as the art world equivalent of the Bernie Madoff investment scandal. Yet for transactional lawyers, the Salander saga is in the same mold as *Haley & Steele* and *Frigon*, although more sizable. Its resolution is following a predictable path in bankruptcy. See *Kraken, supra*. The court approved a Christie's auction in June 2010 of 130 works. Would you be surprised to learn that the bankruptcy trustee secured title insurance for the auctioned works? That insurance would allow purchasers to acquire those auctioned works without fear of financial loss due to conflicting interests that might surface post-auction.

3. *A Consignment Letter*. The Philadelphia Museum of Art consigned two paintings, Maurice Prendergast's *The Harbor* and Arthur B. Davies's *Mountain Landscape*, to Salander-O'Reilly Galleries in 2006. Within two weeks, Salander apparently sold *The Harbor* for $1.5 million but never paid the Museum despite repeated requests. The Museum filed a claim in the Salander bankruptcy litigation (similar to the *Kraken* process) and also proceeded against its insurance carrier, AXA Art. Philadelphia Museum of Art v. AXA Art Insurance Corporation, No. 8:10-cv-00587 (filed D. Md. Mar. 8, 2010). The Museum argued a *Frigon*-type action, that is, its "all risk" policy covers physical loss or damage of the work, "including financial or economic loss." AXA denied coverage for this type of loss. In July 2011, the court dismissed the case, with costs assessed against the Museum. This dual approach was used by many other Salander victims.

The September 15, 2006, consignment agreement between the Museum and Salander-O'Reilly Galleries was in the form of a short letter, letter from the Museum to Salander ("Dear Larry"). The six contractual provisions contained in the letter are described below. The provisions provide a glimpse into the world of museum-dealer art consignments. As you read the following with the priceless advantage of hindsight, determine which provisions were arguably violated by Salander, and consider how you could possibly revise those provisions to better protect the museum consignor. Should consignment agreements include a monthly reporting requirement? Or alternatively, should a consignor, especially an institutional one, do monthly or periodic compliance checks?

a. Consignment and price. The first provision establishes that the arrangement is a consignment of the two works for a period of six months. The minimum aggregate sales price is $1,500,000 with the availability of a discount (not to exceed 10%) for "favored clients." If an offer for a lesser amount is received, Salander is to promptly notify the Museum. The two works "may not be sold in separate transactions" unless the parties "expressly agree."

b. Commission. If there is a successful sale at or above the minimum price, Salander "will be entitled to a dealer's commission of 5%" of the sales price. Sales proceeds less commission are to be sent "immediately" to the Museum.

c. Option to purchase. If the works were not sold at the end of the six month consignment period, Salander "agree(s) to purchase" the art works for "$712,500 ($750,000 less your commission of 5%)" payable in three installments over 90 days. The Museum reserves the right "to terminate this agreement," and the works shall be returned "in which event you will have no obligation, or right" to purchase the art works.

d. Shipping. Costs of shipping are borne by Salander.

e. Insurance. Salander is responsible for "all damage or loss" of the artworks and "must insure" the works for the Museum's benefit for at least $1,500,000. If requested by the Museum, Salander will arrange to have the Museum "named as an additional insured" on its insurance.

f. Duty of care. Salander is to "safeguard" the art in the "same manner as you do with respect to works of art held in your own inventory." Moreover, Salander is not to "do anything that would create or permit any security interest in or lien" on the art works.

B. Disposition at Auction

The choice to sell through a dealer or at auction is not preordained; it is a personal or business decision, not a legal one. Many owners will use a private dealer, but others will prefer to dispose of artworks at auction. Owners are attracted to the auction market because of its perceived transparency, the centuries-old tradition of the major auction houses, their acknowledged expertise, and a belief that a global modern auction will result in the best price. Regardless of whether a dealer or auction house is used, a consignment agreement is necessary. The longevity and worldwide experience of the auction houses is readily apparent in the auction houses' consignment agreements. UCC § 9-102(a)(20) specifically excludes from its definition of consignment transactions with an auctioneer. Consequently, the issues raised in *Haley & Steele* and *Kraken* are not germane to auction consignments. What is the nature of the consignment relationship if the owner uses an auction house? The following case addresses that question in detail.

Cristallina v. Christie, Manson & Woods International, Inc.

Supreme Court of New York, Appellate Division, 1986
502 N.Y.S.2d 165

SULLIVAN, J. At issue is the responsibility, if any, of an auction house to the consignor of works of art for sale at public auction. Cristallina S.A., a Panamanian corporation engaged solely in the purchase and sale of works of art, consigned for sale eight Impressionist paintings to Christie, Manson and Woods International, Inc., the international auction house. The auction was a conceded failure, and as a result Cristallina brought this action against Christie's and its former president, David Bathurst, for monetary redress, including punitive damages. Cristallina claims, *inter alia*, that Christie's and Bathurst intentionally or negligently misrepresented the sum the paintings would bring at auction and failed to advise it of the risks inherent in such a sale. The matter is before us on appeal from a grant of summary judgment dismissing the complaint.

[The edited opinion is reproduced in Chapter 3, *supra*. Review the opinion, concentrating now on the consignment arrangement, and the deviations from that arrangement by Christie's and Cristallina or Jodidio. As you read, consider how you would negotiate the consignment agreement for the seller-consignor.—Ed.]

C. Consignment Agreements

1. *Dealer Consignment Agreement Form.* The following is the template of a consignment agreement prepared by two dealers for use in their gallery. It presupposes that the client will deposit the actual artworks with the dealer for open display or viewing in the gallery for a set period of time. Notice how the agreement details the relationship of client and dealer, and sets specific limits on what the gallery can and can not do with the artwork and proceeds.

Dealer Fine Art Consignment Agreement

The Client	The Gallery
Name:____________________	Name:____________________
Address:_____________,_____	Address:_____________,_____
Phone (home):_____________	Phone (home):_____________

Phone (cell):______________ Phone (cell):______________
Email:__________@_______ Email:__________@_______

Hereby enter into the following Agreement:

1. **Purpose.** The Client ____________________________ appoints the Gallery and their representatives as agent for his/her works of art, consigned under this Agreement, for the sole purpose of sale. The Gallery shall not permit the Artworks to be used for any other purposes without the written consent of the Client.

2. **Consignment.** The Client hereby consigns to the Gallery, and the Gallery accepts on consignment, those Artworks listed on the attached Inventory Sheet, which is a part of this Agreement. Additional Inventory Sheets may be incorporated into this Agreement at such time as both parties agree to the consignment of other works of art. All Inventory Sheets shall be signed by Client and Gallery.

3. **Warranty.** The Client hereby warrants that he/she possesses unencumbered title to the Artworks being presented for sale, and that their descriptions are true and accurate.

4. **Duration of Consignment.** The Client and the Gallery agree that the initial term of consignment for the Artworks is to be ____ months. Thereafter, the consignment shall be returned to the Client *(see item #5, Transportation)*. At that time, the Client's Artworks will no longer be made viewable to the public.

5. **Transportation Responsibilities.** Packing and shipping charges, insurance costs, other handling expenses, and risk of loss or damage incurred in the delivery of Artworks from the Client to the Gallery shall be the responsibility of the Client. Returns: Packing, shipping and insurance costs to return unsold artworks (owned by the Client) shall require a credit card for direct billing to the client. Shipping and Handling charges will be added to the Buyer's purchase price at the time of sale by the Gallery, and are not commissionable as part of the sale of the Artwork.

6. **Fiduciary Responsibilities.** Title to each of the Artworks remains in the Client's name until the Client has been paid the full amount owed to him/her for the Artworks; title then passes directly to the Purchaser. All proceeds from the sale of the Artworks shall be held in trust for the Client. The Gallery shall pay all amounts due the Client before any proceeds of sales can be made available to creditors of the Gallery.

7. **Pricing.** Gallery's Commission; Terms of Payment. The Gallery shall initially offer the Artworks at the Retail Price specified on the Inventory Sheet. Any change in the retail asking price, or in the Gallery's commission, must be agreed to in advance by the Client and the Gallery in writing or via email. Payment to the Client shall be made by the Gallery within thirty days after the Gallery has been paid in full by the Buyer, and Buyer has confirmed approval of purchase.

8. **Promotion.** The Gallery shall use its best efforts to promote the sale of the Artworks. The Gallery agrees to provide adequate webpage coverage of the Artworks, and to undertake other promotional activities on the Client's behalf.

9. **Accounting.** A statement of accounts for all sales of the Artworks shall be furnished by the Gallery to the Client by email and regular mail.

10. **Termination of Agreement.** Notwithstanding any other provision of this Agreement, this Agreement may be terminated at any time by either the Gallery or the Client, by means of written notification of termination from either party to the other. Within thirty days of the notification of termination, all accounts shall be settled and all unsold Artworks shall be removed from the Gallery's website.

11. Procedures for Modification. Amendments to this Agreement must be signed by both Client and Gallery and attached to this Agreement. Both parties must initial any deletions made on this form and any additional provisions written onto it.

12. Miscellany. This Agreement represents the entire agreement between the Client and the Gallery. If any part of this Agreement is held to be illegal, void, or unenforceable for any reason, such holding shall not affect the validity and enforceability of any other part. A waiver of any breach of any of the provisions of this Agreement shall not be construed as a continuing waiver of other breaches of the same provision or other provisions hereof. This Agreement shall not be assigned, nor shall it inure to the benefit of the successors of the Gallery, whether by operation of law or otherwise, without the prior written consent of the Client.

13. Choice of Law. This Agreement shall be governed by the laws of ______________.

Signature Client: _____________ Signature of Gallery: _____________

Date: ___________ Date:___________

Art Inventory:

Title of Artwork:

Detailed Description of Artwork:

____

____

____

Medium: ______________ Dimensions: ______x______

Estimated Sale Price Range: _________to________

Retail Starting Price Agreed Upon by Client/Gallery: ___________

Minimum Net to Client: ________________ Gallery Commission: _____________

Signature of Client:______________________ Date:_________

Signature of Gallery Representative:______________________ Date:_________

2. *Collector's Custom-Drafted Consignment Agreement with Dealer.* The following is a template for a collector's assignment agreement with a dealer involving a work of economic significance. Here is a sense of a discrete, quiet, and private sale, the artwork is not on public display at a gallery, and the consignor drives the majority of the terms.

Art Consignment Agreement

This Art Consignment Agreement is made and entered into as of the ____ day of __________________, by and between ______________________________ (the "Owner") ______________________________ (the "Dealer").

WHEREAS, Dealer is engaged in the business of the sale of works of art;

WHEREAS, Owner is the owner of ________________________ (hereinafter referred to as the "Art Work"); and

WHEREAS, Owner wishes to consign the Art Work to Dealer for sale.

NOW, THEREFORE, Owner and Dealer in consideration of the representations and promises contained herein, agree as follows:

1. **Terms of Consignment.** Owner grants to Dealer the exclusive right, for a period of time commencing immediately and terminating on ____________, 20___ ("the Consignment Period") to offer the Art Work for sale worldwide. The sales price shall be US$__________________, exclusive of any sales tax, and shall be subject to Dealer's commission as provided in Article 6 hereof. During the Consignment Period, Owner shall refer all inquiries regarding the Art Work's sale to Dealer. Dealer may, in its discretion, retain other dealers as it deems necessary or appropriate to assist in the sale of the Art Work, provided, however, that the Owner shall have no responsibility for any payments due such dealers, which payments shall be the sole responsibility of Dealer. Owner and Dealer agree that the Art Work is significant and its value may be negatively impacted by overexposure; therefore, the Art Work is not to be offered or presented to more than _____ potential purchasers, each of whom shall be generally known to the Dealer or its agents through the exercise of due diligence.
2. **Owner's Representations.** Owner represents and warrants that he is the sole and absolute owner of the Art Work, has the full right to sell and transfer the Art Work, and that the Art Work is now free and clear of any and all liens, claims, security interests, or other encumbrances. Owner agrees to indemnify and hold Dealer harmless from any and all demands, claims, suits, judgments or other liability (including professional fees and all expenses incurred by Dealer in connection therewith) awarded any person or entity arising by reason of Owner's ownership, possession, and sale of the Art Work. Title to the Art Work shall pass to a buyer upon payment in full of the Sales Price, less commissions, in good funds to Owner, at which time Owner agrees to transfer ownership and title and to provide such documentation as is reasonably required upon sale.
3. **Costs and Expenses of Sale.** Owner shall not be responsible for any costs which Dealer may incur in connection with its efforts to sell the Art Work. Notwithstanding the foregoing, if Dealer sells the Art Work within the initial Consignment Period, Dealer shall be entitled to receive as reimbursement from Owner costs incurred by Dealer directly attributable to the sale of the Art Work up to a maximum amount of US$____________. Dealer shall provide Owner with an itemized statement of any such costs. If requested by the Dealer, Owner agrees to ship the Art Work at his expense to the Dealer at one location within State ___________ specified by the Dealer for private viewing by one or more qualified potential purchasers. Dealer agrees not to remove the Art Work from State __________.
4. **Insurance.** Dealer shall arrange and pay for insurance for the Art Work against any loss or damage in the amount of the Sales Price, and the Owner shall be named as an additional insured on any such policy. Such insurance shall be provided from the moment the Art Work is shipped to Dealer and until it is returned to Owner or to the buyer upon payment in full. Before any shipment of the Art Work from the Owner, Dealer will specifically inform its insurance carrier of the Art Work, the original location, destination and means of transportation of the Art Work. Such information shall be completely confidential. Dealer agrees to use its best efforts and all due care in handling the Art Work.
5. **Dealer's Representations.** Dealer shall use its best efforts to sell the Art Work for the sales price during the Consignment Period and shall not use the Art Work for any purpose other than a sale pursuant to this agreement. If Dealer receives a bona fide offer to purchase the Art Work for an all cash price equal to or greater than the sales price, Dealer may accept such offer without further authorization from Owner. If Dealer receives a bona fide offer to purchase (i) for a price which is less than the full sales price, or (ii) on terms other than all cash, Dealer shall promptly inform Owner of such offer. Owner shall promptly inform Dealer in writing whether Owner accepts or rejects such offer.

6. **Commission and Payment Terms.** If the Art Work is sold during the Consignment Period, the proceeds of sale shall be paid to Dealer. Dealer shall be entitled to receive ____% of the sales price as a commission in consideration of its services. Dealer shall deduct this commission and the amount as determined under Article 3 above, if any, and forward the balance to Owner within five (5) days of receipt by it of the sales proceeds. Dealer agrees to furnish the Owner with a complete copy of the Dealer's invoice to the Buyer and, if applicable pursuant to Article 3, the itemized statement of its costs directly attributable to the sale of the Art Work. If the Art Work is not sold during the Consignment Period, and the Art Work has been delivered to the Dealer, Dealer shall return the Art Work at its expense to Owner within ten (10) days of the expiration of the Consignment Period.
7. **Noncircumvention.** In the event that Owner sells the Art Work within three (3) months after the termination date of the Consignment Period or its extension, to an individual (or related party or entity) to whom Dealer or its agent(s) has shown the Art Work during the Consignment Period, Dealer shall receive its full commission as provided in Article 6 above. This provision shall not apply after the expiration of such three (3) month period.
8. **UCC Security Interest.** Dealer hereby grants to Owner a security interest in the Art Work (and any proceeds thereof) until sale of the Art Work by Dealer whereupon the proceeds of such sale shall be held by Dealer for Owner and delivered (subject to such commission and expenses as set forth above) to Owner. Upon execution of this agreement, Dealer authorizes Owner to file a Form UCC-1 Financing Statement without the Dealer's signature, indicating Owner's security interest in the Artwork. Dealer agrees to inform (i) any other secured creditor of the Dealer and (ii) any purchaser of the Artwork, of the existence of Owner's security interest in the Artwork (and the proceeds therefrom). In the event of any default under this Agreement by Dealer, Owner shall have all of the rights of a secured party under the Uniform Commercial Code. Owner agrees to file Form UCC-3 terminating Owner's security interest on receipt from Dealer of the sales price less commission and less the amount, if any, pursuant to Article 3.
9. **Integration and Governing Law.** This agreement represents the entire understanding of Owner and Dealer, supersedes any and all other and prior agreements between them, and may not be modified or amended, except in a writing signed by Owner and Dealer. This Agreement shall be governed by the laws of the State of ________________.

IN WITNESS WHEREOF, Owner and Dealer have executed this agreement as of the day and year first above written.

______________________________ ______________________________

Owner Dealer

3. *Museum-Dealer Consignment Letter.* The Philadelphia Museum of Art entered a consignment agreement with the Salander-O'Reilly Galleries through a letter in 2006. It is a distinctive approach, discussed in Note 3 following *Frigon, supra.*

4. *Discussion Points for Consignment Agreements with Dealer.* The following are some of the more common features of art consignment agreements with a dealer or gallery. The ability to negotiate specific terms and conditions depends in large measure on three factors: (1) the desirability and value of the artwork being consigned; (2) the sophistication of the parties, and their prior relationship or potential future business, and (3) the general economic or market conditions.

a. Consignment. The agreement should establish the transaction as a consignment, and clearly vest authority in the dealer as owner's agent for the sale of the properly-described consigned property. Consider stating whether the agreement is exclusive, and whether other dealers may be involved. If others may be involved, specify the commission responsibility. What is the advantage to specifically stating the "sole purpose" is consignment? The time duration of the consignment should be stated, with no ambiguity as to the beginning and end dates, although provision for extension can be made. Six months to a year is usually considered a reasonable period of time for a consignment. Should provision for early termination be made, e.g., in the event of the dealer's disability? or the owner's death? Some agreements also provide a geographic scope, such as worldwide, but many are silent. What is the implication of silence? Could that undermine how the work is promoted?

b. Sales price. Notice how the core economic feature of price was presented so differently in the two dealer consignment agreements and the Philadelphia Museum-Salander consignment. In the Dealer Fine Art Consignment, there is a fluid version of price, with three provisions—an estimated sales range, the agreed starting retail price, and the minimum net. In the Owner Art Consignment, the price is firm, but with a reporting requirement for bona fide offers for a lesser price. The Philadelphia Museum-Salander consignment has multiple prices (also with a reporting requirement) dependent on who the purchaser is—a firm price of $1.5 million for the world at large, subject to a maximum 10% discount for "favored clients," and a whopping 50% discount if the works remain unsold at the end of the consignment period and Salander purchases the work.

Does the grant of a right to the dealer to purchase unsold works, especially at a deep discount, negate the incentive to sell the work during the consignment period? Did you notice that there was no "best efforts" representation by Salander? Unfortunately for the Museum, the terms of the consignment, as opposed to the fact of the consignment, seemed to have mattered little to Salander.

c. Commission and payment. In two agreements, the dealer's commission is a percentage of the sales price, but in *Schulhof* and *Kraken*, there was a set fee. Some agreements provide for a net price to the owner. In such cases, consider capping the dealer's total commission at a percentage of the sales price, e.g., 10%. Also, provide that the owner must be informed of the final sales price. Once a sale has occurred, and the buyer has paid, when does the owner get paid? There is no one answer. The three agreements provide three answers: immediately, within 5 days, and within 30 days. Consider whether to include a notice and verification process for determining the sales proceeds, commission, and any reimbursable expenses.

d. Expenses. The three agreements provide who pays for transportation costs and for insurance. Only the collector's Art Consignment Agreement specifically states the owner is not responsible for any costs incurred by the dealer in connection with its efforts to sell the work. Yet it also incentivizes the dealer by agreeing to reimburse costs (up to a stated maximum) directly attributable to the sale if the work is sold within the original consignment period.

e. Selling methods. By consigning to a dealer, the owner understands that the sale is a private transaction, but a dealer can devise multiple marketing strategies to promote and achieve a sale. How much an owner wants to be involved in setting guidelines may depend on the significance of the work involved. Limited private viewings are vastly different than hosting martini parties during a gallery walk; similarly having the work travel to multiple locations may increase visibility, but definitely increases risk of damage. Recall in *Faggionato* (Chapter 2, *supra*) the prospective U.S. buyer traveled to France for a private viewing at a private location.

If using an image of the artwork in promotional materials, copyright needs to be addressed. The posting of an image on a website should not extend beyond the consignment end date.

f. Owner's representations. At a minimum, the owner needs to warrant good title to the work, free of any claim or encumbrance, and that the owner has the authority to sell. What steps should a consignor who is a fiduciary, without specific knowledge as to these matters, take before making such representations? How do import and export restrictions or cultural property laws affect warranties as to good title, especially if the Owner was not the person who imported the work? Title insurance may be an option for this uncertainty. This might be another appropriate place for the drafter to include "to the best of Owner's knowledge." Should an owner, as opposed to the dealer, give a warranty as to authenticity? If so, consider whether it should be open-ended or, like the auction houses, limited to five years and the original buyer. This might be another appropriate place for the drafter to include "to the best of Owner's knowledge."

g. Dealer's representations. At a minimum, the dealer should be required to use best efforts to sell the work, not to use the artwork for any other purpose other than a sale, and to exercise the same care in the handling of the artwork as the dealer gives property of comparable value. Consider requiring the dealer to maintain the confidentiality of the owner's identity.

h. UCC filings. Any consignment to a dealer raises the question of filing a UCC-1 Financing Statement by the owner. As a corollary, the consignment agreement should provide a specific grant of a security interest from the dealer to the owner. See Notes 3–5 following *Kraken*, *supra*. Neither the Dealer Fine Arts Consignment nor the Philadelphia Museum-Salander Consignment did so. In the first instance, if the dealer is in a *Haley & Steele* type jurisdiction that has taken consumer consignments out of the UCC, the omission of the UCC is understandable; the omission in the second instance is troubling, for the artworks were not consumer goods and the dealer was in a jurisdiction that may require a UCC filing, even for consumer goods. *Kraken* may not provide protection if the loan agreement was revised to specifically cover consignments.

5. *Discussion Points for Auction House Consignment Agreement.* Auction houses have standard consignment agreements that can vary significantly depending on the scope and size of the auction house's market. The standard consignment agreements used by the international auction houses are lengthy, detailed, and evolving, befitting their experience, global reach, and billion-dollar sales. Bonhams, for example, has a 3-columned 11-page Conditions of Business that is the basis for its agreement with the seller. See www.bonhams.com. Smaller auction houses may have a one to two-page form consignment agreement. Regardless of the consignment agreement's length or detail, as the court observed in *Cristallina*, the relationship between the owner-consignor and the auction house is a fiduciary one. Nevertheless, the parties can modify that relationship by contract.

In reviewing any auction house consignment agreement, it is helpful to consider three very broad categories of issues, some of which overlap. First are the economic terms (e.g., reserve and estimates, commission and expenses, auction house's guarantees or advances, and buyer's payment). Second is the discretion that the auction house delineates for itself (e.g., marketing and publicity, conduct of sale, withdrawal from sale, rescission of sale). Third are the representations or warranties that the owner-consignor undertakes (e.g., good marketable title, authenticity, right to photograph and reproduce) and the indemnity given for breach. As in the dealer consignments, the ability to negotiate depends on the desirability of the work, the parties' past relationship and potential for future business, and general art market economic conditions. A consignor should rarely limit its discussion to only one auction house, for having competitive proposals can sharpen the economics and other terms of the deal. The thrust of auction house consignment agreements is to minimize their economic exposure and contract for broad or sole discretion in the auction process. By doing so, their fiduciary obligations are lessened. The following discussion points build from the previous discussion on dealer consignment agreements and will therefore focus on the distinctive nature of the auction.

a. Reserve and estimates. Because a sale at auction fundamentally differs from a dealer sale, pricing the consigned artwork is distinctive. The reserve price is the confidential minimum price acceptable to the seller for that artwork and agreed to by the auction house. Factors beyond the work itself can influence the reserve price (e.g., the seller's economic needs and general economic conditions); consequently, there is legitimate room for differences of opinion. Consignors should listen carefully to the auction experts and consider their own requirements before agreeing to the reserve price. Once agreed, the reserve must be set forth in the consignment agreement in writing to avoid confusion. A consignor could, however, agree to sell without reserve. Under what circumstances would that make sense? Another variation in reserves is granting the auctioneer discretion to reduce the reserve by 10% (or more if given wide discretion) if the auctioneer deems it necessary in order to sell the lot or, as in *Cristallina*, to have a floating reserve. What does this discretion do to the reserve, its concept, and its execution?

Estimates are clearly related to the reserve. By law in New York, the reserve cannot exceed the low estimate. While high estimates may appeal to the consignor, they can dissuade buyers. Some consignment agreements give the auction house discretion in setting estimates, but consignors should insist on being involved. Consignors should listen to the rationale for the auction houses' estimates and affirmatively agree to the estimates. Once agreed upon, the consignment agreement should include those estimates. Recall in *Cristallina* that the estimates changed over time. What does that suggest to you in negotiating the consignment agreement?

In setting estimates, the auction houses may use consultants. If there is an objection to involving any particular person in that process, that must be in the agreement to be actionable. Reale v. Sotheby's, Inc., 718 N.Y.S.2d 37, 38 (N.Y. App. Div. 2000).

b. Commission and expenses. A standard consignment agreement with an auction house includes a seller's commission to be paid to the auction house from the auction proceeds. It is usually set as a declining graduated percentage of the hammer price. Rates can vary, such as 8–15% for lower valued objects and graduate down to 2%. These rates are subject to negotiation and even elimination for highly desirable artworks or for certain institutional consignors, such as museums. For items that do not sell, there is also a fee due the auction house based on the reserve price. Consequently, unless it is negotiated, consignors under standard consignment agreements will pay the auction house for its services whether or not the artwork sells at auction.

In addition, many standard agreements make the seller responsible for a number of costs associated with the consignment, such as transportation, insurance, catalogue, research, promotional efforts, post-auction storage, framing and restoration. Quite often, the consignment agreement is silent as to the cost of these services, yet collectively, these fees can be significant. This is an area where negotiation is common, with many fees split or waived completely for highly desirable works. Another drafting approach may be to impose a cap on the fees or require the consignor's approval for certain fees.

One expense that may take American consignors unaware is the droit de suite, or artist resale right, imposed for auction sales in certain countries, including throughout the EU. Currently capped at 12,500 Euros, an auction house may agree to pay this cost. See Chapter 7, *supra,* for discussion of droit de suite.

c. Guarantees and advances. Commissions and fees represent the traditional form of compensation for an auction house. With competitive markets for highly desirable works, some sellers have been able to sell free of the seller's commission with the auction house relying instead on the buyer's premium. In order to compete for marquee works of art, auction houses have gone further and offered guarantees to some consignors, with advances being paid to some sellers and even sharing the buyer's premium. A guarantee is protection against the piece not selling or not selling well and allows the seller a minimum amount for its economic needs, such as the payment of estate taxes. A guarantee is not free; in exchange for a guarantee, the consignor will pay a fee generally based on the amount by which the sales price at auction exceeds the guarantee (the "overage"). The actual fee can be calculated in multiple ways, e.g., a straight percentage of entire overage or an increasing rate.

Guarantees can be for an individual artwork or for all works in a collection (a "global" guarantee). There is no rule of thumb on whether to have a global guarantee or individual guarantees; it depends on the economics and the desirability of the artworks being offered. If there is a global guarantee, the withdrawal or rescission provisions of the agreement require special attention. The auction house, for example, may desire to terminate the guarantee if a particular artwork is withdrawn from auction. The desirability of having different proposals is obvious.

An advance with or without an underlying guarantee is another incentive used by auction houses. The advance is essentially a loan, and it may be with or without interest. If there is an advance and the works have not been delivered to the auction house, a UCC filing statement may be required to protect the auction house's interest.

For extremely desirable works, some auction houses also offer to share a part of the buyer's premium with the seller. Since its introduction in the 1970s, the buyer's premium has increased substantially over time. One reason may be because that premium is now being shared. When the 2008 economic downturn affected the art market, the auction houses announced their retreat from these incentives. Some thought the incentives might disappear. See, generally, Steven E. Thomas, *Auction Consignment Agreements: Pitfalls and Planning Strategies*, 36 ESTATE PLANNING 23–30 (April 2009); Fred Goldstein, *Nuts and Bolts of Standard Auction House Practices*, ALI-ABA LEGAL ISSUES IN MUSEUM ADMINISTRATION (March 14–16, 2007). That ultimately did not happen, as the competition for unique highly desirable artworks remains intense. What impact the Coronavirus pandemic will have on these incentives remains to be seen.

Another aspect of the financial incentives of guarantees and advances is the ripple effect they can have on other seemingly non-economic terms in the consignment agreement. *Force majeure* clauses, for example, have become more important. Historically, those clauses provided that when an unanticipated and disruptive event occurred outside the control of the parties (an act of God, such as a hurricane or earthquake), the parties may be excused from performance under a contract. Given the nature of a fine arts auction and the 21st century's volatile history, *force majeure* clauses may include references to man-made catastrophic events and substantial decline in world financial markets. Such clauses provide an opportunity to reevaluate the timing of the auction and set forth the monetary consequences if the parties cannot agree on a course of action.

d. Buyer's payment or nonpayment. In the normal course, the agreement should provide for the remittance of the sales proceeds to the seller less commission and expenses within a reasonable period of time (often 35 days). Similarly, the agreement should provide recourse for a buyer's nonpayment. Agreements generally provide in the event of nonpayment, the auction house may proceed against the buyer, but is usually not required to do so. The sale is usually canceled, and the nonpaying buyer is subject to a suit for damages, multiple fees and charges. The seller, however, now has an artwork that did not sell at auction, sometimes referred to as "burnt" in the art market. Consider modifying the agreement to set a timeframe within which the auction house either collects the proceeds from the buyer (through suit or voluntarily), negotiates extended payment terms agreeable to the seller from the buyer, or cancels the sale. Any legal action in the name of the seller should require the seller's specific consent.

e. Research, marketing, and publicity. Standard consignment agreements often give the auction house sole discretion on whether and how to perform research and testing on consigned property. Because works can be damaged by such tests, the consignor should modify the agreement to require information on the tests being proposed and consent to their utilization. Auction house agreements also provide for their sole discretion in marketing and publicity. That is, after all, their business. Nevertheless, publicity that is important to the consignor (e.g., photograph on catalogue cover or sale at particular auction), should be negotiated and set forth explicitly in the consignment agreement. Reliance on initial discussions with the auction house is insufficient.

f. Withdrawal from sale. Sometimes after the consignment agreement is signed, the seller or the auction house may decide not to go forward with the auction. Depending on the circumstances of the withdrawal, a fee plus expenses may be owed by the seller if the seller withdrew in breach of the agreement or if the auction house withdrew because of a breach by the seller. The fee is a percentage of the reserve price (or the mean of the low and high estimates). In many standard agreements, the auction house has the right to withdraw the work for any reason, including an authenticity challenge or the claim to the work by another. See Barnet v. Minister of Culture and Sports of the Hellenic Republic, 961 F.3d 193 (2d Cir. June 9, 2020), Chapter 5, *supra*; Kohler v. Leslie Hindman, Inc., 80 F.3d 1181 (7th Cir. 1996), Chapter 4, *supra*. The *force majeure* clause may be pertinent for some withdrawals. Consider incorporating objective standards into the auction house's discretion to withdraw "for any reason."

g. Rescission. The typical consignment agreement gives the auction house the right to rescind a sale to a buyer at any time if, in the auction house's judgment, the sale may subject the auction house or seller to any liability. See Christie's v. SWCA, 867 N.Y.S.2d 650 (N.Y. Sup. Ct. 2008), Chapter 4, *supra*. The breadth of the agreement's right to rescind demands some scrutiny. Absent such a clause, a buyer could file an action based on title or authenticity challenges. As such, the buyer would be required to prove the challenges and to file within the requisite statutory timeframe. Here the consignment agreement contractually deletes the requirements of proof and perhaps timeliness. Because rescission can have economic consequences, even if there is no proof, the standard provision should be modified. Consider incorporating a deadline for rescission to one year from date of sale and limiting the right to rescind to cases involving the seller's warranties and representations specifically provided for in the consignment agreement. Additionally, requiring advance notification and a process for an independent determination of the pertinent factual issue would restore a measure of fiduciary duty to the seller-principal from the auction house-agent.

h. Seller's representations of title and authenticity. As in the dealer context, the seller's representations as to good title and legal ability to transfer good title free of liens, claims, and encumbrances at the time of auction are nonnegotiable. Standard agreements often require the seller to warrant the work's compliance with import and export restrictions and to provide in writing notice of material alterations and accurate information (including authorship, attribution, and any authenticity-type concerns expressed by third parties) about the work. These representations are more difficult to fulfill and should clearly be limited to "the best of seller's knowledge." In addition, the requirement to notify of accurate information on description and third party comments should be limited to material, written comments of which the seller is aware.

i. Right to reproduce. The standard agreement often has the seller warranting the auction house's right to reproduce, photograph, or illustrate the work, or of any written text submitted by the seller concerning the property. Sellers are often unaware of copyright law and whether or not they are in compliance. Unless the seller is certain as to copyright, the burden should be reversed. See Chapters 7 and 8, *supra*.

j. Seller's indemnity. Broad indemnification clauses are common in consignment agreements. A seller should try to quantitatively limit indemnification to a return of the proceeds received, and qualitatively limit indemnification to actual third party claims against the auction house for the seller's breach or wrongful, negligent acts.

D. Exchanges

1. Art for Art Exchanges

When an owner sells an artwork, the buyer pays the sales price in money; when a transfer of an artwork for an artwork occurs, it is deemed an exchange. Galleries sometimes will give a customer who has acquired a work from the gallery the right to trade the work for another work at a later time, often using the original work's cost as the floor for value. Sometimes collectors will privately exchange works with other collectors. An exchange is a disposition and an acquisition; as such, it should be documented, with both parties agreeing to the economic terms and making the customary buyer's and seller's warranties and representations. The absence of money consideration should not render the transaction casual. Moreover, there are tax considerations. State and local sales may be imposed. The exchange may require the collection and payment of state and federal income taxes.

In a normal sales transaction when an owner sells a painting, the owner must compute the gain on the sale for income tax purposes. If, for example, the owner paid $1,000 for the painting 5 years ago, and now sells it for $10,000, the owner has a gain of $9,000 ($10,000 proceeds minus $1,000 original cost). That $9,000 gain must be reported on the owner's income tax return and it will enter into the owner's tax computation. Prior to 2018, if the owner exchanged the artwork for another artwork that is also worth $10,000, the same gain of $9,000 under certain conditions did not enter into the tax computations. This is known as a like-kind exchange, governed by Section 1031 of the Internal Revenue Code (26 U.S.C. § 1031). Like-kind exchanges are now limited to exchanges of real estate only. Consequently, the $9,000 gain from the art for art exchange is now recognized for income tax purposes and must be reported.

2. Dation en Paiement

If you have been to Paris, you may have visited the Picasso Museum. Its origins, like its art, are unique. The core of the collection came from a French law (referred to as Picasso's Law) enacted in 1968 when Pablo Picasso (1881–1973) was 87. The law provided a mechanism by which heirs of an estate can pay their succession taxes with works of art of high artistic or historic value, instead of money. When Picasso died in 1973, his heirs entered into negotiations with the French government to do just that. The result was 203 paintings, 158 sculptures, 29 relief paintings, 88 ceramics, 1,500 drawings, 1,600 etchings, and various manuscripts and works of pasted paper now housed in the Picasso Museum were used as payment of the Picasso heirs' French succession tax. When his widow Jacqueline died, the heirs again used dation.

The U.K. has a similar statutory mechanism for artistic and historic works to be used as payment of taxes at death. See, e.g., Cultural Gifts Scheme & Acceptance in Lieu Annual Report 2018/19, Sept. 11, 2019, available at www.artscouncil.org.uk. While there is no similar provision in the U.S. for payment of the federal estate tax, there have been several discrete instances in the U.S. where works of historic interest have effectively been used as payment. Technically using works of art to pay an estate tax would not be an exchange; it would presumably be viewed from a tax perspective as a sale. See Anne-Marie Rhodes, *The Medium of Payment: An Option in Estate Tax Reform*, 57 Notre Dame L. Rev. 285 (1981), for additional information on dation en paiement, the U.S. experience, and a template for legislation.

Fifth Drafting Exercise: Art Consignment

To:Junior Associate

From:Senior Partner

Our client Mr. Smith called. Mr. Jones, a longtime friend of Mr. Smith, recently died. Mr. Smith was named the executor of the estate. Mr. Jones is survived by his wife, who is in a nursing home. She is unable to manage her financial affairs due to dementia, but otherwise she is physically healthy. She is the sole heir and beneficiary of Mr. Jones's estate. They had no children. Both Mr. and Mrs. Jones were high school teachers.

Mr. Jones's estate is not large, but it includes one painting, of which Mr. Jones was very proud. It is a small portrait of his wife from many years ago. The artist was one of Mr. and Mrs. Jones's favorite students, whom they encouraged to pursue his art. This student did, and the portrait of Mrs. Jones was included in his first show in a professional gallery. At the end of the wildly successful show, the artist sent the painting to Mr. and Mrs. Jones with a note of thanks for their encouragement. The portrait has been in the Jones's home for over 40 years, quietly appreciating in value as the artist's reputation soared. The artist is still alive.

As executor, Mr. Smith had the work professionally appraised. The range was $80X–120X, with a notation from the appraiser that the value could potentially be greater because of the work's "freshness" to the market. Mr. Smith intends to sell the work, because he is concerned about Mrs. Jones's ongoing financial expenses for healthcare. Mrs. Jones's legal guardian agrees with this plan. He decided not to sell at auction largely because of the timing and expense of the auctions. He hasn't decided which dealer to use, but he's narrowed it to three, one a local/regional gallery, the other two somewhat more national. He'll negotiate with all three. While Mr. Smith understands that the choice of which dealer (as well as selling through a dealer instead of at auction) is a business decision, he would like our input as to the pros and cons. His goal and fiduciary duty is to maximize net sales proceeds for Mr. Jones's estate and for Mrs. Jones. He would like us to draft a dealer consignment agreement that will fully protect Mrs. Jones's interests and the fiduciary responsibilities of her legal guardian and himself. Leave the price open for now. In addition to the dealer consignment agreement, please draft for my review a short memo (no more than two pages) explaining any non-obvious assumptions, optional provisions, or anything for which a heads-up would be helpful.

Chapter 10

Gratuitous Transfers

Disposing of art without receiving consideration involves the legal arena of gifts, trusts, and estates, and the personal aspect of families, friends, and charitable beneficiaries. The owner has three basic decisions to make in transferring ownership of art—to whom (family, friend or charity), when (during life or at death), and how (outright or in trust). Each of these decisions is personal, but often shaped and sometimes effectively determined by legal and tax considerations.

This chapter will explain the basic parameters of gifts and bequests to individual and charitable beneficiaries, address the issue of fiduciary responsibilities of an executor or trustee in the management of art as an asset of an estate or trust, and consider the issue of donor intent in light of changing circumstances. The portfolio value of art, coupled with the varying needs and desires of family members, and the philosophical debate over private property-public benefit, come together in this chapter. It provides the lawyer a rich template for being an attorney as well as a counselor at law.

A. Gifts and Bequests to Individuals

1. Lifetime Gifts

Gifts are made during lifetime by a donor to a donee; bequests are made at death by a decedent to a beneficiary. Both gifts and bequests are commonly made to family and friends. The two cases below involve gifts of art that were later disputed. In *Genecin*, the dispute is between two brothers, and in *Edinburg*, it is between a mother and her children. The legal dispute centers on the effectiveness of the donor's delivery of the art to the donee. From that perspective, these cases deliver sound readable opinions. From the human perspective, however, something else emerges. It is impossible to miss both judges' disappointment at the families' dysfunctional, destructive conduct. When there is a gift of an artwork to one member of a family, lawyers need to pay attention to the family dynamic.

Estate of Genecin v. Genecin

363 F. Supp. 2d 306 (D. Conn. 2005)

KRAVITZ, J. This lawsuit is the result of an unfortunate and bitter dispute between two brothers, Victor Genecin and Paul Genecin, over the rightful ownership of . . . a lithograph . . . that once belonged to their mother, Rita Genecin, who is now deceased. Rita Genecin loved her sons very much and undoubtedly was very proud of them. Both are accomplished; one is a doctor and the other a lawyer. But the Court has no doubt that were she alive today, Rita Genecin would be deeply disappointed in her sons. For they have fought each other viciously over these assets when an amicable resolution was always evident, and in the process, they have leveled distressing allegations against each other—charging each other with fraud, falsifying documents and suborning perjury. Worse yet, in their headstrong battle over these assets, it appears that they may have expended more on legal fees than either could possibly hope to recover.

The court system itself did not fail this family. Magistrate Judge William I. Garfinkel, who has a well deserved reputation for being able to settle tough cases, plaintively urged the brothers "without Court intervention, . . . [to] fashion a resolution that honors Rita's wishes," and he tried to help them toward that goal. This Court itself took the extraordinary action of ordering Paul and Victor to meet with each other, along with their lawyers, during the trial to discuss settlement, because, as the Court observed to them at the time, "you owe it to yourselves, you owe it to your children, and you owe it most of all to the memories of your parents to roll up your sleeves and work as hard as you can to come up with solution that is not a vindication, that is not a victory, but . . . that respects each other and your parents, and that is sensible." Yet, for their own reasons, Paul and Victor Genecin instead inexplicably chose to bring misery and calumny upon each other.

This self-destructive battle need not have happened. And, as the Court noted at trial, it should have been stopped long ago; not for Victor's and Paul's sake, but rather, for the sake of their children—cousins all—and most of all, because of the memory of their loving parents, Rita and Abraham Genecin. Inevitably, this Court's decision, like all judicial resolutions, will disappoint some. Yet, it remains the Court's fervent hope that Victor and Paul can somehow bring themselves to view this decision as marking the end of a tragic period in their lives and that they will seize the opportunity to stop the fighting and begin the healing process.

I.

* * *

Rita Genecin died . . . August 5, 2000 in her home . . . two years following the death of her husband Abraham. Rita Genecin is survived by her two sons—Victor, who resides in New York; and Paul, who resides in Connecticut. Victor Genecin is the sole personal representative of the Estate of Rita Genecin ("the Estate"). In her Will, Rita Genecin divided her residuary Estate as follows: 55% to Victor and 45% to Paul.

Throughout her life, Rita Genecin loved art. She was an artist herself, and . . . was an avid collector of art. Over the years, Abraham and Rita Genecin made gifts [of art] to their sons. . . . The most valuable of the art works Rita Genecin owned in the year preceding her death was an 1897 color lithograph by French artist Henri de Toulouse-Lautrec entitled *Partie de campagne* (*Le chariot anglais*) (the "Lautrec"), which has been appraised as having a value of $150,000. At the time of her death, the Lautrec was hanging in [her] home. . . . Immediately following her death, Paul brought all of the art . . . to Connecticut for safekeeping. . . .

Thereafter, Paul informed his brother Victor . . . that his mother had given him the Lautrec as a Christmas gift . . . in late December 1999, approximately six months before her death. Victor . . . denied that his mother had made a legally valid gift . . . and Victor brought this action. . . . Sadly, in pursuing that claim on the Estate's behalf, Victor has also been compelled to deny the effectiveness of a gift of two lithographs by French artist Edouard Vuillard entitled *Maternite* and *Avenue* that his mother appears to have intended to give him in January 2000 in the same manner that she gave Paul the Lautrec.

* * *

III.

The parties agree that the validity of the Lautrec gift is governed by Maryland law. . . . Under Maryland law, the donee—Paul Genecin—has the burden of establishing every element of a valid gift, he must do so by clear and convincing evidence, and he must establish three elements: "an intention on the part of the donor to transfer the property, a delivery by the donor and an acceptance by the donee." While an admittedly close question . . . Paul has sustained his burden of proof on each element. Therefore, the Court finds that Rita Genecin made a valid gift of the Lautrec to Paul Genecin in December 1999.

A. Donative Intent

"'In order to prove donative intent, it must be shown from the evidence that the donor clearly and unmistakably intended to permanently relinquish all interest in, and control over the gift.'" The Court concludes that Paul Genecin established by clear and convincing evidence that his mother intended to give him the Lautrec in December 1999.

* * *

. . . The admissible evidence presented at trial was overwhelming. . . . First, and most importantly, there is a deed of gift, which was undisputedly executed by Rita Genecin on or about December 1999, which states that "I, Rita Genecin, hereby give, grant, convey and transfer all my right, title and interest in and to the item listed below to you, Paul Genecin in fee simple, absolutely, without any reservations whatsoever." It is difficult for the Court to conceive of a clearer statement of Rita Genecin's intent. . . .

The Court finds it significant that . . . over the years Rita Genecin had made numerous gifts of art to Paul using deeds of gift nearly identical to the one at issue in this case. The Estate does not challenge . . . the validity of Rita Genecin's deed of gift in which she gave to Paul a wood cut print by Japanese artist Shiko Munakata entitled Hawk Woman. The Munakata deed of gift was executed by Rita Genecin on the same date as the identically worded Lautrec deed of gift. Yet, the Estate does not contest it. In fact, in order to find that the Lautrec deed of gift was invalid, the Court would have to conclude from the evidence that Paul Genecin forged the document and committed fraud on the Court by presenting the document in this litigation. Sadly, the Estate advanced precisely this claim at oral argument. The Court emphatically rejects this claim. . . .

Rita Genecin's intent . . . was further evidenced by the testimony of three witnesses. . . . Gregory Genecin . . . testified that after visiting an art museum with his grandmother . . . his grandmother told him that "she gave [the Lautrec] to my dad at Christmas." Ms. Sherlock—who was the only truly disinterested witness to testify—testified that during a visit with her dear friend Rita Genecin in the spring of 2000, Ms. Sherlock observed that the Lautrec had been moved from its usual place in the Genecin home. When Ms. Sherlock noted the move to Rita, Rita explained that she had "given [the Lautrec] to Paul for Christmas." Significantly, Victor Genecin also conceded at trial . . . that his mother had intended to gift the Lautrec to Paul and/or his family. Thus, when asked "I take it it's your understanding that your mother wanted Paul to ultimately own 100 percent of the Lautrec, Paul and/or his family?" Victor testified, "It certainly appears that that was her intention in January of 2000 when she executed those documents."

* * *

For the reasons previously stated, therefore, Court finds that Paul Genecin has established by clear and convincing evidence that Rita Genecin intended to give him the Lautrec in its entirety in December 1999.

B. Acceptance

The Court also finds that Paul Genecin has met his burden of establishing acceptance in this case. To begin with, "[a]cceptance by the donee . . . is presumed, barring evidence to the contrary." The Estate presented no evidence to the contrary at trial. . . .

C. Delivery

In a very real sense, the adequacy of delivery has always been the critical issue. . . . Victor Genecin made this point crystal clear at trial when he was asked to explain why the Estate was not pursuing any claim with respect to . . . Hawk Woman for which Rita Genecin executed a deed of gift to Paul at the same time as the Lautrec. . . . The reason, Victor confirmed, is that "the Hawk Woman was actually delivered to [Paul]; whereas the Lautrec was not."

The facts supporting delivery in this case are undisputed. [A]lthough Rita Genecin did not physically deliver the Lautrec lithograph to Paul, she did execute and deliver to him (as she had often in the past) a very formal looking deed of gift. It is also undisputed that on the advice of her financial advisor . . . , and shortly after giving Paul a deed of gift for the Lautrec, Rita Genecin transferred ownership of her house into the names of herself and her two sons, apparently in the belief that this additional step would aid in perfecting her gifts of art to her sons. . . . [A financial advisor] testified that "I recall Mr. Wagner advising Mrs. Genecin . . . that ownership of the house . . . should be changed to joint ownership with her two sons" in order to perfect her gift of the Lautrec. Thus, although the Lautrec lithograph itself never left the home where it had hung before the Christmas 1999 gift to Paul, after January 2000, the Lautrec hung in a home which Paul jointly owned.

On these facts, there is no question that if the Restatement (Third) of Property: Wills and Other Donative Transfers § 6.2 (2003) governed, the delivery requirement for a completed gift would be satisfied. . . . Section 6.2 of the Restatement provides: "The transfer of personal property, necessary to perfect a gift, may be made (1) by delivering the property to the donee *or* (2) by inter vivos donative document." (emphasis added). Recognizing this latter method of effectuating delivery hardly represents a radical departure from existing law by the Restatement drafters. To the contrary, that method of satisfying the delivery requirement has long been embraced by courts of many jurisdictions. . . .

* * *

Of course, the question in this case is whether a valid delivery has been effected under Maryland law. . . . [N]either the parties nor the Court have been able to identify a Maryland case directly on point. Therefore, the Court must make an "Erie guess" as to whether Maryland courts would adopt the approach espoused by the Restatement. Although the Court candidly admits that the answer to that question is not entirely clear, the Court is nonetheless satisfied that Maryland courts would look to the Restatement . . . [and] adopt the Restatement's approach of recognizing that the delivery requirement can be met by inter vivos delivery of a donative document. The Court reaches this conclusion for several reasons.

First, delivery by donative instrument is simply a natural application of the doctrine of constructive delivery that has long been recognized by Maryland courts. . . .

Maryland courts have acknowledged a wide variety of acts as constituting constructive delivery. Thus, over the years, Maryland courts have embraced constructive delivery of a bank account by transfer of a bankbook, constructive delivery of the contents of a trunk by transfer of a key to the trunk, and constructive delivery of the proceeds of an insurance policy by delivery of the policy documents. These cases demonstrate that Maryland has rejected unduly rigid manual delivery requirements in favor of constructive delivery rules that serve to effectuate the donor's intent and prevent fraud. . . . The Court therefore concludes that the oft-quoted standard that constructive delivery must be "as nearly perfect and complete as the nature of the property and the attendant circumstances and conditions will permit" is a flexible one, and that "[w]hat constitutes delivery depends largely on the intent of the parties." Indeed, Maryland's highest court has cautioned that "hard and fast" rules of delivery "are to be applied in a manner which will not frustrate a clear manifestation of intent." Yet, that is precisely what would happen if the Court rejected Rita Genecin's gift of the Lautrec because Paul did not immediately take the lithograph to Connecticut, as he did the Munakata.

Second, the Court believes (as do the Restatement drafters) that delivery by transfer of a clearly worded donative writing can satisfy the concerns underlying Maryland's delivery requirement. The chief concern . . . is that the donee is simply committing fraud in asserting that a gift was made at all. As Maryland's Court of Appeals has long noted, "the requirement of actual delivery is the only substantial protection [against fraud], and the courts should not weaken it by permitting the substitution of convenient and easily proven devices." Indeed, many Maryland cases in which courts have found gifts to fail for lack of physical delivery address situations in which evidence of the alleged gift is purely oral and the putative donor has done nothing at all to memorialize or evidence his or her donative intent. . . .

However, as the Restatement drafters recognize, the evidentiary function of the delivery requirement can be equally well served by an effective donative instrument. The New York Supreme Court, Appellate Division persuasively made this point in Gruen v. Gruen, 104 A.D.2d 171, 488 N.Y.S.2d 401, 403–04 (N.Y.A.D.1984), a case with facts strikingly similar to this one. The court in *Gruen* held that a father had successfully given a painting by artist Gustav Klimt to his son by sending him a gift letter, stating that "it is the delivery of the [written] instrument itself which fulfills the 'delivery' requirement of a gift inter vivos, and duplicative manual delivery is therefore unnecessary." *Id.* at 403. . . .

Here, the Court finds that there has been no fraud and that Rita Genecin made her intent to give the Lautrec to Paul clear and unmistakable in numerous ways, including taking the rather extraordinary action of transferring ownership of her home to her two sons (to whom she had gifted art that remained hanging in the home). . . .

Another reason to insist on physical delivery is to impress upon the donor that the gift now belongs to the donee and to ensure that the donor intended the gift to be irrevocable. However, a donative writing is certainly capable of serving a similar function. As the court recognized in *Gruen*, "the delivery of a written conveyance . . . requires a high degree of deliberation on the part of the donor, substantially higher than a manual delivery, and affords the clearest and most convincing evidence of the fact that the gift has taken place." *Gruen*, 488 N.Y.S.2d at 404 (quotation marks and citations omitted). . . .

Third, Maryland courts have also recognized that once a valid delivery takes place, a donor's physical retention of gifted property does not necessarily invalidate the gift. . . .

Fourth and finally . . . Maryland courts generally look favorably upon the Restatement and that they have adopted the Restatement's position in many other areas of the law. . . .

For the foregoing reasons, the Court concludes that Maryland courts would adopt the Restatement's position on delivery and would recognize that Rita Genecin's delivery of a deed of gift to Paul Genecin (combined with the virtually immediate conveyance of joint ownership to her home) would satisfy the delivery requirements for a valid inter vivos gift. . . .

* * *

In conclusion, the Court finds and declares that Rita Genecin did make a valid gift of the Lautrec lithograph to her son Paul Genecin in December 1999 and the Lautrec is therefore the lawful property of Paul Genecin. The Clerk is directed to enter final judgment and close this file.

Edinburg v. Edinburg

492 N.E.2d 1164 (App. Ct. Mass. 1986)

GREANY, J. This phase of the Edinburg litigation concerns the ownership of nineteen pieces of art work. . . . The judge concluded that Dorothy B. Edinburg had either made gifts of or sold the disputed artworks to her children's trusts. . . .

. . . Dorothy, as settlor, created on April 3, 1963, three irrevocable inter vivos trusts for the benefit of her three children, [John, Hope and Jo-Ann]. The original trustees were Dorothy's husband, Joseph M. Edinburg; his sister, Golda Edinburg; and Joseph's uncle, Mr. Joseph Talamo, an attorney. In early 1981, Dorothy and Joseph filed . . . for divorce. On May 4, 1982, Dorothy filed an action . . . seeking the filing by Joseph and Golda, the two remaining trustees, of accounts for each of the trusts; the confirmation of their resignations; and the appointment of a bank or some other suitable corporate fiduciary as the successor trustee. On September 12, 1982, Joseph filed accounts. . . . They indicated that Dorothy had withdrawn $33,900 from Jo-Ann's trust but had never accounted for the use of the money. They also indicated that Dorothy had withdrawn $15,400 from Hope's trust and $9,700 from John's trust.

In October, 1982, Dorothy filed objections to the accounts [stating] that the nineteen drawings at issue belonged to the trusts, not to her, and that the accounts inaccurately claimed that Dorothy owed money to the trusts. . . . Dorothy simultaneously took the position in the divorce litigation, in testimony under oath, in written documents, and by her conduct, that the nineteen drawings were properties of the trusts by reason of gifts or sales made by her.

On February 16, 1983, Joseph died, terminating the pending divorce complaints. . . . At about the same time, Dorothy sought to reverse her position as to the nineteen drawings, claiming that she had not made gifts of them or sold them to the trusts. Instead, she contended that she had constructed the appearance of gifts and sales in order to keep the art works from falling into her husband's hands by way of any division of property in the divorce actions under G.L. c. 208, s 34. This reversal led Dorothy to assert that she had committed perjury in prior testimony when she stated under oath that the drawings belonged to the trusts, and to claim that she had falsified documents and made misrepresentations to others in order to deceive the trial court and her husband. Confronted with this situation, the judge conducted a five-day trial.... Following the trial, the judge ... concluded that the nineteen drawings belonged to the children's trusts....

* * *

2. *The question of the gifts of sixteen drawings.* The judge determined that sixteen drawings had been given by Dorothy as gifts to two of the three irrevocable trusts. As a general rule, to sustain a transfer as a gift, there must be evidence of donative intent on the donor's part, combined with evidence of delivery of the property to the donee, or someone acting on the donee's behalf, in a manner that surrenders dominion and control....

Whether Dorothy possessed the necessary donative intent was "essentially a question of fact." In addition to her testimony, under oath, that she had made gifts of the sixteen drawings to the trusts, several independent witnesses testified that Dorothy had made gratuitous and unsolicited statements to her counsel, her husband's counsel, and others that the art works belonged to the trusts. There was evidence that Dorothy had stated to appraisers from Christie's ... that the art works were the property of the trusts. There was further evidence that she had affixed labels to some of the drawings that indicated their ownership by specific trusts; that she had placed stamps on the mats of other drawings, again indicating ownership by specific trusts; and that she had placed drawings that were of appropriate size in solander boxes,[13] which were marked as containing property of specific trusts. Thus, by means of labeling, stamping, or sequestration in solander boxes, each of the sixteen drawings had been identified as the property of a particular trust. Further, the evidence warranted the judge's finding that, in a meeting with her son John in March, 1982, Dorothy directed him to copy down the name of each artist and the title of each drawing given to his and Hope's trusts and other information, so that the ownership of each of the art works by a specific trust would be clear and unequivocal.

Other evidence showed that Dorothy had made gifts of art work to each of the three trusts in the past. This last evidence tended to demonstrate a pattern of giving to her children. Finally, the judge could note that Dorothy's financial statements filed in connection with the divorce litigation did not list the disputed art works as

13. A solander box is a special box employed to protect delicate works of art such as the drawings in this case.

her property. All of the above, which represents a summary of the evidence found credible by the judge, is sufficient to sustain his findings that Dorothy manifested the requisite donative intent.[14]

Dorothy's conduct in effecting gifts by placing the contested art works in the children's trusts, however, makes this a somewhat exceptional case. This is not the typical gift situation, in which physical delivery of the subject matter of the gift by the donor to the donee has clearly occurred. Ordinarily, such a definitive act of delivery confirms that the donor has irrevocably parted with dominion and control over the subject of the gift. Nevertheless, where such actual delivery is impractical, some symbolic or constructive form of delivery may be present and sufficient to warrant a conclusion that a gift has been made.

* * *

Dorothy's arguments [on delivery] overlook the exceptional nature of this case. It is significant here that "[t]angible personal property usually is not placed in a trust." Casner, 2A Estate Planning § 7.1.7 (1985). Without suggesting that traditional concepts of delivery ought to be dispensed with, we think that the judge could properly find a completed gift, despite the absence of delivery in a purely technical sense.

A method of analysis for approaching exceptional gift cases . . . follows: "While delivery is certainly one form of corroborating evidence, it . . . should not be the only acceptable evidence sufficient to corroborate the donee's claim. To insist on delivery as a necessary element of a gift [may be] unreasonable; to state the requirement in terms of the amount of proof necessary to establish the donee's claim, recognizing that delivery is sufficient corroboration in the normal case, is clearly the better approach." . . . This analysis by no means expresses a novel proposition but has been stated by authorities on the law of personal property and has been previously applied by other courts. In essence, the analysis relies upon the principle that evidence of the donor's words and conduct that is sufficiently strong to corroborate the donee's position that a gift has been made will safeguard against fraudulent claims and warrant a conclusion by a fact finder that the gift is valid, notwithstanding equivocal or weak proof of delivery.

Significantly, this case need not turn on statements of future donative intent. Dorothy repeatedly affirmed, in sworn testimony, in documents submitted to the court, and in private conversation, that the transfers of the art works to the trusts were indeed completed gifts. . . . The acts of placing labels and stamps on the drawings and sequestering them in special containers—all in order to specify the donee trust involved—constitute a form of symbolic delivery. The propriety of such a

14. The fact that Dorothy had not filed gift tax returns in connection with these drawings is not dispositive of the issue of her donative intent. . . .

form of symbolic delivery, where the nature of the property militated against giving physical dominion, was noted by the judge.[17]

* * *

All of these circumstances persuade us that the lack of further objective evidence of Dorothy's relinquishment of control should not be deemed decisive.... [O]ur conclusion is fortified by the principle that a court of equity will not look kindly on one who seeks to benefit by his own turpitude.

3. *The question of the sale of three drawings.* There is ample evidence to support the judge's conclusion that Dorothy had acquired three drawings for Jo-Ann's trust. Dorothy acknowledged her practice of purchasing art works in her own name and then subsequently selling them to one of the trusts. The purchase invoice from the foreign gallery... indicates that the drawing was purchased for, and with money from, Jo-Ann's trust. Ten other documents signed by Dorothy confirmed that she had withdrawn funds from Jo-Ann's trust to pay for the three drawings.... The amounts withdrawn by Dorothy from Jo-Ann's trust... corresponded roughly with the sums which had been paid for the pictures. The judge's finding that the three drawings had been sold to Jo-Ann's trust is not clearly erroneous.

* * *

Judgment affirmed.

Brown, J. (concurring): Two less cosmic thoughts occurred to me as I sifted through this voluminous record. The first is that I wish the needy knew how to put the law to work for them as assiduously as the greedy seem to do. Second, why do the poor and the disadvantaged receive different treatment in our courts than the privileged and wealthy? The central figure in this drama, Dorothy B. Edinburg, has admitted committing perjury several times. Given her blatant admission that she had falsified documents and committed perjury in order to deceive the trial court and her husband, I am compelled to conclude that she attempted to manipulate the legal system and make a mockery of our system of justice. Mrs. Edinburg's "conduct constituted both an affront to the court's dignity and a perversion of the court's purposes as an institution for just resolution of legitimate disputes."

If Mrs. Edinburg were poor, black or on welfare, I suspect that she would have been prosecuted to the full extent of the law. When will perjury become a crime for such perpetrators as she—lawyers, entrepreneurs, developers, so-called "wheeler-dealers"

---

17. The judge found that "the delicate nature of these works of art on paper and their high value required that the works be kept in safe places, that Mrs. Edinburg was experienced in this respect, that the trustees of the trusts were not experienced in conservation and security matters, that there were no trustees from 1980 on after the resignation of Joseph M. Edinburg and Golda Edinburg, and that Mrs. Edinburg reasonably and logically provided for the safety and security of these works of art." The fact that Dorothy retained the key to the vault is also not significant. The judge could have inferred from the evidence that Dorothy kept other art works that belonged solely to her in the vault and that her retention of the key was designed to give her access to those art works.

and the like? . . . It cannot be said often enough that doctors, lawyers, merchants, politicians and other professionals must not be encouraged to believe that there is one standard for them and another for the less advantaged citizens among us.

In the instant case, Mrs. Edinburg would have us believe that a lie in pursuit of wealth is not an indictable offense. Perjury is no less a crime when the objective is fortune rather than freedom. How can we still pretend that all persons are treated equally in our legal system? It is a fiction, but we cling to the myth. That old refrain "Don't do the crime, if you can't do the time"—must have application to persons regardless of race, sex or station in life.

Notes and Questions

1. *Ambiguity in Transfer: Inter Vivos Gifts. Genecin* and *Edinburg* present an issue of ambiguity, the ambiguous conduct effecting a delivery for a lifetime gift. In order to make a gift (that is, a gratuitous transfer of ownership during lifetime), the donor must have donative intent, deliver the property (actual or constructive), and the donee must accept (generally assumed, unless rejected or disclaimed). Donative intent and delivery are two separate elements, but in proving a gift, the evidence is often intertwined. Quite simply, the reality of actual delivery is seen as confirming the donor's subjective donative intent; if delivery is constructive, the corroboration of intent is weakened. Questions of donative intent can come up in many contexts, such as in the old loan case of *Escot Church*, discussed in Chapter 8, *supra*, or as here in *Genecin* and *Edinburg*. In each, the judge looked to all the facts and circumstances, including the conduct and statements of the transferor, to resolve this subjective inquiry regarding donative intent.

With respect to delivery, the inquiry is typically more objective: was there some documentation or written record transferring title to the property? Lawyers tend to think of indispensible documents to evidence a transfer of title, such as a deed for a gift of real estate, stock transfer or assignment forms for a gift of stock, a motor vehicle registration form for a gift of a car, a check for a gift of money, and so forth. When it comes to most items of tangible personal property, such as art, the tradition of indispensible documents is not deep. This is especially so in the family and friend context. Many individuals can probably identify with Mrs. Edinburg's putting labels or stickers on the various drawings and her original expectation that those labels would work. This casual tradition of disposing of art within a close circle of family and friends mirrors the casual tradition of acquiring art by handshake in the commercial context. As art values increased, commercial best practices calling for documentation became more common in the acquisition of art. A similar, more formal approach should govern the gratuitous disposition of art as well. Mrs. Genecin's deeds of gift were clearly atypical, but extremely important. Her conveyance of her home into a joint tenancy with both her sons was truly exceptional.

A deed of gift, including an acceptance, for a transfer of an artwork outright to a family member or friend is relatively simple and direct:

DEED of GIFT

I, ________(name)________, of ____________________, ________________, am the sole owner of __________________________, a work of art by the artist ____________________________.

I hereby give, outright and absolutely, all my right, title, and interest in and to such work of art, specifically including any copyright interests and associated rights therein, to my __________, ______________________________________, of ______________, ______________.

IN WITNESS WHEREOF, I have executed this Deed of Gift, this ________ day of _________________________, 20___, in _______________________, ____________________.

____

(Donor-Owner)

Subscribed and sworn to before me this ____ day of ______________, 20___.

____ My commission expires: ______________________

Notary Public

ACCEPTANCE OF GIFT

The undersigned as donee of the above described gift hereby accepts the gift as of the date this Deed of Gift was executed.

____

(Donee)

Given the simplicity of a deed of gift, why is there resistance to formalizing or documenting the transfer?

In the *Edinburg* case, the gifts were to irrevocable trusts for the benefit of her children and were not outright transfers. The court quoted from now-deceased Professor A. James Casner's treatise: "tangible personal property usually is not placed in a trust." This statement did not defeat the gift transfer; rather, it led to an analysis focusing more attention on the donor's words and actions as evidence corroborating the gift. While Professor Casner's statement is probably still true today, many trusts in fact hold tangible personal property as trust assets. When a gift transfer involves a trust, the donee for purposes of the Deed of Gift would technically be the trustee, "John Q. Smith, as Trustee of the Susan B. Smith Trust dated ____________, 20__, and his successor or successors in trust," and not the trust itself.

Regardless of the donee's status as individual or trustee, two additional steps should be considered to substantiate the transfer of the art and to reduce ambiguity in intrafamily gift transfers. Insurance on the property should be changed to the new owner. A gift tax return, even if not technically required, should be filed to further corroborate the gift. These steps, if absent, may raise questions as to the existence or bona fides of the gift transfer, such as for creditor purposes or estate tax purposes.

2. *Structural Parameters of Transfer.* After the owner decides who among his family and friends will be the beneficiary, there are two follow-up questions: when and how? That is, will the transfer of ownership take place during life as an inter vivos gift or at death as a transfer by will or trust? And will the transfer be an outright transfer to the beneficiary of full ownership or a transfer in trust with the beneficiary receiving a defined beneficial interest (but not legal ownership) in the trust that owns the art?

a. During lifetime or at death? The legal construct for an inter vivos gift of an artwork directly to an individual is as familiar to us as a birthday party. It is, therefore, relatively straightforward: the donor with donative intent delivers the artwork to the donee who accepts the gift. The reasons for gift giving during life are generally personal (such as celebrating milestones of birthdays, graduations, weddings; for the pure pleasure of sharing; educating the next generation for stewardship of valuable assets; relief from the burdens of ownership; or downsizing one's residence), but can be shaped by tax considerations. The transfer of property by gift during lifetime is subject to the federal gift tax, perhaps to the federal generation-skipping transfer tax (e.g., the gift is to a grandchild), and depending on the donor's domicile, to a state's gift and generation-skipping transfer tax as well. On the other hand, delaying a gift to the time of death does not generally eliminate taxes; it merely substitutes the federal estate tax regime for that of the federal gift tax, and usually a similar substitution at the state level. Is there any tax advantage or detriment to making a lifetime gift instead of a death time transfer?

Two tax advantages to lifetime gifts are the ability of the donor to use the gift tax annual exclusion and the removal of the artwork from the donor's gross estate for tax purposes, including any post-gift appreciation. The federal gift tax applies to transfers of property by gift (26 U.S.C. § 2501); however, like many taxes, there is an exemption, or de minimus, amount for gifts of present interests. While an outright gift of an artwork should routinely qualify as a gift of a present interest, a gift of that same artwork to a trust may not. See Calder v. Commissioner, 85 T.C. 713 (1985), discussed in Chapter 11, *infra*. In 2020, the gift tax annual exclusion amount on a per donee (not per donor) basis is $15,000. Consequently, if the value of the artwork does not exceed $15,000, the outright gift is free of federal gift tax. If the donor is married at the time of the gift, the spouses can agree to "gift split," meaning the gift will be deemed for gift tax purposes as coming from both spouses. 26 U.S.C. § 2513. Therefore, if the value of the artwork does not exceed $30,000, there is no gift tax. Finally, if the artwork is transferred to two people, such as a wedding gift, and the married donors gift split, the threshold value is now $60,000. The simplicity of the gift tax annual exclusion should not be overlooked.

The second advantage to a lifetime gift is the removal of the artwork from the donor's estate and the removal of any post-gift appreciation. Returning to the wedding gift scenario, if that $60,000 artwork doubles in value by the time the donor dies, the donor's estate has effectively been reduced by $120,000 because of the previous gift. And it was transfer tax free.

A possible tax disadvantage to making a lifetime gift involves the basis of the artwork for income tax purposes. In the wedding gift scenario, if the donor paid $20,000 for the artwork, his basis for income tax purposes would be his cost of $20,000. The significance of basis comes into play if there is a sale or disposition (but not including a gift) of the artwork. A quick example: If, instead of gifting the artwork to the wedding couple, the owner sells it for $60,000, there is gain of $40,000 ($60,000 amount realized—$20,000 basis). That gain would be included in the owner's income for income tax purposes. If we now return to the wedding gift scenario, the donees would take the donor's basis for income tax purposes. Thus, the newlyweds would have the same $20,000 income tax basis as the donor did. If they sell the work for $60,000, they would be the ones to report the $40,000 gain. If the newlyweds, however, were to sell the work at the time of the donor's death when its value is $120,000, their gain would be $100,000 ($120,000 amount realized—$20,000 basis). But, if there had not been a lifetime gift, and the artwork was included in the owner's estate, the traditional rule is that the income tax basis of property acquired from a decedent is the fair market value at the date of death, or the $120,000. 26 U.S.C. § 1014, but see 26 U.S.C. § 1022 for basis of property acquired from a decedent dying in 2010. (A word of caution, eliminating this "step-up" in basis is a frequent topic in tax reform; always double check current tax law.) Consequently, if the newlyweds instead received the work at donor-decedent's death, their basis would be $120,000; and a sale at that point for $120,000 would not create taxable income for them. The trade-off for removing the $120,000 from the owner's estate for estate tax purposes by way of a prior inter vivos gift is the donee's acquiring the donor's basis for income tax purposes. For some taxpayers, that trade-off makes sense. For other taxpayers (especially if their estates are less than the transfer tax free amount), the trade-off does not make sense.

b. Outright or in trust? The third and final parameter in gifting is deciding how the transfer will be structured—as a full, direct, outright transfer to the beneficiary as new owner or to a trust for the benefit of the beneficiary? Three primary determinants will shape the answer: the beneficiary, the property, and the donor, with tax considerations overlaying each factor.

First is a consideration of who the intended beneficiary is and her legal status. If the beneficiary is a 10-year-old grandchild, a 92-year-old incompetent or disabled spouse, a spendthrift, or a creditor-pursued or creditor-attractive beneficiary, it would be foolish, or at the very least unwise, to vest absolute ownership in that beneficiary. A minor or incapacitated beneficiary cannot deal directly with the property in any event, so interposing a trust is not unusual. It is an appropriate reaction to the legal status of the beneficiary. When a beneficiary is a spendthrift, has significant creditor claims, or potential for such claims (such as a highly successful professional who may attract litigation, e.g., a physician), a forward-thinking plan is to avoid giving outright ownership to that beneficiary and instead create a trust for his or her benefit. Properly drafted, a trust created for another person's benefit can insulate the property in the trust from the claims of the person's creditors, a very valuable benefit.

Another scenario where a trust instead of outright ownership could be effective is when there are two beneficiaries, but only one artwork, such as two siblings and one work that has great family attachment. In an appropriate family dynamic, a time-sharing arrangement where the ownership of the artwork is placed in a trust with one child having possession in even years and the other in odd could work. It is hard to know if this technique might have worked in *Genecin*.

The second factor is the nature and extent of the property. A painting worth $500 must be viewed in a different context than a painting worth $50 million. The transactional requirements of creating and maintaining a trust are not worth it for the first, but seem almost mandatory for the second. A somewhat similar concern can exist for a collection of objects, especially when some of the value arises from being part of the collection, the whole being greater than the sum of its parts.

The third factor, often the decisive one, is the donor's desire for control. A gift given outright to a beneficiary is now the beneficiary's, subject only to the beneficiary's desires and wishes for its use and enjoyment, and free of any restraint or restriction of the donor. For some donors with great attachment to the artworks or concern about the beneficiary's situation or judgment (whether valid or not), this is too great a strain. An outright transfer is just unacceptable, and a protective trust is the only answer. This decision of trust or outright transfer is a personal judgment of the donor that must rest on an internal comfort level of her own, sometimes independent of the beneficiary and property factors, and sometimes totally reflective of those two factors. As litigation in the U.S. increases, family structures become more fluid, and tax benefits can be tweaked, many donors opt for trusts instead of outright ownership for valuable or significant art.

Tax considerations may influence the decision of outright or in trust. For example, the owner of an artwork is unmarried and without children. He wants the painting that has been in his family for many years to go to his brother, and then to his brother's child. If the owner gives the work at his death outright to his brother, and then later his brother passes the painting to his child at his death, the painting is subject to tax at two deaths. If, instead, the owner had placed the ownership of the painting in a trust for his brother for his life, with his brother's child having the successive interest in the work at his father's death, there would be only one tax at the original owner's death.

3. *Bitter Disputes and Unseemly Actions.* It is impossible not to notice the courts' dismay with the litigants' behavior and arguments. Surely the strained family relationship is one source of the courts' concern. In this regard, using litigation

as the form of dispute resolution can aggravate, or perhaps permanently rupture, the family relationship, and destroy any hope for reconciliation. Some commentators suggest mediation. See, e.g., Mary F. Radford, *An Introduction to the Uses of Mediation and Other Forms of Dispute Resolution in Probate, Trust and Guardianship Matters*, 34 REAL PROP. PROB. & TR. J. 601 (2000).

Does the uniqueness of the artwork contribute to the family's friction? Think how to raise the issue with a client with an eye towards anticipating and planning for a dispute.

Judge Brown's concurring opinion in *Edinburg* invites discussion of his "cosmic thoughts." If you were representing Mrs. Edinburg, what would you have done? What are your ethical and professional responsibilities? As important as client representation and confidentiality is, a lawyer also has a duty to our system of justice. Knowingly participating in a fraud upon the court is never appropriate.

2. Testamentary Bequests

If the artwork was not transferred during lifetime, the artwork will be part of the decedent's estate at death. The question in contested situations for death time transfers shifts away from the quasi-objective question of delivery to the subjective question of decedent's intent.

Clark v. Greenhalge

582 N.E.2d 949 (Mass. 1991)

NOLAN, J. We consider . . . whether a probate judge correctly concluded that specific, written bequests of personal property contained in a notebook maintained by a testatrix were incorporated by reference into the terms of the testatrix's will. . . . The testatrix, Helen Nesmith, duly executed a will in 1977, which named her cousin, Frederic T. Greenhalge, II, as executor of her estate. The will further identified Greenhalge as the principal beneficiary of the estate, entitling him to receive all of Helen Nesmith's tangible personal property upon her death except those items which she "designate[d] by a memorandum left by [her] and known to [Greenhalge], or in accordance with [her] known wishes," to be given to others living at the time of her death. Among Helen Nesmith's possessions was a large oil painting of a farm scene signed by T.H. Muckley and dated 1833. The value of the painting, as assessed for estate tax purposes, was $1,800.00.

In 1972, Greenhalge assisted Helen Nesmith in drafting a document entitled "MEMORANDUM" and identified as "a list of items of personal property prepared with Miss Helen Nesmith upon September 5, 1972, for the guidance of myself in the distribution of personal tangible property." . . . In 1976, Helen Nesmith modified the 1972 list. . . . Neither edition of the list involved a bequest of the farm scene painting. Ms. Nesmith [also] kept a plastic-covered notebook . . . which bore the title "List to be given Helen Nesmith 1979." One such entry read: "Ginny Clark farm picture hanging over fireplace. Ma's room." . . . Ms. Nesmith's private home care nurses knew of the existence of the notebook and had observed Helen Nesmith write in it. On several occasions, Helen Nesmith orally expressed to these nurses her intentions regarding the disposition of particular pieces of her property upon her death, including the farm scene painting. Helen Nesmith told [her nurses] that the farm scene painting was to be given to Virginia Clark, upon Helen Nesmith's death. Virginia Clark and Helen Nesmith . . . lived next door to each other for approximately ten years (1945 through 1955), during which time they enjoyed a close friendship. The Nesmith-Clark friendship remained constant through the years. . . .

* * *

Ms. Nesmith executed two codicils to her 1977 will: one on May 30, 1980, and a second on October 23, 1980. The codicils amended certain bequests and deleted others, while ratifying the will in all other respects.

Greenhalge received Helen Nesmith's notebook on or shortly after January 28, 1986, the date of Ms. Nesmith's death. Thereafter, Greenhalge, as executor, distributed Ms. Nesmith's property in accordance with the will as amended. . . . Greenhalge refused, however, to deliver the farm scene painting to Virginia Clark because . . . he wanted to keep it. Mr. Greenhalge claimed that he was not bound to give effect to the expressions of Helen Nesmith's wishes and intentions stated in the notebook, particularly as to the disposition of the farm scene painting. . . . Ms. Clark thereafter commenced an action against Mr. Greenhalge. . . .

The probate judge found that Helen Nesmith wanted Ms. Clark to have the farm scene painting [and] that the notebook was incorporated by reference into the terms of the will. The judge awarded the painting to Ms. Clark.

The Appeals Court affirmed the probate judge's decision. . . . We . . . now hold that the probate judge correctly awarded the painting to Ms. Clark.

A properly executed will may incorporate by reference into its provisions any "document or paper not so executed and witnessed, whether the paper referred to be in the form of . . . a mere list or memorandum, . . . if it was in existence at the time of the execution of the will, and is identified by clear and satisfactory proof as the paper referred to therein." The parties agree that the document entitled "memorandum," dated 1972 and amended in 1976, was in existence as of the date of the execution of Helen Nesmith's will. . . . There is no dispute, therefore, that the 1972 memorandum was incorporated by reference into the terms of the will.

The parties do not agree, however, as to whether the documentation contained in the notebook, dated 1979, similarly was incorporated into the will through the language of Article Fifth. Greenhalge advances several arguments. . . . First, Greenhalge contends that the judge wrongly concluded that the notebook could be considered a "memorandum" within the meaning of Article Fifth, because it is not specifically identified as a "memorandum." Such a literal interpretation of the language and meaning of Article Fifth is not appropriate.

"The 'cardinal rule in the interpretation of wills, to which all other rules must bend, is that the intention of the testator shall prevail, provided it is consistent with the rules of law.'" The intent of the testator is ascertained through consideration of "the language which [the testatrix] has used to express [her] testamentary designs," as well as the circumstances existing at the time of the execution of the will. The circumstances existing at the time of the execution of a codicil to a will are equally relevant, because the codicil serves to ratify the language in the will which has not been altered or affected by the terms of the codicil.

Applying these principles in the present case, it appears clear that Helen Nesmith intended by the language used in Article Fifth of her will to retain the right to alter and amend the bequests of tangible personal property in her will, without having to amend formally the will. The text of Article Fifth provides a mechanism by which Helen Nesmith could accomplish the result she desired; i.e., by expressing her wishes "in a memorandum." The statements in the notebook unquestionably reflect Helen Nesmith's exercise of her retained right to restructure the distribution of her tangible personal property upon her death. That the notebook is not entitled "memorandum" is of no consequence.... In this connection, the distinction between the notebook and "a memorandum" is illusory.

The appellant acknowledges that the subject documentation in the notebook establishes that Helen Nesmith wanted Virginia Clark to receive the farm scene painting upon Ms. Nesmith's death. The appellant argues, however, that the notebook cannot take effect as a testamentary instrument under Article Fifth, because the language of Article Fifth limits its application to "a" memorandum, or the 1972 memorandum. We reject this strict construction of Article Fifth.... To construe narrowly Article Fifth and to exclude the possibility that Helen Nesmith drafted the notebook contents as "a memorandum" under that Article, would undermine our long-standing policy of interpreting wills in a manner which best carries out the known wishes of the testatrix. The evidence supports the conclusion that Helen Nesmith intended that the bequests in her notebook be accorded the same power and effect as those contained in the 1972 memorandum under Article Fifth. We conclude, therefore, that the judge properly accepted the notebook as a memorandum of Helen Nesmith's known wishes as referenced in Article Fifth of her will.

* * *

Lastly, the appellant complains that the notebook fails to meet the specific requirements of a memorandum under Article Fifth of the will, because it was not "known to him" until after Helen Nesmith's death. For this reason, Greenhalge states that the judge improperly ruled that the notebook was incorporated into the will. One of Helen Nesmith's nurses testified, however, that Greenhalge was aware of the notebook and its contents, and that he at no time made an effort to determine the validity of the bequest of the farm scene painting to Virginia Clark as stated therein. There is ample support in the record, therefore, to support the judge's conclusion that the notebook met the criteria set forth in Article Fifth regarding memoranda.

We note, as did the Appeals Court, that "one who seeks equity must do equity and that a court will not permit its equitable powers to be employed to accomplish an injustice." To this point, we remark that Greenhalge's conduct in handling this controversy fell short of the standard imposed by common social norms, not to mention the standard of conduct attending his fiduciary responsibility as executor, particularly with respect to his selective distribution of Helen Nesmith's assets. We can discern no reason in the record as to why this matter had to proceed along the protracted and costly route that it did.

Judgment affirmed.

Notes and Questions

1. *Ambiguity in Transfer: Bequests.* Like *Genecin* and *Edinburg*, the *Clark* case involved ambiguity: the ambiguous meaning of "a memorandum" for the testamentary doctrine of incorporation by reference. Was the 1979 notebook maintained by the decedent sufficiently referred to in the 1977 will, as amended by the 1980 codicils? There was no ambiguity as to the particular artwork; its description was sufficiently definite in the context of the estate. To the extent the scope of the incorporation was alleged to be ambiguous or confusing, the court applied the "cardinal rule" in will construction, that of ascertaining and fulfilling the dominant intention of the decedent. Unlike *Edinburg*, where the judge could hear Mrs. Edinburg's direct testimony as to her donative intent and actions, in a testamentary transfer, the opportunity for direct examination is missing. Consequently, experienced estate planners place a premium on careful and precise drafting. There are two drafting scenarios where a bequest of an artwork can create ambiguity.

The first involves a specific bequest of an artwork that is insufficiently or inaccurately described. For example, a specific bequest in a will states: "I give my Robert Motherwell, including any copyright interest, to my son, if he survives me." At the time of death, decedent owned two Motherwells. Alternatively, a specific bequest might provide: "I give my Robert Motherwell painting, including any copyright interest, to my son, if he survives me." The decedent did not own a painting by Motherwell, he owned a lithograph or a drawing. In a similar vein, would the *Clark* result be different if the "farm picture hanging over the fireplace in Ma's room" had been moved to the dining room? Probably not, but using a location to describe a "movable" can carry risk. Consider adding the word "currently."

The second situation where drafting can create ambiguity occurs when there is no specific mention of the artwork in the will. Well-drafted wills usually contain a minimum of two dispositive provisions—the personal and household effects bequest and the residuary bequest. If there is no specific mention of the artwork, does the artwork pass pursuant to the personal and household effects provision or pursuant to the residue? Or perhaps an alternative provision? If the beneficiaries of the provisions are the same, the issue is largely academic, but if there is a difference in beneficiaries, a construction suit may be necessary. See In re Rothko's Estate, 352 N.Y.S.2d 574 (N.Y. Sur. Ct. 1974), where the court determined, over the objections of the executors and residuary charitable beneficiary, that the specific devise of the home "with all of the contents thereof" included the artist's paintings located in his home at the time of his death.

Both of these drafting problems may spring from a common source: the drafting attorney's insufficient information about the client's bequest. Knowledge is power in this context. If the client has a limited number of artworks that are significant to the client, it would be best to draft a specific dispositive provision for those works, specifically describing each such work. For example, "I give my Robert Motherwell lithograph, *Rite of Passage II*, 1979–1980, and my David Hockney lithograph, *Pretty Tulips*, 1969, including any copyright interests, to my son, if he survives me." Alternatively, if the client's art collection is extensive and listing the works is inappropriate or unwieldy, a specific gift of the entire collection should be considered. For clarity, either of these dispositions in a will should precede the personal effects disposition. If the bequest of an art collection is placed after the personal effects provision, the art collection should be specifically excluded from the operation of the personal effects provision. Of course if the bulk of the estate consists of artworks, such as can occur with an artist's estate, the drafting presumptions should be further refined. Successful artists sometimes incorporate their art business and therefore do not own their artworks individually but own stock instead. See, e.g., Priv. Ltr. Rul. 201323029, outlining one such plan that included a charitable component as well.

2. *Additional Drafting Points.* The decision to make the artworks a specific bequest as opposed to a residuary bequest carries along with it two common law doctrines—abatement and ademption. Both doctrines are codified in many jurisdictions and probate codes, and like many common law doctrines, they have extensive interpretative histories. Under the doctrine of abatement, a specific bequest of property receives preferential treatment, and that property can generally not be used to pay the estate's creditors (other than certain claims of a surviving spouse) until all non-specific gifts are exhausted. Under the doctrine of ademption, a specific bequest of property, such as an artwork, will be adeemed (or fail) if that artwork is not part of the estate at the time of death. Thus, if the artwork is sold or transferred during the decedent's lifetime, the specific bequest will fail. Another aspect of a specific bequest is that any liens, charges, or encumbrances against the property (such as a warehouse storage lien) will carry over to the new owner: one accepts the burdens as well as the benefits of ownership. A testator's will can modify the application of any of these doctrines.

Three further drafting issues arise in the context of art bequests in wills or trusts at death. They are the impact of taxes, the effect of valuation changes, and refining the "to be divided among them as they shall agree" clause.

a. Planning for taxes and expenses. The first involves a provision that should be addressed and clarified in any will or trust: who should pay the costs of any estate, inheritance, or succession taxes associated with the transfer of property? When that property includes highly-valuable art, relying on a generic tax provision may cause an unintended distortion in the value of the beneficiaries' bequests and unintended conflict between the beneficiaries. A general tax provision in many wills is: "My executor shall pay from the residue of my estate all estate and inheritance taxes assessed by reason of my death." Consider the example of a father who has two adult children, Lee and Pat, for whom he has equal love and affection, and a taxable estate valued at $100X. Father has one significant artwork valued at $50X, and the remaining $50X is in stocks and cash in bank accounts. If father's will takes the direct approach of a specific bequest of the artwork to Lee, who desires it, and the residue to Pat, who does not desire the artwork, what is the impact of say a 30% estate tax? Lee will receive the $50X artwork as a specific bequest free of the 30% tax, while Pat will receive the residue of $50X, less the $30X in tax (that is the 30% tax on the taxable estate of $100X), or $20X. Is this what their father intended? Probably not. Revising the tax clause to apportion the tax among all beneficiaries relative to their proportionate interests is one solution. A similar concern exists with respect to the payment of the estate's expenses, such as funeral costs, appraisal fees, attorney fees, and so forth. Typically, they are paid out of the residue, further exacerbating the inequality of the legacies. Revising the expense clause to apportion the amounts among the beneficiaries may be the appropriate solution. Drafting for specific bequests of art also raises the issue of packing and transporting those works to the new owner. Many documents provide that the estate will bear these costs as an expense of the estate. If this is not intended or appropriate under the circumstances, the document should be revised accordingly.

b. Anticipating valuation changes. Let us consider the prior hypothetical with one slightly different variant—now father has two artworks, each equally valued at $25X when he comes to his estate planner. His plan is to make a separate specific bequest of one work to Lee, a separate specific bequest of the other work to Pat, and divide the residue equally between Lee and Pat. What could go wrong with this plan? The simple and direct answer is that values could change. One work could increase in value or decrease in value because of market conditions, or more dramatically, one work could be deemed inauthentic, virtually destroying all significant value, or be authenticated as a masterpiece, causing value to skyrocket. Another version of changing values can occur if ownership is challenged by another individual or a government. This can create a drafting dilemma: directly acknowledging this issue might be seen as an admission against ownership, while ignoring the issue can defeat treating the two children equally. One drafting technique is to provide for a compensating cash distribution if (i) the values of the two works differ significantly whether on a percentage basis or absolute dollar amount, or (ii) if one of the works is not owned by father or by the child at the time of the father's death.

c. Setting guidelines for beneficiaries' choosing artworks. When a personal art collection is extensive, or where artworks are included in the personal effects provision, a common technique is to allow the beneficiaries to divide the works among themselves. Most beneficiaries accept the reality that some of their highly desired items may go to another beneficiary; yet for some, as in *Genecin*, the swirl of emotional or personal attachment to a particular item, negative feelings toward another beneficiary, and discrepant values can be overwhelming. Identifying situations that call for more precise guidelines for division of an art collection is itself imprecise. Many experienced estate planners pose the question directly to their client, the person who best knows the situation and her beneficiaries. The following is an example of will language giving more detail to the typical "to be divided among them as they shall agree" provision:

> In the event my children cannot agree as to the division of the artworks, then each then living child of mine shall have the right to select one artwork, in an order initially determined by random selection, such as drawing numbers from a hat. Once each living child has selected an artwork in the order initially determined, the selection process shall continue until all artworks are selected or no child desires to continue to select, except that the order of selection shall be reversed from the previous order each time the selection process repeats.

Think how this would need to be modified to include the descendants of a deceased child of the testator. If a client is especially concerned about the beneficiaries' inability to divide property, it may be appropriate to add a mediation provision to the document. See Mary F. Radford, *An Introduction to the Uses of Mediation and Other Forms of Dispute Resolution in Probate, Trust, and Guardianship Matters*, 34 REAL PROP. PROB. & TR. J. 601 (2000).

3. *Art and Estate Tax—Some Numbers.* The IRS prepares and releases statistical information on tax returns filed, including estate tax returns. Beginning with the 2008 reports, art is one of the reported asset classifications used by the IRS for its statistical purposes. According to the IRS, for estate tax returns filed in 2009, the $2.845 billion of art reported on those returns accounted for approximately 1.5% of all estate assets. For returns filed in 2018, the $3.141 billion of art reported on all returns similarly represented approximately 1.5% of all estate assets.

Almost 9.5% of all returns in 2009 included art, while approximately 14% of all estates in 2018 included art. For 2009 estates of $2–3.5 million, 6% reported art as an asset, while for estates of more than $20 million, 38% included art, which represented approximately 4% of their assets. By 2018, of the largest estates (those over $50 million), 41% included art, which represented approximately 3.2% of their assets. See SOI Tax Stats—Estate Tax Statistics, at www.irs.gov. Interestingly, some investment advisors suggest clients diversify across asset classes, including for high net worth clients, 5% in art.

B. Gifts and Bequests to Museums and other Charitable Organizations

For many individual owners and collectors of art, the goal has always been to transfer the art collection to a museum or a charitable organization. The decision-making process for a charitable transfer follows the same broad outlines as for a transfer to an individual (i.e., who, when, and how), and the need for careful drafting of the deeds of gift and bequests continues, but with significantly higher attention paid to tax incentives and tax requirements. Qualified transfers of property to charities during lifetime can provide income tax and gift tax charitable deductions to the taxpayer, and qualified transfers at death can provide an estate tax charitable deduction. These deductions can be economically significant. The rules for the income, gift, and estate tax charitable deductions for artworks are not intuitive; they are highly complex, interrelated, and constantly subject to change by Congress. Consider this, therefore, a gentle disclaimer and best practices reminder: before embarking on a major gift of art to a charitable organization, consult a tax advisor.

1. *Inter Vivos Gifts of Entire Interest.* When an individual decides to give an artwork to a museum, making that gift during lifetime instead of at death can result in a substantial income tax benefit to the donor. In its simplest form, let us assume a sculpture purchased years ago by the taxpayer for $10,000 is now worth $50,000. Taxpayer donates the sculpture to a qualified charity and is entitled to take a $50,000 charitable deduction on her income tax return. If the taxpayer is in the 35% marginal tax bracket, the tax savings can approach $17,500 (35% of $50,000; however because of possible quantitative limitations on deductions, there can be some loss in actual value to the taxpayer). How does one qualify for this beneficial income tax treatment? There are four basic requirements that a taxpayer donating a tangible artwork must meet in order to claim the fair market value of the artwork as an income tax charitable deduction: the tax status of the recipient organization, the tax status of the type of property being donated, the related use rule, and having a qualified appraisal by a qualified appraiser. 26 U.S.C. § 170. If any of these basic four requirements is not satisfied, the deduction for the full fair market value will be denied. A deduction in the amount of the taxpayer's cost may be allowed instead, but it is also possible that no deduction at all will be allowed. See Conrad Teitell, *No Qualified Appraisal, No Deduction*, 134 TRUSTS & ESTATES 84 (1995); D'Arcangelo v. Commissioner, 68 T.C.M. 1223 (1994); Scheidelman v. Commissioner, 100 T.C.M. (CCH) 24 (2010). In addition, a taxpayer may be limited in the amount of a deduction that can be claimed in any one year because of the general percentage limitations for charitable contributions, which is generally 30% of the taxpayer's contribution base for gifts of appreciated tangible personal property. 26 U.S.C. § 170(b)(1)(B).

a. Status of charitable recipient. There are two types of charitable organizations for tax purposes: public charities and private charities. A public charity is basically an organization that receives part of its support from the general public. To receive the full fair market value deduction, the donee recipient must generally be a public charity. 26 U.S.C. § 170(e)(1)(B). The IRS maintains on its website (www.irs.gov), a cumulative list of exempt organizations. One needs to ascertain that the donee charity is a public charity under § 509(a) of the Internal Revenue Code, not just that it is a § 501(c)(3) tax exempt organization.

b. Type of property donated for tax purposes. In order to take the full fair market value as an income tax deduction, the donated property must be characterized for tax purposes as long term capital gain property. 26 U.S.C. § 170(e)(1). This generally means that the artwork is a capital asset as defined in § 1221 of the Internal Revenue Code in the donor's hands, it has appreciated in value, and it has been held by the donor for more than one year. An artwork is not a capital asset for charitable deduction purposes if the donor created it, if it was received as a gift from the artist-creator, or if it is held as inventory by a dealer. Artists therefore cannot receive a full fair market value deduction for donating their own works to charitable organizations. If a collector received an artwork as a gift from an artist, that work is similarly not a capital asset for the collector. See Carol Vogel, *Thanks for the Memories, Andy Warhol*, N.Y. TIMES, Oct. 30, 2009, at C22, concerning the auction of an Andy Warhol self-portrait which was a gift from Warhol to the owner, who as a high school girl had been a volunteer-secretary at the Factory in 1965.

c. Related use rule. When the charitable donation is of tangible personal property, such as an artwork, the related use rule requires that the charity's actual use of that tangible personal property be related to its purpose or function that constitutes the reason for its tax-exempt status under § 501(c). 26 U.S.C. § 170(e)(1)(B). Thus, for a donation of a work of contemporary art to a public museum of contemporary art, a taxpayer can reasonably assume, absent specific knowledge to the contrary, that the work of contemporary art will not be put to an unrelated use by the museum. But caution is necessary; museums sometimes have galas or fundraisers that raise money by auctioning donated artworks. Those donated artworks do not satisfy the related use rule. See Treas. Regs. § 1.170A-4(b)(3)(ii); also IRS Form 8283 Noncash Charitable Contributions, Section B, Part IV, where the donee charity obligates itself to notify the IRS if it disposes of the donated property within 3 years of the gift.

d. Qualified appraisal by a qualified appraiser. 26 U.S.C. § 170(f)(11). See discussion in Chapter 11, *infra*.

2. *Inter Vivos Gift of Partial Interest*. Gifts of less than all of the donor's interest in an artwork to a charity during lifetime are not encouraged by current federal tax law. In the worst- case scenario, a gift may have been made for gift tax purposes that does not qualify for the gift tax or income tax charitable deduction. This is a result of the split interest rules governing charitable gifts. See 26 U.S.C. §§ 170(a)(3), 170(f)(3)(A), and 2522(c)(2-3), also discussion in Chapter 8, *supra*; Lerner & Bresler, 3 ART LOAN 1573–1604; but cf., Joseph M. Dodge, *Are Gift Demand Loans of Tangible Property Subject to the Gift Tax?*, 30 VA. TAX REV. 181 (2010).

One type of partial gift for artworks that was quite popular for many years was known as the fractional gift. In Winokur v. Commissioner, 90 T.C. 733 (1988), *acq.* 1989 WL 1109340 (1989), the taxpayer had donated a 10% undivided fractional interest in 44 artworks to a publicly supported museum in each of two years. The deed of gift specifically entitled the museum to possess the artworks for 10%, then 20% of the year, with the choice of days being in the museum's discretion. In fact, the museum did not take possession of any of the artworks for the tax years in question, except that the museum did take possession of five artworks when the final 80% was transferred to it. The IRS denied the charitable deduction for income tax purposes under § 170(a)(3), arguing that the undivided 10% interests were gifts of future interests in tangible personal property. The Tax Court found for the taxpayer, holding that it was the right to possess, not actual possession, that made the transfer a present gift. The income tax charitable deductions were therefore allowed, albeit for a lower amount.

With *Winokur* as precedent, many collectors made fractional interest gifts of artworks to museums. Donors of fractional interests were no longer the fee simple owners of the artwork—they effectively were co-owners with a public charity. Why would someone do that? The tax reason was that a fractional gift allowed the taxpayer to avoid the percentage limitations of the income tax charitable deduction that could be triggered with a donation of particularly valuable artworks. For example, assume a collector decides to gift an appreciated artwork that he purchased years ago to a public art museum. The fair market value of the artwork is $1,500,000, and the collector's tax contribution base for the charitable deduction is $500,000. Because the percentage limitation for gifts of appreciated tangible personal property is 30% of the contribution base, the collector could only claim a maximum charitable deduction income tax purposes of $150,000 (30% of $500,000). That, however, is only the equivalent of ten percent of the work's value. The tax efficient method of gifting would have been to make a gift of 60% of the artwork in year one and claim a total deduction of $900,000 (60% of $1,500,000). Because of the percentage limitation as mentioned, only $150,000 would have been allowable in year one, but the excess contribution could be carried forward for the next succeeding five years. 26 U.S.C. §§ 170(d)(1)(A), 170(b)(1)(B). Assuming constant values, a charitable deduction of $150,000 could be claimed for each of the succeeding five years. In year seven, the remaining 40% would be given, with a similar $150,000 deduction for four years. See Anne-Marie Rhodes, *Big Picture, Fine Print: The Intersection of Art and Tax*, 26 COLUM. J.L. & ARTS 179, 193–196 (2003). In 2006, Congress amended § 170 by adding new subsection (o) that curtailed the utility of fractional interest gifts for charitable deduction purposes. 26 U.S.C. § 170(o). See Samuel G. Wieczorek, *Winokur, Lose or Draw: Art Collectors Lose an Important Tax Break*, 8 HOUS. BUS. & TAX L.J. 90 (2007). Why did Congress take this action?

3. *Fractional Interest Gifts under § 170(o).* Despite the constraints imposed by section 170(o), gifts of fractional interests in artworks to museums did not entirely disappear. The availability of an income tax charitable deduction, though limited,

can still be a useful approach to a taxpayer. In documenting the gift, the basics of property law and the requisite tax requirements are of utmost importance. There must be donative intent, delivery, and acceptance for a valid gift for property purposes. When there are co-owners, it is appropriate to spell out the terms regarding what a co-owner can do and what one cannot do. The tax requirements should also be referenced in the gift agreement transfer.

Consider the following template for a gift of a partial interest in an artwork to a tax-qualified museum.

Gift of Partial Interest

1. Transfer

I, ____________, hereby give, assign and transfer to ___________ (the "Museum"), as an absolute and unrestricted gift, a X% undivided fractional interest in the below described object (the "Work"), including an equal percentage of any copyright interests and associated rights as I may have, if any, in the Work:

[Insert description of the Work]

2. Representations and Warranties

I represent and warrant that (a) I am the sole owner of the Work, (b) I have the sole right to convey good title to the Work, and (c) the Work is free and clear of all encumbrances, liens, and restrictions. I further represent and warrant that, to the best of my knowledge, the Work is authentic and conforms to the description provided above; the Work has not been imported into or exported from any country contrary to its laws; and no patrimony or other laws or regulations applicable to the Work have been broken.

3. Sales, Encumbrances, Loans and Conservation

For so long as I possess any ownership interest in the Work, (a) I agree that I shall not sell or encumber the Work without the Museum's prior written consent; (b) neither party shall lend the Work to any third party without the prior written consent of the other party; (c) each party shall notify the other promptly upon receipt of a loan request for the Work so that the parties shall have sufficient time to consult about the proposed loan and make necessary arrangements if they agree the loan should be made; and (d) neither party shall perform any conservation or repairs on the Work without obtaining the prior consent of the other party.

4. Credit Line

I wish this partial gift to be identified to the public and in the records of the Museum as:

[Insert desired credit line]

At such time as I have conveyed my entire ownership interest in the Work to the Museum, I wish this gift to be identified to the public and in the records of the Museum as:

[Insert desired credit line]

5. Possession

The Museum shall be entitled to possession, dominion and control of the Work for that percentage of each calendar year proportionate to the Museum's percentage ownership interest in the Work, and I shall be entitled to possession, dominion and control of the Work for the remainder of the year. The Museum and I shall endeavor to schedule our respective rights of possession of the Work to accommodate each of our needs. I intend that the Museum shall have physical possession of the Work, and shall use it for its exempt purposes, for at least such periods as may be required to avoid the recapture of any tax deduction and the imposition of penalties under the Internal Revenue Code.

When the Work is in my possession, I will carry insurance in an amount sufficient to protect the interests of both the Museum and myself against physical loss or damage to the Work, and I will cause the insurer to furnish to the Museum a certificate of insurance as evidence of such coverage. When the Work is in the Museum's possession, the Museum will insure against physical loss or damage to the Work under the Museum's Fine Arts Insurance Policy. The owner in possession of the Work shall be responsible for the costs of packing and shipping the Work to the other owner.

6. Pledge

I unconditionally and irrevocably pledge that I will give my remaining ownership interest in the Work to the Museum through further gifts of fractional interests in the Work from time to time during my lifetime or through a bequest upon my death. I intend to give my remaining ownership in the Work to the Museum by such date as may be required to avoid the recapture of any tax deduction and the imposition of penalties under the Internal Revenue Code.

I shall provide in my estate planning documents that upon my death any remaining interest in the Work not previously gifted to the Museum shall be gifted to the Museum. However, any failure to include a specific bequest of the Work to the Museum in my estate planning documents shall not release my executors, administrators, trustees, heirs, and assigns from the obligation of delivering the Work, and all right, title and interest thereto, to the Museum in accordance with this Agreement. This Agreement shall extend to and be binding upon my executors, administrators, trustees, heirs, and assigns.

7. Commitment

This Agreement is a definite commitment by me to give the Work to the Museum as set forth herein. I authorize the Museum to make this pledge known to others to encourage them to make similar commitments. I understand that in reliance on this Agreement, the Museum is adjusting its acquisition plans and may also take other steps, such as publicizing the Agreement and adjusting its exhibition and programming plans.

8. Other

This Agreement shall be governed by the laws of ____________.

---

4. *Testamentary Transfers: Estate Tax Overview.* Transfers of property at death are generally subject to the federal estate tax (with the apparent exception for those who died in 2010, the year in which the federal estate tax was not in effect). The estate tax free amount for 2018–2025 is $10 million adjusted for inflation; the amount for 2021 is $11,700,000. 26 U.S.C. § 2010(c)(3)(C). The amount as adjusted for inflation is scheduled to sunset in 2026, at which point $5,000,000 will be the starting amount to be adjusted for inflation. Congress debates the tax-free amount routinely, and changes in the currently scheduled tax-free amounts must be anticipated. Estates that exceed the tax-free amount can generally receive a full estate tax deduction for property left to the surviving spouse and for property given to charity. For estates that exceed the tax free amount, use of the marital and charitable deductions can reduce the federal estate tax to zero. While any particular case can differ, for many clients and their estate planners, significant use of the estate tax charitable deduction is more routine at the death of the second spouse and not at the death of the first spouse. Some estate planners advise married clients who wish to make a charitable

gift at the death of the first spouse to die, to make the gift to the surviving spouse with a request, not a direction, to give the property to charity. Why? The gift to the surviving spouse qualifies for the estate tax marital deduction, and the surviving spouse can take an income tax charitable deduction when the gift is made. A direct bequest from the decedent could qualify for an estate tax charitable deduction, but the estate would not receive an income tax deduction for the charitable gift. Thus, the two-step process is more income tax efficient, assuming the spouse survives, is competent, and is willing and able to make the gift.

Because transfers at death are not governed by the income tax charitable deduction, there are fewer tax restrictions on testamentary transfers of artworks to charities. For example, the distinction between a public charity and a private foundation generally disappears, as do the capital gain property requirement and the related use rule. Clarity in drafting the bequest, anticipating changing values, and allocating the payment of taxes and expenses remain important basic requirements for a testamentary gift to charity. See Notes following *Clark v. Greenhalge*, *supra*.

5. *Testamentary Transfers: The Copyright Issue for Bequests.* Special estate tax rules on retained copyright interests create a drafting concern. To understand the issues, a brief background on tax law's split interest rules and copyright's separate property rule is necessary.

When a decedent bequeaths an interest in property to a charity and another interest in the same property to a non-charitable beneficiary (e.g., a life estate to a brother with remainder to charity), the charitable deduction for estate tax purposes is denied unless the transfer is in a Code-sanctioned form. When the charitable portion is the remainder interest in a split interest gift, the charitable deduction is available only if the transfer is in the form of a charitable remainder annuity trust ("CRAT"), a charitable remainder unitrust ("CRUT"), or a pooled income fund. 26 U.S.C. § 2055(e)(2)(A). Alternatively, if the charitable gift portion is the income or lead interest, then the charitable deduction is only available if it is a guaranteed annuity interest or unitrust interest. 26 U.S.C. § 2055(e)(2)(B). These highly detailed constructs were developed to counteract abuses in charitable deduction planning. Prior to the enactment of the split interest rules in 1969, it was possible for a decedent to create a trust in her will leaving a life estate to her child, with the remainder interest to charity. Her estate would have been entitled to a charitable deduction in her estate equal to the actuarial value of the charity's remainder interest. The only problem was that the charity would not necessarily receive the remainder interest, because the trustee would have also been given discretion to use the principal of the trust for the child's "best interests." Many trustees—often the family members themselves—would decide that it was in the child's best interests for the child to receive the whole trust estate outright, effectively terminating the trust early and thereby defeating the charity's remainder interest. Congress was rightfully protective of the fisc and the integrity of the tax system in enacting the split interest rules.

Within 10 years of enacting the split interest rules for charitable transfers and tax deductions, Congress took up the complex issue of copyright. Congress enacted the Copyright Act of 1976 (17 U.S.C. §§ 101–914) that totally revamped the traditional common law copyright in favor of a statutory form, bringing the United States into greater harmony with international norms. Significantly for artworks, the artwork's copyright is now a separate property. It is separate from the ownership of the tangible artwork. 17 U.S.C. § 202. For purposes of copyright law, they are two separate, distinct properties. Copyright generally stays with the artist after the sale of the physical artwork, but copyright can be transferred. See 17 U.S.C. § 201(a) and (e). A transfer of copyright ownership, other than by operation of law, must be in writing and signed by the owner. 17 U.S.C. § 204.

The traditional tax law view was the artwork and its copyright were two interests in the same property. When copyright law newly held that the work and its copyright were two separate properties, an obvious conflict existed. In practice, this meant that if a decedent were to make a bequest of the artwork to a charity but not also transfer the copyright to the charity, the gift was a split interest gift for tax purposes. And it was a transfer that did not meet any of the statutory safe harbors. Consequently, no estate tax charitable deduction would be allowed. In 1981, Congress addressed this inconsistent treatment retroactively by adding § 2055(e)(4) to the Internal Revenue Code. 26 U.S.C. § 2055(e)(4). It provides rather limited but important relief. Under § 2055(e)(4), a work of art and its copyright will be treated as two separate properties (i.e., not two interests in one property) for purposes of the estate tax split interest rules in the case of a testamentary qualified contribution of a work of art. Three statutory definitions are provided: work of art, qualified contribution, and qualified organization.

A work of art is "any tangible personal property with respect to which there is a copyright under Federal law." Qualified contribution is any transfer of a work of art to a qualified organization if the "use of the property by the organization is related to the purpose or function constituting the basis" for exemption under § 501, the related use rule. Finally, a qualified organization is any organization described in § 501(c)(3), excluding a private foundation under § 509 (but a private operating foundation as defined in § 4942(j)(3) will not be excluded).

How does one apply these rules in estate planning? First, if the decedent collector never had the copyright, the transfer of a work of art will not be subject to the split interest rules. Second, if the decedent does own the copyright at the time of death, a bequest of the work of art to a qualified charity can be made without simultaneously transferring the copyright. It is then very important to provide that the use of the transferred work of art must be related to the purpose or function of the qualified charity's tax exempt status. The practical difficulty is that this condition may not be satisfied post death and an alternative gift needs to be arranged. Consequently, the better drafting technique is to transfer both the work of art and its copyright to the charity, thereby avoiding the impact of the related use rule.

When estate planning for artists who wish to donate works of art to qualified charities but not the copyright, the related use rule in the context of the particular charity must be clearly and critically considered. If the artist does not necessarily wish to retain the copyright for the donated works of art, the drafting lawyer should consider specifically transferring the copyright interest as well in order to avoid the trap posed by the related use rule. Some of the angst caused by the related use rule can and probably should be addressed prospectively with the charity for gifts of significance.

6. *Artist's Right to Terminate Transferred Copyright.* The Copyright Act of 1976 provides artists (or their statutory heirs) the right to terminate previously transferred copyrights, including copyright transfers by gift, sales, or to a trust. There are three statutory rights to terminate based generally on when the transfer occurred: grants made on or after January 1, 1978, grants made pre-1978, and grants made in their renewal window on October 27, 1998. For transfers in 1978 and thereafter, the right to terminate exists in general within a five-year window beginning 35 years after the grant. For transfers in 1978 therefore, the 35-year mark was 2013, at which point the five-year right to terminate began, and it ended in 2018. To exercise this right, the artist (or statutory heirs) must notify the current copyright holder no more than 10 years before the five-year window begins and no later than two years before it ends. Because this right to terminate is relatively new in practice, there is little guidance on the tax implications of the right to terminate. See Bridget J. Crawford & Mitchell Gans, *Sticky Copyrights: Discriminatory Tax Restraints on the Transfer of Intellectual Property*, 67 WASH. & LEE L. REV. 41 (2010).

The tax and economic consequences of Copyright's grant of the inalienable right to terminate can be significant:

> The inalienable right of artists and statutorily defined heirs to claw back transferred copyrights during the statutory termination period should be carefully considered by advisors because it can create unintended windfalls to defined heirs who are not meant to be included in an artist's estate plan, eviscerate a major source of funding for an artist's foundation, make managing an artist's legacy by the artist's foundation a challenge (if not an impossibility), and create unexpected gift and estate tax consequences.

Michael L. Duffy, *Rights That Go Bump in the Night: Planning and Administering Copyrights in an Artist's Estate,* PROB. & PROP. 25 (Sept.-Oct. 2017).

7. *Acceptance by the Museum.* In *Genecin* and *Edinburg*, the question was whether there was a sufficient delivery of the art by the donor to the donee. Acceptance by the donee was generally assumed. When making a testamentary transfer to a museum, however, one should not assume the artwork will in fact be acceptable to, or accepted by, the museum. The professionalization of museums and their collections policies has matured. One can no longer assume that a bequest to a museum will be routinely accepted. Before embarking on an estate plan that is premised on

a significant charitable donation, a client should have a frank conversation with the intended charitable donee.

Four factors predominate in a museum's decision whether to accept or refuse a proffered donation. First and foremost, is the nature of the museum's collection or collections. It is illogical for a museum of contemporary art to be the testamentary beneficiary of 15th century Flemish tapestries. On the other hand, a museum without a tapestry or textile collection, but with a wider collecting focus or desire to expand, may be a receptive beneficiary. Having discussions in advance is a practical way to understand a museum's focus and vision.

The second and third factors are the authenticity of the work and the donor's ability to convey good title, the two core concerns of any acquisition. See Chapters 4 and 5, *supra*. It is with respect to good title that U.S. museums have reformed and reshaped their acquisition policies in the area of looted art and restitution. Guidelines issued by the American Association of Museums (AAM) and the Association of Art Museum Directors (AAMD), in line with the principles developed at the Washington Conference on Holocaust-Era Assets, have created a new emphasis and framework for museums' provenance research. Karen D. Daly, *Provenance Research in Museum Collections*, in MUSEUM REGISTRATION METHODS 62–77 (Rebecca A. Buck & Jean Allman Gilmore eds., 5th ed. 2010). The three primary recommendations (identify, publicize, and research) focus on a museum's current holdings, but naturally, the same professional concerns and scrutiny would apply to acquisitions. The core mandate is to identify pre-1946 objects, acquired after 1932 that underwent a change of ownership in continental Europe between 1932 and 1946. Consequently, if a donor's collection includes any such object, a higher scrutiny and comfort level for the object's provenance should be anticipated for any donation to a museum. A similar emphasis on the provenance of offered antiquities or archeological objects relative to the Cultural Property Implementation Act (CPIA) and the National Stolen Property Act (NSPA) should be anticipated. See Chapter 6, *supra*.

Some museums developed a provenance questionnaire for donors to complete, and some request or require a warranty of title. Consider how an estate fiduciary should respond to such requests. There are difficult ethical issues embedded in these situations. What is the museum's confidentiality protocol if its provenance research discovers unsettling information? Does it inform anyone? Does the estate fiduciary amend the tax returns to reflect the cloud on title? Cf. Doherty v. Commissioner, 63 T.C.M. 2112 (1992), *aff'd*, 16 F.3d 338 (9th Cir. 1994), discussed in Chapter 11, *infra*.

Assuming the three prior factors are satisfied, the final factor concerns the straight-up practicalities of the museum—is the object worthy of inclusion in the collection, in terms of the direct and indirect costs of maintaining, exhibiting, storing, and conservation? If the donor has placed any restriction on the donation, such as permanent exhibition, the museum may decline because of the perceived impracticality, even though the work is otherwise museum worthy and desirable.

Planning for a significant gift or bequest to a museum requires the skills of practical drafting, knowledge of tax incentives and requirements, and awareness of the intended museum's acquisition protocols. In short, it requires the lawyer to broaden her perspective from a focus on the wishes of the donor to include the real world demands and constraints of a modern museum.

8. *Alternative Charitable Beneficiaries.* For some owners of extensive and significant collections, the outright transfer of their collections to an established museum is not consistent with their long term vision for their collection or their family's philanthropic tradition or legacy. A donor can create charitable foundations or charitable trusts to perpetuate the philanthropic mission for the art collection. A self-created private foundation may be the appropriate vehicle for a collector or an artist who wishes more control over the collection. See Anne-Marie Rhodes, *Artist-Endowed Private Foundations in the U.S.: An Overview*, in ARTISTS' ARCHIVES AND ESTATES: CULTURAL MEMORY BETWEEN LAW AND MARKET/ARCHIVI D'ARTISTA E LASCITI: MEMORIE CULTURALI TRA DIRITTO E MERCATO (Alessandra Donati et al. eds., 2018). One such vehicle is a private operating foundation, which is an organization that devotes its assets or income to the active conduct of its charitable purposes, as opposed to making grants to other organizations. With a private operating foundation, the donor may make donations of artworks to it and receive the same fair market value income tax charitable deduction as for a donation to a public charity (assuming the donation meets the same four tax requirements of 26 U.S.C. §§ 170(b)(1)(A)(vi) and 170(b)(1)(E)(i)). The donor may also serve as president of the foundation. There are definite and specific requirements under the tax laws for the organization and operation of the private operating foundation, which are beyond the scope of this note, but one in particular (the private inurement doctrine), deserves mention. The tax exempt status of the foundation will be lost if any personal benefit inures to the donor. In the context of a foundation owning art, a common question is if the artworks can be stored or exhibited at the donor's residence when they are not on exhibition loan. No. The IRS ruled that is an act of self-dealing that would disqualify the tax exempt status of the foundation. See Rev. Rul. 74-600, 1974-2 C.B. 385; also Tech. Adv. Mem. 8824001 (June 17, 1988).

Consider the California art collectors and philanthropists Eli and Edythe Broad and their Broad Art Foundation, created in 1984 after the Broads "ran out of wall space" in their home. Their Foundation's mission is to lend its works of contemporary art to accredited institutions around the world. The Broad's goal was public exhibition of their collection, not storage in a museum. Since its 1984 founding essentially as a lending library of contemporary art, the Broad Art Foundation has made more than 8,000 loans to over 500 museums and university galleries worldwide. Consistent with this desire for public display, the Broads announced in 2008 that their personal art collection and the holdings of the Broad Art Foundation would not be donated upon their deaths to an established museum. It was clear to them that no museum would commit to placing a large part of the collection on permanent display. Instead the Broads built a new museum in Los Angeles to house their collection. The Broad opened in September 2015 with a policy of free admission.

Beyond the forceful personalities of committed collectors on one hand and the financial, political, and legal constraints of museums on the other, is the model of a lending library for art sustainable? Does it represent a new ownership-use model that recalibrates ownership and control in a private foundation with enhanced public access and display at public museums? It is a model that may appeal to other major collectors. Preserving the vision of the original donor over the arc of time and vagaries of life can be a challenge. Drafting for donor intent is difficult. See Part D, *infra*.

C. Administering an Estate that Includes Artworks

There are no special rules for the administration or management of an estate or trust that includes artworks. The executor of the estate or the trustee of the trust is held to the same fiduciary standards governing any estate or trust, including the primary fiduciary duty of loyalty. The *Rothko* case, with its hasty sweetheart deals, represents a spectacular failure of the executors to heed those fiduciary duties.

In re Estate of Rothko, Deceased

372 N.E. 2d 291 (N.Y. 1977)

COOKE, J. Mark Rothko, an abstract expressionist painter whose works through the years gained for him an international reputation of greatness, died testate on February 25, 1970. The principal asset of his estate consisted of 798 paintings of tremendous value, and the dispute underlying this appeal involves the conduct of his three executors in their disposition of these works of art. In sum, that conduct as portrayed in the record and sketched in the opinions was manifestly wrongful and indeed shocking.

Rothkos' will was admitted to probate on April 27, 1970 and letters testamentary were issued to Bernard J. Reis, Theodoros Stamos and Morton Levine. Hastily and within a period of only about three weeks and by virtue of two contracts each dated May 21, 1970, the executors dealt with all 798 paintings.

By a contract of sale, the estate executors agreed to sell to Marlborough A.G., a Liechtenstein corporation (hereinafter MAG), 100 Rothko paintings as listed for $1,800,000, $200,000 to be paid on execution of the agreement and the balance of $1,600,000 in 12 equal interest-free installments over a 12-year period. Under the second agreement, the executors consigned to Marlborough Gallery, Inc., a domestic corporation (hereinafter MNY), "approximately 700 paintings listed on a Schedule to be prepared", the consignee to be responsible for costs covering items such as insurance, storage restoration and promotion. By its provisos, MNY could sell up to 35 paintings a year from each of two groups, pre-1947 and post-1947, for 12 years at the best price obtainable but not less than the appraised estate value, and it would receive a 50% Commission on each painting sold, except for a commission of 40% on those sold to or through other dealers.

Petitioner Kate Rothko, decedent's daughter and a person entitled to share in his estate by virtue of an election under EPTL 5-3.3, instituted this proceeding to remove the executors, to enjoin MNY and MAG from disposing of the paintings, to rescind the aforesaid agreements between the executors and said corporations, for a return of the paintings still in possession of those corporations, and for damages. She was joined by the guardian of her brother Christopher Rothko, likewise interested in the estate, who answered by adopting the allegations of his sister's petition and by demanding the same relief. The Attorney-General of the State, as the representative of the ultimate beneficiaries of the Mark Rothko Foundation, Inc., a charitable corporation and the residuary legatee under decedent's will, joined in requesting relief substantially similar to that prayed for by petitioner. On June 26, 1972 the Surrogate issued a temporary restraining order and on September 26, 1972 a preliminary injunction enjoining MAG, MNY, and the three executors from selling or otherwise disposing of the paintings referred to in the agreements dated May 21, 1970, except for sales or dispositions made with court permission. . . . By a 1974 petition, the Attorney-General, on behalf of the ultimate charitable beneficiaries of the Mark Rothko Foundation, sought the punishment of MNY, MAG, Lloyd and Reis for contempt and other relief.

Following a nonjury trial covering 89 days and in a thorough opinion, the Surrogate found: that Reis was a director, secretary and treasurer of MNY, the consignee art gallery, in addition to being a coexecutor of the estate; that the testator had a 1969 inter vivos contract with MNY to sell Rothko's work at a commission of only 10%; And whether that agreement survived testator's death was a problem that a fiduciary in a dual position could not have impartially faced; that Reis was in a position of serious conflict of interest with respect to the contracts of May 21, 1970 and that his dual role and planned purpose benefited the Marlborough interests to the detriment of the estate; that it was to the advantage of coexecutor Stamos as a "not-too-successful artist, financially", to curry favor with Marlborough and that the contract made by him with MNY within months after signing the estate contracts placed him in a position where his personal interests conflicted with those of the estate, especially leading to lax contract enforcement efforts by Stamos; that Stamos acted negligently and improvidently in view of his own knowledge of the conflict of interest of Reis; that the third coexecutor, Levine, while not acting in self-interest or with bad faith, nonetheless failed to exercise ordinary prudence in the performance of his assumed fiduciary obligations since he was aware of Reis' divided loyalty, believed that Stamos was also seeking personal advantage, possessed personal opinions as to the value of the paintings and yet followed the leadership of his coexecutors without investigation of essential facts or consultation with competent and disinterested appraisers, and that the business transactions of the two Marlborough corporations were admittedly controlled and directed by Francis K. Lloyd. It was concluded that the acts and failures of the three executors were clearly improper to such a substantial extent as to mandate their removal under SCPA 711 as estate fiduciaries. The Surrogate also found that MNY, MAG and Lloyd were guilty of contempt in shipping, disposing of and selling 57 paintings in violation of the temporary restraining order dated June 26, 1972 and of the injunction dated September 26, 1972; that the contracts for sale and consignment of paintings between the executors and MNY and MAG provided inadequate value to the estate, amounting to a lack of mutuality and fairness resulting from conflicts on the part of Reis and Stamos and improvidence on the part of all executors; that said contracts were voidable and were set aside by reason of violation of the duty of loyalty and improvidence of the executors, knowingly participated in and induced by MNY and MAG; that the fact that these agreements were voidable did not revive the 1969 inter vivos agreements since the parties by their conduct evinced an intent to abandon and abrogate these compacts. The Surrogate held that the present value at the time of trial of the paintings sold is the proper measure of damages as to MNY, MAG, Lloyd, Reis and Stamos. He imposed a civil fine of $3,332,000 upon MNY, MAG and Lloyd, same being the appreciated value at the time of trial of the 57 paintings sold in violation of the temporary restraining order and injunction. It was held that Levine was liable for $6,464,880 in damages, as he was not in a dual position acting for his own interest and was thus liable only for the actual value of paintings sold MNY and MAG as of the dates of sale, and that Reis, Stamos, MNY and MAG, apart from being jointly and severally liable for the same damages as Levine for negligence, were liable for the greater sum of $9,252,000 "as appreciation damages less amounts previously paid to the estate with regard to sales of paintings." . . . The liabilities were held to be congruent so that payment of the highest sum would satisfy all lesser liabilities including the civil fines and the liabilities for damages were to be reduced by payment of the fine levied or by return of any of the 57 paintings disposed of, the new fiduciary to have the option in the first instance to specify which paintings the fiduciary would accept.

The Appellate Division . . . modified to the extent of deleting the option given the new fiduciary to specify which paintings he would accept. Except for this modification, the majority affirmed . . . with additional comments. Among others, it was stated that the entire court agreed that executors Reis and Stamos had a conflict of interest and divided loyalty in view of their nexus to MNY and that a majority were in agreement with the Surrogate's assessment of liability as to executor Levine and his findings of liability against MNY, MAG and Lloyd. The majority agreed with the Surrogate's analysis awarding "appreciation damages" and found further support for his rationale in *Menzel v. List*, 24 N.Y.2d 91, 298 N.Y.S.2d 979, 246 N.E.2d 742. . . . Justices Capozzoli and Nunez, in separate dissenting in part opinions, viewed *Menzel v. List* as inapplicable and voted to modify and remit to determine the reasonable value of the paintings as of May, 1970, when estate contracts with MNY and MAG had their inception in writing.

Since the Surrogate's findings of fact as to the conduct of Reis, Stamos, Levine, MNY, MAG and Lloyd and the value of the paintings at different junctures were affirmed by the Appellate Division, if there was evidence to support these findings they are not subject to question in this court and the review here is confined to the legal issues raised.

In seeking a reversal, it is urged that an improper legal standard was applied in voiding the estate contracts of May, 1970, that the "no further inquiry" rule applies only to self-dealing and that in case of a conflict of interest, absent self-dealing, a challenged transaction must be shown to be unfair. The subject of fairness of the contracts is intertwined with the issue of whether Reis and Stamos were guilty of conflicts of interest. . . .

These contentions should be rejected. First, a review of the opinions of the Surrogate and the Appellate Division manifests that they did not rely solely on a "no further inquiry rule", and secondly, there is more than an adequate basis to conclude that the agreements between the Marlborough corporations and the estate were neither fair nor in the best interests of the estate. This is demonstrated, for example, by the comments of the Surrogate concerning the commissions on the consignment of the 698 paintings and those of the Appellate Division concerning the sale of the 100 paintings. The opinions under review demonstrate that neither the Surrogate nor the Appellate Division set aside the contracts by merely applying the no further inquiry rule without regard to fairness. Rather they determined, quite properly indeed, that these agreements were neither fair nor in the best interests of the estate.

To be sure, the assertions that there were no conflicts of interest on the part of Reis or Stamos indulge in sheer fantasy. Besides being a director and officer of MNY, for which there was financial remuneration, however slight, Reis, as noted by the Surrogate, had different inducements to favor the Marlborough interests, including his own aggrandizement of status and financial advantage through sales of almost one million dollars for items from his own and his family's extensive private art collection by the Marlborough interests. Similarly, Stamos benefited as an artist under contract with Marlborough and, interestingly, Marlborough purchased a Stamos painting from a third party for $4,000 during the week in May, 1970 when the estate contract negotiations were pending. The conflicts are manifest. Further, as noted in Bogert, Trusts and Trustees (2d ed.), "The duty of loyalty imposed on the fiduciary prevents him from accepting employment from a third party who is entering into a business transaction with the trust" (s 543, subd. (S), p. 573). "While he (a trustee) is administering the trust he must refrain from placing himself in a position where his personal interest or that of a third person does or may conflict with the interest of the beneficiaries" (Bogert, Trusts (Hornbook Series 5th ed.), p. 343). Here, Reis was employed and Stamos benefited in a manner contemplated by Bogert. In short, one must strain the law rather than follow it to reach the result suggested on behalf of Reis and Stamos.

Levine contends that, having acted prudently and upon the advice of counsel, a complete defense was established. Suffice it to say, an executor who knows that his coexecutor is committing breaches of trust and not only fails to exert efforts directed towards prevention but accedes to them is legally accountable even though he was acting on the advice of counsel. When confronted with the question of whether to enter into the Marlborough contracts, Levine was acting in a business capacity, not a legal one, in which he was required as an executor primarily to employ such diligence and prudence to the care and management of the estate assets and affairs as would prudent persons of discretion and intelligence, accented by "(n)ot honesty alone, but the punctilio of an honor the most sensitive" (*Meinhard v. Salmon*, 249 N.Y. 458, 464, 164 N.E. 545, 546, *supra*). Alleged good faith on the part of a fiduciary forgetful of his duty is not enough. He could not close his eyes, remain passive or move with unconcern in the face of the obvious loss to be visited upon the estate by participation in those business arrangements and then shelter himself behind the claimed counsel of an attorney.

* * *

The measure of damages was the issue that divided the Appellate Division. The contention of Reis, Stamos, MNY and MAG, that the award of appreciation damages was legally erroneous and impermissible, is based on a principle that an executor authorized to sell is not liable for an increase in value if the breach consists only in selling for a figure less than that for which the executor should have sold. For example, Scott states:

> "The beneficiaries are not entitled to the value of the property at the time of the decree if it was not the duty of the trustee to retain the property in the trust and the breach of trust consisted *merely* in selling the property for too low a price" (3 Scott, Trusts (3d ed.), s 208.3, p. 1687 (emphasis added)). . . .

A recitation of similar import appears in Comment d under Restatement, Trusts 2d (§ 205):

> "d. Sale for less than value. If the trustee is authorized to sell trust property, but in breach of trust he sells it for less than he should receive, he is liable for the value of the property at the time of the sale less the amount which he received. If the breach of trust consists *only* in selling it for too little, he is not chargeable with the amount of any subsequent increase in value of the property under the rule stated in Clause (c), as he would be if he were not authorized to sell the property. See § 208." (Emphasis added.)

However, employment of "merely" and "only" as limiting words suggests that where the breach consists of some misfeasance, other than solely for selling "for too low a price" or "for too little", appreciation damages may be appropriate. Under Scott (§ 208.3, pp. 1686–1687) and the Restatement (§ 208), the trustee may be held liable for appreciation damages if it was his or her duty to retain the property, the theory being that the beneficiaries are entitled to be placed in the same position they would have been in had the breach not consisted of a sale of property that should have been retained. The same rule should apply where the breach of trust consists of a serious conflict of interest which is more than merely selling for too little.

The reason for allowing appreciation damages, where there is a duty to retain, and only date of sale damages, where there is authorization to sell, is policy oriented. If a trustee authorized to sell were subjected to a greater measure of damages he might be reluctant to sell (in which event he might run a risk if depreciation ensued). On the other hand, if there is a duty to retain and the trustee sells there is no policy reason to protect the trustee; he has not simply acted imprudently, he has violated an integral condition of the trust.

"If a trustee in breach of trust transfers trust property to a person who takes with notice of the breach of trust, and the transferee has disposed of the property . . . (i)t seems proper to charge him with the value at the time of the decree, since if it had not been for the breach of trust the property would still have been a part of the trust estate" (4 Scott, Trusts (3d ed.), § 291.2. This rule of law which applies to the transferees MNY and MAG also supports the imposition of appreciation damages against Reis and Stamos, since if the Marlborough corporations are liable for such damages either as purchaser or consignees with notice, from one in breach of trust, it is only logical to hold that said executors, as sellers and consignors, are liable also pro tanto.

Contrary to assertions of appellants and the dissenters at the Appellate Division, *Menzel v. List*, 24 N.Y.2d 91, 298 N.Y.S.2d 979, 246 N.E.2d 742, *supra* is authority for the allowance of appreciation damages. There, the damages involved a breach of warranty of title to a painting which at one time had been stolen from plaintiff and her husband and ultimately sold to defendant. Here, the executors, though authorized to sell, did not merely err in the amount they accepted but sold to one with whom Reis and Stamos had a self-interest. To make the injured party whole, in both instances the quantum of damages should be the same. In other words, since the paintings cannot be returned, the estate is therefore entitled to their value at the time of the decree, i.e., appreciation damages. These are not punitive damages in a true sense, rather they are damages intended to make the estate whole. Of course, as to Reis, Stamos, MNY and MAG, these damages might be considered by some to be exemplary in a sense, in that they serve as a warning to others, but their true character is ascertained when viewed in the light of overriding policy considerations and in the realization that the sale and consignment were not merely sales below value but inherently wrongful transfers which should allow the owner to be made whole.

The decree of the Surrogate imposed appreciation damages against Reis, Stamos, MNY and MAG in the amount of $7,339,464.72 computed as $9,252,000 (86 works on canvas at $90,000 each and 54 works on paper at $28,000 each) less the aggregate amounts paid the estate under the two rescinded agreements and interest. . . . Significantly, the Surrogate's factual finding as to the present value of these unreturned paintings was affirmed by the Appellate Division and, since that finding had support in the record and was not legally erroneous, it should not now be subjected to our disturbance.

* * *

The Marlborough corporations and Lloyd contend that there was no violation of either the temporary restraining order or the preliminary injunction by the delivery of paintings sold prior to the court's restraints and that, therefore, the finding of contempt was erroneous. The Attorney-General in response contends that the "group" sales did not pass equitable ownership and that even if the invoices had been typed prior to said order and injunction no sale took place until after the injunction. In support of the latter position, the Uniform Commercial Code (s 2-106, subd. (1); ss 2-307, 2-401, subds. (2), (3)) is cited for the proposition that as a matter of law the questioned sales took place on delivery to the purchasers which in all instances occurred after the injunction, the latter of the two court restraints. MNY, MAG and Lloyd counter with the argument that, under art market custom, invoices of paintings are sales and that the restraining order and preliminary injunction failed to clearly state what acts were prohibited. In any event, the plain and simple import of both the order and the injunction not to sell or otherwise dispose of the paintings was violated by dispositions of them. Consequently, it is immaterial how the applicable Uniform Commercial Code provisions might be interpreted. If MNY, MAG and Lloyd had invoiced paintings and were acting in good faith, they would have advised the court of their prior commitments....

Accordingly, the order of the Appellate Division should be affirmed, with costs to the prevailing parties against appellants, and the question certified answered in the affirmative.

Notes and Questions

1. *Aftermath.* The three executors were removed, and Kate Rothko became the sole administrator of her father's estate. She subsequently sued her attorney over his $7.5 million fee, which was reduced to $2.6 million by the surrogate. Six months after her father died, her mother died, and her young brother, who was then 6 years old, went to live with a maternal aunt. When he was 12, Kate, then in her mid 20s, became his guardian. By 1986, the Rothko Foundation, which received half of the estate, was gradually phased out, as it had fulfilled its core mission—disseminating Rothko works to major museums. The Foundation distributed more than 1,000 works of art to 29 museums in the U.S. and abroad. The largest recipient was the National Gallery of Art in Washington, D.C., which received a core selection of 285 paintings.

Frank Lloyd, the owner of the Marlborough Gallery, was indicted in 1977 on charges of tampering with evidence in the *Rothko* case. A British national, he was not tried until his return to the U.S. in 1982, when he was convicted. He did not serve any jail time; his sentence required him to create a scholarship fund and art education programs at his gallery. He died in 1998 with his reputation shattered. His galleries continued; however, the New York gallery announced its closure in 2020. In May 2012, Rothko's *Orange, Red, Yellow,* sold at auction for $86.9 million, his highest auction price.

In 2008, Kate and Christopher Rothko received court permission to exhume their father's body from his gravesite with the Stamos family and reinter his body in another cemetery.

2. *Other Artists' Difficult Estate Administrations.* Robert Rauschenberg, an acclaimed post-war American artist, well-known for his combines, died in 2008. Like Rothko, he appointed three friends and business associates as trustees to administer his $600 million estate and to protect his charitable foundation. When they claimed a $60 million fee—calculated by an attorney for the foundation to be approximately $40,000 an hour—a lawsuit was commenced in 2013. In August 2014, a judge awarded the three trustees a total fee of $24.6 million, "finding that the Trustees did an exemplary job." The decision was upheld on appeal. Robert Rauschenberg Foundation v. Grutman, 198 So. 3d 685 (Fla. 2d DCA 2016). See also Patricia Cohen, *Foundation Fights Fees for Artist's Trustees*, N.Y. TIMES, Aug. 22, 2013, at C1.

American artist Cy Twombly died in 2011 leaving much of his vast trust to his foundation. Two of the four foundation directors valued his trust at $1 billion, arguably inflating the value to increase their fees. A lawsuit was filed in 2013 and settled confidentially in 2014, although the two directors did resign from the foundation. Randy Kennedy, *Settlement Reached in Cy Twombly Foundation Lawsuit*, N.Y. Times Blog, Mar. 14, 2014, at https://artsbeat.blog.nytimes.com/2014/03/14/settlement-reached-in-cy-twombly-foundation-lawsuit/.

In the Rauschenberg litigation, the trust did not contain a provision regarding trustee compensation. A well-drafted trust will have a trustee compensation provision, even if it merely says the trustee shall be entitled to "reasonable compensation."

3. *Executors, Art Advisors, and No Further Inquiry.* Rothko's prospective selection of his three friends to manage his estate was not unreasonable. Each had a different and important focus—one business, one art, and one general. They would all have to agree on any course of action, and therefore, each would act as a check and balance on the other two. The plan's structural failure, as drafted, was that there was no effective check and balance on the executors as a whole.

In most cases, the beneficiaries of the estate are the ones who serve as the primary enforcers of the plan, simply and directly because they are the ones affected. They've got skin in the game. The value and size of their legacies are at risk with every decision made by the executor. Consequently, they will closely scrutinize the actions of the executors, and executors know that.

In *Rothko*, the family was given the statutory minimum with the balance of Rothko's property going to the Rothko Foundation that the three executors also controlled. The family members' legacy was proportionately minimal and easily paid; therefore, the family's legal standing and influence over the executors were severely circumscribed. On the other hand, the Foundation, the primary beneficiary of the estate, was an entity controlled by the executors; consequently, it offered no independent resistance to the executors' actions. Under most states' laws, the State's

Attorney General has the right and power to enforce charitable legacies. However, for many reasons (generally lack of dedicated resources, competing case loads, and political pressure), AGs' offices are often ineffective and inefficient enforcers of charitable legacies. See Part D, *infra*, for discussion on standing.

The family's escape from Rothko's will was not in the will itself but in a state statute, now repealed, that allowed a spouse or children to elect against the estate plan if more than half went to charity. N.Y. EST., POWER & TRUST LAW §5-3.3 (1967), repealed in 1981. Kate successfully made the election, and therefore, she and her brother became entitled to half the estate. With that one-half interest, which would clearly be affected by the decisions of the executors, the family now had the legal standing necessary to contest the executors' actions.

At common law, a trustee or fiduciary is held to the highest ethical standard, classically formulated by then Judge Cardozo as "Not honesty alone, but the punctilio of an honor the most sensitive." Meinhard v. Salmon, 164 N.E. 545, 546 (1928). After all, the creator of the trust has transferred the legal title to his property to the trustee for the sole benefit of others. The common law's rule therefore was strict and straightforward: a trustee was not to engage in any act of self-dealing with the trust's property. Two defenses were allowed. First, that the creator of the trust specifically authorized the act in the trust instrument. Second, the beneficiaries consented to the act after full disclosure. In either instance, the trustee must also act in good faith and the transaction must be fair to the trust's beneficiaries.

With the professionalization of trustees, certain practical exceptions crept into statutory law. A bank acting as a trustee may deposit trust funds into its own banking department and invest trust funds in its own common trust fund or mutual fund. Similarly, a trustee may receive reasonable compensation for its services from the trust. Is there room for further movement in the no-further-inquiry rule? Some commentators believe the no-further-inquiry rules does more harm than good today and it is time to move to a standard that would judge a self dealing or conflicted transaction by the best interests of the beneficiaries, with the trustee or fiduciary bearing the burden of proof. See John H. Langbein, *Questioning the Trust Law Duty of Loyalty: Sole Interest or Best Interest?*, 114 YALE L.J. 929 (2005). Others believe the common law has it right. Melanie B. Leslie, *In Defense of the No Further Inquiry Rule: A Response to Professor John Langbein*, 47 WM. & MARY L. REV. 541 (2005).

When an estate will include substantial artworks, is it better to have an executor or trustee with no knowledge of the art market or someone with substantial knowledge? As posed, this is an unanswerable question; it is totally dependent on who the person is. Ideally, the person should be trustworthy, professionally competent, and art business savvy. Life is often less than ideal. One middle ground approach is to nominate an art advisor in the will or trust instrument and direct or suggest the executor or trustee to consult with the art advisor for all issues relating to the artworks. This is similar to a common technique when an estate or trust includes an interest in a closely held business—one names a separate business advisor. The decision-making authority resides in the executor or trustee, who is held to fiduciary standards, but would have the benefit of expert art counsel known to and selected by the decedent. Having an art advisor avoids making the executor or trustee an involuntary curator. Would you authorize or direct the executor or trustee to enter into business contracts with the art advisor? Think about how the art advisor would or should be compensated.

4. *The Empty Hook.* When a property owner dies, the legal system governs the transfer of title from the decedent to the next owner of the property. Assuming a competent adult, an owner can leave written instructions for the disposition of his property upon his death in his will or in his revocable trust. The administration of the decedent's estate will be conducted by an executor if there was a will or a trustee if there was a revocable trust. Both are fiduciaries and held to fiduciary standards in the administration of a decedent's estate.

An executor or trustee has three broadly defined duties. First is to collect and take control of all the property of the decedent. The fiduciary's perspective here is to err on the side of including an asset, to maximize the estate. The second duty is to pay all legitimate expenses, debts, and claims against the decedent or the estate. For this duty, the converse holds, with the fiduciary desiring to minimize these payments. The third duty is to make distributions in accordance with the terms of the will or trust. In this duty, the fiduciary's perspective is neutral, an executor or trustee is not to prefer one beneficiary over another.

When an estate includes valuable artworks, the nominated executor should ascertain as soon as possible after death if the works are secure, and if not, quickly move to secure them. If there is an extensive collection, the executor may seek to expedite the issuance of letters testamentary from the court. If the collection is in the decedent's revocable trust and the decedent was acting as trustee during his lifetime, the new successor trustee should accept the office as soon as possible, likewise to secure the assets. An itemization and appraisal of the artworks should be undertaken by the fiduciary relatively soon. When a fiduciary sees the "empty hook" where a prized artwork used to be, the fiduciary, under the first obligation to gather all assets, must investigate the work's whereabouts and its includability in the decedent's estate or trust.

It is possible that the work did not belong to the decedent at the time of death; it could, for example, have been a bona fide gift to a child. See *Genecin*, *supra*. Alternatively, a child could legitimately assume that her parent wanted her to have it then because of a specific bequest of the work to the child in her parent's will or the written memorandum or note. See *Clark*, *supra*. A third possibility is that the child simply wanted it (or more sinisterly, did not want a sibling to have it)—whether or not the parent agreed—and took the work once the parent died. A fourth possibility is that the work could have been stolen by another. In all four scenarios, the fiduciary must ascertain the facts for estate and trust purposes. In addition, whether or not the artwork is owned by the estate or trust at the date of death, it may nevertheless be included in the estate for estate tax purposes. See, e.g., 26 U.S.C. § 2036. As painful as estate taxes can be for illiquid assets, not paying those taxes can create significant future financial liability, including penalties. It also may decrease the later value of the artwork because of the possibility of a tax lien. The fiduciary can also be liable for breach of fiduciary duties and personally surcharged. For a valuable artwork, the new owner-child needs a clean and well-documented provenance. The fiduciary should provide that orderly documentary transition. In what ways does the empty hook scenario implicate the two other basic duties (paying taxes and expenses, and making proper distribution) of the executor or trustee fiduciary? How would you as attorney for the fiduciary deal with the empty hook in a normal grieving family? In a dysfunctional family or a blended, non-aligned family? Although the actual words may be tricky to make your own at first, in dealing with the beneficiaries under those scenarios, the lawyer's duty in representing the fiduciary is crystal clear. All of the decedent's assets for property and for tax purposes must be ascertained and accounted for. Clarity of duty sharpens the focus.

5. *Representing an Estate and Evaluating Unknown Works: A True Story.* Not all valuable artworks are obviously valuable to one and all. Family members, beneficiaries, and fiduciaries may not know the significance of what the decedent owned. A fiduciary is not held to a standard of omniscience, but a fiduciary must act reasonably in the performance of the fiduciary's function. Hitting the right balance between too little investigation and over the top inquiry may be more difficult in practice than anticipated. Consider the following story from the perspective of an attorney advising an executor in fulfilling her fiduciary duties.

In the early 1970s, an estates lawyer represented a husband and wife. When the husband died, his will left his entire estate to his wife, who was his executor and sole heir, as the elderly couple had no children. The wife's health was beginning to fail. The couple was not wealthy. They had fled from Austria to the U.S. during the build up to World War II. Among their possessions in their apartment were two gouaches that the husband, a dentist, had received from a grateful young artist in Austria in exchange for dental services. The husband and wife were able to take the gouaches out of Austria because the border guard, who also happened to be a grateful patient of the dentist, looked the other way. The works were not prominently displayed in their apartment; they were just on the top shelf of a bookcase. When her husband died, the widow told the lawyer that her husband thought the works might be valuable, but she herself did not know. Neither the husband nor wife had mentioned the artworks to the lawyer when he was writing their wills.

The lawyer began the probate process, including appraising the property. The appraiser did not know of the artist. The art reference books in the library did not mention the artist. When the lawyer calls the city's main art museum and speaks with a curator, the curator had not heard of this artist. Two friends of the lawyer who were interested in art had not heard of the artist. The lawyer finds and calls the leading dealer for the artist in the United States. The dealer summarily dismisses the lawyer's inquiries, asserting that the works must be fakes, because the dealer knows all of the artist's works and he has not heard of these. Within a few months, the lawyer is reading a magazine article and notices a photograph of a home's interior that has a painting in the same style. He writes the owners via the author of the magazine article. They eventually respond and indicate they are collectors of this artist's work and ask him to send the works to them for their consideration. The lawyer declines to do so; the lawyer now believes the works may really have monetary value for his client, whose physical health is failing and whose resources are modest. About the same time, the lawyer meets a curator at a cocktail party who had heard of the artist. That curator arranges a private viewing for the head curator of the city's main museum, who upon seeing the works proclaims, "What an addition to the world of art!" Eventually, the collectors from the magazine article and lawyer (and his client) agree that the collectors will pay the airfare for the lawyer to bring the works to them. If the collectors decide to buy and the estate can agree to a sale, the travel costs will be credited to the collectors. The lawyer is met at the airport by the collectors' driver, whisked to their penthouse apartment, where the collectors and an art expert view the work. They make a "one time" on the spot offer of $X, which the lawyer (on client's behalf) rejects. The driver takes the lawyer to his hotel. Another offer of $1.2X from the collector is made the next day. Lawyer returns home, speaks with his client, who also rejects this offer. Sotheby's thinks the works might bring $1.3X at auction before the seller's commission. It is quiet for weeks; then an offer from the dealer (who happens to live in the collectors' city) for $1.6X is made and accepted.

The client is happy, and the funds from the sale of her Egon Schieles helped to support her for the remainder of her life.

Go back through this story and determine at what point the widow as executor fulfilled her duty to ascertain value. Does her status as executor and sole beneficiary lessen her duty? Remember, taxing authorities can play a role in any estate. What about the lawyer? How many contacts are necessary to establish reasonable diligence under the circumstances? Must the lawyer have followed through on the serendipitous magazine article? How far does one need to go to determine value? See Chapter 11, *infra*.

In a postscript to this true story, more than 35 years later, the lawyer visits one of his children who lives and works in another city. His child introduces him to a friend. In the course of congenial conversation, it comes up that the child's friend had purchased (yes, you are correct!) the Egon Schieles. Would the lawyer like to see them?

6. *Fiduciary's Investment Powers and Duties.* An executor or trustee as the legal title holder to the estate or trust property has a recognized duty to administer the assets generally as a prudent person would. See Uniform Prudent Investor Act § 2(a) ("UPIA"); and Restatement (Third) of Trusts § 90(b) (2007). One pertinent aspect of prudent investing is the norm of diversification, which can be excused if the trustee reasonably believes that special circumstances exist such that the trust is better served without diversifying. UPIA § 3. What constitutes special circumstances is not defined, but the decedent's intent, difficult markets, tax considerations, and

other concerns can impact the duty to diversify. An extensive art collection in an estate or trust can present the executor and trustee with just such a difficult investment diversification dilemma—the orderly management of illiquid tangible assets with valuation uncertainties that may or may not bear a special relationship or special value to the purposes of the estate or trust or the beneficiaries. UPIA § 2(c)(8). Beneficiaries with differing investment perspectives, financial needs, and risk tolerances add another dimension to the fiduciary's investment calculations and diversification determination. The boundaries of the duty to diversify are not certain, and art exceptionalism may undermine the fiduciary duty to diversify. The fiduciary must independently evaluate the duty to diversify for each estate or trust. A reasoned analysis must be set in context: (i) the dispositive terms set forth by the decedent, (ii) the extent of the collection, independently viewed and vis-à-vis other assets, (iii) who the beneficiaries are: spouse, minor children, charitable foundations, (iv) the market for the works, and (v) the liquidity needs of the estate or trust, are some factors.

D. Donor Intent and Changing Circumstances

1. Cy Pres and Deviation

There is no more difficult problem in art law than reconciling a deceased owner's intent concerning his gifted artworks with unanticipated, changed circumstances. One such highly charged case is that of the Barnes Foundation, a unique educational institution and gallery founded in 1922 by Dr. Albert Barnes in the Township of Lower Merion, outside of Philadelphia. Dr. Barnes created the Foundation "as an experiment to determine how much practical good to the public of all classes and stations of life may be accomplished by means of the plans and principles learned by (Barnes) from a life-long study of . . . psychology as applied to education and aesthetics." As such, Dr. Barnes directed the Board in the Trust Indenture to "ensure that the plain people, that is, men and women who gain their livelihood by daily toil in shops, factories, schools, stores and similar places, shall have free access." Dr. Barnes had risen from humble beginnings to great wealth, and was reportedly often at odds with Philadelphia art elites, who viewed his educational ideas and art collection with criticism. The Barnes Foundation was funded in part with Dr. Barnes's extraordinary art collection, including 181 Renoirs, 69 Cézannes, 59 Matisses, 46 Picassos, and 7 Van Goghs. The Barnes Foundation collection was housed in Lower Merion in a specially designed building containing 24 galleries, surrounded by landscaped gardens. The paintings and art objects were personally arranged by Dr. Barnes in what some thought a haphazard fashion, but which others believe reflect the educational perspective of John Dewey. In any event, upon Dr. Barnes's death in 1951, the bylaws became irrevocable. The Barnes collection has been estimated to be worth $25–30 billion. It has been a tempting prize for many years, to many people, and subject to much litigation. See http://www

.barnesfoundation.org for official background information on Dr. Barnes and his Foundation.

The Barnes Foundation, a Corporation

Court of Common Pleas of Pennsylvania, 2004

2004 WL 1960204

OTT, J. The next chapter of The Barnes Foundation saga opened on September 24, 2002, when the Board of Trustees of The Foundation (hereinafter "The Foundation") filed a petition to amend its charter and bylaws. A number of individuals and entities filed pleadings seeking to intervene in the matter. Among them were Lincoln University, the Board of Trustees of the Violette de Mazia Trust, and three students currently enrolled in the art education program at The Foundation. By memorandum opinion and order dated February 12, 2003, the Court granted the status of intervenor to Lincoln University only.... The current petition includes provisions that resolved all of the differences between The Foundation and Lincoln University, and the latter has now withdrawn from participation in the case.

At the outset, we must comment on the unprecedented public interest in this case. Since the filing of the original petition, rarely a day has gone by without a letter or phone call arriving at the undersigned's chambers from someone wanting to weigh in on this matter. Politicians, art scholars, financial experts, and former students have sent suggestions for saving The Foundation. Major newspapers have published endless dialogues of letters to the editors, as well as editorials endorsing one outcome or another, as if this were a political race. Even legal scholars, attorneys, and law professors, who know that cases are determined by applying the law to the evidence produced in court and *not* by public opinion, have sent unsolicited opinion letters for our edification. The court has studiously avoided being influenced by these outside forces; however, the experience has been unique.

As this court and higher courts of the Commonwealth have recited on numerous occasions, The Foundation is a Pennsylvania nonprofit corporation created by Dr. Barnes:

> to promote the advancement of education and the appreciation of the fine arts; and for this purpose to erect, found and maintain, in the Township of Lower Merion, County of Montgomery and State of Pennsylvania, an art gallery and other necessary buildings for the exhibition of works of ancient and modern art, and the maintenance in connection therewith of an arboretum, wherein shall be cultivated and maintained trees and shrubs for the study and for the encouragement of arboriculture and forestry....

See Barnes Foundation Charter, approved by decree dated December 4, 1922.

Dr. Barnes and The Foundation entered into a trust indenture under date of December 6, 1922, whereby Dr. Barnes donated his artwork to The Foundation to accomplish its charitable purposes. The collection amassed by Dr. Barnes during his lifetime which is housed at the Lower Merion gallery is large and virtually priceless. Dr. Barnes also funded The Foundation with an initial endowment of approximately six million dollars. The Foundation's bylaws incorporate the December 6, 1922 indenture, as amended, in its entirety.

In the instant petition, The Foundation sets forth its current financial state as follows. Dr. Barnes' initial endowment has been depleted. The Foundation is unable to cover its general operating expenses and to meet its needs in areas such as professional staffing, conservation treatment, fund-raising, collection assessment, facilities care, and public relations. The Foundation's ability to generate revenue from visitors to or fund-raising activities at the Merion gallery is limited by the existing zoning restrictions in Lower Merion Township. The Foundation's ability to raise revenue is also limited by the small size of its Board of Trustees.

The Foundation states that its "current fiscal situation is dire, puts at risk The Foundation's ability to fulfill its primary purpose, and threatens The Foundation's survival." In the hopes of ensuring its ability to continue its purpose in the future and to improve its finances, The Foundation struck an agreement with two of Philadelphia's leading philanthropic institutions, the Pew Charitable Trusts (hereinafter "Pew") and the Lenfest Foundation (hereinafter "Lenfest") whereby Pew and Lenfest promised to help The Foundation raise approximately $150 million. It is the conditions attached to this promise that have catapulted The Foundation back into court. The fund-raising assistance from Pew and Lenfest is predicated upon the relocation of The Foundation's art collection from Merion to a new site to be built in Philadelphia, and upon the expansion of the number of trustees on The Foundation's Board. Both of these proposals run afoul of Dr. Barnes' indenture and The Foundation's charter and bylaws. Accordingly, The Foundation now seeks to amend these documents. . . .

It was decided that the issues raised in the petition should be bifurcated and the court should first determine the following proposed changes to The Foundation's charter and bylaws relating to governance. . . .

The least controversial of the matters presently before us is the proposed change in the size of the Foundation's Board of Trustees. Dr. Barnes' indenture provided for five trustees. The initial Board consisted of Dr. Barnes, his wife, and three other individuals. After the deaths of Dr. and Mrs. Barnes, vacancies in the office of trustee were filled as follows: Girard Trust Company (now Mellon Bank) nominated one trustee, and Lincoln University nominated the other four. The indenture specified that: "no Trustee shall be a member of the faculty or Board of Trustees or Directors of the University of Pennsylvania, Temple University, Bryn Mawr, Haverford or Swarthmore Colleges, or Pennsylvania Academy of the Fine Arts."

Under the changes now being proposed by The Foundation, the Board would consist of fifteen members. Lincoln University would nominate five persons for election. Mellon would no longer be involved. Upon approval of the changes, the current five trustees would immediately elect three additional trustees and Lincoln would immediately nominate three new names for election. A nominating committee chosen from these trustees would then recommend the remaining nominees for election to the Board. For the election of these final trustees on the initial expanded Board, Pew and Lenfest would jointly have the power to approve the nominations, however, the two institutions would have no authority in the nomination or election of trustees thereafter. The petition asserts that a larger Board is necessary because modern nonprofit corporations require larger governing boards consisting of "members who have access to a variety of communities and resources and who can provide governance expertise."

* * *

Testimony on this issue was . . . elicited from Maureen K. Robinson, a consultant for nonprofit organizations. She testified that boards of nonprofits must be large enough to meet their basic responsibilities but not so large that the decision-making process becomes cumbersome. She quoted statistics generated by the National Center for Nonprofit Boards and Stanford University's Graduate School of Business showing that the average size of nonprofit boards for 2002 was nineteen (19) and the median was seventeen (17). Ms. Robinson opined that the current size of the Board of The Foundation is too small to do its work effectively. She stated that the proposal to triple the size would greatly improve the Board's fundraising abilities. She testified that raising millions of dollars " . . . is not a task for a one-man band. It's not even a task for a quintet. You need a pretty full orchestra in order to achieve those kinds of results."

Ms. Robinson also explained that a larger board brings greater participation and accountability. Under the current organization, a quorum is reached with only three trustees, and decisions can be made by a simple majority vote of only two. The witness stated that such a scenario fosters neither accountability nor participation. She also explained that with a larger board, there is a larger pool from which to draw leadership on a continuous basis. Ms. Robinson also commented on the fact that Lincoln University currently has the power to nominate eighty percent (80%) of The Foundation's Board. She noted the inherent conflicts in one nonprofit's having this authority over another's governing body. To paraphrase Ms. Robinson's explanation, Lincoln is in a position to compete with itself for stellar candidates, i.e., it does itself a disservice if it nominates stellar candidates for The Foundation's Board and does not keep them for Lincoln's Board, and does The Foundation a disservice if it keeps such candidates for its own Board.

* * *

In light of the testimony summarized *supra*, we find ample support for the proposal that the Board of Trustees of The Foundation should be expanded. It is clear that the stewardship of a modern-day nonprofit must rest on many shoulders. It is imperative that the trustees have wide-ranging experience, expertise, and contacts, and the ability to attract donors of substance. A board of only five trustees, no matter how talented and dedicated the individuals may be, cannot meet the enormous responsibility of carrying The Foundation into the twenty-first century.

The legal authority for amending Dr. Barnes' indenture on this issue can be found in the doctrine of deviation. This doctrine has played a part in much of the recent litigation involving The Foundation. [In one of those cases—Ed.], the Superior Court stated:

> The doctrine of deviation has been summarized in the *Restatement (Second) of Trusts*:
>
> > [A] court will direct or permit the trustee of a charitable trust to deviate from a term of the trust if it appears to the court that compliance is impossible or illegal, or that owing to circumstances not known to the settlor and not anticipated by him compliance would defeat or substantially impair the accomplishment of the purposes of the trust.
>
> *Restatement (Second) of Trusts* § 381 (1959). Those terms subject to deviation are limited to administrative provisions of the trust, *i.e.*, "the details of administration which the settlor has prescribed in order to secure the more important result of obtaining for the beneficiaries the advantages which the settlor stated he wished them to have." § 561 Bogert, *The Law of Trust and Trustees*, at 27.
>
> In order to permit deviation from the administrative provisions of a trust, courts generally require the presence of two elements: "(1) unforeseen and unforeseeable change in circumstances, and (2) a frustration of the settlor's main objectives by this change, if strict obedience to the settlor [sic] directions were required." Bogert, *supra* at 230. It must be emphasized that the relief afforded by deviation is not based on mere convenience, but on the necessity of effecting a change in a situation where compliance with the terms of the trust "would defeat or substantially impair the accomplishment of the purposes of the trust." *Colin McK. Grant Home v. Medlock*, 292 S.C. 466, 472, 349 S.E.2d 655, 659 (1986).

Barnes Foundation, a Corporation—Estate of Violette de Mazia, Deceased, 453 Pa. Super. 436, 451–52, 684 A.2d 123, 130–31 (1996).

The doctrine of deviation also played a role in another proceeding wherein The Foundation sought permission 1) to hold fundraising events at its Merion facility, and 2) to increase the admission fee to the gallery to $10 and 3) to open the gallery to the public six days a week. The undersigned denied the first request on the grounds that it ran afoul of language in Dr. Barnes' indenture and The Foundation had failed to prove that, because it was impossible to raise adequate funds otherwise, deviation was necessary. This court approved an increase in the admission price to $5 and agreed that the gallery could be open one additional day per week. *Barnes Foundation, a Corporation (No. 6)*, 15 Fiduc. Rep.2d 381 (1995). On appeal by The Foundation, the Superior Court reversed us on the fundraising issue, on the grounds that the events contemplated by The Foundation fell outside the ambit of prohibited activities in Dr. Barnes' indenture, and, as a result, deviation was not an issue. That Court upheld the undersigned on the other two issues, agreeing that The Foundation had failed to show that deviations from the terms of the indenture were necessary. The Superior Court noted:

> The burden of proof is always on the party seeking the deviation because in the case of "an express trust, favorable presumptions arise, and the burden of proof is on the party disputing its validity or terms." 89 C.J.S. Trusts §66, at 845 . . . [The Foundation] argues that it should have prevailed below because the evidence offered was "uncontradicted," and the proposed charges were "approved" by the Attorney General. Such an argument has no foundation in law. The mere fact that evidence is uncontradicted does not automatically imbue that evidence with sufficient weight to sustain one's burden of proof. Additionally, although the law requires the participation of the Attorney General's Office in any proceeding to modify the terms of a charitable trust, [The Foundation] cites no support for the proposition that the Court is bound by the position espoused by the Office of the Attorney General, and a reviewing judge must exercise his or her independent power of review.

Barnes Foundation, a Corporation, 453 Pa.Super. 243, 253, 683 A.2d 894, 899 (1996) (citations omitted.)

This court also approved a deviation from the language in Dr. Barnes' indenture requiring the gallery to be closed entirely for the months of July and August. In that matter, The Foundation produced direct evidence, in the form of a 1949 letter from Dr. Barnes, that attempts to protect the artwork from summer's heat and moisture had been unsuccessful. After determining that modern climate-control technology could not be anticipated by Dr. Barnes, we decreed that year-round access to the gallery was permissible. *See Barnes Foundation, a Corporation* (No.9), 18 Fiduc Rep.2d 393 (1998).

With this authority in mind, we believe it appropriate to permit deviation on this issue. We determine that the provisions in the indenture concerning the structure of the Board of Trustees of The Foundation are administrative in nature. We agree that Dr. Barnes could have foreseen neither the complicated, competitive, and sophisticated world in which nonprofits now operate, nor the range of expertise and influence the members of their governing bodies must now possess. We conclude that maintaining the *status quo* in this regard would substantially impair the accomplishment of the Foundation's charitable purposes, and that approving the expansion of its Board of Trustees is therefore necessary.

The second major issue before us-relocating the art collection to Philadelphia-is far more complex. The pertinent provisions of the December 6, 1922, indenture between Dr. Barnes as donor, and The Foundation as donee, as amended, are as follows:

> 9. At the death of Donor, the collection shall be closed, and thereafter no change therein shall be made by the purchase, bequest or otherwise obtaining of additional pictures, or other works of art, or other objects of whatsoever description. Furthermore, after the death of Donor and his wife, no buildings, for any purpose whatsoever, shall be built or erected on any part of the property of Donee.
>
> 10. After Donor's death no picture belonging to the collection shall ever be loaned, sold or otherwise disposed of except that if any picture passes into a state of actual decay so that it no longer is of any value it may be removed for that reason only from the collection.
>
> 11. Should the said collection ever be destroyed, or should it for any other reason become impossible to administer the trust hereby created concerning said collection of pictures, then the property and funds contributed by Donor to Donee shall be applied to an object as nearly within the scope herein indicated and laid down as shall be possible, such application to be in connection with an existing and organized institution then in being and functioning in Philadelphia, Pennsylvania, or its suburbs.
>
> 13. . . . After the death of Donor and his said wife, the furniture, the rare and valuable collection of rugs, together with the Chinese vases and other objects of art, but exclusive of the paintings, that are located in the administration building, shall be sold as expeditiously as may be found necessary at public auction. All the paintings shall remain in exactly the places they are at the time of the death of Donor and his said wife. . . .

The basis for the proposed relocation is financial necessity. [The bleak financial evidence before the court included the dwindling year-end estimates of assets available for operating expenses and capital improvements, the Foundation's general red ink operations budget, the costs associated with the lengthy litigation, and the late attempts to professionalize the Foundation's operations.—Ed.]

* * *

The Foundation painted a bleak picture of its options for getting out from under this financial crush. As for deaccessioning, that is, selling some of the Foundation's artwork, [Board of Trustees President] Dr. Watson and [Foundation CEO] Ms. Camp testified that this drastic course of action is considered unethical in the art world and would not bring enough money for a long-term solution. . . .

* * *

The Board also sought out benefactors, and enjoyed some success (with Pew, the J. Paul Getty Fund, the Henry Lewis Foundation, and the Mellon Foundation) in obtaining funding for the collection assessment program. However, the attempts to build up the Foundation's endowment were met with negative responses. The potential individual donors and philanthropic organizations alike were unwilling to support The Foundation because of the restrictions imposed by the township and the indenture. Some urged The Foundation to merge with another entity and possibly relocate the collection. The Board was unwilling to relinquish control over The Foundation's future by becoming subservient to another board. Dr. Watson approached Pew and Lenfest who came up with the concept now under consideration. Dr. Watson and the rest of the Board decided to accept the offer from Pew and Lenfest (who were joined by Annenberg) because it allowed The Foundation to maintain its independence.

The particulars of the plan envisioned by Pew, Lenfest, Annenberg, and The Foundation are as follows: the outside organizations will commit to helping raise $150,000,000. The cost of constructing the new facility in Philadelphia is projected to be $100,000,000; and the remaining $50,000,000 will be used to replenish The Foundation's endowment. Ms. Rimel testified Pew has already obtained pledges totaling $100,000,000. . . .

* * *

We begin our analysis of this evidence with the observation that the fact-finding in this case has been seriously hamstrung by the total absence of hard numbers in evaluating these proposals. We have only a preliminary "guesstimate" about the real cost of constructing the new venue. We have no concept of The Foundation's operating expenses at the new space. There have been no feasibility studies or *pro formas* projecting the success of the proposed venture. We don't know how much it would cost to maintain the Merion facility for administrative purposes and for the horticultural course. . . .

On the opposite side of the coin, we have no hard numbers to evaluate options other than the Pew/Lenfest/Annenberg plan. . . . The move to Philadelphia has been floated as the only lifeboat in the entire sea. Since the outside charities are footing The Foundation's legal bills in these hearings, we accept their single-option theory as the product of zealous advocacy. We find nothing, however, to commend the Office of Attorney General's actions in this regard.

The Attorney General, as *parens patriae* for charities, had an absolute duty to probe, challenge and question every aspect of the monumental changes now under consideration. The law of standing, which has been repeated so many times in opinions concerning The Barnes Foundation by this court and Pennsylvania appellate courts, permits only trustees, the Attorney General, and parties with a special interest in the charitable trust to participate in actions involving the trust. In these proceedings, the three students were granted amicus curiae status, but their participation was limited to exploring the impact of the proposals on The Foundation's education programs. Thus, the Attorney General was the only party with the authority to demand, via discovery or otherwise, information about other options.

However, the Attorney General did not proceed on its authority and even indicated its full support for the petition *before* the hearings took place. In court in December, the Attorney General's Office merely sat as second chair to counsel for The Foundation, cheering on its witnesses and undermining the students' attempts to establish their issues. The course of action chosen by the Office of the Attorney General prevented the court from seeing a balanced, objective presentation of the situation, and constituted an abdication of that office's responsibility. Indeed it was left to the court to raise questions relating to the finances of the proposed move and the plan's financial viability.

Having established the record summarized above, The Foundation suggests that it has laid the groundwork for invoking the doctrine of deviation on the issue of relocating the collection. We have set forth the basic concepts of this doctrine, including the language of the *Restatement (Second) of Trusts, supra*. Our Superior Court has cited to *Corpus Juris Secundum* for the proposition that the party seeking the deviation (here The Foundation) has the burden of proof. 453 Pa.Super. at 253, 693 A.2d at 899. We too quote there from as follows:

> In exercising its jurisdiction to modify or alter, the court should ... be exceedingly cautious. Courts will exercise such power only when it clearly appears to be necessary and only in extreme cases.

90 C.J.S. Trusts, § 97 (2002 ed.) This language sets forth a "clear and convincing" standard of evidence in deviation matters. Furthermore, if the court is convinced that deviation is appropriate, it must choose the least drastic modification. In support of its argument, The Foundation cites to Comment e of § 381 of the *Restatement*, which provides:

> If a testator devised land for the purpose of maintaining a school or other charitable institution upon the land, and owing to a change of circumstances, it becomes impracticable to maintain the institution on the land, the court may direct or permit the trustee to sell the land and devote the proceeds to the erection and maintenance of the institution on other land, even though the testator in specific words directed that the land should not be sold and that the institution should not be maintained in any other place.

The Foundation did not set forth the remainder of that comment, to wit:

> If, however, the testator provided that if the institution should not be maintained upon the land devised the charitable trust should cease, the trustee will not be directed or permitted to maintain the institution on other land.
>
> So also, if the maintenance of the institution on the land devised was an essential part of the testator's purpose, the court will not direct or permit the trustee to maintain the institution on other land.

Dr. Barnes' indenture does not specifically state that the gallery must be maintained in Merion or cease to exist. Nevertheless, it is difficult to dismiss Dr. Barnes' choice of venue as a minor detail. Dr. and Mrs. Barnes lived on the site, in the administration building adjacent to the gallery. Dr. Barnes' indenture provided for the administration building to be used as classrooms for the art education program after his and Mrs. Barnes' deaths. The focus of the education program is the ensembles of art in the gallery. The arboretum on the grounds is also an integral part of the educational work that was the goal of Dr. Barnes' experiment. Certainly, a strong argument can be made that these facts fall within the parameters of the last sentence of the comment quoted above ("the maintenance of the institution on the land . . . was an essential part of the testator's purpose").

In resolving this very close question, we turn for guidance to the decisions of the Pennsylvania Superior Court in earlier Barnes Foundation matters. In the two opinions issued in September of 1996 (453 Pa.Super. 436, 684 A.2d 123, and 453 Pa. Super. 243, 683 A.2d 894,) that Court examined cases from other jurisdictions where deviation was allowed, noting:

> In each of the above-cited cases, the respective Court made a thorough effort to avoid the momentary impediment and apply a pragmatic approach to ensuring that the settlor's primary goal be achieved.

453 Pa.Super. at 458, 684 A.2d at 133. In both of these opinions, our Superior Court considered the case of *Colin McK. Grant Home v. Medlock*, 292 S.C. 466, 349 S.E.2d 655 (1986), in which:

> The Supreme Court of South Carolina was confronted with a petition by the trustee of a testamentary trust who wished to sell real estate upon which existed a nursing home which had been provided for the care of "elderly Presbyterians." Because of gradual dilapidation of the surrounding neighborhood, it was the intent of the trustees to sell the existing buildings and use the proceeds of the sale to build another facility in a different part of town. Despite the fact that the by-laws of the home, at the time of death of the remaining trust settlor, specifically provided that "[t]he Colin M.K. Grant [sic] shall always be located and conducted in the property at the corner of Hagen and Meeting Streets in the City of Charleston, as Memorial to the late Colin C.K. [sic] Grant," *id.* at 471–72, 349 S.E.2d at 658, the Court permitted the requested deviation and allowed the sale and the rebuilding of a facility at a separate location.

The Court shared the observation that "[t]here is no reason to doubt that if that particular real estate should become unsuitable for [its] purpose, [settlors] would have wished the funds to be used to provide some other means of housing for the intended beneficiaries of the trust. Thus, the use of the specific home they established was merely one method, convenient at the time of the trusts' establishment, for carrying out this intent." *Id.* at 471–72, 349 S.E.2d at 658. The Court then found because the neighborhood in which the home was located had become so dilapidated and unsafe that the purpose of the trust could no longer be carried out, deviations from the terms of the trust was permissible.

From its favorable reviews of the *Colin McK. Grant Home* case, we gather that our Superior Court would find that the present location of the gallery is not sacrosanct, and relocation may be permitted *if necessary* to achieve the settlor's ultimate purposes. We therefore rule in favor of The Foundation on this preliminary point.

That is not the end of our inquiry, however, because the element of necessity has not been established clearly and convincingly. What has been established beyond peradventure is that The Foundation's finances have reached a critical point. It is unnecessary and probably futile to review the last ten years of The Foundation's administration in order to lay blame for this situation. At the hearings in December, the *amicus curiae* attempted to raise the specter of runaway spending by the present administration as the root cause. However, based on this court's prolonged experience with this organization, we accept its claim that the installation of professional management was necessary, expensive and long overdue. Lower Merion Township certainly bears some of the responsibility for the financial crisis. The Foundation's attempt to raise revenues by increased public access to the gallery was met with hostility, bordering on hysteria, from some of the owners of the adjacent houses. The township reacted to the situation by imposing a series of administrative regulations that have put a stranglehold on The Foundation's admissions policy. The witnesses for The Foundation expressed no hope of winning concessions from the Township; and this Orphans' Court has no jurisdiction to broker or impose any changes to the unfortunate situation.

The financial exigency having been demonstrated, there are still issues of necessity and the least drastic solution. There has not been an adequate showing that sufficient revenue can not be generated by other means. We need to be persuaded that the move to Philadelphia is the least drastic deviation that will stabilize The Foundation's future. As we stated above, there is a dearth of hard evidence on the value of the assets that are not displayed in the gallery and could be sold. We heard from several witnesses about the ethical implications of deaccessioning in art administration. However, we are not here focusing on the gallery collection, and we are not convinced that the prohibition is or should be absolute in a non-museum setting. Otherwise stated, we question whether the same constraints on a museum not to sell its art bind an *educational institution* with works of art among its assets. On these unanswered questions, The Foundation must produce additional evidence.

To that end and pursuant to our broad supervisory powers in the area of charitable trusts, we direct The Foundation to undertake an analysis of its assets other than the works in the gallery in Merion. The goal will be to ascertain whether $50,000,000 or more can be raised for The Foundation's endowment through the sale of non-gallery artwork and/or the real estate in Chester County. If it appears that adequate capital can be produced by deaccessioning, the ethical problems presented thereby may have to yield to the donor's expressed wishes. We take our cue here from Dr. Barnes' mandate in P 13 of the indenture that everything except the paintings in the gallery should be sold "expeditiously" after his and Mrs. Barnes' deaths. The details as to how this assessment will be conducted and what experts will be retained shall be determined after meetings *in camera* with counsel.

In addition to this assessment, the court must insist on some reason to believe that the bold proposals before us will accomplish the desired ends. This will require the submission of a business plan for the Philadelphia operation. The Foundation and its backers chose not to commission a feasibility study of this nature on the grounds such an expense should not be incurred prematurely. However, we are convinced that a *pro forma*, including projections for earned revenue, is a crucial piece of evidence at this stage in the decision-making process.

The petition proposes additional changes relating to Paragraphs 6, 30, 33, and 34 of Dr. Barnes' indenture. We will rule on these proposed amendments after the additional information requested above is made part of the record. At present, the following Decree is appropriate.

Decree

AND NOW, this 29th day of January, 2004, upon consideration of The Foundation's second amended petition and after hearing thereon, the Board of Trustees of The Foundation are hereby granted permission to amend the bylaws of The Foundation as they relate to the Board's powers, trustees' qualification, number, composition and selection, election, term and compensation to conform to ARTICLE V of the proposed bylaws introduced at the hearing as Exh. P-4. The disposition of the remaining requests for relief in the second amended petition is deferred, pending the court's receipt of additional information.

Notes and Questions

1. *Aftermath.* In December 2004, after six days of hearings with an additional 1,200 pages of testimony, Judge Ott ruled that the Barnes Foundation had met its burden of proof under the doctrine of deviation establishing the move to Philadelphia as the least drastic modification of Dr. Barnes's intent. In 2007, Friends of the Barnes Foundation joined by Montgomery County (where Merion is located) petitioned the court to reopen the 2004 case that allowed the move. Following a hearing in March 2008, the judge denied the request to reopen the case, determining that Friends of the Barnes Foundation and Montgomery County lacked standing to contest the action. Neither party appealed the decision. The relocation decision was controversial and divisive in the community. See, e.g., the documentary film "The Art of the Steal," by Don Argott. A groundbreaking ceremony for the new facility

was held on October 15, 2008, and the new Barnes museum opened in Philadelphia in May 2012.

2. *Cy Pres and Deviation.* The law requires charities to follow donors' restrictions on their gifts to charities. In general, this norm of obedience comes from the fiduciary principles of trust law which infuse charitable organizations, whether organized as a charitable trust or as a nonprofit corporation. While there is a degree of uncertainty as to the exact boundaries for restricted gifts in the differing organizational formats of trust or corporation, the central issue of obedience is clear. See Susan N. Gary, *The Problems with Donor Intent: Interpretation, Enforcement, and Doing the Right Thing*, 85 Chi-Kent L. Rev. 977, 995–1001 (2010). When those restrictions become problematic, a charity's legal recourse is to seek application of the doctrines of deviation or cy pres. As the *Barnes* case indicated, the doctrine of deviation applies to administrative provisions, not the core purpose of the gift. Deviation from the donor's express administrative requirements can only come after a court determines that strict compliance with the terms has become impossible, illegal, or owing to an unforeseen and unforeseeable circumstance, compliance would defeat the donor's main purpose. The doctrine of cy pres, on the other hand, concerns the core purpose of the trust. A court in the exercise of its equitable power can allow a charitable organization to vary from its original charitable purpose if the purpose has become illegal, impossible, or impracticable, and in some jurisdictions, wasteful, as long as the donor had a general charitable intent and had not provided for an alternate disposition. Cy pres allows a modification of the purpose to one that is "as near as possible" to the donor's original purpose. Notice that while both doctrines reference donor's intent or purpose, the court's ability to alter or vary a core purpose restriction is more limited than its power with respect to an administrative provision. Yet the dividing line between a mere administrative detail and a core purpose may not be so bright and well-defined. Consider Professor Gary's comments on the *Barnes* litigation:

> The Barnes Foundation case demonstrates the use of deviation to permit a modification that seems to go against the donor's intent. In *Barnes* the court agreed to a sweeping set of changes: moving the gallery and art to downtown Philadelphia, lifting restrictions on public access and social gatherings, changing the structure of the board of trustees so that the trustees Dr. Barnes had chosen would lose control, giving positions on the board of trustees to representatives of the museums Dr. Barnes disliked, and providing that the trustees could amend the bylaws without court oversight, thus making further changes without any protection for donor intent easier. The modifications solve the financial problems faced by the Barnes Foundation, but the changes fairly clearly conflict with donor intent.

Susan N. Gary, *The Problems with Donor Intent: Interpretation, Enforcement, and Doing the Right Thing*, 85 Chi-Kent L. Rev. 977, 1025 (2010).

Was Judge Ott's application of the doctrine of deviation in *Barnes*, instead of cy pres, to the relocation correct? Could one argue that the location of the gallery on the grounds with the arboretum is an integral part of Dr. Barne's educational vision? For those who have been there, this argument has merit. "If there were other places like the Barnes, dispensing with it would not be tragic. But one minus one is zero." Peter Schjeldahl, *Untouchable: The Barnes Foundation and its fate*, THE NEW YORKER (Feb. 16, 2004).

Determining donor intent therefore is key, with the written documentation of the gift being the starting point for analysis. If there is no written record of the restriction or condition of the gift, courts are reluctant to infer one. See, e.g., Abrams v. Maryland Historical Society, No. A-58791, A-513/1979 (Cir. Ct. Baltimore County, Md., June 20, 1979); Rockwell v. Trustees of Berkshire Museum, 2017 WL 6940931 (Mass. 2017), *infra*. The lawyer and her client who desires to make a significant long-term or perpetual gift of an artwork must move beyond thinking about the possibility of change to understanding the *inevitability* of change. The lawyer's job is to document and convey the client's core vision with clarity and precision. Dr. Barnes's trust indenture was drafted by Owen Roberts, later a U.S. Supreme Court Justice and an instrumental figure in the creation of the Monuments Men in World War II. See Chapter 5, *supra*. Reread paragraph 11 of the trust indenture as quoted in the court's opinion. Does it give a sense that the location was sacrosanct?

The line between administrative detail and core purpose has been blurred not only by courts, but by the drafters of the Uniform Trust Code as well. Section 412 of the UTC provides that a court "may modify the administrative or dispositive terms of a trust. . . ." Scholars debate the recalibration of this reform. See Ronald Chester, *Modification and Termination of Trusts in the 21st Century: The Uniform Trust Code Leads Quite a Revolution*, 35 REAL PROP. PROB. & TR. J. 697 (2001); Allison Anna Tait, *The Secret Economy of Charitable Giving*, 95 B.U. L. REV. 1663 (2015); Alberto B. Lopez, *A Revaluation of Cy Pres Redux*, 78 U. CIN. L. REV. 1307 (2010).

3. *Spend-Down Approach.* For some in the philanthropic world, one response to the pragmatic difficulties of a perpetual gift is to vary the timeline and use a spend down approach. The Bill and Melinda Gates Foundation, for example, is not of perpetual duration but will terminate within 50 years of the death of the survivor of Bill and Melinda Gates and Warren Buffett. Is that idea compatible with the gift of significant art intended for public display? Probably not, as the core idea in *Barnes* and for many collectors is not to liquidate or spend down, but to keep the art together for educational and public benefit. The idea of dispersing or selling the art in the private market is the absolute opposite of the donor's intent. Art exceptionalism applies here, as unique artworks are not the equivalent of fungible dollars. Significant gifts of art for charitable purposes will continue to have a longer, perhaps even perpetual, timeline, as opposed to charitable monetary gifts addressing concrete and immediate human needs.

2. Deaccession

The *Barnes* case was a high-profile example of how donor intent can be compromised over time by the very institution charged with honoring that intent. In the context of charitable gifts of art, a far more common occurrence is the deaccessioning of the gifted works. Deaccessioning is the process for the formal removal of an object that was formally accessioned into a collection from that museum's collection. When a work has been donated or gifted to a museum, the deaccessioning of that work can provoke a strong response, including litigation, from the donor, the donor's heirs, or other stakeholders.

Rockwell v. Trustees of the Berkshire Museum

2017 WL 6940932 (Mass. Super. Ct., Nov. 7, 2017)

John A. Agostini, Associate Justice, Superior Court

A. Background

The genesis of the Berkshire Museum goes back to 1903. Philanthropist Zenas Crane donated a building that was located behind the Berkshire Athenaeum to hold and display art and artifacts for the benefit of the public. . . .

In 1932, a citizens' petition resulted in a separate legal existence for the Museum and a formal incorporation of the Trustees of the Berkshire Museum as the overseers of this entity. . . .

Over the years, the Berkshire Museum has matured and evolved into a repository of more than 40,000 items with a large concentration of items in the natural sciences, such as fossils, minerals, and reptiles. Since the seventies, the national economic winds have eroded the Berkshire County business environment. . . . The population has shrunk and, most importantly, generous benefactors have vanished. . . . [T]he County has supplanted its industries with recreational and cultural attractions as it progresses to a tourist-based economy. . . .

There appears to be no dispute that the Museum is in serious financial trouble. It has operated at a deficit for many years . . . the Museum's financial outlook is bleak.

Faced with these consequences, the Trustees initiated discussions, by way of a Master Planning Process ("MPP") to address the financial issues. . . .

. . . [T]he Trustees first considered the issue of deaccession as a possible option in June 2015. . . . At a retreat on October 24, 2016, the Board discussed . . . deaccession and, most importantly, moved forward with this method of financing. A meeting in December 2016, established a timeline. . . . Thus, over the course of two years, the Trustees and its subcommittees held numerous meetings regarding the economic future of the Museum.

On May 22, 2017, the Board voted to authorize . . . a consignment agreement with Sotheby's. . . .

The proposed auction includes forty items, with the two garnering the most attention being the works of renowned artist and Berkshire County resident Norman Rockwell. The paintings identified as "Shuffleton's Barbershop" and "Shaftsbury Blacksmith Shop" were personally donated by Mr. Rockwell to the Museum. . . . [T]hese two paintings are considered his finest works and their value is in the millions.

. . . For all the items submitted to Sotheby's the range . . . is approximately $46,000,000 to $68,000,000. . . .

B. Parties and Claims

1. Rockwell Case

The first three plaintiffs identified in the Rockwell Complaint . . . are the three children of Norman Rockwell and all are principal beneficiaries of the estate through testamentary trusts. . . .

The plaintiff Tom Patti is a prominent artist [who] entered into a contract with the Museum for the creation and installation of two items of glass affixed to the building.

The other plaintiffs in the Rockwell Complaint are . . . members of the Museum [and some] have made "substantial donations to the Museum." . . .

* * *

The defendants in the Rockwell case are the Trustees of the Berkshire Museum and Maura Healey, in her capacity as Attorney General of the Commonwealth of Massachusetts. Initially, there were no counterclaims or cross claims asserted by the defendants; however, after the hearing, the Attorney General filed an emergency motion to "convert from defendant to plaintiff if plaintiffs lack standing" and, if so, to seek a preliminary injunction on behalf of the Commonwealth. This motion was allowed.

* * *

Argument

The legal issue before the court is straightforward and well-traveled; the court must decide whether the plaintiffs are entitled to a preliminary injunction enjoining the Museum from selling or otherwise disposing of the 40 works of art under contract with Sotheby's. A preliminary injunction is an equitable remedy, and thus is not appropriately granted in those circumstances where it would impose an unfair or inequitable advantage on one party.

* * *

Before addressing the merits of a preliminary injunction, a digression is required to put in context a core issue in this case. This case is essentially about art deaccessions. According to the Association of Art Museum Directors (AAMD), deaccession is the practice by which an art museum formally transfers its ownership of an object to another institution or individual by sale, exchange, or grant, or disposes of an object if its physical condition is so poor that it has no aesthetic or academic value. Deaccession is not a pejorative term; it is an integral part of collection management in museums. The failure to periodically both pare down and complement a collection may render the art collection obsolete. Consequently, deaccession involves both artistic and financial decisions that go to the core of its mission.

A conflagration occurs, not with deaccession, but the purpose or reason for the deaccession. If it is used to pay for a greater work of art or to change a collection's focus, deaccession is generally tolerated. However, if it is used for operations or capital expenses, it is discouraged, if not condemned. Deaccessioning items from a museum is neither illegal nor unethical per se and every proposed deaccession must be examined on its own merits.

Generally, the art world has relied on two tools to control deaccession: self-regulation and peer-regulation. Self-regulation is simply the policies and procedures that a museum promulgates to guide its operations. The Berkshire Museum allows deaccession and has enacted specific policies for such an event. Peer-regulations relies on accreditation and professional ethics codes. Accreditation is undertaken by the American Association of Museums and ethical considerations are generally regulated by the AAMD. Peer-regulations often have been a powerful tool in shepherding the herd of museums that are considering deaccession for financial reasons. However, there are numerous examples of museums deaccessioning artwork for operating or capital costs. To date, the courts have played a very limited role and there is scant legal authority, statutory or case law, when a conflict of this nature arises.

The two issues before the court are (1) whether the plaintiffs (other than the AGO) have standing to assert their claims and, if the non-governmental plaintiffs have failed to establish standing, (2) whether the AGO has satisfied the requirements for a preliminary injunction.

A. Standing

It has long been the rule that only the Attorney General has standing "to protect public charitable trusts and to enforce proper application of their funds" and assets. The law presumes that the Attorney General can protect public charitable trusts "more satisfactorily . . . than . . . individuals, however honorable their character and motives may be. Since the law authorizes only the AGO to enforce public rights in a public charity, it falls on would-be plaintiffs to demonstrate that they seek to enforce some kind of private right.

The Rockwell plaintiffs, Norman Rockwell's heirs and the beneficiaries of his trust, argue that their unique right to enforce promises made to their father gives them standing in this case. But the law does not allow them as heirs or beneficiaries to enforce their father's contracts; that responsibility generally belongs to Norman Rockwell's estate or his trust, which are not parties to this litigation.

More fundamentally, even if a legal representative of Norman Rockwell's interests had joined this case, the claim, as presented, nonetheless only seeks to enforce Mr. Rockwell's intent regarding the permanent domain of his two works. That private right, if it exists, is no different from the public right that may be enforced only by the Attorney General. Accordingly, the Rockwell plaintiffs do not have standing to enforce any promise made to their father that would bind a public charity.

Mr. Tom Patti . . . complains that the Sotheby's sale would cause his artwork to be unilaterally moved. . . . Mr. Patti has failed to show any likelihood that his artwork will be unilaterally moved . . . his allegations are too speculative to confer standing upon him to ask the court to enjoin the sale.

The remainder of the Rockwell plaintiffs are all members of the Museum who live in Berkshire County. . . .

As the Attorney General conceded at the hearing, a member does not have standing to sue a public charity except in situations like those described in the *Lopez* case. See *Lopez v. Medford Community Ctr., Inc.*, 384 Mass. 163, 424 N.E.2d 229. . . .

The *Lopez* case perfectly illustrates that members may sue when enforcing a right or remedy only available to them, and that, otherwise, they do not have standing. . . . This claim is similar to the *Lopez* plaintiffs' claim of corporate mismanagement and, under *Lopez*, only the Attorney General has standing to bring it.

The plaintiffs who made substantial donations to the Museum argue that they have a private right to sue. . . . The donors in this case have failed to explain how their interest in enforcing the terms of their gifts is any different from the general public's right to have those terms enforced. Accordingly, they do not have standing because the Attorney General exclusively has that right.

* * *

In sum, none of the Rockwell non-governmental parties have standing to pursue Count I of the complaint and, as such their particular requests for a preliminary injunction with respect to that count will be denied. . . .

B. The Merits

1. The Attorney General's Posture

As should now be clear, the Attorney General does have standing to request that the court enjoin the Sotheby's auction. Yet this court has some threshold concerns.

There is no dispute that the AGO was initially made aware of the proposed sale of art by the Museum on June 23, 2017. A letter from Museum's counsel clearly revealed the plan to deaccession. . . .

The AGO, through the Non-Profit/Public Charities Division, commenced a detailed and thorough review of this process. [T]he Division requested and reviewed numerous documents, conducted over 20 informal interviews, met with Museum officials in Pittsfield, had no fewer than 20 conference calls with Museum counsel and fielded more than 400 contacts by individuals interested in the transaction. Clearly, during the last four months, the AGO was fully engaged in this controversy.

On September 6, Sotheby's announced that November 13, 2017, was the date of the first of a series of auctions. As the clock was ticking down in September and October, the AGO took no steps to intervene or even express dissatisfaction with the planned auctions to the Museum. Ultimately, the non-governmental plaintiffs were forced to file suit on October 20th and 25th, respectively, by asserting claims exclusively within the jurisdiction of the AGO. It was not until October 30, two days before the preliminary injunction hearing, that the AGO entered the fray.

After being dragged into the litigation as a defendant in the Rockwell case, the AGO did not file a cross claim against the Museum and, more importantly, it did not seek an injunction to stop the art sale. Instead, shortly before the injunction hearing, the AGO filed a memorandum supporting the plaintiffs' request to stop the sale. In the memorandum, the AGO does not assert that the Museum breached its fiduciary duties, only that it has "concerns" and needs more time to complete its investigation.

Putting aside the issue of why four months was insufficient to complete this inquiry, at no point does the AGO seek a continuance of the hearing in order to reach a decision on the merits for such a sale; it simply wants the injunction, as asserted by the plaintiffs, to be allowed based on its "concerns." . . . Given the considerable financial consequences that will result in enjoining the sale, this request to enjoin based on concerns is unusual.

At the hearing, the AGO admitted the obvious: that the other plaintiffs do not have standing to assert claims for breach of fiduciary responsibilities against the Museum. It was equally obvious that if the plaintiffs have no standing their motion for an injunction will fail. Consequently, at the close of business that day, the Commonwealth filed an emergency motion to convert the AGO to a plaintiff and assert a preliminary injunction on behalf of the Commonwealth, but *only* if the non-governmental plaintiffs have no standing. This motion was allowed the following day.

In this litigation, the AGO is a reluctant warrior. Most of those concerned find the sale of art in any form to be disconcerting, but conduct that raises concern or is troubling is not the legal standard. Whatever "concerns" remained with the AGO, they were insufficient to initially warn the Board that it intends to prevent the sale, nor were they sufficient to mount an injunction on behalf of the Commonwealth when the first auction became imminent. Instead, the burden of carrying this task fell to the non-governmental plaintiffs. This tactic required the AGO to take an astonishing position in its memorandum, a position that was simply anathema to its very core, i.e., members of a charitable corporation arguably have standing to sue a chapter 180 corporation and its board members for breach of their fiduciary duties. The AGO evinced apprehension to the very end, even when it was forced to file a motion to attain plaintiff status, the injunction request was carefully limited to be operative only if the plaintiffs have no standing. In other words the AGO is making every effort to avoid the issuance of an injunction *under its name*. I suspect that if the other plaintiffs had not filed suit, the AGO would not have initiated any litigation.

Thus, the court once again takes particular note of the *Lopez* case. In *Lopez*, the Attorney General had "considered the allegations of corporate mismanagement and had determined that the public interest would not be served by his participation in the case." Since the Attorney General declined to pursue the matter, the Supreme Judicial Court held that it was inappropriate for the trial court to consider any issues, such as the mismanagement allegations, that only the Attorney General could have litigated. In this case, the AGO's deliberate course of action and general reluctance gives the court pause.

It is obvious that the AGO's lack of aggressiveness speaks volumes to this court. As such, this court takes the AGO at its word that its "concerns," are in fact concerns only, and that, absent these "concerns," the AGO would have no qualms with a museum in severe financial straits deaccessioning and selling some of its most valuable objects to finance a new approach for serving the purposes of its charter. Because the AGO has not argued otherwise, this court is constrained to consider only the arguments before it.

* * *

The AGO's "concerns" are as follows: (1) the Museum may be prohibited from selling artwork acquired before 1932 . . . ; (2) Norman Rockwell may have restricted his gifts by requiring that his artwork remain with the Museum permanently or that it only be used to benefit the Museum's art collection; and (3) the Trustees' plan may contravene its purpose. These three concerns essentially allege a breach of trust. The AGO further argues that the "core issue" is whether the Trustees have breached or will breach their fiduciary duties by selling the objects as planned.

All told, the AGO asserts three grounds in support of her motion for a preliminary injunction to enjoin the sale: (1) the Sotheby's sale could be a breach of fiduciary duty; (2) the sale could be a breach of any of three alleged trusts; and (3) if the sale occurs before the AGO finishes its investigation, the public will have been deprived of the AGO's oversight. The Sotheby's sale must be enjoined if the court concludes it is more likely than not that the Attorney General will prevail on any of these three grounds and that, as a result, the sale would adversely affect the public interest.

2. Breach of Fiduciary Duty

For a preliminary injunction to issue based on a breach of fiduciary duty, the Attorney General must show it is more likely than not that (1) the Trustees had a fiduciary duty to the public; (2) that the Trustees breached or will breach that duty; (3) that the public has been or will be damaged; and (4) that the Trustees' fiduciary breach has caused or will cause the public injury.

The AGO argues that the Trustees breached or will breach their statutory duty of care as a charitable corporation. There is some dispute as to what rule the court should employ to determine whether the Trustees acted with the requisite care. While for-profit businesses are subject to the so-called business judgment rule, the Attorney General suggests that nonprofits should be scrutinized under a heightened standard. . . .

However, the SJC's definition of the private business judgment rule is virtually indistinguishable from the statutory duty of care for nonprofits. . . .

. . . [T]his court scrutinizes the Trustees' actions to confirm that their decisions measure up not only to the standard business judgment rule, but also that their choices reflect their "high degree of accountability to the individual donors as well as the community."

The Attorney General, agreeing that the Museum was in dire straits, conceded at oral argument that the Trustees' decision to deaccession and sell the forty objects was in good faith. As such, she solely contends that the decision was unreasonable under the circumstances. The court addresses each alleged unreasonable aspect of the decision in turn.

First, the Attorney General argues that the Trustees unreasonably chose an exorbitant revitalization plan. It is true that, while the Trustees' consultant found that it needed $25.6 million to stabilize its operations, they opted for a plan costing $60 million—$20 million for upgrades and $40 million toward endowment. But the Trustees made reasonable efforts to consider multiple plans over a two-year investigatory period. Further, adding $40 million to the Museum's endowment is hardly an aggressive choice and demonstrates a commitment to the community to keep the Museum operational. The decision to maximize the Museum's endowment and to improve substantially its facilities was not unreasonable. . . .

Second, the Attorney General contends that the Trustees' decision to deaccession was unreasonable because it violated general museum ethics and would result in sanctions. The Attorney General cites no case, statute, or AGO policy in support of the proposition that, to be reasonable, corporate board decisions must follow the professional ethics of the field. The Trustees evidently considered the ethical implications of their decision and weighed those implications heavily. . . . The Trustees have not spurned the ethical guidelines and exposed the Museum to sanctions without cause: indeed, as a result of the sale, the Museum will garner significant assets to tide it over during the expected freeze-out from the industry during which time the Museum will not be loaned exhibits from most, if not all, accredited museums. While public and professional dissatisfaction is understandable, that is not enough to render the decision unreasonable given the Museum's trying financial circumstances. . . .

Third, the Attorney General argues that the Trustees unreasonably decided to violate the Museum's collections management policy by choosing to deaccession the

Museum's most valuable artwork to pay for operational costs. Yet, as the Trustees explained, they are not bound by this policy. The policy is not referenced in the Museum's charter, its articles of incorporation, nor in its bylaws. . . . The Trustees' decision to override its policy was reasonable in this circumstance in light of the extreme financial concerns before them, which are absent from the day-to-day decisions governed by the policy. . . .

Fourth, the Attorney General faults the Trustees . . . for failing to notify the AGO of [certain geographic] restrictions. The Attorney General believes these failures rendered the decision unreasonable. . . .

As an initial matter, there is no law nor AGO policy requiring museums to notify the AGO when deaccessioning objects. With respect to the supposed restriction that objects donated before 1932 cannot leave Pittsfield, the Trustees take the position that there is no such restriction and that no notice was necessary. Whether or not the Trustees were correct, the potential restriction did not render unreasonable their decision to deaccession these older objects. . . .

* * *

The Trustees' decision was not unreasonable for any reason raised by the Attorney General. . . . [T]hey undertook a deliberate and careful review of the available options and chose what they believed to be the appropriate course. That was their duty. . . . [T]he law does not hold the Trustees to a standard of popular or political approval. Rather, the law requires reasonable care under the circumstances, and there is no evidence that the Trustees afforded this decision less than reasonable care.

3. Breach of Fiduciary Duty by Breach of Trust

The Attorney General also complains that the sale must be stopped because it will breach one of three possible "constructive" trusts: the trust supposedly arising from the pre-1932 restrictions, Norman Rockwell's purported inter vivos trust, and the trust intrinsic to the Museum's charter. . . . As a threshold matter, any breach of trust will depend on whether a trust exists.

The Attorney General submits that the trusts at issue are not based on express declarations of trust, but rather are "constructive trusts." "A constructive trust is an equitable remedy used to avoid the unjust enrichment of one party at the expense of another, where legal title to the property in issue was obtained either by fraud, in violation of a fiduciary relationship, or where information confidentially given or acquired was used to the advantage of the recipient at the expense of the one who disclosed the information." There is no allegation that any of the proposed trusts arose from fraud, a violation of a fiduciary relationship, or unfair use of secret information, so the doctrine of constructive trusts does not apply.

However, elsewhere in her memorandum, the Attorney General refers to the proposed trusts as "implied trusts" . . . . But the term "implied trusts" also does not seem to fit the circumstances.... Each of the trusts proposed by the Attorney General are actually best categorized as simply voluntary inter vivos (that is, lifetime) trusts, which are "direct or express trusts which spring from the agreement of the parties." ...

A gift to a charity usually creates some kind of charitable trust, with terms that are either express or implied based upon the circumstances of the gift. When ... a donor gives property to an existing public charity, the donor can choose to donate with or without restrictions. When there are no restrictions on the gift, the public charity's use is confined "to the purposes for which it was organized." ...

On the other hand, when the donor restricts the gift, the public charity's use is limited to "the particular purpose for which the property was given." Accordingly, in this case, if the charitable trust is alleged to be unrestricted, the court must determine the scope of the corporate purposes to decide whether the Sotheby's sale would be in breach of trust. And if the charitable trust was allegedly restricted by the donor, then the court must determine the breadth of those restrictions to see if the Sotheby's auction would violate them, breaching the trust.

(a) The Pre-1932 Restrictions

The first charitable trust for consideration is that which allegedly governed all donations to the Berkshire Museum before it was separately incorporated in 1932.... Accordingly, the Attorney General argues that these gifts are subject to the restriction in the Berkshire Athenaeum's charter prohibiting "real and personal property, or such gifts, devises or bequests" held by the Berkshire Athenaeum from ever being removed from Pittsfield....

* * *

... [Because the geographic limitation was not found in the purpose section of the statutory charter], the Museum is not restricted from using objects received from the Athenaeum in a manner that removes those objects from Pittsfield.

(b) The Rockwell Charitable Trust

The Attorney General argues that the Rockwell gifts were subject to a charitable trust separate from that governed by the Museum's charter. It is contended, then, that the Rockwell gifts are governed by the second type of charitable trust, in which the donor makes particular restrictions, which, if accepted by the charity, bar the charity from using the gift in contravention of those restrictions.... The donor's intent "is to be ascertained from a study of the instrument as a whole in light of the circumstances attending its execution. Search should be made for a general plan, presumably designed to express a consistent and harmonious purpose." If there is any doubt as to the donor's intent, the court should consider "the circumstances existing and known" to the donor at the time of the gift.

Extrinsic evidence relating to events taking place after the time of the gift cannot be considered when determining the donor's intent, but such evidence may be used "to show facts relevant to his knowledge, state of feelings toward or relation to the claimants." Words should be given their "ordinary meaning" unless it is shown that the parties intended to use them in a different sense.

In 1958 and again in 1966, Norman Rockwell gave certain paintings to the Museum without declaring any trust. Shortly after Rockwell donated the first painting, he received a letter from Stuart Henry, the Museum's director, accepting the paintings and stating that they were to be part of the Museum's "permanent collection." The Museum [states] "permanent collection" is and has long been museum parlance for objects accessioned by the museum and implies no actual permanency. [This persuades] the court that the phrase "permanent collection" should be accorded this specialized meaning, which would have been well-known by Rockwell and second nature to Henry. Accordingly, Henry's letter does not support the existence of a contemporary declaration by Rockwell that the paintings were to stay with the museum forever.

As the parties generally acknowledge, deaccession of artwork was not commonplace at the time of either of Rockwell's gifts. To the extent that may bear on the terms of a purported trust, it gives the court little reason to believe that, by gifting his paintings to the Museum without any express restriction, Rockwell nonetheless restricted the Museum from deaccessioning his work. If deaccessioning was so unheard of that Rockwell would not have thought to have restricted the Museum's right to deaccession his artwork, it suggests he did not restrict the Museum's rights in that fashion. On the other hand, if Rockwell and the Museum generally understood the possibility of deaccessioning, Rockwell's failure to expressly restrict the Museum from doing so suggests that restricting the gifts was not his intent.

Based on the foregoing, the evidence of Rockwell's intent to create a restrictive, stand-alone trust (separate from the Museum's corporate purpose) is insubstantial.... The competent evidence submitted to show that Rockwell affirmatively restricted the Museum's use of his paintings is as follows. First, Thomas Smith, a retired curator of the Museum acquainted with Rockwell averred that it was his understanding, at the time of the donations, that Rockwell donated the paintings in question because "they were his favorite oil paintings and he wanted them to stay on display in the Berkshires." Second, contemporary correspondence between Rockwell and Stuart Henry seems to indicate a close relationship and also shows that Henry sometimes asked Rockwell before loaning out the gifted artwork. Third, the Attorney General submitted Rockwell's trust, which, having been drafted after deaccessioning became more common, conditioned gifts to museums on their promise not to sell his artwork.

With respect to Mr. Smith's affidavit, he provides no evidence to support his belief that these paintings were Rockwell's favorites, or that Rockwell intended them to stay on display in the Berkshires. Indeed . . . , there is no evidence before this court that Rockwell ever said—to anyone, let alone the Museum—that he wanted these paintings to remain with the Museum or to be displayed forever in the

Berkshires. As far as the correspondence between Rockwell and Henry, it does little to move the needle in either direction. Henry had ample reason to seek out Rockwell's approval when dealing with his paintings: Rockwell was his friend, Rockwell was an iconic artist of international renown, and Rockwell had gifted the Museum with very valuable artwork. Henry's thoughtfulness in his dealings with Rockwell and his art was natural under the circumstances and thus is in no way suggestive of some express obligation.

Finally, while Rockwell's trust does tend to show his interest, later in life, in restricting the sale against his artwork, a close reading of the trust reveals that, if all gifts fail, the Museum is the default beneficiary of Rockwell's artwork—again, with no express restrictions. The sum total of the evidence tends to show that Rockwell simply wanted to benefit a museum that he particularly enjoyed. It is public record that, by the time of the gift to the Museum, Rockwell's paintings had been featured on every *Saturday Evening Post* cover for some four decades. Rockwell was likely quite experienced with contracting his artistic rights and there is no reason to infer that he lacked the shrewdness needed to unequivocally restrict the valuable artwork when he gave it to the Museum. As this court is unable to find any likelihood that Rockwell specially restricted his gift to the Museum, the gifts are instead controlled by the corporate purposes provided in the Museum's charter at the time of the gifts.

(c) Charitable Trusts Based on the Museum's Charter

The Attorney General lastly seeks to enjoin the Sotheby's sale because the Museum's "New Vision" plan could contravene its corporate purposes.... The Museum's statutory charter provides that it was to be incorporated "for the purpose of establishing and maintaining in the city of Pittsfield an institution to aid in promoting for the people of Berkshire County and the general public the study of art, natural science, the culture history of mankind and kindred subjects by means of museums and collections...." St. 1932, c. 134, § 3....

The question for this court is whether it is more likely than not that the sale of a substantial portion of the Museum's art would violate its corporate purposes. There is no evidence that the sale of art, alone, is in any way a violation of the Museum's charter.... Because deaccession is neither barred by the Museum's charter, nor by any professional or legal authority, the sale, alone, does not violate the Museum's corporate purpose.

Recognizing this, the Attorney General contends that her problem is not with the sale alone, but rather with the Museum's bold New Vision (which incorporates the sale) because the New Vision allegedly could change the nature of the Museum. But there is scant authority for this court to enjoin a party, let alone a corporate board charged with a duty of reasonable care, from doing a lawful act for the sole reason that it anticipates that party will use that lawful act to springboard into an unlawful one.

... Accordingly, it is unlikely that the Sotheby's sale will breach the Museum's charter and the court has no cause to grant injunctive relief on this ground.

4. The Attorney General's Incomplete Investigation

Lastly, the Attorney General requests injunctive relief because the AGO has not yet finished investigating its concerns. The argument appears to imply that, should the AGO learn the Museum's planned action is more inappropriate than it seems, it would more vigorously protect the public rights at stake. Or, perhaps ... whenever the AGO opens an investigation, the proposed action should be enjoined until the investigation can be concluded as a matter of public interest. Neither argument is persuasive in this case.

The AGO's clear policy is that charities only need to give official notice when they seek to sell substantially all of their assets. The Attorney General Guidelines recommend that boards "submit an informal written explanation" when the transaction is "significant," so the Public Charities Division can evaluate whether "the transaction raises other concerns under the law of public charities."

Here, the Trustees' proposed transaction ... will be significant. However, as already explained, the sale, alone, does not change the asset use, does not modify any donor restriction, and will not be for less than fair market value. The Attorney General has not identified any other theory by which the proposed auction would violate the law of public charities....

Tellingly, the Attorney General Guidelines conclude that "[i]t is in the organization's and the board members' best interest to maintain records of the decision-making process that was followed in the event that questions arise after a transaction is completed *that did not involve notice to the Attorney General.*" ... If the usual course is that a charity might sell an object without informing the Attorney General ..., it is surprising that the AGO would seek to enjoin such a transaction potentially jeopardizing millions of dollars of charitable funds. It is bewildering that the AGO would seek such an injunction, at such a cost, when its investigation has uncovered no evidence of bad faith, no conflict of interest, no breach of loyalty, no express gift restrictions, and yielded unconvincing evidence of implied gift restrictions or a breach of reasonable care during a two-year decision-making process....

In the usual case, it probably promotes the public interest to empower the Attorney General to thoroughly investigate whatever it wishes to investigate on behalf of the public. But all investigations are not cut from the same cloth. This particular investigation has yielded unconvincing evidence of charities violations over a period of four months and the AGO has given this court utterly no reason to expect that convincing evidence will ever be forthcoming. Indeed, the AGO's initial indifference to this litigation, compounded with its later faint-heartedness, strongly suggest that the AGO, too, has little expectation of discovering evidence supporting its concerns. The public's interest in having the AGO continue its tepid investigation pales in comparison to the public interest in ensuring that a public charity does not needlessly lose potentially millions of dollars by canceling a contract that it has every right to make. An injunction permitting the continuation of such an investigation under these circumstances would adversely affect the public and be inconsistent with the requirements for such request.

Conclusion

For the foregoing reasons, the Attorney General's request to preliminarily enjoin the planned auction is denied. This may very well mean that timeless works by an iconic, local artist will be lost to the public in less than a week's time. No doubt many will be disappointed in this outcome, and they may take little comfort knowing that, in their loss, the rights of a charitable board to make thoughtful decisions to steer its charity through troubled times have been vindicated. However, it is the responsibility of the court to act dispassionately and decide cases solely on the legal merits of the claims presented.

Notes and Questions

1. *Aftermath. Shuffleton's Barbershop,* a Rockwell masterpiece, sold in a private Sotheby's sale to the new Lucas Museum of Narrative Art in Los Angeles. That museum is expected to open in 2022 and, until its opening, *Shuffleton's Barbershop* will be on long-term loan, initially at the Norman Rockwell Museum in Stockbridge, Massachusetts. Net proceeds from the first Sotheby's auctions to the Berkshire Museum "disappointed." The museum was "not surprised to fall short of [its] expected goal by close to $13 million." Caroline Goldstein & Eileen Kinsella, *Amid Protests, Berkshire Museum's Deaccession Sales at Sotheby's Fall Short of Expectations,* ARTNET, May 23, 2018, quoting Elizabeth McGraw, board president, at https://news.artnet.com/market/berkshire-museum-au. Do you think the protests over the sales affected the hammer price?

2. *Enforcing Donor Intent: Question of Standing.* Making a charitable gift of art presupposes that the gift is for public benefit and, specifically, not for an ascertainable or identifiable beneficiary. Without an identifiable someone with a particular financial stake in the operation of the charitable organization, who can enforce the donor's intent against the abuse or breach of fiduciary duties by those in charge of the organization? As exemplified by *Rockwell* and *Barnes,* the traditional answer is that enforcement lies with the state's Attorney General, as parens patriae, and not with the settlor. This limited standing rule often surprises the settlor and the settlor's family. It is subject to much academic criticism as being ineffective, inefficient, and political. See, e.g., Evelyn Brody, *From the Dead Hand to the Living Dead: The Conundrum of Charitable-Donor Standing,* 41 GA. L. REV. 1183 (2007). Judges have also expressed frustration. Judge Ott characterized the AG's actions in *Barnes* as merely being a "second chair" and "an abdication of the office's responsibility." Similarly, Judge Agostini described the AGO in *Rockwell* as "a reluctant warrior"

and as acting with "indifference," "faint-heartedness," and being "tepid." Some judges are rethinking the rule against settlor standing. See Smithers v. St. Luke's-Roosevelt Hospital Center, 723 N.Y.S.2d 426 (App. Div. 2001); L.B. Research & Education Foundation v. UCLA Foundation, 29 Cal. Rptr. 3d 710 (Ct. App. 2005). Finally, legislators in states that have adopted Uniform Trust Code § 405(c) have also responded by providing a statutory grant of standing to a settlor of a charitable trust. See Joshua C. Tate, *Should Charitable Trust Enforcement Rights Be Assignable?*, 85 Chi-Kent L. Rev. 1045 (2010). The trend is in the direction of allowing settlor standing, but two limitations are apparent. First is time oriented: what happens when the settlor dies? In this regard, consider Uniform Trust Code § 413(b), which limits remote default provisions. Second is the donee's organizational nature: what of gifts to nonprofit corporations instead of charitable trusts?

3. *Planning for Standing.* Examining standing from a planning perspective leads to two drafting suggestions for clients who do not wish to rely exclusively on the Attorney General for enforcement. In the first instance, if the gift is intended to be an outright transfer to a museum with a condition attached (such as public display), the deed of gift could specifically provide that the museum will not contest the family's standing if they seek to enforce the condition. Note the condition itself could give the donor or his heirs a limited reversionary interest and hence standing (in that a violation of the condition might return the property to the donor or his heirs). Caution is necessary, however, on two fronts. The tax consequence of conditions or other restrictions must be considered. If a breach of the condition results in a forfeiture by the charitable beneficiary, the gifted property will generally be returned to the donor or his heirs (a common law approach) or be transferred to another charitable organization (a modern preference). Keeping the gifted property with a charitable organization keeps the gift a charitable one for tax purposes and therefore lessens income, gift, and estate tax concerns for the donor. If restrictions could defeat the gift to charity, a charitable deduction is allowed only if the possibility of the restrictions occurring are deemed "so remote as to be negligible." But see Priv. Ltr. Rul. 9303007 (Jan. 22, 1993), allowing a gift tax charitable deduction for a conditional gift, noting that the particular conditions had no impact on value because the likelihood of the conditions not being followed was so remote as to be negligible. The Unform Trust Code adds another wrinkle to gifts over. Section 413(b) is a non-waivable provision that limits default gifts over to the donor during the donor's lifetime or to individuals only within 21 years of the trust's creation. Consequently, from a trust law perspective, a donor may mandate the gifted artwork be returned to an individual (other than the donor) only if the charitable gift fails within 21 years of the gift.

The second drafting observation is that a transfer to a settler-created charitable trust may be preferable to an outright transfer to a museum. The terms of the trust can be drafted to be amenable to ongoing family involvement, while clearly protecting the charitable interest. See discussion Part B, *supra*, on the Broad Art Foundation.

For many charitably inclined collectors and their lawyers, decisions against standing are unsettling. In choosing to make a gift via a donor-created charitable trust or foundation, the issue of trustee selection and succession is crucial. The unforgiving reality is that for a perpetual organization, at some point, there will no longer be a living individual known by the donor. If there are family members, they may be a logical choice for trustee succession or for selecting the successor trustees. If not, what other avenues exist? The approaches are finite: the charity itself (or representatives of the nonprofit sector), a judicial approach (in equity, a trust will not fail for want of a trustee—the court will appoint a new trustee), a political approach (for example, the mayor can appoint), the trustees could appoint their own successors, or a combination. In planning for this, safely removed in time from the actual trustee shifting event, all of these approaches seem plausible. Experience tells us that it is not the device but the people chosen who will safeguard the trust. For Barnes, having no professional trustee clearly compromised the management of the trust assets. See Samuel P. King & Randall W. Roth, BROKEN TRUST: GREED, MISMANAGEMENT AND POLITICAL MANIPULATION AT AMERICA'S LARGEST CHARITABLE TRUST (2006), for the story of the scandalous waste and breach of fiduciary duties involved in the administration of Princess Bernice Pauahi Bishop's 1884 charitable trust for the school children of Hawaii. The trustee selection was given to the Justices of the Hawaii Supreme Court, and only the threat of the revocation of tax exempt status by the IRS had any deterrent impact.

4. *Arc of Deaccession in the U.S.* Two very controversial museum sales and dispositions in the 1970s led to serious reflection and review of the deaccessioning process and procedures in the United States. Major art museums now have formal policies in place for the deaccession process. A cardinal rule for those museums is that the sales proceeds from deaccessioning are to be used for acquisition and collections enhancement, not operating expenses. (But see Note 5, *infra,* for temporary suspension of rule.) Collectors who donate to art museums are often motivated by the desire to share their art treasures with the public and courted by the museum to do so. The prospect that the museum may deaccession and sell, i.e., monetize, the donated works can seem a betrayal of trust. The insertion of public display or no sale clauses into the deed of gift may actually reflect the donor's central concern, but the wording of those clauses (precatory or mandatory) and the consequences for a breach (gift over to other charity or reversion) must be carefully considered for tax and standing issues. On the other hand, there is a legitimate need for museums to have the ability to deaccession, to prune as it were, their collections over time. There is no debate, for example, that a museum should have the ability to deaccession works that are inauthentic, have compromised title, or are required by law to be repatriated.

To give some flavor to deaccessioning issues, consider the following four cases as a mini reader of controversial deaccessions. The first two from the 1970s were the impetus for self-regulation in the museum community. The last two from the 2000s show deaccessioning in university settings.

a. In 1972, a series of articles in the New York Times by art critic John Canady exposed the Metropolitan Museum of Art's deaccessioning of a number of works from its permanent collection. Thomas Hoving, Director of the Met, secretly sold through the Marlborough Galleries a Van Gogh and a Rousseau, while publicly pronouncing that if the Met were to sell, there would be an announcement. Many of the works were donations from Adelaide Milton de Groote who died in 1967. Miss de Groote was courted by many museums for her collection, and she decided in 1950 upon the Met. Apparently she did not place any legal restrictions on the gift, although she wrote in her will, in a precatory not mandatory manner, that the Met should give any works it did not want to other museums in New York or Connecticut. When the New York Times article broke, Miss de Groot's cousin wrote that the intention was for the gift to be "held in trust for all the public to see." Nevertheless within five years of her death at age 91, Miss de Groot's donated art collection was largely dispersed, with works by Renoir, Degas, Dufy, Picasso, and other masters returned to private ownership. There was such a tremendous public outcry that the New York Attorney General intervened and the Met agreed to certain procedures for the future disposition of artworks. See Stephen E. Weil, A DEACCESSION READER (1997), for an overview of deaccessioning history, policy, and procedures.

b. The Museum of the American Indian located in New York City was created by George Heye in 1916 through the donation of his collection of artifacts. He was its director for life. In 1973, some 15 years after Heye's death and within the same time frame of the Met's deaccessioning controversy, a new trustee of the Museum contacted the New York Attorney General's office. The trustee was alarmed by museum practices and requested a review of the museum's accession and deaccession policies. One example is illustrative of the museum's rather relaxed approach to fiduciary norms. After deaccessioning items, the trustees would purchase the deaccessioned objects through the museum's gift shop. The Attorney General's investigation and legal action led to the hiring of a professional administrator and to a board composed of independent persons. These changes in turn led to a much reinvigorated museum. One that, with considerable negotiation, patience, and political finesse, became the National Museum of the American Indian in September 2004 located on the National Mall in Washington D.C. It maintains its New York origins with a satellite museum in the renovated Old Customs House in Manhattan. See Merryman, Elsen & Urice, LAW, ETHICS AND THE VISUAL ARTS 1227–1230 (5th ed. 2007).

c. When Georgia O'Keeffe's husband, the famous photographer Alfred Stieglitz, died in 1946, his estate included about 900 artworks, including many photographs. In order to resolve certain contentious issues in his estate and consistent with Stieglitz's will, Georgia O'Keeffe received court authorization to transfer Stieglitz's artwork to six nonprofits, including Fisk University. In making the transfer of 97 works to Fisk in 1948, Ms. O'Keeffe indicated that Fisk was "not at any time [to] sell or exchange any of the objects in the Stieglitz collection," to which Fisk University specifically agreed. In 2005, Fisk filed a lawsuit seeking court permission to sell two works from the collection to generate funds for its endowment, improve academic departments, and build a new science building. Like the Barnes and the Berkshire Museum, Fisk was in financial difficulties. Shortly thereafter, the O'Keeffe Foundation (later succeeded by the O'Keeffe Museum) sought permission to intervene, which was granted. The O'Keeffe Museum argued that the attempt to sell violated the donor's restrictions, and therefore the collection should revert to the O'Keeffe Museum. The Tennessee Attorney General (whose first attempt to intervene was denied) opposed the Museum's reversion argument and disputed the Museum's standing. Meanwhile, another museum came forward to buy a half interest in the collection for $30 million; different settlement options with the O'Keeffe Museum were stymied. The trial court determined that the O'Keeffe Museum had an implied right of reversion, and therefore, standing, and that Fisk had breached one condition but that the breach was insufficient to justify reversion. It issued an injunction against selling and ordered Fisk to again display the works. The Court of Appeals for Tennessee determined in 2009 that the O'Keeffe Museum lacked standing, because Georgia O'Keeffe had only a life estate in the works from her husband; consequently, she had no interest in the works to pass to her Museum upon her death. The court remanded the case on the issue of cy pres. Georgia O'Keeffe Foundation (Museum) v. Fisk University, 312 S.W.3d 1 (Tenn. Ct. App. 2009). On remand, the trial court determined cy pres applied to allow the modification of the restricted gift and approved the sale of a 50% interest in the collection. Appeals by both parties followed. The appellate court confirmed cy pres applicability but reversed with respect to the trial court's allocation of sales proceeds. In re Fisk University, 392 S.W.3d 582 (Tenn. Ct. App. 2011). On April 20, 2012, the Tennessee Supreme Court denied permission to appeal, and the seven-year Fisk litigation was finally over. In August 2012, Fisk finalized an agreement to sell a 50% interest in the collection to Crystal Bridges Museum in Arkansas with the understanding the museum will be able to display the collection two out of every four years. The funds from the sale helped Fisk stay open.

d. On January 26, 2009, Brandeis University announced it would close its Rose Art Museum and sell off the 6,000 plus artworks to bolster the University's finances. The Rose has an impressive collection of American Modernism, American Social Realism, Abstract Expressionism and Surrealism, including works by Jasper Johns, Helen Frankenthaler, Ellsworth Kelly, Andy Warhol, Thomas Hart Benton, and other leading figures in 20th century art. It was valued in 2008 at $350 million. The University's decision met fierce resistance within and without Brandeis, leading to a lawsuit filed by Meryl Rose (daughter of the main benefactors) and the resignation of the Brandeis president. The plaintiffs survived a motion to dismiss in October 2009. A trial, at which the plaintiffs would have the opportunity to demonstrate that "their gifts to the Rose should be returned to them under . . . equitable reversion" and/or "fraud," was set for December 2010. Brandeis explored many monetizing options, including a plan to partner with Sotheby's to rent out works from the Rose. See Mason Kerns, *Selling the Picasso to Fix the Plumbing: An Analysis of Five High Profile Deaccessioning Attempts*, ALI-ABA LEGAL ISSUES IN MUSEUM

Administration (March 24–26, 2010). In June 2011, the plaintiffs settled their lawsuit with Brandeis announcing the Rose is and will remain a university art museum. *Brandeis, plaintiffs settle Rose Art Museum lawsuit*, BrandeisNOW, June 30, 2011, at www.brandeis.edu/now/2011/june/rose.html.

5. *Transactional Takeaway.* What does a transactional lawyer learn from these thumbnail sketches of gifts gone awry? First, one needs to know the institutional practices and policies of the intended donee. Since the 1970s spotlight on the Met and the Museum of the American Indian, the museum community has addressed the issue of deaccessioning as part of a more comprehensive and systematic review of collections management. See, e.g., Association of Art Museum Directors, AAMD Policy on Deaccessioning (June 9, 2010), available at www.aamd.org/papers; American Association of Museums, Code of Ethics for Museums (2000), available at www.aam-us.org/museumresources/ethics/coe.cfm; American Association of State and Local History, Statement of Professional Standards and Ethics (June 2002), available at www.aaslh.org/documents/AASLHProfessionalStandardsandEthics_000.pdf. None of these bodies bans deaccessioning outright, rather transparency and checks and balances in practice and policy is the norm; as is the use of sales proceeds for collections, not operating expenses. For members' violations of the deaccessioning policies, sanctions can be imposed that could result in the violating museum's inability to participate in loans and exhibitions with other members. For example, New York's National Academy Museum was suspended in 2008 as a result of its deaccession of two Hudson River School paintings. Jori Finkel, *Whose Rules Are These, Anyway?*, N.Y. Times, Dec. 28, 2008, at AR28. University of Iowa was put on notice that a sale of its Jackson Pollock *Mural* could violate the museum's ethical obligation not to treat their artworks as disposable financial assets. Jens M. Krogstad, *Gartner again wants to sell U of I painting*, D.M. Register, Feb. 12, 2011, at B1. Deaccessioning practices can also catch the eye of legislators, with proposals to legislatively regulate deaccessioning and the use of those proceeds for operating expenses. See Robin Pogrebin, *Museums and Lawmakers Mull Sales of Art*, N.Y. Times, January 15, 2010, at C29.

Second, one needs to determine the client's comfort level of ceding standing to the Attorney General's office in the event of a future abuse. Overreacting by imposing substantial restrictions must be balanced against the possibility of losing the charitable deduction.

Third, one must understand the very real situation of severe fiscal constraints faced by many museums and other nonprofits; in an economic downturn, those constraints can be life threatening. In *Rockwell*, the judge clearly communicated that the decision to deaccession was one the museum took responsibly. It understood its plan could lead to sanctions and, in fact, sanctions did follow. The effect of those sanctions is debatable. In April 2020, with the world in a pandemic with severe, existentialist economic fallout, the AAMD announced a two-year suspension on censures and sanctions for museums using funds from deaccessions to pay for expenses directly attributable to the care of the collection. *AAMD Board of Trustees Approves Resolution to Provide Additional Financial Flexibility to Art Museums During Pandemic Crisis*, April 15, 2020, at aamd.org/for-the-media/press-release/aamd-board-of-trustees-approves-resolution-to-provide-additional-financial-flexibility-to-art-museums-during-pandemic-crisis. Is the AAMD's resolution an official recognition that sometimes survival requires a deviation without a punitive consequence? How does one balance short-term difficulty with long-term viability?

All three points underscore the importance of determining the client's core purpose: preserving the artworks for the public or supporting the donee's core mission? It is not a decision to be made quickly. See Linda Sugin, *Lifting the Museum's Burden from the Back of the University: Should the Art Collection Be Treated as Part of the Endowment?* 44 New Eng. L. Rev. 541 (2010).

Sixth Drafting Exercise: Art Bequest

To: Junior Associate

From: Senior Partner

I just had lunch with our client, Mr. Smith. He is thinking about the statue he has recently commissioned from the artist Ms. Jameson. He wants to donate the statue sometime in the next five years or so to his deceased wife's alma mater in her memory. Mr. Smith doesn't want to do it right away; he wants to enjoy the statue for a few years first. He also wants to see how the college fares over the next few years.

Mrs. Smith went to a small college, that was then and remains today for women only. It is a very good school, but struggling financially, and Mr. Smith is uncertain of the college's viability. If the college were to close, he would not want the statue to disappear or be sold for the benefit of creditors.

The college has asked him to sign a pledge regarding the statue, but he is disinclined to do so at this time.

In any event, he wants us to draft a protective amendment to his will—in case he should die before he actually donates the work to the college—giving (a) the statue in memory of his wife consistent with his wishes and (b) a gift of $100X as a small endowment fund for maintenance, conservation, and student education about this work of art. He would like his daughter Susan (also an alum of the college) to be involved to some degree in determining how the money is used.

Please draft for my review the language for this new distribution and give me a heads-up on any other matters that might need some attention because of this new gift in his will.

Chapter 11

Valuation

The valuation of an artwork is part of the normal give-and-take process of negotiation for the sale of an artwork between buyer and seller. This chapter explores valuation when there is no buyer and seller, that is, when the transfer of the artwork is gratuitous, such as in a gift or an estate context. Fair market value, the regulatory standard supplied by tax law, is the starting point for the valuation discussion. It is an unruly and imprecise standard that is severely tested when confronted with unique artworks.

A. Fair Market Value

1. General Framework

The cases and materials on fair market value are drawn from the tax side of the world. The technical and fiscal setting does not mean the discussion here is any less important or interesting than other topics. For better or worse, when we "follow the money," it often tells us what society values.

Tax is a land where a healthy dose of skepticism is required. There is something about filing an income tax return that can inspire sensible people to act nonsensically. One such place is the valuation of donated art for the income tax charitable deduction. In general, the higher one's income tax deductions, the lower one's income tax. The push therefore is to increase the amount of deductions. Almost from the inception of the federal income tax, Congress allowed a deduction for contributions to charitable organizations. The requirements for claiming a charitable deduction for a contribution of art are highly complex (see discussion in Chapter 10, *supra*), and in satisfying those requirements, the taxpayer must quantify the value of the gifted artwork. For charitable deductions not limited to the basis or cost of the donated artwork, fair market value is the regulatory and judicial standard.

Fair market value is defined by Treasury Regulations as the "willing buyer-willing seller" test: "the price at which the property would change hands between a willing buyer and a willing seller, neither being under any compulsion to buy or sell and both having reasonable knowledge of the relevant facts." Treas. Reg. § 1.170A-1(c)(2). There is an old quip that fair market value has only three problems. We don't know what's fair, we don't know which market, and we don't know how to value. Other than that, it's a fine test.

As the next cases demonstrate, fair market value is a question of fact, with the burden on the taxpayer to establish the validity of the claimed deduction. Since the time of these cases, Congress made substantial changes in the taxpayer's and appraiser's roles and responsibilities for the valuation process. See discussion in Part B, *infra*.

Biagiotti v. Commissioner

52 T.C.M. (CCH) 588 (1986)

Whitaker, J. On February 25, 1983, respondent issued a statutory notice of deficiency to petitioners. . . . In each of the [five] years in issue petitioners donated pre-Columbian or Mayan art objects to the Duke University Museum of Art (Duke), and claimed charitable contribution deductions which respondent disallowed in whole or in part. [IRS allowed a total of $1,600 for the art contributions over the five years.—Ed.]

After concessions, the issues for decision are:

(1) The amount deductible for charitable contributions in all years in issue . . . [and];

(3) whether petitioners are liable for additions to tax under section 6653(a) for negligence or intentional disregard of rules and regulations.

Findings of Fact

* * *

Biagiotti's interest in Mayan and pre-Columbian art was initiated in 1974 or 1975 when he viewed a collection of pre-Columbian and Mayan art at the home of John Fulling (Fulling), a social acquaintance. Prior to that time he had no exposure to or interest in the art. . . . He has made no formal study of Mayan or pre-Columbian art and has acquired little, if any, expertise in the area.

* * *

Biagiotti's initial intent was to collect pre-Columbian art for his own use, but in 1976 he decided to follow Fulling's example and contribute parts of his collection to Duke. Bill Stars, the museum director, convinced Biagiotti of the University's commitment to acquire a major collection of Mayan art for study and display. Biagiotti donated his first piece of art in 1976 and additional pieces in [1977–1980]. . . . Altogether, Biagiotti purchased approximately 200 pieces of art and contributed 25 to 30 percent of those pieces to Duke.

* * *

All of the appraisals . . . were done by James Silberman (Silberman) who had been recommended by Fulling. Biagiotti reviewed Silberman's credentials . . . and also contacted Bill Stars and asked him to verify that Silberman was a legitimate appraiser with excellent credentials.

Although Biagiotti relied on Silberman's appraisals when completing his returns, [he did not] testify at trial. Silberman entered into an agreement with the

Government subsequent to the years in issue but prior to trial, which prevents him from doing appraisals or testifying about appraisals.... Consequently, none of the appraisals ... were admitted as evidence.... At the time the appraisals were done and relied upon as a basis for the deductions, Biagiotti was not aware of and did not have any reason to be aware of the events leading to Silberman's agreement with the Government. Biagiotti had never heard anything derogatory about Silberman at the times in question. [Silberman's appraisals for the five years' donations totaled $191,825 for tax purposes.—Ed.]

At trial both parties relied on expert testimony and written reports.... However, because of differences in the factors each relied on ... the values arrived at were far apart....

Sales prices of comparable pre-Columbian art vary depending on the type and place of sale. Such art is generally sold in galleries and at auctions, although pieces can be acquired directly from "runners" who bring the art into this country. Fulling acquired his art directly from Guatemala or by traveling to the country of origin and purchasing the art there. The highest prices and most frequent sales are generally found in galleries selling at retail to collectors. Dealers in galleries usually mark up pieces at twice their cost. Collectors, aware of the mark-up, are willing to pay such prices because they rely on the dealer's guarantee of authentic merchandise. In the event authenticity is successfully questioned, galleries will refund the purchase price paid. Gallery owners also advise customers on the development of their personal collections.

Auction sales differ significantly from sales in galleries. Auction houses do not guarantee authenticity and they disclaim liability for statements in their catalogs regarding the condition of objects. Prices at auction depend to a large extent on the level of bidding, and it is difficult to label prices as wholesale or retail since collectors, dealers, and occasionally buyers for museums all acquire pieces there. As a result, items purchased may or may not be resold at a later date. For these reasons, auction sales of pre- Columbian art can only be characterized as a mixture of wholesale and retail prices.

Petitioner's first expert, Paul Clifford (Clifford) based his appraisal of the Biagiotti material on his general knowledge of sales of comparable pieces. Clifford served as curator of pre-Columbian art at Duke from 1973 until 1981....

In order to arrive at sales prices of comparable pieces, Clifford consulted available published information. He also relied on his experiences as a collector of pre-Columbian art, as curator at Duke, and as an appraiser. After seeing "thousands of pieces" he put together "pretty much in his head" the parameters of the value of pieces comparable to the Biagiotti art. From these, he arrived at what he determined to be fair market value. [Clifford's appraisals totaled $187,985.—Ed.]

Petitioners' other expert, Ronald Dammann (Dammann) is an art dealer who specializes in pre-Columbian art. He has been a dealer and appraiser ... since 1969. His grandfather started the family-owned business, and he has literally grown up around pre-Columbian art. About 90 to 95 percent of the art he deals in, both in appraising and in the gallery, is pre-Columbian. He has customers worldwide and obtains information about sales of pre- Columbian art through customer contact, and also through contact with east and west coast dealers. Dammann valued the Biagiotti art using sales prices of comparable objects he had in his gallery or knew of in other galleries. Dammann valued all of the Biagiotti pieces except items 7.19 and 8.27.

Dammann did not consider sales of comparables at auction houses when he valued the Biagiotti gift, although he personally buys and sells pre-Columbian art for his gallery at the Sotheby Parke Bernet (Sotheby) auction in New York City twice a year. In his opinion, and we so find, Sotheby auction sales do not represent a significant portion of pre-Columbian art sales in this country during these years. We also agree that auction prices at Sotheby generally do not accurately represent the average sales price of pre-Columbian art in the United States. [Dammann's appraisals totaled $72,775.—Ed.]

Respondent's expert, Michael Coe (Coe), used auction catalog prices for sales of comparable higher quality pieces, and sales prices in shops and galleries for comparable lower quality pieces. Coe is a professor of anthropology at Yale University. He has been teaching anthropology since 1958, first at the University of Tennessee, and for the last 25 years at Yale. His specialty is pre-Columbian art and the archaeology of Mexico and Central America....

* * *

When determining the value of the Biagiotti contributions Coe began by identifying the history and provenance of each piece. In doing so, he relied on his expertise as an archaeologist and anthropologist. He then constructed a chart of price ranges for sales groups of comparable items. He looked for comparable material or material which was superior to the Biagiottis' in auction house sales catalogs. The catalogs contained photographs of the items he determined were comparable. He then broke the comparables into four categories from "top quality" to "poor quality."

He used Sotheby's catalogs exclusively for price ranges of those items within the top three categories. For the lowest group he based prices on what he had seen at shops and galleries that sold items of similar quality, since auctions generally do not list these items in their catalogs or sell them at their main auctions. Using the price ranges he arrived at, Coe then valued each of the Biagiotti items accordingly. [Coe's appraisals totaled $49,375.—Ed.]

* * *

Opinion

Valuation

Where a charitable contribution is made in property other than money, the amount of the contribution is the fair market value of the property as of the date contributed, reduced when applicable as provided in section 170(e)(1).

Sec. 1.170A-l(c)(l), Income Tax Regs. Fair market value is "the price at which the property would change hands between a willing buyer and a willing seller, neither being under any compulsion to buy or sell and both having reasonable knowledge of the relevant facts." Sec. 1.170A-1(c)(2), Income Tax Regs. Fair market value is a question of fact.... Petitioners bear the burden of proving that the Commissioner's determination of the fair market value of the property ... is in error.

The fair market value of property may vary, depending on the market in which the property is sold. The determination of the proper market for evaluation purposes is also a question of fact. Section 170 and the regulations thereunder are silent as to the market to be used in determining the value of donated property. However, we have recognized that the valuation test for estate and gift tax purposes is generally the same as that used for charitable contribution deduction purposes. The regulations for the estate and gift tax valuation test provide that the fair market value of an item of property is to be determined in the market where such items are "most commonly sold to the public." Sec. 20.2031-1(b), Estate Tax Regs.; sec. 25.2512-1, Gift Tax Regs. In the normal situation, a sale "to the public" refers to a sale to the "retail customer who is the ultimate consumer of the property." The sale to the ultimate consumer is any sale to those persons who do not hold the item for subsequent resale, not necessarily the most expensive sale. The most appropriate comparable market for valuation purposes is the most active retail marketplace for the particular item involved.

In the present case, the expert witnesses ... testified at length regarding the fair market value of the Biagiotti contributions. We must determine which expert presented the most probative evidence. Although opinion evidence is admissible ... such evidence must be weighed in light of the qualifications of the witness and of all other relevant evidence of value. We may reject expert testimony when in our best judgment it is appropriate to do so.

Petitioners' expert Dammann is the most reliable witness.... His sales and pricing experience is far greater than the other two experts' and his disinterested conclusions ... are in our judgment as satisfactory an indication of fair market value as can be obtained from an appraisal. Dammann's extensive experience with both auction and gallery sales makes credible his testimony that auction prices are often lower than gallery prices, and sales at the Sotheby auction represent a small percent of sales in the pre-Columbian art market.

Auction sales of pre-Columbian art in this period, since they were composed of wholesale as well as retail transactions, do not reflect accurately sales prices in the retail market.... Furthermore, ... Sotheby sells only a small portion of pre-Columbian art nationwide. We are convinced that Sotheby is the principal auction house selling pre-Columbian art in the United States but we have no evidence as to what percentage of sales are made at auctions other than Sotheby's. Coe testified that he relied on Sotheby catalogs rather than Christie's catalogs since Sotheby is the major auction house for higher quality pre-Columbian art. However, on this record there is no basis for us to determine what percentage of total United States auction house sales of this art the Sotheby sales represented during this period.

By contrast to Dammann, we did not find Clifford's testimony to be convincing for a number of reasons. First and foremost, Clifford has not provided a sufficient explanation or justification for the values he attributed to the Biagiotti contributions. He valued the art significantly higher . . . but gave only general information about his basis for sales prices of comparable items. . . . Clifford may have had significant exposure to pre-Columbian art during his tenure at the Duke museum. . . . However, he has no sales experience and no formal training or study of pre-Columbian art. . . . We thus reject his testimony as to value.

Dammann's testimony is also far more probative as to value than Professor Coe's. Coe is a well-credentialed expert, and . . . he is one of the world's principal authorities on the anthropological and archaeological aspects of Mayan and pre-Columbian art. However, we are not satisfied that his expertise extends to the appraisal of such art, especially as to medium and low quality pieces. We are not convinced that his values represent retail sales prices of art comparable to the Biagiotti gift.

Coe relied almost exclusively on auction sale catalog prices for approximately one-half of the Biagiotti contributions, and relied on his general knowledge of the retail market (as did Clifford) for those items that were not suitable for auction. Coe testified that in his opinion, auction sale prices represent the retail price of higher quality pre-Columbian art. We are not convinced that this is accurate, at least as to art objects of the quality here involved. Coe testified that dealers only buy at auction those items which they anticipate retaining for a period long enough for the items to appreciate in value. However, Dammann, who regularly attends auctions, testified that dealers buy at auction with the intent to stock their inventory and resell at a profit. He also testified that as a dealer he does not generally sell at auction because he can get a better price if he sells through his gallery. He will typically sell at auction when he is in need of ready cash. Further, Coe himself admitted that auction prices are an incomplete source of price information, given the entire market of pre-Columbian art sales.

* * *

Dammann's testimony in this case is simply reliable, whereas as we have said, we have substantial problems with that of both Coe and Clifford. Based on the record before us, we conclude that the value of each item of the Biagiotti gift is that value attributed by Dammann in his revised expert report.

* * *

Section 6653(a)

The next issue before us is whether petitioners are liable under section 6653(a) for negligence or intentional disregard of rules and regulations. Respondent contends that petitioners were negligent in relying on Silberman's appraisals. . . . Respondent argues that petitioners should have known that the appraised values were inflated in light of the difference between Biagiotti's cost from Fulling and the values Silberman attributed to the art. Secondly, respondent contends that petitioners were negligent . . . by failing to maintain adequate records of the initial cost of the art objects.

Section 6653(a) applies only in the event any part of any underpayment is due to negligence or intentional disregard of rules and regulations. Petitioners have the burden of disproving respondent's determination that the section 6653(a) addition to tax is applicable.

With respect to respondent's first argument, petitioners must show that they acted reasonably and prudently and exercised due care in obtaining the appraisals of fair market value which they used on their tax returns. On the record before us, petitioners have carried their burden. Although Silberman was not called to testify and his appraisals have not been accorded any probative weight in our determination of fair market value, nothing in the record indicates that petitioners were not justified in relying on Silberman and his appraisals at the time their tax returns were filed. As we stated earlier, at the time the appraisals were relied on, Biagiotti was not aware of the events that led to the later agreement between Silberman and the Government which prohibits Silberman from doing appraisals or testifying about them when they involve charitable contributions. Consequently in no way does the agreement or Silberman's failure to testify bear on the issue of negligence.

* * *

Respondent has also urged that we find . . . petitioners' failure to establish their cost basis in each of the contributed objects was due to negligence or intentional disregard of section 1.170A-1(a)(2), Income Tax Regs. Although Biagiotti maintained inadequate records with respect to the cost basis in the objects contributed, we fail to see how his cost basis in any way relates to the underpayment in this case. Petitioners' underpayment is due to an inaccurate valuation at the time of contribution; the cost basis has nothing to do with the determination of said value. Consequently, we see no connection between the inadequate record keeping and the underpayment of tax in these circumstances. Section 6653(a) is simply not applicable on these facts.

Decision will be entered under Rule 155.

Ferrari v. Commissioner

58 T.C.M. (CCH) 221 (1989)

Whitaker, J. [The Ferraris donated 21 pieces of pre-Columbian art to Duke University over four years, 1978–1981, and claimed charitable contribution deductions on their income tax returns for those gifts. The IRS denied portions of the claimed deductions. Taxpayers' expert was the same Mr. Dammann from *Biagiotti*, and the IRS's expert was Claudia Giangola, an art dealer and a member of the IRS Art Advisory Panel. Both sides accepted the qualifications of the experts. — Ed.]

Opinion

This case presents another instance where this Court is called upon to value a relatively obscure collection of art objects on the basis of testimony by well-qualified individuals who unfortunately were able to arrive at a common valuation of only 2 out of the 21 objects. The Court is called upon to exercise its judgment in an area totally foreign to the training and experience of a trial judge. This is a particularly apt example of a valuation controversy where arbitration by a third expert in pre-Columbian art would have been a far more satisfactory method of arriving at valuation for tax purposes.

We note that both appraisers originally valued each object at what that individual thought was the higher end of the valuation range. At the Court's request, Mr. Dammann provided in his testimony values which reflected his judgment of the middle of the range. Ms. Giangola testified that the range, in her judgment, was 15 to 20 percent of the high end value. Mr. Dammann on the other hand seemed to conclude that the range of values was almost infinite. Ms. Giangola's testimony on this point was much more credible and we have accepted it. That has not, however, solved our problem because in most instances Mr. Dammann's median value differed from Ms. Giangola's high value by more than 20 percent.

Petitioners seem to argue that this Court must accept the valuations of one or the other of the two expert witnesses who testified in this case, that only in special circumstances can a court substitute its judgment for that of an expert. . . .

The law applicable to expert testimony was recently summarized by this Court in *Estate of Giselman v. Commissioner*, T.C. Memo. 1988- 391, 55 T.C.M. 1654, 1658, 57 P-H Memo T.C. par. 88,391, 88-1932, 88- 1937 from which we quote:

> Opinion evidence is admissible on the question of value; however, it must be weighed in light of the demonstrated qualifications of the expert and all other evidence of value. * * * We are not bound by the opinion of any expert witness when that opinion is contrary to our own judgment. * * * We may embrace or reject expert testimony, whichever, in our best judgment, is appropriate. * * * We are not restricted to choose one valuation over the other, but may extract relevant findings from each in drawing our conclusions. * * * [Citations omitted.]

We have embraced such portions of the testimony of each of the experts as we found to be proper. Our valuations are based on the entire record and reflect our own best judgment.

* * *

The market in this case is the retail sales market at art galleries dealing in pre-Columbian art. Value is the price a customer would pay the gallery for a piece of this type of art. Comparable retail sales at galleries are the most significant criterion of fair market value. The range of prices arises out of the fact that, as both expert witnesses agreed, galleries have no way of uniformly fixing the price for items which are comparable. Pricing of a pre-Columbian art object is essentially a question of judgment and experience and is a product in part of the price paid by the gallery and its level of markup. The ranges which the experts describe cover, in their judgment, the range of prices among various art galleries which handle pre-Columbian items.

Every price in that range should reflect at least in theory the price which might be realized by an art gallery in a sale of a comparable item to a retail customer. Thus, again in theory, the entire range reflects retail sale prices. Thus, fair market value as defined by the regulations is on this record not a single price but a range of prices.

Charitable contributions must be valued as of the date of the gift. Prices of pre-Columbian art change relatively slowly. The parties have assumed, as we do, that there were no significant price changes during the period 1978–1981. . . .

Reference to one of the items involved reflects the problem faced by this Court. Number 79.10.8 is a carved bowl with circular glyph text and sides depicting two Cauac Monsters. Mr. Dammann's value at the high end of his range is $9,500, his median value is $7,500 and Ms. Giangola's value at the high end of her perceived range is $6,000. The high value assigned by respondent's expert is roughly 65 percent of the value of the high value assigned by petitioners' expert and 80 percent of his median value. As we have already commented, it is astounding that these parties would seek a court solution to such a fact situation rather than arbitration by another expert.

Ms. Giangola's appraisal contains a reasonably detailed description of each piece, including comments about the condition of each piece. None of her descriptions were questioned by petitioners. Ms. Giangola further described this collection as generally 'lower quality material, material of the type which was in every day use rather than being specially made for wealthier and more important citizens.' The record also reflects the fact that in July 1988, in her capacity as a member of the Art Advisory Panel and together with other panel members, Ms. Giangola appraised these 21 pieces on the basis of photographs and other information. While her valuations reflect her own opinion, it is likely that her valuations are at least conservative and probably reflect discussions with other members of the Art Advisory Panel. Taking all of these factors into account, we have . . . redetermined the fair market value of each piece in issue to be a value which lies at the mid point between Mr. Dammann's mean or median value and Ms. Giangola's high value. We are confident that one could find a comparable piece of this art which in some gallery has sold at a value approximately equal to the value we have found.

* * *

Decision will be entered under Rule 155.

Notes and Questions

1. *Fair Market Value—Which Market? What Method?* Judge Whitaker framed the market question (auction or dealer) in *Biagiotti* in a straightforward manner. He marched through the Internal Revenue Code and the Regulations under § 170 for the income tax charitable deduction meaning of fair market value. When he ran into silence under § 170 on which market to use, he merely switched over to the same fair market value standard used in the estate and gift tax arena. Those

regulations filled in the void. The market where the item is "most commonly sold to the public," the "retail market," is the appropriate market. The two main markets for art—auction and dealer—need to be examined from the perspective of the particular property (here pre-Columbian art), to determine which is the most common retail market for the property.

Based on expert testimony in *Biagiotti*, the judge chose the private dealer market as the market where pre-Columbian art is most commonly offered to the public. Because neither Coe nor Clifford was a dealer, the only access each of them had to extensive sales data was auction records. How reliable as indicators of fair market value are such results? Recall Cristallina v. Christie, Manson & Woods International Inc., 502 N.Y.S.2d 165, 170 (App. Div. 1986), Chapter 3, *supra*, where Christie's admitted that its press release falsely reported the results of an auction "for the benefit of [Cristallina] and the art market." Guarantees, buy-ins, and extensive financing offered some buyers at auction may also undermine the integrity of the posted auction results. Moreover, think how you would have argued for an auction model during the time of the criminal antitrust conspiracy. See discussion on auction practices in Chapter 3, *supra*. On the other hand, using the dealer market is not necessarily purer, as a dealer in that type of art may have an inherent incentive to support higher values. It is not unheard of that public pricing information on private sales can be somewhat inflated. See Staechelin & Ors v. ACLBDD Holdings Ltd & Ors (2019) EWCA Civ. 817, where Gauguin's 1892 painting *Nafea faa ipoipo* (*When will you marry?*) was reported privately sold in 2014 for $300 million when the actual price was $210 million. Choice of market is made in the first instance by the appraiser; the lawyer needs to be aware that the marketplace must be defensible.

Judge Whitaker also noted that auction houses do not guarantee authenticity and that the auction audience was a mix of dealers, collectors, and institutions. Now that there is a five-year authenticity guarantee under certain circumstances by major auction houses, should Judge Whitaker rethink his conclusion? A similar rethinking may also be due with respect to the undifferentiated makeup of the auction attendees—some collectors do attend and some dealers at auction are actually representing private clients. Should the result change because of that? The answers may not flow directly from these questions, but from the impact those changes would have on the "retail" market for pre-Columbian art.

The IRS expert in *Biagiotti*, Professor Coe, segmented the works between high quality and those of lesser quality, with different markets for each. The high end would be valued in the auction market and the lesser quality works would be valued in the dealer retail market. This raises the classification question of how finely one defines the property, which is itself a factual question. A similar segmented approach was used by the Tax Court in valuing the artworks in the estate of Georgia O'Keeffe. See Estate of O'Keeffe v. Commissioner, 63 T.C.M. (CCH) 2699 (1992), see Section A.2, *infra*. For works valued on comparable sales data from auction, the pertinent number is the hammer price plus buyer's premium. See Tech. Adv. Mem. 9235005 (Aug. 28, 1992). Presumably, that would now also include the overhead premium.

Note that the method of valuation—comparable sales of art—was not in question in either *Biagiotti* or *Ferrari*. The valuation of hard to value, unique assets can also involve a choice of valuation method. For example, the valuation of shares of stock or other interests in a closely held business enterprise may be based on a business assets approach, an earnings approach, or a combination. The nature of the business enterprise will influence the valuation method. A service business is usually valued on an earnings approach and not an asset approach, while an entity that only owns, say, unimproved real property will usually be valued on an asset approach and not an earnings approach. While not a totally pre-ordained conclusion (see, e.g., Calder v. Commissioner, 85 T.C. 713 (1985), discussed *infra*), it appears that most art is valued on an asset approach using comparable sales data, and not an earnings approach. If, say, artworks were to be rented out by the owner, valuation may need to take the earnings approach into account, to some extent. See Estate of Elkins, *infra*, and discussion in Chapter 10, *supra*, regarding Brandeis University's proposal to have Sotheby's rent artworks from the University's Rose Museum.

2. *Expert Opinions.* Both *Biagiotti* and *Ferrari* proceeded as Tax Court memoranda decisions. This means the case raises no new question of law; rather, the case involves only the application of settled tax law to the facts of the case. Most valuation cases are exactly that: fact driven and fact sensitive, where advocacy is critical. It may be seen as a battle of the experts. In *Biagiotti*, there was a wide range of opinions as to the amount of the charitable deduction for the objects given to Duke. Not surprisingly, the two outliers were the taxpayer at $191,825 on the original returns and the IRS at $1,600 in the notice of deficiency. Some call this the splitting-the-baby approach; better to err on the side of overreaching to protect the middle-of-the-road end result. Once engaged in the audit and litigation process, the taxpayer's experts and the IRS expert occupy the space in between: $49,375 (Coe), $72,775 (Dammann), and $187,985 (Clifford). Judge Whitaker generally adopted Dammann's appraisal.

By the time of the *Ferrari* case, you can sense Judge Whitaker's frustration with the déjà-vu aspects of the case and the inability of two recognized experts, including Dammann from *Biagiotti*, to agree on 19 of 21 values. Judge Whitaker characterized the opinion of the IRS expert (who was then a member of the IRS Art Advisory Panel) in *Ferrari* as "conservative" and probably reflective of internal IRS discussions. The opinion makes it clear that valuation for tax purposes is not a contest where the winner takes all—the judge can come up with an independent determination of value. On appeal, the Fourth Circuit affirmed the careful, item by item, valuation process of the trial court judge, analogizing his process to that which a willing buyer and a willing seller would engage in. Ferrari v. Commissioner, 931 F.2d 54, at * 4 (4th Cir. 1991).

Between the time of *Biagiotti* and *Ferrari*, there is also a noticeable shift in credentials for the art valuation experts. In *Ferrari*, both experts have extensive private market expertise in pre-Columbian art, underscoring that valuation is fundamentally a function of art markets and economics, not academic expertise. The increased competence and expertise of appraisers is now a statutory and regulatory matter for tax purposes. *Biagiotti* and *Ferrari* are fairly tame cases with generally upstanding valuation experts, yet even so, there is a hint at valuation abuse with the IRS's assertion of penalties. This abusive aspect will be more fully explored in Part B, *infra.*

3. *Tax Penalties.* In addition to paying the correct tax amount based on the proper charitable deduction, a taxpayer will also have to pay interest on the underpayment of tax and, in some cases, penalties. The Commissioner in *Biagiotti* asserted a 5% underpayment penalty for negligence or intentional disregard of rules and regulations based on the taxpayer's initial use of Silberman's appraisals in the preparation of Biagiotti's tax returns. Silberman was later disqualified by the IRS as an appraiser. The Court refused, however, to sanction Biagiotti, allowing him the benefit of relying on an "unreliable" appraiser.

Balancing a taxpayer's personal responsibility for a proper tax return against reliance on experts is an ongoing question in tax administration. The complexity of the tax code is well known, and many taxpayers employ professional return preparers and other experts in assembling their returns. Shopping for an appraiser with a well trained eye for art and a well tuned ear to tax, especially against the imprecise backdrop of fair market value, which for art means falling within a range of values, contributes to the game-y nature of tax. Congress has been consistently strengthening the penalty provisions that can be assessed against the taxpayer and others for valuation misstatements. See Part B, *infra.*

4. *Impact of Title and Authenticity on Value.* In the acquisition of art, title and authenticity are the core legal concerns for the buyer. Those two factors are also central to the valuation process and are equally critical to the seller for the price on disposition. Biagiotti's interest in pre-Columbian art was piqued in 1974–75 and he began collecting thereafter. He acquired his first piece in 1975 through his friend Fulling "from a party named 'Estoril.'" The court noted that pieces could "be acquired directly from 'runners' who bring the art" to the U.S. If Biagiotti were your client today and he wished to donate some pieces to Duke, what steps would you take before the donation? See Chapter 6, *supra*, for discussion on the 1970 UNESCO Convention on the Means of Prohibiting and Preventing the Illicit Import, Export and Transfer of Ownership of Cultural Property, and the U.S. Cultural Property Implementation Act (CPIA).

If artworks are determined to be unsaleable at auction or through a dealer in the retail market by virtue of their questionable provenance or acquisition history, does that mean their fair market value is zero? In an interesting estate tax scenario involving medieval artworks and cultural property stolen during the final days of World War II by a U.S. Army officer, the IRS determined that the illicit market, not the auction or dealer market, was the appropriate market for those items. The illicit status of the works did not exempt the works from being included in the gross estate for estate tax purposes (dominion and control over assets, not only legal title, can be the basis for inclusion in the gross estate) nor require a zero valuation. See Tech. Adv. Mem. 91-52-005 (Dec. 27, 1991). While the publicly available TAM redacts name and identifying details, the underlying facts seem to fit the case of Texan Joe T. Meador and the Quedlinburg Treasures from central Germany. See United States v. Meador, 138 F.3d 986 (5th Cir. 1998); William H. Honan, TREASURE HUNT: A NEW YORK TIMES REPORTER TRACKS THE QUEDLINBURG HOARD (1997).

A similar valuation quandary involved Robert Rauschenberg's *Canyon* when its owner died. It was an unusual piece, as it included a complete taxidermied eagle on the canvas. That eagle, however, meant the artwork was not able to be sold, as sales of eagles or parts are strictly prohibited by the U.S. government. That did not stop the IRS from valuing the work at a reported $65 million while the estate valued the artwork at zero. Neither extreme position is defensible. Although sales are forbidden, gratuitous transfers are not. Therefore, there is some value in being able merely to possess the artwork and pass it on. The IRS reportedly recognized the prohibition on legal sale but thought that the illicit market might be pertinent. The Service assessed a $40.9 million deficiency in taxes and penalties. The parties settled their controversy by having the artwork donated to the Museum of Modern Art in New York without claiming a charitable deduction. See Anne-Marie E. Rhodes, *Valuing Art in an Estate: New Concerns*, 31 CARDOZO ARTS & ENT. L. J. 45 (2013).

The following case considered the impact a question of authenticity had on an income tax charitable deduction. Note how the court refused to rule directly on the work's authenticity, but circumscribed its ruling as to the impact on valuation by merely raising a question.

Doherty v. Commissioner

63 T.C.M. (CCH) 2112 (1992)

PARR, J. Respondent determined deficiencies in petitioner's Federal income tax. . . . The sole issue remaining is the valuation of a painting petitioners contributed to the Charles M. Russell Museum.

* * *

In 1969 petitioner bought the painting, which we will refer to as Attacking Stagecoach for purposes of this case, from an antique dealer named David Burnham for $10,000. During tax year 1982, petitioners donated an undivided 40-percent interest in Attacking Stagecoach to the Charles M. Russell Museum in Great Falls, Montana. In tax year 1983, petitioners donated the remaining undivided 60- percent interest in the painting to the museum.

Petitioners determined the painting was an original by Charles M. Russell with a fair market value of $350,000 at the date of the donation. At the beginning of trial, petitioners requested that the Court allow them to amend their petition to decrease the fair market value of the painting, and accordingly their claimed deduction, to $200,000. Respondent determined the painting is a forgery and had a fair market value of no more than $100.

Attacking Stagecoach depicts a cowboy action scene. . . . A square butte is at the horizon of the painting. The bottom left corner bears the initials CMR and a buffalo skull is beneath the initials. Attacking Stagecoach is painted on duck, a rough canvas not normally used for fine paintings. The painting measures 70 by 64 inches and is not sized.[3]

Charles M. Russell is a noted western artist and Montanan for whom the Charles M. Russell Museum is named. Charles M. Russell's works range from the late 1800's through the early 1900's. Since his death in 1926, Charles M. Russell's works have become quite valuable; one oil painting brought $480,000 in the 1970's.

At the outset we reiterate our thoughts in *Messing v. Commissioner,* 48 T.C. 502, 512 (1967), on the issue of valuation:

> Too often in valuation disputes the parties have convinced themselves of the unalterable correctness of their positions and have consequently failed successfully to conclude settlement negotiations—a process clearly more conducive to the proper disposition of disputes such as this. The result is an overzealous effort, during the course of the ensuing litigation, to infuse a talismanic precision into an issue which should frankly be recognized as inherently imprecise and capable of resolution only by a Solomon-like pronouncement. [Citations omitted.]

* * *

There is little doubt that the opposing experts in this case are two of the foremost authorities on the works of Charles M. Russell. Petitioners' expert is Mr. Ray W. Steele and respondent's expert is Mrs. Ginger K. Renner. Mr. Steele worked as a curator for 2 years, and then as the executive director for 18 years at the Charles M. Russell Museum. Mr. Steele retired from the museum in August 1989. While at the museum Mr. Steele authenticated its entire Russell collection of approximately 1,800 works. Mr. Steele testified that Mrs. Renner and he are the top Russell experts in the country. Mrs. Renner owns and maintains the largest archive and library on Russell art and history in the country, and is consulted regularly by Sotheby, Christie's, and Butterfield and Butterfield auction houses to authenticate Russell works of art. Throughout her career, Mrs. Renner has authenticated over 500 Russell pieces.

We will first focus on the few areas in which the experts agree. Both Mr. Steele and Mrs. Renner agree that the scene of a stagecoach being attacked is an appropriate subject matter for a Russell painting. Likewise, a square butte, a low mesalike hill which marks the horizon line, is common in Russell paintings. Both experts agree that Attacking Stagecoach is not a finished painting. And finally, both Mr. Steele

3. Sizing is the placing of a gesso base on a canvas in order to provide the artist with a smoother surface on which to paint. Sizing also prevents undue absorption of the pigment, oil paint in this case, into the canvas.

and Mrs. Renner agree that Attacking Stagecoach is not like any Russell painting they are familiar with.

It would be unfair to categorically say that the two experts agree on nothing else. But instead of listing all the specific instances of disagreement, we will now examine each expert's methodology and conclusion.

Mr. Steele's expert opinion is that Attacking Stagecoach is an authentic Charles M. Russell painting and was worth $200,000 at the time of donation. Mr. Steele bases his conclusion on the following factors. The work appears to have been painted in a fast manner, which according to Mr. Steele, exemplifies the spontaneity of Charles M. Russell. The subject matter and square butte are also characteristic of Russell's work.

The coarse canvas is characteristic of Russell because he painted on virtually everything, including tobacco can lids, tin, and clay. Mr. Steele has seen a crude oil drawing by Russell of a deer painted on a petticoat. Mr. Steele concludes that Attacking Stagecoach is an oil sketch that was not intended to be a masterwork, sold, or displayed. Mr. Steele opines that the signature and buffalo skull are authentic, and while the skull is admittedly not as perfect as on many Russell paintings, it is not a forgery. According to Mr. Steele, the false skulls are usually riddled with particular idiosyncrasies absent in the skull on Attacking Stagecoach.

Mr. Steele also opines that the CMR initials and the skull were applied at the same time the picture was painted. The oil paint seeped through the canvas, which was not sized, and the pigment consistently shows through the painting. Mr. Steele points out that if the signature were fake and placed on the painting at a later date, then the value and the hue of the signature would not match anything in the painting. Additionally, Mr. Steele observed the canvas is weathered with holes, tears, and stains which occurred after Attacking Stagecoach was painted.

Mr. Steele rules out the possibility that Attacking Stagecoach was painted after Russell became famous, because the canvas is so old and is beginning to break down. Additionally, the paint was applied while the canvas was relatively new. In Mr. Steele's opinion, Attacking Stagecoach was painted after 1897, as late as 1910, but closer to 1905.

In Mrs. Renner's expert opinion, Attacking Stagecoach could not possibly be an authentic Russell. Mrs. Renner believes the initials and buffalo skull are easy to forge. The particular signature and logo were not used until 1897 or 1898 which dates the piece sometime after 1897. According to Mrs. Renner, Russell's early work was immature or naive, but never as crude as Attacking Stagecoach, which was painted after 1897 when Russell was a much more talented artist. Additionally, no matter how quickly Russell would have painted a piece, it would contain certain elements of his style and skill which Mrs. Renner does not see in Attacking Stagecoach.

The elements of the composition convince Mrs. Renner that Attacking Stagecoach is not an authentic Russell. The most predominant example is the fallen figure and horse in the foreground. The figure is very undefined and lacks body weight and volume....

The lack of realism in the painting is another element of the composition Mrs. Renner relies on to support her opinion. According to Mrs. Renner, Charles M. Russell liked to paint it "like it was". Attacking Stagecoach has almost no definition in its characters. The gear for controlling the horses is not well defined and is historically incorrect as is the drawing of the stagecoach wheels....

Regarding forgeries, Mrs. Renner testified that some of the earliest forgeries were painted while Russell was still alive. These forgeries were oil paintings and almost inevitably copies of Russell paintings that had been reproduced.

* * *

Both parties want us to rule on the authenticity of Attacking Stagecoach. We decline to do so, particularly when two of the foremost authorities on the works of Charles M. Russell cannot agree on the painting's authenticity. Even though we will not decide whether Attacking Stagecoach is an authentic Charles M. Russell, we recognize that the shadow cast by disputing the authenticity of a painting acts as a depressant on its value.

* * *

The fair market value of Attacking Stagecoach is adversely affected by: (1) The poor quality of the painting; (2) the poor quality of the canvas; and (3) the dispute over the painting's authenticity. The Russell work Kick Over the Morning Coffeepot, described as one of Russell's poorer quality paintings, sold for $55,000 prior to 1981. Upon considering the infirmities of Attacking Stagecoach, the zenith period in which it was donated, and discounting for the doubt about authenticity, we conclude it had a fair market value of $30,000 at the date of donation.

Decision will be entered under Rule 155.

Doherty v. Commissioner

16 F. 3d 338 (9th Cir. 1994)

Canby, J.

* * *

II.

The Dohertys contend that the Tax Court improperly relied upon facts and circumstances occurring after the date of their donation in making its determination of the painting's fair market value.

The Tax Court's determination of Attacking Stagecoach's fair market value at the time of contribution rested in part upon the fact that a painting for which authenticity is in doubt will change hands at a lower price than one for which authenticity is undisputed. The Dohertys assert that this ruling was error because the authenticity of Attacking Stagecoach had not been questioned prior to the time that they donated the painting to the museum. They say that because the doubt as to Attacking Stagecoach's authenticity did not arise until the Commissioner evaluated the validity of their deduction, the doubt cannot be considered in making the fair market value determination. We disagree.

If we were to accept the Dohertys' position, taxpayers would be entitled to undisputed acceptance of their (or their chosen appraiser's) valuation of artwork merely by avoiding others' scrutiny of the work prior to its donation. We decline to adopt this view. It is enough that the facts that form the basis of the doubt that later arises were in existence at the time of the contribution, and would have affected the bid of a willing buyer. The government's expert based his conclusion as to Attacking Stagecoach's authenticity on the condition and quality of the painting itself, not on subsequently revealed information regarding Russell's works. The factual bases of the experts' conclusion existed at the time of the contribution and those bases would have been relevant to a hypothetical buyer and seller at the time of the contribution. Moreover, the Tax Court's determination that reasonable hypothetical buyers and sellers would have been aware of those facts at the time of the contribution is not clearly erroneous. Thus, the Tax Court correctly applied the regulatory directive in determining fair market value.

III.

The Dohertys further argue that the Tax Court's determination of the value of Attacking Stagecoach is clearly erroneous. We begin by noting, as we have previously:

> [C]omplex factual inquiries such as valuation require the trial judge to evaluate a number of facts: whether an expert appraiser's experience and testimony entitle his opinion to more or less weight; whether an alleged comparable sale fairly approximates the subject property's market value; and the overall cogency of each expert's analysis. Trial courts have particularly broad discretion with respect to questions of valuation.

Sammons [*v. Commissioner*], 838 F.2d [330] at 333–34 (quoting *Ebben v. Commissioner*, 783 F.2d 906, 909 (9th Cir.1986)).

The Tax Court in this case was presented with the conflicting views of two experts regarding the value of Attacking Stagecoach. That court's opinion discusses fully the basis for the ultimate determination of fair market value. We decline to disturb the Tax Court's thoughtful determination in this case.

The judgment of the Tax Court is AFFIRMED.

Notes and Questions

1. *Discounting for Doubts on Authenticity or Attribution.* Judge Parr determined the value of the painting by noting the poor quality of the painting, the poor quality of the canvas, and the doubts over its authenticity. He made reference to the sale of

a Russell of poor quality for $55,000. Without further elaboration, he determined the work's value to be $30,000 for the charitable contribution deduction for income tax purposes.

In contrast and twenty-five years after *Doherty*, Kollsman v. Commissioner, T.C. Memo, 2017-40, aff'd, 777 Fed. Appx. 870 (9th Cir. 2019), gave a fuller explanation for discounts. In *Kollsman,* there was also an attribution issue but of a different stripe than in *Doherty*. Decedent owned the 17th Century artwork *Orpheus* asserted to be by Jan Brueghel the Elder, Jan Brueghel the Younger, or the Brueghel studio. There was no assertion of inauthenticity, i.e., it was not a forgery. The estate valued *Orpheus* at $100,000 based on an appraisal that the court rejected. That appraisal did not contain any comparable sales data, and the person valuing the work had a "significant conflict of interest" as he hoped the estate would consign the work to him for sale. *Id.* at *19. The Service asserted a value of $500,000 for the work on the basis that it was likely by Jan Brueghel the Elder, the more valued artist. In determining the estate tax value, the court discounted the Service's $500,000 to $375,000, a discount of 25%. The court, however, specifically broke the discount into component parts, reflecting a 5% discount for risks associated with cleaning, a 10% discount for the physical condition of the work (convex warp or bowing), and a 10% discount for the uncertainty of attribution. Significantly the court wrote "while we found [the Service's expert] largely persuasive regarding *Orpheus*' attribution . . . , an attribution dispute nevertheless exists, rendering a discount appropriate." *Id.* at *40.

2. *Time of Valuation and Impact of Post-Transfer Events.* Valuation is to be timed as of the date of the gift or as of death for the pertinent tax purposes. So easily stated, yet some items of property, like art, may have hidden (or hidden in plain view, unrealized, or unappreciated) valuing-affecting qualities that surface later. Are these post-transfer events or discussions to be taken into account when valuing a gift "as of" the transfer? If so, how long is the post-transfer valuation window kept open? The Ninth Circuit drew a distinction between those facts and circumstances that are actually in existence at the time of the donation and those that arise wholly thereafter. In this regard, the art expert's opinion on authenticity was necessarily based on the existence and quality of the work itself. The Court's distinction therefore may be cold comfort in authenticity and valuation cases. If a doubt as to authenticity came about by reason of a new post-transfer technology, that might be sufficiently different to justify non-consideration for tax purposes. This could be analogized to the *Dawson* reasonableness approach for a dealer's contractual liability for a work's authenticity (no liability for the dealer if there was a reasonable basis for authenticity in fact at the time). Dawson v. G. Malina Inc., 463 F. Supp. 461 (S.D.N.Y. 1978), discussed in Chapter 4, *supra*.

Similar arguments are made with respect to the introduction of post-transfer sales data. Many courts allow such evidence as a way of understanding the vitality of the market for the artist's work. See, e.g., Estate of Smith v. Commissioner, 57 T.C. 650 (1972), *aff'd*, 510 F.2d 479 (2d Cir. 1975) (using a two-year window);

Estate of Newberger v. Commissioner, T.C. Memo 2015-246, involving valuations for three artworks as of July 2009, a low point in the art market, where court viewed post-death sales of seven months (for estate's Picasso oil), and sixteen months (for comparable Motherwell oil), and a pre-death sale of 21 months (for comparable Dubuffet work) as relevant for valuation. Consideration of post-transfer events for valuation purposes is not wholly the domain of the IRS; taxpayers also argue the reality of post-transfer events to support their valuations.

3. *Experts Again.* In *Doherty*, as in *Ferrari*, the experts' expertise on the artist was not in question; their credentials were extensive and impressive to the court. In their testimony, both experts opined on authenticity as well as on value. Two updating points on experts need to be made. First, the Dohertys' expert, Mr. Steele, would not be considered a qualified appraiser for valuation purposes today in a similar case. Why? Mr. Steele was the executive director of the Charles M. Russell Museum, the charitable recipient for the painting in question, at the time of the gift. Holding that position would be deemed a conflict of interest for valuation purposes. See Part B, *infra*. The second update concerns the growing recognition that the expertise for authentication and for valuation can involve significantly different competencies. Recall Judge Whitaker's adoption in *Biagiotti* of the dealer's valuation precisely because of the dealer's experience in the retail market, and the rejection of the academic and curator's valuations.

2. Discounts from Fair Market Value

When artworks are given or bequeathed to family or friends, the gift or bequest is subject to the gift or estate tax. A transfer to a spouse, however, can qualify for an unlimited federal marital deduction, meaning that a spousal gift or bequest can be tax-free. For gifts or bequests to family or friends that are subject to gift or estate tax, the valuation preference of the taxpayer is for a value at the lower end of the range. In the context of a taxable gift or bequest, the lower the value, the lower the tax. Fair market value is the gift and estate tax valuation standard just as it is the income tax standard. Over time, two discounts from the basic fair market value have emerged in the gift and estate tax arena: the blockage discount and the fractional interest discount.

If either of those two discounts is pertinent, valuation becomes a two step process. The first step is a determination of the fair market value for the work or works in the collection. This is followed by a separate determination of the appropriate discount factor to be applied for blockage or the undivided fractional interest. The blockage discount and fractional interest discount are not new; they are recognized discounts in valuing stocks and business interests for tax purposes. The next four cases present the judicial approval of those business valuation discounts for artworks. *Estate of Smith* represents the initial acceptance of the traditional business discounts into the art context, and the *Estate of O'Keeffe* fine tunes the application of the blockage discount. *Scull* tacitly approves a valuation discount for a less than

100% ownership interest in artworks, and the *Estate of Elkins* shows the dramatic impact that discount can have.

Estate of Smith v. Commissioner

57 T.C. 650 (1972)

Tannenwald, J. Respondent determined a deficiency of $2,444,629.17 in the Federal estate tax of the Estate of David Smith (hereinafter referred to as Smith or decedent).

... The following issues remain for decision: (1) The fair market value of 425 sculptures created by Smith and in his possession at the time of his death; and (2) the deductibility of certain commissions incurred and paid by petitioner in the course of selling some of the aforementioned sculptures.

* * *

David Smith, a sculptor, died possessed of 425 pieces of nonrepresentational metal sculptures created by his own efforts. The sculptures were valued at $714,000 in the estate tax return. Respondent, in his deficiency notice, determined that they should be valued at $5,256,918 but now concedes that they should be valued at not more than $4,284,000. It is this issue of valuation, together with a related question involving the deductibility of certain expenses, which the parties have placed before us for decision. We approach the task with considerable circumspection, recognizing that this case involves a highly unusual set of circumstances to which the usual, simplistic valuation approach may not be fully applicable and that, in the final analysis, our ultimate determination of value will necessarily constitute a "Solomon-like pronouncement." See *Morris M. Messing*, 48 T.C. 502, 512 (1967).

Initially, we are faced with certain broad assertions by petitioner, which attack this proceeding in its entirety. First, it argues that the number and nature of the sculptures, coupled with the limited scope and vagaries of the market ... make valuation as of the date of death impossible. Consequently, it argues that we should determine a zero value and that any other determination of value would be a violation of its constitutional rights. We find this argument to be without merit. Valuation has been consistently recognized as an inherently imprecise process. Difficulties encountered in determining value, e.g., the presence of a limited market or other restrictive elements, have never been considered a bar to accomplishment of that task, much less to have acquired a constitutional significance, although such elements are factors to be taken into account. *Publicker v. Commissioner*, 206 F.2d 250 (C.A. 3, 1953). Moreover, the record herein shows clearly that the sculptures had value at the date of Smith's death, so petitioner's assertion that they had a zero value is factually baseless.

* * *

We now turn our attention to the critical issue in this case—the determination of the fair market value of the sculptures at the time of Smith's death. In the final analysis, this is essentially a question of fact. As we view the record herein, . . . the value attached by respondent to each piece of sculpture, if it had been sold separately, is identical with the value established by petitioner on the same basis. Where they part company is with respect to the weight to be accorded to the fact that each item would be sold on a market on which 424 other items would simultaneously be available. Respondent claims that such simultaneous availability would have no adverse impact. . . . Petitioner asserts that this is totally unrealistic in this case; that the problem must be viewed in the context of what could be obtained if all 425 sculptures were offered for sale at the moment of death; that any purchaser under these circumstances could only be a person or syndicate acquiring the bulk of the sculptures for resale; that such person would be required to make a large cash investment which could be recouped with an acceptable profit only over a long period of time; and that such person would pay only 25 percent of the separate "one-at-a-time" value which after a further discounting by one-third to take into account the effect of the contract with Marlborough, results in a valuation of $714,000.

We find it unnecessary, in this unusual case, to make any hard-and-fast choice between the two approaches. . . . On the one hand, we think that the initial 75-percent discount, which petitioner has applied to the "one-at-a-time" value . . . is too high. On the other hand, we think that respondent should have given considerable weight to the fact that each item of sculpture would not be offered in isolation. We think that . . . such simultaneous availability of an extremely large number of items of the same general category is a significant circumstance which should be taken into account. In this connection, the so-called blockage rule utilized in connection with the sale of a large number of securities furnishes a useful analogy. . . . We think that a museum or individual collector of art objects would not completely ignore the resale value of a given item. . . . Moreover, the "retail market" claimed by respondent may well encompass the use of an auction method of disposal . . . ; in such a situation the presence of a large number of pieces on the market at one time would be a most material factor. . . .

We have taken into account certain other elements. . . . These include the fact that Smith's reputation as a sculptor had not fully blossomed; the relatively low level of acceptability of nonrepresentational sculpture in the market place; the distribution of the 425 items according to size, period in Smith's life during which they were created, and their expression, in relative terms, of the quality of Smith's work; Smith's tendency to work in series and whether or not a given item was part of a complete series owned by Smith at his death; the number of sales by Smith (or his agents) in the 25 years before his death and the prices at which sales were made during the period immediately preceding and following death; the fact that the bulk of the items was located at Bolton Landing, N.Y., which was relatively inaccessible, and that a large number of the items could not have been readily transported to a location more accessible to potential buyers.

One element of value which petitioner urges be taken into account relates to its obligation to Marlborough by virtue of the exclusive agency contract which Smith made and which survived his death. Petitioner insists that any value based upon the gross sales price must be reduced by one-third to take into account the commissions to which Marlborough was entitled. We think any reduction in value with respect to this element is precluded by the decided cases. In Publicker v. Commissioner, supra, the court refused to permit the price which could be realized on the sale of a piece of jewelry to be reduced by the Federal excise tax which would have been payable. The measure of value laid down by these cases is what could be received on, not what is retained from, a hypothetical sale. Even if one may question the equating of "price" with the gross price including tax, in situations involving the excise tax, it cannot be gainsaid that the "price" herein is what a purchaser would pay for a piece of sculpture. . . .

Having carefully considered the entire record herein, we conclude that the fair market value of the 405 sculptures at the moment of Smith's death was $2,700,000.

Estate of O'Keeffe v. Commissioner

63 T.C.M. (CCH) 2699 (1992)

Cohen, J.

* * *

The expert reports and the testimony at trial comprise hundreds of pages, containing much repetition, inconsistency, and interesting, but immaterial, information. We do not set forth such details here. We have considered all of the testimony and the exhibits. . . .

Property includable in a decedent's gross estate is generally included at its fair market value on the date of the decedent's death. Sec. 2031(a). Fair market value is the price at which property would change hands between a willing buyer and a willing seller, neither being under any compulsion to buy or to sell and both having reasonable knowledge of relevant facts. *United States v. Cartwright*, 411 U.S. 546, 551 (1973); sec. 20.2031-1(b), Estate Tax Regs.

The parties in this case agree that the total of the individual fair market values of each of [Georgia] O'Keeffe's works in the estate exceeded $72,759,000 on March 6, 1986. They disagree, however, as to the appropriate blockage discount to be applied to the total. . . .

In this case, the opinions of petitioner's experts that O'Keeffe's works in the estate, individually valued in excess of $72 million, could have been sold on the date of her death for $18 million, defies common sense. Our conclusion is based in substantial part on the particular content of the works. The individual values of 44 pieces totaled almost one-half of the agreed value of the whole group! [There were approximately 400 works in O'Keeffe's estate.—Ed.]

Respondent's expert's opinion is erroneous as a matter of law. There is no justification for his exclusion of the bequeathed art from the total subject to discount.

Determination of fair market value assumes that works are in the market and precludes consideration that works are "unavailable for sale." He was not entitled to consider the actual disposition of the works of art of the estate any more than fair market value may be determined by assuming that particular purchasers will purchase works of art from the estate. . . .

* * *

Although each of the experts was qualified to express an opinion on the subject matter on which he or she was called to testify, each of them suffered from the same tendency to ignore relevant facts inconsistent with the position of the party employing the expert and to exaggerate facts consistent with the view espoused. Thus, each conclusion as to the appropriate blockage discount suffers from substantial defects and is patently unreliable. [One of the Estate's experts,] Thaw, for example, in effect assumed a forced sale in bulk of all of the works of the estate to a single buyer.

[The other Estate expert,] Rose's opinion relied on her concern with the condition of certain of the works of art in the estate. . . . Both Thaw and Rose conceded that they would not have recommended to a seller that the works in the estate be sold for the $18 million that they opined was the blocked value of the estate on the date of death.

The discounts that [IRS expert] Adelson applied to what he categorized as "Remaining Art" were inadequate. They were not consistent with IRS material recognizing blockage discount. . . .

Respondent's tiered approach was based solely on individual dollar values, i.e., no discount was applied to works valued at or more than $500,000, and 20-percent and 50-percent discounts were applied to categories of $200,000 to $499,999 and under $200,000, respectively. Respondent's approach of considering the specific segments of the estate and the uniqueness of pieces within the estate makes sense and is supported by the evidence, although the specific percentages used by Adelson do not and are not.

At the Court's urging, respondent included a revised three-tiered proposed discount in her brief, but the percentages suggested would still be applied solely on the basis of individual values. We are persuaded from Thaw's testimony and other evidence that the most valuable works would not necessarily be sold first and that some works of all types and values would be fed into the marketplace at a controlled pace. The most reliable consensus of the experts is that the better works could be sold within 7 years, and sale of the bulk of the estate would take more than 10 years. The record does not support any specific percentages at the levels proposed by respondent.

* * *

From the evidence, it is apparent to us that different works in the estate would be of interest to different segments of the art market. The parties have not reasonably quantified assumptions about the specific markets in which segments of the works in the estate would be salable. Petitioner has erroneously assumed that all of the art would initially be sold to a bulk purchaser, who would purchase for resale. Petitioner thus ignores the market of collectors who, while taking into account resale value, are not primarily interested in the rate of return on the investment.

* * *

We conclude that the respective experts in this case each failed to consider the relevant market for particular works of O'Keeffe or groups of works in the estate. The failure to consider the relevant market undermined the respective positions of the parties. . . .

We cannot rely on the burden of proof in this case. There is evidence from which we can determine a value, although we are frustrated and imposed upon by the lack of reliable expert opinion supporting the discounts claimed by the opposing parties. We are persuaded that O'Keeffe's works in the estate on the date of her death should be segmented, not necessarily by value but by quality, uniqueness, and salability. There should be at least two categories, i.e., works that are salable within a relatively short period of time at approximately their individual values and works that can only be marketed over a long period of years with substantial effort. We believe that petitioner's experts' opinion is valid only as applied to the second category of works. Respondent's argument is meritorious with regard to the first category. For want of a more reliable breakdown, we conclude that one-half of the value of O'Keeffe's works in the estate would be appropriately subjected to petitioner's experts' analysis and should be discounted 75 percent. Using our best judgment on the entire record, we conclude that the other half of the total value of O'Keeffe's works should be discounted 25 percent. After considering the entire record, we conclude that the fair market value of O'Keeffe's works in the estate at the date of death was $36,400,000.

To reflect the agreement of the parties and our conclusion,

Decision will be entered under Rule 155.

Notes and Questions

1. *Estate Tax and the Blockage Discount. Estate of Smith* and *Estate of O'Keeffe* are estate tax valuation cases involving a working artist's estate. *Estate of Smith* established the appropriateness of the blockage discount for valuing the artist's works included in the artist's estate. The case was affirmed on appeal to the Second Circuit. 510 F.2d 479 (2d Cir. 1975). The parties in the *Estate of Smith* at different points in time took extreme litigation positions: the taxpayer asserting a zero value on constitutional grounds and the IRS flatly denying the applicability of the blockage discount. Both, however, embraced $4,284,000 as the undiscounted value for the 425 sculptures based on a sales approach. Notice how the *Estate of Smith* court rejected making a "hard-and-fast" choice between the two positions, but effectively allowed the concept of blockage to be a factor in fair market value at a rate less than the taxpayer's asserted 75% discount. The first paragraph of the court's opinion

perhaps telegraphed the "Solomon-like" outcome. The court's ultimate determination of $2,700,000 as the fair market value for all the works is roughly the agreed-upon undiscounted $4,284,000 value, discounted by about 37% (halfway between taxpayer's 75% discount and IRS's 0% discount).

Twenty years later, *Estate of O'Keeffe* reflected the blockage discount as a given, with the court's discussion focusing on the size of the discount. Taxpayer asserted a generic across-the-board discount of 75%. One of the taxpayer's appraisers, Mr. Thaw, was also involved in *Estate of Smith* and had similarly argued for a 75% discount. The IRS used a segmented approach based on value, with the discounts ranging from 0 to 50%. Both sides agreed the undiscounted value exceeded $72.8 million. Judge Cohen adopted a version of the IRS segmented approach, but she divided the works along a time line of salability, not value. Her division "for want of a more reliable breakdown" was a rough half and half. The discounts are 75% for one-half of the works and 25% for the other half. The end result is $36.4 million, or somewhat skeptically, one-half the agreed upon $72.8 million. Judge Cohen's frustration paralleled Judge Whitaker's in *Biagiotti* and *Ferrari*.

Are art valuation cases inherently Solomon-like because of the uniqueness of art and its market or because of the factual nature of valuation?

2. *Gift Tax and the Blockage Discount*. When Alexander Calder died in November 1976, the IRS agreed with the estate's valuation for 1,292 gouaches included in his estate. The IRS had determined a range of values, applied a 60% blockage discount factor and held that the estate's value was close enough (about 80% of IRS's low range). Before the end of 1976 (presumably because major tax law changes would become effective in 1977), Alexander's widow, Louisa Calder, created irrevocable trusts benefitting their two daughters and four grandchildren. She transferred ownership of 1,226 gouaches to the trusts and filed a federal gift tax return valuing the 1,226 gouaches at $949,750, the same value used for Alexander Calder's estate tax purposes.

Louisa Calder's gift tax return raised two fundamental questions. Was the blockage discount appropriate in a gift tax case? If so, how is it applied? Calder v. Commissioner, 85 T.C. 713 (1985). The IRS denied the extension of the blockage discount to the gift tax, reasoning that a gift, unlike death, is a voluntary and planned transaction that the donor can time to her own tax advantage. The court rejected the IRS argument based on regulations and case law "squarely to the contrary."

Allowing a blockage discount for gift tax purposes raised new practical questions. In the context of the estate tax, the valuation is of the estate's assets; in the gift tax context, the valuation is on a per gift basis. This raised two related questions for the blockage discount. How many gifts were there—four (one to each trust) or six (one for each beneficiary)? This was easily disposed of, as the gift tax rule is that when a gift is to a trust, one considers each beneficiary of the trust as the donee, not the trust itself. Consequently, there were six gifts. Should the blockage discount be applied on a separate basis to each of the six gifts or applied in the aggregate to all six gifts made by the donor? Taxpayer argued that the discount should be determined based on the entire block of gifted gouaches, because that would best reflect the orderly sale of those works over time. The court felt the gift tax regulation that provided the theoretical support for the blockage discount in the first place specifically required valuation be done "with respect to each separate gift." The court applied the regulation based on that underlying principle, even though the pertinent regulation referred to gifts of stock.

Having decided these two preliminary issues, the final task was to determine the appropriate discount factor for each of the six separate gifts. In a radical departure from other cases, the court adopted a novel IRS approach ("We are not prepared to say that . . . theory is unreasonable") that seemed to annuitize the value of the art over an assumed liquidation timeframe. The final number was about 27% higher than the donor's valuation. The annuity valuation approach has not garnered much use and does not seem likely to do so. Its use in *Calder* may have been related to another gift tax issue. Mrs. Calder claimed gift tax annual exclusions for each of the transfers to the trust as gifts of present interests. Each trust provided that the beneficiary was entitled to the income of the trust for life. Generally, the right to receive income for life does qualify as a gift of a present interest. 26 U.S.C. § 2503(b); Treas. Reg. § 25.2503-3(b). The value of the life estate must be determined, and that is done by resort to valuation tables. Perhaps this issue influenced the IRS's annuitized valuation approach for the blockage discount. However, because the artworks were not income producing, the court denied the annual exclusions.

3. *Secondary Consequence of Blockage Discount.* In *Estate of Smith* and *Estate of O'Keeffe*, the Tax Court found the fair market value of the estate's artworks to be $2.7 million and $36.4 million respectively, in the aggregate and not on an individual basis. From a blunt estate tax perspective, this is an unimportant difference, but is that true for other tax purposes?

Two brothers inherited their father's New York art gallery when he died in 1989. When they filed the estate tax return for their father's estate, they reported $12.4 million as the discounted value of the entire art inventory. The estate's return was reviewed by the IRS Art Advisory Panel, which determined a discounted value for the entire art inventory of $14.5 million. The panel specifically agreed with the application of a blockage discount to a gallery's inventory, viewing the underlying principles gleaned from the traditional blockage discount in artists' estates equally applicable to a gallery. The brothers agreed to the adjustments made by the IRS and paid the additional tax.

Meanwhile the brothers continued to operate the gallery and make sales from the gallery's inventory. For income tax purposes, a sale is a realization event, and the taxpayer needs to report any gain from the sale. Gain on a sale is the excess of the amount realized (generally the amount received by the seller for the item) over the seller's adjusted basis (generally the seller's cost of the item). 26 U.S.C. § 1001(a). Under § 1014, the income tax basis of property acquired from a decedent is generally its fair market value as of the decedent's date of death. 26 U.S.C. § 1014. (A special rule applies for decedents who died in 2010.) The brothers used the undiscounted value of the artwork that was sold to compute their gain for income tax purposes. The Tax Court held that the brothers must use the discounted value for each item inherited from their father. That discounted value would be computed by applying the agreed upon discount to the undiscounted value of each item so inherited. They were obliged to do so by the tax principle of consistency. Janis v. Commissioner, 87 T.C.M. (CCH) 1322 (2004), *aff'd*, 461 F.3d 1080 (9th Cir. 2006), and 469 F.3d 256 (2d Cir. 2006).

Might the brothers have been better off economically if they did not take the blockage discount in their father's estate? Probably not. For 1989, the estate tax free amount was $600,000, the top estate tax rate was 55%, and the estate tax was due nine months after death. Income tax rates for the years in question (1995, 1996 and 1997) topped off at 39.6%.

4. *Non-Tax Uses of Blockage Discounts.* The blockage discount for artworks was developed in the estate and gift tax context. As the discount has become established, it has also become recognized beyond its tax purpose. For example, in In re Warhol, 1994 WL 245246, (N.Y. Sur. Ct. 1994), the court applied blockage discounts to the almost 100,000 items in Andy Warhol's estate. This was not for estate tax purposes (his estate was going to charity—the Andy Warhol Foundation for the Visual Arts), but to establish the fee of the former attorney to the executor, which was based on a percentage of the estate.

See also Grosz v. Serge Sabarsky, Inc., 806 N.Y.S.2d 498 (N.Y. App. Div. 2005), where the court remanded the dispute to the trial court to determine if a blockage discount was applicable where only 90 artworks were at issue (the case involved liability for lost artworks).

Scull introduces the possibility of a fractional interest discount from fair market value for artworks that are not wholly owned by the taxpayer and the *Estate of Elkins* applies that discount in a unique fact pattern.

Scull v. Commissioner

67 T.C.M. (CCH) 2953 (1994)

Parker, J. Respondent determined a deficiency in decedent's Federal estate tax of $710,725.82 and an addition to tax under section 6651(a) of $151,303.76. Based upon expert valuation reports, respondent filed an Amendment to Answer on March 11, 1992, resulting in an increased deficiency, from $710,725.82 to $1,745,589, and an increased addition to tax, from $151,303.76 to $358,276.

After concessions, the issues for decision are:

(1) The fair market value, as of January 1, 1986, of decedent's undivided 65-percent interest in the art collection owned by decedent, Robert C. Scull, and his former wife, Ethel Redner Scull. . . .

[Robert Scull died on January 1, 1986, survived by his wife and three children from a prior marriage. Scull's estate included an undivided 65% interest in an art collection with the 35% interest owned by his former wife Ethel. The Sculls were early and prominent collectors of pop and minimalist art from the 1950s onward. They were friends with many artists and became the subject matter of some artworks, e.g., Andy Warhol's *Ethel Scull 36 Times*.

Ethel filed for divorce from Robert in 1975 and they were divorced in 1981. A question of the proper ownership of the art collection was extensively litigated. Sotheby's had prepared an appraisal of the art collection in 1978 during the divorce proceeding and updated it in 1984 (with another revision in 1985) during the pendency of the ownership question. The trial court determined in 1985 that Ethel was entitled to a 35% interest in the collection. Robert appealed the determination two weeks before he died. Ethel also appealed the decision. Thereafter, one of Robert's executors entered into an agreement with Peter Brant (of *Lindholm v. Brant*, 925 A. 2d 1048 (Conn. 2007), discussed in Chapter 2, *supra*) purportedly selling the estate's 65% interest to Brant for a minimum of $5.3 million. Certain works were sold at Sotheby's fall auction in 1986 for $7.8 million.

The majority of the opinion concerns the fair market value of the art collection as of Scull's date of death. The portion dealing with a discount for the undivided interest follows.—Ed.]

5. Entire Scull Collection

The entire Scull collection had a fair market value of $12,228,006 on the date of decedent's death.

6. Decedent's 65-percent Undivided Interest

Decedent had a 65-percent undivided interest in the collection. Petitioner argues that the value of that interest was less than 65 percent of the value of the entire collection. Pursuant to the trial court in the divorce proceeding, Ethel Scull had a 35-percent undivided interest in the collection and the right to an in-kind distribution. Scull had appealed the Appellate Division's determination of constructive trusts to the Court of Appeals (highest court) which affirmed the lower court in April of 1986. In addition, after the valuation date, on January 31, 1986, Ethel Scull had appealed to the Appellate Division, seeking to increase her portion to 50 percent. That appeal was not disposed of until February of 1987. Under the willing buyer/willing seller standard, the willing buyer is assumed to have reasonable knowledge of material facts. Any purchaser of petitioner's interest in the collection as of January 1, 1986, would consider Ethel Scull's rights in the collection and Scull's pending appeal on the date of death. However, since Scull's appeal, if successful, would have increased his share, that appeal does not provide any basis for a reduction. Moreover, since Ethel Scull's appeal came later, it probably should not be taken into account. In any event, given the trial court's detailed explanation of its basis for its determination of the 65-35 split, we think that a purchaser would not require a reduction in excess of 5 percent for any uncertainties involved in acquiring decedent's 65-percent interest, despite one or both appeals. Therefore, we find that the fair market value of decedent's interest in the art collection on the date of death was $7,550,794 ($12,228,006 × 65% = $7,948,204 — $397,410 = $7,550,794).

Estate of Elkins v. Commissioner

767 F.3d 443 (5th Cir. 2014)

WIENER, Circuit Judge:

* * *

Facts and Proceedings

A. Issue on Appeal

Despite the size and complexity of Decedent's estate . . . the single question presented in this appeal is narrow, straightforward, and easily posed:

> Given the parties' stipulation of the FMV of each of the works of art in which Decedent owned fractional interests at his death, is the Estate taxable on Decedent's undiscounted pro rata share of those FMVs, as the Commissioner contended on audit and throughout the Tax Court proceedings, or is it taxable only on those values reduced by fractional-ownership discounts of either (1) a uniform 10 percent each, as held by the Tax Court, or (2) the various percentages that the Estate advanced through the testimony and reports of its expert witnesses?

* * *

B. Background

Over the course of their marriage, the Texas-domiciled Decedent and his wife acquired property, both real and personal, essentially all of which fell into the community that existed between them and thus was owned equally by the spouses. Among their many and varied acquisitions were . . . 64 works of art. Their interests in each of those works were retained for the remainder of their respective lifetimes, and that art was displayed in their home or office, or those of their adult children, or, occasionally, at an art gallery, museum, or other public place, albeit not as one cohesive collection or assemblage.

Decedent and his wife each created an *inter vivos* Grantor Retained Income Trust ("GRIT") that held title to their respective half interests in three of the 64 works (the "GRIT Art"). After the death of his wife during the terms of the GRITs, and for the remainder of his lifetime, Decedent continued to own his 50 percent interest in those three pieces. His three children received his late wife's 50 percent interest, 16.667 percent each.

By virtue of a bequest to him from his wife of her 50 percent interest in each of the remaining works and his subsequent disclaimer of a 26.945 percent interest in each, Decedent owned at his death an aggregate 73.055 percent interest in each of those 61 pieces (the "Disclaimer Art"), comprising his original 50 percent and the 23.055 percent interest from his wife's bequest that remained after deducting the 26.945 percent interest that Decedent disclaimed. That disclaimed interest passed equally to their three children, as their mother's successor legatees, 8.98167 percent each, and was owned by them at his death.

From time to time following the death of his wife, Decedent and his children voluntarily subjected their respective interests in the works of art to various restraints on possession, partition, and alienation. For example, Decedent's three children leased their combined 50 percent interests in two of the three pieces of GRIT Art to Decedent, thereby ensuring his uninterrupted possession of those two works. That lease, which was still in effect at Decedent's death, specified, *inter alia,* that no co-owner could dispose of his or her interest in a leased work unless joined by all co-owners. The lease also provided that none could transfer or assign his or her "rights, duties and obligations" under the lease without the prior consent of all.

Similarly, Decedent and his children encumbered all 61 items of Disclaimer Art with a "Cotenants Agreement." Among other things, it spelled out each co-owner's right of possession for a specified number of days during any 12 month period. More pertinent to this appeal, that agreement prohibited the sale of an interest in any work by a co-owner without the prior consent of all. The one piece of GRIT Art that had not been subjected to the children's lease to Decedent was eventually added to the list of works covered by the Cotenants Agreement.

C. Proceedings Prior to Tax Court Litigation

Decedent died testate in February 2006. . . . The Decedent's Estate Tax Return . . . listed, among other assets, fractional interests in various items of real and personal property, including his 73.005 [sic, 73.055] percent interest in the Disclaimer Art and his 50 percent interest in the GRIT Art.

Following its audit of the estate tax return, the Internal Revenue Service ("IRS") accepted net values that remained after deducting various fractional-ownership discounts on essentially every property, real and personal, in which Decedent owned a fractional interest, *with but one exception:* the 64 works of art. The IRS refused to allow *any* discount against the Decedent's pro rata share-his fractional—ownership interest—of the stipulated FMVs of these works. The IRS assessed an estate tax deficiency of $9,068,266.

D. Tax Court Proceedings

The Estate filed the instant action in Tax Court in July 2010. . . . During th[e] one-day trial, six witnesses testified, five of whom were tendered as experts, three by the Estate and two by the Commissioner. The lone non-expert witness was Mrs. Leslie Keith Sasser, Decedent's daughter and co-executor.

The gist of Mrs. Sasser's responses . . . was that she and the other Elkins heirs are strongly attached to the art work, largely sentimentally; that they do not view those works as business assets, primarily because they simply do not need the money; and that they are determined to retain the art for life, *i.e.*, they would never be sellers. In response to hypothetical questions from the court, Mrs. Sasser did respond—also hypothetically—that she and presumably the other Elkins heirs might be *buyers* of Decedent's interest from a hypothetical willing buyer of that interest, but only if assured by an expert or experts that the price was fair[.] ...

The Estate's three remaining witnesses were tendered as experts in various aspects of the art's values.... The result of the combined, interrelated, and interdependent testimony and reports of these experts was that a proper application of the willing buyer/willing seller test would produce prices for the Decedent's undivided interests in the works of art substantially below his pro rata share of their respective FMVs....

By contrast, the Commissioner adduced no expert testimony or other evidence to establish alternative quantums of fractional-ownership discounts, sticking instead to his no-discount position. He did proffer ... rebuttal witnesses.... Ms. Hanus-McManus's testimony is best summarized by her stated conclusion that "there is no *recognized* market for partial interest[s] in works of modern art and contemporary art within the secondary markets, with the galleries, and with private dealers." She would not state, however, that there had never been, or never could be, sales of undivided interests in such art; only that there was no established or "recognized" market for such fractional interests.

The Tax Court ... ultimately held that such interests are indeed subject to fractional-ownership discounts, but that the price on which the fictitious buyer and seller would finally agree would be the jointly stipulated values reduced by a "nominal" discount of 10 percent only.

II. Analysis

A. Standard of Review

... We have long held that "determination of fair market value is a mixed question of fact and law." As noted in the Estate's appellate brief, *de novo* review is appropriate here because "there is a pure question of law imbedded in the valuation calculus."

B. Framework

* * *

2. Burden of Proof

... The second part of today's inquiry—the correct percentages of fractional-ownership discounts to be applied—presents a somewhat thornier question, at least theoretically. The Tax Court failed to require the Commissioner to bear that burden of proof, even though 26 U.S.C. § 7491 mandates that when, as here, the petitioning taxpayer adduces sufficient evidence to establish the material facts—in this case, the amounts of the discounts—the Commissioner has the burden of refuting such facts and proving different ones. Yet he chose not to adduce any evidence of discount *quantum* whatsoever, sticking instead to his no-discount position....

3. Preponderance of the Evidence

After rejecting the Commissioner's no-discount position, the Tax Court announced . . . it would proceed to determine the appropriate quantum of the discounts based on a *preponderance* of the evidence. In most trials, "[a] determination of where the preponderance lies requires a measuring and weighing of all the evidence, pro and con." But, when, as here, the *only* evidence on an issue is that presented by but one party—and by the one that did not have the burden of proof, at that—there is no "preponderance": It takes two to tango. . . . [T]he Tax Court's error in announcing its use of the preponderance standard to determine the amounts of the discounts ultimately makes no difference. This is because, having put all of his eggs in the one, no-discount basket at trial, the Commissioner cannot be heard on appeal to question the quantity, quality, or sufficiency of the evidence adduced by the Estate to prove the *quantum* of the fractional-ownership discounts to be applied. Likewise, given the total absence of substantive evidence from the Commissioner on the issue of quantum, the Tax Court should have accepted and applied the uncontradicted quantums of the partial-ownership discounts that the Estate proved with much more than substantial evidence.

4. Merits

Just as it was obvious to the Tax Court that the Commissioner had no viable basis for rigidly insisting that no fractional-ownership discount was applicable, it should have been equally obvious that, in the absence of any evidentiary basis whatsoever, there is no viable factual or legal support for the court's own nominal 10 percent discount. . . .

* * *

We repeat for emphasis that the Estate's uncontradicted, unimpeached, and eminently credible evidence in support of its proffered fractional-ownership discounts is not just a "preponderance" of such evidence; it is the *only* such evidence. Nowhere is there any evidentiary support for the Tax Court's unsubstantiated declaration that "a 10% discount would enable a hypothetical buyer to assure himself or herself of a reasonable profit on a resale of those interests to the Elkins children." Besides the error in logic of presuming that the hypothetical willing buyer *must* turn right around and sell his fractional purchases to those heirs, we cannot escape the conclusion that . . . such a determination constitutes reversible error under any standard of review.

5. Correct Quantum of Fractional-Ownership Discounts

* * *

It is principally within the last few pages of its opinion that the Tax Court's reversible error lies. While continuing to advocate the willing buyer/willing seller test that controls this case, the Tax Court inexplicably veers off course, focusing almost exclusively on its perception of the role of "the Elkins children" as owners of the remaining fractional interests in the works of art and giving short shrift to the time and expense that a successful willing buyer would face in litigating the restraints on alienation and possession and otherwise outwaiting those particular co-owners. Moreover, the Elkins heirs are neither *hypothetical* willing buyers nor *hypothetical* willing sellers, any more than the Estate is deemed to be the hypothetical willing seller.

We acknowledge, of course—as did the Estate's experts—that a hypothetical willing buyer would be aware of and take into account *all* aspects of the remaining fractional interests in the art that the Elkins heirs owned, not just the likelihood of their hypothetical desire to acquire the Decedent's fractional interests in the art from any successful hypothetical buyer thereof. An objective reading of the entirety of those experts' written reports and their testimony at trial demonstrates beyond question that the heirs' financial strengths, their out-of-hand rejection of the idea of ever selling their interests, and the time and money that the legal restraints in their arsenal would cost a willing buyer, combine to minimize any effect to the contrary that their "psychic" attachment to the art might otherwise have on the discounts that apply here. To repeat, Mrs. Sasser testified that if, hypothetically, she and her siblings were to purchase such interests, it would only be after first determining *from experts* that any price was fair and reasonable. And the experts consulted would likely be those persons whom the Tax Court accepted at trial; experts whose ultimate values were based on their substantial discounts below FMV.

Furthermore, like the absence of an established market, the subjective characteristics of the Decedent's descendants as the owners of the remaining fractional interests would likely cut the other way: A potential willing buyer would undoubtedly insist that his potential willing seller *further discount* the sales price to account for the virtual impossibility of making an immediate "flip" of the art. Such a fully informed willing buyer would be well aware that, by virtue of becoming a co-owner with the sophisticated, determined, and financially independent Elkins heirs, he could not possibly make such a quick resale—absent a deep discount, that is. And, the situation is only exacerbated by the effect of the various restrictions on partition, alienation, and possession that survived the death of the Decedent.

III. Conclusion

We conclude our review by examining the entire record to see if we can determine the correct quantums of the fractional-ownership discounts and thereby avoid remand. When we do so, we conclude that the discounts determined by the Estate's experts are not just the only ones proved in court; they are eminently correct....

... Accordingly, we (1) affirm the Tax Court's rejection of the Commissioner's insistence that no fractional-ownership discount may be applied in determining the taxable values of Decedent's undivided interests in the subject art work; (2) affirm the Tax Court's holding that the Estate is entitled to apply a fractional-ownership discount to the Decedent's ratable share of the stipulated FMV of each of the 64 works of art; (3) reverse the Tax Court's holding that the appropriate fractional-ownership discount is a nominal 10 percent, uniformly applied to each work of art, regardless of distinguishing features; (4) hold that the correct quantums of the fractional-ownership discounts applicable to the Decedent's pro rata share of the stipulated FMVs of the various works of art are those determined by the Estate's experts and itemized on Exhibit B to the Tax Court's opinion; and (5) render judgment in favor of the Estate for a refund of taxes overpaid in the amount of $14,359,508.21, plus statutory interest in a sum to be agreed on by the parties, based on the timing of the payment of that refund to the Estate, all as jointly stipulated to us by the parties.

AFFIRMED in part; REVERSED in part; and RENDERED.

Notes and Questions

1. *The Elusive Fractional Discount.* If the Sculls were still married at his death in 1986, it is likely that no discount would have been taken on the return. Why? The extent and therefore value of Scull's interest in the art collection was in question because of the divorce litigation. Clearly, the divorce was an external independent factor and not tax motivated. The uncertainties of litigation by itself could affect the value of an asset under the willing buyer-willing seller test. Consequently, it may be appropriate to think of *Scull's* 5% fractional interest discount as wrapped within the uncertainties of litigation.

Twenty years later, *Elkins* allowed a substantially more significant fractional interest discount. Although tempting to view *Elkins* as establishing that as a new, across-the-board valuation norm, it would be a mistake to do so. It is more likely that *Elkins* was a strategic and tactical miscalculation by the Service rather than an unqualified judicial endorsement of significant fractional interest discounts. In addition, the unique facts were enormously important.

Mr. and Mrs. Elkins owned the artworks as community property and, in July 1990, each of them established a GRIT containing his and her respective one-half interest in three artworks. Clearly the GRIT was tax planning. [Note: This type of GRIT is no longer available. See 26 U.S.C. § 2702.] When Mrs. Elkins died in 1999, she bequeathed to her husband her community half interest in the remaining 61 artworks. He filed a qualified partial disclaimer under § 2518 of the Internal Revenue Code effectively giving up 26.945% of the artworks. Therefore, only a 23.055% interest in the artworks passed to him from his wife's estate, resulting in his new ownership interest of 73.055% in the 61 artworks. Elkins' qualified disclaimer allowed his wife's estate to fully utilize her tax-free amount, thereby passing the 26.945% interest in the disclaimed artworks to the three children free of estate tax. Clearly the disclaimer was tax planning. After Mrs. Elkins' death, the Elkins family entered into agreements that restricted the possession, partition, and alienation of the artworks. Under § 2703, these types of restrictions are deemed tax-motivated and not to be considered in valuation. The Tax Court agreed that those restrictions were not relevant for valuation purposes. Nevertheless, that court allowed a nominal 10% discount, reasoning that the hypothetical willing buyer would not be certain of the Elkins children's intent regarding the artworks.

The Fifth Circuit took a decidedly different approach. The court easily agreed that a discount for a fractional interest was appropriate; it was the *quantum* of the discount that was at issue. Noting that under § 7491 of the Internal Revenue Code, once a taxpayer produces sufficient evidence on the pertinent issue, here valuation, the Service bears the burden of proof. Because the Service maintained its zero-discount policy, it did not offer any evidence as to a proper amount. That strategy backfired, as the Fifth Circuit, seeing only the taxpayer's evidence, deemed those valuations "eminently correct." See Philip N. Jones, *Burden of Proof—The Fifth Circuit Muddies the Water*, 122 J. Tx'n 36 (2015), decrying the court's all-or-nothing approach.

2. *A Spirit of Compromise: 5%*. In 2009, the Ninth Circuit, in an unpublished opinion, affirmed a 5% fractional interest valuation discount for a 50% interest in nineteen artworks. Stone v. United States, 2009 WL 766497 (9th Cir., March 24, 2009). The estate had argued for a 44% discount and the IRS initially contended no discount was appropriate. Later, the estate dropped its asserted discount to 36% and the IRS, in a spirit of compromise, offered 5%. Both the trial court and the Ninth Circuit recognized that in a hypothetical willing buyer-willing seller scenario, a fractional interest may trade at a discount. It is up to the taxpayer to prove the discount. On this issue, the taxpayer's expert was not convincing:

> But the taxpayer still bears the burden of proof. In this case, the court simply concluded that the evidence offered by the Estate was neither probative nor convincing. In opting to not credit Hoffman's report and testimony, the district court cited, *inter alia*, Hoffman's total lack of experience with the art market; the dissimilar motives driving purchasers to acquire art, on one hand, and real estate or limited-partnership shares, on the other; and the unreasonably low appreciation rate and unreasonably high present-value discount rates Hoffmann used in his cost-of partition analysis. We cannot say the district court clearly erred in adopting the government's 5% discount rate and rejecting the Estate's.

While numbers are important in tax, what may be more important is that the appropriateness of a fractional interest discount (at least in some circumstances) was conceded by the IRS only five years before *Elkins*. See Wendy C. Gerzog, *Valuing Art in an Estate*, 117 Tax Notes 619 (2007).

3. *Asymmetry in Fractional Interest Discounts*. Perhaps IRS's concession of 5% is a gift? Consider the following text from the IRS Valuation Training for Appeals Officers: Coursebook 5–14 (1998):

> The Art Advisory Panel . . . and Art Appraisal Services . . . do not recommend any discount be applied to the value for a minority ownership or interest in art works for charitable contributions or estate and gift tax cases. . . .

> . . . The purchase of a partial interest in an art object or collection is really without foundation in the marketplace. Art is not fungible. While discounts for minority ownership have been applied to stocks and real estate, art works are very different. Art is not a going concern but a unique asset.

In Rev. Rul. 57-293, 1957-2 C.B. 153, the taxpayer was allowed a charitable income tax deduction for the pro rata value of a fractional interest in an art object donated to a charity. There was no requirement to discount for the donated object's fractional interest status. Consequently, the taxpayer had the benefit of a higher income tax deduction. See also Rev. Rul. 58-455, 1958-2 C.B. 100. Conversely, in *Scull*, *Stone*, and *Elkins*, the taxpayers were allowed the benefit of discounts for estate tax purposes. For the individual taxpayers involved, this is a good result. In *Elkins*, the Service argued these rulings showed the Service's zero-discount position. The Tax Court rejected that argument, noting that revenue rulings are not binding authority and that the rulings did not explain the Service's reasoning. Is there any policy or practice justification for this asymmetrical view of the fractional interest discount?

B. Qualified Appraisal by a Qualified Appraiser

The unruly nature of fair market value is counterbalanced by a discipline newly imposed on those determining fair market values—the appraisers. When involved in a tax matter, appraisers and their appraisals are now subject to detailed standards that reinforce norms of professional competence and disinterestedness. Before examining those statutory and regulatory requirements for a qualified appraisal by a qualified appraiser, it is worthwhile to understand the historic backdrop of accommodating appraisers and the anything-goes appraisals that frustrated the proper administration of the tax system. These cases and practices provide concrete reasons for the Service's traditional skepticism for taxpayers' art valuations.

1. Valuation Abuses—Case Law Background

Fair market value, the standard for valuing artworks for charitable deduction purposes and for estate and gift tax inclusion purposes, is determined by an appraiser and memorialized in an appraisal. The following trio of cases demonstrates the escalating valuation abuses faced by the IRS as charitable deductions for donated artworks morphed into sophisticated tax shelters assisted by lawyer-drafted and appraiser-friendly business models that lacked economic substance. Congressional and regulatory reactions created a much tighter framework for valuation of artworks for tax deduction purposes and increased the scope and severity of penalties for valuation misstatements, as we shall discuss. As you read these cases, think about the role of the lawyers and appraisers in rendering their opinions. Who does the lawyer represent? Is there a public function served by the lawyer as officer of the court? By the appraiser?

Weil v. Commissioner

26 T.C.M. (CCH) 388 (1967)

FORRESTER, J.

* * *

Facts and Opinion

Issue (3)

In 1960 the individual petitioners gave an oil painting entitled "The Mill" by Frederick Ede to the University of Maine, and . . . claimed [a] deduction for a charitable contribution under section 170(a)(1) in the amount of $1,500. . . .

The respondent has disallowed $600 of this claimed deduction . . . contending that the fair market value of the painting at the time of the gift was $900.

This painting had originally been acquired by Joan S. Weil's father. . . . He gave it to Joan in 1952 when he broke up housekeeping. Joan expressed no opinion as to the value of the painting at any time.

Herbert Chase, an appraiser and art dealer since about 1930 and a member of the American Society of Appraisers was called as a witness by petitioner. He described the painting as an oil, about 24 inches by 29-1/2 inches in size (framed size 35 by 39 inches) which he had examined in petitioner's home in about November 1960 and which he had then appraised as "reasonably worth $1,500 in today's market" but he could recall no further details of the picture.

Chase did not know much about Frederick Ede. He did not know his nationality, the usual subjects of his paintings or of any gallery that had ever exhibited any of them or sold any of them, or of any sales whatsoever of any Ede painting. Chase could not describe the subject matter, the shape or color of the painting in question or the manner of its execution (impasto). He had no prospective buyer in mind when he made the appraisal but stated simply that having been asked to appraise it, and having been informed that his appraisal would be used to establish the amount of a charitable deduction, that he had examined the painting and concluded that it was a very nice one, a "home run," with a fair market value of $1,500.

The record contains no evidence of the value of the Ede painting in question other than the opinion of Herbert Chase which is described above.

Under the Tax Court Rules of Practice, Rule No. 32, burden of proof is on petitioners to establish that the Frederick Ede painting in question had a fair market value at the date of gift in excess of $900. Herbert Chase's unfamiliarity with the painting, the artist and his other works allows us to assign no weight to his opinion and consequently the respondent's determination of a $900 value is sustained.

Decision will be entered for the respondent.

Vander Hook v. Commissioner

36 T.C.M. (CCH) 1394 (1977)

WILBUR, J. . . . The sole issue for decision is the valuation of a fractional interest petitioners acquired in six paintings and subsequently donated to Pepperdine University.

Findings of Fact

. . . On February 17, 1972, Legal Dynamics, Inc., a California corporation transferred a fractional interest in six paintings to Dennis M. Vander Hook for a total consideration of $1,200. . . .

* * *

Legal Dynamics, Inc., was incorporated on November 2, 1971, to provide legal services to labor unions, including estate and tax planning services. Its principal office was located in Los Angeles County but was not separate and apart from the offices of the lawyer, Brent Carruth (hereinafter Carruth), who organized Legal Dynamics.

The paintings in question, although transferred by Legal Dynamics, were acquired directly or indirectly from Frederic Stern (hereinafter Stern), who, within a short time after selling the paintings to Legal Dynamics, appraised the paintings at $250,000. In essence, Legal Dynamics, which acquired the art collection for $12,000, acted as an intermediary by arranging to purchase the art collection and sell fractional interests immediately thereafter. Legal Dynamics also secured the charitable donee for the collection and effected the transfer.

Legal Dynamics represented that the collection would be appraised in excess of cost with the resulting tax savings to the purchasers, and secured (. . .) appraisals from Stern and Harry Muir Kurtzworth (hereinafter Kurtzworth) [for $250,000 and $272,000, respectively for the entire collection of paintings.—Ed.].

* * *

Petitioners claimed a charitable contribution of $12,000. . . . Respondent originally disallowed all but $1,200 as a charitable deduction, and, in an amended answer, disallowed all but $47.

Opinion

Petitioner Dennis M. Vander Hook acquired a fractional interest in six paintings which he donated to Pepperdine University. Respondent concedes that the donation was made to an educational institution that qualifies as a charitable organization under section 170 and that the property was used by the donee in a manner functionally related to its exempt purposes. Additionally, respondent concedes that if the property in issue had been sold on the date of the donation the entire gain would have been long-term capital gain making the requirements of section 170(e) inapplicable in the present case. Therefore, the only issue we confront is the fair market value of the property donated to Pepperdine University which is the measure of the deduction allowable in this case.

* * *

Respondent contends that the paintings allegedly done by: David "A Lady of the Court of Napoleon," Murillo "Saint Joseph with Infant Jesus," Master of Saint Antoin "Vision of Szent Antal," Crespi "The Crucifixion," and Zurbaran "Kneeling Figure of a Saint" are not authentic and produced two experts who supported his position. Conversely, petitioners contend that these paintings are authentic and also produced the testimony of two expert witnesses. Thus, the nub of the controversy turns on whether these five paintings are authentic.

We have no hesitancy in sustaining respondent. Kenneth Donahue (hereinafter Donahue) the director of the Los Angeles County Museum of Art, testified that none of these five paintings are authentic. Donahue's knowledge of the various artists involved, including other works they had painted, the historical period during which they worked, and the compositions and manner of execution characteristic of their work, was extremely comprehensive.

Donahue was an articulate witness who carefully analyzed the paintings in issue. For example, a good picture of a representative work by Crespi entitled "The Holy Family" was introduced into evidence and Donahue contrasted this work in detail with one of the paintings here in issue entitled "The Crucifixion," which petitioners contend was also painted by Crespi. When the pictures were compared in the light of the careful analysis of Donahue, the lack of authenticity of "The Crucifixion" was apparent even to the lay person.

Stern's report was stipulated into evidence and Kurtzworth appeared and testified on the paintings for petitioners. Kurtzworth's comments were not specifically directed to the various attributes of the paintings in any detail, and we have little confidence that there was a reasonable basis for his opinion that the paintings were genuine. He exhibited very little familiarity with the specific works of some of the artists alleged to have been responsible for the paintings in issue. He took the position that he was valuing the specific paintings in question, that he was not required to focus on other paintings of the artists in question, and did not see any need to exhibit any familiarity with these other paintings. Even more damaging, Kurtzworth admitted that he raised the valuations above his original estimate at the request of Hewitt of Legal Dynamics because a higher valuation was needed....

Although a xeroxed copy of a "Who's Who" insert on Kurtzworth was included in the record, there is no evidence that significant purchases are being made based on his judgment, or that he is affiliated with any museums, art galleries, or universities in a responsible capacity. Based on the limited information and knowledge he exhibited of the relevant attributes of the paintings in question, and his failure to relate the paintings in question with other works of the purported artists, we do not find Kurtzworth's testimony helpful.[5]

---

5. Since David was a prolific artist and the painting attributed to him alleged to be worth $160,000, the failure to contrast the work in issue with his other works is puzzling. Also, when

In addition to our analysis of the expert testimony there are other factors that make it clear that respondent must be sustained. It seems wholly unlikely that paintings worth $250,000 would be transferred for less than 10 percent of their value as petitioners allege. Additionally, if the paintings had anything more than negligible value Pepperdine University, the donee, would certainly have treated them with a good deal more care. Donahue reviewed and evaluated the paintings at Pepperdine University on April 11. He was told that three of the paintings were not available, two of them having been lost and one of them had been stolen. Two of these paintings were the paintings by Murillo and "The Crucifixion" ostensibly by Crespi.

We also note that when petitioner Dennis Vander Hook and his associates purchased the art the paintings were stored somewhere in the building where Carruth (the lawyer who put the transaction together) had his offices. The paintings were not even insured, nor were any special precautions taken to preclude their loss due to theft or fire. This manner of caring for them is wholly inconsistent with the theory that they had anything like the value attributed to them by petitioners.

For all of these reasons, we feel that the only painting that was authentic was "The Bishop of Emmaus" by H. Harris Brown. . . .

The others not being authentic paintings and many of them being poorly done, were valuable simply as decorative art to be used in a hotel, home or a religious institution. We find that the evidence as a whole supports a deduction of only $1,200 as allowed by respondent in the deficiency notice.

* * *

Decision will be entered under Rule 155.

Rose v. Commissioner

88 T.C. 386 (1987)

Cohen, J. Respondent determined deficiencies of $191,335.00 and $302,451.12 in petitioners' Federal income taxes for 1979 and 1980, respectively. The issues for determination are (1) whether petitioners are entitled to depreciation and miscellaneous deductions and investment tax credit in relation to their purchase from Jackie Fine Arts of photographic transparencies of Picasso paintings and related production rights; (2) whether petitioners are entitled to deduct interest (a) accrued or (b) paid on partial recourse notes used in such purchase; and (3) whether petitioners are liable for additional interest under section 6621(d).

* * *

In late 1979, [petitioners considered alternative investment opportunities and] a securities broker mentioned Jackie Fine Arts (Jackie) to Mr. Rose. Jackie was a

---

asked about Provenance, or the history of the paintings in question, Kurtzworth indicated that that kind of information does not come as far out as California very often.

corporation that had been involved in the marketing of lithograph tax shelters beginning in 1977. In 1979, Herman Finesod (Finesod), on behalf of Jackie and its affiliate, Art Masters International, Inc. (Art Masters), as "Buyer" entered into an agreement with Paraselenes S.A., as "Seller," a company controlled by Marina Picasso (Marina), the granddaughter of Pablo Picasso (Picasso). [Marina would sell Jackie the Reproduction Masters for 1,000 works of Picasso owned by Marina and grant Jackie the worldwide right to exploit the Reproduction Masters for 15 years. Each Reproduction Master was sold to Jackie for $10,000 plus a nonrecourse promissory note for a percentage of sales to ultimate purchasers. Jackie's plan was to market each of the 1,000 Reproduction Masters to others, calling it the Picasso package.—Ed.]

In 1979, Jackie sold 109 Picasso packages to investors. A total of 223 packages were sold over the life of the program.

In marketing the Picasso packages, Jackie provided to prospective purchasers a series of materials, including "Information Memoranda," tax opinions, "Fact Sheets," and letters. Each emphasized at great length the purported tax benefits of the acquisition of art masters. Typical of the marketing materials was an October 1979 Information Memorandum for the Sale of Art Masters, which summarized the program as follows:

> The Product
>
> Jackie Fine Arts markets art masters, each consisting generally of silkscreen mylars, lithographic plates and mylars, or photoscreen negatives of an original work of art, together with related copyrights. The artist has agreed to cooperate in the production of 100 to 300 limited edition graphics from the art master, which will be signed and numbered by the artist. The art master purchaser will pay for the costs of production of these graphics.
>
> Purchase Price
>
> The purchase price of each art master will vary according to a number of factors, such as the prior sales history of the artist's works. Purchase prices for art masters range from $152,000 to $370,000. Each purchaser will receive the opinions of two qualified appraisers that the fair market value of the art master is at least equal to the purchase price.
>
> Tax Considerations
>
> Jackie Fine Arts has received opinions of its counsel, Meserve, Mumper & Hughes, Los Angeles and Chadbourne, Parke, Whiteside & Wolff, New York, concerning tax matters, which are attached as Exhibits. Subject to the discussion contained therein, the opinions conclude that a purchaser is entitled to a 10% investment tax credit and accelerated depreciation deductions based on the entire purchase price of the art master. A purchaser who properly elects the accrual method of accounting for his trade or business of exploiting the art master is also entitled to currently accrue

> interest deductions on his notes, including the partial recourse note, and a cash basis taxpayer is entitled to a deduction for interest when actually paid. The investment credit available to the purchaser of an art master is not affected by the "at risk" limitation contained in the Code; however, losses incurred in the venture are subject to that limitation. A cash payment made by a purchaser, and all notes as to which the purchaser is personally liable, including the recourse portion of the partial recourse note, qualify as amounts at risk. Accordingly, purchasers of art masters will be allowed to deduct losses up to the total of those amounts. The availability of a substantial portion of these tax benefits depends on a factual determination that the purchaser is acquiring the art master with the intent to engage in the business of exploiting the art master in order to make a profit (aside from tax benefits), and that the fair market value of the art master is at least equal to the purchase price. The opinions are therefore issued in reliance on the existence of such facts. The above summary is qualified in its entirety by the detailed information appearing elsewhere in this Information Memorandum.

The Picasso packages were specifically promoted in a letter signed by Finesod, dated December 22, 1979, containing the following paragraphs:

> We are pleased and honored, after two years of negotiations, to announce that Jackie Fine Arts has obtained the exclusive right to market art masters which are images from Picasso's private collection which have never been made available for purchase by the public. This purchase includes a limited edition of 500 plus 1000 posters.
>
> Jackie Fine Arts is also very pleased to present its art master program for 1979, a sound leveraged tax shelter program which complies fully with the Tax Reform Act of 1978 At Risk Ruling (HR 13511).
>
> The economics in art are excellent and participation in the art master program offers a 4 to 1 write-off for this year and approximately 3.7 for next year.
>
> Our two tax opinions, included in the memorandum, are from Chadbourne, Parke, Whiteside & Wolff, New York City, and Meserve, Mumper & Hughes, Los Angeles, both large, prestigious and highly regarded law firms. Legal defense, if ever required, is handled by Friedman & Shaftan, P.C., New York City.
>
> Our staff of in-house attorneys, CPA's and art experts has been expanded to provide all the services that a purchaser will require.
>
> We have enclosed a Fact Sheet for your consideration. Given the brief time left in the 1979 taxable year and as this will be the last opportunity to invest in our 1979 program, it would be advantageous for you to speed your inquiries by telephoning * * *.

Petitioners' Acquisitions

Upon hearing about the Jackie programs, Mr. Rose directed Robert Metry (Metry), a salesman for Jackie, to send information . . . to George Krauser (Krauser), a certified public accountant and tax partner in a large public accounting firm who advised petitioners on tax planning. [Krauser reviewed the material sent by Metry and Jackie and spoke with the New York lawyers about their tax opinion letters. No independent investigation as to value of the images was done, before the Roses purchased two images in 1979 for a total of $550,000 each, $100,000 of which was to be paid over 14 months, the balance by promissory notes due in 1991. They later purchased another image in 1980. Shortly after the original contract between Marina and Jackie, other heirs of Picasso ("VAGA") challenged Marina's right to enter into such contracts. A settlement was reached requiring VAGA's advance approval for any products made from the Reproduction Masters. The Roses submitted such requests to VAGA, which were denied. The Roses in an unrelated act in Kentucky sued Jackie and the appraisers.—Ed.]

Fair Market Value of Picasso Packages

Pablo Picasso was one of the creative geniuses of the twentieth century and an innovator and contributor to many of its major art movements, such as Cubism and Surrealism. Some of his works are considered milestones in twentieth century art. The value of his original works varies greatly, however. He was at the forefront of some of the major art movements of this century, constantly experimenting and trying new ideas. Picasso was a painter, sculptor, and print maker, making contributions in all artistic mediums.

* * *

The reproduction masters involved in the Picasso packages sold by Jackie and purchased by petitioners were different. They were to be made by a variety of different artists and printers and signed by Marina, Picasso's granddaughter. Such reproductions are not the equivalent of prints or lithographs made or signed by the creator of the original work. The signature of Marina would not add materially to the value of any limited edition. . . .

Purchasers of Picasso packages . . . received appraisals of their purchases from F. Peter Rose (F.P. Rose) and Sigmund Rothschild (Rothschild). F.P. Rose and Rothschild prepared approximately 1,500 appraisals for Jackie, of which approximately 200 related to Picasso packages. F.P. Rose received between $150 and $300 per appraisal from Jackie, and Rothschild received $250 per appraisal from Jackie. The appraisals were set up on a fixed format, in which the name of the purchaser and the name of the image were inserted when a Picasso package was sold.

Rothschild placed a value of $750,000 on each Picasso package appraised by him at the beginning of the program but increased the value to $800,000 at a later stage. F.P. Rose appraised each Picasso package sold from 1979 through the summer of 1980 at $675,000; he raised his appraisals to $700,000 from the summer of 1980 to the winter of 1981 and $750,000 from the winter of 1981 until 1982. F.P. Rose's reports were prepared in Rothschild's office on Rothschild's word processor.

* * *

All of the appraisal letters set forth in identical language the credentials of the appraiser, a summary of Picasso's career, and reference to the sales prices of graphic prints directly prepared by other well known artists. . . . [N]either F.P. Rose nor Rothschild expressed any opinion as to the probable selling price of any of the prints or posters to be created from the reproduction master. . . .

F.P. Rose and Rothschild were defendants in the Kentucky action brought by petitioners against Jackie. Nonetheless, they were the only expert witnesses called by petitioners at trial as witnesses to substantiate the claimed values of the Picasso packages . . .

Neither F.P. Rose nor Rothschild provided any data to support their assertions. . . . They merely cited examples of sales of original works by various artists and ignored the distinction between such items and the reproduction masters they purported to appraise. None of the appraisals . . . took account of varying degrees of appeal of the images sold as part of the Picasso packages. None of them took account of the likely effect of simultaneous marketing of the number of reproduction prints and posters anticipated with each Picasso package multiplied by the number of Picasso packages sold by Jackie.

Although both F.P. Rose and Rothschild were qualified by training and experience to appraise (and to testify as expert witnesses), the exaggerated values claimed by them, the total lack of support for their methods, and the manner in which the appraisals were generated rendered their opinions totally unreliable and not worthy of belief.

[The two expert witnesses for the IRS, Karen Carolan and Sylvan Cole, had much lower values, $7,162 and $55,000, respectively—Ed.]

* * *

Although the lack of comparable sales of equivalent products makes valuation of the Picasso packages extremely difficult, respondent's experts' opinions were well reasoned, credible, and persuasive. The fair market value of the three Picasso packages acquired by petitioners, taken together, is necessarily less than the net revenues reasonably projected by Carolan, which were a total of $7,162 over an uncertain period of time. The fair market value of the Picasso packages acquired by petitioners in 1979 and 1980 was for all practical purposes negligible.

Tax Treatment

By letter dated February 25, 1980, Jackie forwarded to petitioners specimen Federal tax forms to assist in the preparation of their 1979 Federal tax returns. . . .

On April 16, 1980, petitioners sent a letter to Friedman & Shaftan, the law firm mentioned in Jackie's December 1979 letter, inquiring as to the services to be provided to petitioners in the event of an Internal Revenue Service audit. By letter dated May 1, 1980, Friedman & Shaftan responded, assuring petitioners that the law firm would assist petitioners. . . .

On Schedule C to their 1979 income tax returns, petitioners reported an art print activity under the business name Lecia Arts, zero income, and depreciation expense of $125,766. . . . In addition, petitioners claimed an investment tax credit on Form 3468, of which $110,000 was attributable to the Picasso packages acquired from Jackie. Petitioners reported 1979 taxable income exceeding $460,000.

On their 1980 joint individual income tax return, petitioners attached a Schedule C reporting art prints activities under the name Lecia Arts. They claimed depreciation of $341,795, interest of $76,331, and miscellaneous expenses totaling $1,144. The depreciation expense related to the three Picasso packages acquired from Jackie. On Form 3468 for 1980, petitioners claimed investment tax credit, of which $55,000 was attributable to the Picasso package acquired in June 1980. Petitioners reported 1980 taxable income exceeding $550,000.

In a statutory notice of deficiency dated June 8, 1983, respondent disallowed all of the Schedule C losses and investment tax credits claimed for 1979 and 1980 relating to the Picasso packages. . . .

Ultimate Findings of Fact

Petitioners' acquisition of Picasso packages from Jackie Fine Arts in 1979 and 1980 was motivated primarily, if not exclusively, by tax considerations. There was no reasonable possibility that items produced from the Picasso packages would generate sales sufficient for petitioners to recoup their cash investment. Petitioners were relying on recovering their cash investment by immediate tax deductions and credits.

Petitioners did not have an actual and honest profit objective in acquiring the Picasso packages, and the transactions were devoid of economic substance.

Opinion

* * *

To qualify for the claimed depreciation deductions . . . petitioners must demonstrate that the packages either were used in a "trade or business" or were held "for the production * * * of income" within the meaning of section 167(a). Under section 48(a)(1), the investment tax credit is allowable only for property with respect to which depreciation (or amortization in lieu thereof) is allowable. Thus petitioners [must show] that their activities with respect to the Picasso packages either constituted a trade or business or were undertaken and carried on for the production of income.

. . . Respondent argues that petitioners' acquisitions from Jackie were part of a tax-avoidance device, not motivated by legitimate business purposes and totally devoid of economic substance, and should therefore be disregarded for tax purposes. Alternatively, respondent argues that petitioners were not engaged in an activity for profit or a trade or business in 1979 or 1980 with respect to the Picasso packages. . . . Under either of the above theories, according to respondent, petitioners would not be entitled to any deductions or credits. . . .

* * *

. . . [W]e conclude that petitioners are not entitled to the investment tax credits claimed or to any deductions other than interest actually paid on the recourse portion of the indebtedness to Jackie. . . .

This case lends itself to comprehensive analysis because (1) petitioners candidly admit that tax motives played a significant part in their decision to purchase Picasso packages; (2) respondent does not challenge petitioners' testimony concerning their reliance on Jackie and those associated with Jackie about salability of the Picasso reproduction prints and posters; (3) petitioners were not totally passive but actually engaged in post-acquisition activities regarding the assets acquired; and (4) the origin and design of the Jackie program can fairly be characterized as a tax shelter arrangement typical to the years in issue.

1. The Dealings Between Jackie and Petitioners

. . . [T]he Picasso packages were sold by Jackie and purchased by petitioners as a tax shelter, without regard to the income that might be produced, the fair market value of the products, or the methods by which the products might be sold by petitioners. Based on the entire record, we conclude that petitioners engaged in the transaction primarily, if not exclusively, to obtain tax deductions and credits and thereby reduce the tax they would otherwise have to pay on their substantial income from other sources.

Petitioners admit that tax considerations played a part in their decision to acquire the Picasso packages. Their advisor . . . was their tax accountant, whose records reflect that he considered his function to be advising petitioners with respect to "tax shelter." The information sought and received from Jackie focused primarily on the tax advantages to be obtained. Petitioners neither sought nor received prior to their acquisitions in December 1979 information on the manner in which they could commercially exploit the property that they were acquiring. At no time did they obtain any independent valuation information or distribution information, and they never entered into distribution agreements with anyone. The evidence indicates that they were indifferent to the real value of the Picasso packages. Petitioners were totally unbusinesslike in their initial dealings with Jackie.

Persuasive evidence of the lack of arm's-length price negotiation is petitioners' blind acceptance of the exaggerated values of the images claimed by Jackie. The evidence of value . . . demonstrates that an inquiry would have readily shown that the claims of value . . . could not be supported in fact. Although they had plenty of time in 1980 . . . to investigate these facts before making the second acquisition, they failed to do so. By the time of the second acquisition, the dispute between Paraselenes S.A. and VAGA was in full swing, and petitioners had not received the products that they had been promised in December 1979. Not surprisingly, they never did (and apparently never will) receive net income from the activity.

* * *

2. Relationship Between Sales Price and Fair Market Value

Petitioners agreed to pay $550,000 for each Picasso package when, according to the best available evidence, the fair market value of the packages was negligible. . . .

* * *

The appraisals of F.P. Rose and Rothschild sent to petitioners in 1980 did not explain the manner in which they arrived at values of $675,000 and $750,000, respectively. In attempting to support those appraisals at the time of trial in 1986, however, F.P. Rose projected the sale of 23,000 products of each image, at prices ranging from $12.50 for a poster to $2,000 for a signed and numbered print. Rothschild assumed sales of over 36,550 for each image, ranging from puzzles and calendars at $6.50 to tapestries at $4,000. Both . . . gave equivalent appraisals, and presumably made equivalent assumptions, for each of the Picasso packages sold by Jackie. Thus, the values . . . assumed the ability of investors such as petitioners to simultaneously sell literally millions of items. No expertise is necessary to recognize that such a volume of sales is improbable and, in any event, would have to be taken into account in establishing a price reflecting fair market value.

. . . [W]e conclude that the opinions of F.P. Rose and Rothschild are not credible because they are unsupported by any independent evidence and can only be attributable to bias resulting from the contract between them and Jackie.

Through April 1980, petitioners paid a total of $85,000 cash in relation to each of the images acquired December 1979. On their 1979 tax return, due April 15, 1980, they claimed investment tax credit of $55,000, plus depreciation of almost $63,000 for each package, reducing income taxable at rates exceeding 50 percent. As of that time, therefore, the tax savings exceeded the cash invested. It defies reason to suggest that the amounts paid by petitioners are indicative of fair market value of the Picasso packages without regard to the anticipated tax benefits. . . .

We do not believe, in any event, that a person with Mr. Rose's business acumen and experience would translate such speculation into a purchase price of $550,000. We do not believe that, absent the assurances that he requested and received concerning the anticipated tax benefits, Mr. Rose would have paid anything for the Picasso packages.

* * *

4. Perceived Congressional Intent

Petitioners suggest that they were merely taking advantage of tax incentives created by Congress. Indeed, Congress created deductions and investment tax credits to encourage certain types of activities, and the taxpayers who engage in those activities are entitled to the attendant benefits. . . .

We are not at all persuaded that Congress intended to encourage activities such as the Jackie program, which, if successful, would at most flood the market with mass-produced reproductions that, according to respondent's expert Cole, would merely denigrate the fine print art market. There is no evidence or reason to believe that the activities engaged in by Jackie and by petitioners in this case are among those favored by Congress. To the contrary, as discussed below in our discussion of section 6621(d), it appears that the transactions in issue are in the category of those that lead to adverse congressional action.[9]

The nature of the dealings between the parties, the total disparity between the purchase price and the fair market value of the property acquired by petitioners, and the illusory nature of the financing of the transactions convinces us that petitioners' acquisition of Picasso packages from Jackie is devoid of economic substance. The transactions, therefore, do not give rise to any depreciation deductions, miscellaneous deductions, or investment tax credits.

* * *

Additional Interest Under Section 6621(d)

* * *

[Section 6621(d) of the Internal Revenue Code increased the amount of interest to be paid by the taxpayer on a "substantial underpayment attributable to tax motivated transactions"—Ed.]

In *Johnson v. Commissioner*, 85 T.C. 469, 483 (1985), we determined that additional interest under section 6621(d) was due, on our own motion, stating:

> In connection with the enactment of this provision, the Conference Committee stated that:
>
> The conferees believe that, with this amendment, the Congress has given the Tax Court sufficient tools to manage its docket, and that the responsibility for effectively managing that docket and reducing the backlog now lies with the Tax Court. * * * The Court should * * * *assert, without hesitancy* in appropriate instances, the penalties that the Congress has provided. [H. Rept. 98-861 (Conf.) (1984), 1984-3 C.B. (Vol. 2) 239. Emphasis added.]

As in *Johnson*, we conclude that the circumstances of this case are among those in which Congress intended us to "assert, without hesitancy" the sanctions of section 6621(d). This is particularly true to the extent that tax motivated transactions giving rise to additional interest under section 6621(d) include "any valuation overstatement (within the meaning of section 6659(c))." . . .

---

9. Overvalued lithographs acquired in tax shelter promotions and donated to charities have led to negative congressional response. See Explanation of the Senate Finance Committee, p. 444, of changes to sec. 6659 made by the Deficit Reduction Act of 1984, Pub. L. 98-369, 98 Stat. 494, 693.

Decision will be entered under Rule 155.

Reviewed by the Court.

Notes and Questions

1. *Aftermath. Rose* was affirmed on appeal to the Sixth Circuit, 868 F.2d 851 (6th Cir. 1989). Jackie Fine Arts, Inc. and Finesod were involved in multiple lawsuits filed by various purchasers as the tax shelter scheme unraveled. The charming and smooth Finesod has been called the King of Tax Shelters, and the Picasso collection was merely one of many he promoted. Finesod's holding company, M & J Holding Corporation, reflected $1.33 billion in assets on its 1986 tax return. See Faircloth v. Finesod, 938 F.2d 513 (4th Cir. 1991).

2. *Tax Incentives and Accommodating Appraisers.* While *Weil, Vander Hook* and *Rose* are different cases, they are linked by the common desire of taxpayers to lower their income tax by way of deductions. In *Weil* and *Vander Hook*, the deduction was simply the charitable deduction for the artwork donated to a receptive university. In *Rose,* the goal was achieved through the multiple deductions and credits allowable for a trade or business, or with respect to activities undertaken for the production of income. Weil already owned the work, while Vander Hook and Rose had to acquire the artworks before engaging in the planned tax strategy. For them, the artworks were essentially commodified tax benefits. Marginal tax rates provide the practical, illuminating light as to why otherwise astute people seem to act somewhat cavalierly on their tax returns. In 1960 (*Weil*), the top marginal income tax rate was 91%, and in each of 1972, 1973 (*Vander Hook*), 1979, and 1980 (*Rose*), it was 70%. Therefore, assuming a taxpayer in the top bracket, a deduction of $100 would save $91 or $70 in tax, respectively. In addition, for Rose, there was a multiplier effect, touted as a 4 to 1 tax write-off for the first year and projected to be 3.7 to 1 for the second year.

The tax positions taken in *Weil, Vander Hook,* and *Rose* were dependent upon appraisers to establish the fair market value. Weil's appraiser, Mr. Chase, appears quaint compared to the appraisers used by Vander Hook and Rose. Mr. Chase actually examined the work that he was appraising at the taxpayer's home. In those pre-internet days, there was no readily available information on the artist Frederic Ede (1865–1943). Was the judge too quick to dismiss Chase's opinion based on his "unfamiliarity with the painting"? Notice that the IRS did not put on any evidence as to value.

Vander Hook and Rose sought out and bought an art-tax package, that included highly-inflated appraisals prepared by accommodating and highly-interested appraisers. For *Vander Hook*, there was a tenfold increase from cost to appraised value ($1,200 cost, $12,000 appraised value). For *Rose*, the increase was less ($550,000 actually paid, $675,000—$750,000 appraised value), but the other tax deductions and credit more than made up for that differential.

The appraisals provided to the purchasers were clearly manufactured as part of the overall tax shelter scheme. Vander Hook's appraiser at trial, Mr. Kurtzworth, did not impress the court with his competence ("Provenance . . . does not come as far out as California very often") or his independent status (for having "raised the valuations above his original estimate" because asked to do so by the marketer). Rose's two appraisers also had competency and independence concerns. They used identical form appraisal letters for all purchasers, except for the purchasers' names and aggregate values, befitting their use of the same office word processer. They essentially operated as an appraisal mill for Jackie. Moreover, neither provided any financial data to support his conclusions.

The twenty-year evolution from *Weil* to *Vander Hook* to *Rose* is dramatic. Mr. and Mrs. Weil merely donated a painting they had owned for years to a charity and claimed a tax deduction. It seems unremarkable. Vander Hook affirmatively buys into a tax deduction that only works if the value of the donated art is much greater than his cost. It is structurally the same as Weil's charitable deduction, except for the original tax motivated acquisition, even down to a university donee. At first, it may seem middle-of-the-road clever but only in the sense of "too good to be true!" On second thought, it is unsettling. *Rose,* on the other hand, is an aggressive tax shelter, light years away from the Weils' mere charitable donation. The tax shelter is highly and slickly promoted as such, with blue-chip law firms providing generic tax opinions. Those types of opinion letters were somewhat facetiously referred to as the get-out-of-jail-free cards for the purchaser of a tax shelter, because the purchaser would rely on the professional advice to prove lack of criminal or fraudulent intent. The amounts involved in the tax shelters are staggering, and the customer base is high-end and financially sophisticated, with access to qualified advisors. Why did Rose not seek independent legal advice even as he sought input from his accountant? The Picasso Collection tax shelter was exploiting the complexity of the tax code with a plan structured to address the literal terms of the tax code. It fell short because the valuations were unsupportable and the plan lacked economic substance. It was all window dressing. The Picasso Collection was also promoted as a way to exploit the growing and unregulated art market, especially the newly developing area of multiples, reproductions, and secondary objects.

3. *Other Art Tax Shelters.* Finesod was not the only one promoting and selling art tax shelters. Richard Gangel, for example, created Master Editions Inc. in 1978, "fashioned after (the) Jackie Fine Art" model. Its selling prospectus was 50 pages long, 27 of which discussed tax, and these "tax advantaged investments" centered on lithographs of contemporary artists. MEI ceased operations in 1986. Mr. Gangel's tax shelters raised over $400 million. Gangel v. Commissioner, 62 T.C.M. (CCH) 319 (1991).

The art tax shelter is also not solely a U.S. technique. In 2004, the Canada Revenue Agency successfully attacked an art-flip donation case, where taxpayers bought a block of paintings at a discount, donated the works to educational organizations in the U.S.(!), and claimed a deduction based on an inflated appraisal. Taxpayers sued their accountant, who recommended the art-flip tax shelter; the taxpayers were especially incensed that the accountant received roughly a 10% commission from the promoter. The accountant was thereafter ordered to pay damages to the taxpayers. The court determined the accountant had breached his fiduciary obligation to the taxpayers by not disclosing the commission. Lemberg v. Perris, [2010] 6 C.T.C. 116 (Can.).

4. *Impetus for Art-Tax Reform.* These types of persistent valuation abuses underlie three particular phases of art-tax reform. The first stage of art-tax reform was during the high tax era of the 1960s. The primary focus was on the recipients of the donations, that is, the museum and charitable organizations sector. The valuation abuses involved in art donations directly led to the creation in 1968 of the Art Advisory Panel of the IRS Commissioner. See Part B.4, *infra*, for discussion. The idea for such a panel emanated not from the IRS but from the art dealer and museum community, as a self-protection measure. "The art museum directors were concerned with the rise in grossly inflated appraisals of art works that were donated to charitable institutions during the early 1960s. These inflated appraisals reached such epidemic proportions that Congress considered removing art donations from the income tax charitable deduction." Jeffrey C. McCarthy, *Federal Income Taxation of Fine Art*, 2 Cardozo Arts & Ent. L.J. 1, 15 (1983). Congress also significantly changed the operating rules for charities and the donations to them in the Tax Reform Act of 1969. Thus the art-tax reform focus in the 1960s was primarily on the recipients of donations, i.e., museums and other charitable organizations.

In the 1980s, the second stage of art-tax reform focused on taxpayers involved in art donations. It imposed new statutory substantiation requirements on taxpayers making non-money charitable donations. For example, the Tax Reform Act of 1984 amended § 170(a)(1) to expressly provide that a charitable contribution must meet the verification requirements prescribed by the IRS to qualify for a deduction. Tax Reform Act of 1984, § 155(a)(2).

By 2006, the focus for the third stage of art-tax reform moved to encompass a taxpayer's advisors and appraisers. The Pension Protection Act of 2006 added new § 170(f)(11) to the Internal Revenue Code to disallow a charitable deduction for contributions over $5,000 unless a qualified appraisal by a qualified appraiser is obtained by the taxpayer. Section 170(f)(11) directly defined those terms. Congress was no longer content to leave their meaning to the regulatory process. Significantly, Congress also strengthened the penalties provision for valuation overstatements and understatements for taxpayers, and extended heightened liability to the taxpayers' tax advisors and appraisers. See, e.g., 26 U.S.C. § 6695A. These three stages show the reactive quality of art-tax reform. Originally, those reforms responded to abusive valuations and schemes by strengthening substantiation requirements. Later art-tax reform placed increasing emphasis on enacting measures with true enforcement bite to the repeat players in the tax planning and preparation process.

2. Statutory and Regulatory Framework

There are two primary scenarios when the valuation of artwork is at issue for tax purposes: (i) a charitable deduction for income tax purposes and (ii) inclusion in either a decedent's estate for estate tax purposes or a donor's gift for gift tax purposes. These two areas are, however, not the only ones where valuation of art may have tax consequences. For example, an artwork may be considered income (e.g., an art gallery compensates an employee, in whole or in part, with an artwork) and would need to be valued as part of gross income (i.e., an inclusion, not a deduction, valuation).

Section 170 of the Internal Revenue Code governs the charitable deduction for income tax purposes. 26 U.S.C. § 170. It does not make reference to fair market value as a statutory standard for valuation of art as a charitable contribution, but the regulations do. Treas. Reg. § 1.170A-1(c)(1). Moreover, the regulations spell out in detail the record keeping and return requirements for an income tax charitable deduction (Treas. Reg. § 1.170A-13(b), -13(c)), including the statutory and regulatory requirements for a qualified appraisal by a qualified appraiser (Treas. Reg. § 1.170A-13(c)(3), -13(c)(5)).

Section 170(f)(11) provides that a charitable deduction for a contribution of property will be denied unless the taxpayer meets the section's substantiation requirements. 26 U.S.C. § 170(f)(11)(A). The section's substantiation requirements depend on the amount of the claimed deduction. The tiers for donated property are threefold: valued at more than \$500, more than \$5,000, and more than \$500,000. 26 U.S.C. § 170(f)(11)(B)-(D). For donations of property ("property and all similar items of property donated to 1 or more donees shall be treated as 1 property" 26 U.S.C. § 170(f)(11)(F)) of more than \$500, the taxpayer must submit with the income tax return a description of the property and such other information as the IRS requires. For donations of property of more than \$5,000, the taxpayer must obtain a qualified appraisal of the property and attach to the return such information as the IRS requires. For donations of more than \$500,000, the taxpayer must attach a qualified appraisal to the return. The statute clearly requires additional regulatory input by the IRS, and the IRS responded. For transfers of art to charity, Form 8283 Noncash Charitable Contribution is the required form. It creates a separate hierarchy for artworks using a modified schedule, significantly less generous at the upper end than the statute. For works valued at more than \$500 but less than or equal to \$5,000, Form 8283 requires an appraisal from a Qualified Appraiser, but that appraisal does not need to be submitted or filed with the tax returns. If the artwork or artworks exceed \$5,000 but not \$20,000, a qualified appraisal must be obtained. For works in excess of \$20,000, a qualified appraisal must be obtained and included with the Form 8283, and a color photograph or high-resolution digital image must be obtained prior to donation but not included with the return. The following chart summarizes the current regulation requirements for a charitable income tax deduction for artworks:

Value of Deduction Claimed	Statutory and Form 8283 Regulatory Filing Requirements
(1) Individual items are less than $500	• No formal appraisal required.
(2) Individual items or groups of similar items valued from $500 to $5,000	• Form 8283, Section A Part I; • Must obtain Appraisal from a Qualified Appraiser but not required to be filed with return
(3) Individual items or groups of items over $5,000 to $19,999	• Form 8283, Section B • Must obtain Qualified Appraisal by Qualified Appraiser
(4) Individual items or groups of items $20,000 or more	• Form 8283, Part B • Qualified Appraisal by Qualified Appraiser must be included with return • Color photos or high-resolution digital image must be available

Section 2031 of the Internal Revenue Code governs the valuation of property included in a decedent's gross estate for federal estate tax purposes, and § 2512 governs the valuation of gifts subject to the gift tax. 26 U.S.C. §§ 2031, 2512. Like § 170, neither § 2031 nor § 2512 makes reference to a statutory standard of valuation, but the pertinent regulations supply the fair market value standard. Treas. Reg. § 20.2031-1(b); Treas. Reg. § 25.2512-1. Those regulations do not have the same level of specificity for appraisals as the income tax regulation. For example, Treas. Reg. § 20.2031-6 requires an appraisal by an expert if the estate includes items of "marked artistic or intrinsic value . . . in excess of $3,000," and the executor is advised to hire an appraiser of "reputable and recognized competency." Yet even without the requirement of obtaining and submitting a qualified appraisal by a qualified appraiser for estate and gift tax purposes, it is best practice to do so and strongly encouraged by the IRS. See, e.g., Treas. Reg. § 301.6501(c)-(f)(3) (the submission of an appraisal with a gift tax return will serve as adequate disclosure of a gift for statute of limitations purposes); Rev. Proc. 96-15 (procedure for IRS advance determination of value of art in excess of $50,000 requires an appraisal prepared by a qualified appraiser). The absence of an appraisal can be the basis for asserting accuracy penalties. Estate of True v. Commissioner, 82 T.C.M. (CCH) 27 (2001), *aff'd*, 390 F.3d 1210 (10th Cir. 2004).

The singular significance of a qualified appraisal and qualified appraiser is obvious for a taxpayer. The statutory definitions provided in § 170(f)(11)(E) are:

> (i) Qualified Appraisal—The term "qualified appraisal" means, with respect to any property, an appraisal of such property which—
>
> > (I) is treated for purposes of this paragraph as a qualified appraisal under regulations or other guidance prescribed by the Secretary, and
> >
> > (II) is conducted by a qualified appraiser in accordance with generally accepted appraisal standards and any regulations or other guidance prescribed under subclause (I).

(ii) Qualified Appraiser—Except as provided in clause (iii), the term "qualified appraiser" means an individual who—

(I) has earned an appraisal designation from a recognized professional appraiser organization or has otherwise met minimum education and experience requirements set forth in regulations prescribed by the Secretary,

(II) regularly performs appraisals for which the individual receives compensation, and

(III) meets such other requirements as may be prescribed by the Secretary in regulations or other guidance.

(iii) Specific appraisals.—An individual shall not be treated as a qualified appraiser with respect to any specific appraisal unless—

(I) the individual demonstrates verifiable education and experience in valuing the type of property subject to the appraisal, and

(II) the individual has not been prohibited from practicing before the Internal Revenue Service by the Secretary under section 330(c) of title 31, United States Code, at any time during the 3-year period ending on the date of the appraisal.

The IRS issued regulatory guidance on the qualified appraisal and qualified appraiser requirements. For a qualified appraisal, the IRS specifies the required content, form, and execution formalities. A nonconforming appraisal will not be a qualified appraisal. Two points deserve particular mention. An appraisal must be made no earlier than 60 days before the gift or later than the due date of the return. Generally accepted appraisal standards will be deemed satisfied if the appraisal is in conformity with the Uniform Standards of Professional Appraiser Practice (USPAP).

3. Enforcement and Penalty Provisions

Taxpayers historically and routinely were subject to penalties for irregularities in their tax returns, ranging from accuracy-related penalties to fraud. 26 U.S.C. §§6662, 6663. Tax return preparers are similarly subject to penalties and sanctions. 26 U.S.C. §§6694, 6701. For appraisers, there was no specific penalty under the tax laws until the Pension Protection Act of 2006 introduced §6695A: Substantial and gross valuation misstatements attributable to incorrect appraisals. 26 U.S.C. §6695A. Consequently, if an appraiser knows that the appraisal will be used with a tax return and the claimed value on the appraisal results in a substantial or gross valuation misstatement for income, estate, or gift tax purposes, then the appraiser shall pay a penalty. Only if the appraiser can prove that the value "was more likely than not the proper value" can the penalty be excused. For income tax purposes, a substantial valuation misstatement occurs if the appraisal valuation is 150% or more than the correct valuation. 26 U.S.C. §6662(e). For estate and gift tax purposes, a substantial valuation understatement occurs when the value claimed is 65% or less of the correct value. 26 U.S.C. §6662(g)(1). Gross misstatements substitute "200%" for "150%" with respect to income tax and "40%" for "65%" for estate and gift taxes. 26 U.S.C. §6662(h)(2)(C). Under these standards, *Weil* would be a substantial valuation misstatement, and *Vander Hook* and *Rose* would involve gross valuation misstatements. *Estate of David Smith* and *Estate of Elkins* would be gross valuation misstatements, while *Estate of Georgia O'Keeffe* would be a substantial valuation misstatement.

Does the existence of this penalty provision that can only be waived on a "more likely than not proper" standard create an imbalance in the appraiser's role? Or is this confirmation that an appraiser, when preparing an appraisal for tax purposes, serves a quasi-public function? When the art market is so fluid and dynamic, and with art values being inherently imprecise, valuation variance is a significant concern. Appraisers may demand higher fees to cover penalties, or they may decline certain appraisal engagements because of the penalty provision. Think how to construct a more-likely-than-not defense for an appraiser once the correct value has been determined. Is it an impossible standard to meet, or is it premised on the appraiser's reasonable and good faith belief that her appraised values were more-likely-than-not proper?

Two additional penalty provisions are arguably relevant for an appraiser. Section 6694 imposes a penalty on a tax return preparer based on the understatement of a taxpayer's liability by the return preparer. The definition of a tax return preparer includes one who prepares a substantial portion of a return, even if the person does not sign the return. 26 U.S.C. §7701(a)(36). Also §6701 assesses a penalty against one who aids or abets in the preparation of a tax return and who knows that the part so prepared would result in an understatement of tax liability for the taxpayer. The aiding and abetting penalty provision was added to the Internal Revenue Code to deal with the abuses afforded tax shelters by the Tax Equity and Fiscal Responsibility Act of 1982.

These three penalty provisions assess monetary penalties, but the Service has a more powerful enforcement tool: the disqualification of an appraiser and her appraisals from tax proceedings. 31 U.S.C. §330(c). Recall in *Biagiotti*, *supra*, the disqualification of the taxpayers' original appraiser by the IRS.

4. Art Advisory Panel

There are two art-specific appraisal resources available internally to the IRS: the Art Appraisals Services and the Art Advisory Panel. Art Appraisal Services is an internal IRS section that provides in-house assistance on art appraisals. The Art Advisory Panel, on the other hand, is a voluntary, appointed group of about 25 outside art experts that has been in existence since 1968. The Art Advisory Panel assists the IRS in determining value for artworks involved in income, estate, and gift tax matters. See Mary Anderson et al., *Art Advisory Panel Helps Courts Sculpt Estate Valuations*, 42 Est. Plan. 20 (2015). There are currently two sections to the panel: Fine Arts for painting and sculpture, and Decorative Arts for decorative arts and antiques. The Panel generally meets twice a year (currently in New York in April and later in the year commonly in Washington, D.C.) to review art valuations claimed on tax returns. The meetings are closed to the public. Any return selected for audit that contains artwork with a claimed value of $50,000 ($20,000 prior to December 2010) or more per item must be referred to the Art Appraisal Services for possible review by the Art Advisory Panel. The information before the Panel relates only to the artwork; the identity of the taxpayer and the tax consequences are not revealed. Each year, the IRS issues a statistical report concerning the Panel's activities. See, e.g., Art Advisory Panel Annual Summary Report for 2019, available at www.irs.gov. For many years, the Panel's determination of fair market value became the position of the IRS as to value. More recently, the policy of the Service is that the "Panel's recommendations are strictly advisory." For example, in fiscal year 2019, the Art Appraisals Services adopted 62% of the Panel's recommendations. See *id.* at 4.

Administrative and structural concerns arose with the operation of the Art Advisory Panel. Some concerns are about confidentiality and conflicts of interest. With respect to confidentiality and conflicts, it is simply impossible to construct a group of well-known and well-connected art experts who would not know about the donation of multi-million dollar artworks to the Met or the death of a prominent artist or collector. In a similar vein, how was it possible to ascertain a valid blockage discount without knowing what is in the block? Now that the Panel is advisory, the blockage discount is determined in the Art Appraisals Service. Other concerns are about the club-like membership, still others about the Panel's submission requirements. For example, a 2009 directive ("Preferred Object Identification") that an appraisal include images of comparable sales raised issues about the negative impact a lack of such images could have. Appraisers pointed out that many sales are done privately and those images may not be publicly or readily available. Will an appraisal without images of comparables be deemed insufficient, and therefore not be deemed a qualified appraisal? In addition, should confidential private sales be part of the valuation process at all? How can one defend against a valuation based in part on private sales that are not discoverable? See Estate of Mitchell v. Commissioner, T.C. Memo 2011-94, where the court rejected such valuations submitted by the Service. Moreover, some expressed concern that the process used to develop Preferred Object Identification relied on informal conversations among a small group instead of a wider public hearing among all stakeholders. As such, the process was nontransparent and questionable. See, e.g., Letter from American Society of Appraisers to IRS (Mar. 5, 2010). Historically, there was a lack of appraisers on the Art Advisory Panel. There is no requirement that the members of the Panel be qualified appraisers, although some now are. In light of the new tax requirements, should there be? One practical downside, however, for the volunteers is that they cannot prepare an appraisal for tax purposes while they are on the panel. Does this undermine the Art Advisory Panel's authority on valuation? Many welcomed changes to the workings of the Panel have occurred in the last decade. See, e.g., Anne-Marie E. Rhodes, *Valuing Art in an Estate: New Concerns*, 31 CARDOZO ARTS & ENT. L.J. 45, 64–75 (2013). Think about the role the Panel's report has in a disputed case. Section 7517 of the Internal Revenue Code requires the IRS to provide a requesting taxpayer with a written statement providing the basis for the IRS's determination of value of an item of property involved in an estate, gift, or generation-skipping tax determination.

Bernardo v. Commissioner

104 T.C. 677 (1995)

WELLS, J. The instant case is before us on . . . petitioners' motion to compel . . . production of documents. Respondent determined deficiencies in petitioners' Federal income taxes for their taxable years 1987, 1988, and 1989, as well as additions to tax and penalties for such years.

Background

. . . On their 1986 Federal income tax return, petitioners claimed a $593,000 charitable contribution deduction for the donation of a 21-foot granite sculpture entitled "Omphalos" to the Massachusetts Bay Transportation Authority (the Authority). The Omphalos sculpture was created by Dimitri Hadzi. It is currently situated in Harvard Square, Cambridge, Massachusetts. Petitioners' contribution base under section 170 was zero for their taxable year 1986. Petitioners claimed carryover charitable contribution deductions in the amounts of $40,406, $262,355, and $188,057 for their taxable years 1987, 1988, and 1989, respectively.

In the notice of deficiency, respondent denied the charitable contribution deductions petitioners claimed on their 1987, 1988, and 1989 Federal income tax returns on the grounds that petitioners failed to establish that they are entitled to a deduction under any section of the Internal Revenue Code. The notice of deficiency alternatively states that, if petitioners are able to establish that they are entitled to claim a deduction for the donation of Omphalos to the Authority, the amount of the deduction petitioners are entitled to claim is limited to $100,000, rather than the $593,000 petitioners claimed on their 1986 Federal income tax return.

* * *

4. Art Advisory Panel Notes

Respondent contends that the Art Advisory Panel's notes are not discoverable because they "contain purely predecisional, deliberative statements that * * *fall directly within the governmental privilege." In *P.T. & L. Constr. Co. v. Commissioner*, [63 T.C. 404, (1974)] *supra* at 410, we held that "executive privilege, unlike the work product doctrine, does not protect all opinions, conclusions, mental impressions, and thought processes of governmental officials." Statements that a governmental official "would hesitate to make for fear of disclosure to the public" may be protected by the doctrine of executive privilege. Id. In holding that the doctrine of executive privilege is not absolute, we stated:

> [executive] privilege is qualified in that it recognizes there are instances in which justice will require disclosure of such material. A balancing of interests is required; the gravity of the individual's need for disclosure must be weighed against the harm that disclosure may do to intragovernmental candor. [*Id.* at 409.]

The Art Advisory Panel (Panel) was first authorized by the Secretary of the Treasury in 1968, and the Panel is now composed of 25 prominent art specialists and authorities who are charged with assisting the IRS in determining the authenticity and fair market value of works of art. According to 2 Audit, Internal Revenue Manual (CCH), sec. 42(16)4.2, at 7347–4, any income tax case involving a claimed value for a single work of art of $20,000 [now $50,000—Ed.] or more must be referred to the National Office for consideration by the Panel. The Panel's meetings are closed to the public in order to prevent the disclosure of confidential tax return information.

As stated above, the executive privilege is designed to protect the candor of intragovernmental communications. The Panel's meetings are closed to the public in order to protect the confidentiality of the information provided to the Panel by taxpayers and not to insure the candor of intragovernmental communications. Accordingly, we hold that the Panel's notes concerning its valuation of Omphalos are not protected by the executive privilege from discovery by the taxpayers whose appraisal is under consideration by the Panel. Consequently, we hold that respondent must provide the Panel's notes to petitioners.

In addition to the documents listed above, respondent has not produced documents, or answered interrogatories, that "are fully responsive" to the following requests for documents or information contained in petitioners' discovery requests:

> 1. All documents referring, regarding or relating to any of Dimitri Hadzi's sculptures, including but not limited to appraisals of the Art Advisory Panel regarding his work.
>
> 2. All appraisals of the Art Advisory Panel of granite sculptures since 1980.
>
> 3. All appraisals of the Art Advisory Panel of so-called monumental works of art since 1980.
>
> 4. Curricula vitae of all members of the Art Advisory Panel who participated in the appraisal of Omphalos.
>
> . . .
>
> 8. Reports since 1980 summarizing the closed meetings of the Art Advisory Panel.

9. The identity of every person who has knowledge of the value of Dimitri Hadzi's sculpture, Omphalos, or any other sculptures, including but not limited to all persons on the Art Advisory Panel, and describing in detail the knowledge of such person.

Respondent contends that petitioners' requests are overly broad, unduly burdensome, not reasonably calculated to lead to the discovery of admissible evidence, protected by executive privilege, and constitute an attempt by petitioners to go behind the notice of deficiency. In support of respondent's contention that satisfying petitioners' requests would be unduly burdensome, respondent submitted an affidavit by Ms. Karen E. Carolan, chief of the IRS's Art Advisory Services Section and chair of the Art Advisory Panel. According to Ms. Carolan's affidavit, the Panel's records are not computerized and the Panel does not index records that identify documents by artist, materials used in the art, or the size of the art. As to petitioners' requests that are not limited to the work of the Panel, Ms. Carolan's affidavit states that the Commissioner keeps no central file or computerized file wherein the information petitioners seek could be readily located. According to Ms. Carolan, complying with petitioners' requests "would entail making a nationwide search of all records, of all examinations, since 1980."

We agree with respondent's contention that petitioners' requests are overly broad and unduly burdensome. Moreover, we do not believe that the furnishing of such information is reasonably calculated to lead to the discovery of admissible evidence. In light of the breadth of the search respondent would have to conduct in order to satisfy petitioners' requests, and the unlikelihood that the production of the documents sought by petitioners would lead to the discovery of admissible evidence, we hold that, with the exception of petitioners' request number 8, respondent is not required to produce the documents or the information sought in the requests listed above. To the extent that the information sought in request number 8 may be provided without disclosure of confidential materials, respondent is directed to provide petitioners with such information.

Based upon the foregoing,

An appropriate order will be issued.

Proctor & Gamble Co. v. United States

2009 WL 5219726 (S.D. Ohio 2009)

Order Re: Motion To Compel (Doc. 46)

Black, J. This civil action is before the Court on Plaintiff Procter & Gamble Company's motion to compel production of documents withheld on claims of the deliberative process privilege.

This tax refund case arises out of the parties' dispute over one billion dollars in tax deductions and credits that Plaintiff claimed. . . . Among the claimed tax benefits were charitable deductions resulting from Plaintiff's donations of certain intellectual property technologies and 80 artwork paintings donated to the Cincinnati Art Museum and the National Underground Railroad Freedom Center. The IRS performed examinations (audits) of the returns and ultimately issued a Notice of Deficiency determining that Plaintiff was not entitled to the tax deductions or credits at issue in this case. Plaintiff paid the disputed taxes and subsequently filed this civil action seeking a refund.

The Present Discovery Dispute.

During discovery, P & G requested that the Government produce documents underlying the IRS's appraisals of the donated artwork and technologies. In response, the Government withheld many documents relating to these appraisals on the basis of the "deliberative process privilege." Consequently, P & G moved to compel the production of the documents, arguing that the deliberative process privilege does not apply because the documents sought are factual and investigative in nature and because the Government has failed to comply with procedural requirements for claiming the privilege.

* * *

Production of the Art Panel's Documents.

The Court's decision as to the production of the Art Panel's documents is simplified because there is a United States Tax Court decision directly on point. In *Bernardo v. Commissioner*, 104 T.C. 677, 693–94, 1995 WL 366003 (1995), the U.S. Tax Court expressly rejected the Government's argument that documents created by the IRS Art Advisory Panel are protected by the deliberative process privilege. In reaching this express conclusion, the Tax Court found that the Art Panel's meetings were closed to the public "in order to protect the confidentiality of the information provided to the Panel by taxpayers and not to insure the candor of intragovernmental communications." *Id.* at 694 (emphasis supplied).

Faced with this express holding of the most specialized tax court in the country, the Government laments that "it appears that the deliberative process privilege was not properly asserted there [in *Bernardo*], since the IRS failed to introduce evidence that the disclosure of the meeting notes would work harm on the agency." In seeking to make this argument in the present case, the Government presents an affidavit which provides that "Panel members have told me that the secrecy of these deliberations is a key to their participation on the Panel." (Doc. 48-1 at p. 3, P 6.) But one would wonder why Panel members assume the proceedings are secret when the Tax Court ruled 14 years ago that the proceedings are not "secret." Moreover, the lament that Panel members would not serve on the Panel if the meetings were "recorded or made public" or if their comments would be "subject to release to the general public" is not implicated here, because the undersigned is not ordering public release of their comments but merely release to the party opposing the IRS in this litigation. Indeed, production of the Art Panel's documents shall be governed by a protective order limiting release to the participants in this lawsuit only.

Accordingly, the undersigned concludes that production of the documents of the Art Panel shall be compelled here, as they were in *Bernardo*.

Aftermath. *Bernardo* did not go to trial; the parties settled. Theodore Payser, *The Commissioner's Art Advisory Panel: A Long Running Success*, BNA Tax & Accounting, October 22, 2010.

Index of Artists

Index of Authors

Subject Index